ALAN TAYLOR

The Divided Ground

Alan Taylor is a professor of history at the University of California at Davis and a contributing editor at *The New Republic*. He is the author *American Colonies: The Settlement of North America* and *William Cooper's Town*, which won the Bancroft and Pulitzer prizes for American history.

The Divided Ground

Joseph Brant (Thayendenegea), by George Romney, 1776. (Courtesy of Library & Archives Canada; C-011092.)

Samuel Kirkland, by Augustus Rockwell. (Courtesy of the Emerson Gallery, Hamilton College.)

The Divided Ground

INDIANS, SETTLERS, AND
THE NORTHERN BORDERLAND OF
THE AMERICAN REVOLUTION

ALAN TAYLOR

VINTAGE BOOKS

A DIVISION OF RANDOM HOUSE, INC.

NEW YORK

FIRST VINTAGE BOOKS EDITION, JANUARY 2007

The Library of Congress has cataloged the Knopf edition as follows:
Taylor, Alan [date]
The divided ground : Indians, settlers, and the northern borderland of the American Revolution /
Alan Taylor.—1st ed.
p. cm.
Includes bibliographical references and index.
1. Iroquois Indians—History—18th century.   2. Iroquois Indians—Government relations.
3. Iroquois Indians—Land tenure.   4. United States—History—Revolution, 1775–1783—
Indians.   5. Northern boundary of the United States—History—18th century.   6. New York
(State)—History—1775–1865.   7. Ontario—History—18th century.   8. Northern
boundary of the United States—Ethnic relations.   9. New York (State)—Ethnic relations.
10. Ontario—Ethnic relations.   I. Title.
E99.I7T299 2006
974.7004'9755—dc22
2005043582

Vintage ISBN: 978-1-4000-7707-6

Author photograph © Dan Vaillancourt
Book design by Robert C. Olsson

www.vintagebooks.com

147468846

For Carole and Marty

Contents

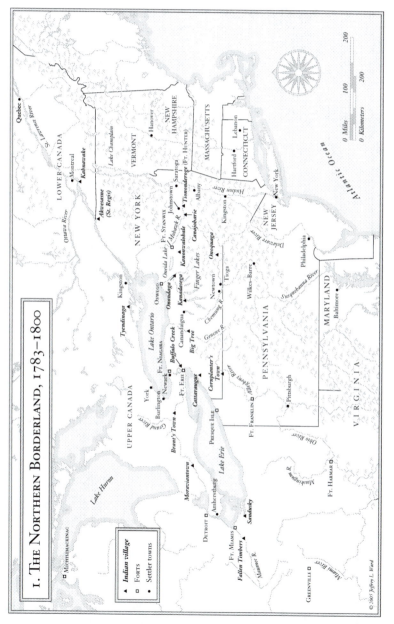

The Northern Borderland, 1783–1800.

The Divided Ground

༉ཞྀ

Wheelock's School

JOSEPH BRANT first met Samuel Kirkland in the summer of 1761. Although raised in radically different cultures, they were both students at a colonial boarding school run by Rev. Eleazar Wheelock in Lebanon, Connecticut. Brant was an eighteen-year-old Mohawk Indian from Canajoharie, a village in the Mohawk Valley, on the northwestern frontier of New York. Originally named Thayendenegea, he became Joseph Brant after his Christian baptism—a double identity common for Mohawks who lived among growing numbers of settlers. A year older, Kirkland felt far more at home at the school because he came from the nearby town of Norwich and was the son of a minister.[1]

Wheelock's controversial school trained colonial and Indian boys to become schoolteachers and missionaries for posting in Indian country. Pious and immensely ambitious, Wheelock pursued a "Grand Design": the conversion of all Indians to Protestant Christianity and to the economic culture of colonial America. The Mohawks were critical to the plan, for they were widely considered the most important and influential natives on the frontier of British colonial America. Success with the Mohawks would, Wheelock anticipated, unlock the minds and souls of all the other Indians deep within the continent. But swaying the Mohawks hinged upon converting and training Brant, Wheelock's first student from that people. In 1761, Wheelock paired Brant with Kirkland for training as an elite missionary team. Brant taught Mohawk to Kirkland, who helped Brant to master English.[2]

SIX NATIONS

Brant enjoyed the patronage of Sir William Johnson, the most famous and powerful colonist on the American frontier of the British Empire. An Irish immigrant of immense charm, cunning, and ambition, Johnson had settled in the Mohawk Valley during the late 1730s. He became wealthy and influential by cultivating the support of Mohawk chiefs and the patronage of royal governors. In 1756, that combination secured his appointment as the king's superintendent for Indian affairs in the northern colonies. Given the importance of the Indians to frontier peace, Johnson held the most difficult and the most powerful position in British America.[3]

By assisting the British conquest of Canada, Johnson enhanced the security and the value of his personal domain of 50,000 acres located on the north side of the Mohawk River. To clear and cultivate that land, Johnson recruited settlers who paid rent as tenants. To honor his royal patron, Johnson named his estate Kingsborough. To flatter himself, Johnson founded a new town called Johnstown, and he built a grand mansion known as Johnson Hall. Befriending the Mohawks had enriched Sir William.[4]

Although only about 400 people, the Mohawks derived extra clout from belonging to a broader Iroquois confederacy known as the Six Nations, which also included (from east to west) Oneidas, Tuscaroras, Onondagas, Cayugas, and Senecas. Especially numerous, the Senecas composed about half of the Iroquois total of 10,000 people. Culturally similar, the Six Nations spoke kindred languages of the Iroquoian family, with the greatest affinities between the Mohawk and Oneida tongues. Their aggregate homeland—"Iroquoia"—extended westward from the Hudson Valley to Lake Erie, and from Lake Ontario and the Adirondack Mountains on the north, into Pennsylvania to the south.[5]

The Mohawks occupied two villages—Canajoharie and Tiononderoge (Fort Hunter)—in the Mohawk Valley, while the Oneidas and Tuscaroras shared the country around Oneida Lake and in the upper Susquehanna Valley. Farther west, the Cayugas and Onondagas held the confederation's heartland around the Finger Lakes. At the western edge of Iroquoia, the Senecas dwelled beside Seneca and Canandaigua lakes and in the valleys of the Genesee and Allegheny rivers.

The Iroquois nations occupied different points on a spectrum of colonial influence, with the eastern villages facing the greatest pressure from settlers. By 1761, the Mohawks were a shrinking minority surrounded by thriving settlements. The Oneidas and Tuscaroras were not yet enveloped, but they lived on the western margins of colonial settlement. To the west, the Cayugas, Onondagas, and Senecas enjoyed greater independence and security because they retained large homelands beyond the colonists—for the time being.[6]

The colonists coveted the Iroquois as allies because they occupied the most strategic position in northeastern North America: along the waterways through the Appalachian Mountains between New York and French Canada, to the north, and between New York and the Great Lakes, to the

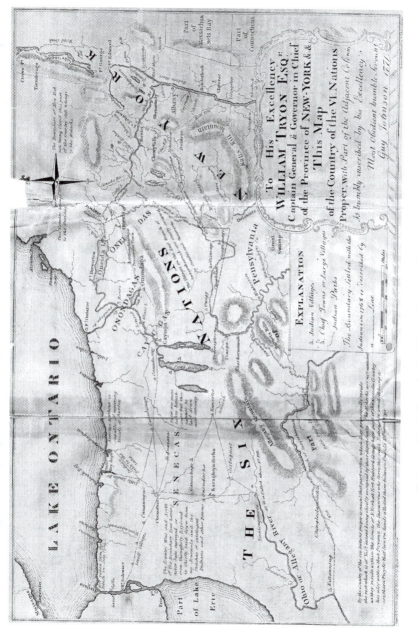

The Country of the Six Nations, by Guy Johnson. (Courtesy of the New York State Library.)

west. Given the impossibility of moving armies with cannon through dense woods and across mountains, British officers needed to control the waterways—at least to defend New York and at best to attack Canada. As raiding enemies, the Iroquois might devastate the colonial frontier, but as allies they could provide an invaluable screen against attacks by more distant Indians allied with the French. The Iroquois location "next to our portages & Frontier Settlements," Sir William Johnson explained, "qualifies them for acting the part of our best friends, or most dangerous enemies."[7]

The Iroquois compounded the power of their position by their formidable reputation as warriors and scouts, as the masters of a forest warfare of sudden raids and deadly ambushes. Indian warriors terrified both by their silent mobility in advance—and by their sudden sound and fury in attack. Their distinctive, piercing screams chilled all but the most hardened foes. An Iroquois warrior also cultivated a formidable appearance by stripping naked except for a loincloth and moccasins; by shaving his head but for a central ridge of hair known as a scalp lock; by tattooing his body with pins and gunpowder to symbolize his kills and captures in combat; by painting his face in some personalized medley of red, black, and blue; and by mutilating his earlobes, weighted with ornaments to drape onto both shoulders.[8]

Warriors intimidated far beyond the proportion of their limited numbers. Veteran British commanders considered 300 Indians more than a match for 1,000 soldiers "in the Woods." Trained from youth in handling firearms, and adept as hunters, the warriors were better shots than almost all colonists or Britons. In hand-to-hand combat, warriors' knives and tomahawks made short work of wounded foes. Most colonists fought only under duress in part-time militias, but for Indian men, war was essential to their survival and their identity. Guy Johnson observed, "As their Natural Genius inclines them to War, and that they consider their happiness as depending on their Military Skill, they use [all] Methods & all things to preserve that Spirit."[9]

During the mid eighteenth century, the New Yorkers and the Iroquois sustained an ambivalent relationship of mutual need and mutual suspicion. During imperial wars, colonial leaders anxiously wooed the Iroquois with presents, flattery, and some limits on settler expansion. During peace, however, those same leaders coveted and finagled the fertile land of Iroquoia, anticipating immense profits from clearing the forest to make thousands of new farms. By 1760, that pressure by land speculators and settlers had already cost the Mohawks most of their land and had taken some from the Oneidas.[10]

Fearing settler expansion, the Six Nations wanted to prolong their valuable position between the British and the French settlements, a position that solicited concessions and presents from both empires. In 1754, a British officer observed, "To preserve the balance between us and the French is the great ruling principle of the modern Indian politics." During the years 1759 to 1761, however, the British routed the French, conquered Canada, and occupied French forts along the Great Lakes. Surprised by the rapid French collapse, the Iroquois feared that their alliance had become redundant to the victorious British, who seemed poised to unleash settlers throughout the continent.[11]

At that troubled moment, Brant traveled eastward to join Wheelock's school in New England, the most populous and expansive region of British America. Called "Yankees" by the Indians, most of the New England colonists descended from seventeenth-century Puritans, religious dissidents who had fled from the mother country to escape the king's official faith, the Church of England. Endowed with a powerful cultural unity and an aggressive sense of religious mission, they felt driven to dominate and transform their new land. By 1761, the 450,000 Yankees had overwhelmed New England's Algonquian Indians, confining the survivors to small enclaves in a landscape of colonial farms and commercial seaports. Sobered by that Algonquian fate, the Iroquois resolved to defend their independence by preserving their strategic position beside, rather than within, the colonial settlements.[12]

BORDERS

At Wheelock's school, Brant and Kirkland began a long and intense relationship that would redefine North America. For nearly fifty years, their lives intertwined, initially as close collaborators but later as bitter foes. By narrating their lives, this book examines the making of twin borders that constituted the new United States: the boundaries between natives and Indians and between the British Empire and the American Republic. To achieve power at their core, new nations must define and control their peripheries. By asserting and displaying political difference at a boundary, regimes consolidate the allegiance and identity of their citizens or subjects within. Loose borders make for weak nations or empires. But attempts to make and to control borders inevitably invite resistance by local people who resent restrictions.[13]

Border-making was especially tangled in North America during the eighteenth and nineteenth centuries, when contending empires projected their ambitions onto the lands of Indians who defended their autonomy and their mobility. By asserting boundaries that overlapped, the rival empires invited natives to seek concessions from both—as the Six Nations did with the

British and the French. The Iroquois defended an alternative vision of political space where natives persisted in autonomy between settler regimes, rather than divided and absorbed by them. After the American Revolution the victors worked to pin Indians down, creating reservations within as a key step to consolidating the larger boundaries of the new nation.[14]

The historians Jeremy Adelman and Stephen Aron distinguish between "borderlands" and "borders." They argue that North America's native peoples defended broad and porous borderlands—until forcibly confined within the borders of Mexico, Canada, and the United States. This book examines the transition of one borderland—Iroquoia—into two bordered lands: the state of New York in the American Republic and the province of Upper Canada in the British Empire. In particular, I will focus on Brant's Mohawks and on the Oneidas who hosted Kirkland's mission.[15]

As a borderland history, this book explores both sides—Canadian and American—of the revolution's contested boundary in search of insights lost by the standard nationalist approach that tells only the American half of the story. American historians often follow Frederick Jackson Turner to narrate the conquest of North America in terms of "the frontier," where American settlement inexorably advanced as Indians rapidly receded. Treating settler expansion and the creation of the United States as natural and inevitable, Turner neglected the creative efforts by Indians to frame alternatives to their dispossession. In his history, both natives and Britons were modest speed bumps in the frontier pursuit of American destiny.[16]

If we treat that American triumph as inevitable, we obscure the fluid contingency of the 1780s and 1790s, when Brant promoted an alternative vision of an enduring Indian confederacy between the empire and the republic. To frustrate American border-making, he championed an earlier boundary that ran from north to south to distinguish an Indian country on the west from the colonial settlements to the east. Sir William Johnson and the Iroquois chiefs framed that alternative boundary in a treaty council at Fort Stanwix in 1768. By drawing a line on a map and surveying it on the land, Johnson hoped to resolve frontier frictions between settlers and natives. He also sought greater power for himself, and his imperial overlords, as the keepers of a defined border between Indians and colonists. But imperial control irritated colonial settlers and land speculators, who wanted a free sway in western expansion. Their irritation fed the American Revolution, which created an independent republic dedicated to facilitating white settlement and Indian dispossession.[17]

To stem the American advance westward during the 1780s and early 1790s, Indians defended a borderland between the new revolutionary line and Johnson's older line.

In contrast to Johnson's line, the revolutionary border separated north from south, distinguishing the new American republic from the lingering British empire in Canada. By pinning the British in Canada, the Americans sought freely and rapidly to expand westward. They insisted that the new border nullified the British network of Indian alliances that stretched south of the Great Lakes into Iroquoia and the Ohio Valley.

By clinging to their British allies, however, Indians defied the new border and the American expansion that it invited. Emboldened by that Indian resistance, the British broke the peace treaty by retaining border forts on the southern shores of the Great Lakes. That retention strengthened native defiance and sustained a cold war between the republic and the empire. To overcome Indian and British resistance to the new border, the Americans worked to divide and separate Indian peoples by isolating their villages on reservations surrounded by settlements.

The new national boundary was the grandest of three types of interdependent lines: property lines, reservation lines, and the border. At the most local and fundamental level, settler society wove a web of property lines to demarcate thousands of farms privately owned. An American state or a British colony derived revenue and power by surveying those lines and selling sovereign title to the enclosed parcels. The recipients returned allegiance to the government that issued their land titles. A state or a colony claimed a sovereign monopoly within to sell land to its supporters—primarily speculators who retailed farms to settlers. Spreading westward, those supporters consolidated a state's sovereignty to the limits of the asserted boundary. In eighteenth-century parlance, a state or colony needed to capture "the interest" of its inhabitants in the security of their property. To understand the development of American (and Canadian) society, we need to examine their foundation: the contested process of acquiring Indian land to make private property.[18]

Once broad, contiguous, and overlapping, during the 1780s and 1790s the Iroquois domains became compact, finite, and distinct—separated and surrounded by settler farms. Restricted by reservation lines, Indians became dependent on state annuities and thereby lost the capacity to flee or to fight. Then the Americans could push forward to claim their boundary along the Great Lakes from the reluctant Britons. Alarmed and inspired by that American consolidation, the British sought enhanced security by tightening their control over the Indians on the Canadian side of the border. Border competition drove both powers to control Indians on reservations, giving meaning to the postrevolutionary boundary between the republic and the empire.[19]

The Iroquois resisted their entanglement within those three interacting layers of lines. Rejecting division and confinement by the peace treaty line, the Iroquois defended their traditional position as autonomous keepers of a perpetual and open-ended borderland, a region of exchange and interdependence. By exploiting the rivalry between the republic and the empire, they hoped to remain intermediate and autonomous. The natives conceived of their borderland as porous for information, trade, and people. The Seneca chief Red Jacket reminded the Americans, "[We] do not give ourselves entirely up to them [the British], nor lean altogether upon you. We mean to stand upright as we live between both." As gatekeepers of a borderland, the Six Nations enjoyed a leverage that would be lost if divided and confined by an artificial border where two Euro-American powers met directly and asserted control over all inhabitants—native and settler—within their respective bounds.[20]

Their most prescient leaders, including Brant, recognized the power of property lines in weaving a settler society. Rather than resisting all settlement, they tried to regulate the creation of new farms to serve Indian ends. They hoped to choose their new neighbors, favoring those who treated Indians generously. They also preferred to lease rather than to sell land. As lessors (rather than sellers), Indians could reap annual rents that would grow as settler labor enhanced land values. As landlords, Indians would also retain sovereign title to the land, preserving their independence.[21]

Of course, native leasing schemes appalled the leaders of New York and Canada as dangerous obstacles to their own power. By asserting a supposed "preemption right," state and colonial leaders declared imminent and inevitable their acquisition of Indian land, diminishing aboriginal title to a temporary possession. By asserting a monopoly to buy Indian land, they reduced the price that Indians could receive for their dispossession. The doctrine of preemption barred Indians from seeking individual buyers or (better still) renters willing to pay market value for aboriginal title. Instead, both New York and Upper Canada bought Indian lands at depressed prices for reallocation to favored land speculators. That reallocation doubly benefited a regime by generating revenue and by securing the "interest" of the powerful and prominent men who speculated in frontier acres by the thousands. And a lower price paid to Indians ensured their poverty and dependence in a settler world.

By repetition in documents and by subsequent historians, the supposed sovereign right of preemption has been naturalized: taken for granted as if it were real. In fact, preemption was imposed to benefit the regimes that invaded Indian country. The dual process of dispossessing Indians and creating private property constructed the state of New York, the United States, and the British Empire in Canada. Their success depended on defeating the

Iroquois alternative of keeping a borderland by enlisting settlers as their tenants.[22]

The Divided Ground plays with the title of Richard White's great work *The Middle Ground,* to which I am immensely indebted. The common ground is the struggle by native peoples to adapt creatively to the transforming power of intruding empires. The substitution of "divided" for "middle" reflects variations in geographic and temporal emphasis. *The Middle Ground* deals primarily with the Algonquian peoples of the Great Lakes and Ohio Valley during the century and a half prior to the American Revolution. *The Divided Ground* tells a later and more eastern story by focusing on the legacies of that revolution for the Iroquois Six Nations of New York and Upper Canada. White reveals an earlier period of mutual accommodations where neither natives nor colonizers could dominate the other, but instead had to craft new customs and rhetoric to deal with each other as equals. *The Divided Ground,* however, attends to the later efforts by natives to cope with an invasion of settlers, coming in great and growing numbers to divide the land into farms, reservations, and nations.

PART ONE

REVOLUTION

Detail from the *Death of General Montgomery in the Attack on Quebec, 31 December 1775*, by John Trumbull. The Indian with raised tomahawk represents Colonel Louis, a Kahnawake Mohawk who supported the Patriots and subsequently joined the Oneidas. (Courtesy of the Yale University Art Gallery.)

View of Fort Niagara from the west, by James Peachey, ca. 1785. At the outlet of the Niagara River into Lake Ontario, the fort occupies the bluff on the east bank, above a riverside cluster of taverns and stores, known as the Bottom. The British employed sailing schooners and ships on Lake Ontario. (Courtesy of the Old Fort Niagara Association, Inc., Youngstown, N.Y.)

View of Fort Niagara from the south, by James Peachey, ca. 1785. (Courtesy of the William L. Clements Library, University of Michigan.)

CHAPTER ONE

Property

Sir William Johnson, by Matthew Pratt, ca. 1770. (Courtesy of the Johnson Hall State Historic Site, Johnstown, N.Y., and the New York State Office of Parks, Recreation, and Historic Preservation; JH. 1971.309.a.)

I N JULY 1761, as Joseph Brant traveled east to join Wheelock's school, Sir William Johnson headed west, ascending the Mohawk River into the country of the Six Nations. His five boats hauled thirty-eight soldiers, their equipment, and presents for the Indians. The traveling party also included his nineteen-year-old son, John, and their cousin and secretary, Guy Johnson. In high spirits, the Johnsons anticipated a victory tour in Indian country to consolidate the recent British conquest of French Canada. With the French banished from North America, British officials expected easily to control the Indians.[1]

Instead, Johnson found pervasive Indian dread and disgust, even among the nearby Mohawks, who had so long cooperated with him. As British allies, the Mohawks had lost about 100 warriors, half of their men, during the recent war with the French. In return for that heavy sacrifice, the Mohawks expected Johnson to protect their villages against conniving land speculators and encroaching settlers. Frustrated in that expectation, the Mohawks complained bitterly to Johnson, who reported that they felt in "danger of being made slaves, and having their lands taken from them at pleasure, which they added would confirm what the French have often told the Six Nations."[2]

Preaching patience, Johnson promised justice to the Mohawks—but New York's leaders and settlers kept breaking his every promise. Fed up, the Mohawks threatened to move away deeper within Indian country. That possibility delighted settlers and speculators who lusted after Mohawk land, but alarmed Johnson, who relied on his special Mohawk connection to influence the Six Nations. Without nearby and content Mohawks as allies, his superintendency would become impotent.[3]

Proceeding upriver beyond the Mohawk country, Johnson reached German Flats, colonial New York's westernmost settlement. There, Johnson met Oneidas, who also bitterly complained of encroaching settlers. The chief Conoghquieson warned Johnson that the Oneida settlers would fight rather than lose their lands. Instead of consolidating British power over the Indians, the conquest of Canada threatened to unravel the alliance with the Six Nations that was essential to frontier security.[4]

In helping the British to attack Canada, the Iroquois had miscalculated, for they had never expected such a rapid and complete collapse by the French forces. No longer could the Indians play off the French against the British to maintain Iroquois independence, to maximize their presents, and to ensure trade competition. A British general explained, "They saw us sole Masters of the Country, the Balance of Power broke, and their own Consequence at an End. Instead of being courted by two Nations, a Profusion of Presents made by both, and two Markets to trade at, they now depend upon one Power." That dependence exposed Iroquoia to land-hungry colonists.[5]

THE SIX NATIONS

The Iroquois pursued a mixed subsistence strategy combining horticulture, gathering, fishing, and hunting. In fields of fertile, alluvial soil, they cultivated mounds of maize topped by climbing beans and surrounded by low-lying squashes and pumpkins. After the fall harvest, the natives dispersed into the hills, occupying many small camps, tended by women, while the men pursued bear, deer, and beaver for meat and pelts. Returning to their villages, they spent the early spring collecting maple sap to make a brown sugar. After planting their crops in May, the Iroquois spent June and July in fishing camps strung along the lakes and streams. Having exhausted the previous year's harvest, the people sought relief by catching eels, salmon, trout, and whitefish. During that hungry season, the women and children also gathered wild onions, followed by strawberries, raspberries, whortleberries, and blackberries. From the forest floor, they also harvested ginseng for sale to colonial merchants.[6]

This mobile, but seasonally patterned, way of life conserved most of the forest and streams—and their wild things—over the generations. Native use contrasted with the colonists' drive to clear most of the forest to provide pastures for cattle and fields for grain. Compared to the colonists, the Iroquois used land extensively rather than intensively. The natives did clear and cultivate compact fields near their villages, but they kept most of their domain as a forest to sustain wild plants and animals. To colonial eyes, the Iroquois peoples wasted their land by keeping a wilderness; but the Indians exploited their domain in ways that the colonists did not understand.[7]

Most colonists disdained the Iroquois as improvident, living from hand to mouth for want of incentives for accumulating private property. Indeed, the Iroquois considered it foolish and demeaning to labor beyond what they needed to subsist. Sir William noted, "The Indians are a Lazy people, & naturally Enemies to Labour." But colonial charges of Indian indolence focused on men seen during the warm months in their villages or on visits to colonial towns: periods and places of male inactivity and heavy drinking. Colonial observers rarely saw Indian men during their strenuous winter hunts, when they endured severe hardships pursuing game for miles over rugged terrain in bitter weather. The colonial view also discounted the evident industry of native women in cultivating and gathering, which the colonists treated as exploitation by lazy husbands and fathers.[8]

They cherished the collective security maintained by expecting generosity from the fortunate to the needy. Instead of storing up wealth, prospering chiefs accumulated prestige by gifts to their kin and to the hungry and ragged. These values of hospitality and reciprocity spread resources through the seasons and across a village, sustaining a rough equality. No one starved in an Iroquois village unless all did so. John Heckewelder, a missionary, noted that the Indians disliked the competitive and acquisitive values of the colonists: "They wonder that the white people are striving so much to get rich, and to heap up treasures in this world which they cannot carry with them to the next."[9]

If paltry by colonial standards, the material wants of the Iroquois exceeded those of their ancestors. The eighteenth-century Iroquois relied

upon traders to provide European manufactured goods that exceeded the
Indian technology to make. In return for furs, the Iroquois procured metal
knives, hatchets, axes, hoes, and kettles—all vastly better than their stone
and wood predecessors. And with cloth, mirrors, glass and silver jewelry, and
alcohol, the traders provided new luxuries to the Indians. Above all, they
needed guns, gunpowder, and metal shot for hunting and war. Dependence
on that imported technology also entailed an Indian reliance on colonial
blacksmiths and gunsmiths to repair metal tools and weapons.[10]

In personal appearance, the Iroquois conveyed a mix of tradition and
adaptation, of America and Europe, of subsistence and commerce, and of
ease and pride. Except for moccasins on their feet, the Iroquois donned more
British cloth than traditional buckskin. In warm weather, men wore little
more than a loose, linen shirt over their shoulders and a loincloth held by a
leather belt. Women's attire consisted of a linen shirt and a cotton petticoat.
In colder weather, both men and women wrapped themselves in woolen
blankets, while men covered their lower limbs with leather leggings. Both
genders delighted in abundant jewelry, especially silver worn as bracelets,
gorgets, rings, and earrings. Women and older men wore their hair long, but
warriors shaved the sides of their head to leave a scalp lock on top. The young
men also plucked their facial hair out by the roots.[11]

Gender and age, rather than social class, structured Iroquois labor.
Assisted by children, women tended the crops and gathered the wild plants,
while men fished, hunted, waged war, and conducted diplomacy. Men's activ-
ities took them deep into the forest and far from the villages. Consequently,
those villages and their fields belonged to the women, the enduring people of
the community. They controlled the harvest and determined the location of
their village.[12]

No land could be forsaken without their consent. In 1763, the Mohawks
explained to Johnson that women were "the Truest Owners, being the persons who labour on the Lands." The Mohawk matrons then assured Johnson
that "they would keep their Land, and did not chuse to part with the same to
be reduced to make Brooms." The Mohawks well knew the Algonquian Indians of the Hudson Valley and New England as negative reference points: as
native peoples who had lost most of their lands and become the impoverished makers of brooms and baskets for colonial consumers.[13]

CHIEFS

The Iroquois dispersed and divided political power from a dread of coercion.
They understood the world as constantly embroiled in a struggle between
the forces of good and evil, of life and death, of peace and war. Because

those conflicts raged within every nation, village, and person, all forms of power had to be dispersed and closely watched to preserve the freedom of a people.[14]

An Iroquois nation was an ethnic and linguistic group divided into several jealous villages and subdivided by internal factions led by rival chiefs. Although one village usually was a bit larger and more prestigious, hosting the council fire of the nation, the chiefs there could only admonish and advise, but never command, their fellow people in other, smaller villages. No nation was united under the rule of a single headman, although one chief might enjoy more honor as the keeper of sacred objects—principally wampum belts—and as the host of public councils. Instead of representing an entire village (much less the collective nation), a chief represented a particular clan, which the Iroquois called "a tribe." Most Iroquois nations had three clans (or tribes): Bear, Wolf, and Turtle. A clan consisted of several extended families, related through the maternal line: matrilineages. Johnson noted that a chief's clout depended on "the number of Warriors under his influence, which are seldom more than his own relations."[15]

The proper chief had been accomplished in war but mellowed by time, becoming eloquent, patient, tactful, dignified, and methodical. The duty of a chief was to keep his head while others were losing theirs. In 1765, Sayenqueraghta, a Seneca, described the ideal chief as "a wise, dispassionate man [who] *thinks much* & thinks *slowly*, with great caution & deliberation, before he speaks his *whole mind.*" A proper chief worked to soothe the discontented, to calm troubles, and to keep the peace by sage advice. Unable to command people, the chief exercised influence through persuasion, which rested upon his prestige, example, and reason. A bullying chief risked his life to assassination by disgruntled warriors.[16]

The clan chiefs (or "sachems") had to share village authority with warriors and matrons. The senior women of the matrilineages chose the chiefs who represented their clan on the village council. Although birth within the proper matrilineage mattered, the clan mothers favored merit and personality in determining their choice. In effect, chiefs were so many male ambassadors, representing matrilineages. Once chosen, a chief ordinarily served for life, but an incompetent could be ousted by the matrons of his clan.[17]

Chiefs promoted harmony and peace, but they could not always succeed—especially beyond the nation among outsiders without kinship ties to the Iroquois. Consequently, the people also needed to summon the darker powers of their young warriors. They could not, and should not, possess the chiefly virtues of calm forbearance. Instead, warriors needed to be decisive, violent, cruel, and proud—quick to take offense and terrible in seeking vengeance. Without formidable warriors, no people could remain free. In theory, chiefs restrained warriors, but ambitious young men longed for the honors of war to demonstrate their courage and prowess. Bristling under restraint by their chiefs, warriors sometimes forced a war by raiding foes or by killing their emissaries. But women could compel the warriors to make peace by withholding the food needed for long-distance raids.[18]

Within their villages, the Iroquois dreaded contention and coercion, preferring the deliberative search for consensus, however elusive. That search led to highly formalized speeches in public council by chiefs closely watched by all the villagers. If those deliberations failed to reach an acceptable consensus, the people agreed to disagree, permitting factions and families to chart varying courses. For example, during the imperial wars, the Oneidas disagreed on a common front, so some helped the French and others the British, while most clung to neutrality.[19]

If a village majority did commit to a provocative decision, the disgruntled voted with their feet by moving away. Over the years, village populations ebbed and surged as some people moved out and others moved in. Driven by the elusive ideal of consensus, this fission helped to sustain that ideal—if not the reality—by temporarily ridding villages of the most discontented.[20]

The lack of coercive power within the Six Nations frustrated colonial officials who hoped to command the Indians by co-opting their chiefs. Early and often, those chiefs tried to explain their limited influence over hotheaded warriors or over another village. Indeed, a chief lost influence if he did colonial bidding by coercing his own people. Johnson eventually gave up trying to mandate head chiefs for each of the Six Nations, explaining that "the extreme jealousy which the Northern Indians entertain of one another would render a particular choice of any one of them unserviceable; and make his Nation pay no regard to him." Noting that chiefs had greater power in the past, or at a distance from the settlements, Johnson concluded that colonial meddling had weakened authority in Indian villages. But, of course, Johnson was the consummate meddler.[21]

The imperial wars diminished the authority of the sachems. Eager to recruit warriors, colonial leaders treated the war chiefs as the real locus of power in an Iroquois village. Consequently, they could drive hard bargains to secure abundant presents including weapons and ammunition. By redistributing this largesse to their followers, war chiefs built their influence at the expense of the sachems. Indeed, warriors and their war chiefs waxed increasingly arrogant. In 1762, the Seneca war chiefs assured Johnson: "We are in fact the People of Consequence for Managing Affairs, Our Sachems being generally a parcell of Old People who say Much, but who Mean or Act very little."[22]

From a colonial perspective, the Iroquois lived in virtual anarchy—owing to the crisscrossing interests of chiefs, warriors, and women; the elusive ideal of consensus; and the powerful animus against coercion. And yet, native villages were remarkably harmonious—except when alcohol abounded. Heckewelder noted, "They have no written laws, but they have usages founded on the most strict principles of equity and justice. . . . They are peaceable, sociable, obliging, charitable, and hospitable among themselves." Their public councils were dignified—in stark contrast to the rancor of colonial politics. Johnson marveled, "All their deliberations are conducted with extraordinary regularity and decorum. They never interrupt him who is speaking, nor use harsh language, whatever may be their thoughts."[23]

Kinship and conversation framed the obligations, duties, and norms of an Indian village. Authority ultimately lay in the constant flow of talk, which regulated reputation through the variations of praise and ridicule, celebration and shaming. The close quarters of Indian villages kept few secrets and enforced moral norms by rendering individuals hypersensitive to their standing in the eyes of kin and neighbors. Humiliated and shunned, a thief or rapist could not endure in an observant, gossiping village. Consequently, theft and rape were virtually unknown among the Iroquois.[24]

The diffusion of power initially helped to frustrate meddling by colonial officials. Multiple factions linked in varying ways to rival outsiders gave Indians options, especially in war. Only after the American Revolution, when

Indian Council at Johnson Hall, by E. L. Henry. (Courtesy of the Albany Institute of History and Art.)

settler numbers surged to envelop the Iroquois, did the diffusion of power become an Indian liability. Thereafter, factionalism provided multiple entry points for state officials to divide and conquer: to secure land cessions by playing off warriors against chiefs, one village against another, women against men, or one chief against another. Once a paradoxical source of strength against outsiders, the dispersion of power later became a grave weakness.[25]

COUNCILS

During the mid eighteenth century, the Six Nations sustained a tenuous alliance with the British colonists of New York. Known as "the Covenant Chain," the alliance bore different meanings for the two sides. Some wishful officials described the Iroquois as dependent wards who submitted their domains to imperial sovereignty in return for British protection and presents. This view imagined the Covenant Chain as a vertical hierarchy where superior Britons commanded and protected the inferior Indians. The Iroquois, however, insisted upon a horizontal alliance of equal brethren. As they saw it, far from creating an obligation for the Iroquois, the colonial gifts paid a partial recompense for the great advantages that colonists reaped from their Indian allies, who provided a valuable trade in furs and who had long screened Pennsylvania and New York from French attack.[26]

To maintain the Covenant Chain, the Iroquois attended councils hosted by colonial leaders. Our knowledge of Indian thoughts and motives largely depends on their council speeches recorded in surprising detail by colonial secretaries. But how reliably "Indian" are these English words? Because the officials employed the interpreters and kept the written record, much Indian nuance got lost in colonial translation. Among the Iroquois, only the Mohawks seem to have had an extensive familiarity with English. And the Mohawks shared the Iroquois conviction that ceremonial occasions, including councils, required Indians to speak precisely in an especially formal version of their traditional languages. Indeed, the Indians usually demanded that a colonist act as an interpreter, as a mark of colonial respect, and as a concession to native sensibilities.[27]

Most colonial interpreters were low-status men who learned a native language either as traders or as adolescents captured and adopted by Indians during war but returned to colonial society in peace. At the Albany council of 1754, a British official complained, "As to the Interpreting, tis most extream bad; at best the Interpreter is a most extream stupid, ignorant & illeterate Person."[28]

Despite the problems with translation and the bias in recording, the best council minutes operate in metaphoric tropes and to a repetitive and ritualistic rhythm evidently defined by Indians because so utterly unlike other forms of colonial writing. And comparing speeches from a common native speaker at multiple councils over the years reveals ideas and styles consistent with a distinctive personality. Where Chief Hendrick (a Mohawk) spoke bluntly, Thomas King (an Oneida) proceeded with tactful circumspection. None of this individual variation (but consistency for each) would characterize their voices if the record was no more than a colonial concoction. Moreover, the Indian speeches often conveyed sentiments unpalatable to colonial leaders, including some eloquent rebukes. By keeping such a full—and often inconvenient—record, officials tried to make sense of Indians. Colonial officials often needed to convey to distant superiors the difficulties of Indian diplomacy and, indeed, the impossibility of governing natives by imperial command. If read with care, a council record usually provides revealing approximations of Indian thoughts.[29]

Indians expected the colonists to respect the natives' ceremonial forms for intertribal diplomacy. Sticklers for tradition, the Indians resented and resisted deviations pressed by hasty officials. Far from feeling inferior in the colonial presence, the Iroquois conveyed utter assurance in their public bearing. One astonished colonist grumbled, "It is really surprizeing to see what an assuming behaviour those Savages put on whilst in Council. . . . smoking with such a confident air of Dignity & Superiority as if they were above all other beings mad[e] and their Authority extended over the whole Earth." A council was their stage.[30]

In contrast to impatient officials, who wanted quickly to get to their point and who stressed a concluding document—the treaty—the Iroquois emphasized the slow process of discussion. From an oral culture, the Iroquois recognized but distrusted the power of written documents. Much harsh experience taught them that colonial writing misrepresented their agreements and stole their lands. To impress memories, Indians preferred the methodical and rhythmic repetition of shared sentiments and histories expressed through prolonged rituals and speeches.[31]

Discounting the power of any document to sustain an alliance, the Indians instead insisted upon orally exchanging the proper words within a ceremonial format to renew a mutual frame of mind. To sustain a peaceful understanding, Indians wanted frequent councils with their British allies, as Johnson noted:

It is highly necessary to convene them in order to repeat their engagements and recommend their observance. This practice, so necessary amongst people who have no letters, is strictly observed by them with one another, and the neglect of it is always considered by them as a disregard to the Treatys themselves.

Without frequent meetings to manifest goodwill, allies would fall prey to evil, contentious, and jealous thoughts, the work of malign spirits.[32]

Colonial officials hosted most of the councils and bore the responsibility of feeding and giving drink to their Indian guests, who usually came by the hundreds—men, women, and children. Given their oral and consensual culture, the Iroquois regarded mass attendance as essential. As witnesses, the warriors and matrons kept chiefs reasonably honest, affirmed their words, and subsequently remembered their collective commitments. Councils also served a didactic function, reiterating key memories and core principles to a younger generation of Indians. A colonial officer explained, "Here they learn the History of their Nation; here they are inflamed with the songs of those who celebrate the Warlike Actions of their Ancestors; and here they are taught what are the interests of their country, & how to pursue them." An Iroquois nation became manifest in mass attendance at a council, where the Indians reproduced their culture.[33]

By arriving slowly and prolonging their speeches and intermissions, the Indians set a deliberate pace, to the frustration of colonial officials. A Quaker observer, James Emlen, noted, "*Time*, the most precious thing in the World, is held with them in little estimation." Initially impatient, Emlen gradually adjusted, concluding, "Perhaps no people are greater masters of their time, hence in their public transactions we often complain of their being tedious, not considering that they & we estimate time with very different judgments." But Emlen did not have to pay the mounting council bills. In 1773, Johnson hosted a council that lasted eighteen days at a cost of £538.2.4 (sterling) to feed and clothe 268 Indians.[34]

Attending Indians ate massive quantities, for they gorged during times of abundance to store calories against periods of scarcity. Officials calculated that at councils an Indian ate twice as much per day as did a colonist. Consuming much food paid Indian respect to colonial productivity, while colonial generosity paid proper tribute to the military importance of their Indian allies. Indians also brought their broken guns and tools to procure repairs at their host's expense. Given the material benefits, natives tended to prolong the proceedings, testing the patience of their hosts. The generous, patient, and imperturbable host rose in estimation as he confirmed his respect for Indian allies.[35]

Upon arriving at the council fire, the visitors entered in ceremonial procession. In welcome, the host conducted the "At the Wood's Edge" ritual, ushering them out of the chaotic world of the forest and into the ordered stability of the council ground. In patient succession, the host cleared eyes, ears, and throats of dust so that the visitors could watch patiently, listen carefully, and speak freely in the coming days. After at least a night's rest, the formal council began with a condolence ceremony that acknowledged recent losses to death, especially of prominent chiefs or colonial officials. The ceremony metaphorically covered graves, dried tears, and cleansed minds of grief, so that all could think and speak peacefully in the coming days.[36]

Only after these preliminaries could a polite host propose substantial business, with each proposal accompanied by a string or belt of wampum passed across the council fire to an Indian spokesman. Made of many small seashell or glass tubes strung in patterns of alternating dark and light color, wampum represented the interplay of death and life, of war and peace. As a sacred substance, wampum confirmed the earnest importance of a message. Without accompanying wampum, words were frivolous.[37]

Devoted to deliberation, the Indians declined any definitive answer to a proposition until at least the next day. No Indian spokesman could make commitments without first consulting his people. Chosen for their eloquence, Iroquois spokesmen were not necessarily the most powerful of their people—although colonists often misunderstood this. Overnight, the attending Iroquois caucused to frame a reply for their spokesman to deliver the following day. Carefully addressing each colonial proposition, the speaker returned the appropriate strings or belts of wampum in proper succession. Only then could the Indian guests introduce their own points, which the colonial hosts were supposed to consider overnight before replying. Such methodical exchanges consumed days and often weeks, for Indians offered polite evasions whenever they could not reach a consensus. Witnessing their deft equivocations, Thomas Pownall remarked, "for the address & management of it, these People, tho we are apt to think them savages & so on, do actually exceed the Europeans."[38]

At the public sessions, colonial officials sat on one side on chairs, with a table for their secretary; the Indians sat on the other, in a big half circle, either on benches or on the ground. Sachems and war chiefs sat in front, with the common warriors and matrons in the back. Colonial speakers ordinarily read from a text while native orators performed more dramatically and extemporaneously, pacing and gesturing while modulating tone and volume. Those skills awed colonial witnesses, astonished at how much they could intuit from an Indian orator's delivery and manner. They often faulted interpreters for failing to capture the majesty and subtlety of an Indian speech.[39]

Both sides employed kinship terms to convey their connection and relative power. Some British officials tried to style themselves "fathers" dictating to Iroquois "children," but the chiefs insistently called the British their "brothers"—meaning their equals. At most, the Iroquois might call the British their "elder brothers," which gave a right to advise but not to command. But an elder brother also had an obligation to give more presents than he received. The Iroquois would, however, address the French as "fathers" because the French behaved more generously, by giving more gifts and by demanding less land than did the British. The Iroquois addressed weaker Indian peoples as "nephews," for in native families the most authoritative man was a mother's brother—an uncle—rather than the father. No good nephew ignored an uncle's advice.[40]

The Iroquois assigned honorific council names to colonial leaders. Attached to roles and invested with symbolic content, these names outlived individuals, passing through the generations. For example, during the 1640s, the Mohawks primarily dealt with a Dutch official, Arent van Curler. Subsequent governors of New Netherland and New York—Dutch and British—became "Corlaer" in councils. Later in that century, the Iroquois met William Penn, the founder of Pennsylvania, naming him Onas (their word for a quill pen). His eighteenth-century successors as governor of Pennsylvania also became Onas.[41]

The Iroquois idealized the original bearer of each name as a paragon of integrity, benevolence, and generosity. By applying such names, and reiterating their glowing reputations, the Iroquois worked to shape the conduct of latter-day governors. This practice expressed the Iroquois sense that history was patterned by repetition. By reiterating names and rituals, they hoped to maintain historical continuity by reproducing its reassuring patterns.[42]

To clarify meanings and assist memories, the Indians employed (and the officials adopted) a system of metaphors. Now rendered stale on dead pages, or distorted by bad Hollywood movies, this language once impressed colonial listeners as remarkably powerful and eloquent. By burying the hatchet in words and pantomime, speakers made peace, particularly if they rhetorically planted a tree to cover the hole. To clear a path meant restoring peaceful trade, while eating from the same bowl entailed sharing a land's resources. Bad birds, however, conveyed irresponsible news threatening to a peaceful understanding.[43]

The strictest decorum usually prevailed during the public sessions, but once a council adjourned for the day, the Indians blew off pent-up steam. Quiet and deliberative at midday, the council grounds became raucous at day's end, often with considerable encouragement from attending colonists. During lingering daylight, young Indian men engaged in a stick-and-ball game akin to lacrosse. Playing as nations, they competed for pride and for a mound of wampum, bracelets, earrings, and necklaces donated by their women or staked by colonial spectators, who marveled at the speed and agility of the competing warriors. In the evening, the Indians convened around bonfires to sing and dance to the rhythm of a drum augmented by sticks struck against posts. Periodically, an especially bold warrior would interrupt the dance to boast of his exploits in war, which then induced others to try to top him.[44]

During the night, colonial hosts privately convened smaller groups of influential chiefs to discuss matters more confidentially. Johnson explained that the public sessions were "a very small part of the Debates, Arguments & Discourses at the private Conferences where the principal Subjects are first Agitated & Determined upon." Private payments greased some cooperation. Thomas Pownall noted that the chiefs "must all be Closetted privately and experience very palpable and solid marks of our friendship for them, or all the Rest we do is doing nothing." Known as speaking "in the bushes," these private conclaves produced provisional agreements subject, however, to review by a caucus of the Indians, followed by formal presentation in public council the next day. Unfortunately, the host rarely recorded the private exchanges which were so critical to the results of a council.[45]

Chiefs delighted in procuring colonial presents, especially fine clothing and silver medals bearing the king's profile. A missionary described one Seneca chief returning from a council: "He was dressed in a scarlet coat turned up with lace, & a high gold laced hat, & made a martial appearance. He had a very sensible countenance & dignity of manners." In genteel attire, a chief displayed his special ability to extract resources from a colonial patron. And yet that clothing also came at a cost, for the colonial host expected some commitment or concession. In a constant cycle, chiefs sought authority within their village by displaying favors from external power. But every token of that favor also implicated the chief in an imperial system beyond Indian control.[46]

Ultimately, the colonial host expected the Indians to mark a concluding document—a treaty—that allegedly codified their understanding. These treaties committed them to assist the British in war or to provide the colonists with more land. Serving colonial interests, such treaties rarely captured Indian intentions with precision. In return for the Indian marks, the host gave a concluding feast accompanied by parting presents. The Indians expected sufficient gifts of cloth and clothing, blankets and bells, tools and weapons, pipes and tobacco, alcohol and jewelry, to provide for everyone attending—as well as for their sick and elderly kin left at home. The host also gave food and drink to sustain the Indians for their journey home—lest hungry Indians prey on the cattle and pigs of intervening settlers. Indians took the measure of their importance and of official sincerity in the quantity and quality of their gifts.[47]

Natives regarded presents as their just deserts for assisting the colonists, but British officials cast those gifts as obligating Indian obedience. In Johnson's words, presents were "His Majesty's bounty and Generosity to all those, who shall study to Deserve his Favor." Unable to agree on a common meaning for presents, the Iroquois and the officials nurtured a creative misunderstanding convenient to both parties.[48]

COVERING THE GRAVE

At German Flats in July 1761, Johnson met the Oneidas in council to deal with a murder. Three weeks earlier, an Oneida had killed a settler in circumstances that revealed the tense mixing of Indian and colonial cultures on the frontier. On the fatal day, about twenty-five Oneidas came to German Flats, seeking a Protestant minister to perform marriages and to baptize children. In celebration, most of the visitors got drunk on traders' rum. En route home, they shot and ate a settler's hog to sate their hunger. The Oneidas believed that the settlers owed them a subsistence in return for Indian lands taken without full payment. But the hog's owner and his son angrily protested. In the ensuing scuffle, an Oneida killed the son, Gustavus Frank, shot through his throat.[49]

The episode expressed the dangerous uncertainty of changing times. So long as the French governed Canada, the German Flats settlers needed Oneida friendship and, so, had to tolerate the occasional pilfered hog. But with Canada conquered, settlers perceived the dead swine as a crime rather than as a price for living in Indian country. They now asked, why should lazy Indians steal the hard-earned fruits of settler labor? In postwar perception, the land and the hogs became completely theirs, rather than partly the Indians' property. Settlers wanted a stricter separation—a clearer demarcation—of their property from Indian claims. But the Oneidas felt betrayed by settlers who had prospered on Indian land and who had been spoiled by military victory over the French. The settlers evidently cared more for their hogs than for their hungry "brethren." With the old rules of their relationship uncertain, the colonists and Oneidas looked to Sir William Johnson to handle the recent murder.

Because natives and newcomers frequently mingled in frontier settings that combined alcohol and weapons, they occasionally quarreled, fought, and killed. After a cross-cultural killing, the response of native chiefs and colonial officials determined whether the violence would escalate into war. To keep the peace, chiefs and officials needed to communicate that a particular homicide was an isolated, atypical event regretted by the killer's people. A violent death had to be mutually categorized and demarcated as a murder, lest it become the first casualty of a war. But whose law—colonial or Indian?—should bring closure to a cross-cultural murder?

British officials longed to impose their sovereignty by applying their law when colonists killed, or were killed by, Indians. Under British law, a murder required a formal trial followed upon conviction by a public execution. But nothing so appalled or alarmed Indians as the public hanging of one of their own people. Nothing more viscerally and immediately threatened Indian autonomy as a free people. To defend their sovereignty, Indians clung to their customary alternative: a ceremony known as "covering the grave."[50]

On July 7, 1761, Conoghquieson tried with ceremony and wampum to cover the grave of Gustavus Frank. The Oneida chief addressed Johnson by his Mohawk name, Warraghiyagey, which meant a man who conducts much important business:

> Brother Warraghiyagey: We are come hither to wipe away your tears, clear your speech, and condole with you for your late loss, & therefore, with this string, we clear the darkness from your Eyes, that you may see clearly, and look upon us as Brethren
> —Gave three Strings of Wampum.
> Brother, We are now assembled together to condole with you according to the antient Agreement between us, that whenever a like mischance should befall either of us, the other should condole with them on their loss, take the Axe out of their Heads, and Cover the deceased's grave so as to bury every thing in an Amicable manner, all [of] which we now perform, and hope it may be understood as we mean it
> —Gave a belt of 9 Rows of Wampum.
> Brother, We acknowledge ourselves extreamly concerned at the late Murder committed by one of our Nation; wherefore we now dig up that great Tree which reaches to the Clouds, beneath whose root runs a stream in which we will bury the late accident, so as it may never more be remembered, & hope that when you recollect that two of our Nation were some time ago murdered by one of your people, for which we never received any redress, you will be the readier induced to bury it in oblivion
> —[Gave] A belt of 9 Rows.

Conoghquieson warned that the Covenant Chain alliance lay in the balance, pending Johnson's acceptance of the wampum, which would end the controversy, preserving peace.[51]

The Iroquois customary law offered two alternatives: revenge killings or covering the grave. The Iroquois possessed neither the state apparatus nor the legal culture collectively to arrest, try, convict, and punish murder. They had no police, no courts, no jail, and no gallows. Instead, revenge belonged to the male relatives of the deceased. Those kin lost face as cowards, and suffered enduring anxiety, if they failed to secure blood revenge, for no spirit of the murdered could rest or give his (or her) kin peace until avenged.[52]

Ideally, the vengeful tracked down and dispatched the actual killer, who might flee but was expected to submit if found. The missionary David McClure saw a confronted Iroquois murderer calmly sit down to sing his death song while the avenger smoked a pipe for twenty minutes before plunging a tomahawk into the singer's skull. But if the original killer proved elusive, his kin might suffer the revenge. This, however, sparked a bloody cycle of further revenge.[53]

No chief could try and punish murderers. Indeed, such meddling made a chief a party to the blood feud, which eroded his prestige and persuasion. Rather than execute a murderer, the chiefs sought to restore harmony by persuading the kin of the dead to accept presents from the kin of the killer. Delivered in public ceremony, such gifts "covered the grave," obscuring the painful memory of the death. Accepting the presents forfeited the right to seek revenge.[54]

Murders involving a killer and killed from different nations were especially dangerous and called for special exertions by the chiefs of both peoples. Otherwise, the feud between families could escalate into a war between nations. During the fifteenth century, such bloody conflicts had nearly consumed the Iroquois nations, inducing them to form their confederacy, which primarily served to cover graves as an alternative to war.[55]

Natives insisted that their legal customs should govern their relationship with the colonists. Even when a settler killed an Indian, the chiefs preferred to cover the grave. Averse to capital punishment, they refused to cooperate with judicial process, urging clemency instead. In 1722, Pennsylvania's governor wanted to execute two colonists for murdering an Indian, but the Iroquois replied that "one life is enough to be lost." Needing Iroquois goodwill, the governor dropped the prosecution and liberated the killers.[56]

Indians hated the coercive instruments of colonial power—the jail, whip, and gallows—even when exercised on colonists. In 1757, Johnson pressed the Mohawks to reveal a colonist suspected of treasonous speech, but "it was, to no purpose, as they said the Man might be hanged." He later noted, "The Indians are so universally averse to our modes of Capital punishment that they would never stand to their Information even against an Enemy, much less a secret friend, from an Apprehension that the Parties must Suffer death." Guy Johnson added, "They are by no means fond of Punishment, and often beg our People, and the soldiers off for offenses committed against them." A missionary concluded, "The whole system of the laws of the white people appear to all free Indians (those not incorporated among white people) to be intolerable, not to say tyrannical. The very word law is odious to them."[57]

Indians found colonial legal proceedings confusing, pointless, and menacing. Although Indians executed enemies by torture (and killed suspected witches among their own people), they balked at assisting in the formal trial and execution of one of their colonial allies. Surely, the natives reasoned, the offended relatives of the executed man would seek revenge; or perhaps the process was a trick meant to provoke a war. The Indians also anticipated that such executions would enable colonial authorities to demand, as an equivalence, the power to try and execute any Indian who killed a colonist. In 1728 after executing two colonists for murdering natives, the governor of Pennsylvania boasted to an Iroquois delegation: "We & you are as one People; we treat you exactly as we do our own People." Although meant to reassure, these words appalled Indians who most assuredly did *not* want to be treated like colonists. In sum, the natives saw nothing to gain and everything to lose if the colonizers substituted executions for covering the grave.[58]

The colonists belonged to a more hierarchical culture that invested the government with the exclusive power to investigate, adjudicate, and punish murder. For colonial officials, only another death could bring closure to a murder; only the government could legitimately kill in revenge; and only after a formal, public, and adversarial process known as a trial. A government's authority became publicly manifest when and where it could try and punish criminals—thereby excluding the operation of private vengeance. The colonists regarded trials and executions as proof that they dwelled in a civilization rather than in savage anarchy. Dismissive of Indian customary law, colonial officials regarded the natives as legal savages.[59]

By imposing British law in cases of cross-cultural murder, colonial officials asserted their sovereignty over native peoples. But any chief who succumbed to imperial pressure and arrested fellow Indians for colonial execution, became, in native eyes, subject to assassination by the kinsmen of the executed. As a result, colonial demands for the surrender of murderers threatened to rupture Indian societies, obliging them to choose between internal strife and external war. For example, in 1759 the British governor of South Carolina provoked a war with the Cherokees by demanding the surrender of Indians accused of murder.[60]

In New York, the colonial officials long avoided legal confrontation with their indispensable allies, the Six Nations, lest they rebel to assist the French. Recognizing the limits of their power, the New Yorkers never judicially executed an Iroquois—despite several murders of colonists. Instead, both sides preserved the Covenant Chain by ceremonially covering the graves as Conoghquieson expected on July 7, 1761.[61]

Although Johnson had previously covered graves, this time he rejected Conoghquieson's wampum. For Johnson had to answer to the British commander in North America, General Jeffrey Amherst, a bullheaded officer with an exaggerated notion of British power. After the conquest of Canada eliminated the French competition, Amherst believed that the Indians had no choice but to accept British dictation. Rejecting Johnson's advice to cover the grave, Amherst instead ordered him to demand the Oneida suspect: "Had one of the Inhabitants Committed a Murder on one of the Indians, I should be for bringing that Inhabitant to Justice in like manner. This is my way of thinking in which I shall never alter."[62]

Johnson explained to the Oneidas that General Amherst did "not understand one Man's murdering another without suffering death for the same." The rules had changed—at least publicly. But Johnson was too shrewd to press the matter to a bloody confrontation. The Oneidas agreed in principle to surrender the suspect, but they regretted that he had fled to parts unknown—an obvious dodge. Rather than rupture the Covenant Chain, Johnson dropped the matter, without informing his commanding general.[63]

But Amherst's stubbornness soon provoked murder controversies with the powerful Senecas in the Genesee country and with the Ottawas, who dwelled near Detroit. In early 1763, those two nations rallied their far-flung Indian allies around the Great Lakes and in the Ohio Valley to mount a bloody rebellion. Called Pontiac's Rebellion, after a charismatic Ottawa chief, the uprising destroyed most of the British forts in Indian country and ravaged the frontier settlements of western Pennsylvania and Virginia.[64]

The rebellion discredited Amherst, who was recalled to England, while Johnson's reputation soared in imperial circles when his negotiations brought the expensive conflict to an end in 1764–1765. Both rebellion and peace vindicated Johnson's policies of treating the Indians, and especially the Iroquois, with relative respect and generosity. In making peace, Johnson overtly trumpeted the legal ideology of the British Empire, but he covertly understood the futility of enforcing it on autonomous Indians. He agreed with a British captain who recognized, "If they are hanged, the savages will look upon it as murder in cool blood, & revenge will ensue."[65]

The failure to impose British murder law also reflected settler resistance. The brutal frontier war hardened animosities along racial lines. Outraged by bloody Indian raids, the Pennsylvania settlers treated all natives, regardless of behavior, as violent brutes best exterminated. In the most notorious episode, in December 1763, armed vigilantes known as the Paxton Boys, surprised their peaceful neighbors, the Conestoga Indians, butchering men, women, and children—and burning their village for good measure.[66]

Johnson's restoration of peace made little difference to the settlers who continued to murder Indians on the frontiers of Pennsylvania and Virginia. Often the victims were Iroquois venturing south to hunt or to trade. Colonial authorities sometimes arrested the murderers, but they almost always escaped punishment. Either mobs broke open jails, or jailers permitted escapes, or jurors refused to convict, in the belief that killing an Indian should be rewarded rather than punished.[67]

Unable to hang their own people, British officials could not hang Indians. Obliged to cover Indian graves, officials had to accept Indian wampum to cover the graves of murdered traders in native country. To defuse conflict, Johnson repeatedly crafted resolutions that saved British face and Indian lives. By procuring the surrender of the Indian suspects, he satisfied the majesty of British law, but on a tacit promise that they would be pardoned, fulfilling Indian expectation. As a further inducement, Johnson rewarded cooperative chiefs with presents, after they endured a pompous speech declaring that in the future, "we would punish with death, every Offender." But that future awaited the next generation.[68]

ALLIES

By covering graves, Johnson conceded that the Iroquois retained a sovereignty begrudged by other British officials. In August 1765, the attorney general of New York, John Tabor Kempe, assured Johnson that aboriginal sovereignty and land title counted for almost nothing in the English law. Kempe insisted, "Wheresoever the King's Dominions extend, he is the Fountain of all Property in Lands, and to deny that Right in the Crown in any Place is in Effect denying his Right to rule there." For Kempe, all of Iroquoia lay within New York, which put the natives entirely within the king's dominion. By sovereign right, Kempe argued, the king's officers could grant frontier land to colonists without Indian consent. Only policy and indulgence—rather than law—induced officials to require paying something to the Indians to give up their mere possession.[69]

In reply, Johnson argued that Iroquoia lay outside of New York's legal jurisdiction because the Iroquois were sovereign allies, rather than subjected peoples:

> I grant it is the policy of our Constitution that Where-so-ever the King's Dominions extend, he is the fountain of all property in Lands, &c. But how can this be made to Extend to the native rights of a people whose

property none of our Kings have claimed a right to invade, & to whom
the Laws have never Extended without which Dominion cannot be said
to be Exercised[?]

Citing some council records, Kempe retorted that the Iroquois had submitted their lands to British rule, becoming British subjects. But Johnson had
attended some of those councils, and he knew that the colonial secretaries
had inserted words never spoken by the Iroquois: "It is necessary to observe
that no Nation of Indians have any word which can express, or convey the
Idea of Subjection." The British commander, General Thomas Gage, agreed,
"As for the Six Nations having acknowledged themselves subjects of the
English, that I conclude must be a very gross mistake and am well satisfied
were they told so, . . . they would on such an attempt very soon resolve to cut
our Throats." So long as the Iroquois sustained warriors, they clung to their
status as allies and resented definition as colonial subjects.[70]

Johnson doubted that Indians could obtain justice as British subjects in
colonial America. Neither the common law courts nor an elected assembly
would protect Indians from fraud and dispossession. In part, the problem
was formal: Indians could not prevail in courts that required written documents and that discounted native testimony as unreliable. And in part, the
problem was substantive: private interest induced assemblymen, councillors,
judges, lawyers, and jurors to deny aboriginal land rights. As an alternative,
Johnson sought the authority "to do the Indians Justice in a Summary wary."
No friend to colonial republicanism, Johnson supported the British Empire's
efforts to tighten control over the restive colonies. As he saw it, Indians
would always suffer from any American government elected by farmers and
led by land speculators.[71]

LAND

Far from providing free land to settlers, colonial governors awarded immense
tracts to wealthy speculators who then profited by retailing, or renting,
smaller parcels to the settlers whose labor made farms. Most colonial fortunes depended upon the real estate appreciation produced by frontier
expansion, Indian dispossession, and settler farm-building. This land system
sustained an unequal distribution of political power, for only grandees
favored by royal governors and their councils could win grants to thousands
of frontier acres to enhance their wealth. Once procured, these large land
grants enjoyed vigorous legal protection from judges and lawyers, who
almost always belonged to the great landholding families.[72]

Colonists thought of natives as wild, roaming hunters with no specific attachments to, or ownership of, any particular place. In 1764, the New York Assembly deemed it "impossible to discover the true Owners of any Lands among unlettered Barbarians, who keep no certain Memorials; Have very indistinct Notions of Private Property; Live by Hunting; Use no Landmarks; Nor have any Inclosures." Colonial ideology systematically obscured Indian cultivation and Indian villages, and the intimate Indian understanding of fishing, hunting, and gathering places.[73]

The Iroquois marked their ownership on the land in forms that colonists dismissed as "savage." The Iroquois country was full of ancient earthen fortifications and burial mounds that marked abandoned towns from a populous past before Indian decimation by epidemic diseases introduced from Europe. Every passing Indian also added a stone to heaps at certain sacred spots. The Iroquois painted prominent rocks, carved trees, and erected posts to mark an important path, the grave of a celebrated warrior, or the site of some great accomplishment in hunting or war. In Seneca country, a traveler reported:

On one large tree I saw an Indian painting, that had been recently done. The figures were Indians, bows and arrows, and deer with arrows pierced through the neck. The colours were chiefly black and red, upon the white ground of the tree where the bark was taken off.

The natives employed a few well-understood pictographs of clan, animals, enemies, and trophies to tell stories of victory and possession.[74]

One of the most famous Iroquois paintings covered a lofty, smooth rock overlooking the Mohawk River. With a red ochre, the Mohawks depicted "a canoe, with seven warriors in it." To maintain its special importance, the Mohawks annually refreshed the painting, even persisting for a generation after the revolution, when they lost their homeland to the Americans. By renewing the painting, the Mohawks signified their continuing cultural possession of the land in defiance of the property laws of their American conquerors.[75]

In 1769, in New York's portion of the Susquehanna Valley, an unusually perceptive traveler, a Quaker named Richard Smith, noted the pervasive signs of Indian occupation. He described striking Indian graves: "One of them was a flat Pyramid of about 3 feet high trenched round, another was platted like a tomb and a third something like our Form." At the juncture of the Unadilla and Susquehanna rivers, Smith saw a large cairn of stones that colonists called "the Indian monument." In the woods, he encountered "deer fences": brush heaped for hundreds of yards to funnel deer driven toward waiting hunters. To facilitate hunting, the Iroquois also shaped a forest of large trees, scant brush, and abundant berries by seasonally setting fire to the undergrowth. Smith recognized what escaped most colonists: a landscape densely marked with native possession.[76]

An Indian domain was far more than an undifferentiated, collective property (as many colonists then believed and as some scholars today assume). On the contrary, the natives had an intricate subset of differential rights to particular places, although their system remains largely opaque because so rarely discerned by colonists. In reply to the New York Assembly, Johnson noted:

> That it is a difficult matter *to discover a true owner of any Lands amongst Indians* is a gross error. . . . Each Nation is perfectly well acquainted with their exact original bounds, the same is again divided into due proportions for each Tribe, and afterwards subdivided into shares to each family, with all [of] which they are most particularly acquainted, neither do they ever infringe upon one another, or invade their neighbours' hunting grounds.

Particular clans (called "tribes" by Johnson) or family lineages held rights to *use* particular alluvial flats and specific streams or watersheds for tilling, fishing, and hunting, year after year and often generation after generation.[77]

But Indian possession was more limited than the colonial mode of exclusive private property. The native ethos of generosity obliged native families to share any abundance with kin and friends in greater need. And native possessors did not own places as commodities for potential sale to others. Only the chiefs convened in public council could legitimately sell any land—and only with the permission of warriors and (especially) matrons. Particular in use, native land became communal in sale.[78]

Indians also had precise notions of their national boundaries. Often an Indian people would share access with another in good diplomatic standing as fictive kin, such as the common rights of the Tuscaroras in Oneida country. But uninvited hunting declared war. The missionary David McClure observed: "To destroy the game of the territory of another nation is, in their view, as much a violation of property, as it would be deemed among us, should one farmer take possession of the land of his neighbour & cultivate it, or carry off part of his harvest."[79]

During the 1760s and early 1770s, the Mohawks of the valley and those of Kahnawake (near Montreal) disputed the intervening hunting territory in the Adirondacks. The valley Mohawks demanded that their Canadian brethren pay a rent of one deer per hunter when they intruded south of Crown Point (on Lake Champlain). In protest, the Kahnawake Mohawks insisted upon a long-standing agreement to share their hunting grounds as "common, and free to one nation as to another, in the same manner as a large Dish of Meat would be to a Company of People." Called upon to mediate, Sir William Johnson favored his old friends the valley Mohawks by instructing the Kahnawakes: "You should abide by your old Limits."[80]

Encroaching settlers depleted the wild resources that Indians relied upon. The newcomers competed for favorite fishing spots, while their roaming livestock consumed wild roots, berries, and nuts. Settlers cut down the forest, curtailing habitat for wildlife, and colonial hunters killed deer and bear faster than they could reproduce. In 1768, Conoghquieson complained to Johnson: "When our Young men wanted to go a hunting the Wild Beasts in our Country they found it covered with fences, so that they were weary crossing them. Neither can they get Venison to Eat, or Bark to make huts, for the Beasts are run away and the Trees cut down."[81]

By killing an occasional pig or calling at colonial farms for bread and meat, the Indians sought shares in settler produce as recompense for the prosperity that colonists reaped from lands procured for a bottle and a song. In alienating land, the Indians sought a long-term, symbiotic relationship with particular settlers. Indians anticipated enduring benefits from helping farmers who should then feed their Indian benefactors when hungry. Johnson noted, "The Grand design of all Indians in such Grants or Cessions is to purchase a better treatment, i.e., provisions sometimes, & a few presents." The Mohawk chief Hendrick more fully explained:

> Let us all be as Brethren as well after as before [our] giving you Deeds for Land. After We have sold our Land We in a little time have nothing to Shew for it; but it is not so with You, Your Grandchildren will get something from it as long as the World stands; our Grandchildren will have no advantage from it; They will say We were Fools for selling so much Land for so small a matter and curse Us; therefore let it be a Part of the present Agreement that We shall treat one another as Brethren to the latest Generation, even after We shall not have left a Foot of Land.

Productive settlers would endure on Indian lands longer than the sale money would last in Indian hands. Let the farmers, then, treat the Iroquois as brethren, generation after generation, feeding the hungry and clothing the ragged. The chiefs understood a land deed as their gift that, by its one-sidedness, created a perpetual debt for the settlers.[82]

By farming the farmers, the Indians hoped to persist within a settler world without adopting colonial gender roles, which required common men to till the fields. Determined to preserve the male role as hunters and warriors, the Mohawks and Oneidas sought farm produce as a sort of rent from colonists. By obligating settlers for Indian land, the natives hoped to reap the productivity of colonial agriculture without themselves succumbing to the drudgery, dishonor, and emasculation that they associated with farming by men.

Indians insisted that they sold only a partial land tenure, *not* a complete and exclusive freehold that entirely deprived them of lingering rights in the premises. They claimed an enduring access to hunt, fish, and gather and to solicit food relief from the new occupants. Where Indians were numerous and powerful, settlers grudgingly accepted the native interpretation of land tenure. But the newcomers longed to substitute their more complete notion of private property that defined returning Indians as trespassers.[83]

During the 1760s, settlers in the Mohawk Valley began to forget their lingering obligations for past land sales. Growing settler numbers and the British conquest of Canada afforded a sense of military security that denied generosity to Indians. Now insisting that Indian land sales had been one-time commercial transactions paid in full, the colonists treated visiting, hungry Indians with contempt as idle beggars, as presumptuous parasites on industrious farmers. In 1767, Johnson reported that "the Inhabitants would not give [the Mohawks] a Morsel since the War, which the Indians thought very hard, they having promised them formerly (when they sold and gave them lands) that they shou'd always be welcome to the Houses, passing and repassing."[84]

Dismayed by stingy and insulting settlers, the Mohawks began to lease some of their land rather than selling it. Leases rendered explicit the Mohawk expectation that settlers would continue to feed Indians—or face eviction. The valley Mohawks cited the precedent of their Kahnawake kin, who prospered by leasing farms to French settlers. By paying a rent in provisions, the leases served the Iroquois goal of pinning down colonists as their agricultural providers—and of saving native men from that fate. Henry R. Schoolcraft later noted:

Adverse to agricultural labor, and always confounding it with slavery, or some form of servitude, at least deeming it derogatory, the first effort of the Iroquois to advance from their original corn-field and garden of beans and vines, is connected with the letting out of their spare lands to white men, who were cast on the frontiers, to cultivate, receiving for it some low remuneration in kind or otherwise, by way of rent. This system, it is true, increased a little their means of subsistence, but nourished their native pride and indolence. It seems to have been particularly a practice of the Iroquois.

Best of all, leases preserved aboriginal title—in contrast to the deeds of cession, which permanently alienated the land into colonial possession.[85]

Colonial grandees worried that native leasing would create a harmony of interest between Indians and poor whites. Indeed, the Mohawks offered better rental terms—cheap and in produce rather than cash—than those charged by New York's or Pennsylvania's great landlords, who feared losing tenants to Indian lease lands. And if poor whites became allies, rather than thorns, to the Indians, the colonial rulers would lose a key pressure that induced natives to sell their lands cheaply and permanently. In sum, Indian leasing alarmed the colonial elite as a double threat: to their designs on Indian lands and to their control over common whites. Conrad Weiser warned Pennsylvania's proprietors that the Iroquois had begun to lease land to poor settlers who "pay them yearly Sums for their Lycence to be there." Weiser warned that "the Proprietors will not only have all the abandoned People of the Province to deal with but the Indians too and . . . they will mutually support each other and do a vast deal of Mischief."[86]

When the Mohawks did sell (rather than lease) land, they drove harder bargains. In 1771, Johnson observed, "The Indians in proportion as their possessions decrease in Quantity raise the price of the rest, and discover much more Interest and Cunning in these matters than they did a few years Since."

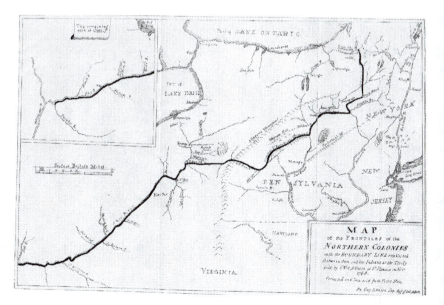

The Fort Stanwix Boundary Line of 1768, by Guy Johnson. (Courtesy of the New York State Library.)

Johnson concluded that the Mohawks had "greater notions of property" and were "better Judges of the Value of Lands than heretofore."[87]

Whether selling or leasing, the Mohawks favored those deemed most reliable and generous—which generally meant Johnson and his friends. Benefiting from their favor, Johnson defended their selectivity: "If the Indians are allowed to be the proprietors of their Lands. . . . They certainly can give the preference to whom they like."[88]

Although Johnson certainly exploited his office to procure Indian lands, his methods compared favorably with other land speculators. Most got a few Indians drunk to procure a surreptitious deed without proper translation, and then they failed to pay its terms, while using creative surveys to inflate the bounds. In sharp contrast, Johnson procured his deeds by dealing publicly and soberly with entire village councils assisted by an interpreter and notarized by a justice. And he scrupulously made his promised payments (although he was not above abusing surveys).[89]

More than the naïve victims of traditional accounts, the Mohawks adapted resourcefully to the colonial pressure for land. By leasing land or selling for higher prices to selected customers with an enduring sense of obligation, the Mohawks sought to preserve their autonomy and enhance their prosperity within a land transformed by growing numbers of settlers.

THE LINE OF PROPERTY

As early as 1758, Johnson proposed establishing a comprehensive, imperial boundary running through all the provinces to demarcate colonial from Indian territory. He sought "a solemn public Treaty to agree upon clear & fixed Boundaries between our Settlements & their Hunting Grounds, so that each Party may know their own & be a mutual Protection to each other of their respective Possessions." Renewing this proposal in 1763, Johnson insisted that a boundary line would curb the dispersed settlements and excessive speculation in Indian lands. It would, he vowed, "encourage the thick settlement of the Frontiers, oblige the Proprietors of large grants to get them Inhabited, and secure the Indians from being further deceived by many who make a practice of imposing on a few Indians with liquor and fair promises to sign Deeds." In sum, a negotiated boundary was supposed neatly to separate the colonists from the Indians, making it easier for Sir William Johnson to control their relationship.[90]

Under the pressure of Pontiac's Rebellion, the Crown embraced Johnson's concept by adopting the famous Royal Proclamation of 1763. Promulgated in October in London, the proclamation sought to mollify the Indian rebels by restraining the colonists from settling or speculating in lands west of the Appalachian Mountains. That prohibition reserved the Ohio Valley and Great Lakes watershed as an Indian country administered by the British military. Within the existing colonies, the proclamation forbade land purchases directly from Indians by speculators. Instead such transactions had to be supervised by the royal governors or the Indian superintendent.[91]

But the Royal Proclamation quickly proved unenforceable. Some settlers and many land grants had already breached the Proclamation Line, especially in western Pennsylvania and western Virginia. During 1763, Indian rebels killed or expelled the intruders, but they returned in swollen numbers after the war. In 1767, British troops tried to remove squatters in western Pennsylvania by burning their cabins, but that experiment failed because the lands were fertile and the flimsy cabins could be quickly rebuilt. And the colonial governments failed to prosecute settlers who trespassed on Indian lands. General Thomas Gage considered "the driving [of] the Settlers off the Lands and destroying a parcel of vile Hutts, to be of little use, for they meet with no Punishment and return again in greater Numbers."[92]

To adjust the Proclamation Line and enhance its legitimacy, Johnson pressed his superiors for the authority and the money to hold a major council, primarily with the Six Nations. Some Iroquois chiefs hoped that a comprehensive boundary would be worth a substantial land cession in the short term. In 1765, the Oneida chief Thomas King proposed:

> Let us make a Line for the benefit of our Children, that they may have lands which can't be taken from them, and let us in doing that shew the King that we are Generous, and that we will leave Him land enough for his people. Then he will regard us, and take better care that his people do not cheat us.

From an Iroquois perspective, the key in all land transactions was to improve their relationship with powerful neighbors. In the king, they detected the consummate patron. Please the king and he would protect the rest of their lands from the colonists. This Indian conviction fed on the council speeches of imperial officials who extolled the "Great King" as the personification of perfect justice, pure power, and consummate generosity.[93]

Johnson played his usual double game, pitching the boundary to the Crown as an Indian idea, while assuring the Indians that the king expected their cooperation. Johnson promised the Indians "a Considerable Present," while he assured his superiors that the Indians would yield up "large tracts" of land beyond the 1763 Proclamation Line. By brokering this exchange of resources, Johnson sought to strengthen his position as the pivotal intermediary between the colonial and the native peoples. While assuring Indians that the boundary would perpetuate their domains, he also promised his superiors, "I can at any time hereafter perswade them to cede to His Majesty more land." Here was his key: a negotiated boundary would make Johnson the indispensable man for procuring Indian land, present and future.[94]

General Gage, however, doubted the wisdom and efficacy of making a comprehensive boundary line given the long, sordid record of colonists invading Indian lands with impunity. Gage concluded, "I am fully convinced that the Boundary Lines never will be observed. The Frontier People are too Numerous, too Lawless and Licentious ever to be restrained." Moreover, "the new Lands would of Course be very soon disposed of to People of Interest, and perhaps in large patents; so that Lands being still dear, the People would have the same Temptation as they have now to emigrate beyond the Boundary." The elite domination of large land grants and the pervasive yearning by common people for homesteads combined to push settlers into Indian country, provoking violence. Given that persistent American tension, Gage opposed squandering British money on a massive Indian council to produce a pointless boundary.[95]

Of course, Johnson was one of those "People of Interest" who expected to reap thousands of acres from a land cession. He needed to extend the boundary westward to legitimize his own land grants from the Mohawks and Oneidas: 130,000 acres along the Charlotte River (a tributary of the Susquehanna) and tracts of 80,000 and 127,000 acres in the upper Mohawk Valley. To sustain his political "interest," Johnson also needed to take care of his powerful friends in high places. He sought to secure Pennsylvania lands for that colony's proprietor, Thomas Penn, and Ohio Valley lands for a set of Philadelphia merchants engaged in the Indian trade. These merchants possessed considerable clout in London, through their lobbyist Benjamin Franklin, and among the Indians, through Johnson's deputy, George Croghan.[96]

In early 1768, the Lords of Trade authorized Johnson to negotiate a comprehensive boundary for the northern colonies "without loss of time." The lords entrusted the southern extension to Johnson's southern counterpart, Colonel John Stuart. A boundary would, Lord Hillsborough hoped, "be finally settled upon such a lasting Basis, as may restore mutual confidence and prevent those abuses of which the Indians have too much reason to complain." Such was the magic promise of a comprehensive boundary: permanently to fix the chronic instability of a violent frontier. Of course, the Royal Proclamation of 1763 had made the same futile promise.[97]

On October 24 at Fort Stanwix, Johnson opened the grand boundary congress with 3,102 Indians in attendance: an unprecedented gathering of natives. Three-quarters were Iroquois, and most of the rest were their purported dependents: Chugnuts, Conoys, Delawares, Minisinks, Nanticokes,

Shawnees, and Tutelos. Of course, Johnson could not publicly negotiate land business with such a diverse throng. After the daily, public, ceremonial meetings en masse, he conducted nocturnal, private meetings at his quarters with the most influential chiefs. In his final accounting, Johnson recorded giving £571 (sterling) in "Private presents to the principal Sachems . . . & to the Chieftains in Cash."[98]

Despite his gifts, Johnson faced hard bargaining with the chiefs. He argued that a large land cession would please the Great King and enable the boundary to endure: "I expect that your Resolutions will be advantageous to us, & that you will make proper allowance for the increase of our People, whereby you will recommend yourselves to the King, and become so pleasing to his subjects that it will greatly contribute to the due observance of the Boundary Line." The chiefs, however, sought a more eastern boundary that kept the colonists far from their villages. Johnson noted that his "difficulties encreased in proportion as we went to the Northward and Came near the Settlements of the Six Nations."[99]

The greatest opposition came from the Oneidas, who felt most directly threatened by Johnson's pressure for a land cession. He especially coveted the nearby portage, which would soar in commercial value once settlers replaced Indians on the upper Mohawk River. Johnson had already begun to plan a mile-long canal across the portage to enhance its commercial potential.[100]

But the Oneida chiefs wanted to retain the portage for their own commercial exploitation. By keeping horses and carts to haul traders' goods for fees, they could earn money to compensate for the declining returns from their hunting. When confronted with Indian schemes to modernize their economic life, Johnson responded with a mix of incredulity and alarm. On the one hand, he dismissed the Oneidas as incapable of conducting a new business. On the other hand, he certainly did not want them to try, lest they succeed, keeping the portage to themselves and out of colonial hands. Playing his trump card, Johnson warned the Oneidas that they risked alienating the Great King. In this particular confrontation, we find a general pattern; by stereotyping Indians as naïve primitives, colonial officials frustrated native attempts to exploit the commercial value of their land. Johnson protected Indians but only from other colonists and only so long as the natives did not aspire to manage their own property in a commercial society.[101]

In a late-night compromise, on October 31, the Oneida chiefs permitted the boundary to run from the Susquehanna River north up the Unadilla River to the juncture of Canada Creek with Wood Creek, about eight miles west of Fort Stanwix. Unable to agree with Johnson on a northern terminus to the boundary, the Oneidas left it incomplete beyond Fort Stanwix, which enabled them to share the portage with the colonists. "This was the Utmost

I could get them to consent to," Johnson concluded. For their concessions, the Oneidas procured an additional $1,000 beyond their share in the general distribution of presents. Shortly after the treaty, Johnson wrote to a partner in land speculation, Goldsbrow Banyar: "I do assure You that the greatest trouble & difficulty I met with was to bring the Oneidaes to allow the Line to run any farther West than Oriskane Creek. This engaged All my interest & Influence [for] three Days & almost 3 Nights."[102]

The Oneida compromise at the northern end of the boundary enabled Johnson to close a deal for the southern end with the other Iroquois chiefs. Johnson agreed to minimize the land cession in Iroquoia while increasing it in the Ohio Valley. By selling distant lands, the Iroquois protected their own homeland, shifting colonial speculators and settlers into a more southern channel that victimized other Indians. On a larger scale, this reflected the long-standing Iroquois practice of making land cessions in Pennsylvania at the expense of their Indian dependents, particularly the Shawnees and Delawares. Recently relocated to the Ohio Valley, they were again made to pay to screen Iroquoia from settler pressure.[103]

Known as "the Line of Property," the new boundary extended only a modest distance beyond New York's settlements but then bulged westward across Pennsylvania and then down the Ohio River as far as the mouth of the Tennessee River. This added the southwestern quarter of Pennsylvania, all of present-day West Virginia, and most of Kentucky to the colonial domain. The bulge provided lands for Johnson's friends, the Philadelphia merchants and George Croghan. The treaty reserved the Mohawk villages of Canajoharie and Tiononderoge and the Oneida village of Oriske as Indian enclaves on the colonial side of the boundary.[104]

Johnson anticipated a future day when the Iroquois would again meet their superintendent to cede more land in another boundary treaty. But the Iroquois spokesman maintained "that no further attempts shall be made on our Lands, but that this Line be considered as final." The Six Nations also insisted upon the right to hunt on the ceded land while denying that colonists could cross the line to pursue game in Indian country.[105]

On November 5, 1768, the Iroquois sachems signed the treaty. Johnson then distributed presents and cash worth £10,460.7.3 (sterling): a massive and unprecedented payment from colonists to Indians. An attending colonist marveled at

the greatest Quantity of Indian Goods and Dollars I ever saw on such an occasion, and they were most judiciously displayed on the Parade [Ground] of the Fort, so that all the Indians might see Them and in the Center of the Parade, circumscribed by the Goods and Dollars on *three*

Sides, [sat] Sir William attended by the Governor of the Jerseys, the Commissioners from Virginia and Pennsylvania, &c., and the Indian Chiefs.

Johnson and his entourage carefully departed before the next morning, when his assistants delivered the concluding rum.[106]

The Fort Stanwix Treaty expressed Johnson's core conviction that the Covenant Chain alliance was essential to British colonial power. In letters and reports to his superiors, Johnson promoted the mystique of the Iroquois as the master warriors and consummate diplomats of North America. And he defined the Mohawks as the most savvy and respected of the Iroquois. According to Johnson, they swayed the Six Nations confederacy, which, in turn, dominated a chain of Indian relationships that reached north into Canada and west into the Ohio Valley and the Great Lakes country. Please the Mohawks and you could control the continent, so he argued. Of course, only Johnson could please the Mohawks—and only if he enjoyed a free hand and a lavish budget for presents. Through repetition the mystique became real in Johnson's mind, and in the opinions of his elite correspondents who shaped imperial policy in London.[107]

But the Iroquois mystique was an increasingly dangerous illusion. At Fort Stanwix the Six Nations sold Ohio Valley lands belonging to Delawares, Shawnees, and Mingos. Infuriated by the cession, they vowed to fight any attempt to settle along the new boundary. At the same time, no border line could restrain the settlers of Virginia and Pennsylvania from penetrating deeper into Indian country. As Gage had warned, the Fort Stanwix Treaty wasted British money without reducing the settler and speculator pressure that troubled the frontier.[108]

CHAPTER TWO

Patrons

Rev. Eleazar Wheelock, by Joseph Steward. (Courtesy of the Hood
Museum of Art, Dartmouth College.)

I N 1761, Joseph Brant and Samuel Kirkland inverted Eleazar Wheelock's
assumption that all Indians were impoverished and inferior to colonists.
At Wheelock's school in Connecticut, Brant arrived riding a horse and wearing fine clothing in the *"Indian*-fashion," while Kirkland walked and wore
plain homespun. While Brant enjoyed a wealthy patron in Sir William Johnson, Kirkland came from a family of downward mobility. Wheelock described Kirkland's father as "a Worthy Minister of the Gospel . . . reduced to
needy Circumstances" by a mental breakdown that led to dismissal from
his parish in Norwich. Thereafter, Daniel Kirtland barely supported his
family on a marginal farm of sixty acres. As the tenth child and fourth son of

an impoverished clergyman, Samuel inherited intellectual aspirations without the property to pursue them.[1]

Earnest and impressionable, he also developed an early passion to convert the Indians to evangelical Christianity. Kirkland later recalled:

> I contracted an affection for Indians from early youth & was always taken notice of by them, especially the families who lived near & usually frequented my Father's house. I conceived a kind of *pity* towards them, from my first remembrance & at length applied myself to learning . . . for the purpose of promoting religious knowledge among them & with an expectation of spending my days with them.

Impressed by that devout purpose, Wheelock accepted Samuel as a charity student and as a favor to his disabled father. Born "Kirtland," Samuel changed his last name to "Kirkland," as a pious play on the Scottish word for church: kirk. While conveying Samuel's devotion to the Calvinist form of Christianity, that name change also sought a distinct identity from his embarrassing father.[2]

Wheelock became Kirkland's surrogate father. Kirkland expressed evangelical self-flagellation and abject deference when Wheelock wrote him a niggardly letter of introduction to Sir William Johnson:

> I had relied too much upon a handsome Recommendation, which had it been given, might have proved fatal to all Success. . . . I desire to bless God if he has given you such knowledge of my wicked heart. Tis almost as easy for you to throw me down as for the Devil to lift me up. This is one of those happy Effects I hope by the Grace of God to receive from the uncommon, strange Confidence I have in you.

A demanding father, Eleazar Wheelock gave scant affection in return.[3]

Both piety and ambition drove Wheelock. Another prominent clergyman, Ezra Stiles, recalled Wheelock with a mix of admiration and suspicion: "He had much of the religious Politician in his Make. It is said that, amidst a great Zeal & Shew of Piety, he was very ambitious & haughty. And yet there was something *piously sweet, amiable, & engaging in his Manner.*" Stiles concluded, "Such a mixture of apparent Piety & eminent Holiness, together with the Love of Riches, Dominion & Family Aggrandizement, is seldom seen."[4]

Brant enjoyed a more amiable and supportive mentor in Sir William, who had taken Joseph's sister, Molly Brant (Konwatsitsiaienni), for his mistress and housekeeper. Molly replaced Johnson's first mistress, Catherine

Weisenberg, a runaway indentured servant originally from Germany. After bearing Johnson three illegitimate children, Catherine died in April 1759, at the age of thirty-seven. By then Johnson had already bedded Molly Brant, who bore their first child, Peter, in September. Although the couple never married, at least not in a colonial ceremony, Sir William treated Molly and their eight children with respect. By conducting his household with grace, intelligence, and determination, Molly charmed genteel visitors, who overlooked the irregularity of her status and the color of her skin.[5]

Equally striking in looks and mind, Molly became Johnson's greatest love in bed and his greatest asset in Indian politics. She came from a prominent family in an Iroquois culture that allowed women considerable influence behind the scenes. Thanks to the matrilineal descent system of the Iroquois, Molly enjoyed a higher status than did her brother. A colonist described her as a "daughter to a sachem, who possessed an uncommonly agreeable person, and good understanding." To be precise, her stepfather (Brant Canagaraduncka) was the sachem of the Turtle clan whose women chose Canajoharie's most prestigious chief: the Tekarihoga. In sum, Molly belonged to the maternal power brokers of Canajoharie. A colonist noted:

> As she is descended from and connected with the most noble families of the Indians, she was of great use to Sir William in his Treaties with those people. He knew that Women govern the Politics of savages as well [as] the refined part of the World and therefore always kept up a good understanding with the brown Ladies.

It was no coincidence that in 1759, when Molly became his mistress, Johnson became much better informed about, and better able to manage, the complex inner workings of Iroquois diplomacy.[6]

As Molly's precocious younger brother, Joseph became Johnson's particular favorite. As an adolescent, Brant served in Johnson's military expeditions against the French in Canada. Overcoming early jitters, Brant became a skilled and ambitious warrior. But Johnson wanted Joseph also to acquire enough English education to become a gentleman, capable of leadership in colonial as well as native society. Johnson sent him off to Wheelock's school to learn colonial words and ways. Noting Johnson's favor for Brant, some colonists mistook the young Mohawk for one of the superintendent's native sons. Apparently sharing that misconception, Wheelock initially recorded Joseph's last name as "Johnson" on a student roll, later substituting "Brant." In fact, Sir William did function as a surrogate father for Joseph, defining his notions of the consummate colonial gentleman, and paralleling the role that Wheelock played for Kirkland.[7]

A MANLY YOUTH

At first, neither Wheelock nor Brant recognized the fundamental contradiction between their goals. Far from seeking a dissolution of Mohawk autonomy and identity, Brant hoped to appropriate elements of British culture to serve Indian ends: to build a syncretic cultural fire wall against colonial domination. As literate Christians, the Mohawks could better fend off cunning and conniving land speculators and could better conduct diplomacy with colonial officials. By preserving their land and their political importance, the Mohawks could prolong their distinct identity as a native people.

Wheelock promoted his school primarily as a benefit to the colonists and only secondarily as an act of charity to the natives. He depicted the Indians as miserable beasts, living in thrall to Satan. They were

> [s]avage almost to the level with the brutal Creation; but fierce and terrible in War. Their Dwellings are eminently Habitations of Cruelty. They have continued from Age to Age, in the grossest Paganism and Idolatry—Strangers to all the Emoluments of Science—but Subtle and skillful in all the arts of Cruelty & Deceit—and on every Consideration their State is, perhaps the most wretched and piteous of all the humane Race.

Converting such brutes to civilization and Christianity was a duty imposed by God upon his favored people: the British Protestants in America. To punish the colonists for neglecting that duty, God sometimes permitted the savages to become "a Scourge and Terror to their English Neighbours—often ravaging and laying wast[e] their Frontiers—butchering—torturing and captivating their Sons—dashing their Children against the Stones—Skillfully devising, and proudly glorying in, all possible methods of Torture and Cruelty within their Power." Wheelock concluded that colonists could best defend themselves by converting the Indians, pleasing God into the bargain.[8]

During the 1750s, Wheelock drew his initial students from small nations of Algonquian-speakers dwelling near the Atlantic coast: Mohegans of Connecticut, Montauks of Long Island, Narragansetts of Rhode Island, and Delawares of New Jersey. Engulfed by settlers, these Algonquians persisted in compact enclaves surrounded by colonial towns. Surviving by partially assimilating to colonial culture, they made and marketed handicrafts, especially baskets and brooms, and they worked for wages as maids, sailors, laborers, and soldiers. They also sought Christian knowledge to resist colonial temptations—especially alcohol.[9]

But Wheelock regarded the enclave Indians as pathetic—as especially poor, ragged, and drunken—as, in sum, hardly worth the effort to save their souls. He longed instead to recruit and educate the Iroquois of the frontier, whom he considered more noble because less exposed to the vices of colonial society. Of course, the farther Indians lived from the colonial settlements, the less they wanted to do with missionaries, perceiving them as the entering wedge of dispossession. Only Indians dwelling among the colonists welcomed Christian conversion from the desperate hope of preserving some autonomy within a colonized domain.[10]

Wheelock shared Sir William Johnson's conviction that the Six Nations were the most powerful and influential of Indians. Through them, he meant to reach and sway the Indians deeper in the continental interior. He also wanted to tap the fund established by the late Admiral Sir Peter Warren (Johnson's uncle and patron) to subsidize the education of Iroquois children. To procure those students and funds, Wheelock needed Johnson's help. Writing to him in 1761, Wheelock promised to counteract "the influence of Jesuits; [to] be an antidote to their idolatrous and savage practices; attach them to the English interest, and induce them to a cordial subjection to the crown of Britain, and it is to be hoped, to a subjection to the king of Zion."[11]

Wheelock's pitch was timely and shrewd. In 1761, Johnson distrusted the lingering French influence promoted by Jesuit missionaries based in Canada. He wanted to substitute British missionaries bearing the Protestant faith: "Ministers & schoolmasters amongst [the Indians] would tend greatly to the Civilizing even the worst of them, after which they could be the Easier managed." Devoted to the official Church of England, Johnson preferred Anglican missionaries, but they were in short supply, which forced him—reluctantly—to cooperate with Wheelock, a New England evangelical.[12]

Brant was the pivotal figure in the uneasy cooperation between Wheelock and Johnson. To curry favor with Sir William, Wheelock spared Brant from the indignities and punishments inflicted on the lowly Algonquian students. Wheelock treated him as the cherished ward of a prestigious and powerful gentleman, who could make or break his Grand Design in Iroquoia. The minister lavished such fine new clothing on Joseph that one of Wheelock's financial sponsors, an association of Massachusetts ministers (known as "the Boston Board"), balked at paying the bill. In November 1761, Wheelock gushed by letter to Johnson: "Joseph appears to be a considerate, Modest, and manly spirited youth. I am much pleased with him." In February 1763, Wheelock extolled Brant as "of a Sprightly Genius, a manly and genteel Deportment, and of a Modest, courteous and benevolent Temper." Praised, rather than humbled, Brant developed a powerful self-esteem that contrasted with the self-abasement demanded of the other students. As a consequence, Brant later expressed a greater fondness for Wheelock and his school than did any other Indian.[13]

At first, Brant's contentment pleased Johnson, who helped Wheelock procure additional Mohawk boys for the school. In printed reports and in letters to donors, Wheelock made much of his special favor from the superintendent. "General Johnson writes me very friendly indeed," Wheelock assured the Boston Board. That news increased donations—including funds from the Sir Peter Warren legacy.[14]

Intelligent and attentive, Joseph mastered speaking and reading English. Fascinated with Christianity, Joseph aspired to become a missionary, which thrilled Wheelock. To train him for the ministry, Wheelock planned to send the young Mohawk to an evangelical college, but Johnson meant for the Church of England to reap the prize: an educated Brant. In May 1763, a letter from Molly Brant abruptly summoned her brother to return home (although Wheelock stalled that departure until July). Without informing Wheelock, Johnson prepared to place Brant at King's College, an Anglican institution in New York City.[15]

But Pontiac's Rebellion of 1763 disrupted the best-laid plans of both Johnson and Wheelock, as reports of native atrocities inflamed colonial public opinion against all Indians. In October, an Anglican minister advised Johnson against sending Brant to New York City, "where he can hardly be a Day without hearing his Countrymen in general heartily cursed as deserving to be all extirpated; and is it not probable the Boys in the Street will be apt to insult him?" At Wheelock's school in peacetime, Brant might pass for a gentleman, but in wartime New York City he would be insulted as a savage. To avoid incidents that would offend and alienate the Mohawks, Johnson kept Brant at home, entrusting his education to an Anglican catechist at nearby Fort Hunter.[16]

The Indian war, however, firmly turned Brant's ambitions away from further education in religion. In early 1764, Brant joined one of the war parties of Iroquois loyalists organized by Johnson to smite the rebellious Delaware Indians residing in the Susquehanna and Chemung valleys. But colonial rumors distorted Brant's role, insisting that he had, in Wheelock's alarmed words, "joyn'd himself with the Enemy, And put himself at the Head of a large party of Indians to fight against the English." If true, Wheelock's school was in deep trouble. For if his most prized student had reverted to brutal savagery, then donating to Wheelock was a bloody waste of money. Because the rumor induced the Massachusetts legislature to suspend further payments from Sir Peter Warren's fund, Wheelock begged Johnson for a letter to discredit the report and to return Joseph to school in Lebanon. Johnson wrote the letter, but Joseph never returned to Wheelock's school, nor did he attend any college.[17]

Instead, Brant remained in the Mohawk Valley, working as an interpreter for Johnson. Wheelock's missionaries and teachers continued to visit and lodge with the genial Brant at Canajoharie, but he preferred the Anglican forms favored by Sir William. In the contest for Brant's mind, Johnson ultimately prevailed over Wheelock.[18]

During the Susquehanna campaign, Brant had passed through the village of Onoquaga, where he met a young Oneida woman named Neggen Aoghyatonghsera. Christened as Margaret, she was the daughter of Isaac Dekayenensere, a leading chief. On July 22, 1765, at Canajoharie, Joseph and Margaret married in a Christian ceremony performed by one of Wheelock's missionaries, Theophilus Chamberlain, who praised the bride as a "handsome, Sober, discreet & a religious young woman." In 1766, she gave birth to their first child, a son named Karaguantier but christened as Isaac to honor his grandfather.[19]

At Canajoharie, Joseph thrived as both a colonial gentleman and a Mohawk chief. With Sir William's help, Brant acquired a large and fertile farm: 80 acres of prime cropland near the village on the Mohawk River's south shore, plus 512 wooded acres on the opposite, northern side of the river. Margaret and Joseph raised corn; kept cattle, sheep, horses, and hogs; tended an orchard; and made maple sugar. In 1769, a visitor described Brant as "a considerable farmer." Drawing upon store credit with colonial merchants, Brant lived in a genteel fashion, acquiring imported clothing, jewelry, bedding, writing paper, a liquor case, and a pleasure sleigh. A visitor noted that Brant dressed in "the English Mode," wearing "a suit of blue Broad Cloth" while Margaret appeared "in a Callicoe or Chintz Gown." In another display of wealth, she wove into her gown an array of silver broaches, worth a shilling apiece and £10 in the aggregate. With Johnson's encouragement, the villagers made Brant a war chief and their primary spokesman.[20]

SENECA FAILURE

Meanwhile, Wheelock sent Kirkland to complete his education at the College of New Jersey (now Princeton). In addition to the president's house and a kitchen, the college consisted of an immense stone building known as Nassau Hall, which housed the approximately 100 students and their library and classrooms. Given credit for advanced studies at Wheelock's school, Kirkland entered as a sophomore during the fall of 1762. Wheelock recruited pious donors, who paid for Kirkland's room, board, and education in return for his commitment subsequently to serve as a missionary to the Indians. Diligent and persistent, Kirkland thrived as a student. In 1764, a New Jersey minister described the tall, slender, and lively Kirkland as "a very pretty, agreeable youth."[21]

He remained at college for only two years, departing in the summer of 1764. A year later, he obtained his degree in absentia in credit for his missionary service in Iroquoia. That service began with seven weeks at Johnson Hall as Sir William's honored guest, learning the diplomacy, politics, mores, and manners of the Senecas, the most distant of the Iroquois. Given the dangers of the Seneca country, the best advice Johnson could have given would have been to stay away. But he hoped to sway the Senecas, in Kirkland's words, "before the *French* have [an] Opportunity to renew and strengthen their Interest."[22]

Undertaking a Seneca mission in early 1765 attested more to Johnson's French obsession, Wheelock's ambition, and Kirkland's devotion than to their common sense. During the rebellion of 1763, the western half of the Senecas had broken with the other Iroquois to attack the British. Only very recently—in August 1764—had they made peace with Sir William. Relatively numerous and distant from colonial settlements, the Senecas also felt little incentive to learn colonial Christianity. The only colonists welcomed in Seneca villages were occasional traders—and two of them had been murdered in 1762 near Kanadasega, which was Kirkland's destination.[23]

Kirkland barely survived his ordeal. During the spring of 1765, Kirkland almost starved to death during a famine caused by a premature frost the preceding September, which curtailed the harvest. In April and in desperation, Kirkland made a harrowing two-week journey east to the Mohawk Valley to procure provisions. Catching sight of the missionary, Sir William blurted, "Good God! Mr. *Kirkland,* you look like a whipping post!" Hunger and dysentery claimed the lives of four Senecas in his traveling party: an adoptive sister, two of her children, and a friend.[24]

He also narrowly escaped assassination by hostile Senecas who suspected Kirkland of sorcery in the sudden and surprising death of a villager who had hosted the missionary. He complained to Johnson that most of the Senecas treated him "with no more respect than they would shew to a dog." Proud of their own culture, they disliked the missionary dogmatism that insisted on a Christian monopoly to spiritual truth. In contrast to the religious absolutism of Christianity, the Senecas sustained dual and relative supernatural truths. In Kirkland's words, they believed that "God has two distinct ways of Government for white people & the Indians, that there are two Roads which lead to Heaven." They clung to their traditional spiritual beliefs as essential to the martial prowess that defended their independence. Indeed, the Senecas blamed Christian conversion for the depopulation, dispossession, and degradation of the New England Algonquians. Kirkland wearily reported, "They imagine [that] all will be well if they keep close to their Traditions."[25]

But this frustration was most inconvenient for Wheelock, who needed news of Kirkland's success to impress potential donors. This need was especially great during 1765–66, when Wheelock launched an ambitious fundraising drive by sending two ministers, Nathaniel Whitaker and Samson Occom, to Great Britain. Wheelock exhorted Kirkland, "Now is the Time if ever to push forward the Grand Affair. If we can send a good Account to Messrs. Whitaker & Occom in England . . . it will greatly help them in their important undertaking." Suppressing the truth, Wheelock invented a missionary triumph among the Senecas, assuring donors that "Mr. *Kirtland* has surprisingly insinuated himself into their Affection and Esteem."[26]

In fact, Kirkland abandoned his Seneca mission and returned home in defeat in May 1766. Prolonged hunger, attempted assassination, and Indian resistance taught him that the Seneca country lay too far beyond the settlements for an effective mission. Distance enabled the Senecas to ignore or threaten the missionary with apparent impunity from colonial retribution. If the Algonquian enclaves of New England lay too close to the colonial world for Wheelock's purposes, the Senecas now seemed far too far away. Perhaps the intervening Oneidas would be just right.[27]

KANONWALOHALE

Two rival villages—Kanonwalohale and Old Oneida—lay at the core of the Oneida country. A cluster of about forty houses, Kanonwalohale occupied a bend in, and a ford across, Oneida Creek, about eight miles south of its outlet into Oneida Lake. "Kanonwalohale" meant "head on a post" in honor of an enemy's skull once displayed at the village entrance. Colonists often called the place Oneida Castle because of a former stockade. Home to about a third of the Oneidas, Kanonwalohale possessed the sacred granite stone that gave the Oneidas their name, which translates as "people of the standing stone." But it was also a walking stone, for legend held that it followed the Oneidas whenever they relocated their principal village. Founded at mid-century, Kanonwalohale eclipsed the former capital village known as Old Oneida: a cluster of about twenty houses located about eight miles southeast of Kanonwalohale.[28]

The ambitions of the local chiefs meshed with Kirkland's mission. By tapping his connections to colonial gentlemen, the chiefs sought a higher standing for Kanonwalohale—at the expense of Old Oneida. In Kirkland, they sought their own equivalent of Sir William Johnson: a colonial patron with external clout. Such a patron enhanced a village's prestige among the Iroquois. A missionary could explain their needs and wishes to the colonial world; and he should draw spiritual power, temporal news, and material assistance into Kanonwalohale.[29]

At Kanonwalohale, Kirkland won the cooperation and influence that had eluded him among the Senecas. In 1768, he marveled, "[I] was treated with great Respect, Love, and Affection." By making Kanonwalohale friends, however, Kirkland made enemies of the jealous chiefs at Old Oneida. They perceived the Christian mission as corroding traditions essential to their authority and to the identity and survival of the Oneidas. Rebuking the Kanonwalohale chiefs for adopting the "white people's religion," the Old Oneida chiefs preached, "You had better revive the old customs & the traditions of the Forefathers & live like true Indians." Reacting against one another, Kanonwalohale and Old Oneida polarized into Christian and traditionalist camps.[30]

Far from passive recipients of Kirkland's preaching, the Indians were demanding catalysts whose long dialogues consumed his days. "Constantly thronged with Company from Morning to Evening," Kirkland often wrote in his journal. Seeking out Kirkland, individuals unburdened their troubled souls: "Their relations are so tedious I know not where to begin. . . . This evening another came upon the same errand with a long story, enough to fill a sheet." Groups did the same. One night, Kirkland recorded that visiting Tuscaroras "flocked in one after another, untill my house was full, discoursed with them till midnight, & then could scarcely get away from them."[31]

Although welcoming and attentive, the Kanonwalohale Oneidas frequently suffered from hunger. Increasing competition from interloping colonial hunters was diminishing the wild game. In 1767, Kirkland reported, "Seldom a wild fowl or Beast is killed under 70 miles." The colonial intrusion also introduced new forms of vermin that attacked the Oneida crops. After the failed harvest of 1766, the Oneidas suffered a famine in the spring of 1767. Seeking relief, they moved to encampments beside Oneida Lake to subsist on eels and fish. Accompanying them, Kirkland reported, "I have lain and slept with them till I am lousy as a Dog—feasted and starved with them as their Luck depends upon Wind & Weather. It should be asked, why they don't support me, the Answer is ready, they can't support themselves."[32]

Guided by an ethos of hospitality and generosity, the Oneidas shared with Kirkland what little they had. Whenever he visited an Oneida house, "such as they had was immediately set before me—a roasted Squash—Samp Pottage, parched Corn, or the like—tho the poor Creatures have not half enough for themselves." In return, they expected Kirkland to relieve Oneida poverty. The chiefs informed Kirkland:

> You are sent here by the Ministers of Christ & good people of God, to teach us the way to heaven, to feed our souls with spiritual food. They (the Ministers) support you, supply the necessities of your Body, and we

must pray you, in a case of extremity, to uphold our *Bodies*, our *lives*, lest
our souls should unexpectedly leave both you and us, before we have time
to set them in the right way.

Kirkland explained to Wheelock that the Oneidas had conceived "from
the Conduct of the French Priests, that a *True* Minister must be a Father
in a double Sense, not only Spiritual but Temporal—[to] supply the wants
of the Widdow & Fatherless." The Oneidas relied upon Kirkland to provide
their safety net against the increasing deprivations brought by colonial
encroachment.[33]

Adapting to native expectations, Kirkland ran into debt buying food and
clothing for the hungry and ragged and for a steady stream of native visitors.

My house has ever been open to all—comings & goings—my situation
on a public road, or path & acquaintances thro' the confederate Nations
exposes me to unknown crowds of Indians. My house has been considered by the Indians, as a *storehouse* for the poor & in a time of distress
[they] immediately betake themselves to me.

These mounting expenditures strained his resources from, and his relationship with, Eleazar Wheelock.[34]

While providing assistance, Kirkland also demanded substantial changes
from the Oneidas. In particular, he sought to suppress the traders' rum that
promoted so much drunken disorder. Unable by tradition to coerce either
traders or drinkers, the Kanonwalohale chiefs welcomed Kirkland as an outsider with the spiritual prestige to enforce new rules. In December 1766, they
empowered Kirkland to appoint native deputies to seize and destroy any
liquor brought into the village. During the ensuing six months, traders tried
to introduce some eighty casks of rum, but the Kanonwalohale Oneidas
accepted none, insisting, "It is contrary to the Minister's Word, and our
agreement with him." But Kirkland faced a constant struggle as the prohibition rankled a minority, producing contentions.[35]

As liquor receded, Kirkland achieved unprecedented success for a Protestant missionary in Iroquoia. Mastering the Oneida language, Kirkland could
preach without an interpreter, which enhanced his standing. He also benefited from an especially devout and savvy Oneida assistant, known to the
colonists as Deacon Thomas. The Oneidas applied to public worship the
solemnity traditional to public councils, bearing a patient and often mourn-
ful attention that astonished colonial visitors. In 1769, a visiting clergyman
declared, "I think it was the most Solemn Assembly I ever Saw." The Oneida
congregation developed a special love for singing sacred hymns with an

exquisite three-part harmony. Wheelock exulted, "This is all new, and beyond what was ever yet known among Indians." He boasted that the Kanonwalohale Oneidas "under Mr. Kirtland are become a people near to God."[36]

In 1769, Kirkland organized a formal church, on the New England model, with 22 members eligible for communion. Far larger numbers—from 200 to 400—attended the services, which attracted Tuscaroras and Onondagas as well as Oneidas. Kirkland assured a correspondent that "it would afford you peculiar pleasure to see such a multitude of tawny, smooty souls flock to the waters or fountain of life, seeking to be cleansed." Overflowing the small church of hewed logs, the Indians listened at the open doors and windows, even in the snow of winter.[37]

As an evangelical Calvinist, Kirkland preached that all humans justly deserved eternal damnation in a fiery hell as their legacy from Adam's original sin. Unable to lift that sentence by good behavior, people could obtain salvation only by utter submission to divine power. By confessing their "total moral depravity," sinners might attract the divine grace that alone saved souls. Only those manifestly saved by grace could be admitted to communion in the church; and only their children could merit baptism. On these principles Kirkland would never compromise lest he imperil his own soul.[38]

As a father both temporal and spiritual, Kirkland became ubiquitous, essential, and exhausted. By 1771, he supervised four grammar schools, and he oversaw evening psalm-singing schools. Kirkland translated hymns and parts of the gospel into Oneida and he instructed natives in the colonial modes of agriculture. Kirkland also consulted with them as individuals and groups on their spiritual concerns. He wrote letters conveying their requests to external authorities, including Sir William Johnson. In the log church, Kirkland conducted two Sabbath services, morning and afternoon, each lasting from two to four hours and featuring sermons based on a passage of Scripture. Village councils required Kirkland's participation, and villagers sought mediation of their disputes: "Every little petty difference in family, or between Relations, must be brot to me, in order to [obtain] reconciliation." He concluded, "The Lord grant [that] I may partake largely to the grace of patience." By making himself an essential authority and source of social discipline, Kirkland became hostage to Oneida expectations.[39]

Why did Kirkland persist in the hard, demanding life of a missionary? In an ordination sermon for a fellow missionary, Kirkland conceded that they dwelled "among a people of a hard language, many of whom are savage [and] ungovernable—like the wild beasts of the desert." But Kirkland found consolation in preparing for Christ's imminent and millennial return to earth:

O! What noble joy is this—what sublime pleasure, what angelic employment to be instrumental of glorifying God, in the salvation of immortal
souls! If it were but of *one* soul, *that* would be well worth studying,
preaching, praying & laboring for all your days. May you have thousands
of these pagan, tawny souls (thro' your instrumentality) washed & made
white in the blood of the lamb as seals of your ministry—which shall be
your glory & joy & crown of rejoicing in the presence of our Lord Jesus
Christ at his coming.

If he could whiten but a single soul in a tawny body, all would be worthwhile,
so Samuel Kirkland preached to himself.[40]

CONTRACTION

While Kirkland triumphed at Kanonwalohale, the rest of Wheelock's missionary program faltered. In 1766–67, he had sent a spate of students to Iroquoia—to serve as missionaries and schoolteachers—but most quit within
two years. Young men or adolescents, they were overmatched by their
demanding roles in an alien culture. Of eight colonists educated by Wheelock during the early 1760s, only Kirkland persisted as a missionary to the
end of the decade. Citing broken health, the others deserted for better
prospects as ministers in the more comfortable colonial towns. [41]

Wheelock's Indian teachers also failed in Iroquoia, either dismissed for
moral lapses (drinking or fornicating) or ran away in despair. Most were Algonquians who suffered from Iroquois contempt for them as defeated people
feminized by colonial domination. Of 43 Indian boys admitted to his Lebanon
school prior to 1766, at least 4 had died, 8 had been dismissed, and almost all
the rest had fled. Warrior pride had frustrated Wheelock's efforts to teach
subordination to the Iroquois students. He complained that one Mohawk
"was so lifted up with his having been in the Wars, and sent to Hell one or two
of the poor Savages with his own hand, that my House was scarcely good
enough for him to live in, or any of the School honourable enough to speak to
him." Other than Samson Occom (a Mohegan), Wheelock could count no
Indian student a success by his demanding standards. And he chronically
wondered when Occom would succumb to his inner Indian.[42]

Although all but one of the white missionaries had deserted him, Wheelock primarily blamed his Indian students for his failing program. Hypersensitive to public criticism, Wheelock felt humiliated by Indians who
rejected his control and faltered in their moral discipline. Wheelock could
not see that he had set up his Indian teachers to fail. Into suspicious Iroquois
communities, he had sent adolescent Algonquians who could not speak the

local language and who lacked financial and moral support from their mentor. Expected to fail by most colonists, by the Iroquois, and even by Wheelock, the Indian teachers had complied.[43]

By late 1768, Wheelock had little to show for his expensive and ambitious program in Indian education and Iroquois missions. The collapse also reflected Sir William Johnson's turn against Wheelock's program. The worldly Johnson preferred the more sacramental, rational, and convivial worship of the Church of England. Disdaining emotional evangelicals, he insisted that their Indian converts displayed

> the greatest Distortion of the features & zealous Belchings of the Spirit, resembling the most bigotted Puritans. Their whole time being spent in Singing psalms amongst the Country people, whereby they neglect their Hunting & most Worldly affairs, & are in short become very Worthless members of Society.

By setting bad examples, Wheelock's Algonquian teachers irritated the Iroquois: "They generally appear so poor . . . and make so many complaints about the loss of their lands, that the [Iroquois] despise them, hate us, as the cause of their misfortunes, and . . . entertain a prejudice against Religion itself." More accepting of traditional Indian ways, Johnson opposed the efforts by "well meaning but gloomy people amongst us, to abolish at once their most innocent customs, Dances, and rejoicings at marriages, &c."[44]

Johnson also distrusted the Calvinist clergymen as radical republicans hostile to the British monarchy and to British rule in America. He associated them with the violent protests against British taxation in New England. Indeed, Wheelock's donors included such conspicuous Patriots as James Otis, John Hancock, and Samuel Adams. Eager to preserve the empire, Johnson blasted the New England clergy as "Enemies to all our Laws & the British Consti[tu]tion . . . Exchanging their Morality for a Sett of Gloomy Ideas, which always renders them worse Subjects but never better Men." Johnson urged a stronger Anglican establishment in the colonies because "the Members of that Church are the Surest Supports of the Constitution" and "the faithfullest Subjects of the Crown." Johnson especially longed for Anglicans to replace Wheelock's missionaries in Iroquoia.[45]

FUTURES

Johnson and Wheelock charted contrasting routes to the Indian future in North America. Both anticipated an inevitable transformation of Indian peoples into cultural facsimiles of colonists and of the Indian country into a colonial landscape of farms and towns. But they radically differed on the appropriate pace and mode of that dual transformation. In a rush, Wheelock longed thoroughly and rapidly to convert the Indians, dissolving their traditional culture and procuring most of their lands for colonial settlement. More patient, Johnson expressed greater solicitude for native traditions and desires, which argued for a slower, multigenerational process of Indian adaptation. Johnson believed that a slower pace would best preserve imperial authority, maximize his own power, and protect Indians from the violence, trauma, and exploitation of hasty colonial expansion.[46]

Wheelock warned: "The Savages of this Land must be cultivated or be destroyed and perish, and that very soon." By quickly remaking Indians, Wheelock promised to diminish their resistance to colonial expansion, a prospect that appealed to colonial donors. Addressing the Iroquois chiefs in 1765, he argued:

> This earth is all God's land, and he will have it all cultivated. So long as there are not people enough to inhabit the earth, God lets the wild beasts have it for their dwelling place; and a few lazy, savage people he suffers to live a hungry miserable life by hunting. But when the children of men grow numerous, and want the earth to cultivate for a living, the wild beasts must give place to them, and men must improve the land for God; if they do not, they are bad tenants and must be turned off as such.

Wheelock expressed the colonial ideology that cited a divine duty to seize and improve the Indian domain.[47]

In missionary discourse, "civilizing" the Indians primarily meant transforming their gender roles to fit colonial norms. Indian women should withdraw from the cornfields to become housekeepers, while Indian men should swap their firearms for hoes and plows. This did not appeal to Iroquois men, who noted that in colonial society slaves worked in the fields while gentlemen did not. In 1765, a Seneca war chief warned that if warriors became field-workers,

> We shall soon lose the spirit of *true men*. The spirit of the brave warrior & the good hunter will no more be discovered among us. We shall be sunk so low as to hoe corn & squashes in the field, chop wood, stoop down & milk cows like *negroes* among the dutch people.

Warriors interpreted the missionary drive as a double threat: to make women of them as a first step toward enslaving them. Without masculine warriors untainted by labor in the earth, the Iroquois would lose their prowess and succumb to colonial domination, joining the Africans at work on the Dutch farms of the Hudson Valley.[48]

Because Johnson valued warriors as British allies, he sympathized with Iroquois men. Inverting Wheelock's conventional wisdom, Sir William insisted that Indians could be, and should be, Christianized *before* they were civilized: "As Hunters I believe they may be as usefull Members of Society as they would be in any other Capacity at Least for a Century to come." As hunters, they could best serve the British economy by providing furs. And Iroquois warriors could assist the British Empire by intimidating other Indians—as in the suppression of the rebellious Delawares in 1764. If instead made into evangelical, psalm-singing, and hoe-wielding pacifists, Iroquois men would become useless to Johnson and his empire. Imperial rule clashed with the colonial ambition quickly to dispossess all Indians.[49]

Johnson regarded Wheelock's crash program for civilizing Indians as a front for New England land speculators. In September 1767, Johnson insisted that the Six Nations dreaded the "design to wean them from their way of living, purely, that they may be the readier induced to part with their lands to the White people, which they expect will reduce them to the distresses, poverty and Rags, that are the constant attendants on almost all the domesticated Tribes of whom they have the least knowledge."[50]

Wheelock did have designs on Iroquois lands, seeking at least 225 square miles by appeals to the Oneidas and to imperial authorities. He planned to subdivide this tract into townships, reserving one-third for Indians, provided they adopted colonial agriculture. In the remaining two-thirds, he would sell farms to settlers but only to "such as Love, and will be Kind to, and Honest in their Dealings with, the Indians"—a most rare and elusive group in colonial America. Wheelock proposed to relocate his school from Connecticut to the very center of such a frontier tract. That central town would also have "manufactures" to train Indian apprentices in colonial crafts as well as "a large farm of several thousand acres" where the students would work to learn husbandry and to support the school.[51]

In 1768, Johnson decisively denounced Wheelock's Grand program in letters to the imperial lords and messages to Oneida chiefs. Johnson also recruited Anglican missionaries to supplant Wheelock's protégés in the Mohawk Valley. By 1773, the Anglicans had established schools and teachers at Canajoharie, Fort Hunter, and Johnstown. They also filled pulpits at Albany, Schenectady, Fort Hunter, and Johnstown. A leading Anglican effused that "although Sir William, like Solomon, has been eminent in his Pleasures with the brown Ladies, yet he may lay the Foundation of a Building in the Mohawk Country that may be of more real use, than the very splendid Temple that Solomon built."[52]

RUPTURE

Kirkland's feats were money in the bank for Wheelock. Assisted by his glorious accounts of Kirkland's missionary triumphs, Nathaniel Whitaker and Samson Occom raised £12,026 in Britain: a fortune for that era. The pious donors gave the money to educate and to convert the American Indians. But by mid-1768, when the fund drive culminated, Wheelock no longer had much of a missionary program to spend the returns on. Most of the Indian students had been dismissed and the lone surviving mission was Kirkland's at Kanonwalohale.[53]

Weary of his Connecticut parishioners and of running an Indian school, Wheelock decided to move his institution to New Hampshire and to convert it into a college. Given land by the leaders of New Hampshire, in 1770 Wheelock removed his family and school to Hanover, a frontier town on the upper Connecticut River. When the school reopened there as Dartmouth College, only two of the thirty students were Indians. To justify the shift in priorities, Wheelock insisted that his colonial students would still serve the Grand Design by becoming missionaries to the Indians. In fact, only one Dartmouth graduate—James Dean—served for more than a year, and he then lapsed to pursue a secular calling.[54]

Donors protested the diversion of funds, meant to educate impoverished Indians, to the college education of young colonial gentlemen. Matthew Graves complained,

'Tis all a farce. Our grand Indian Scheme is too apparently founded upon Self. The Doctor is turned Heretical. . . . I hope the Holy Spirit will direct the Trustees to improve that fine Collection to the designed End & not let our cunning, Scheming, religious pharisees divide the Spoil.

Professing wounded innocence, Wheelock insisted that he would carefully preserve two parallel institutions: the Indian School and Dartmouth College. But in financial practice, Wheelock made no such distinction, drawing upon his charitable funds for Indians to build his college and to educate colonial students. He treated the college and its lands as his personal property and the trustees of the funds as his servants.[55]

Wheelock's diversion of the charitable funds especially outraged Samson Occom. As Wheelock's first and most famous Indian student, Occom had a personal investment in educating and converting his fellow natives. Eloquent, pious, and Indian, Occom was primarily responsible for the phenomenal success of the British fund drive. After spending nearly three years begging for donations, Occom felt betrayed. In July 1771, he rebuked Wheelock:

> I think your College has [been] too much Worked by Grandeur for the Poor Indians. They'll never have much benefit of it. . . . So many of your Missionaries and School Masters and Indian Scholars Leaving you and your Service Confirms me in this opinion. Your having so many White Scholars and so few or no Indian Scholars, gives me great Discouragement. I verily thought once that your Institution was Intended Purely for the poor Indians. With this thought I Cheerfully Ventured my Body & Soul, left my Country, my poor young Family, all my Friends and Relations, to sail over the Boisterous Seas to England, to help forward your School, Hoping that it may be a lasting Benefet to my poor Tawnee Brethren. . . . I was quite willing to become a Gazing Stocke, Yea Even a Laughing Stocke, in Strange Countries to Promote your Cause.

Occom bluntly concluded that "if you had not this Indian Buck you would not [have] Collected a quarter of the Money you did." Wheelock characteristically dismissed Occom's complaint as Indian ingratitude and treachery.[56]

Wheelock's new college also disaffected his only successful missionary, Samuel Kirkland. Wheelock's promotional efforts depended on letters from Kirkland vividly describing his hardships, endurance, piety, and accomplishments. An English donor assured Wheelock: "I've received your last letter giveing an Account of dear Mr. Kirtland's assiduity among the Indians and his hard—very hard liveing. I've scarce set down to a meal since but I've wished Mr. Kirtland had the like." Wheelock benefited by association with the Christian charisma of the suffering Kirkland. But the mentor also suffered by comparison, for Wheelock lived in relative comfort far from Iroquoia. In the same letters that conveyed Kirkland's hunger, Wheelock asked for an English carriage from his English donors. Determined to prolong Kirkland's useful dependence, Wheelock worried at the missionary's growing celebrity. Although eager to bask in Kirkland's reflected glory, Wheelock did not wish to be eclipsed by it.[57]

Wheelock especially disliked suggestions by the donors that he designate Kirkland as his successor. Wheelock meant to keep the Grand Design in the family, to pass after Nathaniel Whitaker's regency into the hands of Wheelock's eldest son, Ralph. "He is in high Spirits for Indian Affairs, he understands the Business, and has a Tallent at Governing Indians beyond any man I can imploy. . . . he will be the man to conduct this Affair when I have done,"

Wheelock declared in 1767. Addicted to nepotism, Wheelock was oblivious to his son's glaring flaws. Overcompensating for his epilepsy with a studied arrogance, Ralph alienated most of his college peers, including Kirkland, who wearied of being treated like a servant. Preferring the lighter duty of teaching in his father's school at Lebanon, Ralph performed only three brief and ineffective (if not disastrous) missionary sojourns. As Kirkland mastered the demanding role of frontier missionary, he bristled at deferring to the pampered Ralph as his superior.[58]

In 1768, their conflict became overt after Ralph's blundering visit to Kanonwalohale during Kirkland's leave to recover from a nearly fatal illness. When an Oneida chief expressed preference for Kirkland's experienced advice, Ralph abruptly retorted, "Who do you think your father is? Do you think his power & authority are equal to *mine*; he is no more than my Father's servant." Ralph announced that his father was "the head of the ministers in New England. . . . & when he dies I shall succeed him, & manage all the affairs of instructing the Indians."[59]

This blustering only discredited Ralph Wheelock, for the Oneidas already resented news from their children at Lebanon of his beatings. In February 1769, the Oneidas embarrassed the Wheelocks by abruptly removing their six students from that school. Humiliated by that public relations disaster, the Wheelocks blamed Kirkland for abetting or even instigating the withdrawal.[60]

Kirkland also resented the elder Wheelock's neglect to provide timely and adequate financial support for the Oneida mission. Fed up with living in Indian attire and on Indian rations, Kirkland concluded that he would command more respect among the natives by eating and appearing in colonial gentility. Kirkland also wanted a regular salary rather than a persistent dependency on irregular payments from the unreliable Wheelock. Noting the infusion of English money, Kirkland believed that Wheelock could provide a more decent support.[61]

Preferring to keep Kirkland dependent, Wheelock detected extravagance in Kirkland's accounts and ingratitude in his complaints. Adding fuel to the fire, Wheelock recklessly charged Kirkland with plotting to destroy the Grand Design by planning to found a rival school. If so, Wheelock informed Kirkland, "I think in justice & honesty you ought to let it be known & not suffer me to wear out the little remains of Life . . . to spend labour & money in pursuing an end which you design to defeat."[62]

In fact, Kirkland wanted to persist in Wheelock's service, only with a better and more reliable income. In September 1769, Kirkland potentially strengthened their ties by marrying Wheelock's devout niece, Jerusha Bingham. Lacking her uncle's money, Jerusha entered the marriage, in Kirkland's words, "with nothing but Grace and good sense." He was twenty-seven and she about two years younger. In August 1770, Jerusha gave birth to their first children, twin boys named after two leading English evangelicals and philanthropists: George Whitefield and John Thornton.[63]

Despite that marital tie, Wheelock persisted in hectoring Kirkland. In vain, key supporters warned that alienating Kirkland would destroy the Grand Design in Iroquoia. Rev. Charles Jeffrey Smith insisted, "He is thought by the public to be the crown & glory of the school, and to have reflected more lustre upon it than the united blaze of all the other pupils."[64]

Fed up with Wheelock's recriminations and late payments, Kirkland bolted from the Grand Design in October 1770. Compounding the wound, he enlisted in the rival missionary effort conducted by the Boston Board, whose members had become Wheelock's enemies. By winning away the most renowned missionary in the colonies, the Boston Board grew stronger while embarrassing its great rival. From his new employer, Kirkland procured a generous annual salary of £130 and a commitment promptly to pay his expenses. Best of all, he would never again have to answer to Ralph Wheelock. With Kirkland's defection, Wheelock lost the last shred of his Grand Design in Iroquoia.[65]

To complete his disassociation from Wheelock, Kirkland publicly disavowed his mentor's bid for Iroquois land. Kirkland's credibility had suffered in 1768, when Sir William Johnson assured the Iroquois that Wheelock and his missionary cared more for their lands than for their souls. In 1770, Kirkland ruefully wrote a colleague, "Our Honored Patron is most injuriously reproached in these parts as a land seeker, &c. in which I take a small share with him." To vindicate his mission, Kirkland formally vowed, at a public council with the Oneida chiefs, that he would never acquire any land in Iroquoia. In 1772, Kirkland noted, "My refusing to accept of the offer of about five hundred Acres from a Gentleman in the vicinity of Albany has done more to establish my character among the Indians than perhaps five hundred pounds in presents to them would have done." But Kirkland would later regret his promise, when he lived long enough to break it.[66]

RESENTMENT

Prior to 1768, Sir William had treated Kirkland with generous condescension, and the missionary had responded with dutiful deference and flattery. Apparently to cultivate that relationship, in 1767 Kirkland joined the Johnstown Masonic lodge, where Sir William presided as the Grand Master. Rarely did an evangelical minister join Freemasonry, a reputed haven for heavy drinking and irreligious speculation. But their relationship soured when Sir William openly denounced Wheelock's Grand Design in 1768. In response, the maturing Kirkland became more assertive and stopped attending the Masonic lodge.[67]

Kirkland also began to express the Oneida longing for greater respect from Johnson and from the other Iroquois nations. The Oneidas felt that Johnson took far better care of the Mohawks (and of himself) than of their interests. They complained that they had to pay a German Flats blacksmith to repair their tools and weapons, while the Mohawks enjoyed free service from a Johnstown blacksmith employed by Johnson at Crown expense. In addition to their cost, the Oneidas disliked Mohawk boasting that the free blacksmith demonstrated their higher status and superior importance.

During the fall of 1770, Kirkland challenged Johnson by championing Oneida requests for external assistance. Without Johnson's permission, Kirkland persuaded the Boston Board to finance a new frame meetinghouse at Kanonwalohale to replace a crude and crowded log structure. A large new church in the colonial style would bolster Oneida prestige within Iroquoia by serving notice that Kanonwalohale enjoyed substantial patrons in the colonial world. In December 1770, again without alerting Johnson, Kirkland framed an Oneida petition to New York's royal governor. Complaining of neglect by Johnson, the Oneidas sought funds for a blacksmith to reside in their village. Prickly and proud, Johnson felt offended when Kirkland helped the Oneidas bypass his authority. A stickler for a hierarchical chain of authority, Johnson expected all Iroquois requests and colonial patronage to flow through him.[68]

To rebuke Kirkland, Johnson rallied the traditional chiefs from Old Oneida in January 1771. Summoned to Johnstown, they heard Johnson's invitation to request Kirkland's replacement by an Anglican missionary. Sir William also insinuated that they should look to the Crown for their new church:

> That it is much better & more honorable to be done by the King & will better please him. That these Boston people are a seditious & Rebellious people, great enemies to government. . . . Tis proper that you should in every thing ask my advice & have my approbation as the King's servant. If you had in the first place petitioned to me for a church, I would have wrote to the King & great ones there, & it would have been granted [to] you at once.

The chiefs welcomed the chance to reap Johnson's favor at the expense of their rivals at Kanonwalohale. But the Old Oneida chiefs failed to persuade the more numerous inhabitants of Kanonwalohale to reject Kirkland.[69]

Glorying too much in this victory, Kirkland indiscreetly repeated Johnson's provocative rhetoric in a report to the Boston Board. Claiming ownership to his own words, Johnson treated Kirkland's report as a form of theft. Writing to Governor Thomas Hutchinson of Massachusetts, Johnson denounced Kirkland as a "missionary who has owed [his] toleration among the Indians to my countenance. The ingratitude of his conduct deserves my keenest resentment." Johnson warned, "On my Countenance & protection there he owes everything, and the moment I withdraw it may prove fatal to his Life." Wary of conflict with the powerful superintendent, the Boston Board apologized to Johnson and corrected Kirkland. But they also stood by their appropriation to build a church for the Oneidas.[70]

Renewing his attack, Sir William challenged Kirkland at his weakest point: his restrictive and unpopular policy on baptism. The Iroquois preferred the looser practice of Jesuit priests and Anglican and Dutch Reformed ministers, who offered baptism to the child of almost any Indian. By reserving that sacrament to the children of parents who met his daunting standards for morality and faith, Kirkland excluded most of the Oneidas. By denouncing the dancing and feasting with which Indians celebrated a baptism, the minister also challenged community bonds. These exclusions seemed needlessly divisive to Indians who believed that the baptism ceremony conveyed a magical power to protect the health and spirit of a child.[71]

Rubbing that sore point, Sir William rallied a Kanonwalohale majority to challenge Kirkland on that one issue. In public council, a chief named Tagawaron informed Kirkland, "We don't think that your way is wrong, nor do we say [that] the old way is wrong, but both right. However, we have chosen the old." The setback angered Kirkland, who announced bitterly, "Religion is very low with us in the wilderness. . . . I have discovered more of Indian deceit, art & hypocrisy this last year than ever during the whole of my residence among them." He weathered the storm by threatening to quit. Rather than lose their missionary, the Kanonwalohale chiefs retreated by publicly endorsing Kirkland's position on baptism.[72]

Kirkland further bolstered his influence by supervising the completion, in 1773–74, of the impressive new meetinghouse: two stories tall, 36 feet long by 28 wide, painted white, festooned with nine glass windows, and featuring a 60-foot-tall steeple. The edifice attested to Oneida importance, commanding, in Kirkland's words, "the attention of the Indians far & near." To contain costs, Kirkland had advised omitting the steeple, but the Oneidas insisted because "it was so generally practised by the white people, especially those whose religion was [of] the royal kind." Determined to compete with the Mohawks, the Oneidas would accept no second-rate structure. Needing to compete with the Anglicans, Kirkland acceded to the Oneida expectation.[73]

As the most impressive structure built and owned by an Iroquois people, the new church was the pride and joy of the Kanonwalohale Oneidas. By attracting and impressing curious natives, the new church bolstered their status and reputation in their competition with other Iroquois villages. The shiny, new church seemed to justify their controversial support for Kirkland's Christian mission. Similarly, for Kirkland, the gleaming church and Oneida pride vindicated his double decision in 1770 to leave Eleazar Wheelock and to defy Sir William Johnson.[74]

The church symbolized the progress that Kirkland detected in Kanonwalohale as a Christian community adopting colonial ways. In 1773, he boasted that at least eight families had built frame and clapboard houses in the colonial style and had begun to cultivate their crops with oxen and plows. A visiting minister praised the Oneidas who sang hymns in their own language "with ravishing sweetness and great solemnity." Most of the Oneidas and many Tuscaroras routinely attended Sabbath services and most abstained from liquor, making Kanonwalohale a singular village in Iroquoia. In February 1774, Kirkland concluded, "Things never wore such a smiling face as they now do." In April he added, "The Cause of religion flourishes. I never knew divine truths [to] take such [a] hold of pagan hearts as the winter past." In July, Occom visited and marveled at the "hopeful Prospect of the Indians' future Happiness. Great alteration has been [made] among these Indians both as to their Temporal and Spiritual Concerns since I was here 12 years ago."[75]

But Kirkland also noted an ominous undercurrent of resistance that periodically surged into view. Rumors of war could ignite a longing—especially among young men—to revive the traditional ways of warriors. In September 1773, some Senecas carried to Kanonwalohale the news that their people had murdered four French traders. Kirkland reported:

> The *scalp* or *death shout* was brought into their town by some of the upper nations. The martial spirit of the young warriors soon waked up from its long slumber & they shouted & hallood till their spirits were raised to a prodigious pitch. Some of the [Christian] professors said it appeared to them as though hell had broke loose & their former pagan state revived full & fresh in their view. Some of the sturdy fellows stave open my door but did not enter the house [and they] soon made their escape.

Such volatility led Kirkland to wonder if he would ever completely reach the hearts and minds of his Oneida hosts.[76]

DEATH

During the early 1770s, aggressive land speculators renewed their pressure on the Mohawk villages. Tiononderoge (Fort Hunter) was threatened by the municipal corporation of Albany, which in 1686 had procured a deed to the village's most valuable lands: 1,000 acres of alluvial flats that sustained their crops. Posing as disinterested trustees, the Albany leaders had persuaded the Mohawks that only this deed could protect those lands against other speculators. Beyond the lavish alcohol served at the signing, the corporation paid nothing for the land, which was to remain in Mohawk possession until they left or died out. Upon sobering up, the Mohawks feared that the Albanians would press for Indian removal. Johnson and a succession of royal governors sought a legislative act permanently protecting the Mohawk title to the Tiononderoge flats. But Albany County's powerful legislators consistently blocked this redress in the assembly—to the deep frustration of the Mohawks.[77]

Canajoharie confronted a similar threat from George Klock, a farmer and trader of German descent, who kept a disreputable store and tavern next to the village. He possessed little education but a powerful will, considerable courage (or gall), and relentless cunning. Beginning in the early 1750s, he pressed his claim to Canajoharie, citing an old Indian deed of dubious legitimacy. Klock stubbornly defied both the menaces of the Mohawks and the commands of Sir William to desist. Expecting deference rather than defiance from commoners, Johnson denounced Klock as "the most troublesome and worst man I ever knew."[78]

Exasperated by two decades of fruitless protests against Klock's machinations, the Mohawks took matters into their own hands. On May 23, 1774, Brant led warriors to Klock's house. Breaking in, Brant stunned Klock with a blow from a pistol butt. He complained, "They said that they would Destroy all what I have and all and everything my Children has and Children's Children after them so long as there was one to be found." The warriors seized his legal papers and forced him to sign a document releasing his claim to the village. Once they left, Klock reneged on his release, and he prosecuted Brant for assault. That prosecution so aggravated the Canajoharie Mohawks that they pressured Johnson by threatening to pack up and move west. They understood that their departure would devastate Johnson's system of managing the Covenant Chain—and, through it, the natives of the interior.[79]

In 1774, Sir William faced a deepening crisis in Indian affairs. War erupted that spring in the Ohio Valley. Atrocities by Virginia settlers reaped bloody retribution by the Mingos and Shawnees, who resented their ouster from the river's southern shore under the terms of Johnson's Treaty of Fort Stanwix. By appealing to the Six Nations for assistance, the Ohio natives threatened to inflame the entire colonial frontier. That appeal tempted the Senecas, who bristled at recent British pressure to surrender murder suspects—despite the persistent murders of Senecas by Pennsylvania settlers. At that moment of crisis, the Canajoharie and Tiononderoge land controversies threatened to alienate the Mohawks, so essential to Johnson's influence in the Iroquois confederacy. Without the Mohawks to champion Johnson's agenda, the Six Nations might act upon Seneca resentment by joining the Ohio Valley rebellion.

In July 1774, Johnson dealt with the crisis by convening about 500 Iroquois chiefs in council at Johnson Hall. The Seneca chief Serihowane angrily complained that colonists murdered Indians and stole their land with impunity: "Brother, We are sorry to observe to you that your People are as ungovernable, or rather more so, than ours." Despite the glowing promises made at the Treaty of Fort Stanwix in 1768, no effective boundary protected the Indians from the settler invasion: "If this is the case, we must look upon every engagement you made with us as void and of no effect, but we hope it is not so, & that you will restrain your people over whom you say you have authority."[80]

In reply, the best Johnson could do was to highlight the equal impotence of the Iroquois confederacy. Sir William challenged the Six Nations to renew their mythic hegemony by ordering their supposed dependents, the Mingos and Shawnees, to make peace. Neither Johnson nor the chiefs seemed to recognize how hollow their mutual words had become—pressing one another to revive pretensions to fictional powers. Neither side could see the impending and related collapse of both the Six Nations confederacy and the British Empire in North America.[81]

Matters worsened for Johnson on July 11, when a Canajoharie chief, Tekarihoga, broached Mohawk grievances before the assembled council. "Brother," he began, "it is with pain I am under the necessity of complaining again, against that old Rogue, the old Disturber of our Village, *George Klock*." Because justice "has often been promised, but never been afforded us," Tekarihoga called upon the Six Nations to "convince the English that we have friends & deserve attention." The other Iroquois muttered "that even those Nations who are most faithful to the English are treated with Injustice."[82]

The Mohawk intervention irritated Johnson, who wanted to focus the council on keeping the Six Nations out of the Ohio Valley war. No longer young, and wracked by ailments, Johnson felt stressed by the demanding hours and precise performances of an Indian council held in the midst of a

Col. Guy Johnson, by an unknown artist, 1775. (Courtesy of
the Fenimore Art Museum, Cooperstown, N.Y.)

crisis. After briefly replying to Tekarihoga's speech, Sir William suffered "a
Fit" and had to be carried away to his bed, where he died two hours later.[83]

HEIRS

With the empire in crisis, the timing of Johnson's death rendered the blow
especially ominous. General Thomas Gage reported: "I should at all times
consider this event as a Publick Loss. I look upon it as a heavy one at this
Juncture, when the frontier People, of Virginia particularly, have taken so
much Pains to bring on an Indian War." Gage also confronted a virtual collapse of British authority in the colonial seaports, where radical leaders
resisted British taxes. Infuriated by that resistance, Parliament and the
Crown resolved to punish Boston by enforcing a blockade with occupying
troops commanded by Gage. That shift withdrew British troops from the
troubled frontier in western Pennsylvania, which Indians and settlers then
drenched in blood. The depth of the frontier crisis also assumed a shocking

new clarity in imperial circles with the loss of Sir William's flair for obscuring unpalatable realities.[84]

Few people felt much confidence in his three favored male heirs: Sir John Johnson, Daniel Claus, and Guy Johnson. In imperial favor and Sir William's will, they trumped the younger mixed-blood children of Molly Brant. Their privilege came from Johnson's original, white mistress, Catherine Weisenberg, who gave birth to Sir John and to the wives of Daniel Claus and Guy Johnson. In 1769, an astute friend had predicted that Sir William's death would "be a great loss to mankind in general, but particularly to this neighborhood, and I don't see that anyone of the Family is capable of keeping up the general applause when he is gone."[85]

Sir William initially hoped that his son, Sir John, would succeed him as the royal superintendent of Indian affairs for the northern colonies. But, as Cadwallader Colden, the lieutenant governor of New York, noted, the indolent and aloof Sir John "showed an entire Disinclination of having anything to do with Indians & their Affairs." He preferred the easier life of inheriting his father's great landed estate worked by tenant farmers paying rent.[86]

When Sir John moved his family into Johnson Hall, Molly Brant returned to Canajoharie, where she became a trader and sustained a mix of native dignity and colonial gentility. In August 1775, a visiting gentleman reported that "she saluted us with an air of ease and politeness. She was dressed after the Indian Manner, but her linen and other Cloathes [were] the finest of their kind." Equally proud of her Mohawk descent and her connection to Sir William, she expressed pique at any sign that her station had fallen in the eyes of colonists. The gentleman saw her upbraid a passing Kirkland for failing to call upon her: "She said there was a time when she had friends enough, but remarked with sensible emotion that the unfortunate and the poor were always neglected." Her aggressive self-pity masked her powerful influence among the Iroquois. A Patriot, the gentleman noted with alarm, "the Indians pay her great respect and I am afraid her influence will give us some trouble . . . being intirely in the Interests of Guy Johnson."[87]

Faced with Sir John's disinterest, Sir William had nominated Guy Johnson to succeed to the superintendency. Although lacking discipline and talent, he charmed Sir William by his conviviality, Irish birth, and a prior family connection (allegedly as a nephew but probably as a cousin). Sir William's death in mid-council helped Guy Johnson, who reassured shocked and anxious chiefs by pledging to perpetuate the patronage and methods of Sir William. Eager for continuity, the chiefs put their support for Guy on the council record for conveyance "to the *Great King,* who, we hope will regard

Sir John Johnson, by Charles St. Memin. (Courtesy of
the Johnson Hall State Historic Site, Johnstown, N.Y.,
and the New York State Office of Parks, Recreation,
and Historic Preservation; JH.1971.173.a.)

our desires, and approve of you as the only person that knows us, and our
affairs, that business may go on as it did formerly." Given the pressing frontier and imperial crises, General Gage and Lord Dartmouth had little choice
but to ratify Guy's succession as acting superintendent.[88]

Guy should have been more careful about what he wished for. A genial
mediocrity, he had been promoted far above his capacities as a dutiful secretary and a drinking companion. Lacking Sir William's energy, cunning, and
theatricality, Guy Johnson could never match his father-in-law's bravura performance in imperial correspondence or Indian council. As superintendent,
Guy struggled to maintain Sir William's illusion of a unique ability to speak
for an apparently powerful Six Nations confederacy. He soon felt overwhelmed by his daunting new responsibilities. A visiting Occom found Guy
Johnson "very Solitary on the account of the Death of Sir William Johnson."
But of course Sir William was primarily to blame for Guy's burdensome
inheritance.[89]

RIVALS

Guy Johnson resented Patriot agitators, who meddled with the Indians. Asserting his official monopoly to conduct Indian relations, Guy exhorted the Iroquois: "I charge you, therefore, to shut your Ears against such reports & I have the fullest Authority to Assure you that His Majesty will be your only true Father, Protector, & Friend." He added that "it was to the Crown [that] they owed their happiness & security & all the favors they received." To preserve those advantages, the Indians must heed only "the King's advice & those in Authority under him." But, as a source of official news, Guy faced a formidable competitor in Samuel Kirkland, who spoke for a new and rival power: an American Congress.[90]

Sir William's death provoked an outpouring of grief from both colonists and Indians, but Kirkland reacted with Calvinist astringency. He pointedly preached to the Oneidas from Jeremiah 9:23–24: "Thus saith the LORD, Let not the wise *man* glory in his wisdom, neither let the mighty *man* glory in his might, let not the rich *man* glory in his riches." Kirkland implied that Sir William's wisdom, might, and riches were worse than worthless when opposed to the righteousness of God. Rather than mourn the death of a powerful man, the Oneidas should reflect on the emptiness of all mortal accomplishment.[91]

During the following winter (1774–75), Kirkland clashed with Guy Johnson over the proper religion for the village of Onoquaga on the Susquehanna River. The villagers divided over the strict policy on baptism demanded by their Calvinist missionary, Aaron Crosby, and supported by his friend and occasional visitor Samuel Kirkland and by a minority, led by the chief Good Peter. Isaac Dekayenensere led the majority in favor of the more indulgent and inclusive practices of the Anglicans. They found powerful allies in Isaac's son-in-law, Joseph Brant, the Johnson family, and Rev. John Stuart, the Anglican missionary at Fort Hunter. The majority vowed "to follow the wholesome advice they had been accustomed to receive from Sir William Johnson & to conform strictly to the Religion which he professed & encouraged, as well as to pay due regard to Col. [Guy] Johnson's advice & direction."[92]

Raised and educated in New England, the hotbed of colonial resistance, Kirkland understood the imperial crisis in Patriot terms. Letters from his New England friends denounced the British troops occupying Boston, announced covert colonial preparations for war, and championed the Continental Congress in Philadelphia. Kirkland observed, "My heart almost bleeds for the distressed situation of poor Boston & the Judgments that are impending." In November 1774, Rev. Stephen West assured Kirkland, "Every thing forbode the next to be a bloody summer."[93]

As Patriots prepared for war, they worried that the British would mobilize devastating assistance from the Iroquois warriors. To help Kirkland neutralize the Six Nations, the Patriots forwarded Congresss resolutions for the missionary to interpret to the Indians. Kirkland plunged into this new assignment with verve and energy. In June 1775, he boasted: "I apprehend my interpreting the doings of the Congress to a number of their Sachems has done more real service to the cause of the Country, or the cause of truth and justice, than five hundred pounds in presents would have effected." Kirkland's political activity outraged the leading chief at Old Oneida, Conoghquieson, who charged that Kirkland had disgraced his sacred office with political intrigue. But once again the Kanonwalohale chiefs defended Kirkland as a cherished source of influence and information. Defying Johnson's monopoly, the Oneidas sought to protect themselves by obtaining as much news, from as many sources, as possible.[94]

Politics alienated Kirkland from his old friend Joseph Brant, who chose an opposite path. In March 1771, his beloved wife Margaret died, darkening Joseph's mind with grief. Seeking consolation, he moved to Fort Hunter to live with Rev. John Stuart. Brant gradually recovered by plunging into activity as Stuart's interpreter, teacher of Mohawk, and collaborator in translating the Anglican catechism and the Gospel of St. Mark. Grateful for Stuart's counsel, Brant became a partisan Anglican at increasing odds with the New England dissenters. Brant later insisted that the Mohawks initially mistook the New England missionaries for "messengers of Peace, but we were soon Surprisingly undeceived when we found Soon after that they came to sow the seeds of discord among our People in order to Alienate our antient attachments and Alliance from the King our Father, and join them in Rebellion against him." Brant looked to the Great King to protect Indian lands from covetous colonists.[95]

Remarrying in 1773, Brant returned to Canajoharie. His new wife, Susanna, was a half sister to the late Margaret, which renewed his kinship ties to their father, Isaac Dekayenensere of Onoquaga. At Canajoharie, Brant served Guy Johnson as an interpreter, an advisor, and a special envoy to Six Nations councils.[96]

Although Kirkland and Brant polarized over the imperial crisis, they retained a residual bond. In May 1775, Guy Johnson detained Kirkland at Johnson's mansion, Guy Park, barring his return to Kanonwalohale. At month's end, Johnson took Kirkland to Fort Stanwix, where an angry Indian lunged with a knife, which Kirkland parried with a chair. Brant intervened, subduing the attacker. Kirkland recalled Brant saying, "We think him ungrateful to our King. He thinks he doth his duty towards his country. Let him then be considered as our enemy, but do not kill him while he is our prisoner." Shaken by the episode, Johnson decided to release Kirkland, lest his death in custody further inflame the public against British rule. But Johnson imposed a parole on Kirkland, compelling his retreat to Cherry Valley, a settlement on the southern margins of the Mohawk Valley, to await further directions—or a revolution for American independence that would invite the missionary to break that parole.[97]

CHAPTER THREE

War

General Philip Schuyler, engraving after Alonzo Chappel. (Courtesy of the American Antiquarian Society.)

D URING 1774, colonial Patriots prepared for armed resistance by organizing local committees of correspondence and safety. Defying royal authority, these committees answered instead to newly formed provincial congresses (in each colony) and to the Continental Congress of delegates from the thirteen colonies of the Atlantic seaboard. The committees shared information, coordinated plans, enforced a boycott on importing or consuming British goods, intimidated Loyalists who refused to cooperate, and seized control of local militias. The committees and congresses formed an alternative, revolutionary government that undermined the royal institutions of British America.

That revolutionary process accelerated after April 1775, when General Thomas Gage's troops provoked war by killing Patriots during a raid on Lexington and Concord in Massachusetts. Two months later, Lieutenant Governor Cadwallader Colden complained that Patriot committees and congresses acted "with all the confidence and authority of a legal Government." By early 1776, the royal governor, assembly, council, and courts of New York no longer exercised any authority. That collapse troubled American Loyalists, who considered legal continuity and the British Empire as essential to social stability and economic prosperity.[1]

In August 1774, local Patriots formed their first committee in Tryon County, which included the Mohawk Valley. That committee acted with a new confidence inspired by the death of Sir William and by the succession of his dithering heirs. By May 1775, the organization of a Patriot militia alarmed Guy Johnson, who dreaded a surprise attack on Guy Park. Losing his nerve, Johnson bolted, heading upriver with 90 Mohawks, including Joseph Brant, and 120 Loyalists. Their pretext lay in a Six Nations council at Oswego on Lake Ontario, where Guy met 1,458 natives, mostly Iroquois. Conspicuous by their absence were the Oneidas, who heeded Kirkland's advice to stay away. At the end of the council, Johnson and his party continued northward to British-held Canada rather than return home to confront the rebels.[2]

Exploiting Guy Johnson's absence, the Patriot militia seized control of Tryon County. In January 1776, General Philip Schuyler of Albany led 3,000 armed Patriots to Johnstown to disarm Sir John Johnson and his Loyalist militia. Once the Patriots withdrew with their plunder, however, Sir John began to stockpile new arms. In May, a regiment of Continental Army troops marched to Johnstown to arrest Sir John, who fled through the woods and across the Adirondacks to refuge in Canada. Occupying Johnson Hall, the victorious Patriot officers played on Sir William's billiard table and pilfered his celebrated collection of Indian curiosities. In Canada, Sir John organized a regiment of fellow Loyalist refugees, the King's Royal Regiment of New York, to seek revenge on their persecutors.[3]

STAKES

The Patriot cause merged a frontier hunger for Indian land with a dread of British power. Patriot leaders despised the Johnsons' alliance with the Iroquois as an unjust impediment to settler expansion. As the Patriots saw it, the Johnsons supported savages for their own selfish manipulation, to enjoy a privileged priority in acquiring their lands. When the Johnsons defended Indian rights, Patriots detected a threat to colonial liberty, which they equated with their own power to make private property from native lands. They considered British taxation and British protection of aboriginal title as common exercises in distant and irresponsible tyranny.[4]

The Patriots insisted that the Johnsons served a corrupt empire by retaining native warriors as enforcers to intimidate colonists defending their liberties. In May 1775, a Patriot committee in the Mohawk Valley denounced "the Indians, whom we dread most" because "they are to be made use of in keeping us in awe." By allying with Indians against white men, the Johnsons betrayed the racial hierarchy favored by the Patriots. They blamed the Johnsons for treating the Iroquois with diplomatic respect, humoring a native pride that seemed absurd and dangerous to most colonists. General Schuyler seethed in a private letter: "*Entre nous*, . . . I would rather be the proprietor of a potato Garden & literally live by the Sweat of my Brow, than be an Indian

John Butler, by Henry Oakley. (Courtesy of Niagara Historical Society and Museum.)

Commissioner at a Time when you cannot prudently resent an Insult given by these haughty princes of the Wilderness." Schuyler longed to humble such assertive Indians.[5]

Noting the Patriots' sense of racial entitlement and lust for native lands, the Mohawks feared dispossession and enslavement. Joseph Brant urged Indians "to defend their Lands & Liberty against the Rebels, who in a great measure begin this Rebellion to be sole Masters of this Continent." Playing on this fear, Guy Johnson asked the Mohawks, "Are you willing to go with them, and suffer them to make horses and oxen of you, to put you into wheelbarrows, and to bring us all into slavery?" In the Mohawk Valley, both political camps dreaded enslavement by the other.[6]

The American Revolution promoted a white man's republic from the ruins of a British "composite" empire. After the conquest of Canada, colonists had imagined a partnership with the British to share in the imperial fruits of victory. But they soon felt bitterly disappointed when the British instead treated them as second-class subjects. Patriots bristled when denied the chief liberty of Englishmen—to pay no tax without legislative representation. The British also tried to protect Indian lands from the colonists, who feared confinement within a boundary patrolled by savage warriors allied to a domineering empire.[7]

The colonists especially resented the Quebec Act adopted by Parliament in June 1774. To please the French Canadians, Parliament endorsed French civil law, protected the Catholic faith, and mandated a provincial government that combined a military governor with an oligarchical council (and without an elected assembly). These measures antagonized British colonists who increasingly saw themselves as the target of every imperial measure. Surely, Patriots reasoned, the British would soon apply the precedent of authoritarian rule and an established church throughout the colonies. The American Declaration of Independence denounced the king "for abolishing the free System of English Laws in a neighbouring Province, establishing therein an arbitrary Government, and enlarging its Boundaries so as to render it at once an example and fit instrument for introducing the same absolute rule into these Colonies."[8]

The Quebec Act also offended Patriot leaders by extending Quebec's boundaries south to the Ohio River and west to the Mississippi, subsuming a vast Indian country coveted by speculators and settlers. An exasperated Parliament sought to restrain the intruding frontiersmen who provoked so much trouble with the Indians. Governed by the military without an elected assembly, Quebec might protect Indians better than Virginia or Pennsylvania ever had. In effect, the British expanded Quebec to bolster the boundary for the Indian country that Sir William had negotiated at Fort Stanwix in 1768. But that expansion alienated powerful colonial politicians who doubled as land speculators, including George Washington and Benjamin Franklin.[9]

In effect, the British increasingly treated their colonists as just another group within a composite empire of diverse peoples. Suspecting the loyalty of the colonists on the Atlantic seaboard, the British sought to check their rising power by bestowing favors on French subjects and Indian allies. In the words of historian Linda Colley, the British haltingly (and for selfish reasons) "evolved a more hybrid construction of their American empire," as a set of ethnic and cultural groups held together by imperial power. Of course, this composite structure dismayed colonists who had counted on their British culture and their white race to bestow superior privileges. If denied dominion over the other peoples of North America—French and Indian— those colonists expected to share in their degradation as the objects of British dominion. Rejected as full partners in the British Empire, the Patriots sought their own "empire of liberty" premised on the majority's rights to hold private property (including slaves) and to make new property by dispossessing Indians.[10]

CONGRESS

During the spring of 1775, the Continental Congress took command of an armed rebellion that spread throughout the thirteen colonies along the Atlantic seaboard. The British, however, preserved a tenuous hold over the northern colonies of Nova Scotia and Quebec, including the Great Lakes country. The Patriots dreaded that the British would exploit their northern strongholds to rally the Indians for raids on the colonial settlements—just as the French had done during the previous war. The Patriots also shared Sir William Johnson's conviction that the Six Nations held the key to Indian relations throughout the northeastern quarter of the continent. Neutralize the Iroquois and all the other Indians would keep quiet, or could be more readily defeated. Operating on that conviction, the Patriots worked desperately through the summer of 1775 to keep the Iroquois out of the war. If the Iroquois remained on the sidelines, the Patriots could invade and conquer Canada, which would then secure the colonies from frontier attacks.[11]

For expert assistance in Iroquois affairs, Congress relied on Samuel Kirkland and James Dean, two former students of Eleazar Wheelock. As masters of Iroquois protocol and languages, Dean and Kirkland could explain the Indians to the Americans—and the Americans to the Six Nations. Born in Connecticut, Dean had grown up at Onoquaga, where he had been adopted by the Oneidas and acquired a linguistic fluency that exceeded Kirkland's. A missionary insisted that by age thirteen Dean had become "a perfect Indian boy in language, manners and dress." Graduating from Dartmouth in 1773, Dean had served Wheelock as a missionary to the Canadian Iroquois for two years.[12]

Kirkland plunged into his new, secular role as Indian agent for Congress with an enthusiasm that reflected an eagerness to transcend his often frustrating mission. Mobilizing Indians to fight was easier than converting them to Calvinist Christianity. And, frankly, Kirkland needed a salary from Congress because the war interrupted his payments from missionary societies in Britain.

But Kirkland had limitations as a frontier diplomat. Although genial and intelligent in conversation, he became wooden in public performance, wanting the charisma of Sir William Johnson or Joseph Brant. Kirkland's flat and halting interpretation failed to do justice to the dramatic mannerisms and vocal virtuosity of compelling native orators. DeWitt Clinton later observed: "Those who have seen [Kirkland] officiate at public treaties must recollect how incompetent he was to infuse the fire of Indian Oratory into his expressions—how he labored for words and how feeble and inelegant his language [was]."[13]

Dean and Kirkland invited the Six Nations to a formal council to renew the Covenant Chain under Patriot auspices. But Dean and Kirkland struggled to teach the rudiments of native diplomacy to the congressional commissioners, for most were inexperienced, brusque, and blundering. The worst, Turbot Francis, obliged Kirkland repeatedly in public council to make "some apology to the Indians for his abruptness." The commissioners' secretary conceded that Kirkland and Dean had to rework a speech and "put it into such Mode & Figure as would make it intelligible to Indians, for in its original form, you might almost as well have read them a Chapter out of [John] Locke."[14]

Heeding Oneida advice, Dean and Kirkland appealed to the Iroquois reverence for tradition by choosing Albany as the council site and by persuading the commissioners to make General Philip Schuyler their primary spokesman. Before Sir William Johnson's rise to power, New York's Indian policy had been conducted at Albany by local commissioners of Dutch ancestry and fur trade experience. At the dawn of the eighteenth century, the leading commissioner had been Philip's great-uncle, Peter Schuyler (1657–1724), fondly known to the Iroquois as "Queder." By Iroquois custom, that council name, with its associations and influence, passed to the general as an heir playing a comparable role. In Iroquois minds, "Queder" inherited an obligation to behave as a generous patron and as a champion of Indian interests. But the latter-day Queder also inherited a powerful prestige and influence among the Six Nations, which Schuyler would exploit.[15]

The commissioners laid claim to the Covenant Chain, rejecting the competing claim of the British Empire. Calling themselves "the descendants of Queder," the commissioners posed as restorers of tradition against the distorting interruption of the upstart Johnsons. Presenting wampum to the Iroquois, the commissioners explained, "By this belt, we the twelve United Colonies renew the old covenant chain by which our forefathers, in their great wisdom, thought proper to bind us and you, our brothers of the Six Nations, together, when they first landed at this place." By claiming that the Covenant Chain properly belonged to the colonists, the commissioners marginalized the Johnsons and their empire as usurpers.[16]

While invoking tradition, the American commissioners also transcended it by championing an emerging federalism. In Six Nations diplomacy, the best way to pitch innovation was to drape it in tradition. The commissioners spoke for the "United Colonies," a federal entity much larger than the old Albany commissioners, who had represented only New York. In addition to Schuyler and Volkert P. Douw from New York, the commissioners also included Oliver Wolcott of Connecticut, Turbot Francis of Pennsylvania, and Major Joseph Hawley of Massachusetts. All the northern colonies, not just New York, had a pressing interest in good relations with the Six Nations. And none of the other colonies trusted New York alone to manage the American relationship with the Iroquois. By renewing the Covenant Chain under American auspices, the commissioners rendered Six Nations relations a federal responsibility—nearly a year before the rebellious colonies formally declared their independence from Britain. On the commissioners' recommendation, Congress also took tangible charge of Iroquois relations by appointing and paying two blacksmiths, as well as Kirkland and Dean as interpreters and agents, all placed under Schuyler's supervision. In sum, at Albany in 1775 the Americans renewed the Covenant Chain by linking the Iroquois to a nascent federal government.[17]

For the moment, Congress wisely asked only for neutrality, which most of the Six Nations chiefs accepted as in their best interest. A Patriot official noted, "It is plain to me that the Indians understand their game, which is to play into both hands." Relatively few in number, the Iroquois needed to find and hold the tipping point in a balance of power between external rivals: formerly the British and the French, now the British and the Americans. It would never do prematurely to embrace a belligerent of uncertain power, lest they gamble their lives and lands on a loser. In the confusion of 1775, with a new Congress asserting power and with the British in retreat—but perhaps able to recover—the Six Nations held aloof from both. But during the ensuing year, the various villages and nations began to choose political positions depending upon their local situation and leadership.[18]

Long favored by the Johnsons as privileged allies, the Mohawks recognized that the Patriots would inevitably treat them with diminished respect. In 1775, they numbered only 406 souls, surrounded and often aggrieved by over 42,000 colonists in Tryon and Albany counties. Captain John Deserontyon explained that his people clung to their Johnson connection because "we thought it would be very hard if we should lose them for it was only them [that] helped us." But the Mohawks had to proceed cautiously because of their vulnerability to Patriot attack—especially at the lower village, Tiononderoge (Fort Hunter). In 1775 and 1776, most of the Tiononderoge Mohawks tried to keep their lands and lives by remaining neutral until the Johnsons could return to the valley to restore order. At Canajoharie, however, the Mohawks acted more aggressively to restore imperial power. During the summer of 1775, Joseph Brant led most of the young warriors from that village to join the British defense of Canada, a necessary prerequisite for recovering the Mohawk Valley from the Patriots. Those warriors left behind most of their wives, children, and elders—including Molly Brant, who acted as a British informant behind Patriot lines.[19]

Leading Patriots felt of two minds about the Mohawks who remained in the valley. On the one hand, they were probable spies and a potential fifth column that might suddenly rise up in support of a British invasion. In May 1776, a Patriot officer assembled the Mohawks to threaten that, if they helped the enemy, "He would burn their upper & lower Castles on the Mohawk River, would burn all their houses, destroy their Towns & Cast the Mohawks with their Wifes & Children off of the face of the Earth." On the other hand, their vulnerable persistence among the Patriots rendered them valuable hostages for the good behavior of their distant kin and allies. Determined to retain the Mohawks, Philip Schuyler warned that any attempt to leave would forfeit their lands and their lives.[20]

Immediately west of the Mohawk Valley dwelled the Oneidas, who had begun to feel the settler encroachment that had already enveloped the Mohawks. To avoid that fate, the Oneidas (and their Tuscarora dependents) adopted an opposing strategy. Unlike the Mohawks, the Oneidas had long felt neglected, and sometimes exploited, by Sir William. Seeking an alternative patron, they cultivated Kirkland as their own leading colonist able to speak for them to external power. Consequently, they resented the threats by some Mohawks against Kirkland's life. By assisting the Patriots, the Oneidas also sought enhanced status among the Six Nations. By replacing the British Empire with the American Congress, the Oneidas expected to supplant the

Mohawks as the most favored and influential Iroquois nation within the Covenant Chain. In effect, the Oneidas jockeyed to become the eastern door of the confederacy: the essential brokers of the Iroquois relationship with the ascendant Americans. Surely the grateful victors would then protect their allies' lands, so the Oneidas reasoned. But by helping the Patriots, the Oneidas and Tuscaroras forsook the alluring presents offered as the king's bounty to loyal Indians.[21]

Farther west, the Onondagas, Cayugas, and Senecas gradually fell under the influence of the British troops and Loyalist refugees who gathered at Fort Niagara. During the fall of 1775, Colonel John Butler (a former deputy to Sir William Johnson) took post at Niagara. Endowed with presents and authority from Governor Sir Guy Carleton, Butler frequently convened the western Iroquois in council to prepare them for war. He cultivated their distrust of the Patriots as an upstart people without the means and the expertise properly to conduct Indian relations. Addressing the chiefs, Butler ridiculed Schuyler's scanty resources as an American commissioner:

> He was born but yesterday; just now, as it were, [he] started up out of the ground and tomorrow will return into the earth, whence he came. It will not be the space of a month before you hear him cry. He has no men, guns, cannon and ammunition, or clothing; and should he survive the summer, he must perish by the cold next winter for want of blankets. But the King wants neither men nor money; there is no computing his numbers. . . . What a wretched situation must you be in when the King . . . comes in earnest to sweep off the *Americans* if he finds you supporting the *Americans!*

Overwhelmingly agricultural, the thirteen colonies lacked the British manufacturing capacity to produce the steel and cloth goods needed by the Iroquois. The Indians also doubted the ability of the untrained and poorly equipped Patriots to compete with the superior discipline and arms of the British regulars. And by assisting the British, the Onondagas, Cayugas, and Senecas hoped to secure their help in protecting Iroquois lands against invading settlers.[22]

Schuyler lacked the presents needed to cultivate Indian support: "My house is daily crowded with them, and I have next to nothing wherewith to relieve their distress." Struggling barely to supply the Oneidas and some Tuscaroras, the Patriots felt ambivalent about winning active support from the other Iroquois. Far better, Congress reasoned, for the other Iroquois to remain neutral, for then "we should not be deemed responsible for any supplies farther than was consistent with our convenience and abilities." But needy Indians could not afford a neutrality that would deprive them of access to essential trade goods.[23]

VOLUNTEERS

Of all the contenders for Sir William's mantle, Joseph Brant had the greatest ability, charisma, and vision. Better than anyone else of his generation, Brant could combine, or shift between, European gentility and Indian culture. Watching Brant's fine appearance and performance at a formal dinner, the Baroness Riedesel marveled,

> He conversed well, possessed polished manners, and was highly es-
> teemed by General Haldimand. . . . He was dressed partly as a military
> man, and partly as an Indian. He had a manly and intelligent cast of
> countenance. His character was very gentle.

But Brant soon discovered that his paramount asset—his cultural hybrid-ity—was also his greatest liability. So long as Brant served imperial designs, Britons cherished Brant as a gentleman able to sway his fellow natives. But Brant became an especially dangerous Indian in British eyes whenever he defied their management. Meanwhile, British favor aroused Iroquois dis-trust, for many Indians worried that Brant's cross-cultural insights would betray Indian secrets to his British handlers. In sum, Brant remained too fully Indian for the Britons and too enmeshed in British culture for jealous rivals in the native world. But a tireless energy drove Brant to probe the lim-its of his cross-cultural leadership to seek Sir William's mastery of border-land communication.[24]

In July 1775, Guy Johnson, Daniel Claus, and Joseph Brant hoped quickly to rally the Canadian Iroquois for raids to reclaim the Mohawk Valley, but the military governor, Sir Guy Carleton, refused to cooperate. Carleton dis-trusted Indian warriors as unreliable, and he feared that, by committing atrocities, they would alienate potential Loyalists among the Americans. Carleton also disliked Johnson and Claus, who returned the favor. In part, the clash was personal, for Carleton was aloof, austere, and disciplined, while the Johnsons were convivial hosts and sloppy administrators.[25]

But the clash also represented British infighting for power over Indian relations, a contest that had begun during Sir William's lifetime. Carleton insisted that Canadian security required vesting Indian policy in his hands as governor rather than entrusting it to a superintendent dwelling in New York. Fond of the French Canadians, Carleton had also advocated their interests in the fur trade, at the expense of the Schenectady merchants favored by Sir William. In addition, the governor had dismissed Sir William's conspiracy theories that blamed French Canadian agents for all unrest among the Indians. Of course, Sir William and his deputies derided Carleton as an arrogant and ignorant meddler too easily duped by the wily French.[26]

During the summer of 1775, Carleton bluntly told Guy Johnson that he had no authority over any Indians within Canada. Worse still, Claus learned that he had been sacked as a deputy superintendent and replaced by Carleton's nominee, Major John Campbell, a former army officer who benefited from marriage into a prominent French Canadian family. During the preceding war, his father-in-law, Luc de La Corne, had been the French partisan working among the Indians against Sir William Johnson, which hardly endeared Campbell to Johnson's heirs. Moreover, they could justly complain that Campbell lacked talent, tact, or any facility with Indian languages.[27]

Claus and Guy Johnson abruptly sailed to London, where they could press their cases directly to the imperial lords. Johnson wanted his superintendency rendered permanent and his authority extended to Canada, while Claus sought restoration as a deputy superintendent. To provide Indian testimony to their abilities and influence, Claus and Johnson took along two Mohawks: Joseph Brant and John Hill (Oteronyente). Of course, Brant and Hill had their own reason for going: to secure Crown guarantees for Mohawk lands. By sailing away from Quebec in November—just ahead of a siege by the invading Americans—Claus and Johnson infuriated Carleton, who considered their departure a selfish desertion during a moment of crisis. Possessed of a long and vindictive memory, he never forgave them. Instead, Carleton developed a countervailing fondness for their lingering subordinate, John Butler, who agreed to assume the arduous duty of Indian agent at strategic Fort Niagara. Smelling opportunity, Butler exploited Carleton's favor to rise at the expense of his former patrons, the Johnsons.[28]

In January, the voyagers reached London to find that the new imperial secretary of state, Lord George Germain, favored a more aggressive policy against the rebellion, including the employment of Indian allies. Seeking his favor, Claus and Johnson laid claim to Sir William's unique mystique as the master of Indian affairs. With an awkward egotism, Guy boasted that, for Indians to show "an attachment to a person who was dear to Sir William Johnson, and for many years particularly conversant in their affairs, was natural enough, & it was my ambition to render this subservient to His Majesty's interests."[29]

Brant spoke with a more forceful clarity on behalf of his people, cast as Britain's best, but much abused, allies:

The Mohocks, our particular Nation, have on all occasions shewn their zeal and loyalty to the Great King; yet they have been very badly treated by his people in that country, the City of Albany laying an unjust claim to the lands on which our Lower Castle is built, as one Klock and others do to those of Conijoharrie, our Upper Village. We have been often assured by our late, great friend Sir William Johnson, who never deceived us, and we know he was told so, that the King and wise men here would do us justice; but this notwithstanding all our applications has never been done, and it makes us very uneasie.... Indeed, it is very hard when we have let the King's subjects have so much of our lands for so little value, they should want to cheat us in this manner of the small spots we have left for our women and children to live on. We are tired out in making complaints & getting no redress.

Because Brant made a far better impression on the imperial elite, his support for Johnson and Claus secured more for them than they could win for themselves.[30]

A smooth politician, Germain offered them each half a loaf. Guy Johnson became the permanent superintendent of Indian affairs for the northern colonies, with the same salary as Sir William Johnson, but without his authority in Canada. That left Johnson without any Indians to manage, unless the British could subdue the rebellious colonies. Claus got only a lesser appointment as a deputy confined to working with Iroquois refugees in Canada—leaving most of the Canadian Indians to Major Campbell's mismanagement. Brant reaped presents, praise, and vague promises of future redress for the Mohawks, but only after the rebellion had been subdued. Germain meant to avoid alienating colonial settlers, who might yet be wavering in their allegiance, while keeping the Mohawks on a British string.[31]

In addition to impressing Germain, Brant dazzled high society in London. Previous colonial promoters had occasionally brought Indians to London to capitalize on their exoticism. But never had a native visitor possessed such a facility with English words and refined manners. Brant presented a hybrid persona—both genteel and native—a persona that seemed utterly natural, entirely lived within. In public, he carefully wore an Indian costume complete with feathered headdress and steel tomahawk, but in that attire he had himself painted in oil by George Romney, a high-fashion artist. For his cultural versatility, Brant could thank his cumulative education by Molly Brant, Sir William Johnson, Eleazar Wheelock, Samuel Kirkland, and John Stuart.[32]

The key first step to Brant's new celebrity came at St. James's Palace on February 29, 1776, when the Great King, George III, formally received the ambitious young Mohawk. Taking a lasting pride in the encounter, Brant later assured Kirkland: "I have had the honour to be introduced to the King of England—a finer man than whom I think it would be a truly difficult task to find." That royal reception rendered Brant welcome at the homes and masked balls of fashionable aristocrats. He also secured initiation into London's most prestigious Masonic lodge and received an array of expensive gifts, including silk shirts, an engraved rifle and pistol, and a silver watch.[33]

In early June, Brant and Guy Johnson set sail for America, bound in an armed convoy to New York City, the target of a British invasion led by Sir William Howe. Given the paucity of Indians on that front, this was an odd destination for the superintendent and a Mohawk war chief. Why not Canada, where Indians abounded? Alas, Sir Guy Carleton still commanded there and still wanted no part of Guy Johnson. So, with bureaucratic wisdom, Germain sent Johnson to where he could do the least harm rather than to where he might do the most good.

After a long and difficult voyage, the convoy reached New York's harbor in late July 1776. The voyagers found significant new developments since their departure from Quebec nine months before. Under Patriot pressure, Sir John Johnson had abandoned Johnson Hall, fleeing to Canada—where Carleton was driving back the American invasion. Despite that Canadian defeat and Howe's impending attack on New York City, the Continental Congress declared an independent United States on July 4, 1776. That declaration soon seemed reckless, for Howe drove George Washington's Continental Army out of New York City and across New Jersey during the fall.[34]

After distinguishing himself for bravery during Howe's campaign, Brant undertook a daring mission meant to rally the Six Nations for the next summer's campaign, when the British hoped to mop up the faltering Patriot rebellion. In November, Brant and a Loyalist friend, Captain Gilbert Tice, left New York City, heading northwest through Patriot territory. Traveling at night and sleeping by day in the woods, Brant and Tice traversed the Catskills, reaching Onoquaga on the Susquehanna River in early December. By month's end they headed westward across Iroquoia to Fort Niagara.[35]

No mere pawn of the British, Brant embraced Loyalism to serve Mohawk interests. Indeed, he challenged Governor Carleton, who opposed Brant's plan immediately to lead Indian raiders into the Mohawk Valley. But promoting military independence contradicted the Indians' material dependence on British trade and presents. The other Iroquois listened politely to Brant's plan but clung to their cautious neutrality, for they meant to wait until the British began their invasion of New York from Canada. Brant blamed that caution on Butler's influence. Of course, Carleton and Butler wanted Iroquois assistance but only on a British schedule, on British terms, and under British leadership. Once the British invasion began, they would call upon the Iroquois for warriors to act as auxiliaries.[36]

The western Iroquois chiefs had their own reasons to balk at Brant's daring plans for unilateral action. Devoted to tradition, lineage, and a deliberate pace, they resented Brant as a boastful and aggressive young man, a minor war chief of obscure origins from a relatively weak people, the Mohawks. As they saw it, Brant assumed improper airs, acting as if he had been commissioned by the Great King to lead all of the Six Nations. Brant's pushy ambition particularly irritated the great old Seneca war chief Sayenqueraghta. Proud and leading a more numerous people, Sayenqueraghta refused to play second fiddle to a Mohawk upstart.[37]

Lacking Brant's colonial education, Johnson patronage, and London visit, Iroquois traditionalists distrusted his emphasis on all three as sources of unique power. Brant's cultural hybridity troubled Iroquois traditionalists. He seemed too fluid, able to flow back and forth between the Indian and the British worlds, depending upon opportunity. That versatility eroded categories that the chiefs wished to keep distinct. Jealous of their political secrets, the Seneca chiefs preferred to deal directly with true Britons—who could be kept in the dark about some things—rather than deal through a fellow Indian who too smoothly shifted between languages and cultures, producing troubling mixtures by breaking down reassuring barriers. To defend Iroquois tradition, the chiefs preferred a cautious alliance with the British rather than gambling on Brant's daring unilateralism, innovative pan-Iroquoian vision, and charismatic leadership. There was plenty of irony to go around. Brant invoked his British contacts and insights to argue for greater Indian autonomy, but traditional chiefs heeded British advice to ignore his aggressive plans for native initiatives because those chiefs saw Brant as too colonial in his ways.

Frustrated at Niagara by British officers and Seneca chiefs, Brant free-lanced by heading to Onoquaga in the spring of 1777. He hoped to set an infectious example for the other Iroquois by conducting the war in his own way. Although most of the Onoquaga villagers cautiously held back from joining Brant, he enjoyed surprising success in recruiting the Loyalists who abounded in the settlements of the upper Susquehanna and Delaware valleys. Small farmers living in frontier hardship, they had hoped to sit out the war, but the Patriots demanded taxes, oaths of allegiance, and militia service—and they plundered those who refused. Seeking an opportunity to strike back, these alienated settlers rallied to Brant when he raised the king's flag at nearby Onoquaga.[38]

Brant formed a distinctive and irregular corps of about 100 men known as "Brant's Volunteers." Only a fifth were Mohawks, with the rest drawn from the Loyalist settlers. More irony: Brant wanted to promote greater Indian autonomy and initiative, but he proved most effective in mustering a company of poor whites who trusted in the personal charisma that so troubled Indian traditionalists. Lacking uniforms, the volunteers dressed and painted themselves as Indian warriors. That role-playing released their inhibitions against attacking rebel neighbors, who became a cultural other. An Indian appearance also compounded the terror of their Patriot targets. But that Indian guise also marked them as race traitors subject to immediate execution when captured by the Patriots, a knowledge that contributed to their desperate effectiveness in combat.

Unpaid by the British, Brant's volunteers relied upon plunder for their compensation and upon Brant's scrounging at Niagara for their rations and clothing. Despite the greater hardships, the volunteers preferred Brant's charismatic, innovative, and spontaneous style over the hierarchy, discipline, and steady pay of a standard regiment. Clinging to Brant, they rebuffed the financial enticements of other Loyalist commanders, including John Butler, who was raising a battalion of rangers. Of course, Brant's irregular unit irritated conventional officers. One Briton complained that the volunteers "refuse to take arms or be under any command. . . . I have been thirty years a soldier, but never had so much trouble as with those fellows." Hated by the Patriots and disdained by British officers, these volunteers developed an especially intense bond to their leader, despite the exceptionally dangerous service that he conducted. Indeed, those dangers compounded his hold, for Brant seemed uniquely capable of guiding them to safety and victory.[39]

In July 1777, Brant led his volunteers north to Oswego, on Lake Ontario, to rendezvous with an advancing army commanded by the British colonel Barry St. Leger, with Sir John Johnson as the second-in-command. At last, the British and the Loyalists had launched their Canadian invasion of the Mohawk Valley. At Oswego, St. Leger and Sir John convened an Indian council that summoned the Six Nations to join the king's cause. Bolstered by Iroquois warriors, the invaders headed southeastward against the Patriot garrison at the renovated Fort Stanwix.[40]

FORT SCHUYLER

During the summer of 1776, General Schuyler had ordered the reconstruction and garrisoning of Fort Stanwix at the critical portage between the Mohawk River and Wood Creek. Renamed Fort Schuyler, the post guarded the western entrance to the Mohawk Valley, which reassured the Oneidas of protection in the event of a British-led invasion from Canada. In Schuyler's words, the fort would "impress on the Indians an idea that we are capable of acting with vigour, and that we do not mean to be trifled with." In August, Schuyler met some Six Nations chiefs in council at German Flats to explain the new policy, to bestow presents, and to promise protection of Oneida lands against encroaching settlers. He pledged that the United States would honor the boundary line established by the 1768 Treaty of Fort Stanwix. In return, the attending chiefs renewed a friendly neutrality that endorsed Schuyler's military plans to defend the valley.[41]

The pretense of Iroquois unity and neutrality collapsed in August 1777, when St. Leger's army advanced from Oswego to attack Fort Schuyler. That diverse force consisted of about 700 Britons and Loyalists joined by 800 Iroquois warriors: a mix of Senecas, Cayugas, Onondagas, and Mohawks. On the other side, Oneidas and some Tuscaroras helped the Patriot defense. At Kahnawake, an Oneida spy, Deacon Thomas, provided an advance warning of the invasion, a warning that facilitated efforts to strengthen Fort Schuyler. Once St. Leger's siege began, about 60 Oneida warriors, led by Honyery (Thawengarakwen) joined the 700 American militia, commanded by General Nicholas Herkimer, who marched from German Flats to relieve the fort.[42]

At Canajoharie, Molly Brant noted the Patriot preparations and sent a secret message of warning to her brother. Tipped off, the Loyalists and Iroquois ambushed Herkimer's men near the Oneida village of Oriske (Oriskany), about five miles southeast of the fort, on August 6. After a bloody, daylong battle in brutal heat, dense gunpowder smoke, and even a brief thunderstorm, the Oneidas and Patriots retreated, leaving behind at least 200 dead. The Patriot losses included five members of the Tryon County Committee of Safety, two state legislators, and General Herkimer. The Loyalists and their Iroquois allies suffered lighter losses but heavy enough by native standards: about 50 dead, including one of Sir William's Indian sons, William Tekawironte. Stunned by their unexpected casualties, the western Iroquois lost interest in further combat, for they longed to return home to conduct condolence ceremonies for the dead. Their desertion grew with news of the approach of another Patriot force commanded by Benedict Arnold. Disheartened by those desertions, St. Leger retreated in haste and disarray to Canada in late August.[43]

The bloody battle at Oriske embittered relations between the Oneidas and the Mohawks. Immediately after the battle, Brant's Mohawks burned Oriske, while the Oneidas (and some Patriots) plundered Tiononderoge and Canajoharie, taking the greatest loot from Molly Brant. Although gratifying to Oneida and settler anger, this plundering weakened the Patriot cause by inducing most of the Mohawks still in the valley to flee to Canada or Niagara, where they strengthened the British with additional warriors. The

Canajoharies, including Molly Brant, headed west to Niagara to reunite with her brother. Led by Captain John Deserontyon, the Tiononderoge refugees fled northward to convene at La Chine near Montreal, where Daniel Claus supplied their needs in return for their military service. Deprived of his Tiononderoge congregation, Rev. John Stuart became a Patriot prisoner, held at Schenectady, while the Patriots converted his Anglican chapel into a tavern and later a stable.[44]

Infuriated by the heavy losses at Oriske, the Patriots increased their persecution of the Loyalists in the Mohawk Valley. Plundered and sometimes horsewhipped, several hundred fled northward to Canada during the winter and spring of 1777–78. Their young men bolstered the Loyalist battalions, including those commanded by John Butler and Sir John Johnson. Meanwhile, the Patriots consolidated their hold on the valley by confiscating Loyalist properties, including the Johnson estates of Kingsborough, Guy Park, and Williamsburgh. Anticipating Loyalist and Indian raids, the Patriots fortified the houses of local leaders with earthworks, palisades, and blockhouses to serve as neighborhood refuges and rallying points. But those preparations did little to ease the destructive Loyalist and Indian raids that surged during the spring. In June 1778, the Niagara commandant reported, "Scalps & Prisoners are coming in every day, which is all the News [that] this Place affords."[45]

BROTHER AND SISTER

Returning to Onoquaga in 1778, Brant became the most active and able of partisan commanders, rustling cattle, burning houses, and killing Patriots. His notoriety led alarmed Patriots to see his hand in every frontier atrocity, although most were committed by other raiders. For example, in July 1778, Butler and Sayenqueraghta destroyed the Yankee settlements at Wyoming on the Susquehanna River in Pennsylvania. When the raiders slaughtered their prisoners, the Patriots blamed Brant, who was in fact far away at Onoquaga. Proud of his genteel restraint that spared civilians and most prisoners, Brant bristled at the Patriot propaganda casting him as the ultimate bloodthirsty savage. Indeed, Brant's Volunteers behaved better than did the Continental soldiers who ravaged Iroquois villages.[46]

In October 1778, Continental soldiers and frontier militia based at Cherry Valley descended the Susquehanna to destroy Onoquaga. Brant and his Volunteers were away on a raid, leaving the village defenseless. Alerted to the approaching danger, most of the villagers fled westward in time. Onoquaga impressed the Patriot commander as "the finest Indian town I ever saw; on both sides [of] the River there was about 40 good houses, square logs, shingles & stone Chimneys, good Floors, glass Windows, &c., &c." The soldiers torched the houses, butchered the cattle, chopped down the apple trees, and mowed and spoiled the growing corn crop—and they killed some native children found hidden in the cornfields.[47]

In November, the Loyalists and Iroquois revenged Onoquaga by surprising Cherry Valley. John Butler's arrogant son, Captain Walter Butler, led the raid, but he lost control of the Seneca warriors, who killed 32 civilians in addition to 16 soldiers. The Cherry Valley Massacre embarrassed British commanders who blamed Butler and exonerated Brant. Indeed, his exertions had saved many civilians from vengeful Senecas. Niagara's commandant assured the governor that Brant "behaved with great humanity to all those who fell into his hands at Cherry Valley. This (I am convinced) will recommend him to your Excellency's notice much more than any thing else I could say in his favour." While becoming a brutal savage in Patriot propaganda, Brant won British applause for a genteel restraint applauded as a triumph over his native nature. Daniel Claus extolled Brant's "singular power and command to resist the Excess of Liquor & whenever a little intoxicated his governing himself from the usual savage madness & frenzy."[48]

In early 1779, Brant visited Quebec to call on General Haldimand, a Swiss-born veteran officer who had supplanted Carleton as the commander and governor in Canada. In seeking favors from Haldimand, Brant obtained eager assistance from Claus, who passionately hated John Butler for profiting at the Johnson's expense by cultivating the favor of their nemesis, Sir Guy Carleton. Claus denounced Butler as indolent, blundering, and corrupt. To make a pointed contrast, Claus described Brant as the true and consummate genius of frontier warfare, possessed of a zeal, activity, ability, honesty, and influence that shamed John Butler.[49]

At Quebec, Brant impressed Haldimand, who praised that "very intelligent and good man" as critical to the British war effort. In addition to presents of fine clothing and silver jewelry, Brant obtained a captain's commission in the royal army with a £100 salary. Haldimand also promised clothing, rations, and medical care (but no pay) for Brant's volunteers. And the governor agreed to support Molly Brant's considerable expenses, observing that "whatever may be done for her is Due to the Memory of Sir William Johnson, to Her Services, and will be a handsome Mark of attention to Joseph." Finally, on April 7, Haldimand pledged in writing that "as soon as the present Troubles were at an end" the Mohawks "should be restored at the Expence of Government, to the state they were in before these broke out." This promise later become problematic, when the British failed to subdue the American rebellion. How were the British to restore the Mohawk situation if their homeland remained in Patriot hands?[50]

In May, Brant returned to Niagara to live in the genteel style permitted by his new salary, plunder from raids, and enhanced credit with merchants. A Patriot prisoner recalled:

> His dress was very fine; he wore a broadcloth blanket over his shoulders in the usual Indian style, of the finest make, with a deep, rich, red border. When he showed himself about the fort, he was always in full and careful costume, glittering with brooches, etc.

On the Niagara River, six miles above the fort, Brant acquired a farm with a stout log house, which he augmented by building a small chapel for Anglican services. To work the farm and serve the household, Brant appropriated slaves captured during his frontier raids. He began to approximate the mode of life he had seen at Johnson Hall.[51]

A new marriage enhanced his prospects. His second wife, Susanna, had died in late 1778, probably of tuberculosis. A year later, Brant married Catharine Croghan (Adonwentishon), the twenty-year-old daughter of George Croghan (one of Sir William's deputies) and a Mohawk woman. As the niece of Tekarihoga, the most prestigious chief of Canajoharie, Catharine dramatically boosted Brant's standing and clout among the Mohawks. Although a love match, the marriage was also as politically shrewd as Sir William's choice of Molly Brant.[52]

By public honors and gifts, Haldimand hoped to enhance Brant's standing and influence among the Six Nations, but the British rewards backfired by provoking the jealousy of rival chiefs, especially Sayenqueraghta. Walter Butler warned that Brant "has been more notice taken of than has been good for his own interest with his own people." A British general opined that, without a royal commission, Brant "would be much happier and would have more weight with the Indians, which he in some measure forfeits by their knowing that he receives pay." Learning this lesson in late 1779, Haldimand quietly retrenched his favor to Brant by pocketing a promotion from captain to colonel offered by Lord Germain. By securing a government pension for Sayenqueraghta, Haldimand also belatedly sought to reward "the man of greatest influence in the whole Six Nations, by whose intrigues Major Butler has been able to carry through many essential points."[53]

But no chief, neither Sayenqueraghta nor Joseph Brant, could match the Iroquois influence of Molly Brant. To an inherited prestige greater than her brother's, she added a formidable will, keen mind, pointed eloquence, and a powerful mystique as Sir William's widow. One British officer considered Molly's influence "far superior to that of all their Chiefs put together." According to Daniel Claus, she publicly rebuked Sayenqueraghta for slighting Seneca obligations to "the late Sir William Johnson, whose memory she never mentioned without tears in her eyes, which affects the Indians greatly." Shamed, Sayenqueraghta and the other Seneca chiefs immediately "promised henceforth truthfully to keep their engagements with her late friend, the Baronet, for she is in every respect considered and esteemed by them as Sir William's Relict, and one word from her is more taken notice of by the Five Nations than a thousand from any white man." Claus added that Molly "prevented many a mischief & much more so than of her Brother Joseph, whose present Zeal & Activity occasioned rather Envy & Jealousy."[54]

In reward for her Loyalist zeal and native connections, Molly expected an almost unlimited respect and generosity from British officers. Collecting an annual pension of £100, she dressed in a calico gown fastened with abundant silver brooches. At Carleton Island, a British base at the northeastern corner of Lake Ontario, the government built a fine mansion for Molly and her family. When that proved inadequate, British officers had another built on the nearby mainland. In addition to her own prodigious consumption, Molly demanded goods to sustain her servants, children, and extensive kin. Guy Johnson grumbled: "Molly used to go to the Stores & take out everything she pleased & give to her particulars. She is certainly, you know, pretty large minded. . . . I fear that any Expense or Attention will fall short of her Desires, though I wish to gratify them." Needing her Iroquois influence, and intimidated by her imperious manner, few officers dared to disappoint Molly Brant.[55]

EVERLASTING FRIENDSHIP

As most of the Iroquois rallied to the British and Loyalists to raid the Mohawk Valley, the Oneidas and Tuscaroras soared in importance to the Patriot cause. As guides and warriors, they became indispensable to the defense of an embattled frontier. Serving as allies, rather than as hired soldiers, the Oneidas conducted the war as they saw best. While fighting the British and Loyalists with verve, the Oneidas avoided (after the battle of Oriske) combat with their fellow Iroquois, who reciprocated the restraint. That mutual caution served the interests of the frontier Patriots, who were on the defensive, better than the British, who complained that their Iroquois allies avoided any area where they might clash with the Oneidas. That mutual restraint also enabled Oneida spies to mingle with their Iroquois friends at Niagara and in Canada, gathering information that alerted the Patriots to impending attacks. And by circulating American overtures and news of Patriot victories, the Oneida agents worked to disaffect Loyalists and their Iroquois allies from the British cause. Ruing the Oneida effectiveness in the shadow war of the northern frontier, Haldimand declared: "The Treachery of the Onidas and [the] constant obstacles they present to our Scouts in any attempt upon the Mohawk River makes it a matter of serious consideration to compel them to relinquish the Rebel Interest, or to cut them off."[56]

Recognizing their crucial importance, General Schuyler carefully wooed the Oneidas. In early 1776, he wrote to them: "Be assured that you will be a happy people whilst you remain in Love and Friendship with us and that I will do my utmost to make you love me as much as I do you." Although desperately short on supplies, Schuyler did everything he could to provide something for the Oneidas. In October 1776, he observed, "They are such good Friends, that I wish to have it in my power to give them some Cloathing." Schuyler also promised American protection for Oneida lands after defeating the British and the Loyalists: "You will then partake of every Blessing we enjoy, and united with a free people, your Liberty and Property will be safe."[57]

Schuyler bolstered Oneida morale by forcefully disseminating news of Patriot victories. After George Washington's Continental Army won the battles of Trenton and Princeton during the winter of 1776–77, Schuyler rushed the news to Kanonwalohale. He sent along barrels of rum, "wishing you to drink Health, peace and Liberty to your American Brethren and everlasting Friendship between you and them." Upon receiving a subsequent keg in early 1779, to celebrate another Patriot victory, the Oneidas assured Schuyler, "It makes us feel happy & wish further Success & greater Victories to your Chief Warrior and all his Men." Alas, the chiefs also reported that a drunken warrior had gotten lost and had frozen to death in the snow outside of Fort Schuyler. Both the British and the Patriots exploited alcohol to try to manage their Iroquois allies. In the process, both promoted an often deadly addiction that they had piously denounced in peacetime.[58]

INVASION

Stung by the frontier raids of 1778, the Patriots counterattacked in 1779, when Washington diverted part of his Continental Army to invade western Iroquoia. Anticipating such an invasion, the Iroquois chiefs begged Haldimand to renovate and garrison the lapsed fortress at Oswego on Lake Ontario. Instead, the governor dithered, citing a lack of men and supplies. Discounting the Patriot offensive capacity, Haldimand worried far more that a French fleet and army might ascend the St. Lawrence River to attack his headquarters at Quebec.[59]

In April, Colonel Goose Van Schaick led the first Patriot probe into Iroquoia. Heading west from Fort Schuyler, his troops surprised and destroyed the main Onondaga village, killing 12 and taking 33 prisoners. Because the most militant Onondagas had already withdrawn to Niagara, the villagers were neutralists and easy pickings for a surprise attack. The Onondagas accused the Patriot soldiers of raping and killing women captured at the village, "yet these Rebels call themselves Christians."[60]

During the summer, the main Patriot invasion advanced in three prongs. From Pittsburgh, Colonel Daniel Broadhead marched north against the Seneca villages in the Allegheny Valley. From the Mohawk Valley, General James Clinton led his brigade down the Susquehanna River to Tioga to meet the main thrust, commanded by General John Sullivan, who marched up that river, past the ruins of Wyoming. Samuel Kirkland joined the Sullivan expedition as a chaplain, mixing Christianity with patriotism to inspire the troops. In mid-August at Tioga, Clinton rendezvoused with Sullivan, creating an army of 3,000 men, more than three times the number of Loyalists and western Iroquois mustered to resist.[61]

At Newtown Point on August 29, Sullivan's soldiers brushed aside resistance led by Brant, Butler, and Sayenqueraghta. The Patriot troops then methodically located, looted, and burned the Iroquois villages around the Finger Lakes and in the Genesee Valley, while Broadhead did the same in the Allegheny Valley. Everywhere, the soldiers marveled at the substantial villages of log cabins, the broad fields of Indian corn, and the extensive orchards of apple, peach, and cherry trees, all of which they systematically destroyed. Patriot torches claimed Kanadasega, Sayenqueraghta's home village that had hosted Kirkland's original mission in 1765. On September 15, Sullivan turned back, returning via the Chemung and Susquehanna rivers to Pennsylvania. In retrospect, he boasted of destroying 40 Iroquois villages and at least 160,000 bushels of corn. Impressed by Iroquoia's fertile soil, many officers and soldiers eagerly anticipated a postwar return as conquering settlers.[62]

In a gratuitous finishing flourish, Clinton's returning soldiers dispossessed the four Mohawk families who still lingered at Tiononderoge, hoping for safety in their neutrality. Arrested and evicted, they lost their homes to envious settlers. Colonel Peter Gansevoort observed, "It is remarked that the Indians live much better than most of the Mohawk River farmers, their Houses [being] very well furnished with all [the] necessary Household utensils, great plenty of Grain, several Horses, cows and waggons." That lost property represented the fruits of their long, profitable alliance with Sir William Johnson. This dispossession troubled Philip Schuyler as a betrayal of the trust that the neutral Mohawks had placed in his public promise of their safety. His protests led Washington to order the Mohawks freed from the Albany jail, but they failed to recover their confiscated homes.[63]

In early September, Haldimand belatedly dispatched Sir John Johnson from Montreal to defend Iroquoia against Sullivan's invasion. In addition to acting far too late, Haldimand sent far too little, entrusting Sir John with only 400 Loyalists and Britons, about 200 Canadian Iroquois, and Guy Johnson. After three years of comfortable inertia in New York City, Guy had at last made his way to his duty in Canada. During the relief expedition, neither Johnson manifested Sir William's initiative and charisma. Advancing slowly and complaining all the way, they did nothing to inspire their Indian allies. Equally reluctant to leave Canada, the Indians drank heavily and displayed a truculence that repeatedly delayed an already laggard expedition. It seemed fitting that the ill-starred Guy Johnson would appear only at the moment of disaster to help lead a long, slow progress from Montreal to futility.[64]

At last, the Johnsons reached Niagara on October 5, three weeks too late to catch Sullivan—a good thing, given their inadequate numbers. At Niagara, they found 5,000 despairing Iroquois refugees, in a straggling, makeshift village that stretched eight miles above Fort Niagara along the river. Desperately ragged and hungry, the disgruntled refugees faced the cold rains of autumn without adequate shelter. They blamed the British for their woes. In a subtle but calculated insult, the Iroquois chiefs initially declined to conduct the customary welcoming ceremony expected by Guy and Sir John, a slight unthinkable in Sir William's day and evidence that the Sullivan expedition had strained the British relationship with their Iroquois allies.[65]

With Butler's and Brant's help, Guy and Sir John tried to distract the Iroquois chiefs by organizing a revenge raid to destroy the Oneida villages. Unenthusiastic, most of the chiefs dragged their heels by getting "very drunk & very troublesome." When the raid did, at last, get under way, only 87 warriors showed up, half of them Mohawks, for Brant was the only chief to show any enthusiasm for the venture. In late October, Sir John halted the farce by canceling the raid.[66]

Returning to Montreal, he left Guy Johnson behind to cope with Iroquois anger through the long, cold, and hungry winter, when hundreds died from malnutrition, exposure, and disease. But far from breaking the western Iroquois—as the Patriots had expected—dispossession and suffering enhanced the survivors' grim determination to renew their raids in the spring of 1780. The Loyalist Richard Cartwright observed, "The rebels must have found that their grand Western Expedition, attended with such vast labour and enormous expense, instead of conquering, had only served to exasperate the Indians."[67]

LOSS

Employing most of their troops to attack Patriots along the Atlantic seaboard, the British could spare only small garrisons to defend Canada and the forts scattered along the Great Lakes. A mere 400 soldiers, mostly Loyalists, guarded Niagara, an extensive fort built for three times that number. To screen undermanned Niagara from Patriot attack, the British procured about 900 Iroquois warriors to raid the settlements in the Mohawk Valley. By putting the frontier Patriots on the defensive, the British preserved their forts, prevented a renewed invasion of Canada, and destroyed farms and gristmills that supplied the Continental Army. Those raids also demoralized the valley Patriots by exposing their vulnerability to a frontier war of surprise and terror. Brant, Sayenqueraghta, the Seneca chief Cornplanter, and Walter Butler led war parties out of Niagara, while Sir John Johnson conducted parallel raids from the St. Lawrence.[68]

This frontier war took an increasingly grim toll on the Oneidas. In July 1779, when Deacon Thomas died resisting arrest at Kahnawake, Haldimand celebrated the death of "the right arm of Parson Kirkland." In February 1780, Schuyler sent the Oneida chiefs Skenandon and Good Peter to Niagara to promote Iroquois defection from the British alliance. But the western Iroquois rejected the overture, and Guy Johnson cast the emissaries into the fort's dungeon, a bitterly cold and windowless "black hole." Held on short rations for 150 days, Good Peter and Skenandon cracked, winning their release by consenting to guide the Loyalist war parties.[69]

During the campaign of 1780, the British and their Indian allies initially targeted the Oneida and Tuscarora country, determined to eliminate that forward base of Patriot influence in Iroquoia. Impending attack intimidated the Tuscaroras of Kanaghsoraga, at the western margin of the Oneida country. Defecting from the Patriot alliance, they fled westward to join the Loyalists at Niagara in early June. Their removal exposed Old Oneida to attack, inducing those villagers also to withdraw to Niagara and to submit to British guidance. From Kanaghsoraga and Old Oneida, the British retrieved 294 Indians, a mix of Tuscaroras, Onondagas, and Oneidas. Guy Johnson gloried in the defections as his greatest coup. In a triumphant speech, he rebuked the defectors for their delay: "What think you would your old Friend, the late Sir William Johnson, have said to you on this Occasion, to whom you were always carrying complaints of the Encroachments made on your Lands & frauds committed by those very People to whom you have been since so much attached[?]"[70]

The evacuation of Kanaghsoraga and Old Oneida left Kanonwalohale isolated and vulnerable. In mid-July, Joseph Brant led another war party out of Niagara against Kanonwalohale, compelling Skenandon and Good Peter to come along to urge their people to surrender. A few Oneidas, including Captain Jacob Reed, did surrender, but most (over 400) instead took refuge at Fort Schuyler, where Kirkland served as the garrison's chaplain. Brant's raiders then systematically destroyed the crops, houses, and meetinghouse that represented the material progress of Kirkland's mission. The Kanonwalohale Oneidas lost about seventy-three houses, as well as almost all of their horses and other personal possessions. That destruction deepened the Oneidas' enmity for Brant, who had acted on his own anger at them for plundering his home (and that of his sister Molly) at Canajoharie. In early 1781, Claus described Brant as "fixed in his Mind to take Revenge on [the Oneidas] ... for sundry insults that he as well as his Sister received from them." [71]

The Oneidas moved their women, children, and old men to a bleak refugee camp near Schenectady. Most of the warriors then returned to Fort Schuyler to assist the Patriot defense of the Mohawk Valley. Because American finances and logistics were a mess, the refugees suffered from ragged clothing, scanty food, and cold, leaky huts. A smallpox epidemic, pervasive poverty, and rambling begging took their toll on Oneida morale. Samuel Kirkland recalled, "The devastation of their towns reduced them to absolute want & dependence & their dispersion among the whites rendered them more than ever idle, intemperate & abject." Cherishing the Oneidas as his best fighters, General Schuyler warned Congress in October 1780:

> In the late incursions of the enemy, they joined with our troops with alacrity and behaved with a spirit which drew the admiration of the officers under whose command they fought and bled, but I fear their virtue will at last yield to a continuation of distress which no human being can endure and that they will renounce an alliance which has exposed them to such abuse.

In British Canada, Haldimand seconded the strategic importance of the Oneidas, urging his subordinates to destroy the Schenectady refugee camp: "This opportunity should, if possible, be taken to extirpate the remaining unfriendly Oneidas who much impede our scouts and recruiting Parties and are in many respects very useful to the Rebels." Fortunately, that British raid fell short. [72]

The destruction of the Oneida villages exposed the Patriot settlements to British and Indian raiders. The raiders' access further improved during the spring of 1781, when the Patriots abandoned Fort Schuyler. Unable to supply the fort adequately or to repair the damages wrought by a flood and a fire in rapid succession, the Patriots withdrew the demoralized garrison. By the end of 1781, the raiders had destroyed most of the Mohawk Valley settlements, making refugees of at least two-thirds of the inhabitants, widowing 380 women, and leaving about 2,000 children without fathers. New York's Patriot governor, George Clinton, lamented, "Schenectady may now be said to become the limits of our western Frontier."[73]

EXTRAVAGANCE

To rally Iroquois raiders, the British multiplied the presents delivered at Fort Niagara. The Iroquois experienced a great boom in rum, guns, ammunition, cloth, clothing, hatchets, hoes, mirrors, and jewelry. In 1781 at the three Great Lakes posts of Niagara, Detroit, and Michilimackinac, the British delivered presents worth £100,000—up dramatically from the £500 given in 1775. The increased presents included massive quantities of alcohol: over 7,000 gallons of rum annually during the early 1780s at Niagara alone. The commander there, General Allan MacLean, marveled that "the People at the head of [the] Indian department seem to Vie with each other who shall expend [the] most Rum, and the great Chiefs are striving [to see] who shall Drink [the] most Rum."[74]

In wartime, the British at last acted with a generosity that impressed their allies. Addressing an Indian council at Niagara in 1779, Sayenqueraghta urged:

> It is also your Business Brothers to exert yourselves in the Defense of this Road by which the King, our Father, so fully supplied our Wants. If this is once stopt we must be a miserable People, and be left exposed to the Resentment of the Rebels, who notwithstanding their fair Speeches, wish for nothing more than to extirpate us from the Earth, that they may possess our Lands, the Desire of attaining which we are convinced is the Cause of the present War between the King and his disobedient Children.

Rather than imposing the British will on the Indians, vulnerable Fort Niagara was a vital Indian asset worth protecting from Patriot attack.[75]

Niagara became notorious for drinking, brawling, whoring, and cheating. Crude taverns, stores, and bordellos sprouted on "the Bottom," the riverside flat below the fort. The Bottom boasted Indian prostitutes infamous for both beauty and drinking. Wartime Niagara also attracted profiteering traders. In 1779, a mercantile clerk marveled that such an isolated post should annually consume £30,000 in merchandise. Dealing with illiterate customers and tricking a distant bureaucracy invited conniving and corruption by officials and merchants. Every post commandant reached General MacLean's conclusion, "It's a maxim I find that has been long adopted in this Part of the World, that what ever can be got from Government, is well got, where no censure can insue."[76]

Two major firms predominated: that of Edward Pollard and the rival partnership of Forsyth & Taylor. To maximize their profits, the firms bought the interest of key officials who swayed the allocation of government contracts. Early in the war, Pollard exploited his friendship with John Butler to secure most of the government business supplying the Indians at Niagara. In return, Butler took a cut of the profits. That profitable understanding came to a crashing halt in October 1779, when Guy Johnson arrived to take charge of the Indian Department at Niagara. To undermine Butler's influence with the Indians, Guy switched government favor to Forsyth & Taylor.[77]

The Johnsons underestimated Butler as a crude bumpkin who had risen far beyond his competence and his class thanks to Sir Guy Carleton's misguided patronage. How dare Butler exercise the government largesse and conduct Indian councils in the manner of Sir William? Once Haldimand replaced Carleton, the Johnsons expected to cut Butler down to size, restoring his subservience. But Haldimand appreciated Butler's talents as an agent to Indians. In addition to speaking the Iroquois languages better than could Sir John or Guy Johnson, the rough-and-ready Butler mixed better, sharing in the hardships and profane humor of the Indians. Loath to sacrifice those talents to the Johnsons' resentment, Haldimand ordered them to collaborate tactfully with Butler. Ignoring Haldimand's advice, Guy Johnson robbed Butler of the fruits of his corruption and spared few chances to insult him.[78]

But Guy made crucial mistakes. Desperate to buy influence among the Iroquois, Guy Johnson spent government money in profligate quantities and kept sloppy records. In both regards, Guy followed Sir William's example— but to a greater degree driven by a sense of inferiority. Lacking Sir William's charisma and cunning, Guy Johnson could never get away with the same excesses, to say nothing of greater ones.

To win Sayenqueraghta away from Butler, Guy Johnson gave "a fine blue Coat, trimmed with Gold-Lace, and a gold-embroidered Waist Coat" supplemented with abundant silver jewelry. Sayenqueraghta's son collected a scarlet coat with gold epaulets and a silver gorget. When Haldimand protested such extravagance, Johnson confessed his inability to resist ambitious chiefs: "Many of the Indians will no longer wear Tinsel Lace and are becoming Good Judges of Gold & Silver." Their families also expected wine, tea, coffee, sugar, chocolate, and fine linens. And the favor bestowed on one chief invited clamors for similar gifts from jealous rivals.[79]

To maintain their own influence, chiefs needed additional gifts for their kin and supporters. Otherwise, how could they persuade warriors to fight for the British? Johnson explained to Haldimand that the war chiefs "must depend on the Superintendent's interest and Indulgence to make up any party of Consequence." Johnson felt helpless to deny Indians who often reminded him that the British had promised to fulfill all of their needs—and that the British had failed to help them during Sullivan's invasion.[80]

While Johnson faulted voracious Indian demand for the mounting costs, the chiefs often felt stinted, blaming corruption by Indian Department officials. In public council at Niagara in 1783, a visiting Sir John Johnson announced a belated economy drive to reduce presents. Sayenqueraghta angrily replied that the Indians expected to "receive the Presents intended for us, & that they may not be applied to the use of the White people, & at the same time charged to us, which has often been the case, & has frequently, & undeservedly given us the Character of being Extravagantly expensive to the King our Father." He then paused to point at the attending Indian Department officers, including Butler.[81]

By 1781, the soaring costs of supplying the Indians alarmed the imperial overlords in London. They pressured Haldimand to do something, especially at Niagara, where the corruption and trickery had become too blatant. Noting the new concern for economy, Butler detected an opportunity to even scores with Johnson. Gathering evidence of the superintendent's corrupt dealings with Forsyth & Taylor, Butler sent it to Haldimand, who ordered General MacLean to investigate. MacLean reported that Johnson's accounts were "Extravagant, Wounderfull & fictitious, and the quality of Articles so Extraordinary, New & Uncommon." One Johnson entry credited Forsyth & Taylor with providing 1,156 kettles—a thousand more than the actual 156. Suspended as superintendent and summoned to Montreal, Johnson faced an angry Haldimand, who blasted Guy's conduct as "reprehensible." In vain, Johnson defended his practices as adhering to Sir William's precedents. Although never convicted, Guy remained in official disgrace and limbo, unable to return to duty and obliged to defend his accounts in London (where he died in 1788). In Guy's absence, Butler took over at Niagara, basking in Haldimand's favor—to the Johnsons' dismay. In corruption and intrigue, they had been defeated by their supposed inferior.[82]

In early 1782, the home government replaced Guy Johnson as superintendent with Sir John Johnson. After Guy's effusive incompetence, Sir John's austere restraint and apparent sense of honor reassured his superiors. Long loath to deal with the Indians, Sir John reluctantly accepted the daunting post as the price of another, coveted benefit: permanent rank and pay as a brigadier general. And Sir John did not mean to work very hard as superintendent. Remaining at Montreal, he delegated the grunt work at the frontier posts to subordinates. At Niagara, the Iroquois celebrated Sir John's ascent as the second coming of the great superintendent: "Our feelings for our friend your Father [Sir William Johnson] were great, and are now renewed at your sight." They hoped that Sir John could conduct their business "without the Interference of others, as has been done formerly by our great friend, Sir William Johnson." But the Iroquois expected more than Sir John could deliver and far more than Haldimand would permit.[83]

Haldimand quickly limited Johnson's power by revoking his vindictive decision to replace John Butler with Dr. John Dease as the head of the Indian Department at Niagara. Although inexperienced in Indian affairs and ignorant of native languages, Dease had the good fortune to be Sir William's nephew (and his personal physician) as well as Sir John's cousin. Appalled by Dease's appointment, Haldimand rebuked Sir John and abruptly restored Butler to office. Thereby the governor denied Sir John the power long enjoyed by Sir William to appoint or dismiss the subordinate officers of the Indian Department. In vain, Sir John protested that such a limitation "will hold me up in a very trifling light, not only to the officers in the Department, but to the Indians." Unlike Sir William, Sir John was subordinated to a colonial governor.[84]

TWO HELLS

In early 1782, Haldimand advanced the British position by ordering Major John Ross to rebuild the fort at Oswego: a base far closer to the Mohawk Valley than Niagara. An enthusiast for the aggressive move, Brant avidly assisted the British reconstruction. Ross reported:

> I cannot say too much in his favor. . . . I can assure your Excellency that we are much indebted to the Indians for assisting us to work. . . . Joseph shewed them the Example. I never saw men work so hard, and it greatly encouraged the Troops.

But like so much in the British war effort, the occupation of Oswego was too little, too late.[85]

In October 1781, at Yorktown in Virginia, the British had suffered a catastrophic defeat when Lord Cornwallis surrendered his army to Washington's forces. That blow toppled the war regime in London, and the new administration opened negotiations for peace in Paris. The new regime also sent Sir Guy Carleton to New York City to assume command of British forces in North America, with instructions to act only on the defensive. In late June, Haldimand learned of the new policy, which he forwarded to Major Ross, who imposed it on the Indians. Brant denounced the defensive policy as a betrayal of loyal allies. Alarmed by Brant's fury, Haldimand's secretary, Captain Robert Mathews, instructed Ross that "the Indians may rest assured they will never be forgotten. The King will always consider and reward them as his faithful Children, who have manfully supported his and their own Rights." In fact, Haldimand privately anticipated that the British negotiators would betray the Six Nations. He warned Carleton: "They are alarmed at the appearance of an accommodation so far short of what our Language, from the beginning has taught them to expect, deprived of their Lands & driven out of their Country, they reproached us with their ruin."[86]

A defiant Brant urged the Indians to persist in their own aggressive war against the Patriots. But the Indians could not sustain raids without British logistical support. Frustrated, Brant despised the British policy of keeping the Iroquois in limbo, as idle wards blamed for the provisions and presents that they consumed: "We think the Rebels will ruin us at last if we go on as we do, one year after another, doing nothing, only Destroying the Government goods & they Crying all the while for the great Expences, so we are, as it were, between two Hells."[87]

Under orders to wind down the war, British officers began to perceive Brant as a problem. No longer understood as a fellow gentleman who had transcended a native nature, Brant reappeared in alarmed British correspondence as an Indian who knew (and asked for) too much. When Brant charged Butler with embezzling Indian goods, Captain Mathews assured a fellow officer,

> *Entre nous*, there is an old Jealousy between Col. Butler & Joseph—the Latter is a Most Excellent fellow but, as he Candidly acknowledges, a thorough Indian, being of a More implacable disposition. The General therefore Wishes that as Little Blame as possible Should appear to fall on Col. Butler.

When push came to shove, British and Loyalist officers defended the reputation of their own against an implacable Indian. In the spring of 1783, General MacLean similarly warned, "Joseph knows too Much and too Little, tho a good fellow in the main, he is a perfect Indian." In May, that commandant shrewdly sent Brant to Quebec for prolonged, distracting discussions with Haldimand. MacLean meant to keep Brant away from Niagara, where "he would be So much More Sensible of the Miserable Situation in which we have left this unfortunate People, that I do believe he would do a great deal of Mischief here at this Time." In particular, MacLean feared Brant's reaction to the recent murder of an Indian friend by Jonathan Pray.[88]

PRAY

In early 1783, Jonathan Pray was an American prisoner living and working in the Niagara household of Dr. John Dease. Niagara officials procured indentured servants by cheaply buying captives taken by the Indians. Nurturing a bitter hatred of his initial captors, Pray spied an easy opportunity for revenge on the night of April 15, 1783, when a drunken Delaware Indian collapsed at the front gate to Dease's yard. Pray boasted to his fellow prisoner-servants "that he would kill every Man that was blacker than a white man." After walking on the insensate Delaware, Pray fetched an ax and struck a fatal blow to the skull. Three days later, General MacLean had Pray arrested and cast into the fort's "Black Hole" pending orders from Haldimand. Brant demanded Pray's conspicuous execution at Niagara because, in MacLean's words, "nothing else will Convince the Indians that they will have redress." Brant's demand did not contradict the traditional Indian aversion to legal execution of colonial allies, for Pray was their war enemy.[89]

MacLean and Haldimand, however, dared not execute an American, for they expected soon to receive news of a conclusive peace treaty. Executing Pray for killing an Indian would further inflame American Anglophobia—complicating British hopes for a reconciliation. Rather than hang Pray at Niagara, MacLean sent him to Montreal, allegedly for trial. But Pray never reached the Montreal jail, apparently escaping en route, perhaps with British collusion to avoid an embarrassing trial.[90]

In subsequent complaint, Brant aptly discerned the racial message in Pray's escape:

> We demanded justice. The Murderer was Confined, and the Earliest opportunity taken of sending him off. This was all we ever heard of it. I don't mention this Circumstance with the least intention of diminishing the Crime committed, only to shew that if a white man kills an Indian, the Crime is passed by with impunity, but if an Indian kills a white man, he is to be instantly delivered up to Justice.

Brant regarded Pray's escape as part of a larger betrayal of the Indians by the British. Brant saw them as appeasing Americans, who treated their victory as an assertion of cultural and racial superiority over the Indians. When Pray claimed a right to kill "every man that was blacker than a white man," he expressed the darker side of the American Revolution. The new republic served its white citizens, who expected to dispossess Indians—deemed inferior and doomed.[91]

Indeed, the Iroquois plight seemed dire by war's end. Whether allied to

the British or to the Patriots, all the Iroquois had suffered devastating raids
that destroyed almost all their villages by 1781. The violent dislocations promoted malnutrition and disease, reducing Iroquois numbers by a third, from
a prewar 9,000 to a postwar 6,000. Becoming refugees either at Schenectady,
on the American frontier, or at Montreal or Niagara, within the British orbit,
the Iroquois left behind a broad and bloody no-man's-land. After the war,
American settlers and speculators meant to fill that vacuum, inspired by
favorable reports from the soldiers in Sullivan's invasion.[92]

PART TWO

LINES

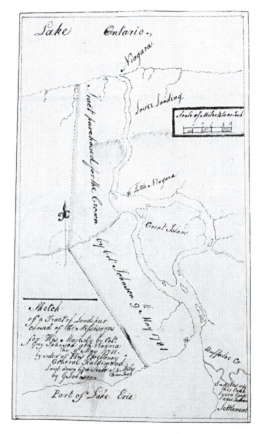

Map of the First Mississauga Land Cession, 1781. Note the mouth of Buffalo Creek to the lower right, with the reference to the new Indian Settlement. Fort Niagara lay at the outlet of the Niagara River into Lake Ontario. Fort Erie lay at the river's inlet, on the west bank. (Courtesy of the Archives of Ontario; RG 1-1, vol. I:67, #3693.)

View of Cataraqui Taken from Captain Brant's House, by James Peachey. In July 1784, Peachey depicts the principal Loyalist settlement in the future province of Upper Canada from the vantage point of Brant's house. (Courtesy of Library and Archives Canada; C-00152.)

CHAPTER FOUR

Peace

Sir Frederick Haldimand, by Mary Ann Knight.
(Courtesy of Library and Archives Canada;
C-018298.)

Aᴛ Qᴜᴇʙᴇᴄ ɪɴ Aᴘʀɪʟ 1783, General Haldimand received distressing
news from London. During the preceding fall, the war-weary imperial
government had concluded a preliminary treaty of peace, granting American
independence within remarkably generous boundaries. The British retained
Canada but accepted a new border through the Great Lakes and the rivers
between them, including the Niagara River, which emptied Lake Erie into
Lake Ontario. The new boundary sacrificed the leading British forts along
the Great Lakes, including Detroit, Michilimackinac, Niagara, and Oswego.
The treaty also abandoned most of Britain's Indian allies, including the Six

Nations, by placing them on the American side of the new border. For the United States, a nation verging on financial collapse and unable to defend its long frontier against Indian raids, the peace treaty was a stunning diplomatic victory. But the native allies of the British suffered a shocking betrayal, for the diplomats treated them as mere pawns passed into American control. Stunned by the terms, Haldimand confided to a friend, "My soul is completely bowed down with grief at seeing that we (with no absolute necessity) have humbled ourselves so much as to accept such humiliating boundaries. I am heartily ashamed and wish I was in the interior of Tartary."[1]

The betrayal of the Indians reflected a propaganda victory for the Patriots, who depicted the Indians as bloodthirsty savages preying upon defenseless civilians. Accepting that view, the new British prime minister, Lord Shelburne, insisted that "the Indian nations were not abandoned to their enemies; they were remitted to the care of neighbours, whose interest it was as much as ours to cultivate friendship with them, and who were certainly the best qualified for softening and humanizing their hearts." In fact, few Americans possessed soft and humanizing hearts for their Indian enemies. The Iroquois bitterly resented their disadvantage in the propaganda of atrocities. In 1783, Sayenqueraghta complained, "If we had the means of publishing to the World the many Acts of Treachery & Cruelty committed by them on our Women & Children, it would appear that the title of Savages would with much greater justice be applied to them than to us."[2]

During the spring of 1783, Haldimand and his post commandants along the Great Lakes tried to keep the Indians from learning the grim terms of the provisional treaty, in the vain hope that the final peace treaty would bring better news. But triumphant Patriot officials and Oneida couriers spread the news along the frontier to demoralize the hostile Indians, and to embarrass the British. In May, the American secretary of war, Benjamin Lincoln, pointedly informed the Indians "that all the Tribes and Nations of Indians who live to the Southward and Westward of the line agreed on [at the peace treaty], must no longer look to the King beyond the water, but they must now look to the Great Council, the Congress of the United States at Philadelphia." This was a sobering proposition for natives who had fought against the Patriots.[3]

The peace treaty and new border outraged the British-allied Iroquois as unjust humiliations that impugned their autonomy. The Mohawk captain John Deserontyon fumed, "Our minds are in pain. . . . The disgrace is almost killing us." At Fort Niagara in May, General MacLean faced a firestorm of Iroquois protest: "They told me they never could believe that our King could pretend to cede to America what was not his own to give." MacLean reported the Iroquois insistence "that the Indians were a free People subject to no

Power upon Earth, that they were faithful allies of the King of England, but not his Subjects—that he had no right Whatever to grant away to the States of America, their Rights or Properties." According to MacLean, Joseph Brant charged, "England had Sold the Indians to Congress."[4]

Fearing the Indian outrage, MacLean procured 1,800 gallons from the merchants lavishly to inebriate the Iroquois. He explained to Haldimand: "We have been under the Necessity of giving something more in the Rum Issues to the Indians this last fortnight, than usual, to keep them in good humour, and upon the whole they have behaved well." MacLean's alcohol was a desperate measure that dramatically reversed his former attempt to reduce Indian drinking.[5]

The rum purchased security for the British at a grave cost to Iroquois morale and morals. Meeting Sayenqueraghta at Niagara, a visiting British officer commented, "He is a sensible old man and has been a very good Warrior in his day but like all the rest is very much addicted to Liquor, for no sooner was the council over than his Majesty was dead drunk rolling in an Outhouse amongst Indians, Squaws, Pigs, Dogs, &c., &c." In a debilitating cycle, warriors drank for a release from an increasingly painful reality, only to compound, by their drinking, the deterioration of their circumstances.[6]

That summer, the British also increased their presents to the Indians at Niagara, reversing a recent economy drive, which again attested to the British dread of a native uprising. Making the best of a bad situation, the chiefs returned grateful speeches for the enhanced presents. That Iroquois acceptance sustained British conceits of Indian dependence. In fact, the dependence was mutual, for the British could not preserve their posts and their fur trade along the Great Lakes without Indian consent. Indeed, during 1783 the British had to make three substantive concessions to mollify the Indians: by retaining the posts, by reviving the Fort Stanwix line of 1768, and by endorsing a new pan-Indian confederacy.[7]

CONCESSIONS

The Indians threatened violence if the British tried to surrender the border posts to the Americans. Badly designed, poorly maintained, and weakly garrisoned, the forts were vulnerable to the superior numbers of nearby Indians. Meant to supply and assist Indian attacks on the American frontier, the posts were ill suited to command and control the natives. The Indian threats hit home because British officers recalled, some from direct experience, that in Pontiac's Rebellion of 1763 the Indians had united to destroy most of the British posts, killing hundreds of soldiers.[8]

By alarming the post commandants and fur trade merchants, the Indians compelled a dramatic shift in British policy. Haldimand refused to surrender the border forts to American emissaries, and he barred American traders from entering the Indian country. Citing a secret (nonexistent, in fact) clause to the peace treaty, Sir John Johnson and John Butler assured the Iroquois that the forts would never be relinquished until the Americans had done justice to the Indians. Haldimand informed his superiors in London that retention alone could "prevent such a disastrous event as an Indian War." He urged the imperial lords permanently to retain the posts by obliging the Americans to accept a broad buffer zone possessed by the Indians. Initiated from fear of the Indians, the proposed borderland also appealed to Canada's premier economic interest, the mercantile firms that traded British manufactures for the furs garnered by Indian hunters around the Great Lakes. British posts and an Indian borderland would combine to keep American traders and settlers away from that valuable trade.[9]

In early 1784, the home government recognized that the peace treaty line compromised both the security and the economy of Canada. Moreover, with growing signs that the American union of republican state governments was faltering, the British wanted to be in a strong position for the anticipated collapse. Finally, the British found principled grounds for retaining the posts by seizing upon two American violations of the peace treaty: the states blocked British merchants from collecting prewar debts and obstructed Loyalists from reclaiming confiscated properties. Loyalists found it especially dangerous to return to New York State, where angry mobs and confiscatory laws made a vindictive combination.[10]

In 1784, the imperial lords tacitly endorsed Haldimand's decision to withhold the posts. The policy shift reflected another new regime in London. In 1782, the relatively liberal administration of Lord Shelburne had indulged the Americans with generous peace terms in the vain hope of wooing their return to some association with the British Empire. By mid-1783, that approach seemed futile and foolish to most British leaders, who toppled the Shelburne administration. A succession of cautious administrations followed, all vaguely suspicious of the Americans and none sufficiently stable to make difficult decisions. Preferring to wait and see as the American confederacy unraveled, the imperial lords retained the forts, without making that a permanent policy. But Americans perceived an insidious plot by Britons determined to reverse the recent revolution. Prone to exaggerate British purpose and power, few Americans recognized the muddled leadership and internal divisions that promoted imperial inertia during the 1780s. An exception was the frustrated American minister to London, John Adams, who explained in 1785, "They have an unconquerable Reluctance to deciding upon any thing, or giving any Answer."[11]

By catalyzing Britain's policy shift, the Indians demonstrated that they possessed initiative and were more than mere pawns in an imperial game. Far from intimidating the Indians, the British troops and their posts were hostages that enabled the Indians to compel concessions. Those concessions exposed the fallacy in the peace treaty: the insistence that a new and artificial boundary could suddenly separate native peoples from their British allies. Interpenetrated and interdependent with the Six Nations, the British could not afford a rupture with their native allies.

The Indians also induced the British to fudge the new peace boundary by asserting the priority of the Fort Stanwix line of 1768. Running east-west, the new international boundary aggressively ignored the native world by abruptly dividing the continent between the British Empire to the north and the American Republic to the south. In stark contrast, the Fort Stanwix line ran north-south, delimiting a native domain to the west from the settler land to the east. Where the peace boundary threatened to erase native land title, the Fort Stanwix line highlighted and preserved a native domain.

As with the retention of the posts, the reiteration of the Fort Stanwix line demonstrated Indian initiative. In May at Niagara, the Iroquois pressed their border theory upon the British. Brant then carried that argument to Haldimand in Quebec. Brant also urged the Iroquois version of a double boundary in a letter to Philip Schuyler. Brant denounced recent, encroaching land surveys by New York as "contrary to the Treaty held at Fort Stanwix in 1768, when a Boundary line was fixed upon and settled by our late, Worthy friend and Brother, Sir William Johnson." As always, Sir William's name invested a precedent with a mythic, compelling power in Iroquois memory.[12]

The Iroquois defense of the Fort Stanwix line proved irresistible to British officials embarrassed by the peace treaty's betrayal of their Indian allies. That treaty became less damning if the Fort Stanwix line survived to preserve Indian lands, so British officials made the Iroquois boundary theory their own. Haldimand assured his superior, Lord North, "These People, my Lord, have as enlightened Ideas of the nature & Obligations of Treaties as the most Civilized Nations have, and know that no infringement of the Treaty of 1768 . . . can be binding upon them without their Express Concurrence & Consent."[13]

The Iroquois insisted that a broad and independent Indian domain persisted between the Fort Stanwix and the Treaty of Paris lines. Neither American nor British, that buffer zone appealed to the Indians, who wished to live between, rather than be divided by, the republic and the empire. Indeed, some chiefs boldly interpreted their exclusion from the 1783 peace treaty as a declaration of native independence. In 1784, Captain Aaron Hill (Mohawk) boldly informed American officials, "We are free and independent and at present under no influence. We have hitherto been bound by the Great King, but he having broke the chain, and left us to ourselves, we are again free and independent."[14]

In a third, related development, the British-allied Iroquois framed a broad new confederation with the Indian nations of the Great Lakes and the Ohio Valley. During the summer of 1783, Brant led forty Iroquois deputies to meet their western counterparts in council at Sandusky on Lake Erie. Forming a loose confederation of thirty-five native nations, the Indians vowed to defend the Fort Stanwix line against American encroachment by denying to any member nation the power to dispose of land without common consent. Although initiated by the Six Nations, leadership soon passed to the Shawnees, Delawares, and Miamis, for they possessed more warriors and won growing prestige by defeating American troops during the 1780s. In 1788, some Iroquois chiefs, including Brant, told Kirkland "that Congress could not blame them for such a conduct, neither ought they to be jealous of them; for what had Congress done, but to unite thirteen states as one."[15]

Far from serving the British Empire, the confederation chiefs sought, as they explained to Kirkland, to "unite as Indians independently of white people." Indeed, the Indian confederation worried British officials, who had long tried to manage Indians by promoting jealousies between their nations. But the fearful British had little choice but to accept what they could not resist. By endorsing, advising, and supplying presents (especially ammunition), they hoped to buy influence.[16]

But that aid persuaded Americans that the Indian confederacy was a plot by insidious and powerful Britons to steal the frontier fruits of the American Revolution. Unable to recognize Indian initiative, Americans reflexively blamed both the buffer zone and the post retention on malicious Britons reneging on their peace treaty by ventriloquizing docile Indians.

In fact, the implementation of British Indian policy was rife with confusion and delay. In theory, the empire was a hierarchy where orders issued from the king's ministers in London to the governor general in Canada, and on to the post commandants around the Great Lakes and their assistants in the Indian Department, for application to the native peoples. In turn, information about Indians returned from the Great Lakes country, descending the St. Lawrence to Quebec and then took ship across the Atlantic to England. But the passage of both orders and information was painfully slow: four months to or from Niagara in the best of circumstances during the short summer. And far worse conditions prevailed during the long Canadian winter, which curtailed transatlantic shipping as ice locked up the St. Lawrence River. Consequently, eight to twelve months elapsed to complete the circuit of information from Niagara with the return of an order from

London. Inertia flourished from the combination of a hierarchical command structure with the long delays in response from either end of the imperial chain.[17]

The delays and the inertia encouraged independent action only by the most distant and least responsible tentacles of empire: the local agents of the Indian Department. Although disdained as disreputable by regular military officers, the Indian Department agents were indispensable because of their rare mastery of native languages, their insights into Indian cultures, and the influence of their kinship connections by informal marriage to native women. Without an Indian Department agent, a British post commander was lost in dealing with Indians. But the native sources of an agent's expertise and influence also compromised his allegiance to imperial orders, which inevitably seemed out of date and misinformed. That tension between native complexity and imperial naïveté bred a selfish cynicism among the Indian Department officers, who often manipulated the information delivered to natives or obtained from them. Seeking extra compensation for their troubles, the agents also embezzled presents meant for the Indians. Struggling to control their expenditures, Lord Dorchester denounced the department's "certain assumed official independence, and much mystery."[18]

BALANCE

The British pleased their Indian allies by keeping the border posts, by endorsing the Fort Stanwix line, and by covertly supporting a broad Indian confederation. But those moves angered the Americans, initiating a state of cold war along the frontier. Although willing to sustain a cold war, the British were by no means eager to renew an expensive hot war with the Americans. Instead of announcing the post retention as permanent, British leaders held out the vague prospect that someday they would deliver the posts, once satisfied on the issues of prewar debts and Loyalist return. In the meantime, the British played for time, to see if the United States would collapse, leaving the posts, the Indians, and the fur trade in the British orbit.[19]

Nor could the Americans afford another war with the British Empire. Financially strapped, the United States was barely able to fight the Indians in the Ohio country. Employing a mere 350 soldiers, the Americans lacked the means to seize the British posts much less to sustain the massive war that would then ensue. Resenting British power and their own weakness, the Americans could only hope to undermine the Indian buffer zone to improve their prospects for a diplomatic solution.[20]

During the 1780s, the Americans worked to pin down the Iroquois within the American boundary as dependent peoples surrounded by settlers. If deprived of an Indian buffer zone, the British posts would become vulnerable to an American surprise attack. To dissolve that buffer, the Americans needed to draw the Iroquois away from Niagara and toward the New York settlements—contrary to our assumption that Americans always tried to drive Indians from their lands, as quickly and as violently as possible.

Despite their posturing as conquerors, the Americans knew all too well, from recent experience, that the Indians were devastating enemies in forest warfare. Adept at long-distance, surprise raids on vulnerable settlements, warriors possessed a prowess disproportionate to their limited numbers. If pushed over the new boundary into Canada, the Six Nations would become especially formidable enemies. Beyond American influence and well stocked with British munitions, they could more securely raid the American settlements. In July 1783, General Schuyler warned Congress, "if driven to reside in the British Territory, they will add strength to those people . . . and in case of a future rupture, expose the western country to the most dreadful extremities."[21]

If instead enticed deep within the American boundary and far away from the British posts, the Iroquois would become militarily impotent. Endorsing Schuyler's reasoning, Congress authorized him to send a message, during the winter of 1783–84, inviting the Iroquois at Niagara to return to their homelands within New York. John Butler reported, "This information has already kindled some Jealousy and [is] very likely to create a good deal of uneasiness." The uneasy were chiefs eager to preserve the power of consolidation in the Niagara corridor.[22]

If the first step was to draw the Iroquois back from the border and deep into New York, the second was patiently to envelop them within new settlements. By reducing Iroquoia to a set of shrinking and disconnected reservations, the Americans could reduce the power of their mobility. Schuyler explained that the Americans could best overwhelm the Six Nations gradually and environmentally, rather than immediately and militarily. Because hunting settlers would steadily destroy the game animals critical to the native economy, Schuyler predicted that the Indians would "dwindle comparatively to nothing, as all Savages have done who . . . live in the vicinity of civilized people, and thus leave us the country without the expense of a purchase, trifling as that will probably be." Because the Iroquois numbered only about 6,000 in 1784, the far more numerous New Yorkers (about 240,000) would dominate Indians lured back into the state and gradually surrounded by new settlements.[23]

Achieving the proper balance between luring and surrounding was tricky. Indeed, aggressive settlement threatened to alarm the Indians, sending them scurrying back to the British line. So long as the Iroquois had an open corridor to flee to Canada, American leaders needed to regulate the pace of encroachment. The proper pace would envelop the Iroquois without spooking them prematurely.[24]

MOHAWKS

Just as the Americans defied conventional wisdom during the 1780s by trying to lure the Six Nations within New York, the British were surprisingly ambivalent about drawing all of the Six Nations within Canadian bounds. Greatly outnumbered by the 2,500,000 Americans in 1783, the 100,000 British subjects in Canada needed Indian allies close at hand to even the odds in any renewed conflict. One British official explained, "We are no longer the first landed power in North America. Therefore [we] cannot have too many Indians under our protection and countenance." Like the French during the 1750s, the British relied on Indian warriors to defend Canada against the more numerous Americans.[25]

But the British commanders preferred to keep most of their Indian allies in a buffer zone on the American side of the boundary line. The British feared that, if the Indians withdrew into Canada, American settlers would promptly fill the vacuum in western New York, facilitating a surprise attack on Niagara. Placed east of the river, however, the Iroquois might keep American settlers at a wary distance. Officials also wanted to limit their costs for the provisions demanded by migrating Indians to tide them over until their first harvest at their new villages.[26]

In addition to keeping Americans out, the British officers also needed borderland Indians to keep their own soldiers in. Already undermanned, the border posts could ill afford desertion by enlisted men weary of the hard service and the harsh discipline in the Royal Army. Desertion to the American settlements also enticed with prospects of ready employment at higher pay and in much better conditions. To deter deserters, British officers employed Indians to pursue them, sometimes with fatal consequences. Skilled trackers, expert in the forest terrain, and possessed of a fearsome reputation, Indian warriors usually got their men—and deterred other soldiers from making the run. Paid $20 for every recaptured man, the Indians found the service rewarding. If withdrawn within Canada, the Indians would be less effective at preserving the Niagara garrison located on the river's east bank.[27]

After Sullivan's expedition of 1779, the Iroquois refugees had established three major clusters of villages in the Niagara corridor. In 1783, about 879 natives lived at Loyal Village, eight miles south of Fort Niagara. The largest refugee cluster lay farther south at Buffalo Creek, near Lake Erie's outlet into the Niagara River. Founded in 1780 to relieve the expensive crush of refugees near Fort Niagara, the Buffalo Creek villages hosted at least 2,100 Indians in 1783. Another 461 dwelled farther southwest at Cattaraugus, beside Lake Erie. Located along major waterways and near the British posts at Fort Niagara or Fort Erie, the three clusters were convenient for the British to deliver the annual presents and trade goods that reiterated their alliance. At Buffalo Creek in 1791, Thomas Proctor found the inhabitants "far better clothed than those Indians were in the towns at a greater distance, owing entirely to the immediate intercourse they have with the British."[28]

In the exception that proved the rule, the British did encourage one Iroquois nation, the Mohawks, to relocate within Canada. The British acted on Sir William Johnson's premise that the Mohawks were the most important and influential of Indians. In theory, the Mohawks swayed the other Six Nations, who, in turn, guided the Indians of the Great Lakes and Ohio country. Clinging to that half-truth, the British persisted in treating the Mohawks as their prime sources of news and conduits for messages and initiatives. To bolster that dual role, the British hoped to secure the Mohawks within the boundary and to provide them with superior presents. General MacLean reasoned, "If we could keep the Mohawks in humour, I think the others might follow their Example." Haldimand agreed that pleasing the Mohawks would "preserve the Friendship & Alliance of the Indians in general, whose Conduct is always governed by that of the Six Nations." Ironically, that imperial belief strengthened the Mohawk reputation for possessing special insights and some influence over the British. In this hall of mirrors, the Mohawks did enjoy more than their share of native influence (and more than their share of native distrust) because the British nurtured a powerful illusion.[29]

By securing the Mohawks, the British especially hoped to control the prodigious talents and volatile charisma of Joseph and Molly Brant. Frustrated by the peace treaty terms, the Brants alarmed their British handlers by conspicuously toying with the idea of returning to the Mohawk Valley. In 1783, General MacLean warned Haldimand, "Capt. Joseph Brant, tho a brave fellow, . . . has been the most troublesome, because he is better instructed & much more intelligent than any other Indian." By inducing the Brants to reside within the Canadian border, the British hoped to ensure their loyalty and secure their influence. In 1783 Haldimand ordered fine houses built for Molly and Joseph at Kingston, a new Loyalist settlement near the outlet of Lake Ontario.[30]

Sparing little expense (despite his tightening budget from the Crown), the governor also purchased land from the local Mississauga Indians for the other Mohawk refugees. He promised to build a sawmill, gristmill, church, and school and to staff them with a miller, blacksmith, minister, and teacher. The governor also assured the leading Mohawks, including the Brants, of financial compensation for their lost homes in the Mohawk Valley. They were the only Indians so compensated. Haldimand informed his British superiors that the Mohawks warranted special exertions and extraordinary expenditures lest they "abandon us, and return to their former settlements, which the Americans already hold out to them in order to detach them from us."[31]

Initially, Haldimand wanted to consolidate the Mohawks on a small reserve at Tyendinaga, on the Bay of Quinte near Kingston. Detached from the other Six Nations and plunked beside new Loyalist settlements, the Mohawks would be more responsive to British influence and less independent in their diplomacy. Reading that geography of power more negatively, Brant preferred a more western location, closer to both the other Six Nations at Niagara and to the Indian confederates around Lake Erie and in the Ohio Valley. In early 1784, Brant selected the Grand River valley, on the Niagara Peninsula, within the British boundary but only a day's travel from Buffalo Creek. Compared to Tyendinaga, the Grand River tract was warmer, larger, more fertile, and less impinged by settlers.[32]

Unable to dissuade Brant, Haldimand reluctantly endorsed his decision. In 1784, John Butler negotiated another land cession from the Mississaugas: six miles on each side of the Grand River, approximately 570,000 acres in total. The governor also shifted to Grand River his promised church, mills, school, clothing, and farm tools. Sir John Johnson hoped that these measures would "Counteract Mr. [Philip] Schuyler's endeavours to draw them Back to their Old Settlements." Brant assured the British that the Americans still hoped "to disappoint our wishes to remain in the English limits, which those Yankees cannot bear."[33]

In 1785, Brant led the Mohawks at Loyal Village, near Fort Niagara, west to settle on the Grand River. Brant hoped to unite all of the Mohawks by also wooing the residents of the other, smaller Mohawk refugee village at La Chine, near Montreal. But they clung to Captain John Deserontyon, an ambitious chief who preferred to lead his own small community at the Bay of Quinte rather than play second fiddle to Brant at Grand River. Sticking to the original plan, Deserontyon and the La Chine Mohawks settled at Tyendinaga. The division exacerbated old village rivalries between the upper and lower Mohawks of the Mohawk Valley, for Grand River primarily attracted Canajoharie Mohawks, while Tyendinaga belonged to former residents of Tiononderoge (Fort Hunter).[34]

The split proved uneven because Brant appealed to more Mohawks than did Deserontyon. Although courageous in war and eloquent in council,

Deserontyon could never match Brant's education, connections, and cunning. Drinking too much too often, Deserontyon behaved erratically, costing him influence with the British, which then diminished his standing among the Mohawks. Making the most of his superior clout, Brant obtained the larger land grant and more presents, which attracted and retained most of the Mohawk refugees. In 1788, about 400 lived at Grand River, compared to only 100 at Tyendinaga. Given that Canajoharie had been only slightly larger than Tiononderoge before the war, the postwar skew in favor of Grand River reveals that Brant had enticed half of the lower Mohawks, led by Captain Isaac Hill, to join the upper Mohawks.[35]

The former Anglican missionary at Fort Hunter, John Stuart, contributed to the Mohawk split by declining to move west to Grand River, which he dreaded as an isolated wilderness. During the war, the Patriots had imprisoned Stuart as a suspected spy. Exchanged in 1781, he moved to Montreal and became a chaplain for Sir John Johnson's regiment. At war's end, the British demobilized the regiment, settling the soldiers on lands in or near Kingston. Cherishing the relative comforts of Kingston, Stuart preferred to visit nearby Tyendinaga rather than join the main body of the Mohawks at distant Grand River. Stuart's inertia enabled Deserontyon to argue that his people should linger at Tyendinaga to benefit from their missionary.[36]

GRAND RIVER

In addition to uniting the Mohawks, Brant wished to consolidate all of the Iroquois at Grand River. This wish defied the British preference to keep most of the Iroquois east of Niagara to hold the contested buffer zone. By uniting the Iroquois along the Grand River, Brant meant to invert the British geographic scheme. Rather than obliging the Six Nations to serve as a tripwire for Fort Niagara and Fort Erie, those posts should screen the Iroquois from American attack. In Brant's political geography, the British Empire would serve the Six Nations, rather than the reverse.

At Buffalo Creek during the fall of 1784, the Six Nations chiefs met in council to consider Brant's invitation. Uniting at Grand River would, Brant argued, increase their power and promote their autonomy from all colonizers, British as well as Americans. A Seneca chief recalled that Brant "wanted the Six Nations would go over to Canada to make [a] parmanent home together with all the Indian Nations to form their own Custom[s] [and] Traditions of the Different tribes of Indians . . . and to live once more indepentante [of] government, &c."[37]

The chiefs entrusted the decision to the clan matrons, who had primary jurisdiction over village location. With Solomon's wisdom, the women

Mohawk schoolchildren at Grand River, by James
Peachey, 1786. (Courtesy of the Metropolitan
Toronto Library Board.)

decided that the Six Nations should divide, with half on each side of the
Niagara boundary. Like Brant's argument, the matrons' reasoning placed no
more trust in the British than in the Americans: "For it may be in future time
the cannadian [Six Nations] may be oblidge[d] to Remove or it may [be]
Drove off their lands, so the cannadian might have a share with us, &c., and
if we Should be Droved off or Deprived of our lands we Shall have a Share
with them." The clan mothers thought that dividing the Six Nation peoples
equally on either side of the border, but close at hand, would best preserve
their mutual security in a porous borderland.[38]

Enough Iroquois did emigrate to make Grand River more than a
Mohawk reserve. In 1789, Mohawks comprised only about a third of the
1,200 total, which also included Cayugas, Onondagas, Tuscaroras, Oneidas
from Onoquaga, and even some Senecas. More even than a Six Nations
reserve, Grand River also attracted some Algonquian-speaking Mohicans,
Delawares, Tutelos, and Nanticokes. Although smaller than Brant's ambitious plans, the Grand River reserve became larger and more diverse than the
British wanted. And, despite opposition from the British and from the Buf-

falo Creek chiefs, Brant continued to urge all of the Iroquois to consolidate at Grand River. In March 1788, Brant explained, "We must, in the first place, get the Mohawks away from the Bay of Quinte. As soon as we can get them here, we shall begin to argue to the Five Nations, and will show our example of getting together ourselves."[39]

Brant also recruited white settlers for Grand River. Most were Loyalists who had served during the war in his volunteers, or in the Indian Department, or in Butler's Rangers. Some had Indian wives and children. By offering large tracts (1,000 acres and more) of fertile, riverside land at a minimal cost, Brant sought experienced farmers. Their rent in produce would help to feed the Indians, and they could teach the natives how to develop farms in the colonial mold. Brant also liked playing the patron. Emulating his mentor, Sir William Johnson, Brant wanted to build an interest in the colonial world by developing a network of dependent white men.[40]

By granting Indian lands to settlers, Brant overplayed his hand, aggravating a substantial Mohawk faction. Opposed to sharing the land with settlers, the dissidents also protested Brant's hasty and arbitrary decisions, so contrary to native conventions of deliberation and consensus. Led by Captain Isaac Hill and Captain Aaron Hill, the opposition derived primarily from the Tiononderoge Mohawks who had settled at Grand River. Bristling at their criticism, Brant blamed insidious meddling by Captain John Deserontyon, who (in Brant's absence) had recently visited Grand River to tell the lower Mohawks that they had become "mere Slaves to Capt. Brant."[41]

Brant provoked a confrontation by pushing for a radical reform of Indian customary law and governance. To stem a recent spate of revenge killings, he urged the Grand River Iroquois to adopt their own coercive system of laws, trials, and punishments. Brant recalled, "My wishing to have Some Laws and regulations Established amongst us was one of Aaron & Isaac's Grievances, thinking that I wanted to introduce too much of the Custom of the Whites." Meddling with the customary law of murder provoked Indians who regarded it as essential to their independence from intrusive whites. Coercive authority appalled Indians, who readily assassinated domineering chiefs. Tempting that fate, in 1788 Brant seized a Mohawk murderer. Brant and his supporters then "applied to the Whites for advice, and wished that an Example might be made. We had not the means within our selves of Confining him, and were at a loss how to Act, being Ignorant of the Steps requisite to be taken."[42]

Appalled by the arrest, and by the settler tenants, Captains Aaron and Isaac tried to assassinate Brant in August. When that failed, the dissidents fled to Tyendinaga, where Deserontyon welcomed them as a boon to his community and as a blow to Brant's ambition. Visiting Montreal in September, the Hills protested to Sir John Johnson and Lord Dorchester: "We wish you to let us know if the Country belongs to him [Brant] and is at his disposal or not." Supporting the dissidents, Sir John declared that Grand River belonged "to the Six Nations in general and the White People have no right to it & must withdraw and if they do not do it forthwith of their own accord, measures will be taken to compel them." And when Brant had the murder suspect sent to Montreal, the British released him.[43]

Given the Mohawk importance to British Indian management, officials dreaded the consequences of a violent rupture within that nation. To heal the rift, John Butler convened both parties in council at Niagara in February 1789. The other Iroquois chiefs vindicated Brant's conduct including his settlement policy at Grand River. Blaming the crisis on Deserontyon, the Iroquois spokesman, a Cayuga chief named Fish Carrier, urged the British to break up Tyendinaga by compelling all of the Mohawks to unite at Grand River. Ultimately, the council proved ineffectual, for the British could neither oblige Deserontyon to move nor oust the settlers at Grand River. Brant retained his power at Grand River, but he had lost the Hills and their followers to Tyendinaga. By recruiting settlers, Brant had provoked a lower Mohawk reaction that weakened his primary goal of uniting the Six Nations at Grand River.[44]

BRANT'S TOWN

The Grand River valley offered a prime setting for Indian villages. Abounding in sturgeon, pike, and whitefish, the river wound through a fertile land of rolling hills covered with hardwood trees. The riverside provided alluvial flats for crops, as well as meadows that grew hay for their cattle. In 1785, a Mohawk named Paulus wrote "that the land where we live at Grand River is exceptionally good. It gives me pleasure to see the crops all growing splendid." Three years later, a visiting Rev. Stuart observed, "I found them conveniently situated on a beautiful river, where the soil is equal in fertility to any I ever saw." In 1792, Patrick Campbell, a Scottish visitor, considered the valley "the finest country I have as yet seen. . . . the soil rich, and a deep clay mold."[45]

Indian cabins were scattered along both banks of the river, occasionally forming village clusters. Campbell noted, "The habitations of the Indians are pretty close on each side of the river as far as I could see, with a very few white people interspersed among them, married to squaws and others of half blood, their offspring." Ascending the river from the mouth at Lake Erie, a traveler first found Delawares and Cayugas. About fifteen miles upstream, on the east bank, lay the Nellis Settlement, named for the principal family of

Brant's Town, Grand River, by Elizabeth Simcoe, ca. 1793. Joseph Brant's large house stands to the left, with a flag in front. To the right, the Anglican church boasts a steeple. The Grand River appears in the foreground. (Courtesy of the Archives of Ontario; F 47-11-1-0-109, #10006349.)

Loyalists favored by Brant. Continuing on, the ascending traveler came, in succession, to villages of Onondagas, Senecas, Tuscaroras, Onoquaga Oneidas, and ultimately Mohawks.[46]

At about forty miles above the lake, a visitor reached the reserve's foremost community, Ohsweken, or Brant's Town, where the Mohawks clustered on a ridge along the east bank near a ford across the river. In 1792, the snug log homes with glass windows impressed Campbell, who observed that the Mohawks were "better and more comfortably lodged than the generality of the poor farmers in my country." Visiting in February, he saw "large quantities of Indian corn in every house a-drying, and suspended in the roofs, and every corner of them." They lived, he concluded, "as happy as the day is long."[47]

With British money and artisans, Brant erected public buildings meant to impress both native and colonial visitors. In 1787, Sir John Johnson reported, "They have a Number of good houses, a Neat little Church, and a good School House." Built of squared logs covered with boards and painted white, the Anglican church was 60 feet long and 45 feet wide. Rev. Stuart reported that it featured "a handsome steeple & bell, a pulpit, reading-desk & Communion-table, with convenient pews." Brant also installed a silver communion service, an organ, and the king's coat of arms. Lacking a resident missionary, the Indians made do with a service read by one of their own and by hymns, all in the Mohawk language. Sacraments, including baptism, required an ordained clergyman, which meant waiting for Stuart, but he never returned after his lone visit in 1788. Although reverential during worship, the Mohawks also struck pious visitors as raucous between services. A Moravian missionary reported that the Mohawks often gathered "in the school-house, played, danced, and drank, and had already smashed nearly all the windows, and thus they live, no better than the savage Indians." The school doubled as a council house for public meetings during cold or inclement weather.[48]

The village's most impressive structure was Brant's genteel mansion. A visiting missionary described "a handsome two story house, built after the manner of the white people. Compared with the other houses, it may be called a palace." A white picket fence surrounded the yard and a British flag flew from a pole beside the entrance.[49]

Brant loved to entertain genteel travelers, usually British officers. Patrick Campbell found that "tea was on the table . . . served up in the handsomest China [with] plate and every other furniture in proportion. After tea was over, we were entertained with the music of an elegant hand organ." Supper followed, "served up in the same genteel stile" by two black slaves dressed in scarlet coats "with silver buckles in their shoes, and ruffles" on their shirts. The guests consumed brandy, port, and Madeira, while Brant led them in toasts to the "King, Queen, Prince of Wales, and all the royal family of England" and "to the brave [Indian] fellows who drubbed the Yankies." He also told stories of his social triumphs in London, especially his reception by the king. After dinner, Brant showed off his prized collection of English gifts, including "a brace of double barrelled pistols, a curious gun, and a silver hilted dagger." That night, Campbell's party settled into "our beds, sheets, and English blankets, equally fine and comfortable." This was rare praise indeed, given the almost universal horror with which British visitors described filthy frontier lodgings.[50]

The house was Brant's stage to perform his hybridity as an Indian gentleman. Brant emulated his mentor, Sir William Johnson, by ingeniously converting his frontier setting and Indian access into genteel assets. Brant performed a distinctive role as a higher sort of gentleman: one uniquely capable of triumphing over a barbarous setting, of living serenely in the midst of Indians. "His deportment at table is perfectly that of a gentleman," marveled one guest. Visitors praised his polite manners, elegant conversation, English fluency, and dapper clothing that mixed gentility with native touches. "Capt. Brant . . . wore an English Coat with a handsome Crimson Silk blanket lined with black & trimmed with gold fringe & wore a Fur Cap, [and] round his neck he had a string of plaited sweet hay," observed Elizabeth Simcoe. The clothing draped an impressive body: "five feet eleven inches—of the finest form and proportions—robust and firm, and possessing great muscular power," a visitor recalled.[51]

Brant also took immense pride in his attractive and dignified wife, Catharine, who "appeared superbly dressed in the Indian fashion." According to Campbell, the "elegance of her person, [and the] grandeur of her looks and deportment" surpassed all others at dinner. She wore a silk blanket bordered with lace over a silk petticoat and scarlet leggings; silk ribbons ornamented her beaded moccasins. Although she understood English, Catharine spoke only Mohawk. In 1792, the Brants also presented three well-dressed children: eight-year-old Joseph, Jr.; six-year-old Jacob; and an infant named Catharine. Joseph's two offspring by his first marriage lived elsewhere in the village. Isaac and Christina had married siblings from a prestigious lower Mohawk family: Mary Hill and the younger Aaron Hill (not the older chief by that name who had tangled with Joseph Brant in 1788), the children of Joseph's dear friend Captain David Hill.[52]

Despite his genteel home, Brant remained engaged with the festive, public life of his Indian village. Indeed, he led the drinking and dancing "frolics," held outdoors in summer and in the schoolhouse in winter. Campbell recalled that Brant summoned the Mohawks to assemble "in their most showy apparel, glittering with silver" to perform native dances while Brant "held the drum, beat time, and often joined in the song, with a certain cadence to which they kept time." After completing a round of native dances, the Mohawks turned to "Scotch reels" and Campbell "was much surprised to see how neatly they danced them," continuing until dawn. Although nearly fifty, Brant danced through the night, and he closely monitored drinking by the young men. In many ways, Brant called the tune at his town.[53]

LOYALISTS AND MISSISSAUGAS

In addition to betraying Indian allies, the British peace negotiators disappointed the American Loyalists. The peace treaty vaguely promised that they could return home to reclaim their properties, but state legislators and local mobs frustrated that promise. Embittered by wartime raids, the Patriots of the Mohawk Valley took special pains to brutalize any Loyalist who reappeared. At Niagara, the British commandant said of his Loyalist troops: "They would rather go to Japan than go among the Americans, where they could never live in Peace."[54]

Instead of Japan, most settled in Britain's North American colonies, which welcomed about 38,000 during the early 1780s. The great majority—

30,000—went to the Maritime Provinces of New Brunswick and Nova Scotia, with smaller numbers heading to Quebec (2,000) and the future province of Upper Canada (6,000), which stretched above Montreal as far as Detroit. In the upper country, most of the Loyalists settled along the upper St. Lawrence or around the Bay of Quinte. Those settlers included Sir John Johnson's troops and their families, primarily former tenants from the Johnson estates in the Mohawk Valley. Another cluster of Loyalist settlements lay along the Niagara River and the north shore of the Niagara Peninsula, which provided homesteads for John Butler's rangers.[55]

To compensate the Loyalists for their service and their suffering, the British provided free land, tools, and provisions for their first two years on the land. Most former soldiers and their families also received farms of 100 to 300 acres, with larger quantities up to 5,000 acres reserved for officers. To further assist the settlers, the British government built and operated gristmills and sawmills. In 1785, a British visitor marveled at the rapid development of new homesteads: "It does one's heart good to see how well they are all going on. . . . The settling [of] the Loyalists is one of the best things [that] George III ever did. You see abundance of fine wheat, Indian corn, and potatoes wherever you go."[56]

The Mohawk and Loyalist movement into Canada imposed upon the Algonquian-speaking Mississaugas, who ranged the land and waters between the St. Lawrence River on the east, Lake Huron to the west, the Ottawa River to the north, and Lakes Erie and Ontario to the south. Numbering about 1,000 souls in 1783, the Mississaugas lived by a seasonally shifting mix of hunting, fishing, and gathering, with little or no horticulture. They lacked political unity beyond their local bands of about a dozen families each. They lived in mobile camps of oval wigwams made of birch bark stretched over cedar boughs. In the spring and early summer, they gathered at the waterfalls in the major rivers to harvest the migrating fish. The Mississaugas were especially adept at making and handling canoes, spears, and nets to take the immense and numerous salmon of their rivers. Elizabeth Simcoe marveled, "To see a Birch Canoe managed with that inexpressible ease & composure which is the characteristic of an Indian is the prettiest sight imaginable." Coveting loaves of bread and jugs of rum, the Mississaugas readily bartered their fish to travelers or colonists.[57]

Cultural and linguistic differences strained relations between the Mississaugas and the Six Nations. During the late seventeenth century, they had waged a bloody war that ousted the Iroquois from the northern shores of Lake Erie and Lake Ontario. During the eighteenth century, relations were more mixed, alternating peaceful trade and diplomacy with sporadic insults and occasional murders. The Mississaugas resented the Six Nations as arrogant deceivers, while the latter dismissed the former as reeking of fish and ignorance.[58]

Perceiving the wider Indian world through an Iroquois prism, the British regarded the Mississaugas as especially dirty, lazy, ignorant, drunken, and savage. The British traveler Isaac Weld observed:

> They are of a much darker complexion than any other Indians I ever met with; some of them being nearly as black as negroes. They are extremely dirty and slovenly in their appearance, and the women are still more so than the men; such indeed is the odour exhaled in a warm day from the rancid grease and fish oil with which the latter daub their hair, necks, and faces profusely, that it is offensive in the highest degree to approach within some yards of them.

While lavishing attention and presents on the Iroquois, British officials usually treated the Mississaugas with contempt or neglect—which they resented. A chief complained, "Can you persuade yourself my Father, to have two children of the same age, and give all your attention to only one of them, leaving the other to the misery to which we are reduced?"[59]

They felt wary about sharing their land with the Mohawks and Loyalists. Living close to hunger, the Mississaugas could ill afford the added pressure on their fish, game, berries, roots, and nuts. The Mohawks seemed especially problematic because, as fellow Indians, they more directly competed with the Mississauga use of the land. Sir John Johnson reported that the Mississaugas "seem to have no Objection to White People settling there, but say that if their Brothers the Six Nations come there, they are so Numerous, they will Overrun their hunting Grounds." White farmers seemed preferable because they raised an agricultural surplus that might help to feed the Mississaugas in hungry seasons, provided the newcomers recognized their obligations as guests on Indian lands.[60]

By welcoming the settlers, the Mississaugas anticipated improving their relationship with British officials, who had been too grudging with their presents. The Mississaugas hoped to teach the British to emulate their French predecessors by behaving as a true Father: just and generous. In return for their gifts of land, the Mississaugas expected increased annual presents of cloth, clothing, gunpowder, shot, and firearms.[61]

Lacking a commercial perspective, the Mississaugas sought a better relationship rather than a particular price for their land. In 1785, a British official reported that, for a land cession, "the Chiefs observed [that] they were poor and Naked, they wanted Cloathing and left it to their Good Father to be a judge of the Quantity." Similarly, in 1788 several Mississauga chiefs explained that they considered their land cession a gift rather than a sale. As they saw it, their present obligated the British to reciprocate in perpetuity. An official reported, "They say now [that] they have given their Lands which their great Father requested, [so] they hope he will take Pity on them as they are very poor and assist them a little in sending them a few Kettles, Tomahawks, Spears, &c., &c., and as it is coming on cold Weather, they hope their Father will try and press his breasts sufficiently to give his Children a good Suck." By this last, mixed metaphor, the Mississaugas sought warming rum.[62]

During the 1780s, the British seemed to respond appropriately by bestowing unprecedented presents and ceremonial respect on the Mississaugas. But, in return, the British procured their marks on deeds bestowing thousands of acres of land. In five transactions—1781, 1783, 1784, 1787, and 1788—British officials secured the Niagara Peninsula and almost all the land along the shores of Lake Erie, Lake Ontario, and the St. Lawrence River. For each cession, the British paid in presents worth from £1,000 to £2,000. British officials then granted the lands to Loyalists, or to the Mohawks and other Iroquois.[63]

To cultivate Mississauga goodwill, Brant framed a unity pact with the band residing near Grand River. In public council in May 1784, the Mississauga chief Pokquan announced:

> We are Indians, and consider ourselves and the Six Nations to be one and the same people, and agreeable to a former, and mutual agreement, we are bound to help each other. Brother Captain Brant, we are happy to hear that you intend to settle at the River with your people. We hope you will keep your young men in good Order, as we shall be in one Neighbourhood, and to live in friendship with each other as Brethren ought to do.

Brant fulfilled his promises by sharing British presents and information with the grateful Mississaugas—as did Captain John Deserontyon at Tyendinaga.[64]

The British, however, disappointed the Mississaugas, who expected continuing, annual payments on a par with what they had received at each deed ceremony. But the British regarded each transaction as a one-shot commercial purchase that extinguished native title within the stipulated boundaries. In subsequent years, the officials delivered only minimal presents—unless the Mississaugas consented to another land cession. In 1794, a chief in the Thames Valley complained "that the English were nearly as bad as the Americans in taking away their Lands."[65]

The settlers also came in greater numbers than the Mississaugas had bargained on, depleting precious fish, game, and plants the Indians needed. The settlers transformed wild habitats by attacking the forest with axes to create pastures for their cattle. Clearing the land increased erosion into the rivers, and sawmills and tanneries further polluted the waters. At Credit River in 1806, Quinepenon complained that "our Waters on this River are so filthy & disturbed by washing with Sope & other dirt that the fish refuse coming into the River as usual for which our families are in great distress for want of food." As the wild game declined in the forest, some hungry Mississaugas began to prey on settler livestock, especially pigs and cattle. In 1794, a Thames Valley chief announced that "they would take Cattle where they could find them, in lieu of Deer." But, by irritating the settlers (known to the Mississaugas as "the People with Hats"), such predation escalated tensions.[66]

Initially, settlers grudgingly fed hungry Mississaugas who called at their cabins, especially in the late winter, spring, and early summer. At York in 1794, Elizabeth Simcoe reported that, as a consequence of a failed deer hunt, "the Indians have been almost starved. A great many of their Women & Children come to our windows every day for bread, which we cannot refuse them, tho'. . . . it is inconvenient to give them what they require."[67]

But as settlers increased in number they increasingly treated the Mississaugas with contempt as idle beggars, driving them away from cabin doors. Rather than accept their status as guests in Indian country, the settlers acted as if they owned the land and had extinguished all native rights. To roust natives, the settlers burned their wigwams, stole their guns, and killed their dogs. In 1793, the Indians sarcastically complained that "the taking or stealing from us is nothing, for we are only Massesagoes & must be Content with all deficultays that we meet with." In 1805, a chief protested:

> Colonel Butler told us the Farmers would help us, but instead of doing so when we encamp on the shore, they drive us off & shoot our dogs and never give us any assistance as was promised to our old Chiefs. Father, the Farmers call us Dogs & threaten to shoot us in the same manner when we go on their Land.

Against mounting evidence, the Mississaugas kept hoping that the newcomers would improve their manners and generosity.[68]

The proliferation of settlements also rendered alcohol cheaper, more common, and more devastating to a native people who initially thought that it would ease their pain and disappointment. Too cheaply and too quickly, the Mississaugas could convert their animal pelts and salmon—and even their government presents and provisions—into rum, whiskey, or brandy. Inebriated Mississaugas were easy marks for traders seeking the kettles and guns so essential to Indian survival. In 1806, an Indian Department official noted that "many of the unthinking Natives return to the Woods in much worse circumstances than when they left them."[69]

Rather than lash out in suicidal raids on the numerous settlers, the Mississaugas tried to make the best of their slowly deteriorating situation. Too often, they had to settle for rebuking the ingratitude of the prospering newcomers. In 1820, a Mississauga chief complained:

> You came as wind blown across the great Lake. The wind wafted you to our shores. We received you—we planted you—we nursed you. We protected you till you became a mighty tree that spread thro[ugh] our Hunting Land. With its branches you now lash us.

In Canada, the Indian experience with settlement differed only in degree, rather than in kind, from the Indian experience on the American side of the border. Although the pace of settlement proceeded more slowly in Canada than in New York, the consequences for native peoples proved remarkably similar in the end.[70]

DISPERSAL

At the end of the war, most of the Iroquois had clustered in refugee villages in the Niagara Valley, primarily at Buffalo Creek. After the peace, however, the Iroquois began to disperse. Some turned westward to Grand River, while others headed east, returning to rebuild their prewar villages in the Genesee and Allegheny valleys and around the Finger Lakes. As Brant had warned, by discouraging Indian access to Canada, the British induced some Iroquois to shift eastward into the American orbit.

The dispersal expressed the dissatisfaction of minorities with Seneca domination. Because the Niagara Valley belonged exclusively to the Senecas, their Cayuga and Onondaga guests felt restive, eager for their own land. Some returned to their old homelands to make their peace with the advancing settlers of New York. That exit strategy especially appealed to ambitious, minor chiefs who preferred to be bigger fish in smaller pools away from the head chiefs at Buffalo Creek. Perhaps the dissident chiefs could obtain presents from the Americans. Authority as chiefs depended upon redistributing largesse from outsiders, but at Buffalo Creek the head chiefs, and especially the Senecas, obtained the British lion's share.[71]

The return eastward also appealed to some clan matrons restive over their diminished authority at Buffalo Creek and Grand River. During the war, British and American officers had lavished their presents and favors on war chiefs, bolstering their prestige and authority. For example, Cornplanter and Brant had been relatively minor figures before the conflict, soaring in influence thereafter. The ascent of war chiefs eclipsed both the sachems and the clan matrons in village politics. In a 1789 speech, the Cayuga clan mothers explained their dismay with their "Uncles," the overly powerful war chiefs at Buffalo Creek:

> Our Ancestors considered it a great Transgression to reject the Council of their Women, particularly the female Governesses. Our Ancestors considered them Mistresses of the Soil. Our Ancestors said, who brings us forth, who cultivates our Lands, who kindles our fires and boils our Pots, but the Women[?] Our Women say, they think their Uncles had of late lost the Power of Thinking and were about sinking their Territory. . . . the Women say let not the Tradition of the Fathers with respect to Women be disregarded; let them not be despised. God is their Maker.

By returning to Cayuga Lake, the matrons reasserted their voice.[72]

By 1791, about 180 Onondagas and 130 Cayugas had rebuilt villages in the Finger Lakes region. Some dissatisfied Senecas also abandoned Buffalo Creek to reclaim traditional hearths in the Allegheny Valley or in the fertile Genesee Valley. At the same time, the pro-American Oneidas (and some Tuscaroras) left their wartime refuge at Schenectady to reoccupy their homeland south of Oneida Lake. The two migration streams—one eastward, the other westward—combined partially to restore a continuum of Six Nations villages, strung in clusters, each about one day's travel from one another, from Kanonwalohale westward to Buffalo Creek.[73]

As Schuyler had predicted, the returning Iroquois were steadily enveloped by settlers. By 1790, New York's frontier counties of Montgomery and Ontario had 29,900 settlers: more than ten times the 2,310 Indians residing east of Niagara at Oneida (900), Onondaga (180), Cayuga (130), Allegheny (300), and Genesee (800). Every year brought more settlers, increasing New York's frontier security, while eroding the autonomy of the Iroquois enclaves. On March 16, 1791, a Genesee settler reported, "People have moved into the Country considerably the winter past & nothing was talked from any fear of Indians." As the settler fears waned, the Indian anxiety waxed. In April, a visitor found that the Genesee Indians anticipated a frontier war and "wished to join the U[nited] States because if they took the other side, they knew that ultimately they must be driven from the[ir] lands."[74]

As Brant had warned, the advancing American settlements compromised the security of British Niagara. Once enveloped by settlers, the Genesee Senecas became prospective scouts and warriors for the Americans, rather than an early warning system for the British. The settlements also raised livestock and provisions in abundance, promising good supplies conveniently located for any American army bound west to attack Niagara. Finally, the thriving settlements attracted and facilitated a surge in desertion by British soldiers who found it easier and safer to run through a shrinking Indian gauntlet. At Niagara in 1792, Robert Hamilton paid a reluctant tribute to the American shrewdness in capturing the Genesee Indians: "In extending their Territory in this quarter, Some degree of moderation and of Justice has been Shewn, in the purchase of the lands from the Native Indians, however inadequate the Sum may be to the value. In this way has the Genesee Country been obtained and their Settlements are thinly Scattered thro' the whole Country to the East of that River."[75]

Brant blamed both British folly and Indian disunity. Raging against all of the Six Nations except the Mohawks, in 1788 Brant insisted, "As for the Five Nations, most of them have sold themselves to the Devil—I mean to the Yankeys. Whatever they do after this, it must be for the Yankeys—not for the Indians or the English." In 1791, Brant warned the British, "The Americans are now daily gaining them over to their Interest and lately drew off several families of the Tuscaroras. This is very prejudicial to the Indians, as it divides and separates them." In 1792, he exhorted the Six Nations chiefs, "We must recollect our speech, that we are not to move in amongst the Americans, but keep ourselves free and not too near them."[76]

Brant pressed the British to reverse their policy of deterring Indian withdrawal into Canada:

[I] have ever disapproved of it's being recommended to the Six Nations to remain on the Lands they are now on, and not to Cross to this side of the [Niagara] River in order to settle.... The Americans in order to Engage them, have had tracts Surveyed on purpose for them to settle amongst them, which is in my opinion lessening the Safeguard that Niagara has always had. If they had been settled on the [Grand River] Lands allotted [to] us by Government, this Settlement might have ever rested in Security, having their frontier well Guarded.

In 1792, Brant threatened a secession by the Grand River Iroquois from their kin within New York:

I believe we shall be intirely independent from the Buffaloe Creek Indians, I mean from the five Nations, for their present measures so widely differ from ours. This is the Consequence of our friends the English stopping those Indians from crossing the River to our side. The Yankees lost no time in confirming them in the mind to keep on that side and making them Enemies to you and us.

Some subordinate British officers conceded that Brant had a point. Alexander McKee, an Indian Department official, concluded, "It was not good policy to prevent the Senecas from settling on the Fort Erie side." Once enveloped and co-opted by the Americans, the Indians became "more dangerous Enemies than all the People the Americans could settle on these Lands."[77]

SETTLERS

On the New York side, the returning Iroquois had to deal with settlers whose treatment varied by their location and numerical strength. They were most powerful and angry in the Mohawk Valley, where the settlers returned in 1783 with bitter memories to a ravaged landscape. Raiders had killed or taken almost all of the livestock and had burned most of the houses, barns, and mills. Bullet-pocked stockades surrounded the few surviving structures. The ruined farms meant hardships for the returning settlers. In May 1784, a traveler noted, "The most beautiful country in the world now presents only the poor cabins of an impoverished population who are nearly without food and upon the verge of starvation."[78]

Every locale sustained a grim memory. The jurist James Kent reported, "The inhabitants point frequently to places where just such a one was killed and scalped." On the battlefield beside Oriskany Creek, where General Herkimer's Patriot army had been crushed by Indians and Loyalists, unburied bones lay scattered through the woods. One visitor saw "a number of skulls, placed in a row on a log in the road." Many bore the marks of tomahawks and scalping knives. Such reminders bred a deep settler hatred for all Indians. In 1784, New York's Indian commissioners advised against attempting an Indian council at German Flats because "the Inhabitants in that Country are generally unruly, and don't like to see Indians since the affair of General Herkermer."[79]

The returning settlers compulsively told stories of death and destruction. French visitors sat down for dinner at the house of Colonel Frederick Visscher, who "begged our permission to eat with his hat on, as he had been scalped by the Indians in the late war, and was left for dead, on his place, with two brothers, whom they had killed after burning his buildings." Another traveler, Elkanah Watson, recalled, "He entered into no family, in which he did not hear thrilling recitals of the massacre of some branch of it, by ferocious barbarians, who carried fire and the sword through their settlements." The grim narration compounded settler anger and conveyed it to newcomers, who often adopted an indiscriminate hatred of Indians.[80]

After hearing too many stories and seeing too many skulls at Oriskany, Watson felt terrified when he stumbled upon an encampment of Indians bound to meet the governor at nearby Fort Schuyler:

> They looked like so many evil spirits, broken loose from Pandemonium. Wild, frantic, almost naked, and frightfully painted, they whooped, yelled, and danced round me in such hideous attitudes, that I was seriously apprehensive, they would end the farce, by taking off my scalp, by way of a joke.

In fact, these Indians were peaceable Oneidas engaged in a harmless dance. Although Patriot allies, the Oneidas increasingly confronted settlers and travelers who blamed all Indians for the bloodshed in the Mohawk Valley.[81]

During the mid-1780s, a more promising relationship (temporarily) developed in the Chemung country in New York's southern tier near the Pennsylvania border. In contrast to the Mohawk Valley, where the settlers returned embittered to ravaged homesteads, the Chemung settlers ventured into an Indian country with some trepidation and restraint.

Most newcomers were poor families with few farm tools and without the means to buy land from a speculator. In 1791, the Dutch traveler John Lincklaen noted that "these people accustomed to live in the woods know none of the comforts of life, whether in their Houses or their Clothing." But they had found an immensely fertile land, especially the broad alluvial flats beside the rivers. Lincklaen marveled, "It is impossible to imagine richer lands." The meadows were "covered with grass as high as a man on horseback." By cultivating such fertile soil, the settlers meant to make property in the Indian country. A former officer in Sullivan's army, Colonel Thomas Proctor, reported meeting an evangelical preacher named Jabez Coolver: "He enjoined me, in a very becoming manner, should I at any time see the Hon[orab]le Gen[era]l Sullivan . . . to tender him the grateful thanks of himself and his parishioners, inhabitants of the district of Tioga, for opening a way into the wilderness, under the guidance of Providence, to the well doing of hundreds of poor families for life."[82]

The newcomers came by river in canoes during summer or overland in sleds during the winter. They built crude log cabins, chinked with mud, without glass for the two holes that served for windows and without a chimney to conduct smoke through a third hole in the roof. They initially avoided the surrounding uplands where a dense forest obliged hard work with axes to make clearings to cultivate grains. Instead, the newcomers favored the fertile and treeless flats beside the rivers. Free from stumps, roots, and stones, the alluvial soil could be easily worked with hoes, which appealed to poor people without oxen and plows, as it had previously attracted Indians. Many such niches remained open for settlement because only a minority of the natives had returned after the war from exile at Niagara.[83]

The newcomers also procured an immediate subsistence by hunting deer and bear, whose populations had surged during the war, when hunters had been kept away. Returning during the 1780s, the hunters found a brief bonanza. A settler recalled, "The deer ran as plenty as sheep. . . . We killed them as we wanted them." The hunters also preyed upon some cattle that had become loose and feral during the confusion of the war.[84]

The Chemung country also attracted a few traders, bearing goods in boats and canoes (or on packhorses). At the junctures of tributaries with the rivers, they built small storehouses for their alcohol, ammunition, tools, and cloth. Dealing with both Indians and settlers, the traders sought furs taken from animals and ginseng dug from the forest floor. Opportunistic, they also employed flattery and alcohol to purchase Indian marks on vague deeds to large tracts of land. Obscure hunters on the move, the mark-makers were rarely the chiefs or matrons with any real authority to dispose of land. Grateful for trade, and longing for patrons, these Indians gave marks to solidify their friendship with the traders, such as Amos Draper of Owego, known as "Qua-see" (Big Man).[85]

During the 1780s, there was, for the time being, enough fish, game, and alluvial land for the small populations of Indians and settlers to coexist in the Chemung and Susquehanna valleys. In July 1786, the surveyor Moses DeWitt reported: "The white People are Settled from the head to Wyoming on this River and the Indians are about here Considerably in Number, a hunting and planting. They are [on] one side of the River, and the white People on the opposite and they never offer the least unbecoming or unfriendly act." DeWitt belonged to a survey party led by General James Clinton, who during Sullivan's expedition had ravaged the local Indian villages. During the 1786 survey, General Clinton met the local Indians, led by Captain Cornelius Sturgeon (an Onondaga) to frame a "Treaty of Friendship." Thereafter, DeWitt reported, the Indians and surveyors were "very merry together, in Shooting at the mark and Chatting about a great many things." Although his survey would hasten Indian dispossession, DeWitt felt perfectly at ease among the natives: "I have been as much as 12 miles back into the Woods in a manner alone, and lay'd out with them and Considered myself (and believe [I] was) as safe as if I had been [back home] in Peenpack."[86]

For a few years, the Chemung settlers and the Indians got along famously despite the recent war. At Tioga in 1786, a surveyor, Andrew Ellicott, reported, "Contrary to our expectations we found the White people and Indians living together in great Harmony in the Neighbourhood of this Place." The family of Captain Sturgeon visited the surveyors to "share in all our Amusements such as Cards and . . . Checkards."[87]

Nineteenth-century antiquarians recorded traditions of Indians and the first settlers meeting festively for foot- and horse races, wrestling and shooting matches, and for dances. At the settlement of Owego, a settler's daughter recalled that Indians "had wigwams near her father's house. They were peaceable and friendly as could be." One of those Indians, a Nanticoke woman named Way-Way, remembered that the settlers were "very good to my people, give us flour, pork & all kinds of provisions."[88]

In 1786, a murder tested the coexistence. A drunken hunter named Collins killed an Indian who chopped wood for the settlers at Coshocton. Sobering up, Collins ran away to save his life, leaving the other settlers in dread of Indian revenge. The local Big Men met the chiefs in council to offer alcohol and to cover the grave with Collins's goods and contributions from the other settlers. By accepting the native customary law, the settlers conceded that local sovereignty remained shared, which lifted the crisis.[89]

A year later, another revealing murder troubled the Chemung country. This time both killer and killed were natives. The victim, Captain Cornelius Sturgeon, had taken the lead in welcoming the Chemung settlers. In 1786, Moses DeWitt praised Sturgeon as "a very likely Indian, looks much like a Soldier, is very Senceable, and a great deal refined." In 1787, Andrew Ellicott reported that the captain "began to adopt the dress and customs of the United States, and introduced them into his family," which "gave great umbrage" to his own people. Behaving like an American, rather than an Indian, Captain Sturgeon "imposed an implicit compliance with his orders—he was punctually obeyed through fear, not love." Such domineering chiefs rarely lived long, for warriors dreaded any sign of authoritarian control especially if exercised on behalf of outsiders. Sturgeon died on the evening that he vowed to send his eldest son to attend an American college. The assassin's many friends appeased Sturgeon's relatives by covering the grave with goods worth £375.[90]

Sturgeon's murder attested both to the anxiety provoked by the settler invasion and to a desperation to keep the peace on the New York frontier. The natives welcomed a parallel, but not an intersecting, friendship with their settler neighbors. Indeed, the Indians dreaded a cultural penetration that touched the core of their identity as especially free peoples. But to police that difference, by the late 1780s they tended to kill their own rather than provoke a war by killing settlers.

On a more daily basis, Indian visitors provoked anxiety among settlers conditioned by childhood stories of bloodthirsty savages. Passing Indians spooked the newcomers by suddenly appearing in the night announced by loud whoops. One antiquarian recorded that settlers "lived in constant alarm—not an inexcusable fear when a score or two of barbarians came whooping to the cabin door, or raised the midnight yell in their camp by the creek-side." The natives sought sleep on the floor, under a roof, and by a warm fire. They also solicited food and drink, which they considered as their due for the lands so cheaply afforded to the settlers. But those natives did not bargain on the growing numbers that would soon follow the welcomed few.[91]

As settler numbers grew so did their sense of security and their resistance to native expectations. In 1787, Moses DeWitt returned to the Chemung country and reported, "The people have settled very much on the Susquehannah River since last Summer. I think . . . that there is ten families to one last year." In 1790, the area hosted about 2,400 settlers—which grew to about 8,700 ten years later. By comparison, the area's postwar natives probably never exceeded 500 during the 1780s. Once settlers became an overwhelming majority, they tended, with cudgels and dogs, to drive away hungry and sleepy Indians. No longer fearing Indians or needing their help, the newcomers could indulge their sense of superiority.[92]

Claiming a belated right to revenge Patriot sufferings from the war, settler bullies destroyed wigwams and plundered the possessions of Indians. A few natives lost their lives after drinking with the most murderous settlers. At Owego, during the 1780s, an Indian named Nicholas and his family thrived by raising cattle and corn on a large alluvial flat, but he felt obliged to move away when settler numbers grew. A neighbor explained, "He was afraid they would take revenge upon him for some past occurrence."[93]

The influx of settlers depleted the wild game, as hunters killed faster than the animals could reproduce. One professional hide-hunter killed 200 deer in two months, a rate that soon doomed the abundance. In Steuben County, where beavers had abounded in 1783, a trapper killed the last in 1794. As game diminished, the white hunters treated their Indian competition more abusively. One imaginative intruder drove away his Indian competition by a cruel practical joke. Near a favorite native campsite, he bored holes in dead branches, filled the cavities with gunpowder, and closed them with wooden plugs. When the Indians returned to build a fire, the wood exploded. Assuming a dangerous witchcraft, they fled from the area, leaving the remaining game to the white hunter.[94]

As settlers poured into Iroquoia by the hundreds, they expanded their settlements beyond the alluvial flats into the surrounding hills, where they worked steadily to effect a radical environmental transformation. Their free-ranging cattle and pigs spread through forest, consuming nuts, roots, and wild plants long gathered and much needed by Indians. The settlers also attacked that forest with axes, oxen, and fire to create clearings for their crops and livestock. Entrepreneurs also dammed the streams to tap their water power for sawmills and gristmills. These changes alienated a native people from the landscape. No longer at home in most of their territory, they retreated into their shrinking reservations.[95]

After most of the Indians moved away, some old-time settlers mourned the lost harmony of the mid-1780s. One recalled:

> People now, friend, ain't a comparison to those Ingens. They were simple creatures, and made their little lodges around by the hills, three hundred Ingens at a time, and never stole a thing. Those Ingens came to our houses, and were around nights, and never stole the first rag. Now that's the truth, friend. They would snap off a pumpkin now and then perhaps, or take an ear of corn to roast, but they were just the simplest and most honest creatures I ever see.

Maintained only by a balance of local power, the Chemung harmony proved short-lived. The surge in settler numbers empowered the pervasive expectation that natives were a primitive people doomed to move away or to die.[96]

On both sides of the peace treaty border, natives tried to adapt to the settler invasion by imposing expectations of generosity. They hoped to farm the farmers by obtaining agricultural produce in seasons of hunger as a sort of rent for the native land. But they belatedly discovered that the commercial and racial imperatives of settler society too quickly overrode the obligations owed to their native hosts.

CHAPTER FIVE

State

George Clinton, by Ezra Ames, 1813. (Courtesy of the
Albany Institute of History and Art.)

DURING THE 1780s, the settler and speculator pressure on Iroquoia
was compounded by bitter competition among the Americans over
who would win the prize. In addition to New York, both Massachusetts and
the United States claimed Iroquoia. Nearly bankrupted by the long, hard,
and expensive war, all three governments desperately needed the revenues
promised by selling Indian land to speculators for development by farmers.
In June 1784, a wary New York congressman worried that "the whole world
seems to look on that W[estern] Country with a wishful eye." To strengthen

a claim, and weaken their rivals, each competitor plotted to secure Indian land cessions and to rush settlers into the contested region. The contenders sought the great vehicle for making property and power in America: control over the acquisition and disposition of Indian land. The victor would reap public revenues by selling the land; would collect taxes on the new farms; and would consolidate authority by interesting speculators and settlers in support of the victorious jurisdiction and its land title.[1]

By expanding westward, New York would become wealthy and powerful, but only if the state could overcome its initial vulnerability to rivals. The great paradox was that the state's short-term prospects appeared dire and, yet, its long-term potential seemed so limitless. The source of both proximate implosion and ultimate power lay in the resources of Iroquoia, riches that could either endow New York or attract despoilers.

During the war, New York adopted a revolutionary new land policy. Colonial-era land grants had generated fees for a few public officials but nothing for the provincial treasury. Under the colonial regime, individual speculators secured licenses to negotiate sales directly from Indians, subject to confirmation at a public council hosted by the governor or by the Crown's superintendent of Indian affairs. In 1777, however, a new republican state constitution reserved to New York a monopoly power to buy Indian land. To generate revenue, the state would survey the land and then resell it with a patent title, at a markup. The purchasers then became dependent upon the state government—a critical means of consolidating the new regime. But the state could not realize that potential revenue and power until the end of the war and the dispossession of the Indians.[2]

Some New York leaders also wanted to reject the colonial legacy, associated with Albany and Sir William Johnson, of bestowing generous presents and diplomatic respect on the Six Nations. These state leaders argued that the supposed treachery of the British-allied Iroquois had demonstrated the expensive futility of treating them as sovereign peoples. Congressman James Duane advised the governor, "If we adopt the disgraceful system of pensioning, courting, and flattering them as great and mighty nations, we shall once more, like the Albanians, be their Fools and Slaves, and this Revolution, in my Eyes, will have lost more than half its Value." Duane understood the revolution as imposing American supremacy on the Indians. He "would never suffer the word nations, or Six Nations, . . . or any other Form which would revive or seem to confirm their former Ideas of Independence." He advised abandoning wampum belts and the term "treaty," which seemed "to[o] much to imply Equality." Instead, Duane favored negotiating "with as much plainness and simplicity as possible—and as if I was actually transacting Business with the Citizens" of New York. Under the new, revolutionary dispensation,

New York should treat the Iroquois bluntly, with minimal ceremony and expense.[3]

Victorious and vindictive, New York's leaders blamed the British-allied Iroquois as "cruel and wanton Aggressors in this War." The state's leaders insisted that only by a massive land cession could the Iroquois atone for their malicious deceit and bloody deeds. Dispossessing the Indians also promised to help New York win Iroquoia away from their federal and Massachusetts competitors. In 1782, without the benefit of a treaty, and in defiance of Congress, the state legislature confiscated 1.5 million acres of Cayuga and Onondaga land to provide bounty lands for New York's soldiers.[4]

But the lands most coveted by New Yorkers belonged to their wartime allies the Oneidas, rather than to their Indian enemies. At the head of the Mohawk Valley and along the upper reaches of the Susquehanna River, the Oneida domain lay in tempting, valuable proximity to New York's settlements. The domains of the hostile Iroquois lay farther west, along the Finger Lakes and in the Genesee, Allegheny, and Niagara valleys. How could settlers get to those distant lands without first occupying and developing the Oneida country? In March 1783, the state legislature defined its ideal solution by urging the Oneidas to move westward onto lands expropriated from the hostile Senecas. By this neat swap, the state would obtain the Oneida country—the best lands for immediate settlement—while inflicting the cost on enemy Iroquois. The Oneidas, however, clung to their ancient, beloved homeland. They wanted no part of moving west to incur the dangerous enmity of the powerful Senecas. Those two nations may have fought for rival sides during the war, but they hoped to restore their previous friendship and alliance.[5]

New York's lust for Oneida lands conflicted with federal promises to protect that domain. To reward the Oneida exertions and sacrifices for the Patriot cause, Congress consistently and carefully distinguished them from the hostile Iroquois. In December 1777, Congress assured the Oneidas,

> It rejoices our hearts, that we have no reason to reproach you in common with the rest of the Six Nations. We have experienced your love, strong as the oak, and your fidelity, unchangeable as truth. . . . While the sun and moon continue to give light to the world, we shall love and respect you. As our trusty friends, we shall protect you; and shall at all times consider your welfare as our own.

In May 1778, General Schuyler assured the Oneidas that, upon defeating the British, "you will then partake of every Blessing we enjoy, and united with a free people, your Liberty and Property will be safe." In October 1783, Congress again promised the Oneidas and Tuscaroras "that the lands which they claim as their inheritance will be reserved for their sole use and benefit." In January 1784, Schuyler reiterated that settlers "have no right at all to settle in the Oneida and Tuscarora country without the leave of these two nations, and none will do this."[6]

Those federal promises alarmed New York leaders, who dreaded the preservation of a large Oneida domain protected by Congress. As a result, the federal assurances intensified the state's drive to subordinate the Oneidas and to procure their land, the better to discredit and defeat the intertwined claims of Massachusetts and the United States to own Iroquoia.

LOAF OF BREAD

During the summer of 1783, the Oneidas returned home to the blackened ruins and overgrown fields of war-ravaged Kanonwalohale, Oriske, and Old Oneida. Samuel Kirkland sadly observed:

> Previous to the revolutionary war, the Oneidas were in a peaceable & flourish[ing] state & many among them had approximated to the first stages of civil society. They had attained some degree of regularity & industry. Their Chiefs had great influence, especially those who sustained a good moral Character & professedly friends to Christianity. The late war proved almost fatal to the nation. A great majority took part with the Americans & lost many of their warriors. . . . In the year 1780 the hostile Indians & [Loyalist] refugees drove them from their villages, burning their church, spreading waste & desolation on every side. . . . When they returned to their desolated villages after the peace, they were wretchedly poor, their land much overgrown, & their reluctance to labour doubled.

Because rebuilding homes and restoring fields proved so hard and slow, hunger afflicted the Oneidas for the rest of the decade, often obliging Kirkland to cut short his missionary visits for want of enough to eat.[7]

In addition to their material losses, the Oneidas suffered socially and psychologically from the stress of war and from increased wartime exposure to alcohol. After the war, the Oneidas drank more heavily and destructively than before. In August 1784, Joseph Brant passed through Kanonwalohale and sarcastically observed, "The Oneidas here are pretty good. They are continually Drunk with Stinking Rum."[8]

Weakened by the war, the Oneidas recognized that their strategic location, large domain (about 6 million acres), small population (about 600), and postwar poverty rendered them especially vulnerable to covetous settlers and speculators. Responding creatively to that intense pressure, the Oneidas sought to channel settlement in ways that would preserve their control, bolster their boundaries, and enhance their income.

To defend their core homeland around Kanonwalohale, the Oneidas developed a buffer zone of dependent communities planted on their eastern margins. Following a long-standing Iroquois custom, the Oneidas recruited Indian dependents from peoples dislocated by colonial settlement. In March 1784, Kirkland reported, "The Oneidas expect in the course of two years to have more than a thousand Indians in their vicinity."[9]

The Oneidas began by renewing the Brothertown project launched in 1774 by Samson Occom. The Brothertown Indians were Christian Algonquians from Mohegan, Groton, Niantic, Pequot, and Farmington in Connecticut; Narragansett in Rhode Island; and Montauk on Long Island. Dispossessed by their colonial neighbors, the Christian Algonquians sought new land and a new start in the Oneida country. Placed along the Line of Property, Brothertown buffered the Oneidas from the settlers to the east in the Mohawk Valley. The Oneidas also hoped to benefit from Indians who, by their familiarity with settler culture, could mediate with the outsiders.[10]

Begun in 1774, Brothertown lapsed during the war, as the pioneers retreated eastward, finding haven with the Mohican Indians of Stockbridge in western Massachusetts. After the war, the Brothertown pioneers returned to the Oneida country, bringing along additional kin from New England. They also recruited their Mohican friends, who desperately needed new land. Although they clung to their national identity and to traditional modes of diplomacy and dress, the Stockbridge Mohicans had adopted sufficient Christianity, the English language, and colonial agriculture and housing to pass for model Indians in colonial eyes. Patriot allies during the revolution, the Mohicans impressed the Patriots as dogged and reliable fighters who suffered heavy casualties. But neither adaptations nor sacrifices spared them from colonial exploitation. With alcohol, fraudulent documents, and surveying tricks, cunning speculators procured almost all of the Mohican domain in eastern New York and western Massachusetts. At war's end, the Stockbridge Mohicans sought a new start in the Oneida country.[11]

In 1783, the Oneidas granted the Mohicans a tract, 6 by 6 miles, located 3 miles south of Kanonwalohale (and west of Brothertown) on the former site of a Tuscarora village with a large apple orchard. By 1790, most of the Mohicans had left Massachusetts to settle their new township, which they called "New Stockbridge." Numbering about 260 people, they struggled with hunger as they labored to clear the forest to make farms.[12]

In addition to recruiting Algonquian dependents, the Oneidas also employed some of their land to strengthen their relationship with prominent "culture brokers" from the colonial world. These were gentlemen like James Dean and Samuel Kirkland: men with the cross-cultural knowledge and linguistic skills to interpret and influence transactions between the Indians and outsiders. Because few Oneidas could speak more than a smattering of English, and fewer New Yorkers knew the Oneida language, the bilingual culture-brokers were rare and, consequently, powerful. The Oneidas desperately needed friends who could honestly assess outsiders' initiatives and who could faithfully explain Indian wishes to the outsiders. By granting them some lands, the Oneidas hoped to "interest" them to defend the Oneida core domain against other settlers and speculators. The Oneidas also felt obliged to help those who had helped them through the dark years of the war, including Dean and Colonel Abraham Wemple, "who turned out an Ox for us and gave Us Bread when We were hungry, Drink when We were dry, and his House was our own." Let Dean have two square miles and Wemple one, next to one another and "on or near the Line of Property" where they could "assist us." In the words of the sachem, the Great Grasshopper, "Our Country is like a Loaf of Bread," from which the Oneidas would cut off and grant pieces to help them keep the rest.[13]

To complete the buffer zone of dependents and mediators, the Oneidas wished to lease lands rather than make wholesale land cessions to the state. In contrast to a one-time purchase payment, which they would spend all too soon, rents promised a steady, annual income. Indeed, that revenue could increase over time as settlement enhanced the land's value. By retaining ultimate title and by obtaining a progressive income, the Oneidas could avoid the dependence imposed by land cessions. In the Brothertown and New Stockbridge refugees from New England, the Oneidas saw the grim consequences of selling land outright. Good Peter explained:

> We look to the Eastward. The Indians who lived there are now settled among us and we have been obliged to give them Lands. This will be our Case should we sell our Lands as they have done.

Without land, the Oneidas would lose respect: "Brothers! While the Indians had all their Lands, they were important; when they met their Friends they could entertain them; but since they have parted with Lands, the Case is altered." But, as prospering landlords, the Oneidas could perpetuate and enhance their prosperity and standing. And if endowed with a substantial income, the Oneidas could attract back to the homeland their people scattered by the war to the west, in the Genesee country and at Grand River.[14]

Leasing made both economic and social sense to the Oneidas, who suffered from the decline of their hunting, which had supplied both meat for subsistence and furs for market. After the war, game animals dwindled in the Oneida country as intruding settlers competed as hunters and cleared the forest as farmers. This transformed environment was especially difficult for Indian men, who could not bring themselves to adopt the female role of tilling the soil, as so many well-meaning missionaries and officials advised. In 1793, some aging warriors explained:

> We are old men and we never learned the art of husbandry when we were young. We were brought up to hunting. This has been our trade. We have learned it well, and while game was plenty it was a good trade to make money by, and we could live well, but now our trade fails us, and we are poor and we are too old to learn a new trade, therefore we wish to *lease* our lands to support us in our old age and benefit our nation. We mean that our boys should learn to till land, and learn to read and write, so that after we are dead perhaps *they* may grow rich by farming like your people but *we* cannot practice what we never learned.

With rents from leased lands, the Oneidas could effect a difficult economic and social transition on their own terms and at their own deliberate pace.[15]

Troubled by the poverty seen in the settlements, as well as in their own villages, the Oneidas also sought an opportunity to patronize needy whites. In 1785, Good Peter explained, "We have many Friends at Albany and Schenectady, who are poor, and have applied to Us for Lands. We wish to gratify them and request they may settle on the Lands along the Line." Rather than becoming dependent wards of New York State, the Oneidas could become patrons to poor white people—a delicious reversal of impending fate. By choosing their own tenants, the Indians might obtain grateful neighbors inclined to avoid frictions. Strategically located on the borders, a tier of renters under Indian influence could provide a firewall against unwanted white intruders—the pressure that drove further land cessions.[16]

The Oneidas favored tenants who had behaved generously. In 1792, they explained their preference for "old Mr. Clock. . . . We esteem him a clever, harmless, old man, and he is of service to us especially when we are out that way a hunting. He supplies us with milk and such things as we want." Similarly, on November 12, 1787, they leased a township (6 by 6 miles) to Jedediah Phelps, a silversmith and merchant based at Fort Stanwix (the former Fort Schuyler), in return for an annual rent paid in ground corn. The Oneidas regarded this lease as a good deed as well as a good deal, explaining:

Our Friend Mr. Phelps has Done us much good. His house is on our fishing and hunting road. There we have had for several years a resting place and a sleeping place when weary and hungry. He has fed and refreshed us more times than we can reckon up. His great benevolence to us must be Considered or we can never hold up our heads.

By rewarding Clock and Phelps, the Oneidas defended their customary expectation that settlers would shelter and feed their Indian benefactors.[17]

Increasingly the Oneidas employed formal written leases to define rents in monetary terms. But their tenants obtained especially good lands at a modest rent. Conrad Klock entered a formal lease of twenty-one years for a 300-acre farm, paying a nominal rent for four years, but £5 ($12.50) annually thereafter. In 1789, the blacksmith Isaac Carpenter obtained a 100-acre homestead for twenty-one years, in return for 12 shillings down ($1.50) and an annual rent of £5 ($12.50), payable in cash or produce delivered at the Kanonwalohale council house. By leasing lands, the Oneidas could make far more money than the pennies per acre offered them by New York for a permanent cession, and they could complete a buffer zone of dependents along the Line of Property.[18]

The Oneidas were willing to provide settlers with some land, provided the Indians received an annual rent and retained ultimate title as landlords. The Oneidas recognized the advantages reaped by the Kahnawake Iroquois in leasing lands with the consent of the Canadian government. Within New York, the Oneidas also noted the material prosperity and political influence enjoyed by the great renting landlords of the Hudson Valley. Why shouldn't Indians derive similar benefit from the future development of their lands?[19]

But Oneida leasing clashed with New York's interest. For if the Oneidas could obtain a secure and increasing revenue by leasing land, the state would lose its leverage to procure land cessions. And, without that Oneida land for subsequent sale to speculators, the state would lose cherished revenue and a coveted means to attract the interest of wealthy men. Moreover, without land cessions, the state could not fill Iroquoia with settlers holding New York title in defiance of Massachusetts. New York leaders also did not like the prospect of rental incomes permitting Oneida men to live in "idleness" when they should, the leaders devoutly believed, become farmers. Moreover, state officials wanted none of the future trouble and expense of policing the tenants who might default on their rents or provoke disputes with the Oneidas.

Insisting that Indians were ignorant and immutable primitives, New York's leaders refused to take seriously the adaptive, new ideas of the Oneidas. Instead, the New York Indian commissioners cast the Oneidas as dummies ventriloquized by cunning whites seeking to bypass the state to lease Indian land. In 1784, the commissioners characteristically blamed "the private artifice of designing Persons who have endeavoured to persuade them into a Belief that this State have it in Contemplation to deprive them of their Lands." By stereotyping Indians as naïve savages, the state leaders asserted their own monopoly to procure native land.[20]

GOOD PETER AND THE GOVERNOR

To defend their lands, the Oneidas relied on their most eloquent and perceptive chief, Gwedelhes Agwelondongwas, known to the Americans as Good Peter, because of his Christian piety and morality. Eleazar Wheelock esteemed Good Peter as "an honest Man, as well as Wise, prudent and steady." Sir William Johnson praised him as "a very faithfull and Pious Indian." Philip Schuyler extolled him as "a man of sense and sobriety." A serene and gray-haired man in his late sixties during the 1780s, Good Peter had grown up along the Susquehanna at Onoquaga, where he converted to Christianity in 1748 under the influence of a New England missionary. Good

Good Peter, by John Trumbull, 1792. (Courtesy of the Yale University Art Gallery.)

Peter assisted worship services by leading psalm-singing, reading Scripture, and preaching in Oneida. He adopted Christianity and cultivated missionaries to gain knowledge and friends to protect his people from outside pressures on their land.[21]

During the war, Good Peter left pro-British Onoquaga for Kanonwalohale, where the Oneidas favored the Patriots. After the 1779 death of his brother, Deacon Thomas, Good Peter became the primary spokesman at Kanonwalohale. Recognizing his importance, Governor Clinton shrewdly advised an agent, "Peter, the Oneida, you must also pay Attention to, and flatter him on Account of his Good Sense and Friendship to Us."[22]

As an orator, Good Peter impressed Americans, even when they could not understand a word of his Oneida. Kirkland regarded him as the most powerful mind and best speaker among the entire Six Nations: "His exhortation far outdid my sermons; I have often thought that if I could speak with as much ease & fluency as he that I would preach every day of my life." Kirkland recalled that Good Peter held his own in debating New York's formidable Governor Clinton, at a council in 1785: "There were some very *smart*, ingenious & really affecting speeches passed at this treaty between the *Governor* & *Good Peter*. Whether they were all put upon the Journals of the Treaty I do not know."[23]

From 1777 to 1795, George Clinton dominated New York's politics. A big bear of a man with bushy eyebrows and a penetrating gaze, Clinton came from a prosperous Scotch-Irish family of farmers and surveyors in Ulster County. During the 1760s, he became a country lawyer and an assembly representative. An early critic of British rule, he embraced the revolution and performed with courage and zeal as a general. In 1777, Clinton won a surprising electoral victory to become the state's first governor under the new republican constitution. A stunned and defeated rival, Philip Schuyler, conceded that Clinton had "played his Cards better than was Expected." The state's most prestigious and wealthy families—the Livingstons, Morrises, Schuylers, and Van Rensselaers—disdained his modest origins and limited education as beneath the proper dignity of a governor. Often underestimated by elitists, Clinton repeatedly defeated them in politics, demonstrating an acumen unmatched in his generation in New York.[24]

Far better than his critics, Clinton understood the republican logic of the American Revolution. He won seven gubernatorial elections by perfecting the popular pose of the principled, egalitarian, and uncompromising Patriot defending the liberties of the common farmers from the greedy ambition of would-be aristocrats: the wealthy, wellborn gentlemen who had dominated colonial politics. He dwelled in a modest cottage, dressed in a plain but dignified manner, and limited his conversation, a contemporary recalled, to "matters of fact—the events of the Revolution, the politics of the day, the useful arts and agriculture." A political rival, Alexander Hamilton, described Clinton as "circumspect and guarded, and seldom acts or speaks without premeditation." A supporter "admired him for his simplicity of manners, ease of access, decision and firmness." After watching Clinton shrewdly maneuver a bill through the legislature, a friend admired "old George with his private Irish ways."[25]

Although populist in style, Clinton was cautious and conservative in public policy. He vigorously supported the great landlords against tenant uprisings, and he tried (in vain) to suppress the secession movement by small farmers that created Vermont during the war. A shrewd judge of men, he appointed many grandees to public offices, so long as their families supported his reelection. While publicly lauding a society of common farmers, Clinton rapidly sold New York's public lands in massive tracts for pennies an acre to wealthy speculators who were, or would become, his political allies. While posing as a man of simple habits, he quietly accumulated an impressive fortune through his own speculations in land. His acquisitions included shares in the controversial Fonda and Oriskany Patents that absorbed Oneida lands at the head of the Mohawk Valley.[26]

Next only to his own interest, Clinton aggressively promoted the state of New York, which he regarded as embattled by powerful and greedy neighbors. Measured by population and economic development, New York in 1783 seemed relatively weak but possessed of immense potential. Long hemmed in by Iroquoia to the west, New York's authority and inhabitants remained virtually confined to the long, narrow corridors of the Hudson and Mohawk valleys. Thinly settled, New York ranked a mediocre sixth in population and prosperity among the original thirteen states, lagging behind even little Connecticut. For enhanced strength, New York needed greater numbers, which required aggressive expansion into Iroquoia. An obstacle if left in Indian hands, that region offered an immense asset if taken and developed by New York. In 1784 Clinton urged the legislature to provide "the utmost encouragement to the speedy settlement of the country. The cultivation of our lands ought to be one of our first cares, since the riches of the state is to be found in the number of its people." With his characteristic persistence, Clinton worked to multiply New York's farms and towns by dispossessing native peoples of their land. That relentless policy expressed both his anxiety and his optimism for New York's future.[27]

Although lacking prior experience in Iroquois relations, Clinton learned quickly during the 1780s. He astutely rejected James Duane's vindictive advice to abandon the traditional ceremonial respect for Iroquois diplomatic customs. Instead, Clinton mastered the use of opening ceremonies, wampum, metaphoric speeches, private conferences and douceurs for chiefs, and concluding presents for all. Like Sir William Johnson, Clinton began to delight in his own theatrical performances as the paternal guardian of the Iroquois peoples and their traditional customs. By pleasing the chiefs with customary performance, however, Clinton softened their resistance to his transforming agenda: the steady transfer of Iroquois lands into state possession for sale and settlement.[28]

Powerful in build and bold in manner, Clinton vividly impressed the Iroquois at councils. Emulating Sir William, the governor commanded attention by his charismatic range and keen sense of timing and mood. As opportunity dictated, he varied from bullying to good-natured banter (and back again). For example, in 1789 the Cayuga clan mothers pressed for a larger reservation, which they called a "Dish." Clinton replied, "The Dish that we will set apart for you shall be sufficiently large, however prolific our Sisters may be, even if they should encrease their Nation to its antient Strength and Number." He confessed, "Sisters: I am advancing in Years and little accustomed to address your Sex in public; you will therefore excuse the Imperfections of this Speech." But he suggested that some of his young aides might "express themselves more agreeably to you upon this Occasion." Some jocular sexual innuendo went a long way with an Iroquois audience. Having broken the council tension with a collective laugh, Clinton imposed a reservation much smaller than the Cayugas wanted. Despite their distrust of state intentions, the chiefs could not help but admire Clinton's manly style and his shrewd appropriation of native protocol. In awe, the Oneidas named him Aquilanda, which meant "Rising Sun."[29]

A cunning judge of human motives and political contentions, Clinton shrewdly worked the factional divisions, village jealousies, and chiefly rivalries that ran fault lines through every Iroquois nation, especially after the divisive war. Consider his handling of Joseph Brant. In preparing for negotiations with the British-allied Iroquois in 1784, Clinton instructed his secret agent, Peter Ryckman to apply flattery and bribery: "To Captain Brandt you will hint that our People in general are pleased with his Generosity to the Prisoners he took during the War, and that he may become a great Man if he conducts himself in such a Manner as will give the Commissioners occasion to believe that he means to be a sincere Friend." But when it became evident that Brant would not sell himself and his people so cheaply, Clinton revised his instructions to Ryckman: "If you find that any Jealousy of, or envy to Brant privails, you will try to discover who are most jealous or envious of him, and promote it as much as you prudently can." Still later, at a council,

Clinton turned on his charm. Lavishing personal attention on Brant, Clinton promised to help his sister Molly gain compensation for her Canajoharie property. Flattered by the attention, Brant effusively thanked the governor, "You obligingly offered your friendly mediation in regard to some family matters which I had the honor to mention to you." Thereafter, Clinton felt that he could manage Brant for the state's advantage.[30]

FORT STANWIX (1784)

The governor distrusted Congress as the tool of the New England states, with malignant ambitions to carve up New York. He cited the wartime loss of Vermont, formerly the northeastern counties of colonial New York. Settled by New England farmers, Vermont had exploited the revolution to become an independent republic. While New York blocked Vermont's bid for admission to the Union, Congress stymied New York's efforts to recover the region.[31]

New Yorkers suspected that the New Englanders meant to produce a second Vermont in Iroquoia, with congressional collusion. Indeed, some congressmen claimed that Sullivan's federal army had conquered Iroquoia for the entire union, putting New York's boundary no farther west than the Line of Property. In 1784, New York's congressional delegation warned Clinton, "Should the Massachusetts People once get [a] footing in that Country, our State, in such case, is to expect but little aid from Congress. . . . The utmost Vigilance ought to be exercised to prevent any encroachment on our Territory as we are to expect no protection otherwise than from our own arm." One New York congressman assured Clinton, "I believe, Sir, a Plan is formed and perhaps wrought into System to take that Country from us." In the heated bickering between the New York and New England delegations, a North Carolina congressman detected "the seeds of dissension which I think will not end without a civil war."[32]

Desperate and defiant, leading New Yorkers prepared forcibly to defend Iroquoia against the New Englanders and Congress. One New York congressman explained, "It is high time for our State to tak[e] the same measures as though it was sorounded with open and avowed Enemies." In early 1784, New York's leaders plotted to push state troops into the British forts at Oswego and Niagara before Congress could do so. Clinton sent a secret emissary to Quebec to seek Governor Haldimand's cooperation, but he refused to surrender the forts either to the state or to Congress.[33]

New York acted aggressively to compensate for a weak legal position. According to the prevailing legal theory, Massachusetts had the stronger claim to Iroquoia because land titles derived from the king. During the seventeenth century, the Crown had vested its sovereign title to American lands in charters granted to favored subjects with colonial ambitions. Where the vague boundaries of colonies overlapped—which was frequent—the earlier charter was supposed to prevail. It was New York's misfortune that Massachusetts held an earlier charter (1630 versus 1663) that projected bounds westward to the Pacific, encompassing Iroquoia. Shortly before the war, Massachusetts had conceded its claim to the Hudson Valley but retained its option subsequently to claim Iroquoia. In October 1783, Massachusetts revived that claim by serving notice in Congress. Like New York, Massachusetts wanted Iroquois lands to sell to speculators to finance the state's enormous war debts.[34]

To counter Massachusetts's charter, New York advanced an unorthodox legal theory that derived land title and jurisdiction primarily from Indian treaties. Governor Clinton reiterated that, under the Covenant Chain alliance, the Iroquois had vested their allegiance and title in New York. To bolster that theory New York pressured the Iroquois to sell their land to facilitate plans to rush settlers onto the contested domain before Massachusetts could react. A Massachusetts congressman feared that New Yorkers would "purchase all our western Territory of the Indians, before we know it. They are really to[o] cunning for M[assachuse]tts in Matters of Land." But New Yorkers worried that Congress would get in the way by claiming an exclusive right to negotiate with the Iroquois.[35]

Constitutional ambiguity clouded whether the federal or a state government had the authority to conduct Indian affairs. Ratified in 1781, the original federal constitution—the Articles of Confederation—gave Congress the power to manage diplomacy, war, and Indian relations on behalf of the thirteen otherwise autonomous states. But the weak Articles also limited Congress's authority to Indians who were "not members of any of the states" and further "provided that the legislative right of any state within its own limits be not infringed or violated." Of course, New Yorkers insisted that the Iroquois were dependent "members" of a state that extended westward across Iroquoia to Lake Erie. And New York's leaders asserted their "legislative right" to procure Iroquois land. But federal leaders considered the Six Nations to possess a sovereignty beyond a New York State that ended at the Line of Property at the head of the Mohawk Valley. Congressman James Monroe of Virginia pointedly asked,

> Whether these Indians are to be considered as members of the State of N. York, or whether the living simply within the bounds of a State, in the exclusion only of an European power, while they acknowledge no obedience to its laws but hold a country over which they do not expect, nor

enjoy the protections, nor any of the rights of citizenship within it, is a situation which will even in the most qualified sense, admit their being held as members of a State?

Answering his own question, Monroe concluded that the Iroquois were autonomous Indians "whose management is committed by the confederation to the U.S. in Congress assembled."[36]

Determined to capture the prized lands, New Yorkers challenged federal oversight in Iroquois relations. In early 1784, James Duane warned Clinton: "And if the Tribes are to be considered as independent nations, detached from the State, and absolutely unconnected with it, the Claim of Congress would be uncontrovertable." To avert that danger, Duane advised,

> There is then an indispensable Necessity that these Tribes should be treated as ancient Dependants on this State, placed under its Protection, with all their territorial Rights, by their own consent publickly manifested in solemn and repeated Treaties. . . . On this ground the Tribes in question may fall under the Character of *Members of the State*, with the Management of whom Congress have no concern.

By asserting a state monopoly over dealings with the Iroquois, the New Yorkers sought a free hand to procure Indian lands before Massachusetts or the United States could.[37]

Much hinged on who, New York or the United States, could bring the Six Nations to negotiate at a peace conference. Excluded from the 1783 Treaty of Paris between Britain and the United States, the Mohawks, Onondagas, Cayugas, and Senecas technically remained at war with the Americans. The Indians were eager for peace but not at the cost of their homelands, while the United States and New York both wanted to make the peace, the better to take Indian lands. During the summer of 1784, Clinton and Congress prepared rival peace councils, one staged by the state and the other by the confederation, both scheduled for Fort Schuyler (Stanwix). Clinton refused to cooperate with the federal commissioners—Arthur Lee of Virginia, Richard Butler of Pennsylvania, and Oliver Wolcott of Connecticut. He forbade them from entering any agreement "with Indians, residing within the Jurisdiction of this State (and with whom only I mean to treat) prejudicial to its Rights." In vain, Lee and Butler urged the state to hold its council "at the same time with, and in Subordination to, the General Treaty," as Pennsylvania had agreed to do.[38]

In the Niagara Valley, the British-allied Iroquois responded warily to Clinton's invitation to a state council. They preferred to make peace at one, big, comprehensive council convened by the federal government and including the entire Indian confederacy. Hedging their bets, the Niagara chiefs sent to Fort Schuyler only a small delegation of "deputies." Drawn from the war chiefs, they lacked the sachems' authority to make peace or to cede land. Brant explained to Clinton that if the deputies liked what they heard at the state's council, the chiefs would attend a subsequent "more general Meeting . . . to establish an everlasting Peace and Friendship between all the [Indian] Nations and the United States."[39]

To deal with a few deputies with limited authority—and as a warm-up act for a federal council—fell far short of Clinton's plan to make peace and renew an alliance on state terms. The governor also wanted an immediate Iroquois land cession that would include the key fortifications at Oswego and Niagara, to strengthen New York's claim against Massachusetts and the United States. But the Iroquois deputies politely declined to make any commitments before hearing from the federal treaty commissioners. Citing the unified precedent of Sir William Johnson's superintendency, Brant replied to Clinton, "Here lies some Difficulty in our Minds, that there should be two separate Bodies to manage these Affairs, for this does not agree with our ancient Customs." The Iroquois preferred to deal with the federal government, as the functional heir of the Crown in Indian affairs, and as the best means to recognize the new Indian confederacy.[40]

The Oneidas (and their Tuscarora dependents) initially balked at attending Clinton's council, suspecting his designs on their land. They belatedly appeared only after officially reassured that the governor would not press them for a land cession. In his opening speech, a defensive Governor Clinton denied that New York had designs on the Oneida lands: "This is not true. You must not believe it. We have no Claim on your Lands; its just extent will ever remain secured to you."[41]

Departing on September 11, with little to show for his efforts, Clinton left behind an agent, Major Peter Schuyler, and an interpreter, Peter Ryckman. They were instructed to observe the impending federal council and should the federal treaty commissioners attempt "any thing that may eventually prove detrimental to the State, you are to use your best Endeavours to counteract and frustrate it." To help foil that federal council, the commissioners provided Schuyler and Ryckman with six barrels and forty-six kegs of rum to ply the Indians as needed.[42]

On October 3, 1784, the federal treaty commissioners opened their peace council with the Iroquois at Fort Stanwix. Burned during the war, the fort was a ramshackle, earthen shell covered with grass and brush. The interior contained two huts with earthen floors and bark roofs; one housed the commissioners and the other stored their supplies and presents. Samuel Kirkland served as the lead interpreter for the council. To impress the Indians, the federal commissioners brought along about 100 armed militiamen from New Jersey.[43]

The Indians constructed their own bark wigwams beyond the walls. Most of the 613 attending were Oneidas (317), their Akwesasne (21) and Kahnawake (20) allies, or their Mohican (65), Tuscarora (33), and Brothertown (4) dependents. Only a few deputies represented the British-allied Cayugas (7), Mohawks (2), Onondagas (5), and Senecas (13). Brant did not attend, called away in mid-September to Quebec for pressing consultations with Governor Haldimand. In his absence, the leading British-allied Iroquois spokesmen were Captain Aaron Hill, a Mohawk, and Cornplanter, a Seneca.[44]

The public meetings convened in a new arbor of pine boughs. The Indian oratory pleasantly surprised Griffith Evans, a Pennsylvania official, who marveled, "I now for the first time hear men, savage in almost every respect, harangue on important subjects with eloquence, force, and coherence." The afternoon lacrosse games and evening dances also impressed Evans, who soon joined in the festivities. He explained to a friend, "[I] am now Just returned from a Grand Dance round a Council fire, Jig my Jole with 'em & am quite hoarse [from] hallowing." The other American officials showed more restraint, for they had come on a serious business: to impose hard terms on the British-allied Iroquois.[45]

The American commissioners asserted federal primacy in Iroquois affairs. In the opening speech, Oliver Wolcott insisted that "without the authority of Congress no business can be valid that may be attempted by particular people or States." He offered peace to the western Six Nations *if* they would recognize federal supremacy in Indian diplomacy, return all Americans taken prisoner during the war (mostly women and children adopted by the Iroquois), and make a land cession. The commissioners sought tracts around the forts at Niagara and Oswego to assure federal rather than state control. The commissioners also wanted all Iroquois lands west of Buffalo Creek, including those along Lake Erie claimed by New York. If the United States could procure Iroquois land, then New York could not, a blow to the state's territorial ambitions.[46]

But the federal council stalled as the chiefs got drunk on the alcohol thoughtfully provided by the New York agents. On October 5 and 12, the federal troops seized and impounded liquor belonging to the state agents or to their allies among the private traders. In retaliation, the agents and traders had the county sheriff arrest the federal officers for theft. The commissioners then had their troops drive away the sheriff, traders, and state agents. Wolcott complained that "the Governor and People of N[ew] York have, from sinister Views, done everything in their power to oppose us." By ousting the state agents and private traders, the commissioners sobered the Iroquois and strengthened the federal hand.[47]

Although shaken by the Federal action, the Niagara deputies remained defiant. On October 17, Captain Aaron Hill declared Iroquois autonomy from both the British and the Americans. Such assertion offended American officials, who could not abide an Indian insistence on equality. Griffith Evans declared, "his assurance was as much as could be borne . . . abounding with ridiculous ostentation and arrogance." Determined to humiliate Hill and the other deputies, Arthur Lee issued a forceful ultimatum on October 20:

> Again you are mistaken in supposing that, having been excluded from the treaty between the United States and the King of England, you are become a free and independent nation and may make what terms you please. It is not so. You are a subdued people.

Driving the point home, the commissioners posted their troops to intimidate the chiefs. Hill furtively informed a passing trader from Niagara that the chiefs "were obliged to comply with whatever the Commissioners dictated— that, in short, they were as Prisoners." One of those commissioners then curtly interrupted the conversation by hustling Hill away from the trader. Lee subsequently boasted, "They are Animals that must be subdued and kept in awe or they will be mischievous, and fear alone will effect this submission."[48]

Overawed, the Iroquois deputies submitted, signing on October 22 the peace treaty dictated by the federal commissioners. As a consolation, the commissioners then doled out presents desperately needed by the Iroquois impoverished by the wartime destruction of their villages. The troops and six hostage chiefs (including Hill) remained at Fort Stanwix through the winter pending the repatriation of the prisoners held by the Iroquois— which proceeded steadily, permitting the hostages to return home during the spring. On October 23, Pennsylvania's emissaries hastily concluded their own treaty, procuring all remaining Iroquois lands within their state for a mere $5,000 in goods.[49]

In addition to securing Oswego, the federal treaty extorted a four-mile-wide strip along the Niagara River and all Six Nations lands *west* of the mouth of Buffalo Creek, at the southwestern edge of the Niagara corridor. It is striking that the Americans demanded land to define the *western* margin of Iroquoia, rather than on the eastern, where settlers were encroaching. From a federal perspective, the critical matter was to affirm that the peace treaty with the British had established a firm international boundary, where American sovereignty ran unchecked up against the British sovereignty, without any intervening Indian borderland. A strip of federal territory along the Niagara River prevented the Six Nations from interposing between British Canada and American New York. Instead, that federal strip separated the Iroquois from their allies, British and native, to the west. The Niagara strip affirmed the insistence by the federal commissioners that the Treaty of Paris made the United States "the sole sovereign within the limits . . . and therefore the sole power to whom the [Indian] nations living within those limits are hereafter to look up to for protection."[50]

The new Fort Stanwix Line ran through the preeminent cluster of Six Nations villages at Buffalo Creek, and (if enforced) dispossessed the Iroquois of their villages at Cattaraugus near Lake Erie. Of course, the Six Nations council at Buffalo Creek promptly disavowed the treaty as dictated by force on their captive delegates. And the general Indian confederacy disavowed the treaty as irregular and unjust. But the Americans refused to recognize those disavowals.[51]

In sharp contrast to the unhappy experience of the British-allied Iroquois deputies, the Oneidas delighted in their special treatment as honored allies. At Fort Stanwix, federal commissioners renewed American promises to safeguard Oneida lands: "It does not become the United States to forget those nations who preserved their faith to, and adhered to their cause, those therefore must be secured in the full and free enjoyment of their possessions." The commissioners also endorsed the Oneida requests for federal funds to rebuild their burned church, support Samuel Kirkland's mission, and to reward James Dean's war services. As the Oneidas saw it, the Fort Stanwix treaty operated as an ideal treaty council should: reaffirming an alliance and providing presents without compelling any land cession from them. The generous treaty seemed to rescue the Oneidas from their postwar poverty and from New York's pressure.[52]

Samson Occom accompanied the Oneidas at Fort Stanwix and left an account of their delight in the federal treaty. At the ceremonial conclusion, "The Indians buried their old Cruel Hatchet very deep in the Ground . . . and the [Americans] broke their Bloody Sword and lay'd it on the grave of the Hatchet . . . and the Burying was attended with Great Pompe, Rejoicing, and Shouting." The chiefs and commissioners exchanged wampum belts and smoked a "Long Pipe of Peace." An aged chief then "ordered the Whole Multitude to Arise, and . . . to form into [a] seven fold Circle" of "the White Brethren and Indians all intermixt together." While some Indians in the middle sang "the Song of Peace and Love," everyone danced in the immense circle, the Indian silver bells and bracelets jingling while the commissioners gleamed in "garments with Broad gold and silver Laces and Large glittering Buttons." This dance of hundreds "made the Earth to Tremble and Rumble." Occom concluded, "Now I think that this Land may truely be call'd the Land of Peace, Unity, Freedom, Liberty, and Independence."[53]

After a long, hard war of dislocation and loss, the Oneidas delighted in their alliance with the federal Congress, which promised to protect their lands from the New Yorkers. A year later, that apparent triumph induced the Onondagas to recognize the Oneidas "as head of the Six late confederated Nations," displacing the Mohawks. A cherished goal of the Oneidas, who had long felt slighted by the special Mohawk relationship with the Johnsons, this new recognition swelled their pride. "The Oneidas esteem this so auspicious an event that they have desired me to communicate the same to Congress," James Dean explained. But Congress slighted the news, which undercut its meaning in an Iroquois world that took its own measure in the reflection offered by external power. Heading the Six Nations meant little without a powerful and engaged partner in the settler world to the east.[54]

The Oneidas struggled to keep the federal government engaged as an ally by sending delegations to visit Congress in New York City in 1785 and 1787. Seeking their own latter-day Sir William, the chiefs urged Philip Schuyler's appointment as an American superintendent for Iroquois affairs. Romanticized by the Oneidas as "Queder," Schuyler seemed to personify the generous concern of the ideal patron. But he refused such a position, having grown doubly weary of dealing with both Indians and Congress. He assured the latter, "I had found the business of attending to the Indians exceedingly irksome & disagreeable." Schuyler also complained of congressional slights, including the failure to refund his wartime expenditures on the Oneidas.[55]

The Oneida delegates also protested that New York aggressively surveyed and sold some of their lands near Fort Stanwix. The federal secretary of war, Henry Knox, sympathized but could do nothing to help. Hamstrung by the weak Articles of Confederation, Congress lacked the funds and the leadership to fulfill its treaty promises to the Oneidas. In 1785, a Connecticut congressman lamented the inability to support Kirkland as a federal agent because "the feeble Finances of the United States give a check to every liberal & enlarged Idea." Unable to levy its own taxes, Congress became virtually bankrupt and largely inconsequential. Governor Clinton and the New York State legislature hastened the federal collapse by blocking a proposed amendment to the Articles of Confederation meant to provide Congress with its own tax revenue (rather than continued dependence on unreliable state requisitions). As the confederation faded into irrelevance, New York could aggressively pursue its Indian policies free from federal oversight.[56]

FORT HERKIMER

In 1784, the immediate threat to the Oneida lands came from Colonel John Harper, a frontier trader and land speculator who had founded the settlement of Harpersfield on the upper Susquehanna River. Originally from Connecticut, Harper had attended Reverend Wheelock's school, where he met Oneida students and learned their language. That rare familiarity and expertise gave Harper a special influence, which he enhanced during the war as a frontier officer who employed Oneida scouts. He picked up an Oneida name—Thaoughweanjawegen—indicating a ceremonial adoption intended to create mutual kinship obligations.[57]

Harper, however, exploited his fictive kinship status in a one-sided manner to procure Oneida lands. In November 1784, Harper visited Kanonwalohale to apply persuasion and rum. After a drunken row that left one Oneida dead, Harper departed with a deed signed by a single sachem and two war chiefs, about an eighth of the full leadership. The deed described a tract six miles wide by twenty-four miles long, sufficient to make four townships. Located on both banks of the Susquehanna below Harpersfield, the tract included the abandoned village of Onoquaga with its fertile alluvial flats. Returning home, Harper began to advertise and to sell lands to settlers.[58]

The Oneidas protested that no deed was valid unless approved by all of their sachems and war chiefs. In 1782, they had "agreed among ourselves that not one Inch of our Land shall be sold. If one, two, or three Sachems or Warriors should get into Liquor and make a sale of any part of our Lands, the rest on finding it out will not agree to it and break the agreement and it shall not stand." In January 1785, a protest delegation headed to New York City, where the legislature met. The State Senate disavowed the deed, but the Assembly sided with John Harper, perhaps because that house included his brother and partner, William Harper. The Assembly recommended granting the entire tract of 92,160 acres to the Harper associates, provided they renegotiated the purchase "when the said Indians are not intoxicated."[59]

Although a clear violation of the state constitution, John Harper's Oneida purchase was potentially useful to a government keen to beat Massachusetts in a race to acquire Iroquoia. After the State Senate rejected the Assembly's proposed solution, the two houses concurred on April 11, 1785, in passing legislation that "required" the governor and Indian commissioners to negotiate an Indian land cession "on reasonable terms" by October 1. The legislature sought Harper's tract to facilitate an aggressive settlement of the Susque-hanna Valley. If occupied by hundreds of New Yorkers willing to defend their land titles by force of arms, the contested domain would elude the grasp of Massachusetts. So the Yankees had taught the New Yorkers in Vermont, so let them learn their own lesson in Iroquoia. To accelerate land sales and settlement, the state legislature set relatively low prices: only 4 shillings per acre for a 500-acre lot and a mere 1 shilling per acre for an entire township of 23,000 acres. And the state exempted the premises from state taxes for at least five years. But all grantees were required to take an oath of allegiance to New York. The state also moved the surveyor general's office from New York City to Albany. A Massachusetts congressman, Rufus King, sputtered, "It is a very unfair mode of procedure."[60]

Caught between rival state governments, the Oneidas would pay in land. In May, New York's Indian commissioners sent Peter Ryckman to Kanon-walohale with a message, discrediting Harper's deed, but putting the onus on the Oneidas for dealing with him. Concluding that they must want to sell the land, the commissioners summoned the Oneidas to meet Governor Clinton in council in June. Clinton and his commissioners converted an Oneida protest against an illicit land sale into an Oneida offer to sell those lands to the state. This forced conversion set a precedent that the state would repeat during the next two decades to procure Oneida lands.[61]

Returning from Kanonwalohale, Ryckman reported that the Indians were starving. The state commissioners concluded that, given the Indians' "Peculiar situation as to Provisions and other Necessaries," the Fort Herkimer council was "well timed for the Advantage of the State." The Oneidas could not afford to boycott a council where the state would, per Covenant Chain custom, feed the participants and bestow any surplus at the end, provided the commissioners got what they came for.[62]

The state also benefited by recruiting James Dean to serve as the coun-cil interpreter. Clinton proposed the move, recognizing that no American possessed a greater influence over the Oneidas or a better mastery of their language. Dean probably accepted because his former employer, the federal government, was collapsing.[63]

The state council convened on June 23, 1785, at Fort Herkimer, near Ger-man Flats. Clinton ostensibly came to protect the Oneidas from the unscru-pulous Harper brothers, but they attended as honored guests of the state commissioners. And Clinton's proposed solution to the crisis was far worse than John Harper's illicit purchase. The governor urged the Oneidas to cede all the land bounded by the Susquehanna River on the south, and by its trib-utaries, the Unadilla River on the east and the Chenango River on the west—nearly five times the area included in Harper's deed. Because that region was "contiguous to the Settlements of the White People," Clinton warned the Oneidas that the land would "soon be of little value for hunting." The convenient pressure of unregulated speculators and hunters served the state's drive to procure Indian lands. According to Good Peter, Clinton "produced a heap of money & told some of our nation to take up a handful but they could not consent to do this; it was too heavy. He then . . . said all this shall be yours, on condition that you will follow my advice."[64]

Despite their desperate need for money, the Oneidas held firm by citing their federal guarantee. Good Peter replied:

> Since last Winter We had determined not to sell any of our Lands, and that the Boundaries fixed should remain. *The United States have informed Us that the Soil of our Lands was our own,* and we wish your Assistance to prevent your People from coming among Us for that Purpose.

As an alternative to the massive land cession sought by the governor, the Oneidas offered to lease a buffer zone:

> We are however willing and ready to lease one Tier of Farms in the Manner they are done by the White People, along the Boundary Line throughout the Extent of our Country, and that People of Influence might be settled on these Farms to prevent Encroachments, and that a Person might be appointed to collect our Rents annually. Brothers! We shall be happy to find that the Proposals We now make will be accepted, as We cannot sell any more of our Lands and this Leasing may be an Income to our Children.

In blunt reply, Clinton denounced Good Peter's "highly disagreeable" proposal as demeaning to the state: "We are sorry that You made an Offer to lease [y]our Lands. We fear You have lost your good Opinion of Us, by making a Proposal which, if accepted, would make the Government of the State tributary to You." Considering Indians as poor, ignorant, and primitive, Clinton could never accept them as prospering landlords with economic power over the state's white citizens. The governor and his commissioners meant for the Indians, instead, to remain tributary to the state, paying in periodic installments of land for occasional relief of their hunger and poverty.[65]

Ultimately, Clinton had the winning card to play. At 600 people, plus another 300 dependents, the Oneidas were no match for the 240,000 New Yorkers. Clinton announced that, without a land cession, there would be no protection, "and that if this is not now done, it is your Fault and not ours." If the state looked the other way as speculators connived and settlers invaded, taking what they wanted, the Oneidas were doomed. Of course, they regarded such protection as their due, given their exertions and suffering as wartime allies and given the past promises of New York governors. But what could the Oneidas do if the state demanded more land as the price to renew those promises? Clinton also undercut and insulted Good Peter as an unfit spokesman given his co-option during the war as a British prisoner at Niagara.[66]

Alarmed, the Oneidas shifted their position overnight. On the morning of June 27, Good Peter abruptly withdrew as spokesman in favor of the more pliant Oneyanha (also known as Peter the Quarter Master), who had signed Harper's deed. The shift apparently registered a swing in Oneida politics, away from the warriors, for whom Good Peter spoke, in favor of the sachems, represented by Oneyanha. Such a switch meant that the clan mothers had intervened. In contrast to the warriors, who cherished the contested tract for deer-hunting, the clan mothers wanted peace and food relief, which hinged upon the state's goodwill. And the sachems wanted the state's presents for redistribution to bolster their own authority weakened by the war.[67]

The Oneidas agreed to sell outright about 460,000 acres for a single payment of $11,500. Pleased with the bargain, the departing state commissioners gave their surplus provisions to the Oneidas, who received ten barrels of pork, twelve of flour, thirteen of corn, three hundred pounds of bread, five bushels of salt, two live cattle, and four barrels and thirty kegs of rum.[68]

At Oneida request, the treaty also stipulated that the state grant patent title for specific tracts to favorites with informal Indian grants: James Dean, Abraham Wemple, and Samuel Kirkland. Because the state commissioners had gotten good value from all three at the council, the legislature granted 2,650 acres to Dean, 640 acres to Wemple, 320 acres to Samuel Kirkland, and another 320 acres for Kirkland to hold in trust for his successor as missionary. As the Oneidas intended, the state located these tracts along the Line of Property, lining up a chain of culture-brokers to help the Indians deal with the settlers to the east. Although the Oneidas initiated the grants, the state legislature, by issuing patent title, had the last word in claiming the allegiance of Dean, Wemple, and Kirkland, for an informal Indian grant had little legal value unless completed by a state patent. Whenever push came to shove, all three proved better friends of the state than to the Oneidas.[69]

Clinton returned to New York City in triumph, for the Fort Herkimer purchase enabled the state to begin advertising and selling lands in the contested region. During the next two years, New York sold 343,594 acres in the cession for $125,955, dwarfing the $11,500 paid to the Oneida. By securing Indian land at a fraction of its value, the state made an enormous profit. Those sales and subsequent settlements weakened the Massachusetts land claim. In vain, Governor James Bowdoin of Massachusetts begged Clinton to stop the sales, pending a legal resolution of the dispute.[70]

At Hartford, Connecticut, in December 1786, agents for New York and Massachusetts compromised their dispute. New York obtained political jurisdiction over the entire contested region, realizing its goal of a western boundary on Lake Erie and the Niagara River. But the two states agreed to split the title to the land, or, more accurately, the "preemption right" to purchase land from the Indians. Massachusetts obtained that supposed right to 6 million acres at the western end of New York beyond the Finger Lakes as far as Lake Erie, as well as 230,400 acres in the Chemung Valley: land taken out of Clinton's Fort Herkimer purchase from the Oneidas. Desperate for cash, in early 1788, Massachusetts sold its land rights to speculators, primarily Oliver Phelps and Nathaniel Gorham, for about 3 cents per acre. The Hartford compromise left the remaining Cayuga, Onondaga, and Oneida lands to New York to obtain and sell.[71]

THE EMPIRE STATE

During the mid-1780s, George Clinton led a remarkable expansion of New York's power. At war's end, New York had possessed no more than a tenuous claim to Iroquoia, a claim contested by the United States, Massachusetts, and the Six Nations. The state's effective title and jurisdiction extended no farther west than the Line of Property at the head of the Mohawk River. By 1787, however, the state had prevailed over its rivals, securing a preemption claim to the lands as far west as Seneca Lake, plus a legal and political jurisdiction that extended all the way to Lake Erie.

New York triumphed by ignoring the United States, by coercing the Oneidas, and by compelling Massachusetts to compromise. But New York's surging prosperity and power alarmed its neighbors in the smaller adjoining states. No longer perceived as weak and vulnerable, New York now seemed too powerful for the confederation to control. In 1788, Oliver Ellsworth of Connecticut worried, "What is to defend us from the ambition and rapacity of New-York, when she has spread over that vast territory, which she claims and holds? Do we not already see in her the seeds of an over-bearing ambition?" In hopes of restraining New York, in 1787 Connecticut quickly ratified a new federal constitution meant to subordinate the states to a more powerful national government. During the subsequent decade, the Six Nations would also look to the revived federal government as a counterweight against the power of New York.[72]

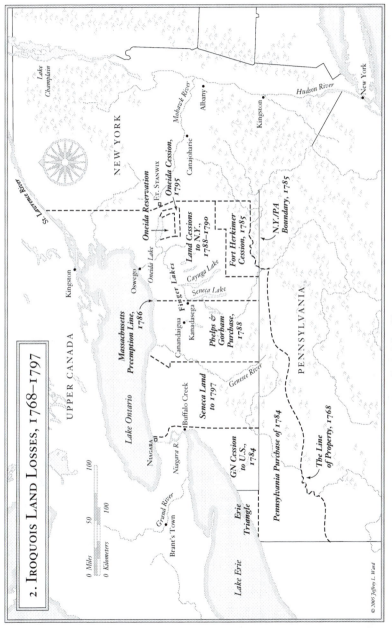

2. IROQUOIS LAND LOSSES, 1768–1797

Lake Champlain

St. Lawrence River

UPPER CANADA

NEW YORK

Lake Ontario

Kingston

Oswego

Oneida Lake

Finger Lakes

Cayuga Lake

Seneca Lake

Mohawk River

Albany

Kingston

Hudson River

New York

Canajoharie

FT. STANWIX

Oneida Cession, 1795

Oneida Reservation

Land Cessions to N.Y., 1788–1790

Fort Herkimer Cession, 1785

N.Y./PA Boundary, 1785

Massachusetts Preemption Line, 1786

Canandaigua

Kanadasega

Phelps & Gorham Purchase, 1788

Genesee River

Seneca Land to 1797

Buffalo Creek

NIAGARA

Niagara R.

GN Cession to U.S., 1784

Erie Triangle

Brant's Town

Grand River

Lake Erie

PENNSYLVANIA

Pennsylvania Purchase of 1784

The Line of Property, 1768

0 Miles   50   100
0 Kilometers   100

© 2005 Jeffrey L. Ward

Iroquois Land Losses, 1768–1797.

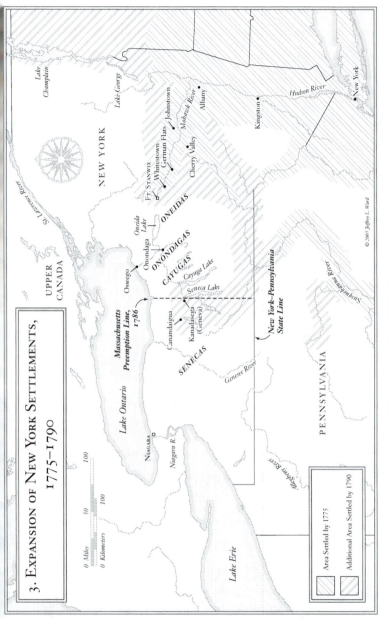

3. EXPANSION OF NEW YORK SETTLEMENTS, 1775–1790

Lake Champlain

Lake George

NEW YORK

Hudson River

New York

Albany

Kingston

Johnstown
German Flats
Mohawk River
Cherry Valley
Whitestown
Ft. Stanwix

ONEIDAS

Oneida Lake

Onondaga
ONONDAGAS

CAYUGAS
Cayuga Lake

Oswego

Seneca Lake

Massachusetts Preemption Line, 1786

Canandaigua
Kanadasega (Geneva)

SENECAS

Genesee River

New York–Pennsylvania State Line

PENNSYLVANIA

Susquehanna River

St. Lawrence River

UPPER CANADA

Lake Ontario

NIAGARA
Niagara R.

Lake Erie

Allegheny River

0 Miles   50   100
0 Kilometers   100

Area Settled by 1775

Additional Area Settled by 1790

© 2005 Jeffrey L. Ward

The Expansion of New York Settlements, 1775–1790.

CHAPTER SIX

Leases

Colonel Louis of the Oneidas, pencil sketch by John Trumbull, ca. 1785. (Courtesy of the Yale University Art Gallery, gift of Mrs. Robert F. Jeffreys, no. 1952.3.4.)

THE ONEIDAS FELT INSULTED by the state's abrupt dismissal of their lease proposal at Fort Herkimer in 1785. But they were intrigued to discover, two years later, that prominent New Yorkers, led by Colonel John Livingston, had formed a company to lease Iroquois land. Livingston and his associates pretended to represent New York, which seemed plausible because so many of them held high state office. At least eight present, and eleven past, members of the legislature invested in the company. Himself an Assembly representative, Livingston belonged to the wealthiest and most powerful family in the state, the owners of thousands of acres worked by dozens of

John Livingston, by John Trumbull, ca. 1816. (Private
Collection.)

tenant farmers, on the east bank of the Hudson River. The associates also
had extensive official expertise in Indian affairs, including Peter Schuyler, a
state Indian commissioner and the nephew of General Philip Schuyler, a kin
connection enormously influential among the Oneidas. Livingston had
served as an associate Indian commissioner at the state's Fort Schuyler council of September 1784. Good Peter observed: "And verily by his appearance
and company, we supposed they came from the Great Council of State and
would not deceive us." At last, the Oneidas concluded, the state leaders recognized that leasing was the best mode for Indians to manage their property.[1]

LIVINGSTON'S LEASES

During the fall of 1787, Livingston and his entourage toured the Chemung
and Finger Lakes districts to construct an extensive and daring "interest." By
financially "interesting" the local traders, who doubled as the local interpreters, Livingston captured the culture brokers of Iroquoia. Almost everyone who spoke both English and an Iroquoian language assured the natives
that they would never get a better deal than Livingston offered. The traders

also provided rum to help Livingston sway the Indians. And a little bribery went a long way with the preeminent Seneca war chief known as Cornplanter, who helped broker the deal. Livingston praised Cornplanter as "a particular friend of mine & is the most influential Man in the Seneka Nation."[2]

In November 1787 at Kanadasega, Livingston concluded a lease with some Seneca, Cayuga, and Onondaga chiefs, securing most of their lands for 999 years. The terms provided virtual ownership while technically evading New York State's constitutional ban on private land purchases from the Indians. Allured by the word "lease," the Iroquois chiefs seem not to have fully understood the 999-year term. Indeed, a leading lessee attested to some confusion by initially reporting that the lease ran for 360 years. Signed on November 30, the "Long Lease" surrendered most of Iroquoia—an estimated 13 million acres—in return for a lump sum of $20,000 due the next spring plus annual payments thereafter of $2,000.[3]

The chiefs probably gave such a massive lease because of a suspicion that New York State meant simply to take their lands with little or no compensation and without providing for the long-term annual income coveted by the Iroquois. Indeed, in 1782 the state legislature had unilaterally annexed Cayuga and Onondaga lands, and in 1785 at Fort Herkimer the governor had coerced an Oneida land cession. By leasing their lands in west-central New York, the Niagara head chiefs also hoped to compel native stragglers to return west to the main center of Iroquois settlement.

After concluding the Kanadasega lease, Livingston's entourage proceeded east to Kanonwalohale to seek a similar deal with the Oneidas in January 1788. Although Livingston sought almost all of their land for a very long time, the Oneidas appreciated his recognition of their power to lease land. Livingston also appealed to the Oneida longing for a powerful patron from the outside world, one with the power to compel justice from New York's settlers and legislators—a latter-day Sir William Johnson. In Good Peter's words, Livingston argued "that it would not be for our advantage to lease a small piece to one and a small piece to another, or to listen to every one that should say to us—*cut me off a slice from your loaf*—it may be better for us that one Great Man should undertake to manage the whole." And, to the impoverished Oneidas, the price seemed impressive. Livingston offered a $1,000 annuity for each of the first ten years, with $100 increases during years eleven through fifteen, when the deal would become fixed at $1,500 annually. Good Peter conceded, "This I must add, that he agreed to give us what I then thought was a great sum." At last, the New Yorkers seemed ready to pay a significant annual rent for Oneida land.[4]

To facilitate the deal, Livingston shrewdly interested all of the culture-brokers in the Oneida country, with partial shares in the company. They included James Dean, Samuel Kirkland, Jedediah Phelps, and Nicholas Jourdan. Kirkland helped by delivering sermons insisting that a smaller reservation would enhance the effectiveness of his mission. Livingston also promised about $2,000 in private payments to Oneida chiefs. By monopolizing the local culture-brokers and bribing key chiefs, Livingston could control the council discourse, which helps to explain why the Oneidas heard the enticing word "lease" more clearly than its 999-year term.[5]

Livingston particularly cultivated the two chiefs who best spoke English: Captain Jacob Reed (Atsiaktatye) and Colonel Louis. Reed had mastered English literacy at Wheelock's school during the mid-1760s. A talented but troubled man, he served as a schoolteacher at Kanonwalohale before succumbing to hard drink. Of bold demeanor but unstable allegiances, he deserted to British Niagara in early 1780 but returned in December. He may have been a double agent: alternately helping both sides with military information. After the war, a traveler reported, "Captain Jacob Reed speaks and writes [English] with tolerable accuracy, shews a bold and courageous appearance and dresses as a white man." Good Peter complained to an American official that Reed was a bright but unstable man "who can talk your language, but we can never fix his attention."[6]

Reed bore the psychological weight of too many overlapping identities: an Indian with a colonial education, a Loyalist and a Patriot, a warrior and a schoolteacher, sometimes a Christian but too often a drunk, an Oneida nationalist and the land speculator's best friend. Rev. Jeremy Belknap reported that Reed "can behave like a Gentleman or turn into a Savage at his pleasure."

Kirkland's son John observed that Reed "hates the white people," which gives complexity to his chronic assistance to land speculators at the expense of his own people. Only by helping the hated outsiders and exploiters could Reed afford the heavy, daily drinking that provided his escape from his painful contradictions and betrayals. As a middle-aged man of squandered abilities and vanished opportunities, he despised himself even more than he hated the whites who exploited him.[7]

Among the Oneidas, Colonel Louis was the other leading supporter of the Livingston lease. A telling figure of the northern borderland, he was born Louis Cook at Saratoga about 1740, the son of a black father and an Abenaki mother. In 1745, he was captured by French-allied Indian raiders. Adopted and renamed Atiatoharongwen, he grew up at the Canadian Mohawk village of Kahnawake. Intelligent, ambitious, and fluent in Mohawk, English, and French, Louis became a prominent chief. Fond of the French, and despising the British conquest and occupation of Canada, he assisted the Patriot invasion of Canada in late 1775. During the next summer, however, the British routed the American invaders from Canada, obliging Louis to flee with them. Assuming command of a company of Oneida and Tuscarora scouts, Louis won a commission from the Continental Congress as a lieutenant colonel in June 1779. Known thereafter as "Colonel Louis," he was probably the only man of African-American descent honored with an officer's commission in the Continental Army.[8]

After the war, he settled with the Oneidas, developing a prosperous farm on Oneida Creek between Oneida Lake and Kanonwalohale. As an Oneida chief, he vigorously promoted leasing, citing the prosperity derived from leases by the Mohawks at Kahnawake. Self-interest seconded that conviction, for Livingston promised Louis a £200 payment.[9]

On January 8, led by Colonel Louis and Jacob Reed, the Oneida chiefs leased almost all of their country (about 5 million acres) to Livingston for 999 years. They reserved the tracts already granted or leased to their clients: to the Brothertown and New Stockbridge Indians and to James Dean, Abraham Wemple, Kirkland's twin sons George and John, Jedediah Phelps, Jean-François Perache, and Archibald Armstrong. The Oneidas retained a reservation of about 250,000 acres located south of Oneida Lake and Wood Creek. They also kept their prime fishing stand, a tract one mile wide on both banks and along the entire length of Fish Creek, which flowed into Wood Creek. In leasing most of their land, the Oneidas gambled their future on Livingston's goodwill and his authority from the state—two dangerous assumptions.[10]

INTERESTS

The Livingston scheme seems astonishing for its nerve: to defy a state government by leasing a vast Indian country for an implausible 999 years. The Lessees even spoke of recruiting armed settlers to secure the land grab by forming a new state in secession from New York and in alliance with British Canada. But the Livingston scheme was all too characteristic of the troubled 1780s, when the new and embattled American union confronted an array of frontier schemers exploiting the recent revolution to defy the old states. Frontier opportunists asserted new land titles based on Indian deeds as the foundation for upstart regimes in Pennsylvania, Kentucky, and Tennessee. These frontier separatist movements allied two distinct but compatible groups: penurious settlers seeking free or cheap homesteads and some especially aggressive land speculators. The opportunists admired and emulated Ethan Allen, who had led Vermont's rebellion against New York. Such new state schemes threatened to hijack the essence of American power: the allocation of frontier lands to construct networks of interest binding influential men to support the issuing government.[11]

During the 1780s, the victorious revolution seemed to open all institutions, boundaries, and land titles to challenge by bold men with visionary plans. In 1787, Timothy Pickering assured Pennsylvania's leaders that their frontier troubles were far from unique: "The peculiar circumstances of the United States have encouraged bad men in several of them to throw off their allegiance, to excite the common people to rebellion & to attempt the erecting of New States." Pickering could not predict "the final issue of the contest in the present weak state of the federal union and general discontent and spirit of revolt so prevalent among the people of these states." No one in 1787 took for granted the stable federal government of secure states that, in retrospect, we now assume was quickly secured by the founding generation.[12]

Relative latecomers to the new state game, the Lessees piggybacked on the nearby land grab in the Susquehanna Valley by New England settlers. Defying Pennsylvania's title and jurisdiction, the Yankee intruders cited Connecticut's sea-to-sea charter, a 1754 Indian deed, and their firearms. Pickering (a Pennsylvania supporter) described the Susquehanna Yankees as "Men destitute of property, who could be tempted by the gratuitous offer of lands, on the single condition that they should enter upon them armed, 'to man their rights,' in the cant phrase of those people." Their munitions and legal advice came from external investors collectively known as the Susquehannah Company. If the Susquehanna Yankees could defeat the sheriffs and militia of Pennsylvania, the investors expected to reap thousands of acres of land for subsequent sale to paying customers.[13]

The Livingston Lessees overlapped in membership, methods, and money with the Susquehannah Company. Both speculations derived leadership from aspiring men in New York's Columbia County. Most in the overlapping inner circles were Freemasons, which provided the bond of a secret brotherhood, enhancing trust in one another as they defied legal authorities. The Lessees and the Susquehanna Proprietors jointly exploited the long, unregulated state border between New York and Pennsylvania. If hounded by the Pennsylvania militia, the Susquehanna Yankees could find safe haven with their kin across the line in New York's Chemung Valley. And the holders of Lessee title could similarly slip south if chased by New York officers. In 1786, a mutual investor celebrated the rapid Yankee settlement on New York's side of the Susquehanna Valley: "The Onaquaguah Country is settling this summer, all pointing to the end proposed. Yankeys will support one another." The "end proposed" was a new borderland state, created by Yankee violence from the ruins of New York and Pennsylvania. As with the peace treaty line between British Canada and the United States, so too with state boundaries on the frontier: all remained in uncertain flux during the 1780s. Whatever surveyors and boundary commissions might decide, true meaning lay in the fluid behavior and expectations of people in the borderland.[14]

Primarily bluster, the new state scheme was meant to intimidate the New York State legislature into accepting a compromise. In February 1788, the Lessees offered to pay the full annual rents and give half of their Iroquois lands to New York in return for state title to the other half. By procuring aboriginal title to almost all of Iroquoia, the Lessees claimed to have saved the state from the bother.[15]

As was the standard practice in an American land grab, the Lessees "interested" at least eight legislators by granting shares in the company and its anticipated profits. Lewis Morris reported, "A great many of the Legislators are concerned and your humble Servant is one. A Share will be about 150,000 acres." Although interesting legislators was good politics, every new share reduced the proportional value of an old share. With at least eighty shareholders, including frontier traders and interpreters, the company soon seemed sufficiently numerous to the leaders. Overestimating their clout, the Lessees took in too few legislators, making too many enemies of the excluded. Morris conceded, "We are much envied and I Suppose we shall meet with most violent opposition." Concentrated in Columbia County, on the upper Hudson River, the Lessees included too few notables from other counties. The excluded legislators championed petitions from dozens of common citizens who feared that such a massive land giveaway would enrich a few to the detriment of the many. Forsaking a great state asset so cheaply would foreclose the future sales revenue needed to keep taxes low.[16]

In politics, most Lessees had opposed Governor Clinton, which hardly endeared them to the most powerful man in the state. The governor bristled at their attempt to force his hand in Indian matters, for he meant to control the dispensation of Iroquois lands within New York, not concede it to John Livingston. On February 20, the state legislature declared both leases invalid because they violated the state constitution. The legislators authorized the governor to employ the militia to oust any settlers introduced by the Livingston Lessees. Clinton assured Joseph Brant, "There never will be an Acknowledgment of the Right to Lands purchased from the Indians without the Consent of the Legislature; but on the contrary, every Intruder claiming under such a Right must be brought to Justice." Indeed, the very essence of state authority lay in its monopoly power over acquiring native land for allocation to powerful citizens.[17]

While nullifying the two long leases as dead letters, New York State held out very different language to the Indians. Seeking advantage in native alarm, the state commissioners insisted that the Iroquois had foolishly lost their lands to con men who would never pay their rent,

> and if they do not pay you, who will help you? And if they say you shall keep a Country to live in [but] afterwards settle White People on it and drive you off, how can you expect Assistance from. . . . the Governor and our Chiefs, for you have brought the Trouble on yourselves.

Only the state could rescue them, but only if the Indians submitted their lands to state control. To that end, the commissioners summoned the chiefs to a council at Fort Schuyler (Stanwix) in June. At the same time, the legislature also promised the Lessees that "if the said leases should be of any advantage to the State, in the negociations with the Indians, that then the said John Livingston should rely on the Justice of the State for a reimbursement of his expences, and such reasonable compensations, as the Legislature may deem proper to make him." While ostensibly disavowing the leases, the state leaders also meant to exploit them as leverage to procure Indian land—and then to reward the Lessees. But Livingston and his associates wanted more than a vague promise of future state rewards.[18]

PARTNERS

The Lessees had better luck in Massachusetts striking a deal with Oliver Phelps and Nathiel Gorham, the New England speculators who had purchased the "preemption right" to western New York. They granted the Lessees a one-sixth interest in their firm to avoid contention and to secure their Indian title and influence. When some minor partners questioned a deal that would offend the powerful Governor Clinton, Phelps explained:

> I am well aware of the Influence of the administration of this State. The Influence of Livingston and associates is not inconsiderable. Which of them would be the most able to impede and embarrass this business is a question. It is pretty evident that a very considerable number of the Natives are strongly in the interest of Livingston and associates. Livingston has all the Interpreters on his side. Major [Peter] Schuyler who has always been the Governor's agent with the Indians [and] also Major [Jelles] Fonda are both . . . conserned with Livingston.

On May 3, Phelps headed west for Iroquoia, announcing grandly, "I am now mounting my horse to go to my Indian world." To realize the benefit of his new partners and their lease, Phelps needed to strike a new deal with the Iroquois chiefs at Buffalo Creek. Those chiefs had so soured on the Long Lease that Joseph Brant threatened to attack the Lessee settlement and headquarters at Kanadasega. By terrifying settlers (and potential settlers), an Indian war would be very bad for the speculators' business.[19]

The western Iroquois felt emboldened by the support promised by the leading trader at Niagara, a Loyalist named Samuel Street, and by his partner, Colonel John Butler. They primarily served themselves rather than the British Empire. When the Buffalo Creek chiefs complained that the Livingston Lease threatened their entire country, the resourceful Butler insisted that the only salvation lay in giving him their "lease of the Country and date it before the date of that given to Livingston." He would then "keep it for them." Of course, he wanted that lease to strengthen his own hand in striking a deal with the American speculators. To make that deal, Phelps and Livingston sent Major Peter Schuyler to Niagara, where Butler and Street agreed to procure Iroquois consent, in return for a one-eighth interest in the increasingly complex partnership. To raise the money for their share of the costs, Butler and Street recruited additional partners among the leading Loyalists and Indian Department officers at Niagara. Each of their fourteen shares would yield at least 20,000 acres. Butler probably retained a double share.[20]

In early July, the various parties convened at Buffalo Creek, the premier postwar cluster of Iroquois villages and the political center for the Six Nations confederacy. The villages included 250 houses and about 2,000 inhabitants, primarily Senecas, Cayugas, and Onondagas. Led by Joseph Brant, the Grand River chiefs also attended the council. Among the capitalists, Oliver Phelps played the leading role, in consultation with John Livingston, Caleb Benton, Ezekiel Gilbert, and Peter Schuyler of the Lessees. Street and Butler also came to sway the Iroquois. Samuel Kirkland attended as an official commissioner for Massachusetts, ostensibly to certify fair treatment of the Indians. That certification was virtually certain because the speculators paid Kirkland's travel expenses and promised him 2,000 acres. This conflict of interest violated his official appointment, which stipulated that Kirkland "should not be interested in the purchase of said lands directly or indirectly."[21]

At Buffalo Creek in 1788, Kirkland, Butler, and Brant buried their wartime differences, finding a common cause in helping land speculators to procure millions of Indian acres. When the Buffalo Creek chiefs balked at Phelps's terms, he shrewdly proposed binding mediation by Butler, Kirkland, and Brant. The chiefs accepted, little realizing that all three had already pledged their assistance to Phelps. Brant received $750 and the promise of an

"Elegant pacing Horse," but he also favored Phelps and Livingston for political reasons. Ceding west-central New York to speculators would uproot the
small, scattered villages of Iroquois, compelling their relocation at Buffalo
Creek or, better still, Grand River. Brant devoutly equated the best interests
of the Iroquois with the Grand River reserve and with his own ambitions to
speak for the entire Six Nations. He also liked playing the deal-maker and
currying favor with powerful gentlemen.[22]

To pressure the Iroquois to accept Phelps's offer, Butler threatened to
withdraw his assistance, assuring the Indians "that the Dish was now offered
them [and] if they did not feed themselves it was their own faults, that before
they called upon him to witness their Bargains, if they did not now determine, he should not attend again, as they had so often made a fool of him."
On July 8, the chiefs accepted Phelps's deal, which replaced the Kanadasega
and the Butler leases of 1787. The new agreement divided the contested 12
million acres into three broad bands, each extending from the Pennsylvania
border to Lake Ontario. The speculators relinquished the western third: the
Seneca domain west of the Genesee River. Close to Buffalo Creek and far
from the New York settlements, that domain could not be settled in defiance
of the powerful Senecas. Phelps and Gorham procured the middle third—
between the Genesee River and Seneca Lake. The Lessees retained the eastern third—between Seneca Lake and the Oneida country. But, to hold that
land, they would have to defeat New York State.[23]

Ultimately, the payment proved more controversial than the acreage conceded to the speculators. The Kanadasega Lease had obliged the Lessees to
pay $20,000 in the spring of 1788 followed by $2,000 in annual rent (for 999
years). Virtually bankrupt, the Lessees failed to meet their big payment that
spring. At Buffalo Creek in July, they obtained an adjustment to reflect the
Genesee acreage that they conceded to Phelps and Gorham. Under the new
deal, Livingston was supposed to pay $10,000 in the spring of 1789 and a
$1,000 rent in perpetuity. Many Senecas insisted that Phelps agreed to pay
the same amounts, but the formal document written by Phelps, and the
memories of Kirkland and Brant, insisted that he pay only $5,000 and $500
respectively: a most paltry return on 2.5 million acres to compensate 2,000
Senecas. Phelps later conceded that, because the rent was "too small to divide
among the Indians," he paid them only every other year, once $1,000 had
accumulated (without interest) "so as to have something worth dividing":
fifty cents per Seneca. "All that our lands came to," Red Jacket bitterly complained, "was but the price of a few hogsheads of tobacco."[24]

In August, Phelps returned home to Connecticut in triumph: "I am well
pleased with the Country. I am sure it is the best I ever saw." He was even
more pleased to find untrue the rumor circulating at home "that the Indians

had killed me." To attract settlers, he needed to stem such alarming reports of frontier violence. So he planted a newspaper story, reporting that the Indians "were highly gratified with the treatment they received, and with the manner in which they had disposed of their lands." The story added (with considerable exaggeration) that some 3,000 settlers had already arrived—security in case the Indians changed their minds.[25]

Meanwhile, John Butler had some explaining to do. As a Crown officer, he was not supposed to help American speculators thrust settlements toward Niagara, compromising the security of the British fort. Instead, he was supposed to keep Americans away, securing Iroquoia as a buffer zone to protect the British posts. Always grasping, Butler had become cynical. Dismayed by the brutality of the war and the betrayal of the peace, he had lost his already scant faith in humanity and no longer believed in anything larger than his own financial interests. Convinced that the Iroquois were doomed to lose their lands to speculators, he wanted to be among the winners.[26]

By delivering British presents and favors, Butler won considerable influence with the Six Nations. Purchased by British taxpayers, that influence now became the capital that Butler parlayed to American speculators, to the detriment of British policy. In 1789, the secretary of state, Lord Grenville, complained that Butler's land deal with Phelps and company was "no less than applying that influence with the Indians which His Majesty maintains at so large an expence and of which his Official Situation gives [Butler] in great measure the direction, to promote the objects of the United States of America, and to further his own private Interest."[27]

Grenville directed the governor general to investigate. He was Lord Dorchester, a new name for Sir Guy Carleton, who had been made a lord of the realm. Of course, that investigation revealed rampant corruption in Indian presents as well as Indian lands. The British problem was that Butler was indispensable, for he remained popular with the chiefs. His alienation might cost the Indian support that the British needed to preserve the posts. A former Niagara commandant explained, "Suspected persons may be displaced, yet they may in revenge create serious discontents among the Indians." Looking the other way at corruption was the price paid to retain Butler's influence among the Indians. At Niagara, the British risked immediate ruin if Butler was cashiered but faced steady decay if he was retained. Characteristically, the British chose delay and decay.[28]

FORT SCHUYLER

Meanwhile, the Lessees clashed with the state in the Finger Lakes country. To rally Indian support, Livingston lavished food, alcohol, and exhortations on the local Cayugas, Onondagas, and Senecas. From his forward base at Kanadasega (at the foot of Seneca Lake), Livingston also talked tough, urging the Iroquois to ignore the governor: "Do not listen to him; he has Warriors, and so have we: if he comes here we will fight it out with him." The Lessees highlighted their comparative advantage in promising a perpetual rental income to the Indians:

> The Governor's Business at this proposed Treaty is to purchase your Lands, but you have leased them to us. He means to pay you all at once for [your lands], and then in a few Years to drive you off and tell you that you have no Property here. But we mean to pay you a great Sum the next Spring, and then pay a certain Sum annually forever, that your Children may have something to live upon.

To intercept Indians bound east for Clinton's council at Fort Schuyler, Livingston convened his own, competing council at Kanadasega, where Lessee agents immobilized the passing Iroquois with lavish quantities of free rum. In June, a surveyor, Colonel Hugh Maxwell, reported finding "many Indians of different tribes and nations, some Oneidas, some Onondagaes, some Jenesee [Senecas], some Tuscaroraes, all getting drunk."[29]

At the foot of Seneca Lake, Kanadasega occupied a strategic crossroads on the east-west Indian path that linked the Oneida country with Niagara and Buffalo Creek. A leading Seneca village before the war, Kanadasega had hosted Samuel Kirkland's first, abortive mission. In 1779, Sullivan's troops burned the village, making Niagara refugees of the Indian inhabitants. By 1787, the chopped orchards had resprouted and the fields cleared by the natives attracted a few returning Indians and a motley crew of squatters and traders. A visitor noted twenty log houses "and as many idle persons as can live in them." Another sleepless traveler felt "troubled, most of the night, by gamblers and fleas—two curses to society." At one crowded tavern, the locals attended "to a silly French conjurer, or trick-player, and his little dancing dog."[30]

By relieving hunger and sating thirst at Kanadasega, the Lessees diminished the Indian willingness to meet Clinton at Fort Schuyler. In June, the state agent John Tayler warned the state commissioners that only the Oneidas were hungry enough to attend Clinton's council. The better-fed Cayugas, Onondagas, and Senecas, he reported, "seem to think that we wish by all Means to deprive them of their Lands." The commissioners postponed their council to September, when they hoped for better numbers of hungry Iroquois.[31]

The high stakes and bitter competition compelled Governor Clinton to seek the largest possible attendance at his council. He exhorted, "Brothers! The Business of the Treaty is of the greatest Importance both to you and to us, and concerns all your Men and all your Women and all your Children, and we could wish that all your People should be there." By a full turnout, Clinton meant to refute any charge that his treaty lacked widespread Indian consent.[32]

When Governor Clinton opened his Indian council in early September, however, the turnout was disappointing. Only the Oneidas came in large numbers, supplemented by a few Onondagas. The Senecas and Cayugas and most of the Onondagas stayed away, preferring the Lessees' rum to the governor's pressure. Visiting Kanadasega, Kirkland reported that the Indians had been "kept in one continual state of Intoxication & Dissipation for three Weeks to prevent their going on to the Treaty." The Lessees had also organized about twenty-five riflemen to intimidate state agents in that vicinity. Phelps noted that any white man who defied the Lessees at Kanadasega would "be tyed up and whiped."[33]

In the first order of business at Fort Schuyler, the state commissioners ousted the uninvited John Livingston, who had come to meddle. They ordered his removal to at least forty miles' distance. Turning to the Onondagas, Clinton struck a quick deal with a few minor chiefs led by Black Cap (Tehonwaghsloweaghte), who led the small community at Onondaga Lake. By dealing with the upstart Black Cap, Clinton stiffed the Onondaga majority, and their head chiefs, at Buffalo Creek. Upon disavowing the Long Lease and ceding most of their national land to the state, Black Cap's minority faction secured a modest reservation of 100 square miles (64,000 acres). The Indians also received a down payment of 1,000 French crowns and £200 in clothing plus a promised annuity of $500 in perpetuity. Of course, the distant Onondaga majority disavowed the treaty as a travesty negotiated with a few unqualified chiefs.[34]

Although Clinton valued the Onondaga deal as a precedent, he especially needed an Oneida treaty to defeat the Lessees. A minority faction led by Captain Jacob Reed clung to their Livingston Lease as a measure of Oneida independence. On March 12, Reed's faction assured the state legislators:

Brothers, We are surprized to hear that you are displeased because others have accepted that which your Chiefs have told us is beneath your Nation. But, Brothers, we are more surprized still, to learn [that] you claim a Right to controll us in the Disposal of our Lands; you acknowledge it to be our own as much as the Game we take in hunting. Why then do you say that we shall not dispose of it as we think best? You may, Brothers, with as much Propriety, when one of our Hunters comes to

your Market with a Pack of Beaver, point out the Person to whom he
shall sell, and to no other.

In early June, Livingston visited Kanonwalohale to offer presents and provi-
sions to dissuade the Oneidas from attending the state's council. Despite the
Oneidas' springtime hunger and James Dean's exertions as interpreter, only
Reed's small faction would accept Livingston's gifts.[35]

Most of the Oneidas had lost faith in the Lessees, thanks to the considerable influence of Peter Penet, a French merchant based at Schenectady. Trading with the Oneidas for furs, Penet also posed as a French official with a
special commission from the king of France and the Marquis de Lafayette to
look after Indian affairs in North America. By endorsing the state's warnings
against the Lessees as tricksters, Penet swayed Colonel Louis, the great
champion of both land leases and French nostalgia among the Oneidas. The
state agent John Tayler helped that conversion by promising to make good
the £200 pledged by the Livingston Lessees to Colonel Louis. Rather than
accept Livingston's provisions, most of the Oneidas looked to the state for
relief, begging for two boats loaded with corn in June: "If not, when you come
up [in September] you will find some of us dead of Hunger." Arriving in
time, that state relief procured a large Oneida turnout in September at Fort
Schuyler.[36]

On September 16, 1788, Clinton opened the council with the Oneidas. To
sway the holdouts, including Jacob Reed, the state commissioners promised
to indemnify them against any lawsuits brought by the Livingston Lessees
for breach of contract after taking their payments. But this state promise
depended on the Oneidas making "a cession of Lands" to New York.[37]

Governor Clinton posed as the savior of Indian lands from unscrupulous
Lessees—provided the Oneidas submitted to his terms. Clinton pitched a
smaller Oneida domain as better suited for state protection against intruders
and speculators. The Indians should be satisfied with a reservation "of such
Extent only that if any of our People should come there it would be immediately discovered. Our People will know that they cannot get any Part of this
Tract and therefore will not attempt it."[38]

While Clinton blamed Indian credulity for the crisis, the Oneida chiefs
faulted the state for rendering them poor and vulnerable. The governor
boasted of his power over the state's citizens, yet he did nothing to prevent
their impositions and intrusions, appearing only after the fact to demand
another land cession from the Indians. Contrary to Clinton's promises, the
state had never punished intruders on Oneida land. For example, John
Harper and his sons continued to bask in the governor's political favor. Consequently, Good Peter doubted that another land cession would, at last, pro-

tect the Oneidas from greedy settlers and speculators: "It is just so with your People. As long as any Spot of our excellent Land remains, they will covet it, and if one dies, another will pursue it, and will never rest till they possess it."[39]

In another reply speech, Colonel Louis blamed the state for withholding a patent title for their land: "You have the Controul of our Land, altho' it is said to be ours. Had you given us a Writing to confirm it as our Property, as the French Governor used to do [in Canada], we should have been in the quiet Enjoyment of it." If possessed of a state patent, as well as aboriginal title, the Oneida would enjoy the legal standing to procure their annual rents from balky tenants by prosecuting them in the courts.[40]

At Fort Schuyler, the Oneidas named Colonel Louis and Peter Otsequette to negotiate with Clinton, but they were no match for the shrewder and more experienced governor. Louis needed state indemnity against the vindictive Lessees, while Otsequette was a callow and flighty youth of eighteen. Adopted by Lafayette in 1784, and subsequently educated in Paris, Otsequette returned from France during the summer of 1788. A fellow traveler, Jean-Pierre Brissot de Warville, recalled: "He danced well, played the flute rather poorly, and spoke both French and English fluently. But he could not produce a single idea. He was a great child, without a thought for tomorrow." Kirkland later remarked, "I find I can't have but little dependance upon *french Peter*, from his natural instability [of] mind." Upon arriving in New York City, Otsequette was quickly befriended by Governor Clinton, who "was about to leave to conclude a treaty about some lands with the Oneidas." Brissot de Warville considered this "lucky" for Otsequette, but the good fortune truly belonged to Clinton, who cultivated the impressionable young man on their journey together to Fort Schuyler.[41]

In the negotiations, Clinton outmaneuvered Otsequette and Colonel Louis, who agreed to dilute the Oneidas' exclusive right to fish in the streams that flowed into Oneida Lake, a right increasingly crucial to their subsistence as hunting became less productive. Clinton asked permission to fish in those streams as a personal favor, playing upon the Oneida eagerness for a personal connection to prominent outsiders. But the state subsequently treated that favor to the governor as a general license for all settlers to fish on the same streams. The equal access promoted the rapid development favored by the state—to the Oneidas' detriment. Within a decade, commercial operations depleted the salmon.[42]

Clinton did make one major concession, as the state at last recognized the Oneida right to lease land to individuals. But New York restricted that right to a four-mile-wide strip along the reservation's southern border and to terms of no longer than twenty-one years. The state even promised to "make Provision by Law to compel the Lessees to pay the Rents, and in every other

Respect to enable the Oneidas and their Posterity to have the full Benefit of their Right so to make Leases and to prevent Frauds on them respecting the same." Had the state fulfilled this promise, the Oneida would have reaped a progressive income from their borderland.[43]

Clinton also permitted the Oneidas to regulate their dispensation of the lands ceded to New York along their eastern margin. The treaty regularized grants or leases previously granted by the Oneidas to favored clients. Because the Brothertown Indians had recently irked the Oneidas, the latter arbitrarily shrank that reserve to just 6 square miles (3 by 2). In better favor, the New Stockbridge Mohicans retained their full township of 36 square miles (6 by 6). The treaty also bestowed tracts on two favored French traders—Jean-François Perache and Peter Penet—and on the twin sons of Samuel Kirkland. But, to Oneida dismay, the state commissioners refused to honor their lease to Jedediah Phelps, apparently because he supported the Livingston Lease. Instead, the commissioners rewarded those who had helped the state, including the two council interpreters: John I. Bleecker, who got 1 square mile (640 acres), and Samuel Kirkland, who was promised 2 square miles (1,280 acres) for his "meritorious Services to the State."[44]

The legislature also took care of Otsequette, who had better served the state than the Oneidas. In 1791, he obtained the rents from 1,000 acres leased in trust for him by state officials. But the land did Otsequette little good, for he had cast off his gentility. At the end of the Fort Stanwix council, an observer marveled, "Ten days ago, I was introduced to him, a polite and well-informed gentleman; today, I beheld him splashing through the mud, in the rain, on horseback, with a young squaw behind him, both comfortably drunk." Thereafter, Americans cited Otsequette as a proof that it was futile to educate Indians, because they would always revert to savagery.[45]

In the Treaty of Fort Schuyler, concluded on September 22, New York secured the Oneida land previously leased to Livingston: about 5 million acres. The Oneidas retained only about 250,000 acres, mostly south of Oneida Lake, but including Fish Creek to the north. In return for the massive land cession, the Oneidas received a $5,000 down payment: $2,000 in cash, $2,000 in clothing and metal goods, and $1,000 in provisions. Clinton also pledged $500 to build a gristmill and a sawmill.[46]

More significantly, the state promised an annual payment of $600 in perpetuity, payable every June 1, at Fort Schuyler. Such an "annuity" appealed to the Oneidas by resembling a rental income in permanence and regularity. With apparent calculation, the state commissioners further fudged the issue by sometimes referring to the annuity as a "rent" and to the cession as a "lease." But a fixed annuity for a permanent cession fell short of a true land lease because the state permanently procured title to the land. Consequently, the Oneidas could not recover the ceded premises from the state and could never increase their rental return as the land grew in value from settlement.[47]

If the principle of an annuity represented a partial Oneida victory, the paltry sum of $600 manifested the state's overwhelming power. Given the Oneida population of about 600, that annuity provided a dollar per capita: an annual pittance for so much land lost forever. Indeed, such small payments delivered in cash encouraged most Oneidas to seek the instant gratification of traders' rum. Far from providing a benefit, during the 1790s the annuity proved a moral bane precisely because it was too small and both literally and figuratively liquid.[48]

Clinton portrayed the Treaty of Fort Schuyler as a benevolent rescue of Oneida lands from the Livingston Lease, as a favor bestowed upon benighted brethren. In fact, the state exploited the Lessee crisis to extract at least as much land for less money than Livingston had promised. Under the terms of the 1788 state treaty, the Oneida would receive, during the first fifteen years, $14,500 from New York: $5,000 down, $500 for the mills, and $9,000 in annuity payments of $600 per year. This compared poorly to the Lessees' promise of $16,500 in annuities during the same period. Moreover, that discrepancy would grow substantially during the subsequent fifteen years as the state's $600 annuity would yield only $9,000, compared to the $22,500 promised by the Livingston Lease's $1,500 annuity at maturity. If the Livingston Lease was a bad deal for the Oneida, the state purchase was far worse. Instead of rescuing the Oneidas, Clinton's treaty abused their trust.

The 1788 Oneida land cession was an extraordinarily good deal for the state. In February 1789, the state legislature began to cash in by carving twenty townships out of the southeastern quarter of the Oneida purchase. The state land office could sell the land either in 250-acre lots to settlers or as entire townships to speculators, at a minimum price of 3 shillings per acre. Given 23,040 acres per township (and 8 New York shillings per dollar), New York would reap at least $172,800 from the twenty townships—nearly twelve times what the state would pay the Oneidas during the initial fifteen years. And those twenty townships represented less than a quarter of the total cession: in future years the state would sell even more land for higher prices from that immense purchase.[49]

SUSPICIOUS TEMPER

As with other land councils, the official record of the Fort Schuyler council omits the private, late-night, informal dickering between Clinton and the

Oneida agents. In a private letter, one state official, Dr. Samuel Latham Mitchell, hinted at the behind-the-scenes intrigue:

> By means of the Suspicious Temper of these Indians, caused by the industrious insinuations of certain of our own people against the State, the business with the Oneydas has been already somewhat retarded, and will in the End be far less easy to accomplish, but the particulars of these matters I must not relate.

The nocturnal secrecy troubled many Oneidas. On September 19, the same day as Mitchell's letter, Good Peter complained, "we chose [that] all should hear what we had to say, as what is transacted secretly has a bad Appearance. All Business relating to the Public should be transacted openly."[50]

Because key decisions occurred in unrecorded late-night conclaves, and because the state commissioners wrote the treaty, the Oneidas and New Yorkers soon disagreed over the terms. The commissioners insisted that they had purchased the land outright, and so stated in the written treaty, but the Oneidas violently disagreed, citing Clinton's speeches. Good Peter remembered: "The Governor of New York said to us; 'You have now leased to me all of your territory, exclusive of the reservation.' . . . He did not say, 'I buy your country.' Nor did we say, 'We sell it to you.' " Given their oral culture, the Indians regarded Clinton's spoken words, confirmed by wampum, as more significant than any written treaty. The distinction between lease and sale was crucial to the Oneidas, who expected to preserve their fundamental title, with the opportunity to reap an increased annuity at twenty-one-year intervals, as settlement enhanced values. Good Peter recalled that Clinton told them, "In twenty-one years we will again converse together on this subject."[51]

The Oneidas did not discover the state's misinterpretation of their intent until June 1, 1789, when the state agent, John Tayler, formally delivered the first annuity payment and explained that it was permanently fixed at just $600. Good Peter recalled,

> This alarmed us in looking forward to our children & grand children, who should come after us. Now see what took place in consequence of this fixed sum, last spring, when the annual payment was made. Behold, we had increased in our numbers, and that stipulated sum seemed to be diminished, it scarcely amounted to a dollar to each individual. In a few years more, should we multiply . . . it may be reduced to a half dollar—to a shilling and even to a penny a piece! How astonishing the contrast.

> While we are thus *sinking* in our interest, our brother of New York has
> every thing springing up in abundance from the ground we leased to him,
> whereby the wealth of his people is greatly increased. He is rising up and
> I am sinking down!

That summer, the Oneidas also discovered that the state surveyors stinted the reservation by running lines that pinched the Indians' expectations on both the east and the west.[52]

In January 1790, the Oneidas sent ten chiefs, accompanied by Samuel Kirkland, to New York City to seek justice from the governor. The chiefs complained, "We find our Hopes and Expectations blasted and disappointed in every particular. Instead of leasing our Country to you for a respectable Rent, we find that we have ceded and granted it forever for the Consideration of the inconsiderable Sum of Six hundred Dollars per Year." They sought, at least, an enhanced annuity "somewhere near to a Compensation for the Cession of so large and fine a Country." The chiefs also wanted a new survey of their reservation to restore the true bounds of their consent at the 1788 treaty. The Oneidas also pressed the state to protect Oriske village from aggressive land speculators, who exploited a suspect royal patent from 1705 to claim that prime tract of alluvial land beside the Mohawk River (between German Flats and Fort Stanwix). The chiefs invoked the 1768 Treaty of Fort Stanwix, which protected a four-square-mile tract around Oriske village, despite its location east of the Line of Property. They also cited General Schuyler's wartime promises "that we should be happy and retain our Property if we conquered the common Enemy." Unfortunately for the Oneidas, George Clinton had invested in the Oriskany Patent.[53]

Clinton and his commissioners rejected all three Oneida appeals: on the fixed annuity, the survey boundaries, and Oriske. Tersely recording that the Oneida protests "were without Foundation," the commissioners implausibly added that the chiefs "appeared fully satisfied" with their defeat. But Henry Brockholst Livingston, a lawyer interested in the Oriskany Patent, attended that meeting and observed that, in fact, the Indians "appeared no ways satisfied with the Explanation." Later that evening, the chiefs confided their dismay to a sympathetic Quaker, who reported that "they knew not but [that] the white people would in time make slaves of them."[54]

Without true ownership of their land, and a fair share in its increasing value, their freedom seemed doomed. The Oneida dream of becoming rentier landlords had been exploited by Livingston and then perverted by the state into a cession and an annuity masquerading as a lease and a rent. But the Indians hoped still to benefit from the state's critical concession, in the

Fort Schuyler Treaty, that they could lease their reservation's southern tier to individuals—and that the state would legally enforce the leases.

CAYUGAS

In late 1788 and early 1789, the Livingston Lessees suffered a discrediting and demoralizing succession of defeats. By concluding treaties at Fort Schuyler with some of the Onondagas and most of the Oneidas, Clinton severely weakened the Lessees, who relied on Indian support. In Montgomery County in September 1788, the state also indicted Livingston and three other Lessee leaders for treason. In January 1789, the Lessees' partnership with Phelps and Gorham collapsed. Nearly bankrupt, the Lessees had failed to pay their share of mutual expenses for treating the Indians, surveying lands, and paying Massachusetts. Sick of their unreliable partners, Phelps and Gorham paid them four townships of land to relinquish their one-sixth interest and go away.[55]

Then the Lessees suffered a crippling defection in February, when a defeatist faction surrendered the two leases to the state, in defiance of Livingston and the hard-liners. In state hands, the documents weakened Lessee efforts to enforce their land claim while strengthening Clinton's leverage with the Indians. In the spring, the Lessees suffered yet another public embarrassment when the governor handily won reelection despite Livingston's conspicuous exertions for the challenger. In the high-stakes test of political interests, George Clinton was routing John Livingston. And a political interest could ill afford a reputation for weakness and defeat. As Livingston looked like a loser, his supporters deserted, seeking refuge in the governor's interest.[56]

The defections included such key culture-brokers as the traders Seth Reed and Peter Ryckman, who resided near Kanadasega and enjoyed a great influence with the local Cayugas. Although barely literate, Ryckman was of Dutch descent, a veteran Indian trader, adopted by the Cayugas, and fluent in their language. During the war, he had been something of a double agent, passing with surprising ease through Iroquoia between British Niagara and Patriot Fort Schuyler. Reed, in contrast, was a Yankee and a former colonel in the Continental Army. Well educated, he possessed better connections at the state capitol. Sizing up the two men, the Lessees considered Reed "the most able to oppose them . . . because he was the most cunning and could give greater information to Government but that Mr. Ryckman was thought to have the most influence with the Indians."[57]

In 1787, the Lessees recruited Reed and Ryckman with a share in the company. In return, they persuaded the local Cayugas to subscribe to the Long Lease. A year later, however, Reed and Ryckman defected in return for Clinton's pledge to provide state title for their Indian land grants. They then employed cattle and rum to entice about thirty Indians to join their sleigh caravan bound to Albany to meet the governor in February 1789. The Indians represented only the little community of about 100 at Cayuga Lake rather than the Cayuga majority of 630 that resided to the west at Buffalo Creek or Grand River. Small in number, the Cayugas at the lake also lacked experienced chiefs. They relied on an Onondaga warrior named Steel Trap (Kanistagea), and on a Seneca spokesman, Toneaghas. In addressing Clinton, Toneaghas blundered, "Brother Governor: You are a Man of Importance. I am afraid of you. I tremble in your Presence." That inept address only whetted Clinton's appetite for Cayuga land. Desperate for an effective spokesman, the Cayuga clan mothers belatedly turned to Good Peter, who had accompanied them to Albany.[58]

By leasing all of the ancestral homeland to Livingston, the western head chiefs had hoped to force their eastern dissidents to return to Buffalo Creek or Grand River. Instead, the Cayugas of the lake turned to the governor to secure a reservation for their homeland. Indeed, they sought enough land to entice the western Cayugas to join them at the lake. A big reservation would enhance their authority within the Cayuga nation by vindicating their controversial decision to return to the homeland. To preserve their access by water to British Canada, the eastern Cayugas also wanted to retain lands extending north all the way to Lake Ontario.[59]

But Clinton did not want a reservation big enough to unite the Cayugas. He preferred a small reservation to keep them divided, with the smaller and weaker party close at hand and beholden to the state. Nor did he relish a Cayuga reservation open at the north to Lake Ontario and so to British influence. Instead, the governor meant to close four state survey lines around a modest Cayuga reservation of 100 square miles (64,000 acres)—a quarter of what the Oneidas had retained. A limited and enclosed reservation served the state's drive to pin down particular Indian nations, isolated by intervening and surrounding settlements. Once divided and surrounded, Indians could be more easily managed for additional cessions whenever the state sought more land. On February 25, the Cayugas of the lake surrendered almost all of their nation's patrimony, a domain stretching from the Pennsylvania border to Lake Ontario, in return for $500 immediately, another $1,625 on June 1, and an annuity thereafter of $500.[60]

The Cayuga minority made the treaty partly to consolidate their symbiotic relationship with Ryckman, a trader who had facilitated their return to

Cayuga Lake. In hard times, he had fed them, while they had granted him a tract of fertile land. Likening their domain to a dish of food, they explained:

> We had long ago all agreed that he should have a Dish in our Country, as we all expected to put our Spoons in it when we were hungry. . . . Our dependence is much upon him for our future Prosperity. Should he be taken from us, we would think some evil Spirit had deprived us of our Hopes.

Endowed with property, Ryckman could continue to feed them and to protect their land from intruders. They expected him to "watch over us" lest "some bad Men may break over the Line you have made round us." As their culture-broker, Ryckman could help the Cayugas cope with the outsiders pressing in all around their reservation. They would surrender much land to keep "their Child" Peter Ryckman.[61]

To reward Reed and Ryckman, the state commissioners awarded them title to 16,000 acres on the west side of Seneca Lake and another 640 acres earmarked for Ryckman at the valuable ferry landing on the east side of Cayuga Lake. But the commissioners mistakenly granted both tracts exclusively in Ryckman's name, trusting him to share the larger one with Reed. But there was no honor among land thieves, for Ryckman meant to have it all. Reed had to muster affidavits from abundant witnesses, including Ryckman's son, that the two men had agreed to divide any lands procured from either the Lessees or the state.[62]

Then Ryckman broke Cayuga hearts by promptly assigning his lands to an agent to sell to land speculators. Far from securing Ryckman as their adopted protector, the Cayuga cession enabled him to cash in and get out, rewarded for manipulating the illusions of his adoptive people. Ultimately, Ryckman's allegiance belonged to a market society that fed on native lands for profit. But that competitive society also ate its own: the conniving agent (another former Lessee) sold the lands for his own benefit, defrauding Ryckman, who had deceived the Cayugas.[63]

CONFRONTATION

During the summer of 1789, the reeling Lessees faced a crucial test when the state sent surveyors to demarcate townships within the Oneida, Onondaga, and Cayuga land cessions. Completed surveys would enable the state to sell farms to loyal settlers, sealing victory in the contested domain. To survive, the Lessees had to stop the state surveys. In desperation, they tried to play their last two cards: armed settlers and Iroquois warriors.[64]

The state's treaties with Cayuga and Onondaga minorities infuriated the head chiefs at Buffalo Creek and Grand River, who preferred to lease the entire Finger Lakes region. The head chiefs despised the state reservations as divisive, as standing invitations for dispersal eastward into New York's clutches, disrupting the security of unity at Buffalo Creek or Grand River. The preeminent Cayuga chief, Fish Carrier (Ojageghte), protested the governor's "Artifice in reserving small tracts of Lands to the Indians, by which he hopes to Divide and Weaken us." Complaining to Clinton, Joseph Brant denounced the eastern Onondagas and Cayugas as "those who remain in the reserved trap and who are entirely in your Power." The western chiefs insisted that no land transaction was valid unless conducted at their Buffalo Creek council fire, "where the business of the Six Nations was done." At Buffalo Creek, Indians prevailed and had access to British officers for alternative sources of interpretation; but at Fort Schuyler (Stanwix) amid the New York settlements and far from Niagara, the governor had every advantage in negotiating with small and weak Indian factions.[65]

The head chiefs felt insulted that the governor would deal with their unqualified inferiors. The chiefs derided the Cayugas at the lake as "a small Number of Boys and Girls headed by an Onondago called Steel-Trap." In June 1789, the head men rebuked Clinton: "We did not expect that you, after advising us to shun private Treaties with Individuals and [to] avoid selling our Lands to your disobedient Children, that you would yourself purchase Lands from a few of our wrong headed young Men, without the Consent or even the Knowledge of the Chiefs." Only at Buffalo Creek could the head men make a land deal binding on the Cayugas or Onondagas.[66]

The proper chiefs especially resented that those disrespectful inferiors were reaping the governor's presents and payments. From the perspective of Buffalo Creek and Grand River, far better to lease the entire Finger Lakes region to the Lessees. Then the true chiefs would be paid and the upstarts compelled to return to their people at Buffalo Creek. The western chiefs instructed Clinton: "We expect to be paid the Money we then agreed for with Dr. Benton [of the Lessees], and to have the Distribution of it ourselves, and not that a few Individuals shall run away with the whole, to the Prejudice of all the Five Nations & to the Disgrace of your Brothers."[67]

During the summer of 1789, the western Iroquois assisted the Lessees with messages of intimidation sent to the Oneidas and to the Cayuga and Onondaga minorities. In late June, the Oneida chiefs alerted the governor, "We are threatened with Destruction, even with total Extermination. The Voice comes from the West; its sound is terrible—it bespeaks our Death." The Buffalo Creek chiefs also sent Fish Carrier east to warn the state's surveyors and agents to leave the Finger Lakes region. But nothing came of these threats, for the western warriors stayed home—perhaps because unable to scrounge up enough food for a prolonged raid during the pervasive hunger of 1789.[68]

But the state also faced resistance from settlers loyal to the Lessees. Most came from Pennsylvania's Susquehanna Valley. To make good their titles from the Lessees, the intruders threatened to uproot the local Cayugas and to attack New York's surveyors. One veteran surveyor, Moses DeWitt, worried: "Our Business for this Season has been more precarious than any that Ever I have been Engaged in."[69]

Bolstered by twenty-five armed guards, DeWitt and the other state surveyors pressed ahead. Their commander, Major Abraham Hardenbergh, explained, "For if we should now be drove off, it will redouble the Strength of the Leasees and put the State to ten times the Expence and Trouble to rectify Matters." Calling the Lessees' bluff, in early September Hardenbergh boldly pushed into their headquarters at Kanadasega to compel the settlers to submit by enrolling in the state militia. Exposed as impotent, the leading Lessees fled to avoid arrest.[70]

In the end, the Lessees displayed more bluster than resolve. Scattering with a whimper rather than a bang, the Lessees lost the critical battle of perceptions, waning in settler support as the state waxed powerful by acting with confidence. In the last analysis, the state successfully banked on the superior legitimacy of its power to transform Indian land into legal title. Routed, the Lessees never paid the rent promised to the Indians, who were left to deal with a state that asserted a monopoly right to buy aboriginal land.

Although the Lessee leadership had been defeated, their settlers persisted within the Cayuga reservation. In creating the reservation, Clinton had promised to oust all intruders—although protecting Indian reservations contradicted the state's fundamental purpose: to facilitate the agricultural development of its public domain. In September 1789, Major Hardenbergh warned Clinton that the Cayuga Lake reservation would

> afford a continual Source of Trouble and Uneasiness . . . since from its pleasing and favorable Situation and goodness of the Soil, it forms an irresistible Inducement for the white People to settle within its Bounds, as well as for greedy and unprincipled Speculators again to form unwarranted Plans for obtaining it independent of Government.

With the Lessees defeated, Hardenbergh cynically advised Clinton to abandon the local Cayugas as no longer useful. Rather than protect a few Indians on so much land, far better to betray them by dealing with the Buffalo Creek chiefs, who wished to reap payment by selling the entire reservation.[71]

But Clinton felt honor-bound to protect the twenty Cayuga families who had helped him by accepting a state reservation at the lake. Although resolute in seeking Indian lands, the governor also took pride in his paternalism toward deferential Indians. In May 1790, Steel Trap invoked the state treaty to request that New York oust the intruders. Clinton promptly issued a proclamation, warning the squatters to depart "on Pain of having their Buildings prostrated and their Improvements laid waste." But Clinton and the Cayugas allowed the intruders to linger through the harvest, provided they paid a rent in corn and agreed in writing to depart in the fall.[72]

To appease the disgruntled Cayuga and Onondaga majorities, Clinton met their deputies in a council in June at Fort Stanwix (which even the state leaders had given up calling Fort Schuyler). Clinton offered only a one-time special payment, called a "benevolence"—$500 for the Onondagas and $1,000 for the Cayugas—in return for ratifying the previous treaties with the local factions. Although the western chiefs so marked and offered polite praise for the deals, as was customary at councils, the western Cayugas at least remained disgruntled.[73]

In 1791, the western Cayuga chiefs struck their own deal with the reservation squatters, who had broken their promises to leave. They were led by John Richardson, an ambitious emigrant from Pennsylvania who had supported the Lessees. Richardson leased for twenty years almost all of the lake reservation (99 square miles) from the western Cayugas for $500 annually (half in cash and half in cattle). The deal reserved a single square mile for Steel Trap's little community. At the federal Indian council held that July at Newtown Point, they pressed the federal commissioner, Timothy Pickering, publicly to certify the lease. Initially reluctant, Pickering agreed upon obtaining a legal opinion from Brinton Paine, a New York state judge, that such leases were valid. Paine, however, was an interested party, having bought a share in the Richardson Lease. But he may have been right. Indeed, Richardson insisted that, at the June 1790 council at Fort Stanwix, Clinton had orally assured the Cayugas that they could lease land to settlers, presumably for up to twenty-one years, as the Oneidas could do with part of their reservation.[74]

Invoking their state treaty, the Cayugas at the lake begged Clinton to remove the intruders. By that fall, about forty squatter families resided on the reservation, compared to twenty Indian families. The latter mourned, "We of the Cayuga nation are in trouble; our peace is broke up;—we have no pleasant days nor quiet nights; our women & children are become disconsolate; joy is no more known in our place of abode." Clinton welcomed the opportunity to make a vivid example meant to deter others from dealing directly with Indians for land. In October, the governor sent William Colbrath, the sheriff of Herkimer County, with 86 armed militiamen to the Cayuga Lake reservation. Surprising the squatters, Colbrath's men quickly arrested Richardson, disarmed his supporters, and burned nineteen cabins. One dispossessed woman recalled cooking "our food by the smouldering ruins of our house." Colbrath temporarily spared four cabins, where the inhabitants were too sick to leave. He gave permanent reprieves to two inns near the ferry across the lake because these assisted travelers and paid a rent in corn to the local Cayugas. At their request, Colbrath also spared the house of a blacksmith and gunsmith, who had been unusually generous and hospitable to the natives.[75]

REPOSE

After securing land cessions from the Oneidas, Cayugas, and Onondagas, Clinton and the state legislature lost interest in punishing the Lessees. In March 1790 the legislature dropped the prosecutions against John Livingston and his leading lieutenants, Caleb Benton, Ezekiel Gilbert, and John McKinstry. Ultimately, the state broke the governor's promise to the Oneidas: "We will severely punish our People for this Act of Disobedience to their own Constitution and Laws."[76]

Far from punishing the Livingston Lessees, in 1793 the legislature rewarded them by granting 100 square miles of state land in Clinton County as compensation for their expenditures in procuring Indian land by lease. Ultimately, the legislature bought the Lessees' argument that they had facilitated the state's efforts to part the Iroquois from their land. A state commissioner, John Hathorn, attested that at the Fort Stanwix council in 1790 the Onondagas and Cayugas had resisted state pressure "to sell their land until they was informed by his Excellency that their former conveyances was delivered into the hands of government—on which information the Indians cheerfully treated."[77]

Ever resourceful, George Clinton could forgive even John Livingston—in return for his political support. In November 1791, shortly after routing the Cayuga squatters, the triumphant but pragmatic governor stopped by Livingston's manor house for breakfast, and he later returned for dinner. Clinton vaguely promised to help Livingston procure lands along the Niagara River. Not coincidentally, the governor faced an especially difficult reelection campaign during the next spring. Anticipating that "the approaching Election may do as much for us in this business as any thing whatever," Livingston engaged his interest to support Clinton, who narrowly won. Livingston's political conversion also reflected his falling out with his former political allies (and Clinton foes) Philip Schuyler and Stephen Van Rensselaer. "I love to Retalliate, and no better opportunity can offer," Livingston explained. Unlike the cool and calculating governor, the choleric Livingston never forgave.[78]

A relic of the turbulent 1780s, John Livingston failed to adapt to the calmer 1790s. In vain, a relative urged, "Moderate your own desires. . . . Have regard to repose & quiet." Instead, Livingston seethed when his Niagara land bid died because Clinton forgot his promise to help. During the fall of 1793, Livingston brazenly revived his secession plot in western New York. He even renewed the anachronistic vow to rally "a Number of armed Troops, collected from Vermont, and elsewhere, in case of Opposition." In fact, Livingston rallied very little support because Clinton had so shrewdly dispensed patronage to reward the frontier's leading men with commissions as justices, county clerks, sheriffs, and militia officers. Led by Oliver Phelps, the frontier leaders quickly and easily suffocated Livingston's revival, putting a belated end to the Lessee scheme.[79]

HUNGRY YEAR

In March 1789, a party of surveyors in the Genesee country suddenly awoke to gunfire piercing their crude cabin, killing one man and wounding another. Bearing knives and tomahawks, four Tuscarora warriors and a woman then broke in, but the surviving surveyors drove them away by wielding clubs and axes. A settler posse tracked the assailants to Newtown Point on the Chemung River. Capturing the suspects, the posse faced a dilemma: what to do with them. The nearest court and jail lay about two hundred miles away, through a dense forest, at Johnstown. Unwilling to hazard the journey, the posse gathered the local settlers to conduct "committee law." After hearing the surveyors' testimony, the settlers declared the two Indians guilty. One died quickly, executed by "the Indian method, with the tomahawk." The other broke away but was quickly caught and beaten to death with stones and pine knots. A nineteenth-century historian commented, "This was the first trial and execution in the Genesee country."[80]

The Indians of the Genesee apparently bristled at this unilateral assertion of settler justice, for the executions broke the custom of consulting with the chiefs and permitting them to atone for a killing by covering the grave with goods. Rather than accept their subordination to settler justice, the Indians took revenge by killing at least one white man, a Dr. Vanderwort near Kanadasega in the spring. In cryptic reply to Oliver Phelps, Nathaniel Gorham wrote, "I have not mentioned the account of the Murder to any Person, not even my Son." Phelps and Gorham kept the secret lest such news scare away the settlers needed as customers for land. Rather than perpetuate the revenge cycle, the Genesee settlers seem to have backed away from again applying their committee law, cooling tensions with the Indians.[81]

But what had motivated the original attack by the Tuscaroras on the surveyors? On an unsuccessful hunt, the Indians were starving. The day before the fatal night, they had begged the surveyors to share their provisions. Apparently denied and insulted, the Tuscaroras returned at night to kill and to take the food, "the object of this bloody attack," according to the original source. Indians expected food from settlers as a customary right for indulging their intrusion into the native world. Indians were especially hungry during the 1780s, for their horticulture had not yet recovered from the wartime devastation. The intrusion of settlers onto valued alluvial flats, and the invasion of settler hogs and cattle into native crops, did not help. To fill their deficit, the Indians relied upon procuring food from the newcomers. Because gifts of food maintained peace between Indians and settlers, withholding provisions invited hostility.[82]

Indian hunger reached crisis proportions in early 1789. In June, when the Oneidas assembled at Fort Stanwix to receive their first annuity payment from New York, Good Peter assured the state agent: "We are so faint that we cannot speak to you, and our Women and Children are come likewise to see you and are very hungry and have no Provisions at home." That month, an Oneida father with five children pleaded with Kirkland for relief: "We are very hungry and almost starved. . . . My family have not tasted any bread, or meat for many days; nothing but herbs and sometimes small fish. I am so weak I can't hoe any corn." Giving as much as he could, Kirkland exhausted his own supplies and became bedridden with fatigue and dysentery brought on by malnutrition.[83]

During the first seven months of 1789, hunger prevailed throughout the northern borderland, in the new settlements as well as the Indian villages. Food was scarce from northern Pennsylvania, across upstate New York, into Canada and western and northern New England. In March, Kirkland reported that "the uncommon scarcity of provisions" prevailed "universally through the territory of the Six Nations, and down the Mohawk-River till we reach Albany." Many hungry settlers abandoned their new farms, fleeing east or south to seek food in older towns. In June, a surveyor reported from the Susquehanna Valley of northern Pennsylvania:

> The people of the Genesee and Niagara Country are crouding in upon
> us every day, owing to the great scarcity of provisions, the most of them

who have gone there lately are starving to death and it is shocking to humanity to hear of the number of families that are dying daily for want of sustenance. . . . The wild roots and herbs that the country affords, boiled & without salt, constitute the whole food of most of the unhappy people who have been decoyed there thro' the flattering account of the quality of the land.

Hungry settlers and surveyors had nothing to spare for the Indians. An Oneida father told Kirkland: "I have been travelling all day among white people, but they can't give me anything."[84]

The hunger of early 1789 derived from four interacting causes: a parasite; a cold, damp climate; settler migration; and panic. In 1788, a wheat parasite, known as the Hessian fly, had devastated the harvest in Canada and much of the American northeast. In Pennsylvania, the British diplomat Phineas Bond reported to his superior, "The ravages here, my Lord, are beyond all conception ruinous;—many farms have had the crops so compleatly cut off as to be left without bread, corn, or even seed corn." That summer's damp, cool weather had favored the spread of the Hessian fly in unprecedented numbers into broad new districts. The unusual weather reflected the global impact of volcanic explosions in Iceland and Japan that blew tons of particulates into the upper atmosphere, reducing the warming sunlight that could reach the earth's surface. The volcanic dust lowered global temperatures, shortened growing seasons, disrupted regional wind patterns, dislocated precipitation, and facilitated parasites.[85]

During 1788, before it became evident that the harvest had failed, settler migration had surged in the northern borderland. Poor newcomers rushed at the worst time into the worst place: the northern settlements gripped by hunger. The next spring, they panicked as the prolonged cold threatened an even bleaker future by postponing the planting of crops and the pasturing of hungry livestock. Deprived of timely new grass, the livestock starved and died, depriving settlers of milk and of oxen needed to plow their fields. Already beleaguered by the failed harvest of 1788, many settlers dreaded a deeper famine in 1789, an alarm that drove up prices and encouraged hoarding.[86]

The starving Indians and settlers sought relief by fishing and by scrounging for small animals and wild plants. Routine for the Indians, this emergency expansion of the food supply disturbed many settlers disgusted by the consumption of tadpoles, robins, beech leaves, sassafras roots, and wild leeks.[87]

During 1788–89, the fortunate few with surplus food possessed a special sway among the hungry peoples of Indian villages and new settlements. The powerful could reward or buy support with food relief. At the first delivery of the state annuity provided by the Treaty of Fort Schuyler, the hungry Oneidas could not reject the payment, although it fell far short of their expectations. That summer, Oliver Phelps similarly exploited the famine to impose his lowball version of the land payment due to the Senecas. In July at Canandaigua, his agent Judah Colt fed hundreds of Indians attending the payment ceremony. Colt recalled,

> They came & went away hungry, nothwithstanding upwards of 100 heads of Cattle was killed for them. Flour was not so plenty. . . . One barrel made up into bread sold for 100 Dollars worth in silver plates of various kind of Indian ornaments. Many horses died distempered during the Treaty. The Indians fed on them freely [and] also the blood and entrails of all the Beef slaughtered.

Weakened by hunger and obligated for the relief, the Senecas grudgingly accepted the half payment presented by Phelps. That precedent weakened their subsequent protests.[88]

The famine also affected the confrontation between the Lessees and New York State. In 1788, the Lessees had held their own in the Finger Lakes country by lavishing food and drink on their Indian and settler supporters. A year later, however, the Lessees faltered as a succession of defeats diminished their resources and curtailed their credit. Measuring the contenders' relative power by their largesse with provisions, the Indians and settlers concluded that the state would defeat the Lessees.

Much of Pennsylvania, Vermont, Connecticut, western Massachusetts, and northern New Hampshire suffered from hunger, but New York was the only state to provide public relief. Of the affected states, New York had the largest supply of frontier lands for sale and settlement; New York also had the largest population of Indians; and New York had to compete with the Lessees for the support of settlers and natives. The hunger presented the state with both an unanticipated crisis and a special opportunity. On the one hand, a failure to feed the natives would weaken the state's moral authority. On June 30, the Oneidas reminded the governor that he needed to fulfill his paternalistic pretenses: "If hunger should kill us while so near our American Brothers, it would be a lamentable story indeed." That sad story would stiffen the opposition to New York among the other Iroquois peoples. On the other hand, by rescuing the Indians from famine, the state could claim a subsequent obligation from the Indians to make further land concessions. Food was power on a starving frontier.[89]

By feeding settlers and Indians, the state also acted to preserve the good reputation of New York's frontier lands. On July 6, Clinton urged the legislature to relieve the "distresses experienced by the failure of the last year's crops, particularly in the exterior settlements, and by the poorer class of people." On July 14, the legislature appropriated £600 to buy 2,000 bushels of corn for distribution on the frontier. The state sent 350 bushels to feed the Oneidas, Mohicans, Tuscaroras, Onondagas, and Cayugas as—in Clinton's words—"a testimony of our Friendship for you." The remaining 1,650 went to feed the settlers as a loan. This display of state largesse proved timely, for in the late summer the state surveyors forged ahead as the Lessee cause collapsed for want of Indian or settler support.[90]

The frontier hunger also helped Clinton to bring the western Cayugas and Onondagas to terms at Fort Schuyler in 1790. Those Indians responded to Joseph Brant's influence, which he employed to curry relief for Grand River from the governor of New York. The severe hunger had induced Brant's people to butcher all of their cattle for relief. Seeking additional provisions and cattle to replenish the herds, in July 1789 Brant struck a deal with Jelles Fonda, a Mohawk Valley merchant. In return for a Mohawk deed to their Canajoharie lands, Fonda agreed to pay £516, advancing a partial payment in provisions and livestock. To obtain the balance of the payment, however, Brant needed the state to clear the title that Fonda had procured from the Mohawks. To secure that end, Brant accepted Clinton's invitation to the Fort Schuyler council in June 1790. Acting as both interpreter and spokesman for the western Cayugas and Onondagas, Brant persuaded them to accept the governor's terms. The famine repeatedly served the interests of the state and its land speculators.[91]

MONOPOLY

After weathering the federal and Massachusetts challenges during the mid-1780s, Governor Clinton faced a greater threat from New York's own aggressive and defiant citizens, the Livingston Lessees. They had exploited the Iroquois longing to lease, rather than sell, their lands. But that unstable alliance only hastened the Indians' dispossession by a state determined to frustrate native leases and disloyal speculators. To defeat the Lessees and to enrich the state, Clinton radically reduced central Iroquoia to just three modest reservations: 250,000 acres for the Oneidas and 64,000 acres each for the Cayugas and Onondagas. That acreage amounted to only about 4 percent of their prewar domains. Before the war, Iroquoia had been a broad Indian country where one native people adjoined another. During the 1780s, however, that domain was reduced to three enclaves surrounded by rapidly

First Sheet, State-Map of New York [The Finger Lakes Region], by Simeon DeWitt, ca. 1792. Produced by the surveyor general of New York, this map vividly illustrates the creation and restriction of Indian reservations by a surrounding grid of lots for private ownership. (Courtesy of the New York State Library; 99-6391.)

growing settlements. The lone major exception was the broad Seneca domain west of the Genesee River within the Massachusetts preemption zone. In addition to their superior numbers, the Senecas benefited from their strategic location on the contested border between the United States and the British Empire. So long as a cold war persisted between republic and empire, the Senecas remained too powerful to be alienated by dispossession.

By frustrating Iroquois efforts to lease land for revenue, the state asserted a monopoly power to purchase Indian lands. State leaders claimed that their monopoly protected Indians from fraudulent purchases by unscrupulous individuals: a legitimate problem. But the state became fiscally dependent on the profits made by procuring and selling Indian land. The state legislators and commissioners minimized what they paid to the Indians and maximized the land extracted from them, goals that clashed with the paternalistic rhetoric of looking after the Indians' best interests. In 1834, the state's surveyor general, Simeon DeWitt, conceded that the state's pre-1829 Indian treaties "were conducted with a view to the benefit of the treasury." In addition to the revenue generated by selling Indian lands, the state annually collected taxes on the farms and other properties established within the cessions.[92]

The state's fiscal benefit peaked during the early to mid-1790s, when the state sold the Oneida lands procured by the 1788 Treaty of Fort Schuyler. From 1790 to 1795, nearly half the state's revenue came from selling land recently obtained from the Indians:

NEW YORK STATE PUBLIC REVENUE FROM LAND SALES, 1790–95[93]

	LAND SALES	PERCENTAGE	ALL OTHER REVENUE	PERCENTAGE
1790:	$3,164	2.5%	$124,484	97.5%
1791:	$123,878	48.3%	$132,552	51.7%
1792:	$325,677	58.2%	$233,823	41.8%
1793:	$224,172	56.7%	$170,877	43.3%
1794:	$293,994	60.7%	$190,334	39.3%
1795:	$142,849	46.8%	$162,169	53.2%
TOTALS:	$1,113,734	52.3%	$1,014,239	47.7%

During that six-year period, the state took in $13.94 in land revenue for every $1.00 it spent on surveys and Indian affairs (including purchases and annuities) combined, making for a net surplus of $1,040,447.

NEW YORK STATE LAND REVENUES COMPARED TO COSTS, 1790–95[94]

YEAR	LAND REVENUE	SURVEYS, ETC.	INDIAN AFFAIRS	SURPLUS/ DEFICIT
1790:	$3,164	$11,813	$7,071	−$15,720
1791:	$123,878	$4,707	$1,657	+$117,514
1792:	$325,677	$1,516	$1,695	+$325,466
1793:	$224,172	$4,763	$5,100	+$214,309
1794:	$293,994	$3,807	$3,106	+$287,079
1795:	$142,849	$5,315	$22,735	+$114,799
TOTALS:	$1,113,734	$31,921	$42,717	+$1,040,447

We see the fruits of monopoly in the state's profits. Under pressure to sell, the Iroquois could find only one legal buyer: the State of New York. The legislature unilaterally set a price per acre, denying its negotiators any leeway to improve the offer. Those negotiators repeatedly told the Indians to accept that stipulated price or risk the state's enmity.

PART THREE

❧❧❧

CONFRONTATION

Red Jacket's silver medal, 1792. Issued to Red Jacket by the United States government during the Philadelphia visit by the Six Nations chiefs, this medal shows the president sharing a peace pipe with an Indian chief who has discarded his war hatchet. The medal conveys the Federalist ideology in Indian relations by depicting the friendly relationship as permitting the agricultural transformation suggested by the oxen, plow, farmer, and farmhouse in the background. (Courtesy of the Buffalo and Erie County Historical Society.)

The Great Indian Council, Buffalo Creek, by Lewis Foy, ca. 1793. This shows the American peace commissioners seated on chairs, listening to an Iroquois orator (probably Red Jacket). British officers and Quaker observers stand behind the American commissioners. For a key to the identities of the represented, see below. (Courtesy of the Montreal Museum of Fine Arts, gift of G. Ronald Jackson and Michael Jackson. Photo by the Montreal Museum of Fine Arts.)

Talk with the Indians at Buffalo Creek in 1793. From William Leete Stone, *Life of Joseph Brant-Thayendenegea* (1838), this sketch provides a key to Lewis Foy's painting of a Six Nations Council at Buffalo Creek in 1793. (Courtesy of the American Antiquarian Society.)

CHAPTER SEVEN

Fathers

Indian Family [Oneidas], by Baroness Hyde de Neuville, ca. 1807. (Courtesy of the New-York Historical Society; 1953.215.)

T HE ONEIDAS ROMANTICIZED the French as generous and selfless patrons, a nostalgia that deepened after the British conquest of Canada in 1760. The Oneidas withheld the diplomatic title of "Father" from the British and Americans, reserving it for the French king (and his representatives). That mystique was sustained by several French prisoners taken during the Seven Years' War. Adopted and married by Oneidas, these former prisoners became influential brokers with the outside world. They included Nicholas Jourdan, captured at Niagara in 1759. Twenty-five years later, his appearance astonished French visitors when they heard him speak their language despite an Oneida appearance: "lead at his ears, bones hung at his nose, and his face was painted with bands of different colors."[1]

During the American Revolutionary War, the embattled Patriots played up their French alliance to impress the Iroquois, and especially the Oneidas. After the war, the Oneidas hoped that the French would remain the alliance's dominant partner, able to protect the Indians by restraining the New Yorkers. Some French officials aspired to just that role, for they sought, through the Oneidas, to recover an influence that reached deep into Indian country. These officials endorsed the Oneidas' conviction that they had supplanted the Mohawks in mediating between the Six Nations and the eastern sources of power and property. The weakness of the American confederacy also induced the French to treat the Americans as junior partners in a lopsided alliance. As a result, during the late 1780s, American officials began to resent the French ambitions to exploit their mystique among the Oneidas.

That context of French ambition, American weakness, and Oneida dreams helps to explain the otherwise mysterious career of Peter Penet. His Oneida popularity outraged Samuel Kirkland, the missionary father who felt eclipsed. But Kirkland had himself to blame for neglecting his Oneida mission as he pursued a new passion for acquiring Indian land.

ALLIES

During the war, to impress the Oneidas, the Patriots highlighted their French connection. In March 1778 at Johnstown, General Philip Schuyler hosted a council for the Oneidas and Tuscaroras, with the Marquis de Lafayette as the featured guest. A handsome young French aristocrat serving as a general in Washington's army, Lafayette dazzled the Oneidas, who adopted him with the name of Kayewla. The new relationship bore immediate fruit when Lafayette ordered, and a French military engineer supervised, the construction of a small fort to defend Kanonwalohale. In gratitude, about 50 Tuscaroras and Oneidas joined Lafayette's brigade in Pennsylvania, where they saw action in May at the Battle of Barren Hill. The Oneida sachem the Great Grasshopper (Ojistalale) urged the warriors to achieve a renown meant to "reach the Ears of our father, the French king." That mission seemed accomplished in May, when the Oneidas learned that France had entered a formal alliance with the United States against the British.[2]

During the summer of 1780, Schuyler again played the French card by arranging for a delegation of Tuscaroras and Oneidas, including Nicholas Jourdan, to visit the French expeditionary force encamped in Rhode Island. The French commander, the Comte de Rochambeau, lavished attention, parades, presents, food, drink, and speeches on his Iroquois guests, evoking again the mystique of the generous French Father. Schuyler calculated that the returning Indians would disseminate news of French prowess and generosity to their contacts in Canada, weakening Indian support there for the British.[3]

But Schuyler did not fully apprehend that the Oneidas believed that their French alliance trumped their dependence on the New York Patriots, who seemed weak, penurious, and grasping by comparison. The Oneidas preferred the French for their superior wealth and theatricality, and for their lack of encroaching settlers. Addressing Rochambeau as the incarnation of the French king, the Oneidas emphasized their "choice" to follow the French lead in the war: "O my Father, whom we have chosen of our own free will to lead us in war, we promise you every assistance." By promoting a French connection, the American leadership underestimated the Indians' capacity to turn it to their own ends.[4]

In September 1784, the French diplomat François de Barbé-Marbois visited Kanonwalohale to woo the Oneidas. A proponent of French strength and American dependence, Marbois hoped through the Oneidas to tap into the network of native diplomacy that carried messages through the Six Nations to the Indians of the Great Lakes and Ohio Valley. The Oneidas welcomed this invitation to become the essential conduit and amplifier for initiatives from the French Father to the native world. Marbois bypassed both federal and New York officials, who disliked his challenge to their domination over native peoples within the bounds claimed by the United States.[5]

The Oneidas, however, relished the French attention. Marbois described the most prestigious Oneida chief, the Great Grasshopper, as "an old man very respected among them, attached to France for sixty years, had an embroidered Uniform of which M. le Chevalier de la Luzerne had made him a present, and he told me he would part with this costume only in death." Marbois explained, "These savages still have great respect for the king of France. They speak of the French nation with reverence."[6]

A month later, Marbois and the celebrated Marquis de Lafayette attended the opening sessions of the federal Indian council at Fort Stanwix. The Oneidas insisted that Lafayette should formally address the council; but the lead American commissioner, Arthur Lee, objected. He aptly feared that Lafayette's speech would encourage the Iroquois conviction that the French dominated their American allies. But the other federal commissioners, Richard Butler and Oliver Wolcott, took Kirkland's advice that such a speech was essential to please the Oneidas and to strengthen their influence among the other Six Nations. Extolling the Oneidas and Tuscaroras for their alliance, while rebuking the other Iroquois for their enmity, Lafayette's vivid speech caused such a sensation that the federal commissioners felt eclipsed. To regain leadership over the council, they quietly encouraged Lafayette and Marbois to leave.[7]

Before departing, Lafayette privately assured the Oneidas that the French Father would soon revive his network of Indian alliances, subordinating both the Americans and the British. Lafayette also took away a teenage Oneida, Peter Otsequette, to educate as an adopted son in France. In private, however, Lafayette confessed himself "very weary of the role of father of the family which has been forced on me here." He expressed "pleasure that I shall depart tomorrow, because all this savagery, despite my popularity, bores me to death." Responding to the public Lafayette, the Oneidas concluded that the French Father would protect their lands from the New Yorkers.[8]

SAMUEL KIRKLAND

While the French were enhancing their mystique, Samuel Kirkland was losing his. The long, hard war had undermined the Oneida mission. To recruit and motivate Indians, Patriot officials provided abundant alcohol and celebrated the warrior ethos, compromising Kirkland's painstaking efforts to transform the Oneidas into temperate and peaceful farmers. And Brant's raiders had reduced to ashes the church, fences, and framed houses that had taken years to build. Driven to a bleak refugee camp, many Oneidas became demoralized by their losses, begging, and alcohol.[9]

By subordinating his religious mission to political ends, Kirkland contributed to the Oneida decline. Forsaking his earlier preaching of temperance and peace, he delivered General Schuyler's alcohol to celebrate Patriot victories. Expressing political rather than evangelical zeal, Kirkland assured Schuyler: "Your seasonable and well adapted Speech to the Indians accompanied with the present of six Barrels of Rum, will . . . do more service to our Cause than a thousand [pounds] expended at a Treaty with them."[10]

During the war, Kirkland neglected his mission at Kanonwalohale by serving as a Continental Army chaplain at Fort Schuyler (Stanwix) and, later, with the Sullivan expedition. Kirkland also spent prolonged leaves with his family at Stockbridge, in western Massachusetts. Matured in years and hardened by the war, Kirkland felt distanced from his youth as the self-sacrificing missionary, full of naïve hopes for transforming Indians. Paid and praised for his native expertise by gentlemen, Kirkland also felt enticed by the secular world of social prestige and material rewards, as Eleazar Wheelock had been.[11]

By war's end, his missionary zeal had faded, but Kirkland blamed the Oneidas. He had not deserted them; they had failed him and God. After the war, he assured Jerusha, "The most of my people are degenerated as much as our paper currency depreciated in the time of the war. . . . They are, in plain English, filthy, dirty, nasty creatures, a few families excepted."[12]

But postwar financial need pressed Kirkland to renew his Oneida mission, for his chaplain's pay expired at war's end. By reviving his mission, Kirkland strengthened appeals to his prewar benefactors to renew their financial support and to provide back pay for the war years. In late 1784, the missionary society in Scotland agreed to provide £300 (sterling) in back pay and to provide £50 as an annual salary. The Harvard Corporation matched it, making for a total salary of £100: a renewal of Kirkland's prewar arrangement.[13]

But Kirkland never recovered his prewar influence at Kanonwalohale. During the war, Kirkland had compromised his moral standing by assisting Sullivan's destructive invasion of western Iroquoia. The native minister Samson Occom explained, "Mr. Kirkland went with an Army against the poor Indians, & he has prejudiced the minds of Indi[a]ns against all Missionaries, especially against White Missionaries, seven Times more than anything that ever was done by the White People or any People what ever." Although the Oneidas certainly celebrated their own warriors, they insisted that a missionary's spiritual power required a strict avoidance of bloodshed. In Kirkland's words, they expected missionaries to be "lovers of universal peace." Visiting Kanonwalohale in 1784, Occom reported, "Mr. Kirkland is but coldly received, his going with the army against the Indians will not be easily forgot."[14]

Compared to his prewar mission, during the 1780s Kirkland spent much less time with the Oneidas and much more with his family at Stockbridge, which his sickly wife was loath to leave. As an older man grown accustomed to the relative comfort of a New England farm, Kirkland also lacked his youthful adaptability to the hardships of an Oneida village. Within a few months, sometimes only weeks, Kirkland returned home, complaining of bad food, scanty shelter, and poor health. His early departures disappointed Indians who remembered the tireless young missionary of the early 1770s.[15]

After the war, Kirkland felt of two minds about the Oneidas. On the one hand, he praised some for "the most undissembled friendship, native kindness & true gratitude & in the critical hour, some have, unasked, step[p]ed forth & offered to receive the hatchet in my stead, & intreated me to retire & compose my mind. . . . Such scenes naturally tend to beget strong attachments & produce permanent friendships." With a few Oneidas, he felt a special bond:

> There is something, to me quite unaccountable, in the affection that sometimes takes place between a white man & an Indian. . . . I am willing to acknowledge [that] there is a *certain something* in my social nature that is really gratified with the *society* of an *Indian*: and there is a certain simplicity & undisguisedness, in some of their manners & mode of expression that is exceedingly pleasing to me.

But, in general, Kirkland had less patience for Indians, blasting "their general course of idleness, and intemperance, stupidity and ingratitude."[16]

Kirkland's diminished energy clashed with the Indians' increased need for his attention and influence. Deeply troubled by their deteriorating circumstances, the Oneidas needed, more than ever, to talk at length with their missionary. Perhaps he could make sense of their anxieties and afflictions, both personal and national, physical and psychological. One Tuscarora warrior confessed an inner turmoil felt by many Indians struggling to achieve the radical transformation demanded by Kirkland's Calvinist theology:

> That it appeared to him that he was *two persons*, or had *two souls* in his body; the one *good*, the other *bad*. That there was a constant struggle within. Sometimes the *bad mind* or soul (as he expressed it) would get the victory over the good mind; and then he had the most fearful apprehensions of death, and seeing his *Maker, God*. And he had no kind of comfort or pleasure in any present enjoyment, or future prospect. Another time, the *good soul* would rise and get the better of the bad one, and pursue it, as a person determined on the destruction of an enemy; and follow it in its windings and crooked paths: and at length all would seem to be melted and little or no life remaining.

If Indians needed more time to talk, Kirkland possessed less patience to listen. In 1787, he grumbled that, in relating "their exercises of mind," the Indian confessors "seem to have no more feeling for me than if I was made of Iron or Brass." When Kirkland balked at conducting a long Sabbath service, the chiefs shamed him by replying "that it was the Lord's day, and they had nothing to do on that day, but attend to God's counsels and the instructions of Jesus Christ. They were not afraid of being weary." Claiming Christianity as their own, these chiefs turned the tables on their weary missionary.[17]

The Oneidas felt deeply discouraged by the destruction of their village and the pressures on their land. Kirkland reported that many Oneidas "mourn and sigh and weep like children in the view of their present miserable state, compared with the white people.... While blessings of every kind flowed down like a river upon the white people, as though God begrudged them nothing, calamity, wretchedness and poverty were the lot of the Indians."[18]

Christianity lost credibility as the Oneidas became painfully familiar with the cheating, drinking, and profanity of most settlers, traders, and land speculators. If Christianity was so good and powerful, why were white people so conniving and hypocritical? Christianity also seemed too abstract to deal with their tangible and increasing afflictions: hunger, exposure, sickness, and violence. Collective stress revived the traditional belief in witchcraft, blaming especially older women with prickly personalities. In 1787, a suspected witch returned to Kanonwalohale from living with the Senecas. Kirkland reported, "This creature was very soon seen by several persons flying through the town in the shape of an overgrown owl; & at another time, running with incredible swiftness in the appearance of a fox." Her threats sickened two Indians. When Kirkland offered the rational explanation of rheumatism, "They appeared to pity my ignorance or incredulity."[19]

The Oneida pagans regarded the missionary as a divisive agent insinuating an alien ideology hostile to the traditional spiritual beliefs best for Indians. They dreaded that the Oneidas "would soon come to ruin which had been the fate of many Indian Nations for adopting the ways of white people." They competed with Kirkland's Sabbath services by holding their dances and feasts at the same time. Some even threatened to kill Kirkland.[20]

Even the ostensibly Christian majority disappointed Kirkland, who described their faith as nominal and utilitarian. Although they attended services regularly, listened intently, and sang beautifully, few Oneidas embraced the thorough moral changes or practiced the evangelical fervor sought by their missionary. In November 1787, Kirkland sadly concluded, "The more I become acquainted with their real sentiments, the more I find this one to prevail among them, viz.—that the Christian religion was not *designed* for *Indians* & must be countenanced no farther than their connexion with Christians renders it necessary." Good Peter tried to console Kirkland: "Father, you know me & I pity you, because so many of the Oneidas have turned back to their old ways."[21]

Kirkland's own faith suffered a devastating blow on January 23, 1788, when his beloved wife Jerusha died in childbirth at the age of forty-four. He had long relied on her unwavering love and consistent piety to stabilize his own more emotional and volatile nature. "She was my guide, my friend, my earthly all, and now I may add [that] my life, my joy, my comfort is dead," he mourned. Something in Kirkland also died, for thereafter the evangelical piety drained from his writings as if his faith grew cold, buried with Jerusha.[22]

Jerusha's death also scattered the family. The eldest two sons went off to college: John to Harvard and George to Dartmouth. Father placed the four younger children (Jerusha, Sarah, Elizabeth, and Samuel Jr.) in the households of family friends in Stockbridge and in Sharon, Connecticut. Neglecting them, Kirkland spent more time on the New York frontier, but less as a missionary than as an agent for land speculators.

GREAT MEN

Kirkland lost moral standing by breaking a solemn and public promise, made to the Oneidas before the war, that he would never acquire any land within Iroquoia. By that promise, Kirkland gained an extraordinary influence at Kanonwalohale during the early 1770s. After the war, however, he felt pressure to build an estate to educate his children in gentility and to endow their inheritance. At the same time, he discovered the financial value of his Indian expertise and influence to governments and land speculators with designs on Iroquois lands. Seizing the new opportunity, Kirkland abandoned his prewar promise as outdated and inconvenient. Moral consistency was a luxury that he could no longer afford. If speculators would inevitably consume Iroquoia, he wanted his share. Kirkland could rationalize that his past exertions, sufferings, and charity as a missionary warranted some land; and that his Indian neighbors would benefit most from his possession of their former land.[23]

Seeking Oneida consent, Kirkland argued that he would attend them more regularly if his family could move onto their own land near Kanonwalohale. The Oneidas recalled that Kirkland "told us that he was very poor [and] had no salary, therefore could not live among us to teach us as a father to his children." He proposed, they remembered, "that if he could have [a] piece [of] Land here he would then instruct us. Then we cut [a] slice for his family." Given the native ethos of reciprocity, and Kirkland's years of charity, the Oneidas could not reject such a direct request. They granted him 320 acres for a farm and another 320 acres to hold in trust for his successors as missionaries, grants approved at the treaty of Fort Herkimer in 1785 and confirmed by the state legislature in 1786.[24]

But by asking for those tracts, Kirkland lost his luster in Oneida eyes. James Dean reported that "Mr. Kirkland, when he first introduced himself among the Oneidas imprudently made a publick and solemn declaration that he never would own a foot of Land [on] this side [of] the Hudson River and [he has since] disappointed them in [so] many promises of faithfullness, that he never can [re]gain their hearty confidence." He became just another minister who succumbed to the allure of native land.[25]

During the late 1780s, Kirkland obtained more land by helping speculators and the state. In early 1788, Kirkland urged the Oneidas to lease almost all of their lands to the Livingston Lessees. His sermon insisted that a smaller reservation would enhance his concentration: "that his Thoughts were too extensive [because] their Country [was] so large that he could not collect himself." If the Oneidas lived more compactly, however, "his Ideas would be more confined and he would preach better." In addition to cash from Livingston, Kirkland secured from the Oneidas a square mile (640 acres) of land in the names of his twin sons, George and John. Then, in a letter to the state legislature, Kirkland praised the Livingston Leases by insisting that "good order" had prevailed at the Indian councils "and that the Indians were perfectly satisfied with the transactions."[26]

That summer, Kirkland helped Oliver Phelps and the Lessees to negotiate with the Buffalo Creek chiefs. Officially, Kirkland served as a Massachusetts state commissioner to certify fair treatment of the Indians, an appointment stipulating that Kirkland "should not be interested in the purchase of said lands directly or indirectly." But, as one of three mediators, Kirkland helped swing a deal that favored Phelps, who then bestowed 2,000 acres on the minister in "consideration of the services rendered to the purchasers of the western Land." A year later, Kirkland visited the Senecas, ostensibly to assess their receptivity to missionaries, but primarily to help Phelps reconcile the Indians to his surveys and to his (low) payment for their lands.[27]

By September 1788, Kirkland had deserted the Lessees to assist Governor Clinton and the state Indian commissioners at the Fort Schuyler treaty council with the Onondagas and Oneidas. Kirkland's timely conversion secured pay as an interpreter and agent plus state title to that square mile of land promised to his sons. To further reward Kirkland's "meritorious Services to the State," the state commissioners added another two square miles near Oriskany Creek. Become mercenary, Kirkland soon complained that the tract was mediocre. Citing his exertions for government, he begged for an additional 1,800 acres, which "would bind me, with an indissoluble bond, to seek the interest of the State." Thinking two square miles sufficient, the commissioners declined to augment their reward.[28]

Despite that one setback, by 1789 Kirkland and his sons had acquired at least 4,560 acres of Indian land. That acquisition excited harsh criticism from Rev. John Cozens Ogden, an Anglican, who assured an English correspondent, "In America we laugh at the pompous magazine reports of Mr. Kirkland's labors among the Indians. Has he told you how many thousand acres of land he has secured from them for his heirs?" Once a critic of Wheelock's land-grasping, Kirkland had become his mentor's landed disciple.[29]

In 1789, Kirkland moved into a new house near the reservation and on land he had once promised never to own. Preoccupied with that new property, he neglected his mission at Kanonwalohale. The Oneidas protested: "[We] Scarcely see him and every time he come[s] to us, he would only renew his promises, but seldom performed them. But when the great people of this state began to hold treaties with us for our Lands, he then attended faithfully in all the treaties—for which we are [uncertain] which of these two are his objects—attending Land or temporal affairs or Spiritual."[30]

Frustrated with their circumstances and disappointed by Kirkland, many Oneidas sought an alternative source of authority and inspiration. They longed for the French king to invigorate his promised protection by sending them a superintendent: a French Sir William Johnson. That longing seemed fulfilled by the arrival of Pierre (Peter) Penet.

PETER PENET

An adept performer, Penet possessed an exquisite sense of timing. He first appeared on his American stage in December 1775, arriving in Rhode Island by sea from St. Domingue (now Haiti), a French colony in the West Indies. Based in Nantes, a French seaport, Penet was a merchant who supplied manufactures and slaves to the plantations of St. Domingue. In the American Revolution, however, the slave-trader spied a golden opportunity to espouse the cause of freedom. He meant to profit as the first French merchant to reach the rebel colonies and to offer his services. Penet and a partner pretended to represent the French government, which thrilled the Americans who desperately needed munitions to fight the British. Penet seemed almost too good to be true: a well-connected French merchant committed to the republican revolution in America. Penet assured Congress that he had "no other Interest than to oblige your Nation, support Liberty, and sacrifice myself for your Country, which I regard as my own." Impressed, George Washington paid Penet's travel expenses to Philadelphia, where congressmen became similarly smitten. In March 1776, Penet sailed for France carrying their wish list for arms and ammunition. His return to France proved as timely as his arrival in America, for in May 1776 the king, Louis XVI, agreed secretly to supply war materials to sustain the American rebellion against the British. At that moment, Penet could tell the royal court exactly what the Americans wanted, which included, of course, working through him.[31]

Although he had not, in fact, been a French official, Penet had leveraged that claim to obtain an official mission from Congress. As a man of lowly origins aspiring to become a grand merchant, Penet understood the power of appearances. Citing his love for the Americans, he asked for an honorary appointment as an aide-de-camp to General Washington. He wanted no pay but coveted "the Honour to wear the uniform and the Ribbon." Eager to cultivate such a promising connection, Washington and Congress approved, adorning Penet with visual proof of his favor in America. Beginning in Rhode Island with nothing but his slick charm, he could reappear in France as George Washington's aide, and so, as the essential man to do business with the rebel colonies. Of course, his triumphant return astonished the other merchants of Nantes, who disdained Penet as an outsider and an upstart, a former gunsmith with excessive ambition. They considered Penet a big talker with too little capital to fulfill his lavish promises. But of course they were jealous men lacking his initiative and cunning. He, not they, had been the first French merchant to tap the promising American market for armaments. And they would never have thought to seek an American uniform and ribbon as Washington's aide. Here then at his American debut, Penet displayed a bold self-assurance that cultivated connections far beyond his means.[32]

But Penet soon revealed another recurrent pattern in his life: the exposure of his excessive claims and promises. During the winter of 1776–77, the American diplomats in Paris discovered that Penet lacked the capital to justify his grandiose taste in clothes, food, and wines, or to fulfill his contracts. "At the same time it is justice to say that he appears to be active, industrious and attentive to your Interests," Benjamin Franklin assured Congress. Even in discrediting Penet, Americans could not stop liking him. For there was something quite American about his social mobility, infectious optimism, and entrepreneurial energy. How could Franklin, a self-made man of so many self-serving poses, entirely disavow Penet?[33]

Although frozen out of business with Congress by the spring of 1777, Penet kept on pitching his French connections to American merchants and states, with surprising success. He dealt in the British ships and cargoes brought to Nantes as prizes by American privateers. Penet also imported Virginia tobacco in exchange for French firearms. Falling short on one contract, Penet infuriated the hot-tempered and arrogant Arthur Lee (later a federal commissioner at the Fort Stanwix council of 1784), but so did almost everyone else in France. Despite that feud, Penet became a favorite with Virginia's governors, first Patrick Henry and then Thomas Jefferson. They commissioned Penet to borrow £100,000 sterling and to build an arms factory near Richmond. Of course, he could neither raise the money for such a massive loan nor recruit the workmen for such an ambitious factory. Another Virginia agent in France, Philip Mazzei, characterized Penet as a "mixture of ambition and vanity, extravagance and generosity."[34]

In late 1782, Franklin sadly reported that Penet was "broke and absconded" to escape his many creditors. Franklin warned Congress, "We have put faith in every adventurer, who pretended to have influence here, and who when he arrived, had none but what your appointment gave him." Seeking German opportunity in French defeat, Penet fled to Hamburg, where he impressed the leading merchants by promising to open the United States to their trade. In early 1783, they eagerly wrote to Congress to plead their favor with "Mr. Penet who in Your Country is honoured with several Offices" and bears "the Character of an intelligent, skillful and . . . well disposed and Zealous Man."[35]

Later in 1783, Penet popped up in Schenectady, New York, where he purchased a substantial house and store for £1,050—a considerable sum, probably borrowed. Entering the fur trade with the Indians, Penet employed two agents, J. P. Lebon and Jean-François Perache. Applying the Marbois plan, they promoted French influence throughout Indian country by beginning with the Oneidas. The chiefs later recalled Penet's introductory speech: "You are now the first Nation I ent[e]red into . . . and for that Reason the westward and all the other Nations of Indians may come and confederate with you and with us." Working through the Oneidas, Penet sought (in Kirkland's words) "an agency or Superintendency over the five Nations, & finally to have the direction & management of all their Landed property."[36]

To prime the pump, during the summer of 1788, Penet sent corn and pork to feed the hungry Oneidas, asking nothing in return (for the moment). To distribute the provisions and his messages, Penet relied on Colonel Louis, a staunch Francophile. According to Kirkland, Penet even invited the Oneidas

> to make out a list of such articles of French manufactory as they wished & Penet would send it home to their Father the French King who would immediately comply with their utmost wishes. An extraordinary list was made out. . . . The feast was made, pipes & tobacco, [and] a kegg of Rum provided.

Like Sir William Johnson, Penet knew the power of theatrical generosity to cultivate Iroquois longing. But before marking this all down to Indian credulity, bear in mind that Penet had done exactly the same to Congress in 1775, procuring their devotion by promising to bear a wish list of munitions to the surprisingly generous French king. In 1788 the Oneidas were no more foolish than George Washington and Benjamin Franklin had been during their own period of desperate need and desire.[37]

After introducing himself, Penet shared his secret with the Oneidas. He represented the French king and the Marquis de Lafayette as their superintendent for Indian affairs in North America. In that role, Penet promised to fulfill an Oneida dream:

> I come not to defraud you about your Lands (as your Brothers the Americans have done already to you these many times) but I am come here to do you good and make you sensible of what you have already

done to yourselves. But if you don't mind what I say to you, your Brothers the Americans will take all your Lands away in a few Days; but if you will obey me you'll flourish & be the happiest People in America.

At last, the Oneidas would receive justice from a powerful patron, who would restore something like Sir William's Line of Property: "The King of France, their old Father, would lift up a Cudgel & say to Congress . . . here is the boundary line betwixt you & the Indians, my dear Children."[38]

The Lessee crisis of 1788 strengthened Penet's hand with the Oneidas and with New York State. During the spring and summer, the state agent John Tayler relied on Penet to persuade the Oneidas, and especially Colonel Louis, to renounce the Livingston Lease. Thereafter, the Oneidas primarily credited Penet, rather than the governor, for rescuing them from the Lessees. As Penet soared in Oneida estimation, Kirkland plunged, blamed for helping Livingston to deceive them. "They have discovered his Views and despise him," Tayler reported. Receiving "abusive treatment" from angry Oneidas that spring, Kirkland avoided Kanonwalohale for most of the ensuing six months. Penet happily filled the vacuum.[39]

In September, the Fort Schuyler council became Penet's victory tour. The Oneidas chose his favorites, Peter Otsequette and Colonel Louis, to negotiate with the governor. Ultimately, the Oneidas accepted the state's terms because Penet promised to reveal "the great secrets of all the advantages arising from the Treaty . . . , which are many, and so beneficial for your Interest and future happiness, as never before was granted or made known to any Indian nation on the Continent." He referred to their new authority to lease their reservation's southern tier, which promised to generate a substantial revenue for the Oneidas.[40]

At the Fort Schuyler council, Penet benefited from the presence of the French minister to the United States, the Comte de Moustier, who had replaced Marbois but who offered no improvement in American eyes. James Madison complained that Moustier was "a cunning disciple of Marbois' politics." In other words, Moustier also treated the United States as properly dependent on France as a sort of passive host for regrowing the French Empire in North America. Indeed, Moustier secretly urged his superiors to press Spain to relinquish the Louisiana Territory, which included New Orleans and the entire western bank of the Mississippi. Such a revived French Empire would keep the United States weak by hemming in westward expansion and by controlling American commerce on the Mississippi.[41]

Renewing the French Empire required rebuilding a network of Indian alliances through the Great Lakes to the Mississippi Valley, which explains Moustier's attendance at Fort Schuyler and his subsequent visit to Kanonwalohale. Kirkland concluded, "They appear to me to be playing the same game over with the Americans since the peace, which they did with the British, at the Close of the French War." Here Kirkland echoed Sir William Johnson's theory that covert French messages had stirred up Pontiac's Rebellion around the Great Lakes in 1763. Although Moustier did not aspire to drench the American frontier in blood, he did wish to prepare for future contingencies, including the reacquisition of Louisiana from Spain. Of course, this French ambition challenged the American determination to control all communications with Indians within the republic's boundaries.[42]

During the council, the minister conspicuously treated Penet as a trusted confidant. That November, Penet shared with the Oneidas a letter from Moustier addressed to him as the "agent general" for Indian affairs. No forgery by Penet, an official copy survives in the archives of the French foreign service. For once, Penet really did have something of an official appointment.[43]

By accepting the Fort Schuyler Treaty, the Oneidas sought to tether New York State to their French alliance. At the close of the conference, Good Peter announced that thereafter all dealings between the state and the Oneidas should flow through their "Father":

> When our Business is compleated and we take Leave of each other, whatever we have to say to you, we will always communicate to you through our Father the French Gentleman (pointing to Mr. Peter Penet), and we request that you'll make him the Channel of Communication of whatever you have to say to us. He is a just and righteous Man; he will deceive us in Nothing, but will always declare to us the very Truth; had it not been for him we should have been ruined.

They hoped that the treaty had placed the Oneidas *and* New York on a par by subordinating both to the French king. Good Peter assured Governor Clinton: "You also my Brother have partaken of the Advantages of an Alliance with that Nation equally with us the Oneidas, his Children." As French children, the Oneidas became elevated to New York's equals, rescued from languishing as its dependents.[44]

Oneida gratitude promised to enrich Penet. To reward "his Benevolence and Services," the Oneidas stipulated that the state grant him a tract of 100 square miles from their cession north of Oneida Lake. Penet promised to recruit 10,000 French emigrants to settle that tract. This promise appealed to the Oneidas, who considered the French the best of all potential neighbors. Governor Clinton, the state Indian commissioners, and the legislature all signed off on this extraordinarily large grant, which attested to Penet's importance. Never before had, and never again would, the state give so much land to a single culture-broker. Compare, for example, Penet's 100 square miles to Samuel Kirkland's mere 3 and you have a measure of their relative importance to the Oneidas and to the state in 1788.[45]

Naturally, Kirkland resented his eclipse by a facile French newcomer who had never done hard service as an Indian missionary:

> But *Penet's* art & address & dissimulation exceeded any Person I ever knew or heard of who had ever any connexion with Indians. By his insinuating manners & almost bewitching *speeches* he soon gained over & compleatly secured most of the Influential characters among the Oneidas.

Kirkland lost even his most able and trusted Oneida allies, Good Peter and Skenandon, to Penet's charm. Long a staunch supporter of Kirkland's Protestant mission, Good Peter astonished the minister by embracing the Catholic priest introduced by Penet during the following spring: "*Good Peter* was so hoodwinked by Penet that he became for a few weeks a curate & servant & Carrier to this Priest—waited upon him every Sabbath morning & carried his images & pontifical Robes to the Church & then carried them back after service." Good Peter could support whatever form of Christianity best promised to unify and to benefit the Oneidas. His consistency lay in his Oneida nationalism rather than in any Christian partisanship.[46]

PLANS

In October, during a Kirkland absence, Penet visited Kanonwalohale to convene the Oneida chiefs in council. He presented a plan for their reform initiated by Moustier. While pursuing French influence and personal gain, Moustier and Penet also nurtured a romantic fondness for the Oneidas as precious children long abused by greedy Americans. The two Frenchmen aspired to rescue and uplift the Oneidas by healing their bitter divisions over land controversies, by reducing their destructive consumption of alcohol, and by promoting their adoption of a European-American mode of agriculture. In an introductory speech on October 19, Penet promised "to make you a great and happy People for ever. I say you will cause all the Nations of the World to admire and rejoice at your prosperity." Here was a heady prospect for a people so discouraged by their diminishing circumstances.[47]

The Penet plan developed Oneida concepts, particularly the importance of clans, the desire to lease for a progressive income, and the drive to retrieve their people scattered to the west. But the plan also promoted Euro-American concepts of bourgeois morality, private property, patriarchal families, and institutional government. Adopting a premise long pushed by the Oneidas, Penet began, "I did look upon you as a Rich people in Lands, but not to your advantage, for you were not your own Masters, either to sell, or hire out, but to your own hurt." They should, he argued, authorize Peter Otsequette and Colonel Louis to survey their reservation bounds and to manage their property. The southern tier, four miles wide, would be leased to settlers to generate a rent to support a new national government for the Oneidas. Additional lands would also be subdivided into lots and rented to settlers for the benefit of particular Oneida families.[48]

The plan also institutionalized an Oneida government, a "Grand Council" of nine chiefs, consisting of two sachems and one war chief from each of the three clans (Bear, Wolf, and Turtle). The councillors would annually explain their decisions to a "Great Assembly" of everyone in the Oneida nation. That Great Assembly had the power to overturn council actions and to choose new councillors for the next year. Endowed by rents for some of their land, this new government would frustrate state efforts to divide the Oneidas along the traditional fault lines of matrons, warriors, and sachems. Of course, the plan concluded by appointing Penet "our true and trusty friend, adopted and chosen Agent forever: to act for us, and for the good and happiness of our nation."[49]

After deliberating for a week, most of the Oneida chiefs and matrons approved the plan on October 25. Triangulating between New York and France, the Oneidas sent one copy to Governor Clinton and another to the Comte de Moustier. The latter wrote to applaud the Oneidas. We do not know Clinton's reaction, but he could not have been pleased to find Penet standing between the state and a more unified Oneida nation. To alert other outsiders, Penet published the plan in at least one newspaper. Anyone seeking a lease of Oneida lands would have to deal with him.[50]

The conventional view interprets this plan as no more than Penet's scam to acquire Oneida land. Looked at more closely, however, the plan reveals a utopian ambition and complexity that could only complicate a mere scheme to defraud. By proposing radical cultural reforms, the plan challenged Iroquoian traditions, which promised to generate resistance. To help the Indians defend their interests in a changing world, Penet sought to narrow the cultural gap between the Oneidas and their settler counterparts. By closely regulating family relations and inheritance, the plan promoted the sort of parental power routine in the settler world but anathema to Indians. Furthermore, to enforce family reform the plan proposed a coercive government, long a great fear of native peoples (witness the assassination of the powerful Onondaga chief Captain Sturgeon in 1787). The Grand Council would appoint a monitor "to overlook the children in town, and see that, in general, they behave well to their parents and superiors." That monitor would also enforce a prohibition against the possession and sale of alcohol on the reservation—a very hard and dangerous job among a people often visited by predatory traders and land speculators.[51]

The council would also fund a school "in the English tongue," which challenged the traditional Oneida preference for learning literacy in their own language, from a fear that English would corrode their culture and reveal their secrets to outsiders. Penet even proposed to send six promising young men "to travel abroad, perhaps, two to England, two to France, and two to some parts of the neighboring states, . . . to learn not only the languages, but to observe their ways and manners." In sum, Penet wanted more than Oneida land; he wanted to be their Father, reshaping them with firm benevolence. More than disingenuous means to a deceptive end, the plan represented Penet's and Moustier's fantasies of paternal power.[52]

Their plan expressed the optimism of the eighteenth-century French Enlightenment, which considered human nature as innately positive and readily improved once rescued from the constraints of irrational tradition. Penet's plan also anticipated the celebrated cultural reforms promoted a decade later by the Seneca prophet Handsome Lake. He too exhorted the Iroquois to adopt private property, patriarchal families, and bourgeois morality to preserve native autonomy and prosperity in a changing world. But Handsome Lake enjoyed far more enduring success by casting cultural change in a religious form. Unlike Penet's secular and rational program, Handsome Lake attached his innovations to the renewal of ancient rituals long neglected by the Six Nations. Moreover, he experienced supernatural visions that demanded innovations but cast them as traditional retrenchment. Lacking similar endorsement from the spirit world, Penet's secular utopia could not survive the factional tensions that it was supposed to transcend.[53]

DIVISIONS

Kirkland and Penet seemed to take turns at Kanonwalohale; as one departed, the other arrived, the two never apparently directly confronting each other. After the October 19–25 deliberations, Penet headed to New York City to consult with Moustier. A month later, Kirkland returned to rally support. Recognizing Kirkland's abilities and external influence, the Oneidas could not bring themselves completely to renounce him even for Penet. During the imperial wars between France and Britain, the Iroquois had developed a perverse strength from factional divisions. By cultivating varying external patrons, and playing them off against one another, these factions provided options for relatively weak peoples surrounded by powerful rivals. This tradition persisted in the competition between Penet and Kirkland for the souls and lands of the Oneidas. Although the Oneidas hoped that Penet could fulfill his promises, many hedged their bets by retaining Kirkland as an alternative Father. As in previous conflicts, it was best to preserve both options and to wait and see how power played out externally, rather than to invest all hopes in a single patron.[54]

The simple explanation advanced by Kirkland and accepted by historians has been that he derived support from the warriors while Penet relied upon the sachems. Indeed, this stark polarity has been invoked as the consistent explanation for all Oneida divisions during the second half of the eighteenth century. But close examination reveals more volatility and complexity. War chiefs and sachems were not stable categories. The most accomplished war chiefs became sachems later in life, as did Good Peter and Skenandon. Moreover, rivalries within each category encouraged alliances of convenience with leaders in the other. On no major issue—Kirkland's mission, the Patriot revolution, the Livingston Lease, or the Penet plan—did all of the sachems unite against all of the war chiefs. Instead, every controversy rearranged congeries of support and opposition, with a mix of warriors and sachems on each side.[55]

There was a kernel of truth to the old explanation, for Penet's plan did mandate twice as many sachems as warriors on the governing council. And the plan's supporters featured the premier sachems, including Good Peter, Skenandon, Beech Tree, and Blacksmith. But the plan also initially enjoyed support from most of the leading warriors, including Peter Otsequette, Colonel Louis, and Colonel Honyery. Of course, the plan's chief early critic, Captain Jacob Reed, was a warrior. Smarting from his disgrace for helping the Lessees, Reed sought to recoup his influence and reputation by supporting Kirkland against Penet.[56]

Particular sachems and warriors could change their minds in response to changing circumstances. The key variable could be as simple as whether Penet or Kirkland was then present at Kanonwalohale. In October 1788, almost all of the Oneida leaders supported Penet's plan. A month later, however, most praised Kirkland's return and attended his Sabbath services. When core members of "the French party" blasted his sermons as insulting to Indians, Good Peter and Beech Tree vindicated Kirkland, although both continued to support Penet's plan. And even Kirkland sometimes noted that the dispute did not always neatly divide warriors from sachems. During the spring of 1791, he observed that clan lines had become the most important division, pitting the sachems and war chiefs of the Bear and Turtle clans against their Wolf counterparts.[57]

In the spring of 1789, Moustier and Penet escalated the confrontation by introducing a Catholic priest, Father Perrot, to the reservation. Perrot set up his chapel at Lake Oneida, probably on the farm of Colonel Louis. Penet apparently hoped that a French priest would provide a religious alternative that could unite the traditionalist and Christian Oneidas. Instead, Perrot produced a tripartite split in spiritual allegiances. Although Good Peter briefly endorsed Perrot, most of the Oneidas balked when the priest expected them to clear his land and build his house.[58]

At the same time, Governor Clinton turned against Penet. His growing ambition alarmed the governor, who meant to manage the Oneidas. In September 1789, Clinton sent a pointed message to them:

> Mr. Penet is only to be considered among you as an adventuring Merchant, pursuing his own private Interest. He holds no Office, nor does he sustain any public Character in this Country; he attempts to deceive you, therefore, when he says he is sent by the King of France and the Marquis Dela Fayette to transact Business with you. You ought not to listen to his Speeches or pay any regard to his Dreams.

Further dashing Oneida hopes, Clinton insisted that the French king had "nothing to do with any particular State or the Indians residing within it." As wards of the state, rather than allies of the French, the Oneidas would suffer a great deflation in status and prospects.[59]

In addition to the controversial priest and the governor's denunciation, Penet's Oneida critics seized upon his failure to deliver the long list of promised presents. They dismissed Penet's excuse that the ships bearing gifts had been delayed or lost at sea. Many Oneidas also balked at Penet's plan, with its daunting expectations for family, economic, and political reform. That summer and fall, business took Penet away to the West Indies, while Kirkland returned to Kanonwalohale—a combination that eroded Penet's influence. Nor did it bode well that Penet had sold both his Schenectady mansion and his 100-square-mile tract to an American land speculator. To the Oneidas' dismay, callous Americans—rather than generous Frenchmen—would settle Penet's northern tract.[60]

Penet also lost his official support from the French Father. Roiled by revolution in 1789, the French government had neither the means nor the resolve to pursue ambitious projects in North America. Moreover, Moustier had worn out his American welcome, primarily by openly living and traveling with his sister-in-law and mistress, Madame de Bréhan. The Oneidas called her "our Mother," but elite American women considered her a harlot. Frozen out of polite society, she soured her paramour's mind against all things American—especially the wretched food. Even their friend Thomas Jefferson recognized that Moustier had lost his effectiveness as a diplomat. Hints to Lafayette invited Moustier's return to France at the end of 1789. [61]

By late 1789, most of the warriors and some of the sachems had disavowed their agent general. But a defiant minority clung to Penet's promises long after their expiration date. Colonel Louis threatened that his Oneida opponents would receive none of the abundant presents expected when Penet returned. Colonel Louis angrily added, "You think you are free People, but I say you are Slaves to the State of New York. . . . Let your Minister, Mr. Kirkland, prove that you are free." For the French party, Penet represented the last, desperate chance for the Oneidas to escape an enslaving domination by New York; but Kirkland's supporters saw Penet as the greater of two evils. [62]

Penet deepened the division by pressing the Oneidas for more land. In 1789, he procured another 5 square miles by lease from a few sachems. His reservation lands included Kanaghsoraga, described by Kirkland as "the best land in all their territory." Formerly a substantial Tuscarora village, Kanaghsoraga had never fully recovered from its wartime evacuation because most of the former inhabitants remained near Niagara. Located on the main east-west path through the Oneida country, Kanaghsoraga promised to become a prosperous way station on the major corridor for settlers bound westward. To request the tract, Penet cited a dream, an irresistible claim in Iroquois culture. And he promised that the tract would permit his relocation from Schenectady to live "where I can keep my eye continually upon my children, and watch over their interest, as my intention is to promote their happiness." [63]

But by procuring the Kanaghsoraga lease from some of the chiefs, Penet overplayed his hand, offending especially the warriors from Oriske village led by the redoubtable Colonel Honyery. Facing eviction by a company of land speculators, who included the governor, the Oriske villagers coveted Kanaghsoraga for their new home. In the spring of 1791, they appealed to the governor, who was happy to evict Penet's agents, both to discredit Penet and to facilitate the Oriske relocation. Because Kanaghsoraga fell within the reservation core, where the Oneidas were debarred by the Treaty of Fort Schuyler from leasing to whites, the state could legally roust Penet's tenants. A posse led by Herkimer County sheriff William Colbrath did so in the fall. [64]

Despite the Kanaghsoraga setback, Penet tried yet again to procure Oneida land. In October 1791, he leased the entire four-mile-wide tract on the southern margin of the reservation. Only nine chiefs marked this lease, but they included Good Peter. Penet planned to sublet to settlers who would pay him rent and who would enhance the value of the land by clearing the forest and cultivating the soil. He promised to deliver to the Oneidas, during the spring of 1792, a dozen oxen and six plows, to help them conduct agriculture in the settler manner. After five years, Penet would begin to pay $250 annually to the Oneidas. And when the lease expired in twenty-one years, he orally promised a $10,000 payment to renew it (although he neglected to include this promise in the written lease).[65]

But Penet defaulted on the lease by never paying the Oneidas. Instead, he fled from his impatient creditors, hastening to the West Indies, never to return. Lavish living had once again compounded debts that ruined Penet's latest grandiose scheme. But he persisted in constructing illusions in the hope that they might yet become real. At St. Domingue, Penet sold Oneida lands to dupes impressed by his grand map displaying an imaginary fortified town, called Fleurville, on the northern shore of Oneida Lake. Meanwhile, Father Perrot had abandoned the priesthood to become a hired laborer among the nearby settlers. The last, lingering vestige of Penet's ambitious scheme was his bed left at Skenandon's house, where it accommodated visitors passing through the reservation.[66]

Penet's debts and evasions undermined his utopian dream of reuniting the Oneidas in prosperity and power. By crystallizing and then dashing Oneida fantasies of rescue by a perfectly benevolent king, Penet deepened their despair. He left a legacy of bitter divisions as Oneida factions traded recriminations. The French party blamed their foes for driving away Penet, their last best hope, while Kirkland's party blasted Penet's friends as credulous fools. In 1791, a young sachem, Captain John (Onondiyo), lamented, "We are at the very brink of ruin." Kirkland sadly explained,

> I find that when Indians are at variance with *Indians* & a deep rooted mutual prejudice has taken place, their dispositions are inexorable, & their spirit of resentment towards each other, much more keen than when offended with a white person. This wrath & strife . . . originated from the remains of the french party, whose minds are exceedingly imbittered by frequent disappointment.

That rancor abated a little in early 1792, when, to Kirkland's pleasant surprise, Colonel Louis abruptly moved north to Akwesasne, a Mohawk community in the St. Lawrence Valley.[67]

DISTANCE

After Penet's defeat, Kirkland again neglected Kanonwalohale to focus on his property a dozen miles to the east. He erected a genteel house boasting a columned portico and a glittering Palladian window. In January 1796, Kirkland married Mary Donnelly, the best friend of his beloved first spouse,

Jerusha. In June, Rev. Jeremy Belknap visited and reported, "He has a large, handsome new house, nearly finished, into which he proposes to move in a few days; thirty acres of wheat growing, besides corn and grass; and thirty head of cattle." Belknap marveled at the enhanced value of Kirkland's lands obtained eight years before: "It was then supposed to be worth not much more than 100 Dollars. It is now worth not less than [$]20,000, or 10 Dollars per acre." That year, an ambitious young lawyer wooed Kirkland's daughter for more than romance: "It is one of the most agreeable Families I ever knew. The old Gentleman is a man of large fortune. I believe him to be worth £2,000 . . . & lives like a Prince." According to a 1799 assessment, among the 803 taxpayers of the town of Paris, only one topped Kirkland's property worth of $8,318. The starving missionary of the 1760s had become a landed prince of the 1790s.[68]

Some fellow ministers faulted Kirkland's shifting priorities and new wealth. By acquiring the large property and worldly values of a gentleman, Kirkland forsook the evangelical purpose and humble means of a dedicated missionary. A minister friend gently warned Kirkland

> of the danger to one's spiritual interest which naturally arises from large
> and extensive business and connexions with the great men of the world,
> whose hearts and views center in present things. And the danger I think

Samuel Kirkland's mansion. (From Walter Pilkington, ed., *The Journals of Samuel Kirkland* [1980]. Courtesy of the Hamilton College Library Archives.)

is that our feelings, our manners, and our reasonings may be assimilated to theirs.

Rejecting such criticism as "the inveterate shafts of envy," Kirkland attributed his good fortune entirely to Divine Providence: "It is nevertheless true that I have considerable property in new, uncultivated land which I must acknowledge as the bounty, the gift of kind heaven! Unsought and undeserved & unmeritted by me." But of course he was far too modest, for he had worked to part that land from the Oneidas.[69]

By forsaking residence at Kanonwalohale, Kirkland hoped to reduce the pressing demands of Indian charity incumbent upon a missionary. But a dozen miles failed to keep away mobile natives who expected traditional hospitality from Kirkland. He complained,

> It matters not what Tribe an Indian belongs to, nor from what parts, or distance he may have travelled, if he can find my house, he feels he has found a *friend* to *Indians* & seems to feel almost as much at *home*, as if at his own house. They all know that I am so well acquainted with the native hospitality of Indians, that I *can't* be so uncivil & rude as to ask an Indian *if he is hungry* (always taking that for granted) but [instead that I will] immediately set before him such as I have for his refreshment.

Built to distance himself from his penurious past in Indian villages, his new mansion instead became a magnet for hungry natives.[70]

Kirkland felt trapped in a paradox generated by his residence on the frontier between a capitalist and a traditional society. He exploited his Indian influence to procure native lands to develop as his own capital, but those Indians gave him that land to pin Kirkland down as their asset, as their safety net. In return for their gifts, they expected succor from his prospering farm and from his connections to governments, speculators, and missionary societies. Those expectations sapped the private property that Kirkland tried to accumulate to buttress his own position in a competitive, commercial society. But if he drove away supplicants (as so many settlers did), Kirkland would sacrifice his special influence among the Indians, which would dry up his value to the great men of New York. That would sacrifice his missionary salary, his cash payments as a state or speculator agent, and any prospect of further gifts of native land. But Kirkland also gave because he had partially internalized the ethos of sharing food after thirty years of living with the Indians.[71]

In a recurrent cycle, Kirkland sought charitable means by procuring more

native land for his patrons among the speculators. In early 1791, after distributing a recent cash windfall to distressed Oneidas, Kirkland explained:

> I received a compensation from some gentlemen in the state of New
> York for some extra services rendered to them (not immediately con-
> nected with the duties of my mission nor interfering with them) which
> furnished me with the means of affording [the Indians] this comfort &
> help.

By helping the great men of New York, Kirkland procured cash that he
partly bestowed in charity on Indians, who needed help more than ever as
land speculation and settlement consumed their domain. To remain their
generous Father, he needed patronage from land speculators like Peter
Smith.[72]

PETER SMITH

A fur trader and storekeeper based at Utica, Smith was short and stout, with
a curved nose and sharp, penetrating eyes. Relentlessly focused on making
and saving money, he dressed plainly and lived frugally. Cunning, tough, and
uncompromising, Smith "grew wealthy very rapidly," according to James
Kent, who considered him "very avaricious." An antiquarian told a "characteristic anecdote" of Peter Smith. One day an aspiring land speculator lodged
with Smith and praised a tract of land, near Oneida Lake, that could be procured from some New York City capitalists for a bargain price. The next
morning, a Sunday, the guest was surprised by Smith's absence. Honoring
the Sabbath, the guest lingered for the day before resuming his journey to
New York City to conclude his bargain. Of course, the poor fool arrived a
day too late, for the capitalists had just sold the coveted tract to Peter
Smith.[73]

In 1792, Smith married Elizabeth Livingston and took in her younger
brother, James, Jr., as a clerk. But the marriage soured as Smith hounded her
poor brother and had him jailed for debt. Even Smith's attorney sympathized
with the young man, reporting: "Your harshness and severity, he insists, from
an early period of your copartnership, your unreasonable requisitions of
labor, and monopolization of advantages have contributed to render his situation unpleasant & his exertions unprofitable and finally have been the parent of his ruin." The attorney warned that further imprisonment "only serves
to embitter the feelings of his relations," including, of course, Elizabeth.
Never one to relinquish an advantage, Smith kept young Livingston in
prison until promised $2,000 to cover questionable debts. When James was

slow to pay, Smith badgered his wife, who responded, "You write so cruel to me that I am almost bereaved of my senses." After years of hearing her family derided as "beggars and thieves," Elizabeth pleaded, "Don't try to make me hate them any more. . . . I must Conclude with the words of Job and curse the day I was born."[74]

So different was Smith's treatment of his Oneida customers bearing furs to his store. A keen student of opportunity, Smith carefully learned some of their language and many of their customs. Although considered a hard-nosed creditor by fellow New Yorkers, he shrewdly indulged his Oneida debtors, cultivating their sense of obligation. In October 1792, Smith traveled to Kanonwalohale to host a dinner for the chiefs. Distributing rum and tobacco, he reminded them, "My house has always been Open to you, my Liquors & Provisions free." Now Smith wanted a favor: a twenty-one-year lease to the lands that Penet had leased a year before. In return for the reservation's four-mile-wide southern tier (45,793 acres), Smith offered $400 on June 1, 1793, followed by $200 for each of the next two years, and $250 annually thereafter until the lease's expiration. He also promised collateral benefits especially appealing to the Oneidas. Smith would sublet only to "peaceable, quiet settlers," and he would establish a large store with low prices for coveted trade goods—his equivalent of Penet's wish list.[75]

Leaving nothing to chance, Smith practiced the tried and true technique of covertly enticing the key culture-brokers in Oneida country. For help in securing the lease, Smith promised present credit and future payments to Captain Jacob Reed, James Dean, Ebenezer Caulkins, and Samuel Kirkland. Four months later, Reed assured Smith,

> It must be very well known to you that promise you made to me that if the Assembly should Confirm your Lease, then you would reward me for what I have done in aiding you to obtain the Lease of our nation. . . . But pray my *friend* don't mention it to no Living Soul . . . But you keep it all in Secrecy.

But Smith proved an unreliable debtor to his secret allies. Eight years later, Kirkland had to remind Smith,

> I have made myself the more easy on acc[oun]t of my small debt to you, from the consideration of *your* soliciting my influence with the Oneidas in behalf of your purchase or lease of land. Were Jacob Reed & Capt. John living (& were it proper to make public) they could witness to my friendly aid & repeated exertions in your favor, even to the risk of my comfort, if not character.

In 1793, Dean and Kirkland had avoided being seen "in private conversation with you, lest it should give such umbrage as wholly to defeat our good wishes for your success."[76]

After tentatively agreeing to the lease in October 1792, the chiefs formally marked the document in January 1793. As with Penet's lease, the primary lessors were sachems—including Skenandon, Beech Tree, and Captain John—but Smith also had a staunch supporter in Captain Reed, a war chief. But Smith's lease also generated opposition, this time led by the war chiefs Colonel Honyery and Captain Peter, the talented but violent son of Good Peter (who had died in 1792). In February and again in May, Oneida warriors intercepted Smith's surveyors, forcing them to desist by smashing their compass and breaking their chain. The opponents begged the state legislature to void the lease: "Brothers you told us that you would protect us. We depend on you for your Protection."[77]

Meanwhile, the Oneida majority also petitioned the legislature, seeking state regulation to ensure that Smith kept his promises. They sought "free liberty to lease our land in such manner & form and to such persons as shall be most for our interests as a people: but we do not wish for liberty to sell it by any means for we think that would tend to ruin us as a nation." Lacking sufficient learning "to make bargains about land," they asked the state to "appoint some good men as agents to assist us in leasing our land that we may not be deceived." By this petition, the Oneidas sought their rights under the Treaty of Fort Schuyler, which obligated the state to "make Provision by Law to compel the Lessees to pay the Rents, and in every other Respect to enable the Oneidas and their Posterity to have the full Benefit of their Right so to make Leases and to prevent Frauds on them respecting the same."[78]

Instead of honoring that leasing clause, the state's leaders again took advantage of a controversial Oneida land transaction. As with John Harper's deed in 1784 and the Livingston Lease of 1788, so too with the Peter Smith lease of 1793: the state legislators exploited Oneida divisions over a private land deal to seek a permanent cession for the state. If the Smith lease was a bad deal for the Indians, at least it would expire in twenty-one years, restoring Oneida ownership. By contrast, a land cession to the state would endure. On March 11, 1793, in response to the Oneida petition for legal assistance in leasing, the legislators instead authorized a new bid to buy Indian lands. Rather than permit a negotiated price, they set a maximum of a $5 increase in annuity for every square mile (640 acres) surrendered. Given the 600 Oneidas on the reservation, they would have to sell 120 square miles (nearly one-third of their remaining land) to increase the annuity by just one dollar per capita.[79]

Rather than support Oneida leasing, the state legislators preferred an Oneida land cession for three reasons. First, the state leaders anticipated trouble and cost from policing Smith's tenants to satisfy Oneida complaints. Second, the state stood to profit immensely by cheaply acquiring Oneida lands in bulk for retail at a substantial markup to settlers. Third, those leaders wanted to improve road and canal transportation through the Oneida reservation to reach the growing settlements in western New York. That east-west link would promote economic development and draw still more settlers westward. Because the Oneidas balked at laboring to improve their paths into roads, the state wanted to introduce settlers along the right-of-way through the reservation.[80]

NEW FATHER

As commissioners, the legislature appointed General John Cantine, and the surveyor general, Simeon DeWitt. Although also empowered to negotiate land cessions from the Onondagas and Cayugas, DeWitt deemed the Oneidas "the most important nation as to Numbers and the Magnitude of our Object." To assure success, Cantine and DeWitt lined up the influence of Dean and Kirkland, whose "connection & acquaintance with the Indian[s] are well known and whose fidelity in cooperating with us left us no doubt that every thing that could consistently be done was done to obtain the Object of the State." Confident of success, the commissioners held their council at Kanonwalohale, to avoid the higher costs of drawing and supporting large numbers of Indians within the settlements. Thereby, however, the commissioners forsook the advantages of hosts, which had proved so powerful at Fort Herkimer in 1785 and Fort Schuyler in 1788. The fall timing also favored autonomy by the Oneidas, who were well fed by the recent harvest.[81]

The council opened on November 4, 1793. DeWitt began by praising New York's superior reliability as a purchaser: "for the State always pays its debts punctually, but individuals often refuse till they are compelled by our Laws." This, of course, missed the point that the Oneida had sought just such a law to compel private individuals to pay their debts as tenants.[82]

The Oneidas recoiled from the state's bid to translate their leasing initiative into another land cession. Captain Reed responded, "Brothers, We were misled in the petition & therefore sink it in the Earth & thus annihilate it." Following up, Captain Peter was unusually blunt and sarcastic, reminding DeWitt and Cantine that in 1788 the governor had promised "that no application should be made again to us for 100s of Years. Perhaps we have misapprehended you, that you meant nights instead of years." Captain Peter concluded, "It is our land and we have a right to do with it as we please."[83]

But DeWitt refused to take no for an answer, tenaciously treating the Oneida petition for a lease law as a "binding" request for a state land purchase: "Whenever any of us signs a petition, we consider ourselves under obligation—we cannot say we annihilate it." He added the standard warning that the Oneidas risked alienating the state legislators. While conceding that individuals often did cheat the Indians, DeWitt insisted that state commissioners always acted honorably: "It is beneath the dignity of the State to use any intrigue to deceive and cheat you out of your lands." Oneida complaints of state mistreatment were, he insisted, base ingratitude given "the destitute condition you would probably now be in had it not been for the paternal interference of the State." That paternalism refused to permit the Oneidas to lease land to individuals: "Would it be in your interest that the State should withdraw its attention from the concerns of Your Nation and leave you to dispose of your lands to whom and in what manner they please and say we care not for our brothers, let them get rid of their property as soon as they please?" But, of course, the Oneidas had not asked to be abandoned; they had petitioned the legislature for three trustees to oversee a twenty-one-year lease.[84]

The commissioners' persistence irritated the Oneidas. In reply Captain John emphasized the state's bleak record of breaking the wartime promises to protect the Oneida lands:

> Now it appears you were very fortunate, you conquered your enemies with our assistance and obtained your Independence and are now rich and happy, as you yourselves confess. Now let us ask you one question. Where are those mighty benefits, those great privileges which we were to receive at the close of the war? It is true that you have gotten almost all our land [for] merely nothing in comparison to the real worth of it, by which means you have enriched yourselves. Was this the[n] the mighty benefit you meant to confer on us? To root us out of the country and reduce us to nothing? We have but a little land left, and if this is gone we shall have nothing, we shall weigh nothing in the scale of nations, and you will pay us no kind of respect. It does not appear that you care anything for us but to get our land. Please to point out to us what advantages we have received for all our sufferings and losses during the late war.

Rejecting the alleged distinction between private speculators and state commissioners, Captain Peter highlighted their connection: "Brothers, It seems as if you wish to entrap us. It seems as if you privately sent out people to bargain with us to lead us into a snare and then you great men come forward & confirm it."[85]

To disrupt Oneida unity, DeWitt and Cantine privately appealed to some older sachems, but the warriors frustrated that nocturnal conference by appearing in numbers, to the commissioners' dismay. Moreover, DeWitt and Cantine exaggerated their sway over the older sachems. Skenandon confided to three French observers, "that his advice, and that of the old men, was to sell nothing, and that the Americans would never be satisfied until they had seized their last acre: that some drunken chiefs had been gained over, but that the great majority would hold fast."[86]

The Oneidas knew that the commissioners were not offering fair market value for the land. The commissioners reported that Captain Peter had observed that "if the Rent which we offered for their lands was a quarter of what our Citizens got for theirs, our proposal might perhaps merit their attention, but [instead] they were trifling to think of." Given that upstate New York landlords usually got $12.50 in annual rent for a new farm of 100 acres, if the state meant to pay fair market value, every 640 acres would have cost $80 in additional annuity. Instead, the legislature fixed its offer at one-sixteenth of that fair market value. Frustrated in their bid, the commissioners returned to Albany—the new state capital.[87]

Trying again, Governor Clinton invited a smaller Oneida delegation to visit Albany in the winter to discuss their lands. As state guests, they would be obligated to their hosts and removed from the scrutiny of their own people. And rather than dealing with mere commissioners, they would receive the governor's personal attention. On February 17, 1794, Clinton met the Oneida delegation in the Albany city hall. To Clinton's surprise, the chiefs did not budge. Captain Peter explained, "We tell you plainly that we are not Inclined to sell or lease any of our Lands, and that was our voice to your Chiefs last fall. . . . We mean to lay our bones where our forefathers' are laid and to keep our Country for our posterity." Unable to have his way this time, Clinton dissolved the council without an agreement.[88]

Something had changed when the Oneidas could openly defy the state commissioners and governor, not once but twice, and despite the influence of Dean and Kirkland. The Oneidas looked to the revived federal government as an ally against New York. In 1787–89, the United States had adopted a new constitution that mandated a national government endowed with greater revenues and with potential power to control the states. In 1793, Captain Peter informed Cantine and DeWitt:

> The U.S. have planted the Tree of Peace in our village. They told us it should be a large, fine, shady tree & advised [us] to watch & cherish it, that this would be the fruit of our struggles [in] the last war. . . . but it seems as if you creep upon the Ground and endeavour to attack its roots and undermine it. . . . All you White People are wise to get lands. Here is P[eter] Smith creeping about us to get lands. He has imposed on us.

We wish now to let all proceedings respecting them to rest here. Be Obed[ien]t to your Great Chief George Washington.

Captain Peter then dramatically flourished a copy of the federal government's Indian Trade and Intercourse Act of 1793. That law mandated that no Indian land cession was valid unless authorized, supervised, and ratified by Congress and the president. Having lost their French Father in the Penet debacle, and Kirkland to his new estate, the Oneidas sought another father in President Washington.[89]

CHAPTER EIGHT

Chiefs

Cornplanter, by F. Bartoli, 1796. (Courtesy of the New-York Historical Society; 1867.314.)

O N JUNE 27, 1790, four settlers killed two Senecas hunting along Pine Creek in northern Pennsylvania. Samuel Doyle and the three Walker brothers—Benjamin, Henry, and Joseph—were hardworking and hard-drinking men of the frontier. The Pennsylvania authorities described the four as "brought up to boating and Farming" but "fond of Company and Strong Liquour." They had met the two Senecas at a local tavern on a break from their hunting in the nearby hills. The Walkers believed that the older Seneca, a chief in his fifties, had killed and scalped their father during the war. The intervening peace had not slaked their thirst for vengeance. That night, the four settlers surprised the sleeping hunters, killing the younger man with a tomahawk blow to the skull and the older with a gunshot to the head. The murderers secreted the dead Indians in the creek, weighted by a layer of stones.[1]

In early July, however, the corpses washed ashore, and people began to talk. The local settlers dreaded that Seneca warriors would seek an indiscriminate revenge. Raised on lurid tales of Indian atrocities, the settlers panicked and fled, vacating a seventeen-mile stretch along Pine Creek. Instead of arresting the suspects, however, the settlers helped them hide, while begging for Pennsylvania state militia to fight off the imagined savage horde. Rather than fight the Senecas, however, Pennsylvania's ruling council sought to arrest, try, convict, and execute the suspects. The council offered rewards totaling $800 for the arrest of the murderers, and sent a conciliatory message to the Seneca chiefs.[2]

But the Senecas were less interested in punishing the suspects than in covering the victims' graves. Their chiefs summoned Pennsylvania to send delegates with presents to the Tioga River "where you will meet the whole of the Tribe of the deceased, and all the Chiefs, and a number of Warriors of our nation, where we will expect you will wash away the Blood of your Brothers and Bury the Hatchet, and put it out of memory as it is yet sticking in our Head." To keep the peace, the Seneca chiefs needed presents for ceremonial distribution to the relatives of the dead. The Senecas also wanted a formal, public renewal of Pennsylvania's attention at the highest level: "Brothers, it is our great brother, your Governor, who must come to see us, as we will never bury the hatchet until our great brother himself comes & brightens the chain of friendship, as it is very rusty." Denied any public council with Pennsylvania since 1784, the Senecas felt neglected and slighted, which degraded the value of their relationship, emboldening frontier killers. Urging the Pennsylvanians to act quickly, the chiefs warned, "Our young warriors are very uneasy." At Canadaigua in August, Oliver Phelps confirmed the Seneca impatience, "I never saw them more enraged than they are at this time."[3]

Taking the hint, the Pennsylvania state legislature appropriated $266 for presents to cover the graves, but the governor asked the newly revived federal government to assume the more expensive responsibility of delivering the presents in a formal, public council attended by hundreds of Indians. President Washington quickly accepted the invitation as an opportunity to demonstrate federal supremacy in Indian affairs. He also hoped to build a more amicable relationship with the Six Nations by healing the strain wrought by the Treaty of Fort Stanwix in 1784 and by subsequent neglect.[4]

In council at Tioga Point in November, the Senecas met a federal commissioner, Timothy Pickering, rather than the governor of Pennsylvania. By teaching Pickering how to cover the graves of murdered Indians, the Senecas helped the federal government to assume the legacy of Sir William Johnson. By accepting Indian customary law, federal officials could assume the Covenant Chain alliance—subordinating the pretensions of New York that threatened both the Six Nations and the federal union.

FEDERALISTS

The new federal constitution mandated a national government with significant *potential* powers to control the states and to regulate individuals, an immense change from the weak confederation that had withered during the mid-1780s. But realizing that potential depended upon establishing precedents despite resistance from the states. The president favored consolidating national power, as did the vice president, John Adams, the secretary of the treasury, Alexander Hamilton, and the secretary of war, Henry Knox. But the cabinet also included a counterweight in favor of states' rights: the secretary of state, Thomas Jefferson. In Congress, a majority called themselves Federalists, to indicate support for a strong national government. During the early 1790s, an opposition gradually emerged under the name of Republicans (not to be confused with the modern party of that name) to suggest their greater devotion to popular government, which they identified with the states.[5]

To realize the nation's potential power, the Federalists needed to gain control over their long and troubled frontier. Henry Knox reported, "The United States have come into existence as a nation, embarrassed with a frontier of immense extent." The frontier arc from Georgia to Maine seemed to dwarf and menace the union of states huddled along the Atlantic seaboard. American settlers had thrust westward, breaching the Appalachians to settle in Tennessee, Kentucky, western Pennsylvania, and Iroquoia. But many easterners doubted the settlers' allegiance, fearing that they would secede to affiliate with the British or Spanish empires. In the lower Mississippi, the Spanish held New Orleans and contested the American claim to its southeastern frontier. Along the Great Lakes, the British clung to forts on the American side of the peace treaty line. Those forts supplied the Indians who resisted aggressive settlers in the Ohio Valley by inflicting defeats that embarrassed the federal government. Small wonder that Knox considered the American frontier to be "critically circumstanced."[6]

To win credibility, the federal government needed to gain control over its frontier. In the federal territory northwest of the Ohio River, the nation sought desperately needed revenue by selling land. In 1787, Congress sold

6.5 million acres primarily to two cartels of land speculators: the Ohio Company of Associates and the Scioto Company. In 1788, James Madison characterized "the Western territory" as potentially "a mine of vast wealth to the United States." Sales ground to a halt in 1788 because speculators could find few retail buyers willing to settle in a war zone. Instead of generating revenue, the region drained the republic's resources for military expeditions against the Indian confederates. From 1790 to 1796, the Ohio country war cost the United States $5 million, almost five-sixths of all federal expenditures for that period. Bleeding money, the United States needed a military victory and a peace treaty to resume land sales. The key was to impose federal control over both settlers and natives. Knox insisted that "Government must keep them both in awe by a strong hand, and compel them to be moderate and just."[7]

The surprising strength of the Indian confederation persuaded the Washington administration to revise the nation's frontier policy. The Federalists set aside the provocative conquest theory advanced by Congress at the end of the war: that by siding with the British the Indians had sacrificed their lands and must accept the dictates of their American conquerors. Operating on that theory, federal Indian commissioners had extorted land cessions from the western Iroquois at Fort Stanwix in 1784 and from the Ohio Valley nations at Fort McIntosh in 1785. Those treaties had infuriated the Indian confederates, who ravaged the new settlements intruding on their side of the Ohio River. To mollify the Indians, Knox conceded that they possessed "the right of the soil" and could not be justly dispossessed except by their own voluntary sale.[8]

As secretary of war, Knox was the key figure in designing and implementing the new Indian policy. The commander of artillery in the Continental Army during the war, Knox had won the friendship and patronage of George Washington. Gregarious, generous, garrulous, flamboyant, and imposing at nearly three hundred pounds, Knox was popular with the gentlemen and ladies of high society in Boston, New York, and Philadelphia. Determined to obscure his modest origins as a bookseller, Knox lived, a friend observed, "in the style of an English nobleman." Rejecting the egalitarian potential of the recent revolution, Knox meant to procure and to enjoy the social distinctions of the colonial elite—to prove to himself and to others that he belonged at society's pinnacle, as a member of a natural aristocracy. Posing as a "father of the people," Knox was a classic paternalist of the Federalist stripe. Distrusting settlers as vicious and turbulent, Knox possessed a patronizing sympathy for native peoples.[9]

To mollify the natives and to save federal money, Knox urged a new "conciliatory system . . . of managing the said Indians and attaching them to the

United States." He insisted that "both policy and justice" urged the new approach. Persisting in the old "system of coercion and oppression" cost too much, while "the blood and injustice which would stain the character of the nation, would be beyond all pecuniary calculation." But he calculated anyway. To defeat the Ohio Indians would require 2,500 soldiers at an annual cost of $200,000—"a sum far exceeding the ability of the United States to advance." By bestowing presents worth only $16,150, Knox hoped to buy a far cheaper peace.[10]

By favoring presents and diplomacy over war, the federal leaders embraced the British (and French) system that the Patriots had previously disdained as corrupt, irrational, and anachronistic. Knox concluded that giving annual presents "was the cheapest and most effectual mode of managing the Indians." But the Federalists disagreed over the proper sort of presents. Knox favored the traditional "practice of making the Indians presents of silver medals and gorgets, uniform clothing, and a sort of military commission," presents that preserved the Indians as martial allies. But Timothy Pickering urged a more transforming range of presents: farm tools and cattle. Rather than sustain the Indians as warriors, Pickering wanted to remake them into farmers in the American mold. In effect, Pickering favored a hybrid system that combined the imperial practice of giving presents with a new republican policy of accelerating Indians' cultural change. President Washington endorsed a mix of both sorts of presents.[11]

Federal leaders also embraced Sir William Johnson's dream of a comprehensive and effective boundary line separating the settler and the native worlds. Along that line, they hoped to interpose federal forts, soldiers, and officials. The new nation would realize its power by creating and controlling a middle zone inserted between settlers and Indians. Knox insisted that "the Indians would be convinced of the justice and good intentions of the United States, and they would soon learn to venerate and obey that power from which they derived security against the avarice and injustice of lawless frontier people."[12]

By controlling the frontier, federal officials meant to regulate the pace at which Indians receded and the settlers advanced. By controlling the settlers, the Federalists sought a moderate frontier expansion meant to strengthen the new nation's bonds. Dreading a violent, unregulated expansion as dissipating the republic's potential, the Federalists wanted to oblige common settlers to live in more cohesive and orderly communities dominated by a genteel elite.[13]

In the short run, the new policy spoke of moderation and coexistence with the Indians, but the ultimate American goal remained the same: to transfer frontier lands from natives to settlers for environmental transformation into a landscape devoted to commercial agriculture. Federal officials simply wanted a more moderate pace for expansion, what General Benjamin Lincoln called "those slow though sure steps which the natural course of things will point out." A regulated and rational pace would avoid war, maintain social control of the settlers, and permit Indians time to adjust to American domination. In due time, the swelling American population would overwhelm the environment that natives needed for their mixed economy of hunting, fishing, gathering, and horticulture. Echoing Philip Schuyler's argument, Knox predicted, "As the settlements of the whites shall approach near to the Indian boundaries established by treaties, the game will be diminished, and the lands being valuable to the Indians only as hunting grounds, they will be willing to sell further tracts for small considerations." Such purchases would cost far less than mustering armies to crush the Indians. Lincoln agreed that Americans should not militarily "precipitate an event which, in the very nature of things, must necessarily take place."[14]

Federal leaders predicted that the Indians would probably die out, at least east of the Mississippi, within fifty years. Only by adopting Christianity and commercial agriculture could the natives avert oblivion. In 1792, Lincoln explained that "the time will come when they will be either civilized or extinct." He reasoned that American civilization "from its very nature must operate to the extirpation of barbarism. . . . Civilized and uncivilized people cannot live in the same territory, or even in the same neighborhood."[15]

Once settled and civilized, the surviving Indians would need far less land than they had as mobile hunters and gatherers. Pickering explained, "They will find their extensive hunting grounds unnecessary; and will then readily listen to a proposition to sell a part of them, for the purpose of procuring, for every family, domestic animals & instruments of husbandry." Consequently, both the federal government and American settlers would benefit from the cultural transformation of Indians.[16]

But first the federal government needed to conclude the expensive war in the Ohio country. Although determined ultimately to procure more native land, leading Americans wanted an immediate end to an Indian war that undercut the value of large, speculative land holdings elsewhere on the frontier. They especially dreaded the possibility that the war would spread, embroiling the Six Nations and threatening the New York settlements. From New York City in 1791, Alexander Hamilton warned the president:

> You are sensible that almost every person here is interested in our Western lands; their value depends upon the settlement of the frontiers, these settlements depend on Peace with the Indians, and indeed the bare possibility of a war with the six Nations, would break up our whole frontier.

It is from this state of things that the war with the Wabash Indians is so much disrelished here.

The Federalist goal was to promote long-term settlements by achieving a short-term peace with the Indians—no easy balancing act.[17]

To win a peace in the Ohio country, the federal leaders needed to cultivate the Six Nations. Already strained by fighting the confederated Miamis, Shawnees, Delawares, Wyandots, Ottawas, Ojibwas, Winnebagos, and Piankashaws, the federal government could ill afford additional Indian enemies on another front. At a minimum, the Americans needed Iroquois neutrality. Better still, the federal leaders hoped to induce the Iroquois chiefs to persuade the Ohio Valley and Great Lakes nations to accept peace on American terms. Or, perhaps some Iroquois would assist the Americans in fighting and subduing the hostile Indians. Federal leaders swallowed the Iroquois mystique, so promoted by Sir William Johnson and so prevalent in the British Indian Department: that, by persuasion or intimidation, the Six Nations could sway all the other Indian nations within a thousand miles to their north and west.[18]

To defeat the Indian confederacy of the Ohio country, the federal government worked to revive and strengthen the Six Nations. That renewed confederacy would possess far more clout than any single Iroquois nation, even the numerous Senecas. A prime reason for reviving the Six Nations confederacy was to include the Oneidas in federal meetings with the other Iroquois. As the most reliably pro-American of the Iroquois, the Oneidas strengthened federal influence among the Six Nations. In 1792, after delivering a federal message to the Seneca chiefs at Genesee, Samuel Kirkland noted, "It is a happy circumstance that the Oneida Chiefs have come up to Genesee. It gives a dignity & weight to the message. Their presence animates the friends to America & lovers of peace." By reviving a special relationship with the Oneidas, the federal government sought a conduit for federal initiatives to reach through the Six Nations deep into the rest of Indian country. This federal approach mirrored what French officials had pursued, at American expense, during the 1780s.[19]

But Governor Clinton balked at the federal policy to bolster the Oneidas and to renew the Six Nations confederacy. Writing to Knox in 1791, Clinton protested that

> those nations are at present disunited by private animosities . . . that this disunion produces impotency and secures inaction, and that, if we should revive their importance, by renewing their union, we may give power and vigor, which we cannot with certainty direct, and over which we shall, with much trouble and expense, have an uncertain control.

The governor preferred to keep the Iroquois divided and dependent, the better to procure their lands for sales and settlement. Having negotiated massive land cessions with weak, individual nations, Clinton did not want to deal, in the future, with a united confederacy allied to the federal government.[20]

To appease Clinton, the Washington administration conceded that New York shared with Massachusetts the exclusive "preemption right" to buy or lease lands from the Iroquois within state bounds. But, to mollify the Iroquois (and especially the Oneidas), the federal government sought to regulate New York's exercise of that preemption power. Knox explained:

> The independent nations and tribes of Indians ought to be considered as foreign nations, not as the subjects of any particular State. Each individual State, indeed, will retain the right of pre-emption of all lands within its limits, which will not be abridged; but the general sovereignty must possess the right of making all treaties, on the execution or violation of which depend peace or war.

By so regulating, the federal government sought fair play for the Indians in order to preserve the peace. For if angered by New York's pressure, the Iroquois might join the Indian confederates in attacking the American settlements, thereby imperiling the entire federal program along the frontier.[21]

The cornerstone of the new federal policy was the Indian Trade and Intercourse Act passed by Congress and signed by the president in July 1790. That pivotal law invalidated any purchase of Indian land, whether by a state or an individual, unless conducted at a treaty council held under federal auspices. Congress renewed and strengthened the law in 1793 by adding criminal penalties: a fine of up to $1,000 or a year's imprisonment. The law mandated the presence and approval of a federal treaty commissioner at a public council; senate approval of the completed treaty; and formal signature and promulgation by the president. The new federal law forbade the sort of unilateral purchases made by New York State with the Oneidas at Fort Herkimer in 1785 and Fort Schuyler in 1788. With good cause, the Oneida warrior Captain Peter waved a copy of the federal act in the faces of New York state commissioners at Kanonwalohale in 1793.[22]

PICKERING

The Pine Creek murders of June 27, 1790, provided a paradoxical opportunity for the federal government to assert its new power and to woo the Six Nations. By covering the graves, the federal government could convert a tragedy into an opportunity, could avert an expanded war in favor of a closer

Timothy Pickering, by Charles Willson Peale, ca. 1792.
(Courtesy of the Independence National Historical Park.)

alliance. The federal government could also assert its monopoly in conducting Indian relations, subordinating the states in the process. All hinged on an apt performance by the federal commissioner entrusted with this immense responsibility at a critical moment.[23]

Initially, that commissioner seemed especially ill suited. Lacking prior experience with Indian diplomacy, Timothy Pickering was an austere and sometimes contentious Yankee, a veteran officer of the Continental Army who had settled on the Susquehanna frontier of northern Pennsylvania. But Pickering proved a quick study with a surprising sympathy for the Indians.[24]

In November, Pickering met about 220 Indians, primarily Senecas, with a few Onondagas, in council at Tioga Point, a small settlement on the Susquehanna River in Pennsylvania, just south of the border with New York State. Noting Pickering's nervous inexperience, the Seneca chiefs offered expert guidance in their diplomatic traditions. Red Jacket, a Buffalo Creek chief, patiently described the appropriate way graves had been covered "in the time of Sir W[illia]m Johnson." Red Jacket explained, "It is the mind of us who are here that the rule of our fore fathers should be observed." He also taught Pickering the ritual forms for renewing the Covenant Chain, enabling the United States to ally with the Six Nations. It helped that Pickering came on a mission entirely satisfactory to the Indians: delivering presents to cover graves; providing polite attention to restore a relationship; but seeking no land (in stark contrast to the land speculators and the state of New York). Little Billy, a Genesee chief, applauded Pickering, "This is the first time we have had an opportunity to brighten the Chain of friendship [since the war]. All the other [council] fires were designed to get away our lands."[25]

Although delighted that the federal government asked for no land, the Senecas wanted a federal review of past transactions, especially Oliver Phelps's controversial purchase made in 1788. The chiefs also sought federal protection for their remaining lands. Promising federal protection in the future, Pickering explained the new Federal Trade and Intercourse Act, giving a copy to the chiefs. But the federal commissioner could do nothing to overturn transactions made before 1790.[26]

When the council dissolved, everyone praised the mood, conduct, and results, so different from the councils of the 1780s. Red Jacket marveled that "ever thing has been done openly." In a letter to the president, Pickering expressed unexpected pleasure over his first treaty council:

> I was an utter stranger to the manners of Indians. But, sir, I have found that they are not difficult to please. A man must be destitute of humanity, of honesty, or of common sense who should send them away disgusted. He must want sensibility if he did not sympathize with them on their recital of the injuries they have experienced from white men.

His superiors expressed similar delight with Pickering's management of a model council that dramatically improved federal relations with the Six Nations. Knox applauded the Tioga council as "conducted with abilities and judgement, and consistently with the Constitution and Laws of the United States—and also with the candor and humanity which ought to characterize all the treaties of the general government with the unenlightened natives of the country." Writing to Pickering, President Washington also offered his "entire Approbation of your conduct in this business."[27]

Unfortunately, Pickering's triumph was clouded by Pennsylvania's failure to punish its murderous settlers. Because local sympathizers hid the Walkers and threatened to kill a key witness, only one of the four Pine Creek suspects, Samuel Doyle, was arrested and tried. And he escaped punishment, acquitted by a jury on November 12. Pickering complained, "It is in the highest degree mortifying to find that the bulk of the frontier inhabitants consider the killing of Indians in time of peace, to be no crime." He warned, "If some examples are not made of those frontier miscreants . . . such meetings as I have held with the Indians will frequently be necessary." Pickering considered the frontier settlers "far more savage & revengeful than the Indians."[28]

State and federal authorities were willing, indeed eager, to prosecute their own settlers who murdered Indians. A public trial and execution was the most tangible proof of a nation's prowess and legitimacy within its asserted boundaries. Moreover, by bringing their own people to justice, authorities could more plausibly require Indians to submit to the courts. But frontier mobs or frontier juries consistently foiled the prosecution of Indian-killers. After Doyle's acquittal, a frustrated American officer wished that such murderers "might be given up to the Indians & be by them burnt at the Stake." In 1793, Pickering suggested abandoning murder jurisdiction as an American goal in its Indian treaties for, "if the Indians fulfil such treaty on their part, it is plain by past experience that the U[nited] States will fail. Either the white offender will not be apprehended or if taken & tried, they will be acquitted, against the clearest evidence, for they will be tried in frontier counties where tis a maxim never to hang a white man for killing an Indian."[29]

Indians preferred covered graves to the trials and executions of murderous settlers, as was manifest in the botched prosecution of Jacob Valentine, a frontier trader. At Oswego Falls on July 27, 1792, Valentine killed an Onondaga chief. Fearing that the Indians might take revenge on nearby settlers, Governor Clinton spent $600 in state funds to track down Valentine in Canada. Brought back to New York's Herkimer County for trial, he was acquitted because the Onondagas refused to testify. Instead, they urged clemency. Rather than a trial and execution, they wanted a condolence ceremony and presents from the judges. One chief later complained to Clinton, "tho' our people did not wish to have this man put to death, yet we expected your [judges] would have spoke to us and taken the hatchet out of our head and wiped away the blood, but they did not do it. The hatchet remains there yet, and it is sore." Irritated by this complaint, Clinton retorted: "The [judges] who went up to try him had no power to speak to the relations of the man who was killed. They brought the murderer to trial. This was all they had power to do." Clinton did not understand that the Onondagas regarded a respect for their ceremonies and a delivery of presents as far more

valuable than watching Valentine hang. And by denying the state an executed settler, the Onondagas avoided setting a precedent that would subsequently expose their necks to state power.[30]

Unable to control or punish their own people for killing Indians, federal
leaders had to keep covering Indian graves at considerable expense. The
murders in western Pennsylvania became so frequent that, in 1796, the secretary of war established $200 as the standard price for an Indian life. Ameri-
can and Pennsylvania authorities apparently accepted a settler's life as of
equivalent value, for Cornplanter paid $200 at Pittsburgh to liberate two
Seneca warriors jailed for murdering a white man. By covering graves, federal
officials could maintain a pretense of power on the frontier. In recognition of
weakness lay an appearance of strength—the lesson that Sir William had
mastered a generation before.[31]

CORNPLANTER

At Tioga Point in 1790, one great Seneca chief was conspicuous by his
absence. Unwilling to share the council stage with the other chiefs, Cornplanter (Kaiutwahku) had remained at his village on the Allegheny River.
Literally and figuratively, Cornplanter was an outlier, an ambitious and eloquent man with a powerful mind, an often overbearing will, and flexible
scruples. The son of a prominent Seneca woman and a trader named John
Abeel, Cornplanter was sometimes called Captain Abeel or Obeal. Deeming
him a person of "uncommon genius," Kirkland concluded, "I think I never
enjoyed more agreeable society with any Indian than *Abeil* has afforded me.
He seems raised up by Providence for the good of his nation." Unlike most
chiefs, Cornplanter rarely drank and never to excess. He also coveted private
property, developing his own substantial farm near his village. A courageous,
resourceful, and accomplished warrior, Cornplanter had garnered respect
and influence by fighting the Patriots during the recent war, but peace cost
him dearly. At the Fort Stanwix Treaty in 1784, Cornplanter reluctantly
accepted the vindictive terms demanded by the American commissioners,
for which he reaped most of the subsequent blame from his fellow Iroquois
at Buffalo Creek and Grand River. Joseph Brant was an especially scathing
critic, deepening an enmity that had begun during the war. Similarly competitive and ambitious, Brant and Cornplanter intrigued against one another
in their rivalry for Iroquois influence.[32]

Unwilling to live where he could not dominate, in 1785 Cornplanter
moved his kin and followers away from Buffalo Creek, resettling in two villages (about nine miles apart) on the Allegheny River near the western end

of the Pennsylvania–New York border. The valley offered a fertile pocket of alluvial flats surrounded by steep, heavily forested hills, where the men hunted deer, bear, and turkeys. Beside the river, the women cultivated about sixty acres, raising corn, squash, pumpkins, beans, and melons. The principal village, Jenuchshadago, consisted of about 350 people dwelling in forty houses. The community's political and ritual life revolved around a council house, beside a clearing that featured a wooden effigy of Tharonhiawagon, a powerful spirit. In 1791 a visitor reported, "This figure is about nine feet in height, and stood on a pedestal of about twelve feet, having on [a] breech-clout, leggings, and a sash over its shoulders, and a very terrible appearance." Most of the houses were single-room log cabins, 16 to 20 feet long, but Cornplanter dwelled in a more traditional longhouse stretching 64 feet to house a composite family of fourteen people related by blood or marriage.[33]

By removing from Buffalo Creek, Cornplanter lost the security of Iroquois numbers as he moved closer to the advancing settlements in Pennsylvania. Descending the river to trade at Pittsburgh, the Allegheny Senecas often suffered thefts and murders by greedy and vindictive settlers. Seeking revenge was tempting, but it would cost Cornplanter's band severely by inviting the Americans once again to destroy the Allegheny villages, as they had done in 1779. And if rousted from the Allegheny Valley, the survivors would have to seek refuge at Buffalo Creek or Grand River, a subordinating humiliation that Cornplanter could not abide. He would make many compromises with the Americans rather than eat crow served by Red Jacket or Joseph Brant.[34]

Given his village's vulnerability to American attack, Cornplanter needed a good understanding with the leaders of the United States. At least they could cover graves; at best they would restrain the settlers, provide regular presents, and restore lands taken at Fort Stanwix in 1784. To maintain his prestige as a chief, Cornplanter also sought American presents to replace the British presents lost when he moved his people away from the Niagara corridor. Eager to cultivate the federal government, in 1787 Cornplanter permitted the American construction of Fort Franklin: a wooden blockhouse, surrounded by a palisade, banked by earth and with four bastions mounting small cannon. The fort lay on a riverside bluff downstream from Jenuchshadago at the juncture of French Creek with the Allegheny River. The local Senecas supported the federal garrison by providing scouts and venison, services that angered the Indian confederates. In January 1789, Cornplanter also subscribed to the Treaty of Fort Harmar, which reaffirmed the controversial terms of the Fort Stanwix Treaty but appeased Cornplanter with a payment. Unfortunately, Pennsylvania ruffians plundered most of the goods from the Senecas on their troubled return home.[35]

Rather than attend the Tioga Point council, as one among many Seneca chiefs, Cornplanter preferred his own visit, with two subordinates, to Philadelphia, where he could deal directly with the American president. Arriving in late November 1790, Cornplanter lingered until mid-February 1791. Kirkland traveled to Philadelphia to assist as a translator. Cornplanter pressed President Washington to relinquish the humiliating land concessions obtained at Fort Stanwix in 1784 and to oblige Oliver Phelps to pay the Seneca version of his obligations incurred in 1788. If successful in both requests, Cornplanter would bolster his influence among the Senecas by vindicating his past conduct. Indeed, Cornplanter angled to become the premier broker of Iroquois relations with the increasingly powerful United States.[36]

In Cornplanter's visit, Knox and Washington saw a precious opportunity. Impressed by his eloquence, sobriety, and intelligence, Knox considered Cornplanter "the fittest person to make use of to manage the six nations— Brandt excepted." The latter, alas, was "almost out of our reach," dwelling within the British line and well rewarded by the British Empire, "besides which, Brandt and the Cornplanter are rivals and sworn enemies; both cannot be embraced warmly at this time by the United States—one is attainable—the other is at least problematical."[37]

But in wooing Cornplanter, the federal leaders had a problem: they could satisfy neither of his principal requests for want of constitutional authority to rectify past treaties. Instead, they promised future federal protection for Iroquois land. Washington reassured Cornplanter:

Here then is the security for the remainder of your lands. No state nor person can purchase your lands, unless at some public treaty held under the Authority of the United States. The general Government will never consent to your being defrauded. But it will protect you in all your just rights.

Washington went further: "You possess the right to sell, and the right of refusing to sell your lands." For a decade, the Iroquois, in general, and the Oneidas, in particular, had been struggling for just that sort of ownership against the threatening doctrine of a preemption "right" held by a state or speculators.[38]

To "attach the Cornplanter by the solid ties of interest," the federal government provided an annual pension of $250 plus a onetime payment of $250 for his two companions. The cash payments and land promises delighted Cornplanter, who felt a new security for his village in his enhanced standing as a federal favorite. He promised to persuade the Indian confederates "to open their Eyes, and look towards the Bed which you have made for us, and to ask of you a bed for themselves, and for their Children, that will not slide from under them."[39]

A month after departing from Philadelphia in delight, Cornplanter wrote from Pittsburgh in sorrow. He informed the president that four Senecas, one of them a woman, had been butchered at Big Beaver Creek, in western Pennsylvania, by patrolling rangers, who killed Indians first and asked questions later. Cornplanter also suffered when frontier ruffians stole most of his federal presents and threatened his life. Cornplanter had to make the best of his uneasy position as the Indian favorite of a federal government unable to control its own people.[40]

RED JACKET

Despite the federal council at Tioga Point and the president's promises to Cornplanter, New York persisted in conducting its own Indian policy. In March 1791, the state legislature authorized emissaries to visit the Senecas for negotiations. Worrying about the impact on the Indians, President Washington raged, "What must this evince to them? Why, that we pursue no system, and that our declarations are not to be regard[ed]. To sum the whole up in a few words—the interferences of States and the speculations of Individuals will be the bane of all our public measures." Federal supremacy in Indian relations remained a tentative work in progress, especially in New York. Although home to the most important Indians for the new federal policy, New York was also run by an especially ambitious state regime led by George Clinton, who meant to control the dispossession of the Iroquois.[41]

In 1791, the federal leaders planned a military offensive, commanded by Arthur St. Clair, against the Indians of the Ohio country. To protect St. Clair's northeastern flank, federal leaders needed to consolidate Iroquois neutrality, which had been shaken in early 1791 by threatening messages sent by the Indian confederates. The messages demanded that the Six Nations join the war by attacking the Americans or face retribution by the confederates. Alarmed by the threats, Knox assured Washington, "Every exertion must be made to prevent the six Nations from joining the Western Indians. The Post at french Creek must be strengthened, and perhaps a party sent to protect the Cornplanter's settlements from the fang of the Whites." By holding a massive council in Iroquoia during the summer, the federal leaders hoped to preoccupy the Six Nations chiefs, keeping them from heading west

Red Jacket, by Baroness Hyde de Neuville, 1807. (Courtesy of the
New-York Historical Society; 1953.206.)

to help the confederates. Better still, a council would secure a public commitment of Iroquois neutrality. Best of all, Knox hoped to recruit some Iroquois
warriors to assist the American offensive.[42]

On April 11, the federal cabinet approved a summer council with the Six
Nations. By inviting all of the Iroquois, the federal leaders included the
friendly Oneidas, who could help sway the powerful Senecas.[43]

In July 1791, Pickering met the Six Nations in council at Newtown Point
(now Elmira, New York). Involving about 1,000 Indians from most of the Six
Nations, this council was far more numerous and complex than his previous
council at Tioga in 1790. And Pickering's prior success at Tioga had bred an
overconfidence in his mastery of Iroquois protocols and politics, which soon
proved to be dangerously superficial.[44]

During the first ten days of the council, Pickering stumbled by broaching
disagreeable issues. Eager to please his superiors, Pickering initially pursued
Knox's misguided instructions to pressure the Iroquois to provide warriors

to assist the Americans in the Ohio war. By so pressing, Pickering ignored Red Jacket's warning, "We wish Congress to be very careful how they speak; and to speak to us of nothing but peace." Instead, Pickering boasted of American numerical and military supremacy, unwittingly insulting his guests. Such vaunting rhetoric did not belong at a public council, which for the Iroquois was meant to nurture a friendly, peaceful frame of mind shared by all. In his journal, Pickering conceded: "Observing their countenances & behavior, I found the foregoing speech of mine was not pleasing to the Indians."[45]

Pickering's errors created an opening for Red Jacket (Shakoyewatha), an ambitious and clever spokesman for the Senecas of Buffalo Creek. The Americans and British called him Red Jacket because of his pride in a British officer's uniform, a prestigious gift from the empire. But Indian critics mocked him as Cow Killer, recalling an embarrassing episode from the war. During Sullivan's invasion, the timorous but sly Red Jacket had covertly slaughtered a cow and covered himself with blood to pretend that he had killed Americans in battle. Detected in the trick, he reaped ridicule rather than the intended applause. Despite such folly, Red Jacket subsequently attained an astonishing influence at Buffalo Creek.[46]

Deceitful, egotistical, intemperate, grasping, and cowardly, Red Jacket lacked the serene and selfless restraint expected of the ideal chief. Thomas Morris, an American land speculator, characterized Red Jacket as "a cunning, talented man without a particle of principle, not in the least confided in by the Indians, but carrying all his measures by dint of talent." His special, indeed extraordinary, talents were for political intrigue and council eloquence. Morris marveled, "He was a very fluent, and the most graceful speaker that I have ever heard address an audience of any description. Of this, he was very sensible, for always before he rose he took great pains to place the blanket round his shoulders and to arrange the silver bracelets on his arms so as to give the most graceful appearance."[47]

Mastering diplomatic customs and grand oratory, Red Jacket performed as the consummate conservator of hallowed traditions, as the classic master of vivid metaphor and dramatic pantomime. But his special popularity derived from a distinctive and innovative style of sarcastic wit that exploited any contradiction or pomposity expressed by a speaker for the other side. His pointed style broke with the serene politeness of traditional Indian speakers. The Senecas relished his skill at poking fun at the pretentious representatives of external power. Yet Red Jacket was also adept at cutting private deals with those he had ridiculed in public council. Red Jacket cultivated Seneca popularity by day that he might drive up his price at night. But his greed was more than selfish. Private payments supported and solidified his standing as a preeminent chief. Most of his presents passed quickly through his hands to kin, bolstering Red Jacket's following, giving him the authority to speak in council. Red Jacket served the Senecas as he served himself.[48]

At Newtown Point, Red Jacket toyed with the honest, blunt, and sometimes obtuse Pickering, who rambled on about American superiority. Living for the very stage that the Newtown Point council provided, Red Jacket mocked Pickering's mistakes in protocol and rhetoric. Easily irritated, Pickering rose to the bait, expressing a public indignation that sealed Red Jacket's triumph. How absurd for Americans to claim superiority, the Senecas concluded, when their Red Jacket could so thoroughly fluster a federal commissioner. At a time of eroding Iroquois power, Red Jacket rhetorically sustained the prowess that was the special pride of the Senecas. When Pickering seemed insufficiently attentive during one speech, Red Jacket blustered that "when a Seneca speaks, he ought to be listened to with attention from one end of this great island . . . to the other."[49]

Pickering felt the council slipping away from him. Retreating from his provocative exploration of differences, he belatedly sought common ground by withdrawing Knox's request for warriors. Instead, Pickering reaffirmed Iroquois amity as neutrals and reiterated the federal protections for Iroquois land. On behalf of the Iroquois, Good Peter responded enthusiastically: " 'Tis the mind of the Six Nations never to sell any more, but to keep it for our warriors for hunting ground forever. . . . Now the U[nited] States have engaged to make our seats easy; we only desire [that] they would fulfil their engagements."[50]

Pickering also considered two controversial requests pressed by the Senecas and Cayugas, who tested their power to control the disposal of their lands. By granting some lands to favorites, they took Washington at his word to Cornplanter: "That you possess the right to sell, and the right of refusing to sell your lands." The Seneca chiefs pressed Pickering to certify their deed of six square miles of Genesee land reserved to the trader Ebenezer Allan to hold in trust for his two daughters by a Seneca wife. The Cayugas of Buffalo Creek similarly sought Pickering's approval of their lease to John Richardson and other settlers of almost all of the reservation at Cayuga Lake.[51]

In both cases, Pickering initially balked. He disdained Allan as disreputable and deceptive, tricking the Senecas into giving an excessive quantity of land. And Pickering doubted the legality of the Cayuga lease. But the Indians insisted, obliging Pickering to consider the cost of refusing: "reviving, or rather exciting their utmost jealousy *as it would have been denying the free enjoyment* of their own lands." Pickering certified the Cayuga lease after obtaining a favorable (but erroneous) legal opinion from Brinton Paine, a New York state judge in attendance. Paine, however, was an interested party, having invested in the Richardson Lease. Pickering approved of the Allan grant only after the Senecas agreed to reduce the size to four square miles.[52]

By changing his tone, and by certifying the two land transactions, Pickering concluded the council on a positive note. On the last day, July 17, he delivered generous presents and assured the chiefs, "Let us make a hole in the ground, scrape together our troubles, & bury them." Responding in kind, the chiefs felt pleased to stand in such good favor with both the United States and the British Empire, for neutrality paid best. Despite his early missteps at Newtown Point, Pickering ultimately secured the primary federal goal by reaffirming Iroquois neutrality. Although still irritated by Red Jacket's mockery, Pickering reported, "we parted as friends; he, his wife & children came to my quarters & shook hands before they set off for home." Red Jacket knew the importance of private parting as well as public posturing.[53]

By delighting the Iroquois chiefs, Pickering unwittingly irritated George Clinton, who opposed any measures to reunite the Six Nations. The governor especially resented Pickering's intervention in the Cayuga land dispute, where Clinton favored the small faction resident at the lake. After his exertions, during the 1780s, to frustrate the federal government and to defeat the Livingston Lessees, Clinton would be damned rather than let any Indians bypass the state government to lease or sell directly to settlers. When the governor protested, Knox and Washington quickly backed away from a confrontation by acknowledging New York's claim to a preemption right as the only legal purchaser of Indian lands within its borders. This federal concession retreated from Washington's promise to Cornplanter that the Indians possessed the full ownership of their lands, a promise that Pickering had tried to fulfill, lest the Indians "think that the solemn assurances of the President were made to amuse & deceive them."[54]

Regarding the Cayuga lease certification as a modest and honest mistake, Knox concluded that on balance "the Commissioner has, with great ability and judgment, carried into effect the objects of his appointment, by cementing the friendships between the United States and the said Indians." In reward for that loyal and able service, the president appointed Pickering to his cabinet as postmaster general. And Washington continued to count on Pickering's advice in Iroquois affairs.[55]

BRANT

Knox and Pickering had invited Joseph Brant and the Mohawks to attend the Newtown Point council. This invitation contradicted the Americans' previous insistence on a strict boundary to separate British from American spheres of Indian management. During the early 1790s, the American and British meddling overlapped, fudging the border and encouraging Iroquois chiefs who hoped to preserve their importance and autonomy by playing off two rival external powers.[56]

Taking their cues from the British, federal leaders regarded Brant as a dominating figure capable of swaying all of the Six Nations and, indeed, the entire Indian confederacy, which the Americans regarded as his creation. A great exaggeration, that conviction derived from Brant's conspicuous talents as a warrior and as a diplomat with a unique ability to negotiate the cultural frontier. Brant alone seemed able to reconcile Iroquois and Algonquians, natives and colonizers, and Americans and Britons. Nor was Brant bashful about promoting his diplomatic prowess, feeding the inflated expectations of his American and British contacts. Officials also preferred to work with a chief who could speak their language and could perform as a fellow gentleman. As a result, few officials noticed that Brant's prodigious ambition and his special cachet in the white world aroused suspicion and opposition among the Indians. The more that officials flattered and wooed Brant, the less that other Indians trusted him.

American officials sensed an opportunity in Brant's growing discontent with British Indian policy. Disgusted by the British betrayal in the peace treaty of 1783, he also felt frustrated as British officials avoided commitments to assist the new Indian confederacy if attacked by the Americans. Fed up with the evasions, Brant had defied the officials in Canada by sailing from Quebec for England in November 1785. Determined to control communication from London to Iroquoia, the officials in Canada feared Brant's bid directly to speak to the Crown ministers. For himself, Brant sought a pension. For the Mohawks, he pressed the ministers to fulfill Haldimand's promise of financial compensation for their property confiscated or plundered by the Patriots. And for the Indians in general, he sought a mutual defense pact to resist American expansion into the Ohio country.[57]

Reaching London in December, Brant renewed his standing as a celebrity entertained by the aristocracy and the urban literati. Living grandly (at great expense to the Crown), Brant delighted in the London social scene in 1786 almost as much as he had a decade before. But he painfully discovered that the evasions in Canada aptly reflected the dithering policy in London. For three months, Brant awaited a formal answer to his requests. Ultimately, Lord Sydney reiterated the British pattern of lavishing money to fulfill Brant's personal requests while denying any policy commitment to the Indians in general. Brant reaped a generous pension worth 5 shillings per day for life, and Lord Sydney agreed fully to compensate the Mohawks for their

Joseph Brant, by Charles Willson Peale, 1797. (Courtesy of
the Independence National Historical Park.)

losses, a total of £15,000, including £1,112 for Joseph Brant and £1,206 for his
sister Molly. This generosity contrasted with that extended to the Loyalists,
who received compensation for only a fraction of their losses. But Lord Sydney would make no promises to help the Indian confederacy. In disgust,
Brant departed England bearing exotic purchases that included two canaries,
a parrot, and a monkey.[58]

In June 1786, he returned to Canada seething with discontent. From Quebec, Robert Mathews reported that Brant "did not hesitate in all Companies
to reprobate the weakness & folly of our Ministers," especially Lord Sydney,
dismissed as "a stupid Blockhead." Careless in his anger, Brant vented to officials eager to bring him down a notch. Irritated that Brant had defied their
authority by visiting London, the Canadian officials also felt threatened by
Brant's ambitions to enhance Indian unity and autonomy. Quebec's acting
governor, Henry Hope, warned Lord Sydney, "I was sorry to observe that his
attachment to Great Britain does not appear to me to have increas'd by his
voyage to England, notwithstanding the liberality of Government to the
Mohawks, and particularly to himself and Sister."[59]

In July, Brant returned to Niagara, where he alarmed British officials by his pointed speeches in Indian councils. Denouncing Brant's "Subtlety & Craft," an Indian Department official insisted that British policy should no longer "add to Joseph's vanity, or put any thing in his power that may call forth that restless ambition which you know him to be possessed of." Niagara's commandant, Major Campbell, warned of Brant's "very great share of Ambition to become a man of the first consequence among the Nations." Campbell concluded, "I cannot help thinking him deep and designing with a stronger attachment to his own Interest than to any Country or People." Faulting Brant's pursuit of interest sounded hypocritical after the pains that British officials took to buy his loyalty with pensions and presents.[60]

Brant felt the strain of resenting British manipulation of the Indians while personally depending upon British patronage. He also struggled to unite disparate Indians subject to intense, countervailing pressures from the British and the Americans. Striving to reconcile those jarring interests, Brant had to play the diplomat rather than the warrior. His restraint also reflected the concerns of a family man with several young children. But it still hurt when Shawnees called Brant a coward for failing to help them attack the Americans. In September 1789, Brant confessed to Robert Mathews,

> Dear friend, it is a critical time for us here. I mean we the Indians. I felt very unhappy often times of late. The most difficult Part for me is of having many children, which concerns me about them very much. . . . If I have not got so many children, I would soon do some thing to drown my unhappiness & Leave more marks behind me than what my father did. I think you [have] done right of not having a Wife & Children, other ways [you] would be [a] dam coward like myself.

Frustrated by the tangle of conflicting interests on the borderland, Brant longed to lose himself in the supposedly simpler choices of war.[61]

Brant's mood further darkened that fall when he was insulted by an obtuse new commandant at Niagara. Spooked by wild rumors of a pending Indian uprising against the British posts, the commandant ordered the sentinels to stop, search, and disarm any Indians entering Fort Niagara. In public, Brant bore arms as a sign of his standing and prowess as a war chief. Used to visiting the fort without challenge, Brant resisted when confronted by a soldier at the fort's gate. Proud and prickly, Brant bristled at the incident as an especially telling sign that the British neither trusted nor respected him.[62]

Brant decided to explore his options on the American side of the border, beginning with New York's Governor Clinton. In 1790, Brant attended the state council with the Cayugas and Onondagas at Fort Schuyler (Stanwix).

Clinton also plied Brant with genteel gifts, including a racehorse. Upon returning home, he wrote to thank Clinton: "I am at a loss for Words to express my gratitude for the civility and attention I received from your Excellency and the rest of the Gentlemen when at Fort Stanwix." Writing to President Washington, Clinton described Brant as "a Man of very considerable information, influence, and enterprize, and in my humble opinion, his Friendship is worthy of cultivation at some Expense."[63]

Washington assigned the courtship of Brant to Henry Knox, who counted on money, flattery, and the personal touch of the chief's old friend (but wartime foe) Samuel Kirkland. That sly minister renewed a friendly correspondence, which Brant immediately saw had a larger purpose. At the same time, Knox also sought Clinton's influence: "Your Excellency will please to hold out such inducements to Brant as you may judge most proper, with respect to money." By flattering Clinton as well as Brant, Knox also hoped to improve New York's cooperation with the federal government. In reply, Clinton boasted that his "friendly and familiar intercourse" with Brant would "enable me to procure an interview with him, at any time and place not particularly inconvenient."[64]

But neither friends nor money could sway Brant without some mutual interest in the politics of the borderland. Both Brant and the Federalists wanted to resolve the Ohio conflict peacefully, but for radically different reasons. Longing to find common ground, both Brant and the Federalists turned blind eyes to their crucial differences. To win a peace on their own terms, the federal leaders sought to divide and disrupt the Indian confederacy, while Brant wanted to strengthen and perpetuate that confederacy by achieving peace under its auspices. Replying to Kirkland, Brant advised the Americans to "call a general Treaty with the United Nations. . . . Abandon that wicked mode of calling them out in separate Nations, or parties, to treat with them, which only serves to irritate and inflame their minds, instead of healing the sore, and removing the prevailing prejudices." If the Americans had to make peace at a general council of the nations, the Indian confederacy would gain legitimacy and strength. To entice the Americans to make such a general peace, Brant urged the confederates to accept moderate terms. Indeed, he worried that recent victories would strengthen Indian hard-liners, who would miss their last, best chance to make the compromise peace needed to preserve and consolidate the confederacy. Recognizing the latent American strength, Brant rued a prolonged war as likely to unravel the confederacy.[65]

Brant also welcomed American attention to enhance his leverage with the British. Playing a cunning game, Brant was careful to inform British officials of *most* of his American contacts. He quickly alerted Sir John Johnson of the

revived correspondence "from the Revd. Mr. Kirtland, that deep, dark Presbiterian." Brant's apparent transparency sustained his claims of persistent
loyalty as it also subtly warned against taking his allegiance for granted. By
reporting American offers of private payments, Brant also enhanced the
value of his loyalty to the British.[66]

Although tempted by the federal invitation to the Newtown Point council, Brant first had to attend a confederation council at the Maumee Rapids
in the Ohio country. There his policy of moderation suffered when militia
from Kentucky, with federal permission, raided deep into the Indian country.
By combining a show of force with an offer of peace, the Americans hoped
simultaneously to intimidate and to woo the Indian confederates. Instead,
that dual approach struck the confederates as double-dealing. At the
Maumee council in June, the emboldened hard-liners confronted Brant by
ritually offering a war hatchet. If Brant rejected the hatchet at that moment
of crisis, he risked his credibility and perhaps his life to assassination as a
traitor to Indian solidarity. By accepting, he promised to join the warriors
rallying against the invaders from Kentucky. Spreading fast, this news caused
a sensation at Grand River, Buffalo Creek, Niagara, the Allegheny, the Genesee, Quebec, and Philadelphia. Carefully scrutinized, Brant's every move
seemed to determine war or peace in the borderland.[67]

But Brant did not want an expanded war without British assistance. If
plunged into combat against the Americans, Brant would lose his clout as a
mediator between them and the Indian confederation. He could only make
that sacrifice if assured of overt British support for the Indians. Seeking that
assurance, Brant led a delegation of chiefs to Quebec to press the governor
general, Lord Dorchester, to provide troops to fight the Americans. By heading to Quebec during July, Brant avoided immediate entanglement in the
Ohio fighting, but he also lost his chance to meet Pickering at Newtown
Point. Not even Joseph Brant could be in two places at once.[68]

At Quebec in August, Brant pressured Dorchester by arguing: "It is a
Grievous thing to us that the Americans always insist that our Country was
given to them by the King, . . . making that a pretence for taking possession
of it, and fixing such lines as they think proper." Let the British make
amends, then, by sending troops to fight beside the confederates against the
American invaders of the Indian country. Lord Dorchester listened politely
and gave the usual presents, but he made no commitments, for want of any
authority to bend the policy of inertia dictated in London. The British
would defend their posts, if attacked, but they would not march to the Indians' assistance. To reassure the Americans, Dorchester hastened a copy of
this speech to the federal cabinet in Philadelphia.[69]

Frustrated anew, Brant returned home to Grand River in early October.

This detour broke his promise to rejoin the confederates in the Ohio country to fight the Americans. Embarrassed by the Quebec setback, Brant did not even bother to stop at Buffalo Creek to recount the speeches to the other chiefs, as custom required. Because sharing news was an essential mark of friendship, withholding it insulted the Buffalo Creek chiefs. Worse still, at Fort Niagara, on his way home, Brant publicly denounced the Seneca chiefs as sellouts to the Americans. He even suggested that the British reduce their presents, advice that John Butler maliciously conveyed to the Buffalo Creek chiefs. Butler's tattling widened a double rift: between Butler and Brant, and between the chiefs of Buffalo Creek and Grand River.[70]

Meanwhile, in the Ohio country the Indian confederates won a stunning victory by crushing an American army commanded by Arthur St. Clair. Shortly before dawn on November 4, about 1,000 warriors, led by Little Turtle, a Miami war chief, approached the slumbering American camp of 1,400 men. The warriors were primarily Shawnees, Miamis, and Delawares, supplemented by Wyandots, Ojibwas, Ottawas, Potawatomis, Cherokees, and even a dozen Senecas and Cayugas. Most of the sleeping Americans were raw recruits from the eastern states, and they were badly led by St. Clair. Surprised and overwhelmed, the Americans broke and fled, losing over 600 dead—the greatest single defeat inflicted by Indians on Americans in their long history of conflict (nearly three times as many Americans died in St. Clair's defeat as at George Custer's more famous "last stand" in 1876). The dead included the army's second-in-command, Richard Butler, formerly a federal commissioner at the treaty of Fort Stanwix in 1784. To humiliate the dead Americans, the Indians stuffed their mouths with soil, to mock their fatal lust for Indian land.[71]

This sweeping victory strengthened the hard-liners among the Indian confederates. Vindictive as well as vindicated, they sent emissaries to Grand River to embarrass Brant for his broken commitment to join them in battle against the Americans. The emissaries delivered a provocative gift, Richard Butler's bloody scalp, along with a rebuking speech:

> You chief Mohawk, what are you doing? Time was when you roused us to war, & told us that if all the Indians would join with the King they should be a happy people & become independent. In a very short time you changed your voice & went to sleep & left us in the lurch. . . . Know [that] it is not good for you [to] lie still any longer. Arise & bestir yourself!

The bloody gift also implied a threat: join the confederates or risk losing his own scalp. In January 1792, Kirkland reported the Indian gossip that Brant, long famous for his sobriety, had begun to drink heavily to cope with the stress of his dangerous position: "I am credibly informed that Brant has lately indulged himself too freely with the *intoxicating draught*—which is ascribed to his having lost so much of his influence among the Indians & being exposed to the resent[ment] particularly [of] the western Confederacy." Brant also felt alienated from the British who mishandled a surprising murder crisis at Grand River.[72]

MURDER

Upon Brant's return from Quebec to Grand River, he found a crisis provoked in late September by the drunken murder of a French Canadian trader by two Mohawks named Hendrick and Kellayhun. Colonel Andrew Gordon, the British commander at Fort Niagara, provocatively demanded that the Grand River chiefs surrender the suspects for imprisonment pending a trial under British law. Refusing, the chiefs instead proposed to cover the grave with gifts for the kin of the deceased. Brant explained, "We have forms and Ancient Customs which we look upon as Necessary to be gone through as the Proceedings in any Court of Justice."[73]

The Iroquois would lose their sovereignty if they accepted British legal jurisdiction. Whether colonial law or Indian customary law prevailed in murder cases was a critical marker of the relative degree of colonial power and native sovereignty. Gordon assured Brant:

> Had the murder been committed by any European, though he had been one of the first Men in the Province, he must have been delivered up to Justice and remained in confinement 'till a Court could be assembled for his Tryal. We asked nothing more of your Nation than we should have imposed upon ourselves.

But that was the very point at issue. The Iroquois did not wish to be treated like British subjects, for they considered themselves independent allies. Adding injury to insult, Gordon suspended the delivery of all presents to the Grand River Indians until they delivered the suspects. Bristling at this treatment, Brant retorted:

> This is by no means the Method of Treating Indians, as must be known to every Person Acquainted with our Customs. Gentle Steps would have had the desired effect, compulsory ones never will. From this late, hasty, injurious order we cannot now think of delivering them up, although no doubt but many of our women & children will Suffer by it.

Gordon had to learn the hard way that empires could not govern Indians by command.[74]

Gordon insisted that, in a treaty made with Sir William Johnson, the Six Nations had promised to surrender murder suspects whenever the victim was a British subject. But Gordon could find no copy of the supposed treaty and could not even specify when and where it had been made. He apparently misunderstood episodes in which Sir William appeared to have obtained such an Iroquois concession in principle but never in practice.[75]

The primary example came in April 1764, when Johnson induced the Genesee Senecas to sign a preliminary peace treaty obligating them to surrender two murderers from the village of Kanestio. That preliminary treaty also stipulated that, in the future,

> should any Indian commit Murder, or rob any of His Majesty's subjects,
> he shall be immediately delivered up to be tried, and punished according
> to the equitable Laws of England, and should any white man be guilty of
> the like crime towards the Indians, he shall be immediately tried and
> punished if guilty.

But Johnson framed this language to impress his imperial superiors in London, for he knew that the clause was unenforceable on the frontier. In the final version of the treaty, made in August 1764, Johnson quietly dropped the demand for future murderers, and he accepted the Indians' insistence that one of the Kanestio murderers was dead and the other vanished. To save face, Johnson "pardoned" the absent murderer in return for a land concession from the Senecas.[76]

In subsequent years, Johnson routinely pardoned Indian murder suspects, all the while insisting that such clemency would never be repeated, although invariably it soon was. For example, in 1774 he released a Seneca jailed for murdering four French Canadian traders at Irondequoit Bay (on the south shore of Lake Ontario). During his long career as the Crown superintendent, Johnson never secured the legal conviction and execution of an Indian for murder.[77]

In Gordon's skewed memory, Johnson's preliminary treaty with the Genesee Senecas became abstracted from its context and his subsequent equivocations. A misleading and provisional treaty with part of one nation was distorted by Gordon into a final treaty binding all of the Six Nations. Perhaps Gordon also recalled the subsequent surrender of the Irondequoit suspect, but not the ultimate failure to prosecute him. Of course, Brant better understood his mentor's handling of cross-cultural murders:

> What gives rise to the report of this agreement is that a party of Senecas Robbed and Murdered a French Man at Arontaquat. The Murderers were demanded and delivered up to Sir William. They were confined but afterwards Liberated.

Not for the first time, Iroquois memory proved more reliable than the paper trail produced by colonial officials. Indeed, a cunning document by Johnson, designed to gull his superiors, had deceived Gordon.[78]

Brant appealed to Sir John Johnson, who also understood his father's deceptions and equivocations, both so essential in borderland diplomacy. Johnson advised General Alured Clarke to restore the presents and provisions to the Grand River Indians and to suspend the demand for the suspects. When Clarke agreed, Brant thanked Johnson for showing a "confidence in us" that would permit the Six Nations "to Exercise our just intentions, without the appearance of Compulsion."[79]

Tensions further abated when the British removed Gordon from Niagara to Montreal, but the case against Hendrick and Kellayhun remained suspended rather than dropped. The institution of a civil government for the new province of Upper Canada revived the possibility of their trial. In June 1792, on his way down the St. Lawrence River to Montreal, Gordon passed the ascending boat of the new colony's new attorney general, John White, who confided that the prosecution of

> two Iroquois Indians does not lay very lightly on my mind. The fact is that when they take a prejudice they rarely forgive and, being the ostensible person that brings them to justice, they may do me the favour to remember me when we meet. And indeed the prosecution will require some management, for it seems that, although they are certainly guilty, we must not hang them.

Apparently, General Clarke had advised White and the new colony's lieutenant governor, John Graves Simcoe, to follow the true Sir William precedent: to pardon the Mohawks after a pro forma surrender.[80]

But Simcoe was far more intrepid than John White and far less pragmatic than General Clarke. A man of extraordinary energy and compulsive "system" (one of his favorite terms), Simcoe meant rapidly to reshape his weak frontier colony into a copy of England capable of confronting the Americans, whom he especially loathed. Imbued with elite paternalism and imperial mission, Simcoe vowed immediately to impose English law uniformly throughout his new province. He lectured the Six Nations:

Brothers, . . . if any of the King's Subjects commits a Crime against any Person of what nation soever living under his Protection, that Person may have recourse to the Laws; & that the King's subjects have also the same Right against all other Persons. Brothers, the King's Justice must flow Impartially to every Person living under his Protection—all men have a Right to avail themselves of his Justice & by the Laws of the Land he can refuse it to no One.

A veteran army officer in the Gordon mold, Simcoe meant to treat Indians as military auxiliaries rather than as autonomous peoples. And he believed as devoutly as Gordon in the myth of Sir William Johnson's murder treaty.[81]

To enforce his doctrine on Indians, Simcoe first had to prove that he could convict and execute whites who killed natives. Fortunately for his purposes, British subjects conveniently provided two test cases, one at each distant end of Upper Canada during the month that Simcoe arrived. On June 25, two off-duty soldiers killed a Mississauga chief known as the Snake in a drunken brawl at Kingston, in eastern Upper Canada. Four days later, and far to the west at Michilimackinac, an enraged mob of fur traders "kicked & stomped upon and with divers weapons, beat, cut, stabbed & murdered" an Ojibwa named Wawanisse, who earlier in the day had slashed several traders with a knife.[82]

Simcoe cherished both cases as opportunities to establish English law throughout Upper Canada. Taking a direct interest, Simcoe cajoled magistrates and judges, urging vigorous prosecutions and death sentences. He dismissed from office the magistrates at Michilimackinac, for releasing the suspects on bail, and he threatened to declare martial law if the grand jury failed to indict them. In the case of the Kingston soldiers, Simcoe had no compunctions about assuring the presiding judge, "I am sorry to say there is little doubt of their guilt and conviction." And Simcoe announced that he would execute the guilty.[83]

But his zeal came to naught because convictions depended upon cooperation from common colonists. Wawanisse's killers evaded trial by escaping with the help of their many sympathizers at Michilimackinac, and a Kingston jury acquitted the soldiers charged with killing the Snake. As in Pennsylvania with the Pine Creek murderers, settlers as well as Indians frustrated the official drive to adjudicate cross-cultural murder. Unable to convict their own people for killing natives, the colonial authorities could hardly resist Indian demands to cover graves.[84]

The case against Hendrick and Kellayhun remained formally unresolved in January 1793, when Simcoe met Brant and the other Grand River chiefs in council at Niagara. Weary of the controversy, Brant challenged Simcoe by delivering a wampum belt. Simcoe reported that the accompanying speech,

> upon being interpreted to me by Colonel Butler, to my great surprise, I understood was to cover the grave of the Person who had been murdered, according to the Ancient Indian Custom, but which has for some years been obsolete in all transactions between His Majesty's Subjects and the Mohawks, who in a Treaty held by Sir William Johnson, as I am informed, had many years ago, agreed to deliver up all their People who should commit any murders, to the Justice of the British Laws. I refused this Belt and left the Council House. The Indians, I apprehend, were in great astonishment, and the Affair began to wear a serious aspect.

That evening, Butler warned Simcoe that he risked alienating the Six Nations, who were essential to the colony's security. Citing "the worthlessness of the Person who had fallen the victim of a drunken quarrel," Butler advised Simcoe to reconvene the council in the morning to accept Brant's wampum. Beating a hasty and uncharacteristic retreat, Simcoe deemed it "most prudent that I should accept the Belt, which was accordingly done [the] next day." Brant had prevailed, affirming the Iroquois autonomy by covering the grave. No doubt John White was relieved that he no longer had to prosecute the two Indians. Rather than dying by Indian vengeance, White succumbed in 1800 to a bullet fired in a duel with a white man.[85]

INVERSION

Two murders, one at Pine Creek in 1790 and the other at Grand River in 1791, bookend an apparent inversion in the American and the British treatment of the Iroquois during the early 1790s. In the first, the murder of Senecas by settlers gave the federal government an opportunity to develop a better relationship with the Six Nations. In the second, the Mohawk murder of a trader invited the British to seek greater control over the Indians within their border. Federal officials practiced restraint because they recognized the desperate need to retrieve the embattled American position among the Indians of the frontier. Rejecting the conquest theory and the abrupt conduct of councils during the 1780s, federal leaders followed Iroquois advice to adopt Sir William Johnson's sophisticated and theatrical conduct of diplomacy. At the same time, some British officials nearly ruptured their relationship with the Six Nations by asserting a bureaucratic misunderstanding of Sir William's true practices. The British of the 1790s were fooled by Johnson's own skill at leaving a paper trail meant to distract his superiors from the evasions he practiced to mollify the Indians. In the paradoxical borderland, the Americans temporarily found appearances of strength by covering graves at public councils, a recourse dictated by their weakness at controlling their own people. Conversely, in 1791–92 some British officials felt overly confident in their power over both settlers and Indians, thereby provoking a bitter controversy that reiterated their true vulnerability.

Although ultimately resolved to Brant's satisfaction, the murder crisis infuriated him as unnecessary and foolish. Determined to preserve the Iroquois status as allies, he resented the British attempts to treat them as dependents. Added to Brant's growing list of British slights, the murder crisis persuaded him to visit the American leaders at Philadelphia.

CHAPTER NINE

Crisis

John Graves Simcoe, by Jean Laurent Mosiner, 1791. (Courtesy of the Metropolitan Toronto Library Board.)

Aᴠᴛᴇʀ ᴛʜᴇ Iɴᴅɪᴀɴ ᴄᴏɴꜰᴇᴅᴇʀᴀᴛᴇꜱ destroyed St. Clair's army, British leaders pressed the Washington administration to accept their mediation of the conflict. By bringing peace to the Indian country on British terms, they hoped to preserve their Indian alliances while averting their own war with the Americans. In addition to imposing enormous new expenses in blood and money, a renewed American war would curtail the valuable transatlantic commerce essential to the British economy.[1]

But as their price for brokering peace, the British expected the Americans to accept a revision of the boundary established by the treaty of 1783. That boundary threatened the fur trade and menaced Canada by inviting American traders and troops to the Great Lakes, on the very doorstep of the British colonies. If Britain surrendered the border posts and abandoned the Indian confederacy, Montreal's merchants worried that "in place of having a Wilderness for a Barrier against the Attempts of an insidious and restless Neighbour, which they could not easily traverse with the implements of regular War, we would then have them at our own doors in force, protected by Forts, aided by a naval Force, and ready to avail themselves of every advantage." Far better, the British thought, to preserve an Indian borderland between the United States and Canada as a screen against the numerous and aggressive Americans.[2]

In early 1792, the British minister to the United States, George Hammond, hinted that his government would welcome the opportunity to mediate the conflict. Federal leaders resented that hint as insulting American dignity by compromising American sovereignty. Because the fundamental purpose of the United States was to manage the steady westward expansion of settlement, the new nation would become a nullity if denied control over Indians within its asserted boundaries. President Washington bristled, "The United States will never have occasion, I hope, to ask for the interposition of that Power, or any other, to establish peace within their own territory."[3]

If the British truly wanted peace, federal officials argued, let them curtail presents to the Indians and deliver up the border forts, rendering further native resistance futile. American leaders abruptly dismissed British claims that they needed to mollify natives with generous presents and retention of the posts. Regarding the Indians as primitive pawns, federal officials could not see their power to pressure the British.[4]

In 1792, the American rejection of British mediation seemed more proud than wise given the destruction of St. Clair's army, and the surprising effectiveness of the Indian confederacy. And another humiliating defeat would cripple the credibility of the new nation both at home and abroad. The Americans needed time to recruit and train a larger and better army. "Another conflict with the savages with raw recruits is to be avoided by all means," Knox explained. Moreover, public opinion in the northeastern states had turned against the war as unjust and expensive. To reduce costs and buy time, the Washington administration hoped to persuade the Indian confederates to negotiate.[5]

During 1792 and 1793, the United States pursued a double track: conspicuously offering peace while preparing for renewed war. To revive and improve the army, Washington and Knox chose an aggressive and able commander, General Anthony Wayne, who openly dismissed the diplomatic initiative as a waste of time and money. But Knox regarded the two tracks as mutually reinforcing, with the drilling soldiers and new forts pressuring the Indians to make peace on American terms. But the confederates saw American policy as two-faced, as they assured Washington: "You hold good in one hand and evil in the other."[6]

The United States recruited native emissaries to woo the Indian confederates. Federal officials particularly favored Iroquois mediators, which reflected the persistent conviction that the Six Nations were the most powerful and influential of Indians. At least such employment would keep the Iroquois from joining the war. And if rejected by the confederates in an insulting manner, the Iroquois might subsequently help the Americans in their renewed warfare.

But in sending peace messages to the western confederates, the United States faced a geographic complication. In the spring of 1792, federal officials had tried to dispense with Indian middlemen by sending two American officers direct from their Ohio Valley forts to the hostile villages. But the Indian confederates ambushed and killed them. The federal government learned why from the redoubtable Colonel Louis, the Mohawk who had left the Oneidas to reside at Akwesasne (St. Regis) in the St. Lawrence Valley. During a visit to Philadelphia, he explained that sending a peace message via a warpath was a grave violation of Indian diplomatic custom. Instead, "runners with such messages must always go round, & come in at the back door." Alas, the back door to the Maumee villages (at the heart of the confederacy) ran through the British forts around Lakes Ontario and Erie. To reach the confederates, American peace emissaries would need some cooperation from the British whom they were trying to bypass. And little help could be anticipated from John Graves Simcoe.[7]

SIMCOE

During the spring of 1792, at the height of the border tension, Simcoe commenced his controversial administration of Upper Canada. During the preceding year, Parliament had divided the old province of Quebec to create two new colonies: Lower Canada and Upper Canada. Based in the St. Lawrence Valley, Lower Canada featured the commercial towns of Montreal and Quebec. Upper Canada ran along the Great Lakes to embrace Detroit and Niagara, which put that new province at the center of the borderland conflict, which the confrontational Simcoe meant to exploit. During the war, as the aggressive commander of a Loyalist regiment, the Queen's Rangers, he had engaged in brutal, partisan warfare. He developed a passionate and enduring hatred for the revolutionaries and a deep empathy for the Loyalists. Unwilling to concede defeat in the last war, Simcoe still hoped to restore the British Empire in North America by undermining the American republic. In 1791, he vowed, "I am one of those who know all the consequence of our late American Dominions. . . . I would die by more than Indian torture to restore my King and his Family to their just Inheritance."[8]

A visionary of empire, Simcoe saw Upper Canada for what it might become rather than for what it was in 1791: a smattering of small settlements and ramshackle forts strung along the Great Lakes, dangerously near the dynamic and populous American republic. In examining a map of Upper Canada, a peninsula thrusting southward amid the Great Lakes, most people saw a vulnerable and underdeveloped limb of empire, ripe for amputation by the aggressive Americans. But Simcoe perceived the mighty arm of a revived empire that could thrust its economic and military power deep into the continent to halt American expansion, which would, he predicted, suffocate the new republic.[9]

As with the Loyalists, Simcoe empathized with the Indians as fellow victims of American aggression. He denounced the Americans for their

> great Swindling Transactions of selling the Indians' Lands to pay off the Debts of the United States; the Right of Preemption, or Speculation, two words of great Swindling Extent; all prove that the United States are rapacious to Seize upon the Indian Lands and to annihilate the whole race of those unfortunate People!

Simcoe meant to help them while bolstering Canada's security. By meddling with Indians south of the Great Lakes, Simcoe denied the legal existence of a boundary with the United States. For justification, he insisted that American violations had nullified the peace treaty of 1783.[10]

While professing a paternalistic sympathy for Indians, Simcoe meant to control those who resided within Upper Canada. He disliked dissent and unpredictability, and he meant to employ the Indians as military auxiliaries in his aggressive game with the Americans. Seeking greater control, Simcoe pressed his superiors to give him command over the Indian Department within his province. That proposal sought to marginalize the authority of Sir John Johnson, whom Simcoe disdained as a political rival and disliked as a dithering temporizer. Playing music to his superiors' ears, Simcoe promised to cut costs and to dissolve the local power of the wayward agents of the Indian Department. To impress the Indians, Simcoe would personally dispense presents at his capital "with all due form & solemnity under his Majesty's Picture." Looking up at a picture of George III, the Indians would learn "to repose in Security on their great Father, [to] consider Him, & not his Officers or Agents as their benevolent Benefactor."[11]

Joseph Brant welcomed Simcoe's willingness to confront the United States but not his attempts to command the Indians as if they were British pawns. Brant defended the traditional Iroquois role as distinct allies, separate and equal. British officials retorted that their presents obligated Indians to behave deferentially as dutiful dependents. Brant countered that, in fact, the British owed presents to Indians in payment for past services in war and for present concessions of forts, trading posts, and settlements permitted in Indian country. In Brant's growing irritation with British meddling, the federal leaders saw an opportunity to seek a separate peace with the Indians of the borderland.[12]

PHILADELPHIA

In July 1791, Pickering had invited the Six Nations chiefs to visit the national capital, Philadelphia, to meet the president during the ensuing winter. In addition to impressing them with American goodwill, Pickering hoped to awe the Iroquois with American wealth and power:

> I have no doubt that they have often heard the United States vilified by the British & represented as poor, mean & contemptible. The dignity of the President & the splendor of his house—the number of attendants, the magnificence of entertainments . . . cannot fail to strike them with surprize and to excite their reverence. The public buildings in Philadelphia—the extent & populousness of the city, the vast quantities of goods in every street, and the shipping at the wharves will so much exceed any thing they have before seen, and so far surpass their present ideas that they cannot fail to wonder and admire.

Such a visit grew in American importance after the crushing defeat of St. Clair's army in November 1791.[13]

St. Clair's debacle provoked panic along the New York and Pennsylvania frontier, as settlers concluded that the news would induce the Iroquois to join the confederates in attacking Americans. The victorious confederates did send renewed threats to the Iroquois at Grand River, Buffalo Creek, and Genesee: join the war against the Americans or suffer attack as traitors to the native cause. From the Genesee country, Othniel Taylor observed, "I think it of the utmost importance that government does something immediately not only to satisfy our Indians but to Protect them as I think they are in danger." Without that security, he expected the Genesee Indians to protect themselves by joining the war, lashing out against the settlers. "You must know," Taylor warned Oliver Phelps, that "a few [hostile] Indians would ruin the Settlement."[14]

To calm settler panic and to reassure the Iroquois, federal leaders commissioned Samuel Kirkland to bring the leading chiefs to Philadelphia for consultation. Accompanied by the Oneidas Skenandon, Peter Otsequette, Good Peter, and Jacob Reed and the Mohican chief Captain Hendrick Aupaumut, Kirkland hastened west to Genesee to recruit Seneca, Cayuga, and Onondaga chiefs. Most proved eager "to see the Great Council of the 13 fires, & to get a peep at the great American Chief," George Washington. Indeed, given the many curious and jealous chiefs, Kirkland struggled (in vain) to restrict the Iroquois numbers and their cost to his federal employers. Few chiefs of any influence or aspiration would accept exclusion. And some sought enhanced dignity by bringing along a warrior or two as assistants. Kirkland's gathering host included the preeminent Senecas Red Jacket, Farmer's Brother, and Little Billy. But neither Cornplanter nor Brant deigned to join a throng of lesser chiefs, lest either sacrifice his pretensions to superiority.[15]

In early March, Kirkland led about fifty Iroquois, a mix of chiefs and warriors, southeast down the Susquehanna Valley and through the settlements of northern Pennsylvania. On March 13, the party reached Philadelphia, where the chiefs were welcomed as honored dignitaries of enormous importance but uncertain loyalties. On March 19, the festive visit turned somber with the sudden death of Peter Otsequette. A weak young man, "French Peter" had struggled to fulfill the exaggerated expectations of his people and of his American patrons. His greatest achievement came in dying, occasioning a massive funeral on March 20, attended by 10,000, which impressed the chiefs with American numbers and goodwill.[16]

To strengthen the Covenant Chain alliance, the president proposed, and the Senate agreed, to stipulate $1,500 annually for presents to the Iroquois. In addition to providing clothing, livestock, and farm tools, the fund would support farmers, teachers, and artisans posted at a few villages to promote, in Pickering's words, "the knowledge of farming—of smith's & carpenter's work—of spinning & weaving—and of reading and writing." Once that fund had been established, Pickering and Knox turned to persuading the chiefs to exert their influence to induce the Indian confederates to make peace with the United States.[17]

Of course, the Iroquois had their own agenda in visiting the federal capital. In formal reply to Washington's opening speech, Red Jacket shrewdly spun out more meaning than the president had intended. The chief recapitulated,

> The President has in effect told us that we were freemen; the sole propri-
> etors of the soil on which we live. This is the source of the joy; which we
> feel— How can two brothers speak freely together, unless they feel that
> they are on equal ground.

Red Jacket sought a federal rejection of the preemption right asserted by New York or by the assignees of Massachusetts. It baffled and irritated the Iroquois that outsiders could claim a future right to Indian property, that they could even buy and sell that alleged right as if it was already a tangible property—as Oliver Phelps and Nathaniel Gorham and Robert Morris had already done. The chiefs well understood that speculators who bought a "preemption right" would, to recoup their investment, relentlessly pressure the Indians to forsake possession. Salvation lay in a federal recognition of a sole and complete Indian proprietorship in their land. Only as federally rec- ognized "freemen" and "the sole proprietors of the soil" could the Iroquois fend off the insidious threat of preemption, which entailed a future property in Indian dispossession.[18]

Red Jacket revived the implications of Washington's speech delivered to Cornplanter on December 29, 1790. But the administration had backed away from that position in 1791 to mollify Governor Clinton, who insisted on pre- emption. In Philadelphia in March 1792, however, no federal leader seems to have challenged Red Jacket's revival of the president's promise, lest contra- diction dampen the Iroquois enthusiasm for assisting federal diplomacy in Indian country.[19]

In late April, laden with presents and impressed with their treatment, the Iroquois chiefs departed from Philadelphia. Kirkland credited the Oneidas for promoting a more pro-American perspective among the other chiefs: "The manners & sentiments of the Senekas, Onondagas, & Cayugas gradu- ally assimilated to those of the Oneidas by their intercourse with each other for about four months." Above all, Good Peter had improved the group's mood: "The Senekas felt & acknowledged his superior talents as well as elo- quence. His rigid temperance & strict piety have gained him much esteem." Here then were the fruits of the federal policy of reconstituting the Covenant Chain and the Six Nations: through the Oneidas, federal leaders could sway the powerful Senecas far more successfully than by dealing with them in isolation.[20]

The Philadelphia visit by the chiefs reassured the settlers on the Genesee frontier. In April, a leading settler joked, "Indian disturbances are hardly thot of unless it is when we find from the New England [news]papers [that] we are all killed." In July at Canandaigua, Israel Chapin reported, "The chiefs that went to Congress are our zealous Friends." He concluded, "The five Nations are perfectly reconciled so that we have nothing to fear from them at present."[21]

But the enhanced Iroquois confidence in federal protection troubled Governor Clinton's supporters. In August, William Colbrath, the Herkimer County sheriff, warned the governor, "The Indians of the different Tribes are Very Saucy since their Return from Philadelphia this Spring." [22]

CHAPIN

To administer federal relations with the Iroquois, the United States needed a superintendent resident in Iroquoia, preferably in proximity to the powerful Senecas. The position's requirements were daunting. The right man would possess the patience to attend prolonged Indian councils and to cope with repeated Indian requests for presents and favors. He would also possess an integrity unknown among the speculators drawn to Indians and their lands like ants to a picnic. Pickering explained that the president wanted "one who was no speculator in Indian lands, and who had too much honesty ever to be made the instrument of deception." To one candidate, he elaborated, "You know what swarms of villains are always ready to take advantage of them. These harpies are ever watching for opportunities to make them their prey." And yet the proper agent also had to be acceptable to the archspeculator in Iroquois lands, Governor Clinton, for the federal leaders hoped to lull his opposition to their Indian policy.[23]

In January 1791, the president offered the position to Samuel Kirkland, who declined "on account of my Clerical character & duties of a Missionary." Increasingly impatient in dealing with Indians, Kirkland also disliked the "troublesome & perplexing business" of such "an ungrateful office." Kirkland proposed James Dean, but he was unacceptable to Clinton. Kirkland concluded, "Gen[era]l Knox tells me it is a matter of importance that the Agent stands well with Governor Clinton. I expect Mr. Pickering will be the man." But Pickering declined, rather than relocate his family from Pennsylvania.[24]

On April 23, 1792, the president appointed General Israel Chapin, a veteran officer from western Massachusetts who had settled at Canandaigua in the Genesee country. A visitor described Chapin as "an agreeable facetious man" who dressed "plain, homely as any farmer . . . but his wife and two daughters [were] extremely handsome and genteelly dressed." Raising cattle on a commercial scale, Chapin possessed substantial property, which attracted Indian visitors seeking food and other presents. In February, he sought the Iroquois superintendency as "a Reasonable compensation for the trouble and Expence which I cannot avoid in my present situation." As a friend of Oliver Phelps, the great land speculator of the Genesee, Chapin was also acceptable to George Clinton.[25]

To Chapin's dismay, his new position only enhanced Iroquois expectations, as they increased their visits to enjoy his hospitality. In July, Chapin complained: "I am continually surrounded by a crowd of them, since my appointment. They all expect to be fed from my table, and made glad from my cellar." Chapin needed more presents to compete with the British at Fort Niagara. He warned Pickering, "Be persuaded Sir that as long as they are able to make them more presents than they receive from us they will have the most with them." Currying Iroquois favor proved more expensive than federal leaders had anticipated.[26]

During the early 1790s, Six Nations chiefs were courted by two ardent and generous suitors. Recognizing the centrality of property to Americans and Britons, Indians regarded generosity as the measure of their sincerity. Chapin explained to his superiors that a recent present of clothing "Confirmed them in oppinion of your Friendly Disposition towards them & that your friendship did not appear by words only but by actions also." The enhanced federal attention and presents obliged British officials to respond in kind. In April 1793, Simcoe sighed, "I observed with regret the expensive dress that the Farmer's Brother had received at Philadelphia, as it adds to that expense, which it is inevitable and proper that we should be at during the present negotiation, to support our credit with the Indians." In turn, enhanced British generosity inspired the chiefs to expect even more from the Americans. In April 1794, Chapin lamented, "The Expences of the Indians increase very fast. Their demands increase with the importance [that] they suppose their friendship to be of to us."[27]

The federal presents to the Buffalo Creek chiefs irritated some American army officers, who were impatient to act more aggressively. At Fort Franklin, the commander, Lieutenant John Jeffers, worked well with Cornplanter's people, but he hated the superior airs assumed by the Buffalo Creek chiefs: "The Black Rascals will walk about with all the pomposity in the world. I had rather wade up to my ankles in blood than to be so insulted." He considered it "only flinging away public Money to send Commissioners or any other person to speak to the Indians at Buffaloe Creek while the English are in possession of Niagara."[28]

BRANT

The federal leaders still pined for Joseph Brant, regarded as the paramount chief who could sway both the Six Nations and the Indian confederacy. Kirkland insisted, "I should esteem the acquisition [worth] more than £10,000 towards the protection of the frontiers & almost believe we might have a peace with the western Indians in the space of six or eight months." Kirkland warned Knox not to underestimate Brant's gentility and wealth: "There are few Gentlemen in Canada who can set more plate upon the Table than Capt. Brant when he makes an entertainment."[29]

Through the winter of 1791–92, Pickering, Knox, and Kirkland flattered Brant in effusive letters, begging him to come to Philadelphia. Pledging "my honor or even my life for your safety," Kirkland signed, "Your affectionate Friend & Father." Contrasting federal benevolence with New York's encroachments, Kirkland assured Brant that "the general government . . . bears a very different complexion from the State governments in regard to the Indians." Knox promised that Brant's reception would "be as flattering to him as may be." On those terms, he ventured to Philadelphia in late May, shortly after Kirkland's delegation returned home.[30]

Brant's trip defied British officials. Writing to Alexander McKee of the Indian Department, Brant explained that he had to visit the Americans after "the evasive answers we received from the Officers of Government, when applied to for assistance. . . . If Great Britain wishes us to defend our Country why not tell us so in plain language[?]" Perhaps the American leaders would prove more candid, enabling a comprehensive peace that would preserve and enhance the Indian confederacy.[31]

Accompanied by a servant and an American friend, Brant headed east to Canandaigua, where he spent a week visiting Israel Chapin. Then Brant traversed the Finger Lakes country and the Mohawk Valley to Albany, accompanied by Chapin's son to provide additional protection from vengeful settlers. After descending the Hudson River to New York City, he proceeded on to Philadelphia, arriving on June 20, nearly a month after his departure from Grand River. The president and his cabinet wined and dined their coveted guest, who delighted, he assured Knox, in "the politeness and attention shewn me by your officers of Government."[32]

That politeness included the proffer of a secret pension of about $1,500, six times what the federal government paid Cornplanter, a ratio that must have delighted Brant. Knox also offered him a personal tract of frontier land valued at $50,000, plus a reservation for the Mohawks to lure them across the border into the United States. Although flattered, Brant politely declined—or so he told the British. In December 1793, Knox secretly sent $400 to Chapin to compensate Brant for "services rendered to the United States." At Chapin's death in 1795, his accounts revealed mysterious expenditures without receipts; Pickering explained that these were cash payments to Brant; "I know enough of Capt. Brant to believe that he would not have received the present but in absolute privacy."[33]

On June 28, Brant left Philadelphia, persuaded that the Indian confederation could make a deal with the Americans. Retracing his steps to Niagara, Brant again bypassed Kirkland. After all of his exertions to facilitate the trip, Kirkland felt slighted: "No Person, in the U.S., has been more friendly to his character & person . . . than myself, but he must act the Indian sometimes." Brant, however, had his reasons for hastening home. In New York City, he had narrowly dodged assassination by a settler come from the Mohawk Valley to seek vengeance for relatives killed during the war. Besides, Brant still did not trust Kirkland, deemed "that deep, dark Presbiterian."[34]

Federal leaders felt that they had reached an understanding with the one man who could bring the Indian confederates to accept American terms. Brant's old friend Rev. John Stuart proved more prescient. Writing from the Canadian side of Lake Ontario, he warned an American friend: "I fear his Interest will be over-rated by People on your side of the Water." Moreover, Brant was no one's pawn, for he served himself and his people rather than any republic or empire. In October, he visited the confederate council to warn, "General Washington is very cunning, he will try to fool us if he can. He speaks very smooth, will tell you fair stories, and at the same time want to ruin us. . . . We must be all at it, as we are all united as one man." Although Brant truly wanted peace, he felt that only Indian unity could procure the right terms from the tricky Americans, who preferred to divide the natives. After warning the confederates, however, Brant set up a secret meeting with Chapin to discuss that Indian council.[35]

Brant was playing a dangerous game by flirting with the Americans while warning the Indians and while alerting the British to some of his flirtation. By triangulating between the parties, Brant sought enhanced leverage. Instead, no one fully trusted him. Determined to control Indians within Upper Canada, Simcoe insisted that Brant should obey British orders rather than correspond and meet with American leaders. Holding fast to the Ohio line, Simcoe resented Brant's willingness to compromise with the Americans. In January 1793, Simcoe complained, "This Cunning and self-interested Savage *chooses* not to understand the difference between a fair Peace, and one upon any terms. I have much to complain of his behaviour of late." Mixing defiance and defensiveness, Brant retorted, "I have [a] good right and as it is my business to get what intelligence I could from the yankys as an Indian chief. His excellency can have the copys of the Letters I have wrote any time he pleases. . . . I think every thing of what I did [was] above board."[36]

As an Indian patriot, Brant trusted neither the Britons nor the Americans. In 1792, he curried American favor as a tactical move to pressure the British. Simcoe belatedly discerned the truth: "I believe that He considers the Indian Interests as the first Object—that as a second, tho' very inferior one, He prefers the British, in a certain degree, to the people of the States." Determined to control the Indians within his province, Simcoe resolved to undermine Brant's influence. Contrary to Brant's expectations, his American flirtation had weakened, rather than strengthened, his influence with the British.[37]

NEGOTIATION

At the end of 1792, the federal government detected a misleading glimmer of hope from its peace offensive. In the fall, the Seneca chiefs Red Jacket, Cornplanter, and Farmer's Brother had attended the confederate council, where they reaped public ridicule from their hosts, who called them "very coward Red men" for helping the Americans. When Red Jacket presented a written copy of American peace proposals, a Shawnee contemptuously hurled the document into the council fire. In reporting back to the Americans, however, the Seneca chiefs obscured their setback by insisting that the confederates would welcome a peace conference during the ensuing summer, provided the meeting was held in their country, at Sandusky on Lake Erie.[38]

In December, Knox agreed to a Sandusky peace council, reasoning that it would, at least, allow more time for General Wayne to organize and discipline his army. The administration promised $50,000 in goods and an annuity of $10,000—if the Indians would accept the land cessions made by the controversial treaties of the 1780s. If that payment did not suffice, the federal government even authorized the commissioners to offer the previously unthinkable: to relinquish some lands previously acquired by treaty from Indians. On February 24, the president's cabinet (with Thomas Jefferson's dissent) conceded that authority to the commissioners, but only as a last resort to save imperiled negotiations. Moreover, they could recede only those lands still held by the federal government, and not those already granted to land speculators and settlers. This ruled out accepting the confederates' long-standing demand that the Americans entirely withdraw behind the Ohio River. Although the federal government offered unprecedented concessions in cash and some land, the terms still fell short of Indian expectations, so swollen by their great victory over St. Clair.[39]

For peace commissioners, the administration also chose able and distinguished men of moderation: Beverly Randolph of Virginia, General Benjamin Lincoln of Massachusetts, and Timothy Pickering of Pennsylvania. These appointments followed Red Jacket's advice that the commissioners should be "sensible, proper people, no Land Jobbers, but such as Colonel Pickering." Although Red Jacket had delighted in publicly tweaking the prickly Pickering, the chief respected his integrity. To further impress the Indians, the commissioners brought along, as official observers, six Quakers and a Moravian missionary. These Christian pacifists promoted a more just and conciliatory Indian policy. The American party also included Mohican and Six Nations chiefs.[40]

Once gathered on a schooner to cross Lake Erie, the sojourners suggested a diversity and forbearance that might make a lasting peace. The Quaker Jacob Lindley marveled:

> There were representatives of five different Indian nations on board; some French, British, German, Scotch, and American United States men: some soldiers, sailors, merchants, mechanics, and farmers. Yet notwithstanding all the variety of prospects and interests, a perfect harmony and decorum were observed.

But the lake voyage inspired very different sentiments from Benjamin Lincoln, who focused on the future of the fertile shore rather than the present of the diverse passengers:

> I cannot persuade myself that it will remain long in so uncultivated a state; especially when I consider that to people fully the earth was in the original plan of the benevolent Deity. I am confident that sooner or later . . . no men will be suffered to live by hunting on lands capable of improvement, and which would support more people under a state of cultivation. So that if the savages cannot be civilized and quit their present pursuits, they will, in consequence of their stubbornness, dwindle and moulder away, from causes perhaps imperceptible to us, until the whole race shall become extinct.

Although embarked on a mission of peace and compromise, Lincoln understood it as a short-term correction meant to facilitate the long-term triumph of his race and culture.[41]

To reach the Indian confederacy, the American commissioners wisely took the "back door" via Niagara. That route obligated them to seek British assistance. During June and early July, they lingered at Niagara as Simcoe's guests, impatiently awaiting word that the Indian confederates would, in fact, agree to meet with them. Simcoe impressed his American guests as the most generous and gregarious of hosts, but he denounced them in private letters as possessed "of that low Craft which distinguishes, and is held for Wisdom, by People who like the Subjects of the United States, naturally self-opinionated, have a very trifling share of Education." In late July, Simcoe confided, "You may be sure I was glad to be rid of the commissioners after six weeks of their company."[42]

Simcoe wanted the Indians to make peace only if the Americans met their boundary demand: the Ohio River. To help the Indians deal with paper-bearing Americans, Simcoe provided copies of maps and documents from Sir William Johnson's records kept by the Indian Department. Acting on Brant's advice, Simcoe also refused to facilitate the shipment of American provisions to feed the Indians at the prospective council, for a feeding host could pressure the native participants. To preserve British influence, Simcoe insisted that he, rather than the Americans, would provision the council. Food was power in the borderland.[43]

In late July, the commissioners sailed across Lake Erie to encamp at the mouth of the Detroit River, where they hoped soon to receive a summons to the confederate council. But the confederates still refused to meet them unless the commissioners first promised to concede the Ohio River as the boundary. As more days dragged by, drunken Indian visitors, rumors of impending attack, a dank heat, and biting insects took a toll on the encamped and frustrated Americans.[44]

Begging a council with the confederates, the commissioners promised to pay "such a large sum, in money or goods, as was never given at one time, for any quantity of Indian lands, since the white people first set their foot on this island." In addition, the United States would "every year, deliver you a large quantity of such goods as are best suited to the wants of yourselves, your women, and children." And the government would return some trans-Ohio lands, but not those already sold by Congress:

> You are men of understanding, and if you consider the customs of white people, the great expenses which attend their settling in a new country, the nature of their improvements in building houses, and barns, and clearing and fencing their lands, how valuable the lands are thus rendered, and thence how dear they are to them, you will see that it is now impracticable to remove our people from the northern side of the Ohio.

By emphasizing actual settlers (who, in fact, numbered only 3,220 in 1793), the commissioners obscured the fact that most of the granted lands were still unimproved and belonged to nonresident land speculators, wealthy men of great clout in American politics.[45]

Disdaining a large payment in goods or a limited restoration of land, the confederate chiefs wished instead to break the process of American expansion. On August 13, they replied:

> You have talked to us about concessions. It appears strange that you should expect any from us, who have only been defending our just rights against your invasions. We want peace. Restore to us our country, and we shall be enemies no longer.

Instead of taking American money for Indian land, the chiefs proposed a provocative alternative to accommodate the displaced settlers:

> As no consideration whatever can induce us to sell the lands on which we get sustenance for our women and children, we hope we may be allowed to point out a mode by which your settlers may be easily removed and peace thereby obtained. Brothers: We know that these settlers are poor, or they would never have ventured to live in a country which has been in continual trouble ever since they crossed the Ohio. Divide, therefore, this large sum of money, which you have offered to us, among these people: give to each, also a proportion of what you say you would give to us, annually, over and above this very large sum of money: and we are persuaded, they would most readily accept of it, in lieu of the lands you sold them. If you add, also the great sums you must expend in raising and paying armies, with a view to force us to yield you our country, you will certainly have more than sufficient for the purposes of repaying these settlers for all their labor and their improvements.

This proposal sought to break the dynamic by which American society transformed class conflict into westward expansion. The Indians recognized that the inequality of white society shunted the poorest to the frontier margins to make property at native expense. Americans considered it far more legitimate for poor white men to dispossess the natives than to demand a redistribution of the wealth held by their leading men. As a radical alternative, the Indians demanded that American rulers pay the frontier poor to withdraw to the southern and eastern banks of the Ohio.[46]

Of course, this Indian proposal was far too radical for the American commissioners to consider. Their nation depended on continued expansion, on the multiplication of family farms producing for the market and integrated into the republic's politics. Expansion built the wealth and population that the new union needed to consolidate control over its member states and to fend off interference from the British and Spanish empires.

Only continued public land sales could generate the revenue needed to sustain the nation's government and to fund its Revolutionary War debt. And that expansion preserved social peace between the classes by providing an outlet for poor families seeking property and the liberty it afforded. Without territorial expansion, American leaders dreaded that some medley of class or civil war and foreign intervention would destroy their risky experiment in American independence, republican government, and federal union. Only the continued consumption of Indian land to make private property could sustain the American social order that combined inequality with opportunity.[47]

Breaking off contact with the confederates, the commissioners hastened back to Philadelphia. In light of their failure, the Washington administration empowered General Wayne to mount an offensive against the confederates during the spring of 1794. A Detroit trader marveled, "The Americans must certainly be a restless People, for no sooner is one army destroyed than another springs up in its place."[48]

The ruptured negotiations divided the Indian confederacy because the defiant final message represented the views of the hard-liners at the expense of the moderates. Led by Brant, the moderates favored a compromise boundary along the Muskingum River (which flowed into the Ohio): a line that conceded the eastern quarter of Ohio already partially settled by the Americans. Brant regarded that compromise as the last chance for making a deal with the Americans that would preserve the Indian confederacy. But Brant lacked sufficient clout to sway the confederation, having alienated the hard-liners, particularly the Shawnees, by his absence from the attack on St. Clair and by his subsequent visit to Philadelphia to consort with American leaders. In 1793, the hard-liners excluded Brant from important meetings and treated him with public contempt. Insulted and frustrated, he lashed back: "I was in a Great measure Blamed for every thing and . . . they were pissing away the time and did not wish to come to any Point whatever."[49]

Brant blamed Alexander McKee of the Indian Department for encouraging the hard-liners. McKee possessed a powerful influence, thanks to his keen intelligence, Simcoe's patronage, and Shawnee kinship by mother (an adopted white captive), wife, and children. The Indian confederates believed that McKee had promised them overt British military assistance during the next military campaign if they rebuffed the American peace overture in 1793.[50]

In response, McKee blasted Brant for creating a divisive misunderstanding. As a translator and go-between for the Americans and the confederates, Brant had fudged key messages, misleading each side to expect concessions that the other could not make. He obscured fundamental disagreements in

Sir Guy Carleton, Lord Dorchester, by Mable B. Messer.
(Courtesy of Library and Archives Canada; C-002833.)

the desperate hope that, once brought together, the two sides might make surprising compromises. But McKee considered Brant's deceptions both foolish and dangerous, for the Americans would never accept the Muskingum compromise line. By missing that point, McKee argued, Brant had foolishly divided the confederation that should have rallied around the hardliners.[51]

Simcoe firmly vindicated McKee, who had followed Simcoe's confidential orders. Simcoe suspected that Brant sought to draw the British into the war with the Americans by so publicly blaming McKee for the ruptured negotiations. Respecting Brant's goals, Simcoe conceded that "he is true to the Indian Interest, and honorable in his Attachment, . . . [for] he sees the Calamities which in all probability must ultimately attend the Continuance of the War, unless by some means or other Great Britain shall take a direct part [in] the protection of the Indians." The next year, however, seemed to promise the overt British assistance that Brant had so long sought against the Americans.[52]

THE BRINK

In 1794, a crisis in Anglo-American relations threatened war. In 1793, France and Great Britain had renewed their chronic warfare, leading the British to seize 250 American merchant ships trading with the French West Indies. American outrage compounded resentments over the withheld border posts and the Indian war. Sympathy for the French Revolution also promoted boisterous public celebrations of French victories over the British. Taking his cue from the hostile American press and public, Lord Dorchester anticipated that the United States would honor its treaty of alliance with France by attacking the British posts and by invading Canada. When some Vermont settlers harassed a small border post, Dorchester feared that a general American attack was imminent. He also suspected that General Wayne's army meant not only to attack the Indians, but to sweep through them to seize Detroit.[53]

In a provocative speech in February 1794, Dorchester urged the Indians of Lower Canada to prepare for war. He refused to recognize American claims beyond their settlements held at war's end in 1783: "All their approaches towards us since that time, and the Purchases made by them, I consider as an Infringement on the King's Rights." Investing British sovereignty in Indian independence, Dorchester also denounced Wayne's new forts in the Ohio country as aggression against "the King's Rights in the Indian Country." Given the abrupt shift by the usually cautious Dorchester, everyone—Canadian, American, and Indian—assumed that he had secret orders from London to prepare for war. Although he did not, the pervasive assumption took on a life of its own, as everyone prepared for a war that the imperial overlords did not want.[54]

In February, Dorchester directed Simcoe to rally the Indians and to arm his vessels on the Great Lakes. Most provocatively of all, in April Dorchester sent Simcoe to build a new fort on the Maumee River—Fort Miamis—to supply the Indians and to guard the southern approaches to Detroit. Delighted by the aggressive new policy, Simcoe pressured the Buffalo Creek chiefs to abandon the Americans and to assist the British in the anticipated war. Israel Chapin reported that John Butler and other Indian Department officers "took pains on all occasions to represent a War between their Government and ours as inevitable." While rallying the Indians, Simcoe also tried to intimidate the Genesee settlers who had pressed perilously close to Niagara. In August, he warned them to retreat eastward or face attack. The apparent turn in British policy thrilled the Indian confederates. McKee reported that the new fort on the Maumee River "has given great spirits to the Indians and impressed them with the hope of our ultimately acting with them and affording a security for their families, should their Enemy penetrate to their Villages."[55]

Federal leaders denounced Dorchester and Simcoe as aggressors for meddling with Indians and settlements within the border claimed by the United States. Washington denounced the "irregular and high-handed proceeding of Mr. Simcoe" as "the most open and daring act of the British agents in America." The president concluded that "all the difficulties we encounter with the Indians, their hostilities, the murders of helpless women and innocent children along our frontiers, result from the conduct of the agents of Great Britain in this country." War was inevitable, he concluded, unless the British promptly surrendered the border posts.[56]

That spring, Governor Thomas Mifflin deepened the crisis by asserting Pennsylvania's claim to "the Erie Triangle," a tract of 800,000 acres fronting on Lake Erie and including the valuable harbor at Presque Isle. Pennsylvania had bought the triangle from the United States in September 1788. To extinguish Indian claims, the state also paid a mere $2,000 to Cornplanter at Fort Harmar in January 1789. Excluded from the payment, the Buffalo Creek and Grand River chiefs denied the purchase, which Cornplanter also regretted shortly after frontier ruffians stole the goods paid to him for it. The controversy escalated during the spring of 1794, when Pennsylvania troops entered the disputed triangle to build forts meant to protect surveyors and road builders.[57]

The Six Nations chiefs dreaded that the new forts and projected settlements would separate Iroquoia from the Indian confederates of the Ohio country. Blasting the Pennsylvania advance as a threat to Indian sovereignty, Brant protested to the president:

> Brother, We are of the same opinion with the People of the United States. You consider yourselves as Independent People. We, as the Original inhabitants of this Country & Sovereigns of the Soil, look upon ourselves as equally independent & free as any other Nation or Nations. This Country was gave to us by the Great Spirit above, we wish to enjoy it—and have an open passage . . . within the line we have pointed out.

By diminishing diplomatic contacts (which traveled along the south shore of Lake Erie) and by blocking the Six Nations' option to flee west to join the confederates, if duress so dictated, the intrusive forts reduced the Iroquois leverage with the Americans. Why bestow concessions and presents on peoples confined by fortified settlements? Military force would then suffice to intimidate them. Urging the fortification of Presque Isle, a Pennsylvania official, Andrew Ellicott, predicted that the Iroquois

> would find themselves cut off from the western Indians, their principal Towns liable to be destroyed at any time in three days, and their very existence as a people depending on their preserving peace with the United States. They foresee all these consequences, and are, therefore by their present menacing and management, endeavouring to prevent an establishment, which they are sensible must command their fears, and awe them into peace, without purchasing at an extravagant price their good will.

Ellicott agreed with Brant that the Erie occupation would produce Iroquois dependency, but the Pennsylvanian celebrated what the Mohawk dreaded.[58]

Infuriated by Pennsylvania's advance, Cornplanter abandoned his pro-American position and instead cooperated with Simcoe, who bestowed generous presents and promised a pension. In July, John Adlum, a Pennsylvania surveyor, visited Cornplanter's village to urge restraint, but he found the inhabitants soured against the Americans. When Adlum tried to address the village council, he experienced a new form of hostility: "The young Indians on the beams above, saluted me with an univer[sal] roar, *vulgarly called farting.*"[59]

During Wayne's critical offensive against the confederates, the federal government could not afford to alienate the Iroquois. In April, Washington directed Knox, "General Chapin should be instructed to leave no means unessayed to keep the Six Nations well disposed towards the U.S." In late May, the president (through Knox) urged Governor Mifflin to withdraw his troops from the Erie Triangle, pending resolution of the diplomatic crisis. Mifflin grudgingly and partially agreed. His troops stopped short of Presque Isle, but they held their ground at Le Boeuf, fifteen miles south of the lake, where they built a blockhouse.[60]

Meanwhile, British agents invited the Iroquois within New York to withdraw to Grand River, reversing the former policy of the 1780s, which had tried to constitute a buffer zone by keeping most of the Iroquois east of the Niagara River. By 1794, that policy had clearly failed, for expanding American settlements had enveloped the Iroquois enclaves as far west as the Genesee River. Subject to settler pressure, those Iroquois villages might supply invaluable scouts and warriors to assist the Americans against the British. "Admitting these Indians into the King's Territories [is]," Simcoe concluded, "the only means of preventing their being turned against us."[61]

Brant delighted in the new policy, which endorsed his long-standing goal of reuniting the Six Nations behind the British line. Abandoning his flirtation with American officials, Brant sent secret messages to the Iroquois within New York. By withdrawing behind the British line, they could become "more Compact and Connected; this we mean to do as Privately as Possible to Prevent the Americans suspecting our designs until . . . the Business be Effected." He sent twenty warriors to the Allegheny to protect the removal of Cornplanter's people to Grand River. Adlum reported, "I think Capt. Brandt has a very great hand in it, and his policy is to get the whole of the Six Nations on the North side of the Lakes, as it will make him the more consequential."[62]

Fearing the impending war, many Onondagas, Tuscaroras, and Cayugas within New York accepted Brant's invitation and Simcoe's presents. Their exodus alarmed New York's settlers as ominous. Kirkland discovered that Simcoe and Brant even enticed the Oneidas with secret messages, promising protection and presents: "two suits ready for the Sachems & head warriors & one suit for every individual and a plenty of guns & ammunition for all their young warriors." About a dozen Oneida families vowed to move, but only if war did break out.[63]

Settlers found reassurance in the persistence of genial Indians—or felt alarmed by their sullen words or sudden disappearance. Consequently, the Washington administration denounced the British enticement of the Iroquois. Jefferson's successor as secretary of state, Edmund Randolph, insisted, "It has grown into a maxim, that the affairs of the Indians within the boundaries of any nation, exclusively belong to that nation." Simcoe retorted that such exclusivity was "incompatible with the natural rights and injurious to the acknowledged Independency of the Indian Americans."[64]

Anticipating war, the British in Canada desperately needed Indian help to even the odds against the numerous Americans. In 1794, the federal army of 4,000 tripled the 1,325 British regulars in Upper Canada. Consequently, British officials on the border could ill afford to watch and wait as Wayne overwhelmed the Indian confederacy that buffered Canada from invasion. But those officials lacked authority from their London superiors openly to assist the Indians against the Americans. To their deep frustration, Simcoe, Butler, and McKee could offer only ammunition, provisions, and vague suggestions of something more.[65]

As the summer progressed, and Wayne's army advanced, many of the confederated Indians grew impatient with the British. Lacking orders to advance, the British troops clung to their own forts at Detroit, Miamis, and Niagara. An Ojibwa chief protested that the British "set on the Indians and the states, one against the other, like two dogs, and that they merely looked on and did nothing." In early August, the Wyandot chiefs exhorted Colonel

Richard England, Detroit's commandant: "We hope you will now fulfill your promise; rise upon your feet and stand by us." But England could do nothing but await new orders as Wayne relentlessly advanced.[66]

Despising this limbo between peace and war, Simcoe urged his superiors in London to declare war and to unleash him upon the Americans. He fantasized about invading the republic to reverse the American Revolution. While Dorchester sensibly planned for only the defensive war appropriate to the scanty forces in Upper Canada, Simcoe recklessly schemed to conquer the United States. Despising the ramshackle border forts as useless, he declared, "Upper Canada is not to be defended by remaining within the Boundary Line." By erasing that line, he promised within three months to rout Wayne's army, destroy the American forts in Ohio and Pennsylvania, burn the Genesee settlements, and neutralize Kentucky. During the following year, he offered to sweep across Pennsylvania to rout Washington at Philadelphia.[67]

While the crisis heated up in the borderland and in Simcoe's correspondence, however, it cooled down in London diplomacy. Faring badly in war with France, the British could ill afford another conflict in North America. That summer British leaders also discovered that they could do business with John Jay, the conciliatory special envoy sent to London by Washington. On July 4, the British secretary of state, Henry Dundas, sent dispatches directing Simcoe to avoid any military action. Dundas explained that he expected Jay's negotiations to culminate in "a perfect good understanding between this Country and the States of America." But the long lag in transatlantic communication played a cruel trick on Simcoe, who persisted in writing bellicose letters during the ten weeks that elapsed between the dispatch of Dundas's letter and its arrival in Upper Canada.[68]

FALLEN TIMBERS

The borderland crisis culminated in August, when Wayne's army pushed northward into the Maumee Valley, the heartland of the confederacy. At Fallen Timbers on August 20, Wayne defeated the Indians and a company of British traders conscripted by the natives and obliged to wear the paint and attire of warriors. Enraged at finding whites in Indian disguise, the victorious Americans summarily hung four captured traders. After defeating the Indians, Wayne menaced the nearby Fort Miamis. The British commander, Major Campbell, coldly refused either to admit the retreating Indians or to fire on the Americans. Demoralized, the natives abandoned their large villages and vast cornfields—which Wayne systematically destroyed.[69]

Although the Indians had suffered relatively light casualties at Fallen Timbers, they were triply demoralized by the loss of their homes, their crops, and their faith in British assistance. Put to the test by Wayne's advancing army, the British alliance had failed. Bitter recriminations followed, reminiscent of those that followed the British betrayal in the peace treaty of 1783. In October, a Delaware chief publicly rebuked the British:

> Thou hast always hitherto urged us to go to war against the States. We have followed thee to our great loss. Look at the graves on the [Maumee River] . . . Thou art the cause of their death. Thou hast always preached to us and said, "Behold, the States are taking away your land. Be brave, act like men. Let not your land be taken from you. Fight for your land." But now we have got at the truth. The States have struck thee to the ground and overcome thee. Therefore hast thou given them our land in order to have peace from them, but thou tellest us to fight for it, so that we may all be blotted out. See, this is the truth. Thou urgest us to war, but sittest still thyself, and mayest not raise thy hand. So hast thou deceived us for many years.

British passivity at the critical moment in 1794 discredited their border theory: that the peace treaty of 1783 had done nothing to weaken Indian autonomy or to undermine their possession of the land. Instead, the Americans' victory vindicated their own border theory: that Indians must become their dependents within a boundary fixed by the 1783 treaty. To make peace and retain some of their country, the Indians of the Ohio country had to accept the American border, which meant forsaking their confederacy and the British alliance.[70]

Recognizing the Indian's importance to Canadian security and the fur trade, McKee and Simcoe had longed to send British troops to assist the confederates. But borderland officials could not set policy for a vast empire with diverse, global interests clumsily coordinated from distant London. When push came to shove, they had to follow orders from the imperial overlords, who chose peace with the Americans. As in 1783, the borderland officials tried in late 1794 to cool Indian fury by increasing their provisions and presents.[71]

CANANDAIGUA

During the spring and summer of 1794, the American officials had desperately worked to preserve Iroquois neutrality to protect General Wayne's advance. The federal leaders invited the Iroquois to attend a council in September, with Timothy Pickering, an Iroquois favorite, as the federal treaty commissioner. The federal administration also reassured the Iroquois by inviting Quakers to attend as official observers. The promise of a council pacified the Iroquois within New York through the critical summer, permitting Wayne's march to victory at Fallen Timbers.[72]

Most of the Iroquois chiefs preferred to meet the Americans at Buffalo Creek, where British influence could counterbalance American pressure. With a similar reading of the political geography, Pickering insisted upon Canandaigua, an American settlement in the Genesee country. To attract the chiefs, he promised to remove "all your Grievances" and to provide plenty of provisions and presents. Writing from Canandaigua, Pickering cited the precedent

> that when Sir William Johnson had the care of all the Indians, he had a Council Fire at his house and when he had any Business with the Six Nations, he sent for them to attend his fire place. As General Chapin has now the Care of you, it will be proper to attend the Council Fire at this place.

Rather than lose the chance to meet Pickering, the chiefs agreed to meet at Canandaigua. Invoking Sir William's name defined the authority of tradition in Iroquois diplomacy.[73]

Beautifully situated at the foot of a long (20 miles) and narrow (1.5 miles) lake, Canandaigua displayed the rapid transformation of the New York frontier by speculators' capital and settlers' labor. An abandoned Indian village in 1784, a decade later Canandaigua possessed a courthouse and jail, plus forty framed houses, including the elegant mansions of Thomas Morris and Oliver Phelps. Most of the settlers were New England emigrants of more property and propriety than normal for the frontier.[74]

Although the Indians manifested genial goodwill, they also made a show of their martial prowess upon arriving. William Savery, a Quaker observer, reported that Cornplanter's warriors "drew up in three sides of a square, the Oneidas, Onondagoes, &c., facing them; each fired three rounds and performed some maneuvers; all in full Indian dress and painted in an extraordinary manner." Savery concluded, "They made a truly terrific and warlike appearance." The Iroquois meant to be taken seriously as negotiating partners. By mid-October, about 1,600 Iroquois had assembled for the largest council since Sir William Johnson's treaty at Fort Stanwix in 1768.[75]

On October 18, Pickering opened the council by conducting the mutual condolence ceremony needed to prepare minds for peace. Savery reported, "He wiped the blood from their beds and the tears from their eyes, and opened the path of peace, which the Indians were requested to keep open at one end and the United States at the other, as long as the sun shone." This

perpetual definition of their relationship delighted the Iroquois as the antidote to the dissolution of their sovereignty by New York's speculators and
settlers.[76]

Because Iroquois independence lay in positioning themselves equally
between the two great powers, the Buffalo Creek chiefs had invited the
attendance of William Johnston, an Indian Department officer who resided
with them. The chiefs explained, "We think the British have as good a right
to be present at our Council as the Americans." Pickering, however, meant to
conduct a council without British meddling, which he blamed for the failure
of the Sandusky peace initiative of 1793. Federal officials had resolved never
again to accept any British interest in Indian affairs on the American side of
their border. In a fiery speech delivered on October 25, Pickering demanded
Johnston's ouster: "Brothers, we had long patiently endured the insolence of
the British, but we shall endure it no longer." Rather than break up the council, the chiefs reluctantly accepted Johnston's ejection, for they had serious
land matters to discuss with Pickering.[77]

The Six Nations wanted federal protection for their lands and the restoration of two tracts that, if left in American hands, threatened to restrict
them to the west. In addition to claiming Pennsylvania's Erie Triangle, the
Iroquois contested the 1784 Treaty of Fort Stanwix cession to the federal
government of lands along the Niagara River and west of Buffalo Creek.
Early in the council, Pickering conceded that "there was too much reason for
their complaints of harsh treatment at the treaty of Fort Stanwix." The
offending tracts threatened to confine and diminish the Iroquois. They
feared, in Pickering's words, that "if they suffer the United States to inclose
them, on all sides, they will become, like other tribes in the interior of the
states, mere makers of baskets and brooms." The Seneca matrons complained that "they had found themselves much distressed by being hemmed
in, but if the request was granted they should feel themselves much relieved
& more at liberty." To be free, the Six Nations needed an open border to their
west with British Canada and with their kin at Grand River.[78]

Per his official instructions, Pickering could offer no concession on the
Erie Triangle, but if the Six Nations conceded that tract to Pennsylvania, he
agreed to surrender most of the Niagara River tract. The United States
would retain the four-mile-wide strip from Fort Niagara to Fort Schlosser,
including the strategic portage around the celebrated waterfalls. But Pickering agreed to limit American occupation of the rest of the riverside strip,
above Fort Schlosser, to no more than a right-of-way as far as Buffalo Creek.
And he conceded about 1 million acres beyond Buffalo Creek as far as the
western terminus of New York State at the Erie Triangle. This latter concession relieved the villagers of Cattaraugus and Buffalo Creek, which had been

imperiled by the federal claim. Although acceptable to the Buffalo Creek and Genesee chiefs, this deal outraged Cornplanter, who wanted recession of the Erie Triangle, which lay closer to his Allegheny village. But his Iroquois influence had suffered from Pickering's revelation that Cornplanter had already taken Pennsylvania's money twice for the Triangle, sharing none with his peers.[79]

On November 11, 1794, Pickering concluded the Treaty of Canandaigua and distributed the final presents to Iroquois satisfaction. Unlike preceding treaties, this time the Iroquois recovered some land. The federal government also gave goods worth $10,000 and tripled its annuity to $4,500. Recognized as allies of the United States, the Six Nations became more than dependent "members" of New York State. The treaty acknowledged the Massachusetts and New York preemption claims to Iroquois lands, but required federal oversight to any future Indian cessions by stipulating that the native reservations would endure "until they choose to sell the same to the people of the United States, who have the right to purchase."[80]

This, the Iroquois felt, was how a treaty council should conclude: in a closer relationship with a generous partner. Three months later, Chapin reported to Pickering: "Our treaty last fall has given Universal satisfaction to the Six Nations. It's remarkable to observe the happiness & good Understanding it has caused throughout the Frontier settlement, especially on the part of the Indians." Pickering also liked the treaty that he had made for the United States: "The great object is obtained: an express renunciation which takes in all the lands in Pennsylvania, including the Triangle which comprehends Presqu'Isle." And he had done so in a way that improved a relationship critical to federal Indian policy.[81]

Pickering treated the Iroquois with relative generosity because the military dimensions and political consequences of the Battle of Fallen Timbers still remained unclear. On October 27, the tenth day of the council, William Savery observed, "The Indians appear cautious of letting out the particulars, probably from the fear that they may operate to their disadvantage at this critical juncture of the treaty; and the accounts being very various, nothing can be clearly ascertained." Given the small casualties of the battle, its real significance was political: in the disunity promoted by disaffection with the British. And those political consequences emerged gradually, over the course of the winter and spring of 1795, when the confederation slowly unraveled. During the preceding fall of 1794, the prevailing news actually weakened American clout, for the settlers in western Pennsylvania had risen in violent rebellion against a federal whiskey tax.[82]

As of November 1794, the Ohio country war and the Whiskey Rebellion both remained unresolved, so the Six Nations retained their critical importance to federal frontier policy. Mollifying them made abundant good sense, as the United States Senate and President Washington showed by promptly ratifying the treaty in January 1795. Washington also rewarded Pickering with a promotion to replace Knox as secretary of war, which the Senate also quickly approved.[83]

Notifying the Six Nations of federal ratification, Pickering emphasized the treaty's importance as a model meant to induce the Ohio confederates to come to terms. The treaty offered, he explained,

> an evidence of the just and humane sentiments of the United States towards all the Indian Nations on our Borders, and [the treaty] should induce those also, who have long been hostile, to come forward with confidence that with them also the United States will negociate and establish treaties of Peace and Friendship on the Principles of Justice, and humanity.

To understand the Treaty of Canandaigua, we need to place it in the middle of a gradual process of pacifying the Indian country, a process incomplete until August 1795.[84]

In a dig at the British, the Treaty of Canandaigua limited the federal annuity to those Iroquois resident "within the boundaries of the United States: for the United States do not interfere with nations, tribes, or families of Indians, elsewhere resident." In fact, however, Pickering had tried to draw Joseph Brant and the Grand River Iroquois across the British boundary to attend the Canandaigua council. Troubled by that location, Brant had declined the invitation, instead heading west to Detroit to try to rally the defeated Indian confederates. He also tried to dissuade the other Iroquois from going to Canandaigua. And Brant resented Pickering's eviction of William Johnston as a further blow to Iroquois perquisites at a council: "As a Free and Independent People, we will join in our Councils who[m] we Please."[85]

Nonetheless, Pickering persisted in considering Brant essential to completing the peace process in the borderland. In friendly letters to Brant, Pickering even insisted, contrary to the treaty's overt language, that it did not exclude the Mohawks in Canada: "As one of the Six Nations, I did not think it proper to name it as not included in the Treaty; nor to omit it, by enumerating the other five. For general concerns, I consider the whole Six as forming one Confederate Nation." Unable to ship bulky presents to Grand River, Pickering instead offered to send a cash equivalent. But Pickering's letter represented a last hurrah for federal recognition of a transborder Six Nations.[86]

Within a year, the triumphant Americans began to take their Iroquois allies for granted. In 1795, the Pennsylvanians developed settlements in the Erie Triangle, including a fort at Presque Isle. At that new fort in September, Andrew Ellicott reported: "We have little or no news in this quarter, and what little we have, is concerning Mr. Jay's Treaty. The Indians continue peaceable, and well disposed; the military establishment here will have a powerful effect in keeping them quiet."[87]

GREENVILLE

The spring of 1795 brought to North America the news that, during the preceding fall, the British in London had concluded the Jay Treaty with the United States, resolving the border crisis. Eager for peace, the British agreed to evacuate the border forts within two years. That prospect accelerated the crumbling of the Indian confederation, already weakened by British passivity at the Maumee River in 1794. Despairing of further resistance, individual villages scrambled to seek their separate peace with the victorious Americans. The spring news of the Jay Treaty rendered the Battle of Fallen Timbers more decisive than it had appeared during the preceding fall.[88]

The dissolution of the confederacy culminated in the Treaty of Greenville in August 1795, when General Wayne dictated American terms to the Ohio country natives. He achieved a primary American goal by dealing with the Shawnees, Miamis, Delawares, and Wyandots as separate nations rather than as a unified confederacy. The treaty obliged the Indians to concede the southern two-thirds of Ohio (and southeastern Indiana)—a bit more than the Americans had claimed by their controversial treaty of Fort Harmar in 1789. They also asserted the right to build forts wherever they chose within the remaining Indian country. In return, the United States paid $20,000 in goods and pledged a perpetual annuity of $9,500. Settlers who crossed the boundary to squat on Indian lands were placed "out of the protection of the United States."[89]

The treaty manifested the Federalist principles of federal supremacy over settlers; a defined boundary with Indian country; payment for Indian lands; and a federal preemption for future purchases from particular nations (rather than from a native confederacy). By setting precedents, the Treaty of Greenville was meant to facilitate later, larger Indian land cessions to the United States. In April, Pickering had explained to Wayne, "When a peace shall once be established, and we also take possession of the posts now held by the British, we can obtain every thing we shall want with a tenth part of the trouble and difficulty which you would now have to encounter." The national republic had prevailed by shattering the parallel effort by Indians to build an effective confederation. In 1796, Joseph Brant mourned "the distressed condition of the poor Indians in general" because the confederacy "seemed entirely at an end and gone too far ever to think of repairing the damage."[90]

Peace between the British Empire and the American Republic eroded the Iroquois importance to both. In succession and combination, the Battle of Fallen Timbers (August 1794), the Jay Treaty (November 1794), and the Treaty of Greenville (August 1795) set new bounds around the Six Nations. With the confederated Indians defeated and the British in retreat, the Americans took command along their border with Canada. Once the British surrendered Fort Niagara to the Americans in 1796, the two powers directly faced one another at the Niagara River boundary. This had ominous implications for the Iroquois claim to live between the empire and the republic.[91]

PART FOUR

✿

LIMITS

Old Fort Erie, with Migration of Wild Pigeons, by Edward Walsh, 1804. A British flag flies over the small fort at the outlet of Lake Erie (background) into the Niagara River (at the left). Settlers blast away at immense flocks of passenger pigeons—which are now extinct. A farm to the right attests to the environmental transformation wrought by settlement. (Courtesy of the Royal Ontario Museum; 952.218.)

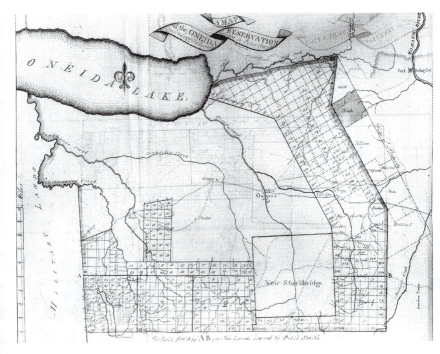

Map of the Oneida Reservation, ca. 1795. The lotted portions on the south and the east margins represent lands procured by New York State in 1795. Note the Genesee Road passing through the reservation, including the main village of Oneida (Kanonwalohale) on Oneida Creek. Note also Van Eps's store to the east and Klock's and Wemp's taverns to the west. The Mohican township of New Stockbridge lies to the south and Brothertown in the southeast corner just below Samuel Kirkland's property. (From Franklin B. Hough, comp., *Notices of Peter Penet and His Operations among the Oneida Indians* [1866]. Courtesy of the American Antiquarian Society.)

CHAPTER TEN

ໍ໌ຈໍໍ

Bounds

Settler's Cabin, Angelica, New York, by Baroness Hyde de Neuville, 1808. (Courtesy of the New-York Historical Society; 1953.240.)

I N AUGUST 1796, American troops occupied Fort Niagara after the British withdrew across the Niagara River to Fort George on the western shore. On September 21, Niagara's new American commandant, Captain James Bruff, met the Buffalo Creek chiefs in council to explain their new situation within an American boundary: "Lines are fixed, and so strongly marked between us [the British and the Americans], that they cannot be mistaken, and every precaution [has been] taken to prevent a misunderstanding." Citing the boundary, Bruff announced new restrictions on the Indians. They must cease tracking British deserters for British pay within the new American line, and the chiefs could no longer cross the border to visit British officials without his permission. He also declared that the Americans would cease the British practice of freely feeding Indian visitors at Fort Niagara. Bruff's speech alarmed the Indians as an assault on three customary rights: rewards for deserters, open communication with both powers, and official hospitality to visiting chiefs.[1]

In a pointed reply, Red Jacket argued that the Six Nations remained autonomous peoples situated *between* the British and the Americans:

> You are a cunning People without Sincerity, and not to be trusted, for after making Professions of your Regard, and saying every thing favorable to us, you . . . tell us that our Country is within the lines of the States. This surprizes us, for we had thought our Lands were our own, not within your Boundaries, but joining the British, and between you and them. But now you have got round us and next [to] the British, you tell us we are inside your Lines. . . . We had always thought that we [ad]joined the British and were outside your lines.

Red Jacket understood that the Six Nations risked losing their sovereignty if the Americans and the British directly met along a shared international border that divided the Iroquois between the empire and the republic. In response to Bruff's demands, the chiefs compromised. The Indians stopped tracking British deserters on the American side, but persisted in crossing the line to receive advice and presents from British officials.[2]

Long the keepers of a broad and porous borderland, the Iroquois now confronted a double set of restricting boundaries: first, the international border along the Niagara River and, second, the private property lines run by surveyors demarcating Indian reservations as pockets surrounded by settlers. The two sets of lines interacted, reinforcing the constriction of the native world. Emboldened by Fort Niagara in American hands, settlers pressed across the Genesee River into western New York after 1796. In turn, their settlements constricted the Indians, confirming American control of the international border run down the Niagara River.[3]

The double set of boundaries also emboldened state and colonial officials to challenge native sovereignty by imposing their law of murder. Having made peace with one another, the British in Upper Canada and the Americans in New York could press their law upon the Indians on each side of the boundary. Rejecting the Indian customary law that covered graves, officials wanted trials and executions to manifest that times had changed, that settler government and colonial law prevailed on both sides of the boundary.

PICKERING'S ADVICE

The Oneidas worried that the federal government would devalue their friendship if the border became fixed. They recognized that Indians lost clout once they became pinned down on reservations delimited by surrounding settlements. In May 1795, Captain Israel Chapin, Jr., who had recently succeeded his late father as the federal agent for the Iroquois, reported:

> The Oneidas observed to me the other day [that] the U.S. believed them to be like beaver, as a beaver's legs are short and cannot run fast, therefore the people of the States supposed they could not run away and do them any mischief on the frontiers, &c. I told them the U.S. had a disposition to [do] as well by them as those at the westward and that their past Services would be rewarded.

If trapped by settlements and a newly effective border, the Oneidas would lose their value as allies as they lost their prowess as potential foes. "Once we coveted their friendship either from fear or policy," two missionaries reported from the Oneida country in 1796, "but neither of these motives can now have any influence; they are rather objects of pity." And American pity was far less generous than American fear.[4]

To defend their importance, the Oneidas counted on the Americans to remember their shared sacrifices and exertions during the revolution. Timothy Pickering agreed that the federal government bore a special responsibility to protect the Oneidas from New York's settlers, speculators, and officials. In late 1793, Pickering assured Kirkland: "Something more must be done than has yet been done for the Oneidas; and tho' their concerns have been delayed, I will not forget them. Their affairs are not on a footing satisfactory to me." To rectify their affairs, Pickering held special meetings with the Oneida chiefs at the Canandaigua council in October 1794.[5]

The Oneida factionalism had, at last, become more clearly a split between the warriors and the sachems. John Thornton Kirkland explained, "The origin of these parties is generally the contests of rival chiefs for preeminence; the sale and division of territory, and the intrigues and the bribes of landjobbers and traders." The warriors blamed the sachems for leasing land, on such poor terms, first to Peter Penet and then to Peter Smith. Of course, the sachems did so in the desperate hope of recruiting a benevolent father with power in the settler world to protect the rest of the Oneida domain.[6]

Captain John (Onondiyo) led the sachems, and Captain Peter (Sautagauliches), rallied the warriors. Although Captain Peter was Good Peter's son, he had been raised by an uncle who opposed Oneida adaptation to American culture. Rejecting his father's Christian faith and morality, Captain Peter advocated traditional practices deemed pagan by Samuel Kirkland. Hard-drinking and violent, Captain Peter committed several drunken murders, but his bold manner and stirring eloquence won great influence.

Captain John was far more temperate, peaceable, and Christian, but prone to depression over the declining status of the Oneidas in a land dominated by prospering settlers. Kirkland declared "that Capt. John possessed uncommon abilities with a very discerning mind, at least for an Indian." Both Oneida captains defended their remaining lands, but they bickered over past failures, present strategies, and future prospects.[7]

To heal their division, the Oneidas sought Pickering's help in recovering some of their lost lands. Captain John explained, "The restoration of our lands would restore peace to our nation. The want of harmony among ourselves affects us more than the loss of our lands." Drawing a stark contrast with New York State, he lauded federal policy: "We really believe the Government of the United States are our friends. You have often advised us to keep our lands."[8]

Pickering sought to reunite the Oneidas and, so, to strengthen their pro-American influence among the other Iroquois at the full council then pending, but that federal goal clashed with the state's efforts to keep the warriors and the sachems divided. He acknowledged that the state's agents and speculators had deceived and cheated the Oneidas in land transactions:

> They pretend to a great deal of generosity and provide a plenty of liquor: and when your hearts become cheerful, and your heads grow giddy, then they make their bargains with you, and get your Chiefs to sign their papers. But as soon as you are sober, you find, to your sorrow, that your beds have slipped from under you. Another misfortune, Brothers, attends these bargains, that true interpretations are not always given of the papers you sign. Perhaps sometimes the interpreters purposely deceive you, but at other times the interpretations are not exact because you have no words in your language by which the meaning of the English can be expressed.

He doubly faulted the Peter Smith lease for failing to provide fair market value and for the absence of a federal treaty commissioner at the transaction. Pickering vividly explained that Smith could carve his lease into three hundred farms, but "for every such farm, which would support a large family in plenty of all good things, a whole year, you are to receive two thirds of a dollar, or what will every year buy you a quart of rum! So you see that for a quart of rum you give away a farm!"[9]

Those flaws also invalidated a more recent Oneida deal: the lease of a township (about 23,000 acres) for $650 a year to Abraham Van Eps, a storekeeper dwelling near the reservation. As Pickering noted, this was the best deal yet offered to the Oneidas: far better than the $200 to $250 per year offered by Smith for a tract twice as large, to say nothing of the $600 annuity paid by the state after acquiring 5 million acres in 1788. But Pickering felt that even the Van Eps deal fell short of justice: "I am well informed that good men stand ready to give you twice that sum, for a smaller piece of land." Pickering endorsed the Oneida efforts to secure a fair market value for their land, in defiance of the state's attempts to impose a monopoly price.[10]

Pickering favored the Oneida leasing initiative—within limits. After recovering the lands procured by Smith, the Oneidas should confine their leases to their southern tier and to terms of no more than twenty-one years, and they should never lease without federal oversight at the transaction. The missionary to the Mohicans in the Oneida country, Rev. John Sergeant, Jr., similarly concluded: "As to the reserved Lands of the Indians in this vicinity, why is it not right that they might have the privilege of leasing some small part of their lands, under the direction of a certain Trustee or Trustees appointed by the superintendent[?] In this case, they will obtain the whole of their rents with the same advantage of an English Landholder."[11]

Pickering warned the Oneidas to avoid any land transactions with New Yorkers without a federal treaty commissioner in attendance: "I know you will be told the state has all the power over your lands, and that the President and his Council have nothing to do with them." He denounced such state proponents "as deceivers, who want to take your beds from under you." He concluded,

> The land is yours and the State cannot take it from you without your own consent. And if any agents come to you to buy it, tell them plainly, that you will make no bargain but in the presence of the faithful men whom the President shall appoint. . . . Speak strong and be not afraid. Follow this advice, and nobody can hurt you, for the United States will protect you.

Pickering recognized that his "advice may offend some white people," but it was exactly what the Oneidas had hoped to hear.[12]

In November and December 1794, Pickering strengthened the federal relationship with the Oneidas in two treaties: the Treaty of Canandaigua (with the Six Nations) and the subsequent Treaty of Kanonwalohale (with the Oneidas, Tuscaroras, and Mohicans). The first treaty renewed the federal commitment to protect the Iroquois land rights by regulating state attempts to purchase. In the second treaty, Pickering promised $5,000 in federal compensation for losses by particular Oneidas, Tuscaroras, and Mohicans during the war, plus another $1,000 to rebuild the Oneida church burned by Brant's raiders in 1780. The federal government also pledged to build (and to operate for three years) a sawmill and gristmill.[13]

ALBANY

Strengthened by their federal treaties of 1794, the Oneidas petitioned the state legislature in February 1795. They sought a law to abrogate Peter Smith's suspect lease and to authorize them to make new legally enforceable leases for a fair market rent. To oversee the leasing and to collect the rents, they sought state-appointed trustees, preferably Philip Schuyler and James Dean. To assess offers made to lease some of their lands, some Oneida chiefs visited Canandaigua to seek the opinion of their federal superintendent, Captain Chapin, on the true rental value of their property. With both state and federal help, the Oneidas hoped, at last, to procure the substantial rental income needed to sustain their autonomy within New York.[14]

The state, however, responded in its usual way to an Oneida request for help in leasing land: by instead passing another law to purchase Indian land outright. On March 31, the Assembly considered but quickly rejected (18 yes to 32 no) an amendment to solicit the presence of a federal treaty commissioner, as required by federal law.[15]

In a further challenge to the federal Indian Trade and Intercourse Act, the legislature endorsed Peter Smith's lease by granting him a preemption right once the state obtained that tract from the Oneidas. An economic and political force in Herkimer County, Smith possessed considerable clout in the state legislature. Noting Smith's influence over his many debtors, politicians competed for his favor, especially with an election looming in the spring. When Smith volunteered to deliver the state's annuity payments to the Oneidas, Onondagas, and Cayugas, George Clinton's nephew and secretary, DeWitt Clinton, eagerly replied: "The Governor accepts your proffered services with pleasure." By delivering the annuity, Smith ingratiated himself to the governor while enhancing his sway with the Indians.[16]

Euphemistically titling their work "An Act for the Better Support of the Oneida, Onondaga, and Cayuga Indians," the legislators asserted that the state's purchase would be for the "sole benefit" of the Indians. But the law mandated paying the Indians no more than 4 shillings per acre for lands that the legislature would sell for at least 16 shillings per acre. Given that predetermined markup of at least 12 shillings per acre, the law should have been entitled "An Act for the Better Enrichment of the State of New York." The law was too blatant for the lame-duck governor, George Clinton, never previously bashful about procuring Indian land. He concluded of the ultimate sales revenue: "three-fourths of which at least will be for the benefit of the *State*, and consequently not a *disposition* for the sole benefit of the Indians." Following his lead, the state's Council of Revision vetoed the act, but the legislature promptly overrode that veto on April 9. The law did no credit to the state's reputation. The Herkimer County clerk, Jonas Platt, denounced the law "as a Stain upon our public Records."[17]

Although busy with his demanding new position as secretary of war, Pickering tried, from the distant national capital, to protect the Oneidas from New York's renewed pressure. On April 26, Rev. Sergeant warned Pickering: "Unless by your kind and friendly interposition, somehow warning the Indians of their danger, they will now by Smith and other designing tools be still cheated out of their Lands." In mid-June, Pickering procured a legal opinion from the federal attorney general, William Bradford, that aboriginal title "cannot be extinguished but by a treaty holden under the authority of the United States, and in the manner prescribed by the laws of Congress." To halt the state's land bid, Pickering forwarded copies of this opinion to the governor of New York and to Captain Chapin. Owing to the slow communications by bad frontier roads, Chapin did not receive Pickering's letter until July 31, three and four days after the state commissioners had concluded land purchases with the Cayugas and Onondagas. But Chapin did travel to Kanonwalohale in time to warn the Oneidas against dealing with the state commissioners.[18]

Those commissioners were led by Philip Schuyler, an inspired choice by the state legislators, for the Oneidas revered him as "Queder," the heir to generations of Schuyler generosity to Indians. They felt particular gratitude for his assistance during the hard years of war. Schuyler also knew how to exploit his insights into Oneida culture. For example, after an Oneida drowned in a favorite fishing creek, the Indians concluded that his spirit would scare away the salmon. Hearing of this belief, Schuyler announced that he had put a magical object in the river to counteract the ghost and to restore the salmon. Testing his claim, the Oneidas found the salmon abundant, which enhanced their respect for Schuyler's power.[19]

After the war, Schuyler withdrew from Indian affairs despite repeated Oneida pleas for his help in their difficult dealings with New York. In 1786, he assured Congress, "I had found the business of attending to the Indians exceedingly irksome & disagreeable." Why then did he consent in 1795 to lead the state commission to procure Oneida land? Schuyler hoped to assist his political party, the Federalists, who had taken charge of the legislature from Clinton's Republicans. And he longed to acquire the Oneida lands along Wood Creek, lands needed for the Western Inland Lock Navigation Company, his enterprise that would construct a canal to link the Mohawk River with Lake Ontario.[20]

Opening the council on August 6, with James Dean's invaluable assistance as interpreter, Schuyler urged the Oneidas to ignore Chapin's and Pickering's warnings. In reply, Captain John dwelled on the absence of a federal treaty commissioner: "We hoped Brothers when you came that you had with you an agent from the United States; but we find that you come only from the state of New York." However, given Queder's exalted standing in Oneida eyes, and Oneida pride in their council manners, they agreed politely to hear his proposition. In return for assigning to the state the tract leased to Peter Smith (45,793 acres), the Oneidas would receive a $1,200 boost in their annuity, a sixfold increase over Smith's rent. For an additional land cession, the state would boost the Oneidas' annuity by $691 per township.[21]

Although better terms than ever before proposed by the state, Schuyler's offer fell far short of the fair market value of Oneida land, which had been much enhanced by the swelling numbers and manifest prosperity of the settlers in Herkimer County. Watching that growth with a keen interest, the Oneidas had grown savvy to the operations of the land market. Captain John explained to Schuyler that they wanted to keep most of their land and to receive a competitive price for what little they might sell:

> Brother, Land is become valuable to us as well as to you—our Lands are almost all gone, and what remains we esteem highly. And we would wish to keep our seats pretty large, as a number of our Brothers, who left us during the War are returning to us and we are glad to see them, and wish to give them a place amongst us.

By keeping most of their land—and by getting a fair price for some of it to augment their annuity—the Oneidas hoped to render themselves whole again, completing the repatriation of their people scattered by the war.[22]

The Oneidas agreed to sell the Peter Smith tract for the $1,200 boost in annuity and to cede another single long, narrow township (three by twelve miles) strung along the Line of Property but only if the state paid "the full value as you give to one another—you know lands near settlements are valuable." Citing a rival offer from a private speculator, Captain John sought at least an $800 boost in annuity for this one township. But Schuyler wanted multiple townships and the state would pay no more than the $691 per township authorized by the state legislature. On August 11, the Oneidas broke up the council. After two days vainly trying to restart the negotiations, the commissioners departed for Albany.[23]

But they left behind James Dean and Abraham Van Eps to recoup the deal. Both had plenty of motivation, for they held informal Oneida land grants that needed state patents for legitimacy, which hinged upon including their tracts in an Oneida cession. On August 16, Dean sent good news to Schuyler. The Oneida clan mothers had "asserted their right to the Lands of the Nation, observing that as the cultivation of the Soil came within their province, so also that the disposal of it rested at their option." Fearing alienation from the state, they obliged the sachems and warriors to embrace the state's last offer, with some modest adjustments to the boundaries. The female intervention had the hallmarks of Dean's influence behind the scenes, for he had a special influence among the matrons thanks to his own devoted, adoptive mother. For the Oneida turnaround, the state commissioners also credited Van Eps, who kept a store near Kanonwalohale and reminded the Oneidas of their many debts.[24]

The reversal wrought a coup in Oneida politics, displacing Captain John as council speaker in favor of a hitherto obscure chief known as Tall William (Taghtaghgivijere). In 1796, John Thornton Kirkland recalled, "Captain John . . . last summer became abandoned to drunkenness & was not allowed by the Chiefs to sit in Council. His expulsion produced violent contention." Apparently, Captain John's ouster was powerfully divisive, alienating a considerable minority. Given the heavy drinking common among Iroquois chiefs, Captain John's lapse was probably more consequence than cause of his ouster: a destructive solace for the shock of defeat at a critical moment for the Oneidas. With Captain John marginalized, they stood scant chance of defying the combined interests of Dean, Van Eps, and Schuyler.[25]

Lest the Oneidas change their minds again, Dean urged "dispatch" upon Schuyler, who promptly summoned them to send deputies to Albany to close the deal on September 10. To preclude later trouble, Schuyler provided Dean with a power of attorney for the Oneidas at home to mark, affording their deputies unlimited power to sell land. Conducted expeditiously by Dean and Van Eps, twelve deputies—and twenty other Oneidas—arrived on schedule, virtually unheard of for an Indian council. That haste precluded intervention by the federal officials, who did not learn of the state's renewed negotiations in Albany until the treaty was a fait accompli.[26]

Accepting the state's terms, the deputies ceded about 132,000 acres—more than half of the Oneida reservation. By including the southern tier leased to Peter Smith, the Oneidas lost the only lands where, by state treaty, they could legally lease, killing their dream of managing their own property. The Oneidas also forsook land along the Genesee path, which the state coveted for improving into a road to facilitate western settlement. And the cession included the Wood Creek lands that Schuyler coveted for his canal. In return, the Oneidas received $2,952 down and $2,952 added in perpetuity to their annuity. That increased annuity reflected a principal price of $.50 per acre (as preset by the legislature), which was easily covered out of the $3.53 average price per acre at which the state subsequently sold the lands. In those sales, the state made an even greater profit than the legislature had stipulated in the enabling act of April which had set a minimum sales price of 16 shillings, or $2.00, per acre.[27]

The Oneidas concluded this treaty on September 15, which was also the day that Captain John died in Albany. It is striking that the commissioners did not permit the hiatus in a public council long customary upon the death of a leading chief. By comparison, at Philadelphia in March 1792, federal officers had allowed three days for Peter Otsequette's funeral before resuming business with the Iroquois chiefs. "All business must be laid by on such occasions till the ceremonies of condolence are performed, which take several days," Samuel Kirkland explained. As power shifted decisively toward the state, however, its mode of business supplanted the Indian customs of the Covenant Chain. In the only acknowledgment of the death by the commissioners, on the morning of September 16, they offered hasty condolences and a single black stroud (a piece of cloth) to the widow. Then the commissioners proceeded with business, signing the treaty and delivering the down payment. Later that day, Captain John was buried in Albany's Presbyterian cemetery: a funeral for Oneida autonomy as well as for its able defender.[28]

The state rewarded those, both Oneida and settler, who brokered the deal. On September 16, the most cooperative delegates—including Skenandon, Tall William, and Jacob Reed—received cash "douceurs" ranging from $125 to $250. The white "conductors" of the enterprise took their reward in land: Van Eps got 2 square miles, while James Dean and Colonel Abraham Wemple procured a square mile each. The biggest individual winner was Peter Smith, rewarded for his critical role in breaking open the Oneida reservation. In 1796, a Quaker visitor to the Oneida country noted:

Some of the Indian lands in this government of New York . . . were by them rented to some white people who settled thereon. After thus obtaining possession, it appears that these white settlers, professed Christians, refused to go off those rented lands: and that some who were in stations of the government supposing, or pretending, they could not easily remove them, even if the Indians were the sufferers, therefore advised the Indians to sell the lands to the government . . . [for] much less than the real value of the lands.

Released from paying rent to the Oneidas, Smith instead bought all the land within his lease that he had not yet sublet to settlers. For $3.53 per acre, Smith procured 22,300 acres of superior-quality land, which he retailed for a hefty profit to become his county's wealthiest man. In 1810, DeWitt Clinton observed, "Peter Smith . . . by wheedling the Legislature, as well as the Indians, he has succeeded in acquiring an immense body of excellent land at a low price, and he is now very opulent."[29]

COMPLIANCE

That summer, Washington and Pickering had hoped that the state's new governor, John Jay, would immediately bring state policy into line with the federal Indian Trade and Intercourse Act. As a Federalist, Jay might be expected to recognize federal supremacy in Indian policy. But Jay was also the proud author of the state constitution, and it gave no authority for a governor to overturn an act of the legislature once it had survived a veto by the Council of Revision. In a letter to Pickering written on July 13, Jay declined to halt the state's bid to purchase Indian lands under the law of April 9, but the governor did agree to seek federal supervision for subsequent state land deals with the Indians. Indeed, on July 18, Jay requested a federal treaty commissioner to help the state treat with the Akwesasne (St. Regis) Iroquois of the St. Lawrence Valley.[30]

Faced with a governor determined to proceed with Indian land purchases that summer, but willing to accept federal oversight in *future* transactions, the Washington administration backed away from a fight. Still new and weak, the federal government could ill afford a confrontation with New York. To endure and thrive, the United States of the 1790s needed patiently to develop precedents of state cooperation. New York's purchase of Cayuga, Onondaga, and Oneida land seemed inevitable to the president on July 27, when Washington reluctantly informed Pickering that "any further sentiment *now* on the unconstitutionality of the measure would be rec[eive]d too late." Taking that point, on August 26, Pickering assured Chapin that he had been quite "right to inform the Indians of the [federal] law and of the illegality of such purchase [by New York]. But having done this much, the business might there be left. . . . You may content yourself with giving the Oneidas the information above proposed, & there to leave the matter." This instruction put the burden of enforcing the federal law on the Oneidas, a weak party that desperately needed help in dealing with the powerful state of New York.[31]

In 1795, the Oneidas suffered as the federal government began to retreat from its active engagement with the Six Nations. With the Indian war won in the Ohio country, Americans no longer dreaded Iroquois intervention and no longer needed Iroquois help. Only the Senecas in western New York continued to receive much federal attention. Because of their larger population and their strategic proximity to the Canadian border, they enjoyed greater solicitude from the federal superintendent, Captain Chapin, who dwelled at nearby Canandaigua. But Chapin rarely visited the Oneidas and generally neglected their complaints. Frustrated by Chapin's indifference, in 1802 the Oneidas petitioned Congress to appoint a federal agent resident in their vicinity, but nothing came of it. Located deep within New York and enveloped by settlements, the Oneidas became taken for granted. In the Oneida parlance, they had become like short-legged beavers who could neither flee nor fight.[32]

Once federal attention diminished, state officials acceded to the letter, if not the spirit, of federal Indian Trade and Intercourse Act. During the balance of his tenure as governor, Jay initiated three more Indian land cessions, all conducted in compliance with the federal law by including a federal treaty commissioner and by submitting the treaty to the United States Senate for approval and to the president for ratification. In the third of those transactions, the state purchased more land from the Oneidas in June 1798. Governor Jay set a precedent that George Clinton could live with upon his return to the governorship in 1801. A year later, Clinton requested (and got) a federal treaty commissioner to supervise a further purchase of Oneida lands. At last, it seemed that New York accepted federal supervision over Indian relations. But that acceptance had become relatively painless because federal supervision had become nominal, limited to certifying state land deals already made.[33]

The 1798 and 1802 cessions to the state cut deeply into the Oneida reservation by extracting prime lands along the Genesee road that traversed the very center of the dwindling Oneida homeland. The state coveted that route to facilitate settlement of, and commerce with, western New York. And lands along a major highway could be sold to settlers at a premium. In the 1798 cession, the state procured about 30,000 acres, in return for a $500 down payment, plus a $700 augmentation to their annuity. In the 1802 cession, New York acquired another 11,000 acres in exchange for $900 down plus a perpetual $300 augmentation to the state annuity. Valuations by state surveyors reveal the state's advantage as a monopoly purchaser. In 1802 the state paid the Indians only $.54 per acre, but surveyors appraised most of the land at $4.15 per acre. After the two cessions, the Oneidas retained only about 75,000 acres, less than a third of their reservation of early 1795 and a mere 2 percent of their homeland at the end of the war.[34]

The period between 1790 and 1795 was critical to the fate of the Oneida domain. During that time, the federal government best attended to its responsibilities to the Iroquois by pressing New York State to adhere to the Indian Trade and Intercourse Act. But the state outlasted that interlude of direct federal engagement in Iroquois affairs. By frustrating federal law during that critical period, the state avoided setting precedents where a federal treaty commissioner obliged New York to pay fair market value for Indian lands. Instead, the critical Oneida cession of 1795 set a very different precedent: of thorough state control over a treaty process that took most of the reservation for a fraction of its true value. The fate of the Oneida lands proved ominous for the Senecas to the west.

INTERPRETERS

In 1796, the American occupation of Fort Niagara invited settlers to press westward across the Genesee River onto Seneca lands. Those settlers promised to enrich Robert Morris, a speculator who had purchased the Massachusetts preemption claim to 4 million acres in western New York, if he could extinguish the Indians' title to the land. A man of voracious appetites, for food as well as land, Morris was known by the Senecas as "the great Eater, with the big Belly." In 1796, they begged federal officials "that he may not be permitted to come and devour their lands."[35]

A Philadelphia merchant and banker and United States senator, Robert Morris was the nation's wealthiest and most ambitious land speculator. "He has more men under his Patronage & [more] moneyed Influence than any other Man in the Union," James Kent noted in 1793. Manic in accumulating lands, Morris purchased millions of frontier acres in scattered tracts from New York to Georgia. He bought too much, too fast, with borrowed money. Shady titles, ill-defined boundaries, and complex partnerships produced such a tangle that Morris had no clear idea of what he owned, but still he kept buying more land.[36]

Facing bankruptcy by 1796, he needed to sell his western New York claim, but it had little value until cleared by a federal treaty of its aboriginal title. He had found a buyer—a cartel of Dutch capitalists known as the Holland Land Company—but the sale was conditional on Morris's success in extinguishing the Indian title at his own expense. He needed to buy as quickly and as cheaply as possible, so that he could turn the land into Dutch gold to save himself from a debtor's prison.[37]

Morris and his son Thomas (who lived at Canandaigua) weakened Seneca opposition by "interesting" all of the traders and interpreters who spoke both English and Seneca. Gilbert Berry, Horatio Jones, Joseph Nicholson, Jasper Parrish, Nicholas Rosencrantz, and Joseph Smith began their careers unwillingly as adolescents taken captive during the Revolutionary War and then adopted by the Senecas as their kin. The adopted captives developed a bicultural expertise valuable to the Indians. By adding Seneca words and ways to their English language and American culture, the adopted adolescents could offer insights and advice about the outsiders.[38]

Through the alchemy of adoption and adaptation, a few captives became especially influential interpreters. After the war, some Seneca chiefs explained to New York's leaders:

> Brothers, you will recollect the late contest between you and your father, the Great King of England. This contest threw the Inhabitants of this whole Island [of North America] into a great tumult and commotion, like a raging whirlwind which tears up the trees, and tosses to and fro the leaves so that no one knows from whence they come or where they will fall. Brothers, this whirlwind was so ordered and directed by the Great Spirit above, as to throw into our arms two of your Infant-Children, Jasper Parrish and Horatio Jones. We adopted them into our families, and made them our Children. We loved them, and nourished them.

At war's end, the Senecas feared losing their adopted children. They "wished them to remain among us, and promised, if they would return and live in our Country, we would give them each a Seat of Land for them and their Children to Sit down upon."[39]

Jones became the preeminent interpreter for the Senecas. A gunsmith's son on the Pennsylvania frontier, he was eighteen years old and serving in a ranger company in 1781 when Loyalist and Seneca raiders overwhelmed his unit. One of the few Americans to survive the skirmish, Jones appealed to the Senecas, who admired his good looks, nimble body, and keen mind. Adopted by Cornplanter's sister to replace a lost son, Jones reaped an influential identity and invaluable kinship connections. He impressed his new kin by becoming a consummate hunter and by cultivating the serene stoicism expected of the ideal warrior. Challenged to a wrestling match, Jones threw a warrior to the ground, wounding his pride. When the loser reached for his tomahawk, Jones held his ground and calmly said: "Cousin, this was a trial of strength and you challenged me. I was the victor, but if my cousin thinks me worthy of death, here I am." Of course, the warrior desisted and Jones's status soared in the eyes of the Senecas.[40]

The Indians cherished their adoptive kin. Warmth and longing suffuse a letter that Pickering wrote in 1790 at the earnest request of a young Seneca named Heautenhtonk, who addressed his adoptive uncle, Jonathan DeLong. Although DeLong had escaped from captivity, his kinship retained its Seneca power; indeed, no relationship between males commanded greater importance than that of an uncle with a nephew. Through Pickering, Heautenhtonk appealed to DeLong:

> When my uncle lived with us at Buffaloe Creek, there was a house full of us: but since the peace we have met with much trouble, and I am almost left alone. Seven of the family have died since you left us. As I had this opportunity of speaking to you on paper, I felt a desire to inform you of the misfortunes of the family. Of the whole family you belonged to, only nine are left. We all wish to see you, to have a little talk with you. If you could come to see us next spring, about planting time, you would make us all very happy. I want to know whether my uncle has made me any more relations, and if any one of them is big enough to travel, and has learnt to read and write, I wish my uncle would bring him along with him, to live in my family, and learn the tongue. I will take a kind care of him. . . . As you made your escape from us without our knowledge, perhaps you may suspect you will be in danger by coming to see us, but be assured you have nothing to fear.

During a time of traumatic changes for the Iroquois, they especially needed the help of those special kin who possessed the powers of reading, writing, and interpreting. Despite all the pressures pulling Indians and settlers apart, some Iroquois families desperately tried to sustain kinship ties across the cultural frontier.[41]

At war's end, Americans compelled the Senecas to release their adopted prisoners, but some bolted back to Iroquoia. Jones preferred a Seneca life for "its unrestrained liberty—its comparative freedom from want and care" and its superior hunting and fishing. But Jones remained sufficiently American to seek commercial advantage in his double identity. He returned not simply as a chief, but also as a trader, profiting by linking his Schenectady suppliers to Seneca customers. By creating dependencies on his goods, trading added a third dimension to Jones's clout as an adopted Seneca and a skilled linguist. His new wife, Sally Whitmoyer, shared his cultural duality as a former captive who had mastered the Seneca culture.[42]

The interpreters' cross-cultural skills and Indian kinship soared in value during the postwar transformation of Iroquoia by settlers and speculators. The Senecas needed help to understand and analyze the newcomers and their proposals, while speculators coveted the interpreters' special ability to bring the Indians to terms. Seeing the American triumph as inexorable, the interpreters meant to profit from the coming submergence of Iroquoia beneath waves of American settlers and speculators. The canny interpreter and trader sought the right moment to sell his Indian influence to the importunate outsiders, to convert his cultural duality into a cash asset. But the astute culture broker also tried to retain the affection of his Indian kin, by pitching a land cession as making the best of a bad situation.

In partnership with Joseph Smith, a fellow captive turned trader and interpreter, Jones established a trading post at Kanadasega, at the head of Seneca Lake. This proved a most strategic location in 1787, when John Livingston's Lessees made Kanadasega their headquarters. By offering cash and shares, Livingston recruited Jones and Smith to help secure the Long Lease from the Six Nations.[43]

And yet they retained the Indians' trust. In 1789, the Senecas appointed them their lead interpreters. As a retainer, the Indians gave them 6 square miles on the west bank of the Genesee River, so "that Smith & Jones might go and live with them and do their business for them." On this gift land, Smith and Jones prospered by developing farms and by selling produce to arriving settlers. Meant to retain the interpreters' allegiance to the Indians, the gift tract instead became a magnet that attracted more Americans into the Genesee Valley.[44]

During the early 1790s, Jones and Smith also seized the opportunity presented by the revived federal role in Iroquois diplomacy. For federal pay they assisted Pickering's councils at Tioga Point and Newtown Point and the chiefs' visit to Philadelphia.[45]

The adopted war captives gave the Americans a peculiar advantage over the British in their postwar competition to sway the Iroquois. In 1794, John Graves Simcoe rued that prolonged alliance with the Indians had denied the British of a generation of potential interpreters while the Americans reaped an ironic benefit from their people captured during the revolution. Simcoe had to rely on an aging and diminishing cohort of interpreters and agents, like John Butler, who was sixty-six in 1794. Simcoe lamented that his interpreters were "hourly growing more scarce" because "Prisoners who are adopted by the Indian Nations, and by that mode given a means of acquiring an interest in their affections & a knowledge of their Language, are now entirely of the Inhabitants of the United States, and not of the British Colonies." During the early 1790s, that advantage in interpreters helped the Americans to detach the Senecas from the British interest. Later in the decade, those interpreters also became the wedge that broke open the Seneca country for exploitation by American speculators and settlers.[46]

BIG TREE

In 1796, Thomas Morris recruited Jones to induce the Senecas to sell most of their land. Morris appealed to Jones's longing for a freehold title for the Genesee land given to him by the Senecas. The natives had meant to secure his interest, but their gift backfired because the tract gave Jones a powerful incentive to assist the land speculator with the preemption right under American law. Once settlement seemed inevitable, Jones needed to secure his own land by brokering the transfer of the Seneca domain into Morris's hands. The speculator offered Jones both a deed and a cash retainer, but vowed that "he shall see no money until the Extinguishment of the Indian Title. I know him too well to trust to his honor. Nothing but Interest [can] bind him to his duty." In May 1797, Morris and Jones persuaded the Buffalo Creek chiefs to attend a land council held under federal auspices.[47]

Fearing arrest for debt, Robert Morris dared not leave his Philadelphia estate, so he entrusted the pending land council to his son Thomas. Desperate for money, Robert Morris anticipated that "the moment the Indian title is obtained there will be a rush of People into that Country that will raise the price of land beyond that of any other part of America." In late August, the council opened at Big Tree on the Genesee River. Thomas Morris conducted the council with assistance from his friend Israel Chapin, Jr., the federal superintendent, and from James Wadsworth, the federal treaty commissioner. During the preceding three years, the Morrises had laid the groundwork for this council by generously bestowing food and drink and polite attention on chiefs who visited Canandaigua or Philadelphia. Now the Morrises meant to capitalize on the Indian sense of obligation.[48]

At Big Tree, Thomas Morris offered $100,000, an aggregate sum unprecedented in land purchases from the Iroquois. In return, he wanted almost all of the Seneca domain of 4 million acres, which meant a price of only about 3 cents per acre. Although eager for the money, the Senecas dreaded losing their importance as a landed nation. Red Jacket observed, "We are still a great People and much respected by all the western Indians, which is still owing to having Lands of our own." If limited to a few reservations, "we could not say we were a free People." As a pointed alternative, Red Jacket offered only a little land for a much higher price: a single township (approximately 23,000 acres) for $1 per acre. But a single township was less than 1 percent of the land that Robert Morris had promised to the Holland Land Company. If he fell so far short, Morris faced ruin. When Thomas Morris violently protested the Seneca counteroffer as an insult, Red Jacket suddenly dissolved the council.[49]

Aided by Chapin and Jones, Morris shrewdly revived the council by convening the clan mothers, the Iroquois element most willing to swap hunting ground for cash and goods. Giving the matrons a belt of wampum, Morris "told them that whenever hereafter they experienced the hardships of poverty to shew it to their Chiefs and tell them that with that Belt they had been offered Wealth, which the Chiefs rejected." Morris noted, "This had an excellent effect, the Women at once declared themselves for selling & the business began to wear a better aspect." He clinched their understanding by giving the clan mothers a herd of cows. Exercising their prerogative, the matrons transferred the land issue from the sachems to the warriors, who renewed the council.[50]

Assisted by Chapin and the interpreters, Morris diminished the Seneca retention to just 200,000 acres in the treaty concluded on September 16. Six of the ten reservations were small—from 1,280 to 10,240 acres—and scattered along the Genesee River. The treaty made four more substantial reservations at Allegheny (26,880 acres), Cattaraugus (26,880), Tonawanda (46,080), and Buffalo Creek (81,920). Determining those relative sizes excited bitter competition by rival chiefs. Morris explained,

> The importance of a Chief, and his influence with his Nation, is, in a great measure, proportionate to the number of his followers; and that number is either increased or diminished, by the extent of land annexed to the Chief's residence. Hence the struggle on the part of every Sachem and Chief Warrior, both to increase his own bounds, and to lessen those of a rival Chief. This contest was more violent between Red Jacket and Cornplanter, than any of the others; the first wanting the principal reservation at Buffaloe Creek, and the second, at his residence at the Alleghany.

Red Jacket won, securing the largest reservation for Buffalo Creek. That triumph promised to draw Senecas from the small Genesee reservations to Buffalo Creek, where they would be consolidated under his leadership—to Cornplanter's dismay. Red Jacket also walked away with the largest private payment: $600 plus a lifetime annuity of $100. Cornplanter had to make do with $300 down and $250 annually.[51]

How had Red Jacket prevailed in a treaty that he had publicly opposed? The chief played a cunning double game. By day in open council, he gave uncompromising speeches, compounding his popularity. At night, however, he privately met with Morris to provide covert advice. On the last evening of the council, Red Jacket explained that he could not mark the treaty in front of his people "because he had pretended to them that he was opposed to it." But he persuaded Morris to save a blank space near the top of the treaty parchment for his subsequent mark in private. Red Jacket explained "that it would not do for the Treaty to go to Philadelphia without his name [on it] as General Washington, when he examined it, and found his Signature wanting, might imagine that he had been degraded and had lost his rank and influence among the Senecas." Red Jacket's formidable pride could not stand such a misunderstanding.[52]

In securing the treaty, Morris also benefited from the key culture-brokers who managed the council discourse. The Dutch capitalist Theophile Cazenove observed, "Such complete success is due chiefly to the pains taken to interest the chiefs and those interpreters who were known to have a great influence with the Indians." Cazenove explained that Morris promised the interpreters "gratifications which were not to be paid if the Indians reserved to themselves more than 200,000 acres. This stimulus had a great effect." Assisted with Dutch funds, Morris paid $2,000 each to the interpreters William Johnston (of 1794 notoriety at the Treaty of Canandaigua) and Horatio Jones and another $2,500 to a third interpreter, Jasper Parrish. The champion payment of $5,000 went to Chapin. For three weeks of service to Morris at Big Tree, Chapin collected ten times his annual salary from the United States.[53]

The Big Tree land cession came too late to rescue Robert Morris from financial ruin. In February 1798, creditors arrested and jailed him. "I may truly Say, that I am a Martyr to the times," he lamented. Bankruptcy proceedings revealed that he owed $2.9 million—an astonishing amount for that generation—to sixty-one creditors. Released in August 1801, Morris lived five more years in genteel poverty, subsidized by the Holland Land Company in gratitude for their riches in Seneca land.[54]

By selling, the Senecas lost their distinction as the last of the Six Nations with a large homeland. After the Treaty of Big Tree, they too lived on enclaves in a landscape primarily owned, and increasingly settled, by whites. In return, the Senecas received a principal of $100,000 invested in a Philadelphia bank, which yielded an annual interest payment of $6,000. This initially seemed impressive until divided among 1,500 Senecas to provide a modest $4 per capita per year.[55]

By claiming the entire payment, the Senecas denied any to their Onondaga and Cayuga guests at Buffalo Creek. Dismayed at their exclusion, many moved across the border to resettle at Grand River, to the delight of Joseph Brant, who was ever eager to augment the Iroquois numbers that bolstered his power. As a consequence of the shifts, the Grand River reserve became more multiethnic, while Senecas consolidated their majority at Buffalo Creek.[56]

Soon even the Buffalo Creek Senecas felt the pinch of settler envelopment, as the Holland Land Company developed a commercial village on their doorstep. The town of Buffalo grew around the trading post of William Johnston. Born in 1742, Johnston was the Loyalist son of a Seneca woman and an Indian Department officer. Fluent in Seneca, Johnston compounded his kinship connections by marrying a woman of that nation. During the 1780s, Johnston worked for the Indian Department and served the Indians as gunsmith, interpreter, and trader. Inheritance, kinship, and ability secured his influence among natives eager for a patron with external connections. Anticipating Indian dispossession, Johnston sought the right moment to capitalize on his native influence to obtain a lucrative property recognized by American society. Like Horatio Jones, Johnston persuaded the Senecas to grant him valuable lands: two square miles near the mouth of Buffalo Creek. Then, to secure a title under American law, Johnston struck a deal with the Holland Land Company in 1798. The company recognized the value of Johnston's influence and of his tract as a prime location for developing a commercial village. The company would give him a deed for a third of his native tract, provided that they got the rest from the Senecas with Johnston's help.[57]

The new village enhanced the profits reaped by both Johnston and the Dutch capitalists. Johnston erected a sawmill that produced the lumber to build Buffalo from the forest once owned by the Senecas. In 1800, he possessed improved property worth $2,034, ranking as the richest settler on the Holland Purchase.[58]

Located on a ridge overlooking Lake Erie, the new town became the great conduit for settler emigration to points west. By 1810, half-acre lots sold for $100 to $250, revealing the appreciation wrought by commercial development. By then, five hundred people occupied about one hundred houses, some of brick or stone. Buffalo sustained four taverns, eight stores, a newspaper, post office, courthouse, jail, and five lawyers but no church, a ratio considered revealing and damning by visitors. The village economy benefited from Indian customers for alcohol and cloth, a trade fueled by the annuity payment generated by the Big Tree land cession. Although the Senecas initially welcomed the commercial advent of cheaper goods at Buffalo, they soon paid dearly for their increased exposure to alcohol.[59]

The Big Tree cession committed the Senecas to American domination, for they became dependent upon the annuity paid from the Bank of the United States and disbursed by the federal superintendent. Chapin explained that the sale "has united their interest with the United States, which we conceive . . . will render us more secure from difficulties that might arise from them." Fearing the loss of their annuity, the Senecas were unlikely to make any trouble or to move across the line to become British allies.[60]

Americans noted a marked change in Seneca demeanor, a decay of their formidable pride in their martial prowess. During the early 1790s, Thomas Morris recalled that "the Indians would come among us, painted for war; their deportment was fierce and arrogant." By 1800, however, they "became completely cowed." For that change, Morris could claim much of the credit because observers linked the Senecas' demoralization to their envelopment by domineering settlers. In June 1798, James Kent, noted, "The melancholy Sedateness of their Squaws inspires Pity & Sympathy. The Senecas are sensible their Nation is dwindling & that the whites are surrounding them. . . . They are now crowded into the Western Extremity of the State." Four years later, Kent added, "They are a harmless race, & perfectly mild & obedient, & I never can look on them but with Pity & Compassion for their degeneracy from the proud Superiority of their Ancestors." As intemperance became common and suicides frequent, a missionary blamed Seneca "despondency." He explained, "Their circumstances are peculiarly calculated to depress their spirits, especially these contiguous to white settlements."[61]

Like William Johnston, Horatio Jones became a wealthy man from his exquisite timing in selling his intercultural skills to land speculators. He acquired an estate worth $100,000 at his death in 1836. But he never fully relinquished the native half of his identity. In 1836, an English visitor remarked,

> I found that the old man was at heart more than half Indian. He spoke of many of the red men with an affection quite fraternal, and his general impression of their qualities was much more favorable than that which I received during my residence among them.

Although enriched by the consumption of Iroquoia, Jones nurtured an uneasy nostalgia for an earlier time of Seneca power.[62]

MURDER

Imposing the common law of murder also constricted the Indian world— and expanded the state's power at federal expense. In New York's Herkimer County, magistrates launched a legal offensive against cross-cultural murder during the summer of 1796—just as the border posts passed into American hands—a revealing timing. In August, a local newspaper observed, "It is as much a duty we owe to the human race to subject [the Indians] to the government of our laws, as to confine a madman in society." No longer dreading Indian enmity, New Yorkers meant to seize jurisdiction over murders by natives.[63]

The magistrates reacted to a surge in Indians killing one another, a surge that was also related to the changing of the guard at the border. In September 1796, Chapin noted a new and demoralizing sense of confinement among the Six Nations:

> And the Americans have their line of Forts all around them and settle-ments advancing upon their Country, so that they have given up all National honor which they ever have had, and have become given to indolence, drunkenness and . . . killing each other. There have been five murdered among themselves within six months.

As settlers and their taverns gathered around the Indian enclaves, liquor became dangerously common. The abundant liquor inflamed resentful recriminations, as Indians blamed one another for lost lands. As an alien and hostile world pressed in around them, natives lashed out at one another and, sometimes, at a settler in or near a tavern.[64]

The New York drive for murder jurisdiction challenged the understand-ing worked out between the Six Nations and the federal government during the early 1790s. By covering the graves of murdered Indians (and by quietly permitting natives to do the same when they killed settlers), the federal gov-ernment kept the peace and asserted a primacy over the states in Indian pol-icy. In 1794, the Treaty of Canandaigua promised to prolong federal responsibility in cases of cross-cultural murder:

> The United States and Six Nations agree, that, for injuries done by indi-viduals, on either side, no private revenge or retaliation shall take place; but, instead thereof, complaint shall be made by the party injured, to the other: by the Six Nations, or any of them, to the President of the United States, or the superintendent by him appointed.

That stipulation recognized that the Iroquois were United States allies—rather than dependent members of New York.[65]

Averse to that recognition, in 1796 New York prosecuted three Indians for murder. In Herkimer County, the magistrates arrested an Oneida named Saucy Nick, a Tuscarora known as Ayamonte, and a Cayuga called Captain Kee. Notoriously defiant, Saucy Nick had killed a settler named Henry Grafts at Myndert Wemp's tavern on the Oneida reservation. The other two cases were still more intrusive, for Ayamonte and Captain Kee stood accused of killing fellow Indians rather than citizens of New York. On behalf of the Cayugas, Brant protested to Chapin that, as Captain Kee "belongs to their nation and is not of your people, they think you should not pass any sentence on him." If their kinsman was executed, the Cayugas threatened vengeance: "that the next murder they should be confined for should be for that of a White Man." Some Oneidas similarly warned that if Saucy Nick swung from the gallows they would kill the next white man to pass through their village.[66]

Some leading New Yorkers doubted the legality and wisdom of the three prosecutions. The attorney general confessed, "It is a question of some delicacy how far it would be prudent to render Capt. Kee amenable to our Laws, and it is . . . subject to some doubt in a legal point of View." As a Herkimer County judge, James Dean insisted that native murder cases "should be settled and satisfaction made to the injured party agreeable to the Indian mode of satisfaction." He noted that the Treaty of Canandaigua submitted jurisdiction over cross-cultural murder to the federal government, which favored covering the grave. As a judge, Dean worried that he would be considered a deadly enemy by the kin of any executed Indian, "and that in the course of years their spirit of retaliation might cost the life of one of his Children or Family."[67]

Although the Herkimer County prosecutor pressed ahead with the cases, juries acquitted Saucy Nick and Ayamonte (and probably Captain Kee). New York's first legal victory in an Indian murder case had to wait another five years, when the culprit was George Peters, a Brothertown Indian accused of killing his wife with a club to the head. In 1801 in Oneida County (recently carved out of Herkimer County), the magistrates arrested, tried, and convicted Peters. On appeal, the State Supreme Court ruled narrowly that the state had murder jurisdiction over the Brothertown Indians because they were an especially small, weak, and vulnerable people unable to defend their autonomy. But that decision left uncertain the state's power over the more numerous Six Nations, particularly the Senecas. Hung on March 26, 1802, Peters was the first Indian executed by the State of New York.[68]

Later that year, the state obtained a new and especially important case because the accused was a Seneca. If New York could try this suspect, then every Indian within its boundaries was subject to state law. On July 25, 1802, a warrior known to settlers as Stiff-Armed George or Seneca George got into a drunken fracas outside a tavern in the frontier village adjacent to the Buffalo Creek reservation. Pursued and beaten, George pulled a knife and stabbed two white men, one fatally. Under pressure from the settler magistrates, the Seneca chiefs reluctantly surrendered George for jailing at Canandaigua, pending trial.[69]

The chiefs recognized that the arrest threatened their sovereignty. Addressing the magistrates, Red Jacket denied that the Senecas had ever accepted the state's legal jurisdiction:

> Did we ever make a treaty with the state of New-York, and agree to conform to its laws? No. We are independent of the state of New-York. It was the will of the Great Spirit to create us different in color; we have different laws, habits, and customs from the white people. We shall never consent that the government of this state shall try our brother. We appeal to the government of the United States.

Citing several murders by whites of Senecas that had been resolved by covering the grave, Red Jacket insisted, "We now crave the same privilege in making restitution to you, that you adopted toward us in a similar situation." Proceeding east to Albany, Red Jacket delivered a similar message to Governor Clinton:

> We always thought that we were answerable to the United States only, under our existing treaties with them. We were always told so by the Commissioners of the President. Five instances have heretofore happened where the White People have committed murders on our people, and in every instance we have applied to the United States and not to the States in which the acts were committed, for redress; and we have always received satisfaction by presents sent to us and particularly to the injured family, but in no instance have they been punished with death. Now, therefore, altho it is true that this crime was committed within the Limits of your State, we know of no Treaty with the state by which we are bound to give satisfaction; but we are perfectly willing to treat with the United States and to give them satisfaction in the same manner we have heretofore received when we were the injured party.

Asserting federal supremacy in Indian affairs, Red Jacket presented a copy of the Treaty of Canandaigua to Clinton. This raised the ante, and the governor's hackles, for Clinton meant to prove state jurisdiction over all the Indians within New York. He replied that settling a murder with presents was "repugnant" to the laws of New York, which he meant to enforce throughout its bounds.[70]

The national government disappointed the Senecas by declining to intervene. In 1801, a new Republican administration led by Thomas Jefferson had swept the Federalists from national power. Unlike the Federalists, who had asserted national supremacy, the Republicans favored states' rights. Where the Federalists were willing (in the short term) to treat Indian sovereignty with some respect, the Republicans were eager, wherever possible, to dissolve diplomatic relations and to subject natives to the laws of particular states. With the Indian confederacy in ruins, the new president saw little reason to consult native wishes. In 1803, Jefferson explained, "We presume that our strength and their weakness is now so visible, that they must see we have only to shut our hand to crush them."[71]

At Canandaigua on February 22, 1803, jurors found Seneca George guilty of murder, but they worried that executing the sentence would lead the Senecas to seek revenge. Conceding that he had killed in self-defense and that "the White inhabitants of Buffaloe Creek have committed wanton & unprovoked attacks on several of the Indians of the Seneca Nation," the jurors sought a pardon. Henry Dearborn, Jefferson's secretary of war, agreed. He noted that Seneca George was related to a chief "killed a few years since in time of peace by white men, one of whom, it is said, was tried and acquitted," an apparent reference to the Pine Creek murders of 1790. Worried about frontier security, Dearborn believed that a pardon would "have a good effect on the minds of the Indian Nations generally." On March 5, Governor Clinton suspended the execution and recommended a pardon to the state legislature, citing "extenuating circumstances which attended the commission of the crime" and "considerations of a political nature for extending the mercy of government to the culprit." A week later, the legislators pardoned Seneca George, provided that he left the state, never to return. The New Yorkers could afford to be magnanimous, having established the critical legal point by arresting, trying, and convicting a Seneca of murder.[72]

But the state's legal power over murder on a reservation remained clouded in cases where the victim was another Indian. In 1821, the state prosecuted a Seneca chief named Tommy-Jemmy (Soonongize) for killing a woman named Kauquatou. Convicted by a tribal council of deadly sorcery, she had her throat cut by Tommy-Jemmy, acting on behalf of the Seneca nation. Red Jacket and court-appointed lawyers argued that Kauquatou's death was no murder under New York law because it was properly considered a legal execution under Seneca law, on Seneca land, by the sovereign Seneca people. Anticipating that the local jurors would agree with the defense, the circuit court referred the case to the New York State Supreme Court. Noting that no law extended state murder jurisdiction over the Iroquois, the Supreme Court judges passed the hot potato to the governor, who promptly tossed it to the state legislature. On April 22, 1822, the legislators passed the needed law giving New York "sole and exclusive jurisdiction" over cross-cultural murders within its boundaries. But they had to pardon Tommy-Jemmy, for the new law could not retrospectively apply to his killing of Kauquatou. Like Stiff-Armed George, Tommy-Jemmy escaped execution after providing a case that helped the state extend its legal powers.[73]

Cross-cultural murder tested the relative power of the natives and of the governments, state and federal, contending with one another to exercise jurisdiction. When authorities had to cover graves, they accepted the limits of their power over both Indians and their own settlers. On the other hand, when Indians had to surrender their own for formal trial, they also relinquished their freedom as a sovereign people. Whether formal law or Indian customary law prevailed in murder cases was a critical marker of the relative degree of state power and native sovereignty. Beginning in 1796, New York gradually accumulated legal power in a process that froze out the federal government, which by covering graves had treated the Iroquois diplomatically as sovereign peoples.

RESTRICTION

The post-1796 boundary along the Niagara River constricted the mobility of the Iroquois on the American side. In government sailing vessels, the British had allowed the Indians free passage across the Niagara River and along the Great Lakes. The American skippers, however, were private entrepreneurs lacking the same generosity. The resourceful Buffalo Creek chiefs sought a partial substitute by contracting with an American ferryman to convey them freely to and fro across the river in return for their land grant to accommodate his home and ferry. But he could not compete with a rival based on the Canadian side, who could charge whites less by refusing to carry Indians for free. In 1802, the chiefs tried again by striking a treaty with the State of New York. In return for some Seneca land along the river, the state promised to mandate a ferry monopoly that would provide free passage to Indians. Prior to 1807, however, the state neglected its end of the bargain, leasing the ferry without stipulating the free Indian passage.[74]

The new boundary also diminished the access to Buffalo Creek by traders on the British side of the border. In May 1802, an American customs collector seized the goods of a petty trader, Mrs. Elisabeth Thompson, from the British side. Chapin characterized her as a "lame Widow woman, who . . . has been fiddling among the Six Nations for a livelyhood." Disliking her lower prices, American competitors complained that Thompson violated American customs regulations in crossing the new border to conduct her old trade at Buffalo Creek. Their complaint induced the American customs officer to seize her wares. Chapin reported, "The Indians, thinking it was altogether oppression in the traders, thought they might assist their old friend who was selling low for cash in hand." They broke open the government warehouse, liberated her goods, and spirited them to safety across the border to Upper Canada.[75]

As a sovereign people, the Senecas insisted that they should control trade on their reservation. But secretary of war Dearborn trumped native sovereignty with his nation's control over the boundary with Canada. Denouncing the "glaring outrage on the laws of the United States," Dearborn demanded that the Senecas pledge never again to interfere with American customs officers. Otherwise, he would withhold the value of the liberated goods from their Big Tree annuity payment. Their dependence on that annuity afforded the federal government a powerful leverage to compel Indian compliance. The chiefs grudgingly conceded that the boundary gave federal control over their trade with Canada.[76]

While constraining the Indians, the boundary empowered thieving settlers who preyed on native property. In 1812, Red Jacket bitterly complained that settlers committed twice as many thefts on Indians as the latter did on the whites. Between 1805 and 1810, the Tuscaroras dwelling near Fort Niagara counted seventeen cattle and two horses stolen by settlers. Exploiting the nearby border, the thieves conveyed the rustled animals into Upper Canada for sale beyond the jurisdiction of American magistrates. In sum, the settler encroachment around the reservations combined with the nearby national boundary to facilitate thefts. That predation compounded the growing sense of social claustrophobia felt by the enclave Indians. Worse still, officials and missionaries concluded that it would be easier to move the Indians west than to protect them from their vicious neighbors. Indian removal seemed a humanitarian measure to New York's leaders, if not to the Indians, who preferred the enforcement of their treaty rights.[77]

In August 1802 at Albany, Governor Clinton pressed Red Jacket and the other visiting Seneca chiefs for another land cession: a one-mile-wide strip of shoreline beside the Niagara River above the falls, as well as the islands in the middle. This land had been restored to the Indians by the United States at the Treaty of Canandaigua. The governor wanted the tract to promote commerce along the river and to permit construction of a new fort at Black Rock, near the mouth of Buffalo Creek, to oppose Fort Erie on the British shore. Clinton also sought to strengthen the American claim to the islands, which the British counterclaimed. And procuring the riverside strip would push the Buffalo Creek reservation back from the international boundary, killing the Senecas' residual claim to live between the Americans and the British.[78]

For $6,000, the governor secured the shoreline but not the islands. Clinton insisted that the Senecas accept that a Black Rock fort would serve "for our mutual protection and defense." By defining the defense of New York and the Buffalo Creek Indians as "mutual," Clinton hoped to alienate them from their kin within the British lines. By intruding a fort between Buffalo Creek and the British line, the Americans meant to divide and isolate the two great centers of the Six Nations—Grand River and Buffalo Creek—in anticipation of a future war with the British.[79]

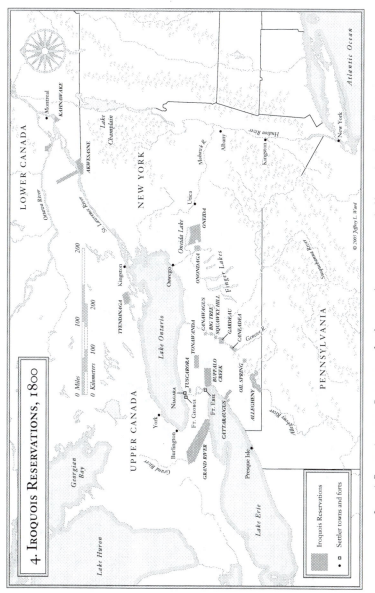

4. IROQUOIS RESERVATIONS, 1800

LOWER CANADA

Ottawa River

KAHNAWAKE
Montreal

AKWESASNE

Lake Champlain

St. Lawrence River

TYENDINAGA

Kingston

Lake Ontario

Oswego

Onondaga Lake

ONONDAGA

ONEIDA

Utica

Mohawk R.

Finger Lakes

NEW YORK

Albany

Kingston

Hudson River

New York

Atlantic Ocean

0 Miles   100   200
0 Kilometers 100 200

UPPER CANADA

York

Burlington

Niagara

TUSCARORA

Ft. George

TONAWANDA

CANAWAGUS
BIG TREE
SQUAWKY HILL
GARDEAU
CANEADEA

Genesee R.

BUFFALO CREEK

Ft. Erie

OIL SPRING

CATTARAUGUS

ALLEGHENY

GRAND RIVER

Grand River

Georgian Bay

Lake Huron

Lake Erie

Presque Isle

Allegheny River

Susquehanna River

PENNSYLVANIA

© 2005 Jeffrey L. Ward

Iroquois Reservations

Settler towns and forts

Iroquois Reservations, 1800. By a process of settlement and cessions, Iroquoia had been reduced to small pockets within a landscape dominated by newcomers.

CHAPTER ELEVEN

Blocks

Joseph Brant, by Ezra Ames, ca. 1806. (Courtesy of Fenimore
Art Museum, Cooperstown, N.Y.; N-421.55.)

DESPITE THE JAY TREATY, few British officials expected the peace to
last. By surrendering the border forts in 1796, the British alleviated the
immediate crisis, but at the cost of bringing American troops and settlers
onto the southern shores of the Great Lakes, to the very margins of Upper
Canada. That advance secured American power over the Iroquois enclaves
within New York, a development that doubled the British desperation to
control the Indians on their side of the border: to determine when, where,
and whom they would fight in the event of renewed war.

Compared to New York, in Upper Canada there was less settler pressure on Indian lands but more official meddling in Indian politics. Relative population size made the difference. In 1800, Upper Canada had only 35,000 settlers, compared to 586,750 in New York. Fearing the American numbers, British officials needed Indian warriors to help defend Canada. Moreover, unless secured as allies, the Indians might instead become the most dangerous of enemies. In John Graves Simcoe's nightmare, American agents would bribe the Indians to attack Upper Canada's small and scattered forts and settlements. He concluded, "All proper attention should be paid to the Indians. The existence of this Province may be said to depend upon it."[1]

Valuing the Indians as military allies, the British did not share the American haste to dispossess and to transform them. Like Sir William Johnson, Simcoe favored a gradual, multigenerational process of adaptation, so that "habits of Civilization may be induced among the Indians without prematurely taking from them their hunting State." He reasoned that hunters made the best warriors, and that the British needed the Indians as warriors. Indeed, the officials distrusted schemes to promote Indian agriculture, even when an Indian, Joseph Brant, was the promoter.[2]

To gain greater control over the Grand River Six Nations, in 1795 the British renewed their pressure to subordinate all Indians to the rule of British law in cases of murder. The convenient victim was a deserter from the American army, a man named Lowell, who had settled at Grand River to ply his trade making saddles and harness. The killer was Brant's eldest son, Isaac.[3]

Young Brant possessed a ferocious temper, especially while drinking. When Lowell failed to complete a promised saddle on time, Brant buried a tomahawk in his victim's brain. A settler grand jury indicted the murderer, but the Grand River chiefs instead insisted upon covering the victim's grave. Determined to win this time, Simcoe sought permission from Lord Dorchester to send soldiers into the Grand River reserve to arrest Isaac Brant. Anticipating that provocative move, Joseph Brant boasted that in a confrontation "it would be seen who had [the] most Interest with the Militia, and that the Governor would not be able to make them Act against him." Brant's confidence reflected years of cultivating good relations with the militia officers in the neighboring settlements. Many had served with Brant during the war.[4]

Fortunately, cooler heads than Simcoe's prevailed. William Dummer Powell, a prominent judge, urged restraint, "as my personal opinion was ever in favour of the entire Independence of the Indians in their Villages, and as the deceased was a vagabond, who preferred their society to that of his own People." Determined to avoid bloodshed, Lord Dorchester procrastinated

York (Olim Toronto), Upper Canada, by Edward Walsh, 1803. The harbor lies to the right, with a fortified blockhouse beneath a British flag in the background. The houses of prominent government officials, including that of Peter Russell, appear to the left. Note the British soldier and the Indians in the stumpy foreground: a common combination in Upper Canada. (Courtesy of the William L. Clements Library, University of Michigan.)

long enough for Isaac Brant to solve the crisis. In early November, in another drunken rage, young Brant attacked his father with a knife. In self-defense, Joseph mortally wounded his son with a dagger stroke to the head. The loss plunged Joseph into a lingering despair that sapped his once formidable energy and enthusiasm.[5]

PETER RUSSELL

By 1796, Simcoe had grown weary and sour as his grandiose plans for Upper Canada crumbled. Instead of dissolving the United States and reversing the American Revolution, Simcoe now faced the triumphant republic on his Canadian doorstep. Sick and irritable, Simcoe had been depleted and yellowed by multiple bouts with the "ague and fever," a malaria endemic to Upper Canada. Wary subordinates found him "peevish beyond description." Obtaining permission to return home, Simcoe departed in July 1796, on the eve of the British surrender of Fort Niagara to an American garrison. His hasty departure spared Simcoe from the hated sight of the American flag flying over Fort Niagara. Sailing away across Lake Ontario, bound for Quebec and on to England, Simcoe left administration of the colony to his deputy, Peter Russell.[6]

Born in Ireland of English parents in 1733, Russell had served as an army officer during the Seven Years' War. During the 1760s, he left the army and settled in Virginia, where he ran a tobacco plantation to financial ruin. Returning to the British army during the revolution, he became an assistant secretary to General Sir Henry Clinton. In occupied New York City, Russell found a friend and patron in Simcoe, then in command of a Loyalist regiment. In 1791, when Simcoe became the lieutenant governor of Upper Canada, he appointed Russell as receiver and auditor general, key fiscal offices, which entitled him to a seat on the colony's Executive Council.[7]

Upon Simcoe's departure, Russell proved timid and vacillating as the colony's interim administrator. Anxious, and more elderly than his years (sixty-three in 1796), Russell got no respect from the other colonial officials. Jealous, greedy, petty, and weary of Canada, they spent much of their time carping and sniping and intriguing against the new administrator. As Simcoe's caretaker, Russell also lacked the clout of a formal appointment as lieutenant governor.[8]

It was also Russell's misfortune to administer the colony during the difficult changes that followed the Jay Treaty. To replace the old forts lost to the Americans, the British built nearby replacements on their own side of the border: Fort George at Newark on the west bank of the Niagara River; Fort Amherstburg on the east bank of the Detroit River; and Fort St. Joseph at the mouth of the St. Mary's River. At the same time, the British withdrew most of their troops from Upper Canada, to reduce costs and to shift men to fight the French in Europe and in the West Indies. In Upper Canada, the evacuation left only 461 soldiers divided and scattered at distant posts. In the event of renewed war with the Americans or new trouble from the Indians, Russell would have to rely on the undisciplined militia of the province, a discouraging prospect.[9]

On the eve of the American occupation of Fort Niagara, Simcoe had ordered the removal of Upper Canada's capital from nearby Newark. It would not do for the capital of a British colony to lay exposed to the cannon fire of an American fort. Conducting that difficult move fell to Russell, who faced stiff resistance from his grumbling subordinates. It took nearly three years for them to shift their homes and their offices to York (now Toronto), a raw new settlement at the mouth of the Humber River on the northwest shore of Lake Ontario.[10]

Although removed from the American menace, the new capital exposed the officials to high costs, chronic isolation, and potential trouble from the local Indians. Where Newark was surrounded by prospering Loyalist settlements, York had Mississauga neighbors, who seemed mysterious and volatile to the anxious newcomers. For want of roads, only the lake offered access to the colony's two main clusters of settlement: to the south on the Niagara Peninsula and to the northeast around the Bay of Quinte and along the St. Lawrence River. During the winter, ice locked up the lake, isolating the new capital from most of its people. Isolation also meant scarce and expensive trade goods, which deterred potential settlers. Consequently, York grew slowly, from just 241 people in 1797 to 336 in 1801. Already unhappy at Newark, the official elite became miserable at York as they stewed in frustration and rancor at their enforced exile. Their bad morale, toxic gossip, and petty feuds compounded Russell's difficulties.[11]

Russell also had to cope with a rearrangement of the Indian Department. With the American threat receding, and the French war escalating, the imperial lords in London wanted to reduce Indian expenditures and to impose a more bureaucratic mode of management. Lobbying in London, Simcoe persuaded the lords to reduce the power of Sir John Johnson as superintendent by transferring control over Indian relations within Upper Canada to the lieutenant governor (or his administrator). Insulted by the change, Sir John blasted the new chain of command as the work of "an Invidious, interested Man." Characteristically, Sir John then retreated still further into passivity, collecting his salary while rarely leaving his country estate near Montreal. His further withdrawal troubled the Iroquois, who cherished their connection to the family of Sir William Johnson.[12]

The shift failed to save money, and it saddled Russell with an impossible and unwanted responsibility. Used to a free hand and generous budgets, the veteran officers of the Indian Department resisted the new regulations that demanded stricter oversight over their expenditures. And Russell lacked the confidence to discipline the restive officers. Without experience in Indian affairs, he could not afford to alienate the agents. The Indians also resented any change in their management, especially one that reduced the presents and provisions that an agent could provide. Led by Brant, the Iroquois complained that the government had introduced a dangerous innovation that slighted the Indians and offended Sir John.[13]

In public council with the Six Nations, Russell bungled when he tried to explain the new system by posing as the king's "immediate representative. . . . His Majesty brings you nearer to him. You now in a Manner speak face to face." Fine, Red Jacket shrewdly replied, "As we now are, as it were, Face to Face with the King our Father, any business we may have to do or any thing we may have to say will now be decided and settled in a moment." No longer would they have to endure months and years of frustrating delays awaiting dispatches from London. Of course, Russell then had to beat a hasty retreat, for he remained hamstrung by his official instructions from distant officials only dimly aware of conditions in North America. In fact, his new responsibility added another delaying layer to the bureaucracy between Indian requests and London decisions.[14]

In addition to the general restructuring, the Indian Department in Upper Canada suffered from jarring changes in key personnel, as the generation trained by Sir William Johnson passed away. In May 1796, death claimed the deputy superintendent, John Butler. Aged, deaf, weary, and cynical, Butler had become ineffectual during the preceding three years. To maintain some continuity, Brant recommended filling the vacancy with William Claus, the thirty-year-old son of Daniel Claus and the grandson of Sir William. During the war, young Claus had ably served in Sir Johnson's provincial regiment and on frontier raids led by Brant. Claus also possessed a rare and valuable mastery of the Mohawk language and customs.[15]

In January 1799, Alexander McKee followed Butler to the grave. After Detroit's evacuation by the British, McKee remained responsible for the diverse native peoples straddling the province's western border, including Delawares, Shawnees, Ojibwas, Ottawas, and Wyandots. Aging and ailing, he devolved most of the daily management of his agency to his close friend and trusted subordinate Matthew Elliott, who resided near the new British post at Amherstburg on the eastern shore of the Detroit River. When McKee died, he was replaced by his son Thomas, but only in a nominal sense. Lazy and often drunk, Thomas McKee could never truly replace his cunning father.[16]

GRAND RIVER

From Simcoe, Russell inherited a land controversy with Brant and the Grand River Six Nations. At issue was the vague certificate given to them by Governor General Haldimand in 1784. That certificate promised eventually to provide a formal deed, but, before doing so, Haldimand gave up his post and returned to England in late 1784. And his successors limited the property rights awarded to the Six Nations by narrowly reading Haldimand's grant. Professing paternalism, these officials insisted that the Indians could not be trusted with the land unless barred from leasing or selling it to anyone (except the government). The restrictions served the British plan to preserve the tract as a haven in a future war for anticipated Iroquois refugees from the United States.[17]

Brant countered that Haldimand had promised the Indians a freehold land tenure equal to that enjoyed by the colony's Loyalist settlers. Rejecting any preemption right, Brant demanded something "better than the Yanky Deeds to their Indian friends." As freeholders, the Indians could lease or sell land to the highest bidder, just as the settlers did.[18]

Simcoe, however, dreaded the prospect of white tenants becoming dependents to native landlords, compromising their allegiance to his government. At Niagara in January 1793, Simcoe presented a limited deed to the Six Nations chiefs in public council: "Brothers, I will tell you fairly I do not believe that it will ever be granted to you in any other Manner, because no British Subject can hold a lease of any Land under the King's Allegiance & Protection, but from a British Subject." Led by Brant, the chiefs angrily rejected the deed, causing, in Simcoe's words, "a great tumult."[19]

Proud of his gentility, Brant seethed when treated as a mere savage who could not manage property. When Simcoe insisted that Indians had always mishandled their land, Brant replied that "the Indians were not always to be fools because they had once been such." Having already leased some land to settlers, he felt humiliated by a deed undercutting that power. "It hurt my pride and feelings extremely [on] this occasion. I cannot hardly reconcile myself to Live [in] Such [a] Situation. ... I am totally dispirited," Brant lamented. He concluded that the British officials coveted the lands for themselves for a song: "It seems natural to Whites to look on lands in the possession of Indians with an aching heart, and never to rest 'till they have planned them out of them."[20]

Brant believed that a restrictive deed would trap the Grand River Indians in deepening poverty and dependence on the government. As settlements expanded around them, the Indians' hunting territory would shrink, curtailing their cash income from selling venison and deer pelts to the garrisons and traders. That disturbing trend would undermine the reserve's respectable standing in the colony and in the eyes of other Indians. In seeking an alternative income, Brant explained,

> My sole and only wish is to support the dignity & credit of the Five Nations and to keep them upon as respectable a footing as the other Nations. Without some Fund this can not be done. We must grow poor & then of course we fall into disrepute.

From Brant's perspective, the Iroquois within the American line possessed a better income and more respect thanks to their rent from Oliver Phelps, to their annuities from the State of New York, and to their presents from the United States. "I hope our [British] Friends would not wish to see us in a worse situation than our Brethren there," Brant observed to Sir John.[21]

To stem economic decline, Brant leased land to settlers. The rental income would enable his people to take care of "their Women, Old Men, and Children." That revenue would also buy time for Iroquois men to effect a gradual, rather than a precipitous, transition to the settler mode of agriculture that featured livestock and plows. Colonial landlords often used leases to develop frontier land by renting for low prices to settlers experienced at making new farms. By felling the forest to create fields and to erect fences, the initial tenant greatly enhanced the value of the lot when recouped by the landlord at the expiration of the lease. Brant's protégé John Norton explained that by "leasing a small tract of land to the indigent farmer," some Grand River Mohawks "received a rent, and at the expiration of the lease had a considerable portion improved." By leasing to settlers, the Indians also hoped to control the apparently inevitable settlement of their surplus lands by outsiders. Without tenants, their lands would fall prey to squatters.[22]

By procuring a rental income, Brant competed with Tyendinaga and Buffalo Creek for Iroquois residents. An American land speculator explained, "His Great Object is to render himself as formidable and as consequential as possible. His Consequence as a great Leader depends upon the Number he can attach to him, and the Means he makes Use of is of no Consequence if he obtains his Object." Grand River was losing population as some inhabitants returned to Buffalo Creek to tap the annuities paid there. Brant hoped to reverse that flow by procuring rental income for annual distribution among the residents.[23]

Ultimately, Brant regarded the right to lease or to sell land as a litmus test for Indian sovereignty. When British officials denied the right "to have King's subjects as tenants," Brant "supposed their real meaning was, [that] we should in a manner, be but tenants ourselves." Evidently, the British sought "to tie us down in such a manner, as to have us entirely at their disposal for what services they may in future want from us, and that in case we should be warned out & obliged to remove, the lands would then fall to them with our improvements & labour." Only by selling or leasing some peripheral land, Brant argued, could the Grand River Iroquois preserve their independence and prosperity on the core of their domain.[24]

The land controversy simmered as Simcoe did his "utmost to procrastinate any decision." In early 1795, Brant became fed up with Simcoe's delays: "I have been too Long plagued [by] that cursed Lands. My patience is most worn out." To break the stalemate, the Grand River chiefs empowered Brant to sell large blocks of land for no money down, for they wanted to take their payment entirely in future years as annual interest on the principal value.[25]

Bypassing the government, Brant sold directly to speculators who lusted after the fertile land, described by one as "like the Gardon of Eden." They paid an average of 4 shillings and 6 pence per acre (the equivalent of 57 cents):

eighteen times better than the 3 pence per acre offered by Simcoe. Beginning in 1795 and culminating in 1797, Brant sold 381,480 acres for a principal value of £85,332. The interest on that principal promised an annuity of £5,119.18.0 (or $12,800): far more than any other Iroquois people then received. For example, after their 1795 cession the Oneidas received $3,552, while the Senecas secured a $6,000 annual income from their Big Tree sale of 1797.[26]

Located north of Brant's Town, the alienated blocks conveyed a hunting territory of diminishing value, while the Indians kept their most fertile lands, located downstream around their villages. Brant considered the retained lands as sufficient "even should the whole of the Six Nations move over to this side [of] the American line." Indeed, attracting them was Brant's primary goal in seeking an annual income for Grand River. By 1797, the size of an annuity mattered most in enticing Iroquois residents.[27]

To limit Simcoe's grounds for complaint, Brant chose Loyalists of property and standing to lead the cartels that purchased the blocks. The buyers included Philip Stedman, a former British army officer who conducted the commercial portage around Niagara Falls. Richard Beasley was a trader, miller, and innkeeper based at the head of Lake Ontario. Benjamin Canby owned mills on the Welland River and operated a ferry across the Niagara River. Jean Baptiste Rousseau was an Indian trader and miller. William Jarvis served as the secretary of the provincial government. As millers, portage and ferry operators, and innkeepers, they were in prime positions to recruit potential settlers. Although these buyers were Upper Canadians of sound loyalty to the empire, it was a poorly kept secret that they had covert partners who were Americans. Consequently, Simcoe opposed the sales, for he vowed to control the disposition of land at Grand River, not concede it to an Indian chief.[28]

In early 1796, Lord Dorchester tried to resolve the controversy by proposing a compromise deed that would permit leases (for terms of up to one thousand years) by the Indians, provided the colonial government had the option to acquire the property by matching the price. Citing the precedent established in Lower Canada, Dorchester observed, "I see no reason why the Indians being patentees of those lands, may not lease them, as those of the Sault St. Louis have done theirs."[29]

Simcoe grudgingly accepted the compromise, but Brant balked because he wanted no restriction on his management of the land and because Dorchester's proposed deed named the legal owners as the "Six Nations." Brant feared that the Oneidas or the Buffalo Creek chiefs might claim a share of the rents or interest without actually moving to Grand River. Because his whole point was to entice Iroquois families to his reserve, Brant wanted ownership restricted "to the Five Nations Settled on the Grand River, their Heirs and Descendants." He explained that "any [who] Chose to Settle . . . have an equal right with the rest for the Profits of the Rents, &c., but until they do live there they have nothing to do with it."[30]

RUMORS

Upon assuming power, Russell upheld Simcoe's opposition to Brant's land sales to speculators. He suspected that American speculators sought land "in the very heart" of the colony to "throw open a wide door by the mouth of that River to the introduction of their countrymen, whenever they shall form the design of wresting this country from us." He also felt threatened by the persistence of "so large an extra-judicial Territory" held by Indians (or by tenants under Indian title) in the heart of Upper Canada. And he especially dreaded Brant's construction of an interest that united Indian warriors with American settlers. Russell warned, "If Brant, therefore, felt himself sufficiently bold to insult Government when he had only his Mohawks to back him, how much more so will he feel when strengthened by a number of Aliens whose interest it will be to support him."[31]

Offended by Russell's opposition, Brant blasted the "great men" of Upper Canada for hypocrisy. Meeting them in a public council at Newark, he demanded,

> As many of the great men here have large Tracts of Land, we would wish to ask them what do they intend to do with their Tracts? Do they mean that they should lay waste and useless? . . . Suppose a present was made to any of them, and the person making the present should say, you are not to make use of what I have now given you; would they not be astonished?

Brant sought the equal right for Indians to behave as land speculators, realizing profits from the commercial potential of their land if settled by farmers.[32]

To pressure Russell, Brant traveled to Philadelphia in early 1797. By calling on the British minister, Robert Liston, Brant sought to convey his complaints to the imperial lords by a channel that bypassed the Canadian officials. In an interview with Liston, Brant accused Russell and his executive councillors of plotting to procure the Grand River lands for themselves.[33]

To add alarm to those complaints, Brant conspicuously cultivated dangerous company in Philadelphia. He attended a dinner party hosted by the intriguing republican politician Aaron Burr, who speculated in Canadian lands and Canadian rebellion schemes. Brant impressed Burr, who wrote to his daughter Theodosia Burr Alston:

He is a man of education—speaks and writes the English perfectly—
and has seen much of Europe and America. Receive him with respect
and hospitality. He is not one of those Indians who drink rum, but is
quite a gentleman; not one who will make you fine bows, but one who
understands and practices what belongs to propriety and good breeding.

The dinner party also included the French minister, Pierre August Adet,
dreaded by the British for his scheming to provoke a revolt by the French
Canadians. Full of drink and bluster, Brant subsequently boasted at a tavern
that, unless quickly satisfied by British redress, "he would offer his Services
to the French Minister Adet, and march his Mohawks to assist in effecting a
Revolution, & overturning the British Government in the Province." Perhaps by design, this threat reached and alarmed Liston, who urged his superiors in London and Quebec to mollify Brant.[34]

After a week in Philadelphia, Brant began his return via Albany, where he
met with New York's Indian commissioners to resolve the Mohawk land
controversy with that state. They were joined by Captain John Deserontyon,
the leader of the Tyendinaga Mohawks. In a rare show of cooperation, Brant
and Deserontyon accepted a $1,000 payment and $600 in travel expenses to
extinguish Mohawk land claims within New York.[35]

By accepting such a paltry payment for such valuable land, Brant sought
to improve Grand River's relations with the leaders of New York. Expressing
regret for his role in the past war, Brant assured prominent New Yorkers that
he "would never again take up the tomahawk against these United States."
But he had to proceed home via the Mohawk Valley, where many settlers
possessed long and vindictive memories. Their murderous threats obliged
Governor Jay to provide a bodyguard to escort Brant. Turning west, he
bypassed the Oneida country, once again declining to visit Samuel Kirkland
or the Oneidas.[36]

Instead, Brant hastened to meet Thomas Morris at Canandaigua, where
he expressed outrage at having been neglected by the federal officials in
Philadelphia. This was an odd complaint given that Brant had rebuffed invitations from the secretary of war, James McHenry, and even from the outgo-
ing president, George Washington. Because the federal leaders had made
their peace with the British, Brant considered Adet and Burr far more useful
dinner companions for alarming the officials in Canada. Brant's preferred
company also concerned federal leaders, who suspected and feared French
intrigues on their frontiers. The mere hint that Brant was dissatisfied
induced McHenry to rush $400 to Chapin to mollify the chief and to secure
his latest information from the Indian world. In 1797, the borderland

remained sufficiently unsettled for federal officials to worry and to pay when Brant became mysteriously discontented.[37]

In mid-April, Brant returned home to find wild rumors that French and Spanish agents were arming and instigating the Indians in the Mississippi Valley to strike eastward across the Great Lakes to smite the British in Canada. Allegedly, that strike would coincide with a French Canadian uprising in Lower Canada, assisted by the appearance of a French fleet bearing troops. "In such Case we shall be between two Guillotines and I think probably have the Tom[a]hawk raised over our Heads," lamented William Dummer Powell. In that context, Brant's dinner with Adet appeared especially ominous, for Upper Canada seemed doomed if the Grand River Six Nations joined the supposed plot, particularly given the few regular troops remaining in the colony.[38]

Brant did not start these rumors, but he shrewdly exploited them, for he recognized that British and American officials properly valued Indians only in a time of war. He set to work confirming and ramifying the alarming reports from his Indian contacts around the Great Lakes. Confirmation also came from the Indian Department official Matthew Elliott, who was friendly with Brant. Elliott's alarming rumors also served his own interest as an agent seeking increased resources and revived autonomy from his anxious superiors.[39]

The rumors certainly spooked Russell, who suddenly dreaded Iroquois disaffection over the Grand River land controversy. In early June, he wrote to Brant, promising "to adjust all matters to your entire satisfaction." Pressing his Executive Council for authority to act without waiting for instructions from London, Russell cited

> the present alarming aspect of affairs—when we are threatened with an Invasion by the French and Spaniards from the Mississippi, and the information we have received of Emissaries being dispersed among the Indian Tribes to incite them to take up the Hatchet against the King's Subjects, which calls for the most conciliatory Conduct on the part of this Government to all the Indian Nations in alliance with us, to prevent their defection.

Although the council unanimously approved Russell's request, he then wavered, gripped by anxiety: "This is the most Consequential Act of my Administration & [it] fills my mind with apprehension."[40]

Russell found powerful grounds to delay on July 15, when he received a troubling dispatch (dated March 10) from his superior in London, the Duke of Portland. Opposing any leases or sales by the Grand River Indians, the duke instead favored granting them a government annuity. Wringing his hands, Russell lamented, "the Dangerous dilemma to which I am reduced, *Disobedience of His Maj[esty's] Commands*—or an *Indian War* . . . for it appears to me from the offence Joseph Brant has taken without Cause, that he means to pick a German quarrel with us; and only seeks a feasible excuse for Joining the French, should they invade this Province." At a private meeting on July 21, Russell informed Brant of the duke's position. Brant erupted, indignantly refusing the annuity alternative, for the very point of selling or leasing land was to reduce Indian dependence on the government. In a letter to the duke, Russell reported Brant's rage:

> I confess, my Lord, that I felt very unpleasantly at this Moment. I was well aware that this Man was deeply committed; that he had great Influence not only with his own Tribe, but with the rest of the five Nations, and most of the neighboring Indians; and that he was very capable of doing much mischief.

Terrified by that prospect, Russell quickly agreed to issue the desired deeds without fees, provided the buyers took an oath of allegiance to the king. "This Speech operated like a Charm," Russell observed, "The Chief's Countenance cleared up on the Instant." Brant and Russell confirmed their private deal at a public council at Niagara on July 24–26. Taking Russell by the hand, Brant "declared that they would now all fight for the King to the last drop of their Blood."[41]

DEEDS

Despite the apparent agreement, the legal paperwork dragged on. Russell required trustees to handle the mortgage security and the payments from the speculators, and these trustees had to be British subjects rather than Indians. Agreeing, Brant named David W. Smith, the province's surveyor general; William Claus of the Indian Department; and Alexander Stewart, Brant's lawyer, who had married a granddaughter of Sir William Johnson's. At last on February 5, 1798, Brant met Russell in York to complete the deeds from the province to the assignees of the Indians. British officials regarded this transaction as exceptional and never to be repeated, but Brant considered the sale as merely a half step toward his ultimate goal: a complete freedom to lease and sell land directly to purchasers without relying on the government to issue the deeds.[42]

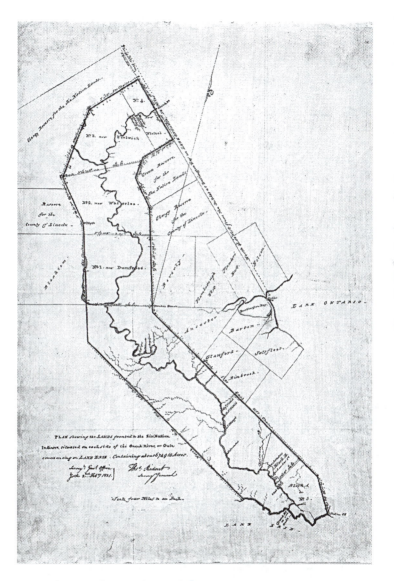

Grand River Lands, survey plan by Thomas Ridout, 1821. The blocks sold by Brant in 1797 include those numbered 1 through 4, in the northern half of the reserve, and those labeled A and B at the mouth of the river on the northern shore of Lake Erie. Note the core cluster of villages at midriver. Brant's new home lay on the shores of Burlington Bay to the east. (Courtesy of Library and Archives Canada; NMC-3115.)

British critics blasted Brant's land deals as driven by his own greed. From the gossip of officials in York, the visiting Lord Selkirk concluded that Brant was "a complete rogue," who had taken kickbacks from the speculators of one-tenth of the lands. In fact, Brant probably retained no more than the £500 that he could justly claim in compensation for his heavy expenses while engaged in official business for the Six Nations. Certainly, neither kickback lands nor extra monies appear in the will that he made in 1805. But some historians still follow Selkirk's lead to fault Brant's sales as selfish and corrupt. Like Selkirk, these scholars hold Brant to a higher standard than they do the colonial officials who avidly speculated in land. According to Brant's critics, a true Indian was supposed to be too naïve or too selfless to outwit white men at their own commercial game. They could only be victims, never victors in market transactions.[43]

In fact, Brant's land sales helped the Grand River Six Nations by enhancing their revenue and independence. Although the buyers lagged in their payments, Brant still collected enough to reduce the Iroquois dependence on government largesse. When the Grand River gristmill burned down in 1803, Brant contracted for its reconstruction with funds from the interest payments, rather than seeking another government favor with the inevitable strings attached. One of the land buyers, the master carpenter William Wallace, paid by building a more substantial council house at Grand River. Brant also assumed from the government the payments to the reserve's blacksmith, schoolteacher, doctor, surveyors, and lawyer. And Brant established an account at Rousseau's store, where traveling Indians could draw on his credit for meals, drinks, shoes, and fodder for their horses. Brant also sustained his popularity at Grand River by funding periodic "Festivals": feasts accompanied by dancing and drinking. By hosting drinking parties on the reserve, Brant hoped to keep the Indians from seeking alcohol in the settlements, where they would be cheated and abused.[44]

The prospect of a generous annual income, divided among the residents, enabled Grand River to compete for Iroquois residents, reversing the former outflow. Dozens of Cayugas and Onondagas came from Buffalo Creek, where they were dismayed by their exclusion from the Seneca annuity provided by the Treaty of Big Tree. Grand River also enticed growing numbers of Mohawks away from Tyendinaga at the Bay of Quinte. John Stuart, the Kingston missionary, conceded that Brant was "a sensible & enterprising chief" for promising "to divide the interest annually among his people, which will naturally operate to the advantage of his Settlement, & depopulate that of the Bay of Quinti." Stuart concluded that the Grand River reserve had "been so judiciously managed by Captain Brant, as to induce many from other tribes to incorporate with them."[45]

On May 1, 1798, Brant celebrated his land sales by convening a festive military muster of the Grand River peoples; 400 Indian warriors and a settler militia company performed for "a surrounding multitude." A visiting missionary noted, "On muster days the white people living on his territory must also arrange themselves under his banners." Proud of the martial display, Brant had a story printed in the province's lone newspaper, the better to advertise his military importance to the colony. Hosting local militia officers for a dinner after the muster, Brant led them in "many loyal TOASTS" to the royal family, "together with all those loyalists who were fellow sufferers with the 6 nations, during the late American war." Brant presented the Grand River Iroquois as equal partners with the Loyalists in defending a shared province.[46]

But British officials rejected Brant's vision of partnership. Distrusting Indians as volatile savages (and Brant as a cunning intriguer), those officials wanted to subordinate the natives at the end of a hierarchical chain directed from London. By that standard, there was much to alarm the British in the newspaper account of Brant's military muster. Officials could not have been reassured to read that the "firing was conducted with such exactness as was thought not to be exceeded by the best disciplined troops." Nor did they like the attendance of Mississaugas "by particular invitation," for the British promoted tensions between the Mississaugas and the Iroquois as part of a policy of divide and rule. And it was especially troubling that Brant could command a company of white men, weakening a racial distinction of particular importance to the empire. Here were the ominous fruits of permitting Brant to lease or sell land to white settlers: they became his dependents willing to serve his ambitions under arms. Officials feared that, in a crisis, Brant would possess more power than the government of Upper Canada.[47]

AGENCY

The Mississauga chief Wabakinine was an elderly peacemaker who sacrificed much land to satisfy the officials and colonists of Upper Canada, but he would not consent to the rape of his sister by a drunken soldier at York. On the night of August 20, 1796, that soldier, Charles McEwan, scuffled with Wabakinine, knocking him senseless with a stone's blow to the head. Other Mississaugas then carried their wounded chief into the forest, where he died two days later.[48]

In response to the crisis, Russell pursued a dual strategy. To satisfy native customary law, he honored the dead chief by convening the local Mississaugas for a condolence ceremony with presents to cover the grave. To fulfill English common law, Russell had McEwan arrested and had evidence gathered for consideration by a grand jury. When the Mississaugas failed to attend the hearing, the grand jurors promptly rejected the indictment against McEwan, alleging "it not having been proven that the Chief with whose murder he was charged is dead." Placing little value on an Indian life, the colonists balked at trying a white man for murdering a Mississauga.[49]

One historian offers the conspiracy theory that Russell sabotaged the case against McEwan by getting the Indians drunk to prevent them from testifying. According to this theory, the Mississaugas wanted justice from the colonial court. In fact, Indians had a powerful aversion to colonial legal process, which they considered confusing and menacing. The Mississaugas rightly suspected that the British would dispense with the trouble and expense of covering graves if they could, instead, convict and execute colonial killers. Worse still, the British would subsequently demand the surrender of Mississaugas accused of murder, for colonial trial and execution.[50]

The conspiracy theory also miscasts the culture of the empire. Because class mattered as much as race to British officials, they felt no solidarity with a common soldier and no reluctance to hang one to consolidate the rule of colonial law over all the peoples of Upper Canada, native as well as settler. Far from sabotaging his own case, Russell longed for a precedent to bind the Indians, so he regretted the lost opportunity to hang McEwan.[51]

Wabakinine's murder created a new opportunity for Brant to expand his influence among the Mississaugas. Weary of being cheated in land deals, slighted in presents, and neglected by officials, the Mississaugas wanted some of the greater respect enjoyed by the Six Nations, so they named Brant to replace Wabakinine as their spokesman. "They say that Brant is the fittest to be their Chief because he alone knows the value of Land," William Dummer Powell reported. Indeed, Brant observed, "I do not think it reasonable that the land should be taken from the *Poor* Mississagues for a shilling an Acre, only to give away to Individuals to make money of." Rather than further enrich colonial land speculators, let the needy Mississaugas make that money.[52]

Brant's new role threatened the British bid cheaply to acquire the last remaining Mississauga lands fronting on Lake Ontario: a strategic stretch west of York as far as Burlington Bay at the head of the lake. Left in Indian hands, this thirty-six-mile-long tract interrupted land communications and colonial legal jurisdiction between the provincial capital and the settlements on the Niagara Peninsula. In October 1797, Russell had William Claus convene the Mississaugas to offer presents worth 3 pence per acre for the coveted tract. Brant countered by demanding at least 3 shillings per acre. Twelve times greater than the government offer, Brant's demand shocked British officials, who liked to think of themselves as paternalists and of the Mississaugas as naïve children.[53]

The following May, the Mississaugas attended Joseph Brant's muster at Grand River, where they vowed to "become one people by merging with the Mohawks." To make that point, the Mississauga warriors began "shaving their Heads and dressing like Mohawks." The Mississaugas named Brant "the sole guardian of our Nation," with exclusive authority to "transact and negotiate all & every such matters as we may have occasion to do and transact with the white people." This power alarmed Russell, who dreaded Brant's ambition "to be at the Head of all the Indian Tribes within this Province."[54]

Noting the enhanced Mississauga demands, the province's chief justice, John Elmsley, regretted, "that the Aborigines of this Part of His Majesty's American Dominions are beginning to appreciate their lands not so much by the[ir] use . . . as by the value at which they see them estimated by those who purchase them." Elmsley insisted that paying the Indians a higher price would do them more harm than good: "Slow as their progress is towards civilization, they are perfectly apprised of the value of money, and of its use, in maintaining them in those habits of indolence and intemperance to which most of them are more or less inclined." If instead paid a trifling price for land, they would have to work harder and drink less to survive as laborers for colonial employers. Of course, paying the Indians less would also permit the government and land speculators to make more money. Elmsley understood that the colony was premised on profiteering from the appreciating value of Indian lands procured cheaply. If Indians competed as speculators, the provincial great men would suffer in their portfolios and in their power. Fearing "that foresight which our Indian neighbours are but beginning to learn," he concluded that "it certainly cannot be our interest to promote their improvement."[55]

Upper Canada's officials also dreaded Brant's Mississauga connection as a security threat. By promoting tensions between native peoples, British policy obliged them all to look to the Indian Department for mediation and union. Lumping the Mississaugas and Ojibwas as "Chippewas," Simcoe advised promoting "the jealousy & separation of the Six Nations (& particularly of the Mohawks conducted by Brant & the Land-Jobbers) from the Chippewas, . . . & yet to have such a hold of the Affections of both those Nations, as at any time to be able to lead them to the defence of the King's possessions against his Foreign & especially, [his] *domestic* enemies." Americans on the borders, and potential rebels within the province, would be cowed by an Indian alliance that needed British leadership for cohesion. But if Mississaugas, Ojibwas, and the Six Nations framed their own alliance, they would not need the British and might turn upon them. Although Brant sought no war with the British, he did want them to fear that possibility when he pressed for concessions.[56]

The British vowed to reduce Brant's power by restoring the Mississaugas to their assigned role as especially tractable and deferential Indians. Simcoe worried that Brant had been "nurtured by [British] impolicy & indecision into dangerous consequence." Powell warned of "the Mischiefs hourly to be expected from these Hordes, if once they are satisfied that our Conduct towards them is influenced by apprehension of their Resentment." Reporting to the Duke of Portland, Russell observed that "Captain Brant's conduct also serves to evince the Wisdom of your Grace's Policy in preventing all Coalition between the Indian Nations within this Government."[57]

To disrupt that coalition, Russell established at York a separate agency for the Mississaugas conducted by a young army officer, Lieutenant James Givens, who had learned their language. Previously, the British had delivered presents jointly to the Mississaugas and Iroquois at the head of Lake Ontario, with Brant acting as the master of ceremonies. To diminish Brant and to discourage cooperation between those peoples, Givens separately delivered the Mississauga presents at the Credit River near York in the spring of 1798. A Mississauga chief protested the new policy: "We have taken our Brothers the five Nations by the hand—and we wish to hold them fast, and not be separated from them."[58]

In disputes with the British or Americans, the Iroquois claimed tradition as the moral high ground, defining their relationship as best conducted in ancient and immutable forms. In this vein, Brant denounced the new Mississauga agency and the recently enhanced power of the government of Upper Canada over the Indian Department. Brant observed to Joseph Chew, "Dear friend, what hurts me most is to see so many new things and Changes taking place, and our Customs getting done away with these [past] few years." Of course, this was an ironic stand given Brant's radical innovations. He acted as a sachem although properly only a war chief, adopted a commercial land program for Grand River, and represented the Mississaugas in land negotiations. Noting the contradictions, Russell retorted, "That Indians being ever inclined to express strong attachments to old usages, ought assuredly [to] be the last in attempting thus to introduce new ways in their Transactions with us."[59]

SKIN FLINTS

To divide the Mississaugas from the Iroquois, Givens and Russell also exploited a land feud between the Grand River Mohawks and their Catholic kin at Kahnawake and Akwesasne (St. Regis). Kahnawake occupied the south shore of the St. Lawrence River near Montreal, while Akwesasne lay upstream at the mouth of the St. Regis River and along the boundary between Canada and New York. The two villages belonged to a Canadian confederation of Catholic Indians known as "The Seven Nations." Predicting a war, Givens warned the Mississaugas to steer clear of the Mohawks and to avoid dressing like them, lest they fall prey to their enemies.[60]

The land feud involved the right to sell lands in northern New York. During the 1780s, New York State claimed to have procured those lands from the Mohawks of Grand River and Tyendinaga. This claim angered the Seven Nations chiefs who, on six occasions between 1792 and 1796, sent delegations led by Colonel Louis to New York to seek either restoration of the contested lands, or at least a fair compensation. In May 1796, their chiefs assured New York's commissioners, "Those Mohawks had as good a Right to sell as they have to come and dispose of the City of New York." When the New Yorkers called the Grand River Mohawks "a just people," the Seven Nations chiefs bluntly replied, "but what makes them just in your Eyes we expect is because they stole from us and sold to you."[61]

To bolster their case, New York's commissioners cynically displayed the Long Lease granted by some Six Nations chiefs to John Livingston and associates in 1787. Although declared void by the state legislature in 1788, that lease served the state's commissioners eight years later as a proof that the contested lands had belonged to the valley Mohawks. Best of all, from the state's perspective, that lease had been witnessed by Colonel Louis, who had been an Oneida leader in 1787. The state commissioners also presented the deed of July 9, 1788, from the Six Nations to Oliver Phelps and associates, a deed signed by Joseph Brant. Meant to convey lands in western and central New York, the two documents were forced by the state to work against the Seven Nations in northern New York. Stunned by the documents, the Akwesasne and Kahnawake chiefs agreed to terms favorable to New York. They procured a $3,180 down payment and an annuity of $533, but kept only a six-square-mile reserve for Akwesasne and some nearby meadows and mill sites on the Salmon and Grass rivers.[62]

Once again, the state's aggression divided Indians who exchanged bitter recriminations over who was to blame for the lost lands. By a cunning deployment of misleading documents, New York's commissioners diverted the anger of Akwesasne and Kahnawake toward their fellow Mohawks and especially to Joseph Brant. That distraction also fed on the bitter rivalry between Brant and Colonel Louis, who had been partisans for opposing sides during the war. Their enmity revived during the early 1790s when each angled to become the key diplomat in resolving the Indian war in the Ohio country. Visiting Philadelphia in 1793, Colonel Louis denounced the federal favors bestowed on his rival. Blasting Brant as "my enemy and the enemy of peace," Colonel Louis complained, "but my father has raised him up. This makes me sick. My Father has struck me." Brant returned the favor by deriding the mulatto Colonel Louis as "that Black fellow."[63]

In 1798, Brant struggled to avert a Mohawk civil war by seeking copies of the controversial documents from the government of New York, but the governor kept finding excuses to delay complying. In 1798, Brant complained that "the backwardness of Gov. Jay to give us the information we sought after makes this appear rather suspicious on their parts." Indeed, Jay entrusted the matter to the commissioner Egbert Benson, "who I know," Brant observed, "would skin a flint if it was possible, should it belong to the Indians." Having created a crisis potentially deadly for Mohawks, New York's leaders prolonged that crisis by withholding the documents that Brant needed for vindication.[64]

After all of his genteel repartee and hospitality with New York's leaders at past councils, Brant had not anticipated that they would hang him out to dry, exposed to the fury of the Seven Nations. At Kahnawake in July 1799, Brant narrowly averted the crisis by meeting the chiefs of the Seven Nations in council. Persuaded that New York had cheated them, the chiefs exonerated Brant, lifting the threat of war, but this did nothing to retrieve their lost lands.[65]

WOLF

In 1799, Brant hoped to strengthen his position by befriending the Comte de Puisaye, a royalist refugee from the French Revolution. A veteran military officer who had assisted a failed British attempt to invade France, Puisaye sought a haven in Upper Canada with the support of Simcoe and the Duke of Portland. Arriving in 1798 with forty-one followers, he obtained a government grant to wilderness land about fifteen miles north of York, where Russell hoped that the French settlement would screen the capital from a potential Indian attack.[66]

Struggling with frontier hardships, the neophyte settlers soon longed for a more accessible location on Lake Ontario. That longing led Puisaye to visit Brant at Grand River. Fond of military aristocrats, Brant took a great liking to the tall and graceful count. Brant also saw an opportunity for increased leverage by providing Mississauga land at Burlington Bay to Puisaye. Given his powerful friends in London, the provincial officials might have to accept such a deal, which would acknowledge Brant's authority over Mississauga land. Vested in Puisaye's hands, the strategic tract would belong to a Brant ally rather than fall to speculators preferred by government officials. To sweeten the bait, Brant persuaded the Mississaugas to lower their price to

1 shilling, 3 pence per acre, which the government would pay them before bestowing the land on Puisaye.[67]

But the proposed deal was not sweet enough to entice Russell and his Executive Council. Five times higher than what they wished to pay for the lands, the price "would certainly prevent our ever hereafter being able to obtain them cheaper." Russell insisted that the Mississaugas ought to follow tradition by donating land to the king and "chearfully accept from him whatever Presents he has been pleased to make them in return." The officials also resented Brant's restriction of the acreage to just 69,120 acres, entirely reserved for Puisaye. They wanted much more land, some for Puisaye but most for themselves.[68]

The councillors saw the tract as critical and the moment as pivotal for the fate of their colony. If they could cheaply secure enough Mississauga land for a hundred townships, the councillors meant to fill them with settlers, swamping the Indian numbers. Thereafter, the natives would be so intimidated by the colonists that, Elmsley explained, the government could "dictate instead of soliciting the terms on which future acquisitions are to be made." In May the Executive Council unanimously refused any "assent to the Right claimed by the Indians of giving their lands to whom they please by permitting their grants to His Majesty to be clogged with Conditions."[69]

To overcome the council's opposition Brant revived the alarming rumors of an impending French and Indian invasion. Brant assured Russell that "a very dangerous cloud hangs ready to burst over this Province." In January 1799, a spooked Executive Council prepared 1,500 provincial militia for emergency service. Russell was so unnerved that he abruptly abandoned his policy of dividing the Indians and of undercutting Brant. Indeed, he proposed to place all of Upper Canada's "Indian Allies under the lead of Captain Brant with such Provincial Rank as may flatter his ambition and excite his Zeal in the service."[70]

But cooler heads soon noted that the renewed alarm coincided with Brant's push for the Puisaye transaction. In late March and early April, a flurry of new reports debunked the rumors of western invasion. Trying to hide his embarrassment, Russell pretended that the latest news "only confirmed me in what I suspected before that it was only the old story dished up in a different form to answer some interested purpose." The punctured rumor stiffened the resolve by the Executive Council to reject Brant's Puisaye proposal.[71]

Having cried wolf once too often, Brant lost credibility in official circles. After the death of his son in 1795, Brant also drank more often and more heavily, which led him to speak with a reckless anger in public. "Altho very cunning in the main," Russell noted, "[Brant] is at times thrown off his guard either by liquor or his extreme impatience of Controul. He then utters sentiments little corresponding with his usual professions of Loyalty & attachment to the King's Interests."[72]

Troubled by these reports, the Duke of Portland replaced Russell by appointing General Peter Hunter, a tough military officer, to govern the colony. During the summer of 1799, Hunter arrived to take command of Upper Canada. Portland directed Hunter to rein in Brant, who had made so much trouble for the overmatched Russell:

> Whatever credit is to be given to Mr. Brandt for his loyalty and attachment to this country (upon which I am not inclined to place any great reliance) it is unquestionably evident that he omits no opportunity of consolidating the Indian Interests with a view to form an Indian Confederacy and to place himself at the head of it, than which nothing can be more directly contrary to our Interests.

Portland instructed Hunter to keep the Indians "as separate and disunited as possible."[73]

HUNTER AND CLAUS

Born in 1746, Peter Hunter came from the landed gentry of Scotland. Entering the royal army as an ensign at age twenty-one, Hunter rose steadily to the rank of lieutenant colonel by the end of the American Revolutionary War, when he served primarily in the West Indies. After the war, he was posted in Canada. Commanding at Fort Niagara in 1788–89, he won settler gratitude by providing food relief during "the hungry year." But he also winked at John Butler's corrupt dealings in Indian presents and Seneca land. During the early and mid 1790s, Hunter won promotion to general by serving his king in British Honduras, on the European continent, and in the West Indies. In 1798, Hunter became the military governor of County Wexford, where he helped to suppress an Irish insurrection by hanging rebel leaders. He impaled their heads on iron spikes for public display outside the county courthouse. As a reward, the Duke of Portland appointed Hunter to command the military in both Canadian provinces and to conduct the civil government of Upper Canada (a lieutenant governor administered the province of Lower Canada).[74]

A military martinet who governed by command, Hunter lacked patience for fools or foes. The merchant Isaac Todd observed, "Gen[era]l Hunter is verry exact and wishes all under him to be so." Brutally frank and demanding, he terrified most of the civil officials, but especially William Jarvis, the

William Claus, by an unknown artist, ca. 1800. (Courtesy of the Niagara Historical Society and Museum.)

secretary of Upper Canada. Critics noted that Hunter especially wanted land grants processed rapidly so that he could reap the official fees. During his last three years in office, he collected £4,393 in land fees, a fortune for his time and place. Hunter immensely improved the hitherto slapdash civil administration, but his sharp tongue, brusque manner, and uncompromising expectations made many enemies. Few, however, dared to say so in public until Hunter was safely dead. Hannah Jarvis, the wife of William Jarvis, then wrote, "For my part, I think the Ministry must have scraped all the fishing Towns of Scotland to have found so great a Devil."[75]

In August 1799, Hunter visited Newark to inspect the troops and to meet the Iroquois chiefs. Determined to manage Indians by division and dependence, Hunter privately rebuked Brant for meddling in Mississauga affairs. Hunter assured the Duke of Portland: "Captain Brant's aim at consolidating the Indian Interests with a view to form an Indian Confederacy, and to place himself at the head of it, shall be resisted by me on every occasion." To that end, Hunter personally supervised the separate delivery of presents to the Mississaugas in 1800. Recognizing defeat, the Comte de Puisaye gave up and returned to England in April 1802, subtracting from Brant's dwindling number of colonial supporters.[76]

By rupturing the Mississauga alliance with Brant, Hunter could impose British terms to buy their land. At the Credit River in the summer of 1805, William Claus procured the long-coveted tract of 250,880 acres at the head of Lake Ontario. As Hunter expected, the Mississaugas couched their concession in traditional deference to the British king. Quinepenon declared: "Although we & our Women think it hard to part with it, yet as our Father wants it he will of course do better with it than we can do ourselves. We therefore have altogether agreed to give all you ask, to do as our Father pleases with it."[77]

In another reversion to tradition, the Mississaugas left the price entirely "to the generosity of our Father." That generosity proved paltry, indeed, as Claus promised goods worth only £1,000. A mere 1 pence per acre, the price was a third of what the British had offered the Mississaugas during the late 1790s and a pittance of the 3 shillings per acre that Brant had demanded on their behalf. Claus conceded that "in former purchases of Indian lands much larger sums have been paid for smaller Tracts." Claus subsequently felt some buyer's remorse at the unjust price. Citing "the pitiyful situation of these poor people, the Mississagas," he proposed doubling the payment by adding another £1,000 in goods. Even this would have raised the price to just 2 pence per acre, but Claus's superiors declined to enhance the payment.[78]

Hunter also moved to constrain Brant's management of the Grand River lands. The general denounced Russell's deeds to Brant's speculators as "highly disgraceful to the Executive Government of this Province." Although he could not undo those deeds, Hunter forbade any further land sales by the Six Nations. In a personal interview with Claus and Hunter, Brant learned "that we are not to be permitted to have any white people settled within our limits or to do anything farther with our lands than living on them."[79]

Claus ably served Hunter's determination to undermine Brant's power. His aggressive challenge stunned Brant, who had expected to dominate the son of his old friend Daniel Claus. Indeed, Brant had pushed for William Claus's appointment as a deputy superintendent and as a trustee for the Grand River land sales. Feeling betrayed, Brant erupted, "When I find I am reduced by the deceptions of a friend, of a brother, whom I confided in, what will not my mind suggest for me to say in my anger[?]" Brant's protégé John Norton later recalled, "His latter Days were sorely disturbed by the parties excited against him among his own People;—those whose youth he had protected were influenced to turn against him, and an *Old Friend* . . . was the first to accuse him, in Whispers to the people, of having embezzled their Money."[80]

Claus was an especially formidable rival for Iroquois allegiance. In control of the Indian agency at Fort George in Newark, Claus could reward or punish chiefs by giving or withholding presents. As a trustee of the Grand River lands, he could block Brant's attempts to manage the revenue from the land sales of 1798. Claus also benefited from, in the words of Sir John Johnson, "the uncommon Affection and regard [the Iroquois] retain for the memory of the Grand Father of Captain Claus, the late Sir William Johnson." In speeches to the Indians, Claus played up his status. As "one of the last of that Great Man's family," he sought "the same marks of friendship that you always professed & shewed to your friend Sir William Johnson." Birth enabled Claus to trump Brant's association with the legendary Sir William.[81]

Shrewdly posing as tradition's defender, Claus faulted Brant as a dangerous innovator. When Brant proposed dividing up Indian lands into private holdings, Claus abruptly rejected the notion: "The manner in which all Indian Land is held, is in common, the idea of subdividing their property and giving to each individual a Share, is a thing not possible." When Brant sought to introduce written recordkeeping by the Indians to manage their lands, Claus discouraged any deviation from the old customs of illiteracy. And when Brant sought written copies of Claus's speeches, the deputy superintendent refused. It better served colonial interests to frustrate Brant's reforms and to preserve the British advantage in literacy.[82]

To sow Iroquois dissension, Claus exploited the shortfall in the anticipated revenues from Brant's land sales to land speculators. Lacking the resources to make their large payments, they had counted on quickly retailing farm-sized lots to many settlers. But retail buyers proved too few and too poor to pay much in the short term. By 1801, the speculators had all fallen into arrears, which emboldened Claus to insinuate that Brant had embezzled payments.[83]

Many young warriors turned against Brant, who, by acting arbitrarily, roused them to challenge an overly mighty chief. Growing irritable and imperious with age, Brant dismissed his young critics as ingrates. He reminded them of "the many important services I have rendered you, the many privations I have suffered on your account, and the journies I have undertaken for your benefit—for the time and expenses of which you have never paid me one penny."[84]

With generous presents and favors, Claus bolstered Brant's young critics at Grand River. Older warriors stuck by Brant and faulted Claus for creating a generational divide. One complained, "The divisions existing among us, and the attempts of the young men to put the Chiefs aside, have no other origin than the Indian [Department] store. It is there [that] the young men receive from his Majesty's bounty that which was designed for those who fought and suffered in his cause, and who are now treated with neglect."[85]

The generational rift also reflected a revival of traditional "pagan" practices at Grand River. In 1798, a young Mohawk warrior fell into a trance that lasted for more than a day. He emerged to describe a visionary encounter with Tharonhiawagon, the "Upholder of the Skies or Heavens," who urged the restoration of traditional Iroquois ceremonies, especially the annual sacrifice of a white dog. The revival challenged Brant's promotion of Christianity and other colonial ways. Seeing the white dog's remains covered with ribbons and hanging from a pole, Brant angrily ordered the pole toppled. When this action increased murmurings against him, Brant wisely reconsidered. Thereafter, he facilitated the revived ceremonies, so long as the traditionalists tolerated the Anglican church in Brant's Town, but the uneasy truce suggested considerable resistance to Brant's promotion of settler ways.[86]

CONSPIRACY

In January 1802, an anonymous informant alerted the Executive Council of Upper Canada to a sensational plot to overthrow British rule and create a republican state that would join the United States. The conspiracy was financed by American land speculators, who lusted after the frontier lands of Upper Canada. They claimed support at the highest levels of the republic. "The American Government," the informant insisted, "is at the bottom of the plan but will not be seen. Col. [Aaron] Burr and Mr. [George] Clinton are ostensibly the principal leaders." In 1802, Clinton was once again the governor of New York, while Burr had recently been elected vice president of the United States. Conveying the informant's shocking news to Peter Hunter at Quebec, Chief Justice Elmsley elaborated,

> That the plan is to assemble a considerable force on the frontiers, & at a given signal to enter the Province: that both the men & the Arms necessary for the purpose are ready & can be brought forward at a Moment's warning & that the Invaders will be immediately joined by between One & two thousand of the Inhabitants of this Country.

Such a plot seemed plausible because British officials expected the worst from the new American president, Thomas Jefferson, whom they considered a reckless radical.[87]

Within Upper Canada, most of the suspects were entrepreneurial immigrants from the United States. During the late 1790s, these aspiring men had aroused the distrust of the executive councillors, who revoked their contracts for land. Threatened with financial ruin, some began to plot a republican revolution. The colony's principal plotter was Asa Danforth, a petty land speculator, road contractor, and political partisan of Governor Clinton.[88]

Another suspect was the versatile Davenport Phelps from New Hampshire. A former merchant, occasional lawyer, and frustrated land speculator, Phelps found a friend and patron in Brant, who cherished his genteel education, Freemasonry, and status as the grandson of Eleazar Wheelock, who had been Brant's teacher. In 1797–98, Brant promoted Phelps's bid for Anglican ordination to become a missionary at Grand River. Deeming Phelps seditious, Peter Russell objected. The Anglican bishop of Quebec agreed that the Six Nations were too crucial to the security of Upper Canada to risk upon a "Spiritual Instructor who would be disposed to unsettle their notions of loyalty & obedience & weaken their attachment to the Government under which it is their happiness to live."[89]

Offended by the British rejection, Brant sought Aaron Burr's help in arranging Phelps's ordination by the Anglican bishop of New York. Brant insisted that "religion and morality respect mankind at large, without any reference to the boundaries of civil governments." But British officials insisted upon close control over any mission to the Indians on their side of the boundary. The Duke of Portland declared that, in the choice of missionaries, Indians "neither have been, nor ever will be, consulted on the Subject."[90]

Frustrated by the Hunter administration, Brant made one last bid to work within the British system by appealing to Sir John Johnson for help. But Johnson was far too cautious and passive to tangle with Peter Hunter or his patron, the Duke of Portland. Furious at Johnson's advice to accept diminished power, Brant broke off their correspondence. He had lost his last significant friend among the colonial officials, who closed ranks against him.[91]

Before plunging into rebellion, however, Brant had to ascertain how much support he could secure from the Americans. In late 1800 and early 1801, Brant wrote "Secret and Confidential" letters to Israel Chapin, Jr., to Governor Clinton, and to Thomas Morris, then in Congress. Brant wanted their help to secure a large tract of federal land near Sandusky on Lake Erie. Ostensibly, the reservation would sustain a mission to encourage Christianity and agricultural progress among any Indians who chose to live there, but that tract could also provide a refuge should the Grand River Indians rebel but suffer defeat. Seeking "the protection of the United States," Brant urged secrecy because of "the great jealousy of the British."[92]

To further explore his American options, Brant sent his adolescent sons Joseph, Jr., and Jacob to study at Dartmouth College. By choosing an American college, Brant pointedly rejected an alternative invitation to educate the boys in England at government expense, an invitation meant to render him more tractable. Instead, Brant drew upon the help of Phelps, a Dartmouth graduate and a cousin of the college's president, John Wheelock, the son of Eleazar Wheelock. Unlike almost every other Indian student, Brant nurtured fond memories of Wheelock, for Brant had reaped special treatment as the favorite of the powerful Sir William Johnson.[93]

In October 1800, Brant's sons traveled to Dartmouth, conducted by Colonel Benjamin Sumner, one of the shadowy American speculators who had invested in Grand River lands. Securing charitable scholarships for the Brant boys, President Wheelock lodged them in his own home. Appreciating the promotional value of educating the sons of the celebrated Brant, Wheelock hoped to persuade the missionary society in Scotland to restore funds long withheld because Dartmouth had defaulted on his father's obligation to educate Indians.[94]

Brant's sons apparently conveyed a provocative proposal to Wheelock, who passed it on to a New Hampshire congressman, Jonathan Freeman. In early December 1800, Wheelock wrote him a cryptic yet suggestive letter:

> In regard to the other affair, it is of so delicate a nature that I need not express much upon it, especially as I had the pleasure to communicate to you fully in our last conversation, the facts relating to it. It appears to me of very great & interesting consequence to our federal government, considering the character that will be concerned in it; [and] the great body of numerous tribes on the western lakes that it will influence. Will not the adoption of the measure of encouraging a few of the natives to incorporate with the United States, by resigning a small tract, lying westerly of Lake Erie, to be formed into a government under the union be the best barrier to these states in future time? Will it not draw an immense fur trade into our country? The government to be so formed, admitting people from our country & others to become settlers & citizens with the red. But I will not now enlarge. You are acquainted with the particulars of the Subject. It is interesting & momentous and it seems that Providence has now opened a door for an incalculable advantage to the United States and there may never be such another opportunity if the present juncture is not embraced. The affair is of such consequence that I had thoughts of writing to the President on the same. If you think best, I will do it. But you will be able better to communicate orally every thing to him that could be done in a letter.

Wheelock concluded, "Pray consider this letter as in utmost confidence." A month later, he added that the subject was "of great magnitude to the interests of the United States and more especially in the contingence of war" by placing "under their control the main force of the *aborigenes*."[95]

Given the content and timing, shortly after the Brant boys reached Dartmouth, the two letters refer to Brant's Sandusky scheme. Evidently, Brant wanted his own quasi-sovereign territory on the American side of the line in association with the United States. Detecting security implications that required great secrecy, Wheelock sought a prompt response from the American president. The timing, however, was inauspicious because President John Adams was a weak lame duck, while Jefferson would not take office until March.

Ominous rumors of Brant's correspondence troubled British officials. They also noted with alarm that Brant received two especially suspicious visitors at Grand River during the spring of 1801: Theodosia Burr Alston and her husband, Joseph Alston. What sinister message, wondered the officials, had the Alstons brought from Aaron Burr, the archrepublican of New York?[96]

That alarm intensified during the following summer, when the officials learned that Brant had covertly visited the Indians dwelling along the Detroit River. If Brant planned to rebel, he had to secure his flank to the west. Secretly addressing a mix of Ottawas, Ojibwas, Potawatomis, and Wyandots, Brant denounced Great Britain as "an ungrateful nation" that "had constantly deceived the Indians." He also boasted:

> I have traveled among white People, and have become perfectly acquainted with their policy, and views towards Indians: The Commander-in-Chief does not know them better. Brothers, I am a greater Man than them all, the Commander in Chief not excepted.

That boasting conveyed Brant's desperation to trump the Indian reliance on British information and advice. But the Ojibwa chief Makonce preferred to curry British favor by revealing Brant's seditious message to Thomas McKee, who conveyed the alarming news to the Executive Council at York.[97]

While invoking secrecy on his correspondents, Brant became dangerously indiscreet when drinking and when challenged by critics. In September 1801, two prominent warriors informed Claus that Brant had recently threatened to move

> to the States, which he will return no more in this Country. He says he will go away, yet the Grand River Lands will [still] be in his hands, that

no man shall meddle with it amongst us. He says the British Government shall not get it, but the American[s] shall and will have it, the
Grand River Lands, because the War is very close to break out.

Brant's loose lips undermined his prowess as a conspirator, for he had to
devote his energies to denying his reckless words and the widespread rumors
of traitorous letters. In public council at Grand River on May 1, 1802, Brant
assured his people:

> It is said, I have made a Speech to the Chippawas, in which I treated very
> disrespectfully the British Government, and since that, wrote to Con-
> gress, requesting their protection to remove within their line. I assure you
> this is a falsehood. Had I done so, I would not deny it; but I never wrote
> to that quarter on any such Subject.

But of course he had written on that very subject to Chapin, Morris, Clinton, and Wheelock, if not directly to Congress. By denying that correspondence in public council, Brant neutralized himself, for he could no longer try
to rally the Indians against the British. Closely watched by Claus and by suspicious warriors, Brant dared not accept Asa Danforth's invitation to attend
a plotting session at Albany in February 1802, although Brant did send his
confidant and protégé John Norton.[98]

Ultimately nothing but more dangerous talk came of that Albany meeting, for the proposed rebellion was a folly. Few colonists would risk their lives
and properties on overt rebellion unless assured of a major American incur-
sion likely to win the war without them. And no American invasion was
forthcoming, for want of support from the nation's leaders. In fact, only Burr
showed much interest in the plot, and his power was waning after a failed bid
to steal the presidency from Jefferson in March 1801.[99]

Given the military weakness of the United States, President Jefferson
could ill afford to provoke an expensive war with the powerful British
Empire. When informed of Brant's provocative bid for a safe haven, Jefferson
informed his secretary of state, James Madison: "I think it shall be better to
postpone an answer to Govr. Clinton on Brant's proposition till we can be
together at Washington. In fact it belongs to the War department." Brant
probably never got an official answer to his request.[100]

The September 1802 date for the American invasion and Canadian
uprising passed uneventfully. By then, the plot had become, in Peter Russell's words, "a tissue of Absurdity & Improbability." Most of the Canadian
conspirators slipped back to New York, where Phelps at last obtained an

Joseph Brant's mansion at the Head of Lake Ontario, by Edward Walsh, 1804. The artist included two Indians in the foreground, next to a settler fence, to convey the hybridity of Brant's identity. (Courtesy of the William L. Clements Library, University of Michigan.)

Anglican ministry. Meanwhile, Brant stuck it out in Upper Canada, loudly protesting his loyalty while denouncing the officials who suspected it.[101]

NORTON

Dismayed by his diminished support and increased danger at Grand River, Brant moved to a new mansion built at Burlington Bay on a 3,450-acre tract given to him by the Mississaugas and confirmed by the government in 1796.[102]

By displaying genteel wealth, Brant emulated his mentor, Sir William Johnson. Observers noted that his new mansion was a half-scale model of Johnson Hall, complete with a portico and a Palladian window. One visitor recalled entering "a spacious hall" and turning right into "a large, old fashioned drawing room," decorated with Brant's life-sized portrait significantly placed next to similar images "of Sir William Johnson and members of his family, in stiff wigs and scarlet coats richly laced." On the mantel sat the dagger "which drank the blood of his ruffianly son Isaac." The front windows looked out over the long, sandy beach where the Indian Department delivered presents to the Six Nations—and where Brant had stabbed Isaac. Facing inland, the visitor saw a prosperous farm in the colonial style, with an orchard and 100 acres in crops.[103]

Like most colonial settlements, Brant's new mansion overlay an ancient landscape of Indian occupation. A visitor reported,

> In this immediate vicinity the soil was mingled with vast quantities of human bones, stones, arrowheads, hatchets, &c., the weapons of ancient Indian warfare. In sight of the mansion, and in plain view of the road, was a large mound of earth filled with human bones.

Hatchets or arrowheads stuck in many of the skulls, attesting that Brant's new home had been the site of an ancient conflict—no good omen.[104]

In November 1802, Hunter escalated the confrontation with Brant by issuing a proclamation invalidating any lease given by Indians, a severe blow to Brant, who had recruited many tenants to Grand River. He bitterly complained:

> Should we be deprived of leasing our Lands, how are we to subsist? Our Tract of land is now surrounded by white people so that our hunting is done away [with]. Many in our Nations [are] perfect Strangers to farming, and should we be deprived of making the most of our landed property, many must Starve, many must go Naked.

The ban reduced the Indians, Brant insisted, "to a line worse than Slavery, [for] our words will be nothing thought of, [and] our writings no better." In 1804, Lord Selkirk visited Grand River to find some "fine improvements . . . abandoned" by tenants discouraged by the proclamation.[105]

The ban on Indian leasing coincided with a strict restriction on Brant's access to provincial leaders and their documents. In February 1803, Brant traveled to York to protest the proclamation, but Hunter refused to meet him. Instead, Hunter's secretary, James Green, conveyed the insulting directive that Brant should convey all requests to Claus, his great enemy. In January 1804, Green informed Claus that Hunter felt nothing but contempt for Brant's revived threats to visit London to seek redress: "that the less notice taken of him, the better—and it is a matter of perfect Indifference to the Lieut. General whether he goes to England, or stays here." Long flattered and wooed by governors, Brant felt demoted and insulted by his new treatment.[106]

Nor did Brant get much response from Claus. Through Green, Hunter assured Claus "that Captain Brandt has no Right to call on you to answer any

Questions he may think proper to ask you." He was to keep a written record of all his meetings with Brant, but was not to provide the chief with a copy. By losing access to the British information that had boosted his standing in the eyes of other Indians, Brant could no longer boast of his unparalleled insights into the outside world.[107]

At a dead end with the government in Upper Canada, Brant longed to break out by making a third trip to London, where he might again make his case directly to the imperial lords. But he could not afford a year or two away from his complicated personal and public business, especially with the payments from the land sales so entangled. Instead, in early 1804, he sent his talented and controversial protégé, John Norton.[108]

Norton claimed that his father was a Cherokee Indian, captured as a boy by a Scottish soldier during the early 1760s. Adopted and taken to Scotland, Norton's father allegedly married a Scottish woman named Anderson. Young Norton served an apprenticeship as a printer but ran away to enlist in the army in 1784. A year later, his regiment went to Canada. Posted at Fort Niagara in 1787, Norton deserted to live among the Mohawks, who took a liking to him. Apparently pardoned by the British, he won a regular discharge in early 1788. Moving to the Bay of Quinte, Norton taught school at the Tyendinaga reserve for a year or two, but he neglected his duties, preferring to hunt and fish with the young men, who taught Norton their language. In 1791, he headed west to work as a fur trader at Detroit. After Wayne's victory in 1794, Norton returned to Niagara, to serve as an interpreter for the Indian Department. Bright, handsome, graceful, inquisitive, and gregarious, Norton charmed Brant, who became his patron. Adopted by the Mohawks, with Brant as his uncle, Norton moved to Grand River, where he married an Iroquois woman, donned native attire, and assumed the name of Teyoninhokarawen. Resigning from the Indian Department in 1800, Norton became a Mohawk war chief.[109]

Scoffing at Norton's assertion of Cherokee paternity, hostile officials saw him as a fraud. In July 1801, Green pointedly informed Norton: "With respect to your being adopted an Indian Chief, it is a matter [that] the Lieut. General can have nothing to do with, as he cannot possibly recognize any Person in that Character but Native Indians." Historians have divided on the issue of Norton's Indian paternity. Supporters cite his dark complexion and expertise in Cherokee culture recorded during a visit to their country in 1809. Doubters note the improbability that a captured Cherokee boy of the early 1760s could grow up in time to sire a son old enough to enlist in 1784. In either case, there can be no doubt that Norton assiduously mastered Mohawk culture—winning acceptance by that people.[110]

In February 1804, Norton departed for England via New York City. By choosing an American port, Norton evaded surveillance and obstruction by British officials at Quebec. As a cover story, Norton insisted that he went to England from a patriotic zeal to enlist in the royal army fighting the French. He carried a letter of introduction from Brant to prominent British aristocrats who had befriended Brant during the revolution, particularly the Duke of Northumberland and the Earl of Moira. Norton also dazzled them with an exotic combination of Christian piety, genteel manners, and Indian appearance.[111]

The aristocrats' romantic notions proved a mixed blessing to Norton. Although their enthusiasm for Indians opened important official doors, they did not understand the pressures that Indians faced to adapt to settler ways. The Duke of Northumberland took far too seriously his ritual adoption, during the war in America, as a Mohawk. Speaking as a fellow Indian, the duke urged Brant to defy reformers bent on "converting us from hunters and warriors into husbandmen. . . . Let our young men never exchange their liberty, and manly exercises, to become hewers of wood and drawers of water." The loss of the warrior ethos would render the Mohawks "less than women." Of course, the duke did not recognize that Brant was one of those reformers and that his opponents were warriors balking at social and cultural change.[112]

The duke and the earl introduced Norton to the new secretary of state for the colonies, Lord Camden. On Brant's behalf, Norton sought a Crown deed of freehold title for the Grand River reserve. Such a deed would cut out the middlemen of empire: the colonial officials of Upper and Lower Canada, who had created so many difficulties and delays. Possessed of a freehold title, the Indians could manage their reserve as a commercial property without restrictions on their right to lease or to sell.[113]

Because colonial power depended on managing the flow of information to superiors in London, Hunter felt threatened by Norton's success in reaching the imperial capital to charm the imperial lords. He and Brant had to be discredited, and quickly. On Hunter's order Claus gathered documents damning Brant as seditious. Hunter forwarded them to London, while Claus convened a Six Nations council to review Norton's mission. Claus warned the chiefs that "a White man under the Mask of being a Mohawk Chief was in England representing Grievances of the 6 Nations without their knowledge, approbation, or consent." In April 1805, Claus packed the council with Brant's rivals and enemies: Grand River warriors and Buffalo Creek chiefs. Smelling a setup, Brant refused to attend.[114]

In the intrigue, Red Jacket played a leading role, for he despised Brant, having heard too many of his jibes about wartime cowardice as "the Cow-

John Norton (Teyoninhokarawen), by Mary Ann Knight. (Courtesy of the Library and Archives Canada; C-123832.)

Killer." In addition to personal spite, Red Jacket pursued a political agenda by asserting that Grand River belonged to all of the Iroquois, including those within the American line, and not just to those who presently resided there. Red Jacket also wanted Buffalo Creek affirmed as the primary council fire for the Six Nations (a claim challenged by Brant on behalf of Grand River). Ordinarily, Hunter and Claus would never concede that superiority to a village within the American line, but in 1805 they were desperate for allies to bring down Brant and Norton.[115]

As Claus intended, this unorthodox Six Nations council disavowed Norton's mission as unauthorized and inappropriate. The attending chiefs also denounced land sales or leases to settlers at Grand River. Red Jacket explained, "We the Six Nations cannot consent to have what the King gave to us in common disposed of in the way it is; we have too much regard for our Posterity to whom we wish it to be preserved for." In Red Jacket's words, the attending chiefs also "put Captain Brant down . . . and hereafter nobody must hear what he says."[116]

Forwarded by Claus to Hunter and across the Atlantic, the council record discredited Norton in London. In July, Lord Camden promptly closed his doors and his mind to Norton's requests. Broke and frustrated, Norton returned to Canada after almost two futile years in England.[117]

Meanwhile, Brant fought his deposition by convening his own council at Grand River on May 1, 1805. By excluding the young warriors and any Iroquois living within the American line, Brant ensured the predominance of his supporters, the chiefs and matrons of Grand River. They disavowed Claus's council as irresponsible meddling by Senecas assisted by a few callow young Mohawks. The dueling councils of 1805 divided the Six Nations into rival American and Canadian confederacies, a bitter fruit of the tightening border between the republic and the empire. Never again would Brant attend a council at Buffalo Creek. In July 1806, he announced that the Onondaga village at the Grand River was the only true council fire for the Six Nations.[118]

Brant also continued to grant Grand River lands to white settlers with leases of 999 years. A list of thirty-nine recipients documents Brant's land management, which displayed a mix of political cunning, commercial ambition, and noblesse oblige. Large grants of 1,200 acres each went to six favorites, including his secretary Ephratus L. Phelps; his favorite surveyor, Augustus Jones; and Dr. Robert Kerr, a surgeon in the Indian Department. Most of the settlers procured farm-sized tracts of 100 to 400 acres, paying an average of 11 shillings per acre—far more than the government would pay for Indian land. These settlers gave such a premium price because the reserve offered exceptionally fertile and accessible lands. Because Brant took special care of his fellow soldiers, at least seven tenants got land "for being a volunteer in the Indian Department." He also used the land to hire skilled labor to develop the reserve; three tenants obtained farms for erecting mills and other public buildings.[119]

DEATH

On August 21, 1805, Hunter died, leaving the administration of Upper Canada to Alexander Grant, the senior member of the Executive Council. A plump old Scot (seventy-one) of scant education and little tact, Grant acted as a caretaker, pending the appointment in London of Hunter's formal successor. Grant persisted in Hunter's policy of restricting Brant's access and influence by requiring his subordination to Claus.[120]

Brant's marginalization deepened after August 1806, when a new lieutenant governor, Francis Gore, replaced Grant. Thoroughly conservative,

Gore suspected any opposition as seditious. Supporting Claus, Gore bluntly rebuked Brant.[121]

Brant turned to an opposition faction in the colony's elected assembly led by Robert Thorpe, an ambitious Irish-born judge newly arrived in Upper Canada. Adopting a novel approach for an imperial functionary, Thorpe sought power by fomenting popular ferment and then by posing, in letters to his superiors, as the one man who could calm the popular discontent. Thorpe rallied public support by posing as a tribune of constitutional liberty against a tyrannical cabal of greedy officials.[122]

By helping Brant, Thorpe made trouble for Grant and Gore. Thorpe encouraged Brant to petition the legislators to investigate the Grand River land controversy. And Brant and Thorpe held a public council to demand Claus's ouster for allegedly embezzling land payments due to the Indians.[123]

In return, Brant helped Thorpe to defeat Gore's favored candidate in an assembly election. Brant led opposition voters from Burlington Bay to York, the district's lone official polling place. Outraged that an Indian chief could swing a colonial election, Gore redoubled his determination to deny freehold title to the Grand River reserve. Gore warned Lord Castlereagh:

> if they are eligible to hold lands by that Tenure, they become subject to His Majesty and entitled to all the privileges of Natural Born Subjects, they will then become electors, and qualified to be chosen Members of the House of Assembly. Are we prepared, My Lord, for such a change? We have already seen Brant, in virtue of a Grant of Land, made to him some years ago for his Military Services, at the head of an Electioneering party to place one of the most worthless and dangerous men (Mr. Thorpe) perhaps in the King's Dominions, in the House of Assembly. What may not be expected when every Savage in the Country becomes possessed of the same privilege?

In fact, few Indians aspired to the electoral role that Brant had played to Gore's special horror.[124]

To Gore's relief and Brant's dismay, Thorpe proved to be an ineffectual legislator in an assembly that lacked the constitutional power to challenge the lieutenant governor. But Thorpe's rants offended Gore, who suspended the judge during the summer of 1807. Seeking vindication, Thorpe departed for England to argue his case, in vain, to the imperial overlords. By gambling on Thorpe, Brant had bet on a loser, compounding the formidable enmity of Francis Gore.[125]

Brant suffered another blow from a surprising direction, as John Norton prematurely grasped for power at Grand River. In late 1806, Brant's failing health, heavy drinking, and erratic behavior led Norton to make important political decisions without consulting his mentor. Upon discovering what Norton had done, Brant erupted with wounded pride in April 1807. Blinded by rage, he foolishly complained to Claus and Gore, who delighted in widening the new division at Grand River.[126]

That spring, a weakened Brant meekly accepted the order that Claus belatedly brought to the long-tangled Grand River land sales of 1798. Of the original buyers, only Richard Beasley had made significant payments, primarily by recruiting settlers from Pennsylvania to make farms and assume the debt. Most of the other original buyers had sold out to American land speculators. Refusing their payments, Claus compelled them to sell out to approved buyers from Upper Canada or Great Britain. Much of the contested land passed to Lord Selkirk, an aristocrat with grand and benevolent ambitions for settling impoverished Scots in Canada. Claus invested the payments in London funds, generating a 3 percent interest delivered annually to the Grand River Indians. In return for that security, the Indians accepted dependence on Great Britain, just as the Senecas had become dependent on the United States by vesting their funds in that nation's bank. When Britain and the United States went to war in 1812, the Senecas and the Mohawks would fight one another as stockholders in rival nations.[127]

On November 24, while completing Selkirk's deed, Brant suddenly died at the age of sixty-three. He had led a hard and increasingly contentious life compounded by deep frustration and heavy drinking in his waning years. Norton reflected that Brant had once been "an Example of Temperance & sobriety;—(which could not be said of him in his latter Days.)" Rev. Robert Addison, an Anglican friend, reported that Brant "fell a victim to drunkenness."[128]

In Montreal, Sir John Johnson "was really sorry to hear of my Poor old friend Brant's Death." Death had beat his resolution "to write to my old friend and fellow Warrior" in search of reconciliation. Johnson, however, was pleased that Brant had recently submitted to Claus's terms: "He had been brought to a Sense of his errors, and had made Peace with all his former friends."[129]

But Brant also had a deathbed reconciliation with Claus's great enemy, John Norton, who recorded Brant's last known words: "Have pity on the poor Indians: if you can get any influence with the great, endeavor to do them all the good you can." These words offer a perfect epitaph for a life devoted to influencing great men so that Brant could help his people. For a time, Brant nearly pulled off his dangerous and double balancing act:

between native and genteel ways, and between Britons and Americans. That time had been during the late 1780s and early 1790s, when the empire and the republic had competed to control a borderland. But, as the apparently pre-eminent chief of the borderland, Brant had suffered from its partition by Americans and Britons into two bordered lands. That partition owed much to Samuel Kirkland, who outlived his old friend and recent rival.[130]

CHAPTER TWELVE

Ends

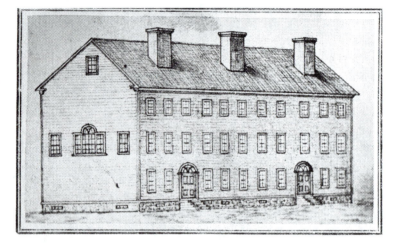

Hamilton Oneida Academy, ca. 1800. (From Walter Pilkington, ed., *The Journals of Samuel Kirkland* [1980]. Courtesy of the Hamilton College Library Archives.)

DURING THE MID-1790S, a crucial period for the Oneidas and their lands, Samuel Kirkland receded from their dealings with the federal and state governments. In 1794, Kirkland did facilitate the federal treaty at Kanonwalohale, but he had not participated in the more important treaty council at Canandaigua. A year later, Kirkland also abstained from New York's land negotiations with the Oneidas, leaving James Dean to serve as the state's chief interpreter and deal-broker. Kirkland's retreat was especially striking because he had been so ubiquitous and pivotal in previous meetings.

Why did Kirkland retreat from cross-cultural diplomacy? During the Philadelphia visit in 1792, Kirkland had irritated Henry Knox, the secretary of war, who found fault with the missionary's accounts, reimbursing them only in part. Infuriated, Kirkland blasted Knox for lacking "order, *System, application, economy,* and *impartial Justice.*" Balking at any further service to government, Kirkland shifted his focus to developing a prosperous farm around his new mansion in the town of Paris, about a dozen miles east of Kanonwalohale.[1]

Kirkland also became preoccupied with founding the Hamilton Oneida Academy, named to honor his fellow Federalist Alexander Hamilton. In 1791, Kirkland drafted a "Plan of Education for the Indians, Particularly of the Five Nations." It subscribed to the American conviction that Indians were doomed unless they transformed their culture by adopting private property, patriarchal families, temperance in alcohol, education in English, and the settler mode of agriculture. In a Federalist vein, Kirkland insisted that Indians were capable of reforming if placed under paternalistic guidance:

> After more than twenty years' observation, I am not able to discover any other repugnancy in the Indian mind to civilization, than what arises from the mere force of an *Indian* or *pagan* education. That they want capacity cannot be urged, for they discover in many things great ingenuity and address, and some marks of original genius are found among them.

Emphasizing nurture over nature, Kirkland rejected the then emerging insistence on a racial, biological inferiority that considered Indians unfit for civilization.[2]

Compared to their Jeffersonian Republican opponents, Federalists like Kirkland reduced the relative power of race, by emphasizing class distinctions. In that spirit, Kirkland defined his academy in elitist terms. Slighting the alternative of many common schools scattered on the Indian reservations, he proposed to educate only the sons of a few preeminent chiefs: two each from the Cayugas, Oneidas, Onondagas, Senecas, and Tuscaroras. Kirkland insisted that the "Education of the first Class" would best "introduce the manners & customs of the white people among them, which the famous Capt. Brant has affected in a very considerable degree among the Mohawks." Endowed with a genteel education, an elite few could become "politicians" and schoolmasters to distill and convey their learning to the common Indians.[3]

Derived entirely from Kirkland's culture, the proposed curriculum sought to transform Indians into gentlemen. In addition to reading, writing, and arithmetic, the students would master Latin, Greek, music, and metaphysics. Above all, Kirkland would teach them "the principles of human nature, and the history of civil society . . . that they may be able clearly to discern the difference between a *state* of *nature* and a *state* of *civilization*." Of course, the pupils would also study "the doctrines of revealed religion" in the Calvinist mode. And the boys would learn agriculture by enforced work on the master's property, as at Eleazar Wheelock's school before the war.[4]

Kirkland's plan ominously echoed Wheelock's ill-fated school for Indian youth. In 1767, Wheelock had dismissed most of his native students to found a college for white boys. A younger Kirkland had then blamed Wheelock's college for diverting charitable funds meant for Indians. By 1791, however, an older Kirkland remembered his old patron differently, as "the worthy founder of that most useful Institution," Dartmouth College. Forgetting his former feud with Wheelock, Kirkland lamented that his mentor's "laudable efforts" had become "a mark for the envenomed shafts of envy." Following Wheelock's lead, Kirkland considered it "necessary to admit into the school" American boys "who shall bear the charges of their own education." In addition to their financial contributions, the settler youth would, in theory, help their Indian classmates to learn English.[5]

Kirkland sited the academy on his own land in the town of Paris, where, he argued, Indian students would find abundant models in the English-speaking, Christ-worshiping settlers. But the location was also self-serving, for the school enhanced the value of his adjoining lands. And he could raise money and building materials from the leading local settlers, eager for an academy that would primarily educate their own sons. In 1792, Kirkland led the subscription drive by donating £10 in money and 300 acres of land.[6]

He procured additional large subscriptions from his land-speculator friends: Oliver Phelps, Jedediah Sanger, Peter Smith, and the State of New York (through the Board of Regents). Kirkland promised that his academy would soften up the Indians to part with more lands by subduing "those prejudices which too naturally arise against the present occupants of an extensive, luxuriant Country, which tradition informs the credulous Indian was given to his beloved Forefathers by the beneficent creator of all things, & of which he is too prone to believe them to have been unjustly despoiled." At the academy, Indians would learn that they should forsake lands needed by a state of civilization. In effect, the subscription converted some of the speculators' profits from procuring Iroquois lands into cultural capital to educate the sons of leading settlers. By also educating a few influential Indians, the school promised a return on the speculators' investment by facilitating future land cessions from deferential natives.[7]

Initially enthusiastic for the proposed academy, the Oneidas soured upon learning that Kirkland meant to educate only two of their sons at a time. They resented being used to attract charitable donations that Kirkland then applied primarily to educate white boys. The Oneidas also protested when Kirkland diverted Ebenezer Caulkins from his proper duty as a school-teacher at Kanonwalohale to serve instead as the master of the new academy.

Dismissing the Oneida complaints as ingratitude, Kirkland blamed "envious and unprincipled white people, who have suggested that I have acted from selfish, interested motives."[8]

Those critics included Rev. John Sergeant, Jr., the missionary at nearby New Stockbridge. Recognizing that the academy would never serve Indian needs, Sergeant favored a more decentralized and egalitarian program of grammar schools dispersed among the Indian villages. Forsaking the liberal arts, these schools would teach rudimentary reading, writing, and arithmetic, as well as farming or an artisinal trade. Timothy Pickering also tried to persuade Kirkland that a "school of plain learning and husbandry, should bound their first attempts. By plain learning, I mean such as that which in New England is acquired by the sons of common farmers." But Kirkland forged ahead with his academy.[9]

Hubris soon cost Kirkland dearly. He designed a grand edifice—three stories tall, 88 feet long, and 42 feet wide—that he could not afford to complete. With funds exhausted, construction ground to a halt in late 1795. The following June, Rev. Jeremy Belknap sadly reported that the academy consisted of "nothing more than a frame, partly covered. The work has ceased and no school is kept." That fall the county sheriff advertised the land and frame for forced sale to cover debts of $1,000. Only the intervention of twenty local gentlemen rescued the academy from auction and enabled completion of the construction in 1798.[10]

As Sergeant and Pickering had feared, Kirkland's academy failed to serve the Indians. In 1799, it had fifty-two white students but only a single native, a Tuscarora named David Cusick. The academy lacked charity scholarships for Indians because the trustees had spent their money constructing a massive edifice. During the next decade, the school grew to 121 students, but Kirkland educated only two more Indians. In the end, Kirkland emulated the folly of Eleazar Wheelock, who had also exploited Indians to raise money that subsequently educated the sons of settlers.[11]

COMPLAINT

Kirkland also retreated from public service because of deteriorating health. In October 1792, while riding through the forest the switch of a branch cost him most of his sight in one eye, which pained his attempts to read and write. He later suffered frostbite and recurrent bouts of pleurisy. In 1795, a horse compounded Kirkland's misery by throwing him onto a "hard, stony ground," battering his right side. Excessive doses of opium brought temporary relief but afflicted his digestion and mind. Kirkland attributed his ailments to "the peculiar sacrifices & Suffering annexed to my [missionary] office, the banishment from Society & the incessant hardship assigned to me in this Savage wilderness."[12]

Distracted by new priorities and poor health, Kirkland grew impatient with the Oneidas, who drank more often and more loudly than ever. On a visit to Kanonwalohale, he reported, "The whole night they were hallooing & yelping from one end of the town to the other." Fed up with the public drunkenness, Kirkland rebuked the Oneidas: "You have almost *broken* my *very heart.*"[13]

But Kirkland bore at least half the blame for their soured relationship by neglecting his mission. At Kanonwalohale in December 1792, Caulkins complained to Chapin that Kirkland was "absent most of the time and leaves the whole burthen of the Indians and his affairs among them upon me, for it is a fact, Sir, that he has preached here but two Sabbaths & two half Sabbaths since you was here in September."[14]

Disappointed with one another, the Oneidas and Kirkland exchanged bitter recriminations. They neglected to repair the Kanonwalohale log church, which became a bone of contention. In December 1793, Kirkland found the seats and floor covered with snow and ice because of the broken windows. Catching a bad cold while preaching, Kirkland blasted the Oneidas for their neglect: "I may add to this, [that] jealousy and ingratitude . . . are characteristic of you as a nation." Why should he preach to a people who would not repair his church? A month later, the chiefs retorted, "Our father seems pretty discouraged by reason of our wickedness. We [are] also discouraged concerning him. For how can a man expect to receive much fruit when he neglect[s that] which he once planted in a garden?" During the preceding five months, Kirkland had visited Kanonwalohale for only three Sabbaths. Why should they repair a church when their missionary so rarely visited them?[15]

In January 1794, the Oneida chiefs complained to his superiors, the Boston Board of ministers. Inverting his rebuke of Indians as lazy, the chiefs made a cutting observation: "We believe indolent teachers may find a thousand excuses." Seeking Kirkland's replacement, the Oneidas pointedly asked the board members "whether you are well satisfied for the little labour he has done among us?" Rev. Sergeant sadly confirmed the Oneida charges by observing that if Kirkland "would faithfully attend to them, [and] have a home among them, that he might yet be very useful. But how to make his duty his pleasure is the difficulty."[16]

The Boston Board forwarded the Oneida complaint to the board's financial sponsor, the Society in Scotland for Promoting Christian Knowledge. The Oneida petition compounded the society's alarm over a recent report from Rev. John McDonald, a Presbyterian minister who had visited Kanonwalohale and Kirkland during the summer of 1792. Convinced that they had enjoyed a most pleasant meeting, Kirkland was subsequently shocked to read McDonald's scathing report to the Society in Scotland:

> I cannot help being of [the] opinion that Indians, (or what are called Redmen) never were intended to live in a state of civil society. There never was, I believe, an instance of an Indian forsaking his habits and savage manners, any more than a bear his ferocity. The Rev. Mr. Kirkland, who acts as missionary among the Oneidas, has taken all the pains that man can take, but his whole flock are Indians still, and like the bear, which you can muffle and lead out to dance to the sound of musick, becomes again a bear when his muffler is removed and the musick ceases. The Indians will attend public worship and sing extremely well, following Mr. Kirkland's notes; but whenever the service is over, they wrap themselves in their blankets, and either stand like cattle on the sunny side of a house, or lie before a fire. This is their mode of passing life.

Why, the Scots ministers wondered, should they throw more good money after bad if preaching to the Indians was hopeless? In early 1794, the Society in Scotland directed its Boston correspondents to investigate Kirkland's mission and file a report.[17]

The Oneida complaints outraged Kirkland as a betrayal. Citing his former exertions and sufferings as a young missionary, he felt properly exempted from any Indian criticism ever. And he derided his critics as a minority of malicious and drunken pagans or Peter Penet's former supporters. In fact, Kirkland's critics included some former supporters, principally Skenandon, the most pious and temperate of Oneida chiefs.[18]

During the summer of 1796, the Boston Board sent two distinguished ministers, Jeremy Belknap and Jedediah Morse, west to investigate Kirkland's mission. In preparation, Belknap read Wheelock's celebrated narratives, which revealed "the warm, enthusiastic manner in which the business of converting Indians had been conducted, and the changes which appeared in the conduct of the persons concerned when the ardor abated." Of course, that moral applied as well to Kirkland as to Wheelock.[19]

In their report, Belknap and Morse painted a depressing picture of Oneidas barely affected by years of missionary attention. Kirkland conceded that "the *influence* of *Christian principles* amongst those Indians who have had Missionaries bears little proportion to the expense & labor." The sweeping cultural changes demanded by missionaries tended to depress Indians who dreaded being reduced to laboring for their American neighbors. Such a fate seemed worse than death to Indian men who had long derided settlers as grubby and grabby people without the honor of warriors. Once serene in their superiority, the Oneidas now worried, John Thornton Kirkland reported, that "they shall be poor, despised, and dependent, gradually dwindling, till they become extinct."[20]

Despite years of missionary exhortation, most of the Oneidas retained their gender roles, which assigned working the earth to women. When Philip Schuyler exhorted the young Oneida men to become farmers

> They answered that it was the work of women; that *man* was not made to work in the Earth like a hedge hog, but to go to war & hunting. Thus there is a contempt for labour which arises from Pride & is with most of them invincible.

Persuaded that the Oneidas must change to survive, Schuyler considered perverse their tenacious resistance to a settler culture premised on individual competition, male labor, and private property. But that tenacity reflected the Oneida desperation to avoid submergence by the enveloping culture of their American neighbors.[21]

Most Oneidas also clung to their traditional ethos of charity and generosity, which favored a minimal security for all over the competitive pursuit of superior prosperity for a few. Schuyler complained,

> They allow any of their tribe to cultivate as much Land as they please; but it is still the common property. They do not pretend to claim the Crops raised on the Land, but if any of their Number raises a Crop, they will continue to *visit* him & expect to be *treated* with his Corn & meat as long as he has any, which is a great discouragement to those who are disposed to work, of which, however, the Number is small, not more than 4 in the Oneida Tribe. *John Skanandogh* is one of them, he keeps tavern at Oneida & is a respectable Character.

After a spring flood ruined the harvest of 1802, starving neighbors exhausted Skenandon's means, which Kirkland considered "an instance of persevering charity rarely to be met with among white people." By August 1803, Skenandon's own family was "perishing with hunger" until relieved by Kirkland.[22]

Belknap and Morse found superficial the Oneida commitment to Christianity. In 1796, overt pagans were few—only about eight adults—but most Oneidas mixed Christian and traditional spiritual beliefs. Belknap sadly reported, "The Oneidas, notwithstanding their opportunities for Improvement, are still influenced by their old mythology—are firm believers in Witchcraft & the power of invisible agency. Like the Samaritans, [they] worship the Lord & serve other Gods." John Thornton Kirkland confirmed, "Their villages are sometimes in the utmost consternation with the accounts of strange sights, apparitions, and possessions, which crafty or credulous persons circulate."[23]

The Oneida morality similarly disappointed Belknap and Morse and their informants. Although marital monogamy had become the norm, heavy and raucous drinking was more rampant than ever. Samuel Kirkland considered sober only about 40 of the approximately 320 adult Oneidas, and almost all of the temperate were women. Belknap reported that Skenandon was the only Oneida man "who never indulges himself in drinking to excess." Because Kirkland demanded strict morality for church membership, many Oneidas attended services but few became formal members eligible for the sacraments. In 1796, the Oneida church counted only 40 members, 36 of them women. Setting his sights low, Kirkland concluded, "If once in a while some poor Squaw worn out with hard labour & hard usage comes & takes refuge in a hope of future happiness 'tis as much as can be expected."[24]

Belknap and Morse sought explanations for the missionary failure to transform the Oneidas. The minister of the nearby town of Clinton, Rev. Asahel Norton, blamed white racial prejudice for discouraging Indian efforts at acculturation. An Oneida boy sent to live and study in a settler town suffered from a corrosive combination of condescension and insult:

> His new friends talk much of their love to him and of their ardent wishes for the salvation of his Soul; but are careful in the mean time to make him fully sensible of his inferiority. To treat him as an equal is impossible. It would bring a stain upon our character. Consequently, he must not be admitted to our tables; he cannot make one in our parties of pleasure. From all intercourse with our females he is debarred unless perhaps they employ him in some menial office. Every day, every hour he has the degrading memorials of his inferiority before his eyes. It is impossible that he should love us. . . . The manners and the habits of his own Country, where he was free and equal to his associates will always be dearer.

Moreover, education invited "the ridicule and brutality of the most ignorant and worthless of the white people." Upon returning home, this Indian boy would revert to his native ways and would encourage resistance to missionaries and schoolteachers.[25]

Norton's criticism of settler society was unusual. Belknap's and Morse's other informants blamed the Indians for stubbornly clinging to their traditional ways. In this view, the problem was not the excessive humiliation of Indian students but their inordinate pride. Despite the growing hardships and indignities wrought by settler envelopment, the Oneidas clung to their distinctive identity as a native people. Sergeant marveled, "As an Independent Nation they have no existence & yet their national pride is so great that they affect to hold themselves as independent as ever—tho at the same time they must know, if they reflect at all, that they depend on the whites who surround them for their subsistence."[26]

But was Kirkland's negligence to blame for the Oneidas' backwardness? Impressed by the difficulties of preaching to the Indians, Belknap and Morse sympathized with the missionary's deteriorating health. Visiting Kirkland's home, Belknap

> found him very weak, both in body and mind. His disorder is an ulcerated jaw, which causes a constant discharge into his throat and stomach, and produces nausea and frequent faintings. His pain has been extreme, and extends up to his eye on the right side. He has taken many anodynes, which have weakened his nerves.

Returning home in late August 1796, Belknap and Morse reported in Kirkland's favor to the Boston Board. Rallying around a fellow minister, the Boston clergy unanimously dismissed the Oneida complaints as "groundless."[27]

But the sponsoring ministers in Scotland reached a different conclusion: that the Oneida mission was an expensive failure. "We are deeply disappointed in Mr. Kirkland," the Scots explained as they withdrew their half of his salary. In disgust, Kirkland resigned his mission in the spring of 1797. After thirty-three years of service, he was no longer a missionary.[28]

AFFLICTION

When Kirkland resigned, he "calculated upon having the means of a comfortable living without their Stipend." Within a year, however, a succession of family and financial setbacks humbled Kirkland. During the preceding decade he had helped an expanding commercial society to consume Indian lands for profit, but now that society turned upon him with a vengeance, and two of his own children helped to drive his downfall.[29]

As an old-school patriarch, Kirkland rebuked his two eldest sons, the twins George and John, then attending college at Dartmouth and Harvard, as ungrateful spendthrifts. Writing to George in 1789, the patriarch lamented "their abuse of my parental kindness & almost unbounded love to them. But I do not give them up for lost. . . . They are yet capable of affording me much pleasure & contributing largely to my happiness." He similarly assured John that it should be a delightful *task* (if it may be called a *task*) to an ingenuous Child to render that tribute of gratitude which he owes to an aged parent. . . . What can be more pleasing to an ingenuous temper than to soothe the declining years of those, by whom their infant days were sustained, their feeble childhood supported, and their giddy youth moderated and directed.

In promoting their guilt, Kirkland again showed the influence of his own surrogate father, Eleazar Wheelock, who had so treated his young protégé.[30]

The studious twin, John, pursued the more cautious path, emulating his father by preparing for the ministry, achieving ordination in Boston in early 1794. George was more secular, energetic, flamboyant, and gregarious. After graduating from Dartmouth in 1792, George returned to Herkimer County, where he dabbled in the law and speculated in land. Delighting in parades, George procured an officer's commission in the militia and organized a light horse company. Eager for public applause, he sought election to the state legislature. Samuel felt a special and surprising pleasure in George's worldly talents and vaunting ambitions. When John faulted his twin as fiscally reckless, Samuel retorted, "George has been very kind & attentive to the Interest & happiness of the family. Should he be prosperous, agreeable to his expectation, I don't know but he will turn out a second *Joseph*."[31]

Alas, George's excessive expectations were the problem. A compulsive gambler, he borrowed money for manic investments in land speculation and for expensive living as a public gentleman—a widespread affliction in the early republic, as Robert Morris attested. Inevitably, George's lands retailed too slowly to pay his impatient creditors. In early 1796, they began to complain that George was increasingly and suspiciously absent, pursuing new speculations elsewhere instead of paying what he already owed. Once again, Samuel made excuses for his favorite son, insisting that all would be set right upon his return.[32]

By the fall of 1796, however, George's mounting debts threatened his father, who had indulgently cosigned his notes to creditors. Seeking assets for foreclosure, the county sheriff attached the land and building materials for Hamilton Oneida Academy. An alarmed John exhorted his absent brother, "Where are you, that you don't stir in the business[?] & [do] not let this mighty scheme end in a farce that will mortify & disgrace the family."[33]

Hiding out in Connecticut from his New York creditors, George responded to the crisis with the desperate confidence of a gambler doubling his bets. Although unable to return home, he was "about to close certain negociations to the amount of $250,000." But six months later, fear of a New York debtor's cell still kept George at a distance: "My usefulness to myself & friends & the world is not to be lost. I was never made to waste my days in a prison." Bombastic and delusional, George blamed his creditors for preying upon his supposed sense of honor: "My enemies must rejoice while the slanderous aspersions of an envious world I despise! I spurn at their malignity, with *triumphant exultation*." In the spring of 1797, he bought two townships on the Maine frontier for another $40,000 that he did not have, leading the seller to demand payment from father Samuel.[34]

At last, in the fall of 1797, George returned to his father's home, where he lived in seclusion, fearing to venture out lest he be arrested for debt. Virtually bankrupt, he confessed, "If I am once sent to prison, I shall never expect to be liberated." In early 1799, George sought relief by procuring an officer's commission in the United States Army, then expanding in anticipation of a war with France. Military service took him away to Pennsylvania and New Jersey, but creditors pursued, provoking mental and physical distress. In March 1800, his commanding officer expected Kirkland to die "in a few months" and considered it "humane to let him die as easy as possible." But George lived to seek a further escape by enlisting as a soldier of fortune in General Francisco Miranda's foolhardy bid to overthrow Spanish rule in Venezuela. Bloodied in defeat, Kirkland died of his wounds and a tropical fever.[35]

George's flight exposed his father to his impatient creditors, who included his former patrons in land speculation, Oliver Phelps and Peter Smith. No sentimentalists, they obliged Samuel Kirkland to sell almost all of his real estate at a fraction of its estimated value, retaining only his home farm. Still, Samuel confessed, a fear of arrest "keeps me looking out 50 times in a day."[36]

Shamed by the financial collapse, he lamented, "The sorest trial, I have ever known is the embarrassments of my Son's affairs. . . . I *love* my dear family & I still Love my *prodigal, imprudent, & unfortunate Son George*." A long life of sacrifice and danger now seemed futile by any material calculus:

> To be arrested & harrassed in law, and especially for demands for which I have never ate, nor drank, or even smoaked a pipe of tobacco, in the going down of my son, would be more grievous than all the hardships, fatigues, & difficulties I have undergone for near 40 years in the wilderness.

He had endured it all to seek a genteel life for himself and his children, but that dream turned to ashes in the late 1790s. In 1800, a local trader balked when Kirkland asked to borrow some tea and sugar: "I find it's his genteel way of Begging without the least Idea of returning."[37]

One of George's aggrieved creditors was Thomas Herring, a young merchant who served as Peter Smith's business correspondent in New York City.

In 1798, a dunning trip to the Kirkland household produced an odd twist. Although George failed to pay, Herring collected something else: an engagement to the debtor's sister, Sarah (Sally) Kirkland, then twenty years old. They married in New York City on November 22, 1799—but the couple did not live happily every after.[38]

Samuel saw Sarah as the reflection of her late mother, the blessed Jerusha: "a tender, affectionate daughter, who resembles in every feature & complexion of the mind the once fair original with whom I was blessed." Her brother John had regretted Sarah's adolescent "love of solitude & seclusion" and her lack of "talents for society." But as a newlywed, she showed far too many social talents and far too little resemblance to her saintly mother. Just three days after their marriage, Thomas Herring sailed for England on business. When he returned the following spring, he charged Sarah with adultery with multiple partners. Her notorious affairs had unleashed gossip as far as Boston, where William Eustis pressed Aaron Burr (an expert in adultery) for the juicy details: "Please name to me the personages connected with her. . . . On parting from Mr. H. to whom did she first attach herself—who next & so on—what was the affair of the camp[?]"[39]

The gossip tormented her clergyman father, who noted "the indescribable affliction & distress I have been called to endure in regard to my family." But Samuel stood by his daughter in negotiations for a divorce, which Herring considered "in perfect consonance with their craft." No longer enamored, Herring considered the Kirklands to be pious hypocrites. Despite the scandal, in 1808 she made a reputable second marriage to a Boston merchant, Francis Amory, while Herring never remarried.[40]

REVIVAL

In the spring of 1798, Kirkland suddenly and surprisingly renewed his missionary visits to Kanonwalohale, citing better health and a revived sense of Christian purpose. His health benefited from visiting the mineral baths at Ballstown Springs. "Oh how delightful & pleasant it is to enjoy ease & tranquility after such pain and so many tossings as I have endured," he effused. During 1800, Kirkland resumed living at Kanonwalohale for about half of every year, something he had not done since the war. From Good Peter's widow, Kirkland rented a small and smoky cabin that combined kitchen, sleeping quarters, and study in a single room. Lacking a bed, he slept in the Indian mode on a blanket atop a wooden bunk, which he considered "a *kind of Martyrdom.*"[41]

In the fall of 1804, his health suffered a relapse, as he experienced great pain, and the loss of hearing, in his left ear. Eight months later, a physician belatedly discovered and extracted the cause: "a large black bug with glazed wings, nearly half an inch long." Kirkland recalled, "This animal I suppose crept into my ear at a time when I slept on the floor at Oneida . . . when I observed great numbers of them in the ceiling & on the walls & from which time I had suffered violent and almost unceasing pain." Extraction eased the pain and revived his spirits.[42]

In returning to the Oneidas, Kirkland initially acted at his own expense and initiative, without authorization or payment from any missionary society. But by returning, Kirkland strengthened his bid to recover his salary, which he desperately needed to cope with his debts. Impressed by his selfless activity, in 1800 the Harvard trustees restored their half of his salary (£50, or $125). Although the Society in Scotland balked at renewing the other half, Kirkland got some new support from the Northern Missionary Society, based in Albany.[43]

Although the renewed mission tested his aging body, it soothed his troubled mind and agitated soul. Battered by family and financial disasters, Kirkland no longer could find a reassuring measure of his worth in the prosperity of his estate. As a Calvinist, Kirkland had to attribute his setbacks to God's purposeful wrath: "trials the most singular, sorrows the most pungent & heartfelt, in the course of a holy & righteous providence, have been alotted [to] me." Apparently, he had angered God by straying from his proper calling as a missionary. Only by returning to his duty could Kirkland merit divine favor and renew his purpose and worth. After a long absence, religious sentiments returned to his letters: "May I trust in the living God, be thankful, & give him praise continually." In sum, his revived mission appeased his psychological and spiritual hunger at least as much as it served his financial need.[44]

By renewing the devotion of his evangelical youth, Kirkland sought to rescue something from three decades already invested as the Oneida missionary. But he could not retrieve a vanishing past, for he noted with pain the dying generation of chiefs who had been his closest collaborators. No longer could he work with Deacon Thomas, Jacob Reed, Captain John, or Good Peter. "Alas!" Kirkland sighed, "what would I give for the influence and eloquence of good Peter. He is no more!" Some of that eloquence lived on in Good Peter's son, Captain Peter, but it argued against Christianity. And the Oneida church had dwindled to just twenty-one members (at least seventeen of them women), half of its level when Kirkland had left the mission in 1796.[45]

Of Kirkland's staunchest supporters, only Skenandon remained, and he was about ninety years old. Once a tall and robust warrior, Skenandon drank heavily until 1755, when he awoke one morning in an Albany street having lost his clothes in a drunken barter for more rum. Deeply embarrassed, he kept his vow never again to drink, a resolution so often made but so rarely kept by Iroquois chiefs. Embracing Christianity and the settler mode of agriculture, Skenandon became the model Oneida patriarch for Kirkland's mission. Rev. John Sergeant, Jr., praised Skenandon as "very industrious, raises all kind of grain, has a good number of horses, cows, hogs, &c., owns a sleigh and waggon." Kirkland extolled the chief as "a man of good sense, ready invention & quick wit, not an eloquent speaker, but [a] good Counsellor."[46]

But Skenandon remained an Oneida nationalist, making some cultural changes in hopes of preserving an Indian domain. He preached temperance in a desperate attempt to unite his people against losing more land: "Drink no strong water. It makes you mice for white men, who are cats. Many a meal have they eaten of you." It is also revealing that, despite his extensive dealings with outsiders, Skenandon resisted learning more than a few English words and clung to his native attire and adornment. For all of his adaptations to the settler world, Skenandon never wished to become a white cat.[47]

PAGANS

During his renewed mission, Kirkland faced greater competition from Quakers who had established a school, a blacksmith's shop, and a model farm on the reservation during his absence. The Quakers became popular by treating traditional Oneida beliefs with respect and by abstaining from the lust for Indian land that had soured Kirkland's former mission. An elderly chief known as Blacksmith (Aughweehstanis) explained that previous missionaries were "friendly to us, till they get our trees and lands, and then they are no more our friends; but the Quakers are good people, and do not serve us so; I love the Quakers." In January 1800, the Quakers dissolved their Oneida compound and shifted their operation westward to Cornplanter's village on the Allegheny, but they left behind a popular legacy that Kirkland had to deal with.[48]

Although he disliked Quaker theology, Kirkland respected its influence in favor of agriculture and temperance. And rather than offend his Oneida hosts, Kirkland patiently cooperated when itinerant Quaker preachers returned to renew their ties. Kirkland even assisted the controversial female preachers authorized by the Quakers. In July 1805, Dorothy Ripley, an English Quaker, reported that Kirkland "acted as a kind brother to me, interpreting for me." His respect contrasted with the behavior of a fellow Calvinist minister, Jacob Cram, who tried to block her from preaching to the Oneidas. But the matrons of the Oneida church defied Cram "with great indignation," for they considered Ripley to be "their sympathizing sister." She expected that "the next woman whom the Lord sendeth, he will not dare to insult." Taking her side, Kirkland praised Ripley for addressing the Indians "in a judicious and affectionate manner" that "much pleased & animated" them.[49]

Kirkland also faced a "pagan revival" as the Oneida champions of traditional spirituality grew in numbers and confidence. At the core of the so-called "pagan party" were four refugee families from Oriske. Kirkland considered them "a mongrel breed, having most of them some mixture of French-Dutch or African blood." As mixed-bloods, they apparently found a validating source of authenticity by vociferously championing Oneida traditions. From that seed group, the traditionalists had expanded steadily by allying with the Quaker sojourners. As believers in the "inner light" within every soul, the Quakers treated native mysticism sympathetically as compatible with Christianity—in stark contrast to the contempt expressed by their Calvinist rivals.[50]

The Oneida traditionalists also felt inspired by news that the Grand River Six Nations had revived traditional ceremonies, particularly the white dog sacrificial feast. In the spring of 1799, the Kanonwalohale pagans, led by Blacksmith and his nephew Captain Peter, ceremonially sacrificed a white dog for the first time in a generation. They concluded with a great feast and lacrosse game, generating a festivity that attracted more adherents. The traditionalists also benefited from Blacksmith's possession of the sacred and wandering stone that gave the Oneidas their identity. From only about four families in 1796, the pagans surged to about a third of the 750 Oneidas by 1805.[51]

Kirkland became far more tolerant of traditional beliefs and ceremonies during his renewed mission. In 1800, he described the pagan revival with more ethnographic curiosity than evangelical intolerance, noting that "their feasts & sacrifices bore ... resemblance to the Christian sacrament." Kirkland applauded the pagans for reducing drinking and violence at Kanonwalohale. In return, Blacksmith and his supporters often attended Kirkland's services and held "serious & interesting conversation" with the missionary. He marveled, "Most of the Pagans now treat me with as much respect & Indian civility as the Christian Indians." This comity reflected the considerable Christian influence on the beliefs of the so-called pagans, as well as Kirkland's new respect for alternative paths to morality.[52]

The Oneida traditionalists also felt the influence of a Seneca prophet, Handsome Lake, who was Cornplanter's half brother. In 1799, Handsome

Lake dramatically repented his alcoholism and experienced visions of divine messengers. He then exhorted the Iroquois to avert a fiery apocalypse by adopting spiritual and material reforms that combined elements of Christianity and settler culture with renewed ceremonies drawn from Iroquois tradition. Although Handsome Lake claimed to revitalize an ancient system of beliefs, he rejected the Iroquois sky spirit, Tharonhiawagon, in favor of a Creator who demanded most of the social program long advocated by Christian missionaries: temperance, marital monogamy, and settler-style agriculture. Handsome Lake endorsed Christianity as a parallel gospel meant for white people but worthy of Indian respect. During visits to the Onondagas in 1803 and 1804, Handsome Lake received delegations of Oneida traditionalists, who embraced his message.[53]

Handsome Lake's way also had a dark side: a mania for exposing and killing supposed witches. He blamed witchcraft for the many diseases and disappointments afflicting the Iroquois as they lost their lands and their prestige. Heeding his example, the Oneida traditionalists began to hunt witches in their midst. In August 1804, the village council convicted two women, who confessed and revealed poisonous powders and magic fetishes. Acting on that council's order, a chief promptly killed both women with tomahawk blows to their skulls.[54]

In addition to Handsome Lake's message, the witch executions also revealed the influence of the state's new power to try and execute Indians. At Whitestown on March 26, 1802, many Oneidas attended the state's execution of George Peters, a Brothertown Indian, for murdering his wife. As the presiding clergyman at the gallows ceremony, Kirkland "exhorted the Indians & spoke to the Oneidas in their own language. . . . After which I made the prayer & he was then swung off." The scene profoundly moved and troubled the Indians, for they thronged to Kirkland's subsequent sermons on the execution. On April 17, Kirkland reported,

> A general collection of the Indians notwithstanding the rain. They came from several Villages—some from Kaghnightola nearly seven miles—all in expectation of hearing my discourse upon the nature of murder & its punishment—the dying speech of the unfortunate George Peters.

After the crowd listened intently through a three-hour service, Kirkland concluded: "the most solemn assembly of Indians I have addressed for many years." The biblical text for his sermon (Numbers 35:33) is suggestive: "for blood it defiles the land & the land cannot be cleansed of the blood that is shed therein, but by the blood of him that shed it." The same reasoning informed the Iroquois drive to purge their village of deadly witches by public trial and execution, which suggests that Peters's execution served as a precedent.[55]

By executing the two witches in 1804, the Oneidas both emulated and resisted the power of the New Yorkers all around them. They adapted to their changing circumstances in selective ways that tried to preserve their distinctive identity as Oneidas. By conducting a public investigation and execution, the Oneidas sought their own, parallel form of coercive power, but they limited its exercise to witchcraft. That preoccupation distinguished them from their settler neighbors, who no longer considered witchcraft deadly enough to handle judicially. It is also revealing that the Oneidas con-

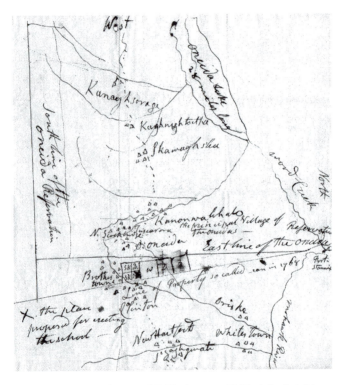

The Oneida Country, by Samuel Kirkland, ca. 1792. Kirkland sketched this map to promote his proposed academy, which he locates on his property ("SK") along the Line of Property from 1768. This map foreshortens the distance of his property from the native villages of Old Oneida, New Stockbridge (Tuscarora), and Kanonwalohale to the west. Farther west lie the hamlets of Skawaghslea, Kaghneghtotha, and Kanaghsoraga, all on the path to the Genesee country. (Courtesy of the Dartmouth College Library; 792900.1.)

tinued to reject any change in handling murder cases—the preoccupation of the state. The Oneidas would neither try murderers nor surrender suspects to state jurisdiction. Instead, they persisted in entrusting revenge to the kin of the victim.[56]

DISRUPTION

Kirkland had returned to a shrinking reservation. The cessions of 1798 and 1802 disrupted the reservation's cohesion by taking land along the Genesee Road that bisected the Oneida domain on an east-west axis. Visiting the reservation in June 1798, the jurist James Kent predicted: "The Oneidas from a widespread Dominion are narrowing their Lands constantly. The Axe will soon be heard all around them, & like the Rhine they will dwindle in the Sands before they are lost in the Ocean."[57]

Prior to 1798 outsiders had experienced the reservation as a plunge deep into a wilderness and a fall backward in time. Kent recalled,

> The Forests were majestic, the Timber tall, thick & enormously large, consisting of Hemlock, Ash, Bass, Maple, &c. . . . The Forests stood on each Side [of the path] like an high, impervious wall. Such a venerable Wilderness where the Trees carry back our Thoughts to the last century & the dreary dominion of Indians fill the mind with Seriousness & Reverence.

In 1790, an Italian visitor shuddered in passing through "dark and dense forests, in which we constantly meet bears and rattlesnakes." Only a few visitors examined the forest more closely to detect the gradations of human impact over time. In 1793, three French travelers observed, "We can trace the remains of orchards, and even of ancient clearings, in places now lying waste." They aptly concluded that the Indian population had once been much larger.[58]

Visitors found the thick forest immediately depressing but prospectively inspiring. In 1796, Jeremy Belknap remarked, "Were the country in a state of cultivation, nothing could be more charming than such a prospect; but it is melancholy to see so fine a tract of land in such a savage state." Travellers imagined a brighter future when laboring settlers would improve the land's immense potential for commercial agriculture. The French visitors extolled the Oneida lands as "the best in this part of America."[59]

While marveling at the fertility of the red clay soil, the visitors also cursed as it clogged their boots, wagon wheels, and horses' legs in wet seasons. In November 1793, the French complained:

The Indians have no occasion for roads, and never do any thing for them, the state has not yet undertaken any, and this route is therefore almost impassable. It could scarcely be traced through the woods by some trees marked here and there; the streams had no bridges, the swamps no causeways, and the oft used stepping places were nearly impassable. Yet this is the great route to the Genesee, and to all the western country.

That same week, a frustrated Alexander Coventry got tangled in the forest and bogged in the mud seeking his way westward. In 1798, James Kent described the route through the Oneida reservation as "one vast quagmire" and "the worst road I ever rode in my Life. It is new & from the excessive wet Season abominably miry. It is a bed of clay almost impassable for a Horse, & also full of roots & Stumps & Causeways."[60]

After the dark forest and dank path, travelers felt arrival at Kanonwalohale as a burst into the open sunshine and as the discovery of an oasis of humanity. Kent effused, "The Entrance to the *Castle* from the woods was pleasant—a champaign Country burst upon us & the Sun breaking out from the Clouds added Spirit & Interest to the occasion." Set beside a meandering stream, the village occupied an elevated, cleared plateau of about 150 acres with an impressive view southward toward distant hills. "The Plains look cleared & old & are without fence & have Cattle & Horses grazing in common," Kent noted. In addition to the ruined palisade of the small fort built during the war, Kanonwalohale had twenty-five houses clustered at the center, with another forty strung along the path, approaching or receding "over a compass of near three-quarters of a mile long, and half as wide, and detached from each other in a loose, irregular manner." So said a Quaker visitor of 1795. Such visitors lamented the absence of the systematic order that they preferred in their own world.[61]

Most Oneida homes were single-room and single-story cabins built of logs, with dried mud to plaster the chinks, roofed with sheets of hemlock bark, and featuring a small porch and a glazed window or two. A few dwellings were traditional wigwams made of bark stretched over an oblong framework of poles. Within both cabins and wigwams, visitors found scant and crude possessions: benches and cribs for sleeping; wooden bowls, spoons, and baskets; and some iron kettles and pottery dishes procured from traders. After the harvest, drying corn hung from the poles or rafters. A hearth (or two) lay at the center of the earthen floor beneath a hole (or two) in the bark roof to vent the smoke. The village's most striking and exceptional house belonged to Skenandon, who kept an inn for travelers. Dorothy Ripley described it as "a good, framed building of wood, painted red, two stories high and two rooms on a floor." His red house and prosperous farm stood out in a village of log cabins embraced by a few apple trees and small gardens for corn, beans, peas, potatoes, and squashes.[62]

By proceeding a dozen miles west of Kanonwalohale on the Genesee path, travelers came to the village of Kanaghsoraga at the western margin of the reservation. A small village of about twenty Oneida families and some Dutch and German tenants, Kanaghsoraga displayed a greater mixing of settler and native cultures. Drawing a contrast with Kanonwalohale, the traveler John Maude reported that the Kanaghsoraga villagers "dress as the Whites, and many speak a little English." The village featured a prosperous farm and inn kept by John Denny, of mixed French and Oneida descent. After suffering other frontier inns, travelers extolled Denny's as remarkably clean, comfortable, and commodious.[63]

After the land cession of 1798, settlers proliferated along the Genesee route, transforming the Oneida country. In 1790, only one settler town abutted the reservation on the east—the aptly named Whitestown—with a population of 1,891. By 1810 the core of the Oneida country had become two New York counties, named Madison and Oneida, with thirty-two towns and a population of 55,778, making a local ratio of about sixty settlers per Indian.[64]

More settlers meant more labor to upgrade the path into a road, which enhanced land values and facilitated travel, further accelerating the settler flow. After an initial boost with state funds and taxed labor, in 1800 the road became an incorporated turnpike capitalized by private investors. To recoup their investment, the owners speculated in adjoining lands and collected tolls at periodic gates. Boosters celebrated the turnpike as emblematic of their cultural superiority over the Indians. In 1807, Benjamin DeWitt insisted that "the contrast between our present turnpike roads and the dismal footpaths of the aborigines, is not greater than between our state of civilization and refinement, and their condition of rudeness and barbarity."[65]

The Genesee turnpike became New York's main conduit for settlers heading west and for their farm produce coming east to market. The road eclipsed Philip Schuyler's canal, which suffered from unstable water levels in the Mohawk River and Wood Creek. While benefiting the road, settlement weakened the waterway, for deforestation diminished the land's retention of water, hastening spring's runoff, which reduced water levels in summer below the minimum needed for boat traffic. The stagnation of the canal undercut the growth of Rome, the commercial village built on the site of Fort Stanwix. Instead, regional superiority passed to its rival village, Utica, which benefited as the eastern terminus of the Genesee turnpike. In 1811, Utica boasted 2,000 inhabitants, 400 houses, 15 stores, 6 taverns, 4 churches, 2 breweries, and an academy. Village lots sold for $200 to $1,000.[66]

American observers delighted in the transformation of the Oneida landscape along the Genesee road. In September of 1808, James Kent returned to exult:

> [T]he alteration on the road within the last ten Years is astonishing. The face of the Country is so altered that it can no longer be recognized. A well made *Turnpike road* goes thro' the whole Country. The Oneida reservation is contracted to 1 Mile E[ast] & say 3 or 4 W[est] of the Castle & the country is well settled & cleared along the road.

Praising the thriving new fields of wheat and hay, Kent insisted that the area "resembled a terrestrial Paradise. I suppose the Country around here for 30 miles surpasses any in this State for good land & prosperous Settlement."[67]

At the former western end of the reservation, the Indian village of Kanaghsoraga had vanished, replaced by Canaseraga, a commercial center with twenty frame houses painted white. In a double sense, the landscape had whitened. Village land sold for $100 to $125 per acre, while farms back from the road fetched $16 per acre: a considerable advance from the 50 cents per acre paid by the state to the Oneidas.[68]

In 1806, Alexander Coventry returned to marvel at the broad turnpike through a settled landscape, where he had gotten miserably lost in a deep forest fifteen years earlier. In 1791, he had complained that Indian markings on the trees had rendered it "difficult, or perplexing to find the right" path. Fifteen years later, he could note his progress by stone markers placed by the turnpike company at mile intervals: symbols of a systematized land. Where New Yorkers celebrated a blossoming, the Oneidas experienced deforestation and settlement as constriction by a cold, intruding culture. Settlers and travelers felt more comfortable as the landscape became more alien to the Oneidas. Coventry's reassuring milestones were tombstones for the traditional topography long nurtured by the Indians.[69]

Where settlers felt unleashed by the turnpike, the Indians felt trapped by the new toll gates and toll bridges. In February 1802, the Oneida and Onondaga chiefs explained, "We are pouer and not always furnishead with money as white peopeal ar[e], nor never was usead to pay for goin on the Roads or Crossing Rivers or Lackes." What good were their treaties granting free passage to hunt and fish on their ceded lands if they had to pay tolls coming and going? Petitioning Congress, the chiefs insisted,

> Brothers we Sepos that you must know that we ar[e] free Born and not Exposied to your Laws as there is now a making a Turonpick Roade and a bri[d]ge already maid across the Caiugey Lack[e] and all Natives in this

Contiannant has to pay for Crossing that Bri[d]ge and as soon as the turnpick is finnishead we sepose that will be the saim. Brothers that makes all Nations think verrey harde.

Citing their Indian sovereignty and their American alliance, the chiefs sought a federal law exempting Indians from paying tolls at any gates or bridges throughout the nation. But they sought in vain.[70]

Cutting through Kanonwalohale, the turnpike turned Skenandon into a tourist attraction, as growing numbers of genteel travelers passed through the village bound west to see Niagara Falls. Rarely spending more than a single day on the reservation, they formed superficial impressions of the Oneidas from two scenes: drunken young men gathered around a roadside tavern and wizened and blind Skenandon within his red house. The visitors described him as an ancient and ineffectual shell of a once formidable warrior ignored by his people and dependent on visitors' charity. A common trope was to mock Skenandon as an Indian "king" with rustic trappings. Julian Niemcewicz, a Polish gentleman, wrote,

> In front of the door we found two royal princesses who were washing down two sorry little horses. There were some pigs and dogs; these made up the palace guard. On entering the room, we found wooden beds all around, without any mattresses, only the same woolen blankets, which serve as clothing. His Majesty the King had been sitting on one of these beds and was just getting up. He was an old man of 86, tattooed on his chest and hands, and with enormous ears.

These travelers depicted Skenandon as the last of the Oneidas, as a symbol for a decaying people destined for extinction. That convenient convention exonerated the victors by assigning the dispossession of the Oneidas to the interplay of Indian folly with divine providence.[71]

CONTEMPT

The growing number and power of the settlers bred contempt for the Oneida minority. Formerly feared and treated with some restraint, the Oneidas now reaped insults to compound their injuries. Expecting the persistence of traditional generosity, they called at settler farms for food and drink only to reap abuse instead. In 1800, Kirkland reported that a chief, "a very peaceable man, had been beaten with a pair of fire tongs by a white man, & that his head was so broken they despaired of his life." In 1804, Captain Peter protested,

Whiteskins have whipped & beaten some of us poor despised Indians
because of our frailties & follies & chased us from their houses with such
whips as they used upon refractory horses. Alas! How times are changed.
In the days of the glory of our forefathers it was not so.

Other settlers gave the Oneidas too much alcohol, the better to cheat them
in bargains for their livestock, timber, pastures, and homes. Captain Peter
concluded: "I don't think it is right for the White people to give so much rum
to the Indians when they know the weakness of Indians. . . . And if we Indians must bear this reproach of *loving Rum*, the White Man certainly *loves
monney*." The reservation margins attracted particularly predatory men. Rev.
Asahel Norton wrote of the Oneidas: "With a very few exceptions they have
dealt with men of vicious hearts, artful, lavish of promises & perfidious."[72]

No longer dreading Indian vengeance, the neighboring settlers stole
Oneida lands and timber. Those squatters undercut the Oneida bargaining
position, for the state did nothing to oust the intruders. On the contrary, the
legislature rewarded them with a preemption right to buy their lots, at the
appraised value, once the state extinguished the aboriginal title. Given a
powerful state more solicitous of squatters' votes than of Indians' rights, the
Oneidas had to accept pennies on the dollar from New York for their land.
Otherwise, they would get nothing for lands overrun by squatters.[73]

The improved Genesee Road and growing settlements promoted two
institutions especially detrimental to Indians: taverns and sawmills. Interacting, both further weakened the Oneida hold on their embattled self-esteem
and their dwindling land base. Considered a necessity for emigrating settlers
and traveling gentlemen, the roadside taverns brought increased misery to
the Indians. Alcohol became too cheap, too abundant, and all too handy for a
people especially vulnerable to its addiction. In 1802, Ann Mifflin, a Quaker
visitor, explained: "Their sale of lands on the state road for the accommodation of Taverns gives them ready access to spiritous liquors which keeps
them poor & miserable, and brings them into this besotted state. This sale
was opposed by some of more regular lives." Heavy drinking especially
afflicted the young men, who felt betwixt and between. Although raised by a
culture that celebrated war and hunting, they reached manhood within a
radically transformed environment that left them with precious little to
do—except drink. In their cups at a tavern or a store, young men could
immediately, albeit briefly, bolster their masculine pride. Sobering up only
compounded their misery, which renewed their longing for escape into a bottle of rum.[74]

But those bottles had to be paid for. Young men procured money or alcohol by marking releases proffered by settler lumbermen. In the despairing

words of Skenandon, the young warriors "drank the trees!" The upgraded Genesee turnpike improved access to eastern markets, rendering the immense trees of the reservation marketable and coveted. By denuding the reservation of large trees, the lumbering exposed the soil to erosion and littered the ground with branches and tops, lowering the agricultural value of the land, to the detriment of the entire nation. Skenandon denounced the logging as "not only a theft against the nation at the present time, but it was a robbery against their Children & grand Children, who, when they should come upon the stage, would not be able to build themselves houses to shelter them from the cold & storms." What little cash the Oneidas did acquire flowed into taverns, which poured despair and violence back into their lives.[75]

The county's district attorney, Nathan Williams, neglected his duty to prosecute timber trespassers. In 1810, the Oneidas complained

> that the white people were daily Trespassing on their Land by cutting and destroying the Timber, that they had done every thing in their power to prevent it, that they complained to Mr. Williams, but no mean has been taken to prevent it—that those trespassers frequently assert that some one Indian has given them liberty to cut the timber which sometimes may be so as liquor has great influence on them.

Such unchecked lumbering pressured the Oneidas to sell more land to the state before they lost more trees and more land value.[76]

The settler encroachment undermined the Oneidas' traditional economy, which mixed horticulture with hunting, fishing, and gathering of wild roots, nuts, plants, and berries. The fish dwindled as the newcomers dammed the streams for mills and excessively harvested salmon and whitefish for commercial sale. Settlers also depleted the game by competing with the Indians as hunters, and they reduced habitat by clearing the forest for farms. The diminished forest also constrained gathering. And the Indians' vegetable gardens suffered from the settlers' roaming livestock and from vermin that accompanied the settler invasion. In 1805, Blacksmith "thought the white people devils" because the Indians "never were infested with rats, or crows, till they settled round them."[77]

Losing their broad, forested domain, the confined Oneidas became too dependent on their limited gardens beside the creek and more vulnerable to nature's oscillations. In 1802, a spring flood wiped out their recently planted crops, producing a short harvest that fall and widespread hunger during the next year. The following year, a summer drought diminished the hay yield, which meant starving and dying cattle during the next winter. Another drought in 1805 obliged the Oneidas to disperse in search of roots and whortleberries. A year later, Kirkland reported, "Many of them for about two months past have been reduced next door to a state of starvation."[78]

Hungry Indians were in no position to resist pressures from the state to make new land cessions that promised an immediate infusion of cash. Although only a fraction of the land's value, the infusions helped the chiefs to provide charity to the poorest of their people. In sum, the Oneidas experienced a vicious cycle as a shrinking reservation led to deprivation, which induced further sales of land by desperate chiefs.

The diminished respect for the Oneidas transformed the treaty councils conducted with them by the state. After 1800, New York dispensed with the traditional, large-scale, long-lasting, and expensive councils of the Covenant Chain. Subsequent councils stuck to the business agenda and moved to the rapid rhythm set by a state determined to contain costs. Most councils involved only about a dozen chiefs brought to Albany for a few days that kept to a tight schedule and a close focus on procuring land. The new mode dismayed most of the Oneidas, who no longer participated in councils as witnesses. Distance screened the quick and small-scale councils in Albany from the collective scrutiny of the people, which invited abuse by, and bribery of, the few chiefs involved. In vain, Oneidas complained of losing their homesteads by land cessions that they had neither known about nor consented to. And the state no longer bothered to document the give-and-take at the councils, impoverishing the record left for historians. Formerly rich in the exchange of views, the state's council records became terse and pro forma as the councils became shorter and smaller affairs.[79]

After 1802, New York ceased adhering to federal law by neglecting to request a federal treaty commissioner or to submit subsequent treaties to the president and the Senate for ratification. In 1805, the governor rejected an Oneida appeal for a federal treaty commissioner to help the feuding "Pagan" and "Christian" factions to divide the reservation between them. Instead, the New Yorkers alone conducted the partition council that awarded the lands west of Oneida Creek to the Christian Party, while the Pagan Party received those to the east, with the exception of the Fish Creek tract, which went to the Christians. The treaty even divided the village of Kanonwalohale, with the Pagans clustered at the east end and the Christians on the west.[80]

Although this 1805 treaty secured no land for the state, it facilitated subsequent acquisitions, for the division increased the Oneidas' vulnerability to pressure from the overlapping ranks of tavern-keepers, lumbermen, squatters, land speculators, and state officials. By extending credit beyond the Oneida capacity to repay, and by applying liquor beyond their ability to resist, local entrepreneurs created debts. Seeking payment in land, they conducted indebted chiefs to Albany to make further land cessions to New York, with stipulated set-asides for the creditors. During the years 1807 to 1809, the state procured at least 33,000 acres in three transactions, two with the Christian Party and another with the Pagans. The state paid 50 to 75 cents per acre—fractions of the land's growing value.[81]

In early 1810, Skenandon and the other Christian Party chiefs protested to the governor against cessions conducted in distant obscurity by a few chiefs beholden to their creditor conductors:

> [A] number of White men, by giving a few of our Warriors Drink, money, or Cloth[e]s, have greatly imposed upon us, by leading our men to Albany against our will and there bribing them, to sell our lands, that they themselves may be made rich. Would, Sir, you like that we should buy the town of Albany from a few of any White men we could persuade to sell it[?] And we, then, come and take it, whether you be willing or not. You would not like this, and we do not like it.

The chiefs sadly conceded that they had initially mistaken their creditors for friends, "But at last we have found out that they got our property not for us but for themselves, and that we got nothing, but a little drink and good words from them. By their gathering our property, they have grown rich, and we have grown poor."[82]

New York built wealth and power by dispossessing and confining the Iroquois. By 1800, the state had established three counties—Chenango, Herkimer, and Oneida—on lands wrested from the Oneidas. In that year in those three counties, the state appraised the real estate as worth $8,904,202—more than 407 times the $21,852 paid to the Oneidas. Anticipating that appreciation from settler labor, the Oneidas had fought long and hard (but ultimately in vain) to preserve their title as landlords, who could collect growing rents from their prospering settler-tenants.[83]

Instead, the state had procured Oneida lands at a fraction of their market value by insisting upon a preemption right as a monopoly buyer. Obliged to sell for paltry annuities, the Indians lost the means to develop farms and to build schools and churches, to the dismay of their missionaries. In 1818, John Sergeant, Jr., complained of New York's leaders: "They buy out the Indian title for one price, which they fix without consulting the Indians; and sell it at another and advanced price, thus making a gain, often a large one, out of the Indians." Jedediah Morse similarly concluded that the Six Nations

> are so far under the control, of the Legislature of New-York, in respect to their lands, as that they are not permitted to sell them to private individuals, or companies, but to the State only, who claim the right of preemp-

tion and of disposing of this right, to whom they please. The Indians are thus deprived of the privilege, common to free men, of going into the market with their lands, and of course, of obtaining their fair and full value.

Had the Iroquois received the "fair and full value" for leased or sold lands, they would have fared far better in their difficult economic and social transition, while still providing farms for the growing settler population.[84]

REPENTANCE

Attending the 1799 payment of the state annuity to the Oneidas, Kirkland noted the traders who "flocked in at this market day for their gains in great numbers." Because the traders primarily offered alcohol, Kirkland reported a frightening night: "It was a lamentable & shocking sight to see a number of intoxicated Indians, half-naked, yelping & hallooing, challenging & fighting with each other, like so many wild bulls or rather like infernal spirits in human shape: it seemed as tho Satan was let loose among them." He considered it lucky that only one man got stabbed.[85]

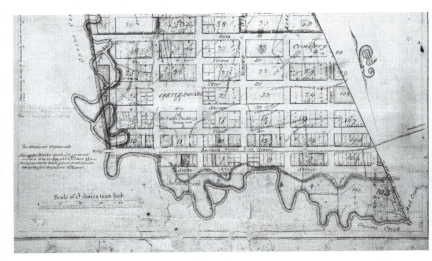

Village of Oneida Castle, survey plan by John Randel, 1813. A surveyor employed by New York State prepared this map that projects a rectilinear grid of streets and lots over the rounded forms of nature and the ghostly vestiges of the suppressed Indian landscape, including the property of Skenandon, the old fort from Lafayette's day, and the meeting-house of Samuel Kirkland. (Courtesy of New York State Archives; A-0273, #131B.)

Kirkland came to see cynicism in the state's policy of paying no more than would permit the Indians to undertake an annual drinking binge: "The State have paid them all they mean to pay as the price of their lands & of the annuity, which is about five or six dollars a person annually, none will think the Indians, all poor & suffering & some wedded to liquor, will or *can* spare any at present for maintaining religion." Struggling for funds to sustain his mission, Kirkland regretted that, despite New York's windfall from selling Oneida lands, the state legislators declined to appropriate funds to advance the "Civilization & national happiness" of the Indians. They rebuffed an Oneida request for money to rebuild their church.[86]

New York's stinginess toward Kirkland's mission was remarkable given his exertions to facilitate Oneida land cessions and given how much money the state reaped by retailing that land. By selling a single 100-acre lot carved out of the 1795 cession, the state made more than enough money to cover Kirkland's annual salary of $250—and that cession contained enough land for more than 1,000 such farms. But even New York's Federalist leaders had come to deem missionary efforts a waste of time and money, as they concluded that Indians were immutable barbarians. John Jay and Philip Schuyler dissented from the enthusiasm of their national counterparts Henry Knox and Timothy Pickering for funding programs to promote Indian acculturation. Of course, the more jaundiced view served New York's drive to render the Iroquois dependent, the better to oblige further land cessions at the lowest possible price.[87]

Kirkland also lamented that the state legislature ignored pleas from the Oneida and Mohican chiefs for a law to prohibit selling alcohol to Indians. The author of those petitions, Captain Hendrick Aupaumut, detected hypocrisy when the state's leaders preached temperance to Indians: "For every time they held Treaties, they would bring several barrels of rum to pour down the throats of the Indians; and when they advised us to break off from drinking, the Indians could not receive their advice, because they gave the liquor themselves." In 1799, the chiefs complained to the state legislators: "We united our Voices two years ago for your assistance that you might bound this Tyrant [rum]. But you refused to give that Assistance which one brother had [a] right to expect from another."[88]

In 1800, the legislature belatedly enacted a law, effective July 1, prohibiting liquor sales to the Indians of Oneida County on pain of a fine of $5 to $20. But if the chiefs and matrons sought that law, many of the young warriors resented it. "Poor Skenendon's life has already been threatened," Kirkland reported in May, "by one of his young warriors, on account of his forwardness in procuring the act." With apparent help from liquor traders, many warriors petitioned the legislature, complaining that the law infantalized them: "We are able to take care of ourselves. We are not Children. We would wish to be like other People and have it in our power to drink a little Rum if we pay for it." The liquor traders and county magistrates liked the profits of their trade far more than the hassles of turning away warriors eager to drink and infuriated by refusal. They insisted that the law "has Created Grate Disturbences Between the Inhabitants and the Indians and that the Law is Continualy Avoided." Although the state kept the law on the books, the county magistrates failed to enforce it.[89]

For assisting the state and its speculators, Kirkland had to share in their blame. In August 1805, his unusual spiritual friend Dorothy Ripley elicited an emotional confession. After preaching together at Kanonwalohale, they had "a very solemn ride" back to his home. En route, she "remarked, that if he had been more faithful, the Lord then would have blessed his labours more abundantly, which he with tears acknowledged [that] he believed." She added, "if thou hadst only taken thought for the Indians, God would have cared for thee and thy children; and I am fully sensible that no one will ever profit the Indians unless they can lay aside their own interest. . . . My aged brother, with tears, said he 'Would take my advice: for what I had advanced was the truth.' " Having won and then lost a great estate, Kirkland could now see his folly in neglecting Oneida souls, when they had most needed his help.[90]

Although most of the Oneidas continued respectfully, indeed earnestly, to attend Kirkland's sermons, they still disappointed his moral hopes. Periods of pious devotion and temperance resolutions alternated with outbursts of drunken violence. In 1806, he sighed, "They are wavering & unstable even when *sincere*. They begin well but do not persevere."[91]

Through all the oscillations by the majority, a pious minority clung to Kirkland as an essential source of strength during trying times. In 1805, the Oneida Christians assured the Boston Board:

> We need his help, his counsel & his instructions *every day*, as well as on Sabbath days, and never did we require his labours & his constant watch over us more than at this period. When we duly consider our situation, it seems to us that we must inevitably go to ruin should he leave us.

Wary of change, they felt reassured by their long relationship with Kirkland. In adhering to Kirkland, the Oneidas heeded the same stubborn traditionalism that so often frustrated his exhortations that they change.[92]

That pious minority gave Kirkland a new sense of inner peace. "I know of no part of my Missionary life when I engaged in its duties with more fidelity & application than during the years 1801 & 1802," Kirkland reflected. Humbled by financial loss and wayward children, Kirkland had become less self-righteous and more forgiving of his Indian flock. No longer expecting a thorough transformation of all Oneidas, he found sufficient victory in the persistence of his close relationship with a few.[93]

Although Kirkland had strayed in pursuit of mammon in midlife, he ultimately felt a renewed devotion for his Oneida congregation, a community of love that he had never known elsewhere. In 1806, he had explained, "I love them, & they love me. The attachment is strong, the affection subsisting betwixt us (the little handful of worthy communicants) is indissoluble." If he had lived less well than Brant, Kirkland died in a far better spirit—which is what mattered most to an evangelical missionary. At the age of sixty-six, he died of pleurisy on February 28, 1808—just three months after Brant, his old schoolmate.[94]

Sarah Ainse

Mary, an Oneida Woman, by Baroness Hyde de Neuville, 1807.
(Courtesy of the New-York Historical Society; 1953.207.)

S ARAH AINSE remains a mysterious presence despite her recurrence in
the historical record. Let's begin with her name. Baptized as "Sarah,"
she usually went by the more familiar "Sally," but both mask her original,
unknown, native first name. "Ainse" is probably a corruption of "Hance" (or
Hands), a common surname among the Oneidas. As an adult, she also spo-
radically went by the last names of three husbands: Montour, Maxwell, and
Willson.[1]

We do not know where she was born or the identity of her parents. She
called herself an Oneida—and was the half sister of Skenandon. But histori-

ans sometimes label her a Conoy, Shawnee, Mohawk, or Ojibwa because she traded with them and knew their languages. In fact, individual Indians often possessed multiple and shifting ethnic identities, owing to marriage, adoption, and changing residence over the years. Assigning her a single ethnic identity matters more to historians than it did to Sarah Ainse or to her diverse relatives and neighbors in a fluid borderland.[2]

She was probably born in the mid-1730s, for she married at age seventeen and prior to 1753. Her literacy in English suggests an early education in a colonial school. She also mastered an array of native tongues, for a Moravian missionary later observed: "She understands and reads most of the Indian languages."[3]

Possessed of a versatile mind and a powerful will, Ainse also cut a striking figure: tall and graceful. She caught the eye of Andrew Montour, an influential and flamboyant cross-cultural diplomat on the Pennsylvania and New York frontier of the 1740s and 1750s. Although the son of an Oneida warrior, Andrew Montour took his colonial name from his more famous mother, "Madame [Isabelle] Montour." Of mixed French and native ancestry, Madame Montour was a prominent trader and interpreter during the early eighteenth century. Combining colonial gentility with native customs, she taught cultural fluidity to her son, who learned French and English as well as Oneida, Delaware, Shawnee, and Miami. In addition to becoming an Oneida chief, Andrew Montour served the colonists as a scout, interpreter, and consultant in native affairs. Initially employed by Pennsylvania, Montour entered Sir William Johnson's service in 1756. Usually based at the village of Shamokin on the Susquehanna River, Montour ranged widely, visiting Philadelphia, the Ohio Valley, and Iroquoia. By 1753, Sarah Ainse became his second wife, succeeding a deceased Delaware woman.[4]

Montour's land ambitions anticipated Joseph Brant's vision for Grand River. Straddling the frontier, Montour sought from the Six Nations a tract of land on Sherman's Creek, a tributary of the Susquehanna, where he planned a composite community of natives and settlers. From the latter, he would collect rents to sustain his family. But colonial officials were horrified by the prospect of tenant farmers consolidating a native title on lands coveted by Pennsylvania's proprietors. Instead of reserving the land for Montour, they secured it for themselves by purchase from the Iroquois in 1754. That purchase infuriated Montour, who felt betrayed by officials he had served so well for so long. The interpreter Conrad Weiser reported, "[Montour] Says he will now Kill any white men that will pretent to Setle on his Creek." Swearing at Weiser, the drunken Montour wore on one leg "a Stocking and no Shoe, on the other a Shoe and no Stocking."[5]

His marriage to Ainse was short-lived and probably tempestuous, for he drank too much, and she spent too freely. In 1753, a Pennsylvania official observed, "Andrew [Montour] has been arrested for fifty pounds, . . . for he is an expensive man having a wife who takes up goods at any rate and to any value." Three years later, she left him to live with Oneida relatives, including Skenandon, at Kanonwalohale. She took along Nicholas, the youngest of her three children with Montour, who placed the older two, Polly (but sometimes Debby) and Andrew, Jr., in colonial homes in Philadelphia. During the late 1750s and early 1760s, Andrew occasionally visited Sarah at Kanonwalohale. In 1766, he moved away to the vicinity of Fort Pitt, in the Ohio Valley, where he died in 1772, murdered by a Seneca guest during a drinking bout. Unable to sustain a middle position on the settler frontier, Andrew Montour left a dream for his widow to pursue.[6]

LAND

Ainse became a trader at Fort Stanwix in 1758, when the British established that post at the strategic carrying place between the Mohawk River and Wood Creek. There, in April 1765, she met and befriended the young missionary Samuel Kirkland, providing him with a night's lodging on Skenandon's recommendation.[7]

Savvy about the colonial property system, Ainse pressed the Oneidas to grant her a tract of 6 square miles near Fort Stanwix, a prime location for commercial development. In her words, "being a little accustomed to civilized ways of living," she "requested of the said nation to give her the portion of land she was entitled to in order to improve upon it in the manner of white people." In August 1762, an Oneida chief informed Sir William Johnson that "Sarah Montour came from Fort Stanwix, with a Barrel of Wine, and desired a Meeting with all our Sachems, in order to get some Land from them for her Child (which She was desirous should be near the old Oneida Castle as thereby the English would be prevented from taking it) which being granted, She Treated our Sachems with Wine."[8]

The chiefs favored Ainse as their best hope of sustaining an Oneida interest in a tract particularly coveted by colonists. Chiefs tried to steer vulnerable tracts into the hands of favored patrons, who could be trusted to provide future generosity. But it was her misfortune that powerful colonists sought the same land. Rejecting her Oneida deed, Sir William in 1772 procured the land for a cartel of friends, including New York's royal governor, William Tryon.[9]

Frustrated within New York, Ainse followed the fur trade into the Great Lakes country. In 1766, she began trading with the Mississaugas on the north shore of Lake Erie. A year later, she moved northwest to Michilimackinac, at the entrance of Lake Michigan, where she lived with, and perhaps married, a colonial trader named William Maxwell. In late 1774, Ainse shifted her operation to Detroit, where she traded on a large scale, borrowing over £3,000— a testament to her good credit and to her extensive contacts in Indian villages. Prospering, she bought a town lot and several slaves. In 1783, she picked up another short-term husband, John Willson, who paid off at least £1,256 of her debts before they parted.[10]

Attentive to opportunities, she again sought Indian title to a prime tract of land, this time on the lower Thames River (then known as the River La Tranche). The location was superb: fertile land, fronting on a river navigable by boats, and close to Detroit, a thriving commercial center. In 1780, she agreed to pay £500 in goods to the local Ojibwas for about 150 square miles stretching along both banks of the river. The Ojibwas explained that they favored "their sister Sally Ainse" because "she had always used them well." Like the Oneidas, the Ojibwas employed their land to cultivate a beneficial relationship with a patron who had helped Indians—which seemed the best predictor of ongoing, future benefit.[11]

By acquiring the Thames tract, while reasserting her Oneida land claim, Ainse played both sides of the uncertain boundary spawned by the American Revolution. Like the Seneca matrons who counseled dividing the Six Nations between Grand River and Buffalo Creek, Ainse hedged her bets by seeking refuges on both sides of the new border. Good Peter and Skenandon urged Governor Clinton to protect her Fort Stanwix tract, but he was not about to recognize an Indian right to create land titles valid in a settler society. Meanwhile, she urged her Oneida relatives to join her on the Thames, for she meant her tract to accommodate "her friends, who were loyalists and Indians." During the spring of 1794, at the peak of the borderland crisis, Skenandon nearly accepted Ainse's offer of a haven in Upper Canada.[12]

In 1787, Ainse moved onto her Thames tract, where she erected a house, fenced in an old Indian field, and planted an orchard. Thriving as both farmer and trader, Ainse made a vivid impression a decade later on the visiting Alexander Coventry:

> Going down the [Thames] River, we stopt a little while at Mrs. Hands, an "Oneida Squaw," who has a good farm here and a tolerable good house with furniture in the English style, having several pictures and a considerable plate. She is almost the only instance I have met with, of the native American preferring or approaching civilized life. Mrs. Hands seems to be a full blooded native, but is remarkably tall and elegant in her person. Her features are by no means disagreeable, although I suppose

she is nearly 50 years old. She was dressed fully in [the] English mode with a long gown and her hair flowing loose behind. She has been [a] temporary wife to several white men (eminent merchants), [and] has at one time traded largely in merchandize in Detroit.... She has lived in fashion: her household furniture is now worth £500. In fact she has been a bon vivant and spent her thousands.

Coventry underestimated her enduring charm, for she was probably sixty in 1797. As he hinted, Ainse's property was doubly anomalous in a colonial society that reserved property rights to settler men, for she was both a native and a woman. That so few Indians accumulated the property of civilization attested to the obstacles placed by colonial law and settler aggression.[13]

Indeed, squatters invaded her land. Treating Ainse's Indian title with contempt, the Detroit land board granted certificates that entitled the squatters to procure legal deeds from the colonial government. The board reserved a mere 200 acres for her. In protest, she supposed "one Indian to have a right of conveying to another." But the board rejected the right of natives to grant private property to individuals of their choice. Her primary foe was Alexander McKee, the local Indian Department agent and a member of the land board. In 1790, he purchased the valley for the Crown from the Ojibwas, ignoring their stipulation of a reserve for Ainse. When at least eighteen chiefs subsequently certified that reserve, McKee still denied it.[14]

In 1792, she appealed to the Executive Council of Upper Canada for justice. Traveling to Newark to plead her case, Ainse impressed John Graves Simcoe, who became her champion. In October, the council ordered a compromise by directing the Detroit land board to award Ainse 1,600 acres, including her farm. The board, however, protested that the order set a precedent ominous to all of their certificates—the foundation for settler land titles in the Thames Valley. The board's leader, Colonel Richard England, complained that the council's ruling would "occasion a general Alarm of insecurity in the Settlement and a want of confidence in the Board, who have strictly acted as directed by Government." Procrastinating in enforcing the council's decision, the board members instead wrote letters to belittle Ainse's title, improvements, and character.[15]

Weary of the board's obstruction, Simcoe ordered the surveyor general, David W. Smith, and the attorney general, John White, to issue her a deed for all 1,600 acres. "I am so determined that she shall have Justice," Simcoe explained, "that if it be necessary, the Persons who withhold her Lands from her shall be prosecuted by the Attorney General." But a deed needed an accurate description of the bounds, which necessitated a survey. The Executive Council directed the Detroit land board to employ Patrick McNiff for that purpose. But this invited further delay, for McNiff clouded the issue by reporting:

> I do not know any such person as Sally Ainse; nor do I know of any Lots or Farms claimed by any person of that name on River la Tranche. Sarah Willson an Indian woman has laid her claim to a large Tract . . . if it can be said [that] she has any just claim to land there, the land cannot justly be deemed her property alone, as her husband, Mr. Wilson, is now living and at Niagara or near it.

Under the common law, no married woman could hold legal title to real estate—in stark contrast to Iroquois villages, where women controlled the land. As legal sticklers, the Detroit land board punished Ainse for seeking property rights within colonial society.[16]

Furious at the delays, Ainse charged Smith with dragging his feet to assist his friends on the Detroit board and among the squatters. In a pointed letter, she blistered Smith for colluding in McKee's deception: "Though I am an Indian Woman (& guilty of a great indecorum in presuming to write to you in this manner), I see no reason why I should be openly plundered of my property; of what cost me dear; . . . but as it is allowed, for one Gentleman's word to be taken, & to overthrow the Oaths of Eighteen or Twenty Indian Chiefs, I have a poor chance to go to Law."[17]

Her friend Joseph Brant pressed Simcoe and the councillors to enforce their ruling. Brant understood the larger stakes involved, for vindicating Ainse's native title would establish a precedent invaluable to his push to lease or sell land without colonial interference. Writing from Grand River, Brant pressed Smith:

> You very well know that Sally Ainse's land was her right, before the purchase was made by Government [in 1790], and that the land board cut it in pieces afterwards. Since it has been promised . . . to be restored to her, and is not restored yet notwithstanding, I really must confess that I begin to think it too hard to see our friends the English so very strict about Indian lands—as for instance the great trouble we have had about this land here, and yet cannot learn whether it will end to our satisfaction or not. It grieves me to observe that it seems natural to Whites to look on lands in the possession of Indians with an aching heart, and never to rest 'till they have planned them out of them.

In return, Ainse helped Brant by gathering information from, and conveying his messages to, the Indians in the Thames and Detroit valleys.[18]

But by allying with Brant, Ainse reaped his foes. In 1795, Simcoe resented Brant's charges that McKee had betrayed the Indians by undermining the American peace bid of 1793. By helping Brant to substantiate and spread those charges, Ainse offended British officials determined to control communication among the Indians. Lord Dorchester complained that Brant had "opened a Correspondence with Miss Sally Ainse; has held Council & sent Messengers without communicating at all or consulting with Col. McKee." Simcoe's support for Ainse also cooled once he recognized that Brant's Grand River land title claims would benefit from her success. As Simcoe looked the other way, the squatters began to sell her land for their profit. Upon his return to England in 1796, she renewed her formal complaint, but the Executive Council had wearied of her pleas. With the borderland crisis in remission, the councillors saw no reason to curry favor with Brant or Ainse. In 1798, they abruptly reversed their former resolution, dismissing her claim to more than a single farm of 200 acres.[19]

That year brought another disaster, when fire consumed Ainse's harvest-filled barn, compelling her to seek relief at the Moravian mission on the Thames. In November, the missionary reported: "She came here in need and got help. Having heard of the mishap, our people felt great empathy and collected twenty bushels of corn of their own accord." By 1806, she was a charity case who procured a quart of whiskey, worth four shillings, from a merchant who indulgently wrote next to the entry, "I don't mean to ask payment." This was a long fall from the £3,000 credit she had once enjoyed from that same merchant.[20]

Frustrated in her material ambitions, Ainse sought consolation in Christianity. In 1798, the Moravian missionary noted: "She visited our daily meetings and was very moved. She declared herself a sinner.... She was convinced that ours was the only way to salvation and, had her circumstances allowed it, she would have moved here a long time ago." That visit renewed a family connection, for her late husband Andrew Montour had assisted the Moravians in Pennsylvania. More recently, his sister and her sister-in-law, Mary Montour, had joined the Moravian community that moved to the Thames.[21]

An ecumenical Christian, Ainse hosted clergymen touring the Thames Valley to preach to the settlers. The itinerants included the Baptist Nathan Bangs, who reported lodging

in the house of an Indian woman, the widow of a French Canadian, who had left her considerable property. She was a good, simple-hearted, earnest creature.... She never asked me to sit at the table with her, deeming herself unworthy, but prepared my food and put it on the table in my room. She considered herself highly honored by having the Gospel preached in her house.

Once a young bon vivant, she became an elderly penitent burdened by a sense of loss and sin. In 1803, the Moravian missionary noted her physical decline: "She is very old." Just six years before, she had struck Coventry as elegant and striking.[22]

But she persisted in seeking her property rights within a colonial society that denied them to natives. In 1808, 1809, 1813, and 1815, she pressed the Executive Council for compensation in wild land for the tract that she had lost during the 1790s. But the councillors repeatedly rejected her. On the last occasion, they insisted that Ainse was dead, but that was their wishful thinking. She lived until late 1823, expiring when she was almost ninety, having outlived her children and her property.[23]

LINES

Frustrated in her bid for property rights in settler society, Ainse represents the general dilemma of Indians on the frontier in the wake of the American Revolution. Like her friends Joseph Brant and Good Peter, Ainse asserted a native right fully to own land, including the option to sell or lease parcels to preferred neighbors. In writing the history of settler expansion (and native dispossession), we tend to cast Indians as defiant but doomed traditionalists, as noble but futile defenders of ancient modes of land use and ownership. We see them as adamant primitives who bravely but hopelessly resisted the inevitable. Through this distorted prism, Ainse, Brant, and Good Peter appear as strange exceptions and as tragic examples of cultural limbo: trapped between native tradition and colonial dynamism.

We have inherited this limiting view of Indian property, and of native adaptability, from the colonizers who dispossessed them. Consider, for example, Samuel Kirkland's revealing account of the Oneidas at the Fort Herkimer treaty council of 1785 with New York's governor and commissioners:

> The Indians could never get any clear, determinate idea of this *right of pre-emption* as either inherent in the State or how conveyed to them. Much pains have been taken by interpreters & others to explain this matter. But either their language is deficient, not sufficiently copious, or the capacity of the Indians not equal to comprehending such a mystery. *Good Peter*, an extraordinary Character among the Indians, once proposed a discussion

of the subject with Judge Benson, but he very prudently declined it, fore-seeing that the issue would not accelerate or facilitate the Object of the Treaty.

Regarding that supposed preemption right as a complex truth, Kirkland faulted Indian language or native intellect for the Oneida resistance. But, as the Oneidas saw it, a preemption right was an illogical menace that contra-dicted the New Yorkers' repeated promises to treat their native allies as brethren by protecting their property. That Judge Egbert Benson would not debate the subject affirmed the Oneida suspicion that preemption could not bear close scrutiny. By refusing, Benson revealed that it was the New Yorkers who lacked the language or the capacity to comprehend the property rights asserted by natives. Scholars become Kirkland's heirs when they treat pre-emption as anything more than a partisan fiction asserted to dispossess native people.[24]

Brant, Good Peter, and Ainse (and other creative native leaders) tried to appropriate and invert a colonial system of property meant to dispossess and marginalize them. Resisting the perverse logic of preemption, native innova-tors pressed for recognition of their aboriginal title as complete, as the equiv-alent of a freehold, which afforded the right to sell or lease directly to individuals of their own choice.

Realistic about the power of settler numbers, these native leaders tried to manage, rather than entirely to block, the process of settlement. They did so in three ways meant to preserve Indian autonomy and prosperity. First, by selling or leasing directly to chosen buyers or tenants, the natives evaded the debilitating control of a government acting as a monopoly buyer to enforce native dependence. Second, they sought to choose their new neighbors, favoring the relatively peaceable and generous to constitute a mediating buffer between the Indian homelands and settler society. Third, Indian lead-ers sought an annual revenue to soften the loss of their traditional resources in fish and game, smoothing their gradual transition to market agriculture. To preserve their sovereignty over the land, they preferred to lease land to tenants, thereby asserting an enduring interest in the land and its benefits.

As with all cultural appropriations by natives, these Indians selectively adapted new property notions to serve their own priorities. By innovating, they sought in classic native fashion to preserve a valuable tradition. They nurtured special relationships with selected settlers and gentlemen: those who seemed most apt to honor the traditional obligation to treat Indians with generosity and respect. They hoped to build a buffer of friends, drawn from settler society but committed to softening its power. In effect, these Iro-quois leaders sought latter-day equivalents of Sir William Johnson, whom they romanticized as a protecting paragon meant to instruct his successors in how properly to treat natives. This longing, however, remained unrequited because no gentleman could long resist exploiting the Indian search for a reliable patron. So the Oneidas discovered with John Livingston, Peter Penet, Peter Smith, Samuel Kirkland, Philip Schuyler, and George Clinton.

While innovating in property relations, the Iroquois clung tenaciously to their traditional mode of handling murders. By covering graves, instead of submitting to trials and executions, natives defended their sovereignty as peoples distinct from the settlers. By shaping the settlement of North America, Indians hoped to preserve a place, in principle if not always in geography, beyond control by the continent's rival powers.

That hope clashed with the American drive to perfect the national unity and power promised by their victory in the Revolutionary War. In the peace treaty of 1783, the Americans reaped a favorable boundary with the British Empire. During the subsequent decade, however, Indian resistance and British delays threatened American expansion westward. To secure that promised boundary and to give it their preferred meaning, as reducing the Indians within to dependents, the Americans worked to pin down the Six Nations on delimited reservations surrounded by settlements. So restricted, they would lose their capacity to resist. Instead, they would become useful military auxiliaries for deployment against other Indians and the British in a future rupture. Once pinned down on American terms, natives could no longer broker war and peace between the republic and the empire.

By enveloping the Iroquois of New York with settlements, the Americans weakened the Indian buffer that screened the British posts on the Great Lakes. Backing down from military confrontation, British leaders reconciled with the Americans in 1794. By surrendering the border posts two years later, the British belatedly conceded the peace boundary of 1783. Once the Americans gained a secure perch on the Great Lakes, they were in an even stronger position to subordinate the Indians within the boundary by restricting their movements, regulating their trade, demanding further land cessions, and enforcing legal jurisdiction over murder.

The new boundary pinched the Indians on both sides. Alarmed by the American hegemony over valuable warriors, the British sought tighter control over the Indians within Upper Canada. As Americans grew in power and proximity, the British became more obsessed with restricting native communication, diplomacy, and property on their side of the line. By managing Indians, the British sought predictable military auxiliaries for a future war with the Americans.

In competition with one another, the republic and the empire defined a border that controlled the Indians. That division cost the Iroquois their place as the keepers of a borderland between. Formerly a middle ground, Iroquoia became a divided ground: partitioned between the republic and the empire. During the War of 1812, the Iroquois would fight one another in service to the two powers that had divided them.[25]

That process of native division and subordination helped to consolidate the American republic as a formidable nation. By securing a northern boundary and procuring Indian land, the overlapping federal and state governments impressed their citizens, who could see the benefits of state and nation in frontier farms and boundary fortifications. In Iroquoia, as throughout North America, the limitation of native peoples within the boundaries of nation and the subordinate lines of reservations realized the continental potential of the United States.

Ultimately, the interdependent lines of nation and reservation depended upon a third set of bounds: the private property lines of thousands of farms. That thicket of private holdings surrounded and delimited the native reservations. Wielding axes, fire, hoes, plows, and guns, the settlers transformed the environment that had sustained native peoples in autonomy. In sum, the making of private landholdings and the defining of Indian reservations were reciprocal processes.[26]

Those intertwined processes of line-making constructed the public power of states, nations, and empires in North America. In border competition with the British, the Americans prevailed by filling their side of the boundary with more settlers holding property titles that bound them to the republic. Those titles interested the holders in the fortunes of the issuing government. By asserting a monopoly over granting lands within specified boundaries, a state or a colony claimed allegiance from the settlers as the price for legally protecting their property. For example, during the 1780s, New York State defeated Massachusetts in the competition to bind the interest of the settlers moving into Iroquoia.

The parallel (but contentious) construction of an American state (New York) and a British colony (Upper Canada) dashed the innovative dreams of Ainse, Brant, and Good Peter for Indian management in the settlement of their lands. In 1792, Good Peter explained to Timothy Pickering that New York State had frustrated the hopes that the Oneidas had nurtured at the end of the war:

> Brother, I did not then expect that I should be reduced to our present situation. We then thought we should be the sole proprietors of our own land; and that our disposal of it should be optional with us, in case of a successful issue [to the war]. Brother, It seems to us that we are not really freemen; nor have [we] had the real disposal of our property. If we under-

stand what is meant by a person's being free and independent, as to his own property, he may either lend, or sell his property, or any portion of it as he pleases.

Settlers certainly understood that property endowed freedom, but they maximized their own prosperity and liberty by denying that combination to the Indians in their way. By building state power from a web of private properties, New York and Upper Canada systematically consumed native land and foreclosed the alternatives envisioned by Ainse, Brant, and Good Peter.[27]

By concluding in the early nineteenth century, this book ends on a bleak note for Iroquois prospects. In recent decades, however, native activists revived their challenge to the dividing international boundary, to the attempted dissolution of native sovereignty, and to the land cessions that constricted their reservations in the name of preemption. Citing the Jay Treaty of 1794, native activists assert their rights freely to cross the international boundary without acknowledging the restricting control of the United States and Canada. In effect, they reclaim their mobility as prior and superior to the intrusion of those governments. During the 1920s, Six Nations peoples, led by Chief Clinton Rickard (a Tuscarora), organized the Indian Defense League of America to protest restrictive American immigration and naturalization laws. Winning a test case in 1927, the Indian Defense League began an annual march of celebration across the border at the Niagara Falls Bridge. In 1995, Chief Rickard's granddaughter Jolene Rickard wrote that the enduring march gave her

> a sense of freedom, [of] my inherent right to move freely in Iroquoian territories and that is what the fight is all about for Indian people. It made me realize the border checkpoints I pass everyday as a Tuscarora woman. It takes guts to keep crossing those borders and to not let those barriers become our "Indian" prison.

Rickard imagines restoring the middle position lost when Iroquoia became a divided ground during the 1790s. She reminds us that borders are artificial and lack the permanence asserted by politicians and maps. Requiring belief and cooperation, boundaries survive or lapse depending on how people behave in their vicinity. We tend to see this fluidity more clearly along the American border with Mexico, which invites such massive and conspicuous defiance, while we mistakenly assume that the boundary with Canada is both natural and settled.[28]

Notes

ABBREVIATIONS

AAS American Antiquarian Society (Worcester, Mass.)

AO Archives of Ontario (Toronto)

ASPIA *American State Papers: Documents, Legislative and Executive, of the Congress of the United States, Class II: Indian Affairs*

CHS Connecticut Historical Society (Hartford)

DCA Dartmouth College Archives (Hanover, N.H.)

DCB *Dictionary of Canadian Biography*

DCLSC Dartmouth College Library, Special Collections (Hanover, N.H.)

DHSNY *The Documentary History of the State of New York*

DWFP DeWitt Family Papers (Syracuse University Library, Special Collections)

HCA Hamilton College Archives (Clinton, N.Y.)

HGWAIP Harvard Grants for Work Among the Indians Papers (Harvard University Archives)

HL Huntington Library (San Marino, Calif.)

HORC Henry O'Reilly Collection (New-York Historical Society)

HSP Historical Society of Pennsylvania (Philadelphia)

HUA Harvard University Archives (Cambridge, Mass.)

JBP Jeremy Belknap Papers (Massachusetts Historical Society)

JKP James Kent Papers (Library of Congress)

LC Library of Congress (Washington, D.C.)

LCP Library Company of Philadelphia

LFP Lothrop Family Papers (Dartmouth College, Special Collections Library)

MHS Massachusetts Historical Society (Boston)

MSL Military Secretary's Letterbook (NAC)

MTL Metropolitan Toronto Library

NA National Archives (United States) (Washington, D.C.)

NAC National Archives of Canada (Ottawa)

NYCD *Documents Relative to the Colonial History of the State of New York*

NYHS New-York Historical Society (New York City)

NYPL New York Public Library (New York City)

NYSA New York State Archives (Albany)

NYSHA New York State Historical Association (Cooperstown)

NYSL New York State Library (Albany)

OCHS   Ontario County Historical Society (Canandaigua, N.Y.)

PCC   Papers of the Continental Congress (Library of Congress)

PEI   Peabody-Essex Institute (Salem, Mass.)

PGP   Phelps and Gorham Papers (New York State Library)

PGW-PS   *The Papers of George Washington, Presidential Series* (W. W. Abbott et al., eds.)

PSGIA   Papers of the Superintendent General of Indian Affairs (National Archives of Canada)

PSP   Philip Schuyler Papers (New York Public Library)

PSmP   Peter Smith Papers (Syracuse University Library, Special Collections)

PSWJ   *The Papers of Sir William Johnson*

PYMICR   Philadelphia Yearly Meeting Indian Committee Records (Haverford College)

RRLP   Robert R. Livingston Papers (New-York Historical Society)

SKP   Samuel Kirkland Papers (Hamilton College Archives)

SPG   Society for Propagating the Gospel (Anglican)

SPGP   Society for Propagating the Gospel Papers (Congregational)

SULSC   Syracuse University Library, Special Collections (Syracuse, N.Y.)

TPP   Timothy Pickering Papers (Massachusetts Historical Society)

INTRODUCTION: WHEELOCK'S SCHOOL

1. Patrick, "Life and Times of Samuel Kirkland," 4–9; Pilkington, ed., *Journals of Samuel Kirkland*, xv; Eleazar Wheelock to Samuel Mather, Feb. 3, 1761, and Wheelock to George Whitefield, July 4, 1761, EWP #761153 and #761404, DCLSC.

2. McClure and Parish, *Memoirs of the Rev. Eleazar Wheelock*, 15–20, 26–27; McCallum, *Eleazar Wheelock*, 79–82; Wheelock, *Plain and Faithful Narrative* (1763), 15–16, 20–29; McCallum, ed., *Letters of Eleazar Wheelock's Indians*, 16–17; Axtell, *The Invasion Within*, 204–15.

3. Julian Gwyn, "Sir William Johnson," *DCB*, IV: 394–98; Hamilton, *Sir William Johnson*; Guzzardo, "Sir William Johnson's Official Family."

4. Hamilton, *Sir William Johnson*, 3, 6–7, 11–18, 70, 115–18, 195–96, 245–59, 276–77, 302, 312–19; Guzzardo, "Sir William Johnson's Official Family," 8, 28–31, 43–45, 64–68, 74, 153–59; Shannon, *Indians and Colonists*, 221–24; Allen, *His Majesty's Indian Allies*, 23; Stone, *Life and Times of Sir William Johnson*, II: 163; *PSWJ*, III: viii–xii; Johnson to Samuel Fuller, Jan. 5, 1763, in *PSWJ*, XIII: 282.

5. Fenton, *Great Law and the Longhouse*, 4–9, 19–20; Tiro, "People of the Standing Stone," 17; Tanner, ed., *Atlas of Great Lakes Indian History*, 74–78; Snow, *The Iroquois*, 53, 60–61, 141–57. For Iroquois languages, see Sir William Johnson to Arthur Lee, Feb. 28, 1771, in Edmund O'Callaghan, ed., *DHSNY*, IV: 435; Hamilton, ed., "Guy Johnson's Opinions on the American Indian," 324; Timothy Pickering, "Memorandum on Indian Language," ca. 1794, TPP, LXII: 260. For Iroquois numbers, see William Tryon, "Report . . . on the State of the Province of New York," 1774, in O'Callaghan, ed., *DHSNY*, I: 766.

6. Tooker, "The League of the Iroquois," 418–41; Fenton and Tooker, "Mohawk," 466–80; Snow, *The Iroquois*, 131–50.

7. Sir William Johnson to Lord Dartmouth, Apr. 22, 1773 ("next to"), in O'Callaghan, ed., *NYCD*, VIII: 361.

8. Grant, "Journal from New York to Canada, 1767," 187; Warren Johnson, "Journal," 259; Lender and Martin, eds., *Citizen-Soldier*, 83.

9. Hamilton, ed., "Guy Johnson's Opinions," 322 ("Natural Genius"); Sir William Johnson to Gen. Thomas Gage, Nov. 8, 1770, and Johnson to Arthur Lee, Mar. 28, 1772, *PSWJ*, VII: 993,

XII (1957): 955; Warren Johnson, "Journal," 255–56 ("the Woods"); Sir William Johnson to the Lords of Trade, Nov. 13, 1763, in O'Callaghan, ed., *NYCD*, VII: 574.

10. Aquila, *The Iroquois Restoration*, 233–45; Fenton, *Great Law and the Longhouse*, 363–513; Richter, *Ordeal of the Longhouse*, 255–80; Nammack, *Fraud, Politics, and the Dispossession of the Indians*.

11. Richter, *Facing East from Indian Country*, 151; Wraxall, *Abridgment of the Indian Affairs*, 219n ("to preserve"); Fenton, *Great Law and the Longhouse*, 517–32.

12. A. Taylor, *American Colonies*, 158–203; McCusker and Menard, *Economy of British America*, 103; Gross, *Minutemen and their World*, 68–108.

13. For the contested and contingent nature of boundaries, see Sahlins, *Boundaries*, xv–xvi, 1–9, 269–76; Anderson, *Imagined Communities*, 15; Herzog, *Where North Meets South*, 13–20.

14. For North American borders and Indian resistance, see Weber, "Turner, the Boltonians, and the Borderlands," 66–81; White, "The Nationalization of Nature," 976–86; Clayton, *Islands of Truth*, 69–72, 77–82, 165–67, 231–32, 235–40; Eliades, "Two Worlds Collide," 33–46; Resendez, *Changing National Identities at the Frontier*, 1–55; Albers and Kay, "Sharing the Land," 47–92.

15. Adelman and Aron, "From Borderlands to Borders," 814–41. See also Haefeli, "A Note on the Use of North American Borderlands," 1222–25; Wunder and Hamalainen, "Of Lethal Places and Lethal Essays," 1229–34; and Adelman and Aron, "Of Lively Exchanges and Larger Perspectives," 1235–39.

16. Turner, "Significance of the Frontier," 1–38. For criticism of Turner's frontier concept, see Limerick, *The Legacy of Conquest*, 17–32. I am indebted to three other recent borderland histories of Canada and the United States: LaDow, *The Medicine Line*; Lecker, ed., *Borderlands: Essays in Canadian-American Relations*; Stuart, *United States Expansionism and British North America*.

17. Hinderaker, *Elusive Empires*, 189, 268–70; White, *The Middle Ground*, 413–68; Sosin, *Whitehall and the Wilderness*, 239–41; Colley, *Captives*, 230–36; Countryman, "Indians, the Colonial Order, and the Social Significance of the American Revolution," 342–62.

18. A. Taylor, "Land and Liberty on the Post-Revolutionary Frontier," 81–108; A. Taylor, " 'To Man Their Rights': The Frontier Revolution," 231–57.

19. Cronon, *Changes in the Land*; A. Taylor, " 'The Great Change Begins,' " 265–90.

20. Red Jacket speech, Nov. 21, 1790 ("that we may pass"), TPP, LXI: 86, MHS; Red Jacket, speech, July 10, 1791 ("do not give"), TPP, LX: 92A, MHS. See also the Young King's speech, May 21, 1791, *ASPIA*, I: 165.

21. For successful leasing by the Catawbas of the Carolinas, see Merrell, *The Indians' New World*, 209–10, 230–31.

22. For recent examinations of New York's growth at Iroquois expense, see Hauptman, *Conspiracy of Interests*; Mintz, *Seeds of Empire*.

CHAPTER ONE: PROPERTY

1. Hamilton, *Sir William Johnson*, 284–86.

2. Little Abraham, speech, Mar. 1, 1761, and Sir William Johnson, speech, Mar. 1, 1761, RG 10 (Indian Affairs), Records of the Superintendent, VI: 13–15, NAC; Johnson to Cadwallader Colden, June 18, 1761 ("danger"), and Guy Johnson, Council Minutes, July 4–5, 1761, *PSWJ*, III: 409, 428–30; Sir William Johnson, "Journal to Detroit," July 4–6, 1761, *PSWJ*: XIII, 215–16. For Mohawk losses in war, see Johnson, "Review of the Trade and Affairs of the Indians in the Northern District of America," Sept. 22, 1767, in O'Callaghan, ed., *NYCD*, VII: 957.

3. Teyawarunte (Onondaga speaker), speech, Apr. 23, 1762, *PSWJ*, III: 700; Sir William Johnson to Thomas Gage, Mar. 9, 1765, *PSWJ*, XI: 625; Johnson, "Review of the Trade and Affairs of America," Sept. 22, 1767, in O'Callaghan, ed., *NYCD*, VII: 966.

4. Conoghquieson, speech, July 7, 1761, in Guy Johnson, Council Minutes, *PSWJ*, III: 431–33.

5. Hamilton, *Sir William Johnson*, 283–84, 294; Sir William Johnson, "Review of the Trade and Affairs of the Indians in the Northern District of America," Sept. 22, 1767, in O'Callaghan, ed., *NYCD*, VII: 958; Thomas Gage to Lord Halifax, Jan. 7, 1764 ("They saw"), in Carter, ed., *Correspondence of General Thomas Gage*, I: 10–11.

6. Snow, *The Iroquois*, 67–70; Fenton, "Northern Iroquoian Culture Patterns," 297–300; Recht, "Role of Fishing," 452; Vanderkemp, "Extracts from the Vanderkemp Papers," 72; Tiro, "People of the Standing Stone," 24; Starna, "Aboriginal Title and Traditional Iroquois Land Use," 31–33; Starna, "Oneida Homeland in the Seventeenth Century," 15. For hunting seasons, see also Samuel Kirkland to Jerusha Kirkland, Dec. 15, 1774, SKP, Folder 53, HCA; and Pilkington, ed., *Journals of Samuel Kirkland*, 104, 267. For ginseng, see Hamilton, *Sir William Johnson*, 86–87.

7. Fenton, "Northern Iroquoian Culture Patterns," 296–300; Recht, "Role of Fishing," 453; Starna, "Aboriginal Title and Traditional Iroquois Land Use," 43. Starna calculates that 1,000 Indians required 1,360 square miles to fulfill their needs for venison and deer hides while sustaining the herd (which meant no more than a 31 percent annual kill rate). For settler land use, see Taylor, "The Great Change Begins," 265–90.

8. Snow, *The Iroquois*, 69; Richard Smith, "Notes of a Tour," 75, LCP; Sir William Johnson to Lord Hillsborough, Dec. 20, 1768 ("The Indians"), in O'Callaghan, ed., *DHSNY*, II: 920; Johnson, "Journal of Warren Johnson," 259; Hamilton, ed., "Guy Johnson's Opinions," 316, 322.

9. Lender and Martin, eds., *Citizen-Soldier*, 85; Hamilton, ed., "Guy Johnson's Opinions," 322–23; Heckewelder, *History, Manners, and Customs of the Indian Nations*, 101, 189 ("They wonder"); Onoquaga Chiefs to Sir William Johnson, Jan. 22, 1770, *PSWJ*, VII: 348–49; Pilkington, ed., *Journals of Samuel Kirkland*, 29; Wainwright, ed., "Opinions of George Croghan," 156, 158.

10. Richard Smith, "Notes of a Tour," in Du Simitière MSS, 75, LCP; Shannon, "Dressing for Success," 17–18; Fenton, *Great Law and the Longhouse*, 9; Gahswanyaroras, speech, Apr. 2, 1763, RG 10 (Indian Affairs), IX: 313 (Reel C-1223), NAC; Richter, *Facing East*, 174–79.

11. Lender and Martin, eds., *Citizen-Soldier*, 83; Smith, *Tour of Four Great Rivers*, 68–69; Richard Smith, "Notes of a Tour," in Du Simitière MSS, 75, LCP; Grant, "Journal from New York to Canada," 187; Hamilton, ed., "Guy Johnson's Opinions," 316; Shannon, "Dressing for Success," 20–26; Warren Johnson, "Journal," 265.

12. Wallace, *Death and Rebirth of the Seneca*, 29; Shoemaker, *Strange Likeness*, 18–19.

13. Tiro, "People of the Standing Stone," 31–32; Fenton, *Great Law and the Longhouse*, 10; Canajoharie Mohawk, speech, Mar. 10, 1763 ("the Truest" and "would keep"), *PSWJ*, IV: 56; speech of Seneca matrons to Pennsylvania Commissioners, 1796, in Society of Friends, "Correspondence with the Indians of New York and those Northwest of Ohio River, 1795–1812," 9, NYPL.

14. Snow, *The Iroquois*, xiv.

15. Sir William Johnson to Arthur Lee, Mar. 28, 1772, *PSWJ*, XII: 951–52; Tiro, "People of the Standing Stone," 35–36; Hamilton, ed., "Guy Johnson's Opinions," 321; Sir William Johnson to the Lords of Trade, Oct. 8, 1764 ("the number"), in O'Callaghan, ed., *NYCD*, VII: 663.

16. Wainwright, ed., "Opinions of George Croghan," 157; Sir William Johnson to Arthur Lee, Feb. 28, 1771, in O'Callaghan, ed., *DHSNY*, IV: 433; Sayenqueraghta (spelled "Sagwaenwaraghton" by Kirkland) quoted in Samuel Kirkland, journal, n.d. [April 1765] ("a wise"), in

Pilkington, ed., *Journals of Samuel Kirkland*, 25. For such an assassination (of Kindarunty, a Seneca), see Thomas McKee to Johnson, Nov. 2, 1762, *PSWJ*, III: 924.

17. Campisi, "Iroquois and the Euro-American Concept of a Tribe," 455–62; Fenton, *Great Law and the Longhouse*, 10.

18. Campisi, "Fur Trade and Factionalism," 38; Tiro, "People of the Standing Stone," 35–36. For the role of women, see Thomas King, speech, Sept. 13, 1763, in Sir William Johnson, "Journal of Indian Affairs" (hereafter, Indian Journal), RG 10 (Indian Affairs), IX: 368 (Reel C-1223), NAC; Cayuga Speaker, Feb. 28, 1775, in Guy Johnson, Indian Journal, RG 10 (Indian Affairs), XI: 73 (Reel C-1223), NAC; Heckewelder, *History, Manners, and Customs*, 56–57.

19. Richter, "Ordeals of the Longhouse," 15; Campisi, "Fur Trade and Factionalism," 38; Sir William Johnson to Gen. James Abercromby, May 17, 1758, *PSWJ*, IX: 903.

20. Sir William Johnson to Gen. James Abercromby, May 17, 1758, *PSWJ*, IX: 904; Tiro, "People of the Standing Stone," 35.

21. Sir William Johnson to Lords of Trade, Oct. 8, 1764, ("extreme jealousy") in O'Callaghan, ed., *NYCD*, VII: 663; Johnson to Arthur Lee, Feb. 28, 1772, in O'Callaghan, ed., *DHSNY*, IV: 433.

22. Campisi, "Fur Trade and Factionalism," 39; Tiro, "People of the Standing Stone," 37–38; Campisi, "The Iroquois and the Euro-American Concept of Tribe," 460; Tagawaron speech, Aug. 6, 1763, *PSWJ*: X: 796; Kanadiohora, speech, Apr. 23, 1762 ("We are"), *PSWJ*, III: 697; Sir William Johnson to Arthur Lee, Mar. 28, 1772, *PSWJ*, XII: 952.

23. Gideon Hawley, journal, May 31, 1753, in O'Callaghan, ed., *DHSNY*, III: 1044; Heckewelder, *History, Manners, and Customs*, 329–30 ("They have no"); Sir William Johnson to Arthur Lee, Feb. 28, 1771 ("All their"), in O'Callaghan, ed., *DHSNY*, IV: 434; Johnson to Lee, Mar. 28, 1772, *PSWJ*, XII: 953.

24. Wallace, *Death and Rebirth of the Seneca*, 25–26; Smith, *Tour of Four Great Rivers*, 84.

25. Richter, *Facing East*, 164, 171; Campisi, "Oneida Treaty Period," 60.

26. Richter, *Ordeal of the Longhouse*, 134–42, 208–12; Richter, *Facing East*, 147–50; Jennings, "Iroquois Alliances," 38. For the role of "creative misunderstanding" in Indian-European diplomacy, see White, *Middle Ground*, 50–53; and Shannon, *Indians and Colonists*, 19–24, 44.

27. Merrell, *Into the American Woods*, 57–58, 186–87; Hamilton, ed., "Guy Johnson's Opinions," 324.

28. Merrell, *Into the American Woods*, 92–95, 210–14; Shannon, *Indians and Colonists*, 136–37; Pilkington, ed., *Journals of Samuel Kirkland*, 15 (Mar. 1765); Thomas Pownall to Earl of Halifax, July 23, 1754 ("As to the interpreting"), in McAnear, ed., "Personal Accounts of the Albany Congress," 742.

29. Shoemaker, *Strange Likeness*, 9–10; Fenton, "Structure, Continuity, and Change," 26; Richter, *Facing East*, 133; Shannon, *Indians and Colonists*, 127.

30. Druke, "Linking Arms," 33; Lender and Martin, eds., *Citizen-Soldier*, 49 ("really surprizeing").

31. Richter, *Facing East*, 135; Williams, *Linking Arms Together*, 32; Fenton, "Structure, Continuity, and Change," 6–7; Merrell, *Into the American Woods*, 125–26; Shannon, *Indians and Colonists*, 138.

32. Sir William Johnson to the Lords of Trade, Aug. 20, 1766 ("highly necessary"), in O'Callaghan, *NYCD*: VII: 852; Snow, *The Iroquois*, 65; Druke, "Linking Arms," 29–30, 36; Williams, *Linking Arms Together*, 38, 45–48, 59.

33. Williams, *Linking Arms Together*, 81; Richter, *Facing East*, 139; Lender and Martin, eds., *Citizen-Soldier*, 84 ("Here they learn"); Steele, *Betrayals*, 32.

34. Fenton, ed., "Journal of James Emlen," 291 ("*Time*" and "Perhaps"); Sir William Johnson, Account with the Crown, Nov. 2–20, 1773, *PSWJ*, VIII: 1092.

35. Hamilton, ed., "Guy Johnson's Opinions," 319; Sir William Johnson, Council Minutes, Apr. 26–27, 1762, *PSWJ*, III: 713; Johnson to Henry Bouquet, June 18, 1764, *PSWJ*, IV: 451; Johnson to Lord Hillsborough, Oct. 23, 1768, in O'Callaghan, ed., *NYCD*, VIII: 104–5; Johnson to Rev. Richard Peters, Jan. 3, 1769, *PSWJ*, VI: 563; Shannon, *Indians and Colonists*, 143.

36. Druke, "Linking Arms," 36; Richter, *Facing East*, 135–36; Williams, *Linking Arms Together*, 54–56; Merrell, *Into the American Woods*, 20–22; Guy Johnson, Council Minutes, Mar. 4, 1768, and Conoghquieson, speech, July 18, 1770, in O'Callaghan, ed., *NYCD*, VIII: 38, 229–30.

37. Williams, *Linking Arms Together*, 52, 76–77; Francis Jennings, "Introduction," xv; Druke, "Iroquois Treaties," 88–89; Richter, *Facing East*, 136–37; Snow, *The Iroquois*, 66–67.

38. Richter, *Facing East*, 136–37; Druke, "Linking Arms," 36–38; Fenton, *Great Law and the Longhouse*, 7; Fenton, "Structure, Continuity, and Change," 24; Thomas Pownall quoted in McAnear, "Personal Accounts of the Albany Congress," 730 ("for the address"). For polite evasion, see also Merrell, *Into the American Woods*, 183–84.

39. Merrell, *Into the American Woods*, 259; Fenton, "Structure, Continuity, and Change," 24; Theodore Atkinson, diary, June 29, 1754, in McAnear, ed., "Personal Accounts of the Albany Congress," 735–36.

40. Williams, *Linking Arms Together*, 71–72.

41. Richter, "Onas, the Long Knife," 129; Richter, *Ordeal of the Longhouse*, 140–41, 201–4; Williams, *Linking Arms Together*, 73–74; Theodore Atkinson, diary, July 6, 1754, in McAnear, ed., "Personal Accounts of the Albany Congress," 738–39.

42. Williams, *Linking Arms Together*, 73–74; Richter, "Onas, the Long Knife," 129.

43. Williams, *Linking Arms Together*, 36.

44. Lender and Martin, eds., *Citizen-Soldier*, 82–83, 91–92.

45. Fenton, "Structure, Continuity, and Change," 23; Druke, "Iroquois Treaties," 87; Johnson to Thomas Gage, Aug. 22, 1770 ("a very small part"), *PSWJ*, VII: 852; Shannon, *Indians and Colonists*, 127, 130 (Pownall quoted: "must all be"); Shannon, "Dressing for Success," 22, 31.

46. Shannon, "Dressing for Success," 22, 25; Dexter, ed., *Diary of David McClure*, 42 ("He was dressed").

47. Shannon, "Dressing for Success," 22, 30, 36–37; Johnson to Gage, Mar. 22, 1769, *PSWJ*, VI: 653; Daniel Claus, "Remarks on the Management of the Northern Indian Nations," Mar. 1777, in O'Callaghan, ed., *NYCD*, VIII: 701.

48. Druke, "Iroquois Treaties," 86–87; Richter, *Facing East*, 137; Johnson, Council Minutes, Apr. 24 ("bounty"), and 26–27, 1762, *PSWJ*, III: 704, 713. For the notion of "creative misunderstanding," see White, *Middle Ground*, 50–93.

49. Hans Jost Herkimer and Conrad Frank to Sir William Johnson, June 17, 1761, *PSWJ*, III: 407; Johnson, "Journal to Detroit," *PSWJ*, XIII: 216. The first source gives the victim's name as "Justice," probably a misreading by the editor, and the second as "Gustavus," which is more plausible.

50. White, "Although I am Dead," 414–17.

51. Conoghquieson, speech, July 7, 1761 ("Brother Warraghiyagey"), *PSWJ*, III: 430–31.

52. Warren Johnson, "Journal," 254; Sir William Johnson to Arthur Lee, Feb. 28, 1771, in O'Callaghan, ed., *DHSNY*, IV: 434; Hamilton, ed., "Guy Johnson's Opinions," 322; Cometti, ed., *American Journals of Lt. John Enys*, 89; Jacobs, *Wilderness Politics and Indian Gifts*, 75; Smith, *Tour of Four Great Rivers*, 84. For similar legal customs of revenge elsewhere in North America, see Reid, *Patterns of Vengeance*.

53. Dexter, ed., *Diary of David McClure*, 69–70; *New-York Journal* (New York City), July 2, 1788; Gray, ed., "From Fairfield to Schonbrun—1798," 83; Pilkington, ed., *Journals of Samuel Kirkland*, 355.

54. For assassinations of meddling chiefs, see Thomas McKee to Sir William Johnson, Nov. 2, 1762, *PSWJ*, III: 924; Kent and Deardorff, eds., "John Adlum on the Allegheny," 471–72; *Albany Gazette*, Sept. 6, 1787.

55. Richter, *Ordeal of the Longhouse*, 30–49; Snow, *The Iroquois*, 52–65; Wallace, *Death and Rebirth of the Seneca*, 39–44.

56. Merrell, *Into the American Woods*, 120–21; and Hinderaker, *Elusive Empires*, 123–24 (Iroquois quoted: "one life"); Smolenski, "Death of Sawantaeny," 104–28.

57. Hamilton, ed., "Guy Johnson's Opinions," 322 ("They are"); Johnson, Indian Journal, July 5, 1757 ("to no purpose"), *PSWJ*, IX: 795; Johnson to Earl of Dartmouth, May 2, 1774 ("universally averse"), *PSWJ*, VIII: 1146; Benjamin Mortimer quoted in Gray and Gray, *Wilderness Christians*, 165 ("whole system").

58. Ogista (Seneca), speech, June 16, 1765, MG 19 F35 (PSGIA), 1st Ser., Lot 632, NAC; Governor Patrick Gordon quoted in Hinderaker, *Elusive Empires*, 123–24 ("We & you"). For Indian dismay, see Smolenski, "The Death of Sawantaeny," 119–22.

59. Bushman, *King and People*, 55–60; Reid, *Patterns of Vengeance*, 53–55.

60. Kawashima, *Puritan Justice and the Indian*, 233–39; Salisbury, *Manitou and Providence*, 123–24, 186–87, 215–28; Lepore, *Name of War*, 21–47, 182–85; Steele, *Warpaths*, 228–29.

61. For the importance of the Iroquois, see Snow, *The Iroquois*, 121–40. The New Yorkers could and did bully the smaller, weaker Indian nations of Long Island and the Hudson Valley, who were quickly outnumbered by the newcomers. But the New Yorkers recognized the limits of their power beyond the Hudson Valley. For the want of colonial executions of Six Nations Indians, see Hearn, *Legal Executions in New York State*, 5–14. The colony did execute an Indian in 1708, but he was an indentured Long Island Indian who did not belong to the Six Nations.

62. Jeffrey Amherst to Sir William Johnson, June 24, 1761 ("Had one"), RG 10 (Indian Affairs), Records of the Superintendent, VI: 38, NAC.

63. Sir William Johnson, speech, July 7, 1761 ("not understand"), and Jeffrey Amherst to Johnson, July 11, 1761, *PSWJ*, III: 434, 506; Johnson to Amherst, July 7, 1761, *PSWJ*, X: 312.

64. Jeffrey Amherst to Sir William Johnson, May 29, 1763, *PSWJ*, X: 689; Anderson, *Crucible of War*, 538–41, 544, 550–51; Dowd, *War Under Heaven*, 127–30, 137–38.

65. Treaty of Peace with the Delaware Nation, May 8, 1765, and Johnson, speech, July 24, 1765, in O'Callaghan, ed., *NYCD*, VII: 739, 856; Gage to Johnson, Dec. 14, 1767, in O'Callaghan, ed., *DHSNY*, II: 890; Capt. James Stevenson to Johnson, Dec. 18, 1770 ("If they are hanged"), *PSWJ*, VII: 1041.

66. Merrell, *Into the American Woods*, 284–88; Anderson, *Crucible of War*, 611–12; Richter, *Facing East*, 203–6; Dowd, *War Under Heaven*, 198.

67. White, *Middle Ground*, 344–46; Heckewelder, *History, Manners, and Customs of the Indians*, 337.

68. Johnson followed French precedent. See White, *Middle Ground*, 349–50; White, "Although I Am Dead," 417. For an example of surrender and pardon at Fort Pitt in 1765, see Ogista, speech, June 16, 1765; Lt. Col. John Reid, speech, June 17, 1765; Gage to Johnson, July 8, 1765; and Johnson to Gage, July 20, 1765, *PSWJ*, XI: 791, 792, 834, 862. For Johnson's release of two Potawatomis who had killed two soldiers near Detroit in 1766, see Johnson, speech, July 24, 1766, in O'Callaghan, ed., *NYCD*, VII: 855–56. For another episode near Detroit in 1767, see Johnson to Gage, July 11, Aug. 6, and Aug. 21, 1767, in O'Callaghan, ed., *DHSNY*, II: 858, 861, 862; Guy Johnson, Indian Journal, Sept. 14, 1767, and George Croghan, speech, Nov. 22, 1767 ("we would"), *PSWJ*, XII: 364, XIII: 441. For a soldier murdered near Fort Erie, see John Brown to Johnson, Oct. 17 and 18, and Nov. 2 and 4, 1770; Johnson to Gage, Nov. 8, 1770; Gage to Johnson, Jan. 14, 1771; and Johnson to Gage, Jan. 31, 1771, *PSWJ*, VII: 942, 943, 985,

986–87, 994, 1076, 1117. For an episode near Detroit in late 1772, see Johnson to Gage, Jan. 1, 1773, Gage to Johnson, Mar. 31, 1773, Major Henry Bassett, speech, May 10, 1773, Sakikabowe, speech, May 12, 1773, and Bassett to Gen. Frederick Haldimand, June 14, 1773, *PSWJ*, VIII: 688, 749, 791–92, 795–96, 819–20.

69. John Tabor Kempe to Sir William Johnson, Aug. 12, 1765 ("wheresoever"), *PSWJ*, XI: 888.

70. Sir William Johnson to Thomas Gage, Oct. 31, 1764 ("necessary"), and Johnson to John Tabor Kempe, Sept. 7, 1765 ("I grant"), *PSWJ*, XI: 394, 925; Thomas Gage to Johnson, Oct. 7, 1772 ("As far"), William Leland Thompson Coll., Box 1, Albany Institute.

71. Sir William Johnson to Cadwallader Colden, Oct. 9 and Dec. 11, 1764, and Johnson to John Tabor Kempe, Nov. 6, 1765 ("Justice"), *PSWJ*, IV: 566, 615, 863–64; Johnson to Lords of Trade, Aug. 20, 1766, in O'Callaghan, ed., *NYCD*, VII: 852; John Watts to Johnson, Oct. 29, 1767, *PSWJ*, V: 768; Johnson to Lord Dartmouth, May 2, 1774, *PSWJ*, VIII: 1145.

72. Bonomi, *Factious People*, 188, 204–11.

73. Williams, *Linking Arms Together*, 16–17; New York Assembly, resolution, Oct. 5, 1764 ("impossible"), in "Letters and Papers of Cadwallader Colden," New-York Historical Society, *Collections . . . for the Year 1922* (New York: New-York Historical Society, 1923), 356–58.

74. Sutcliff, *Travels in Some Parts of North America*, 175 ("one large tree"); Shoemaker, *Strange Likeness*, 13–34; Tiro, "People of the Standing Stone," 47; Perkins, *Early Times on the Susquehanna*, 78; McMaster, *History of the Settlement of Steuben County*, 51; Dexter, ed., *Literary Diary of Ezra Stiles*, I: 162; Samuel Kirkland, diary, May 7, 1788, LFP, DCLSC; Campbell, ed., *Life and Writings of DeWitt Clinton*, 150, 173–74; Macauley, *Natural, Statistical, and Civil History of the State of New York*, II: 109, 114; Gray, ed., "From Fairfield to Schonburn—1798," 79–80; O'Callaghan, ed., *DHSNY*, III: 1040; Coventry, *Memoirs of an Emigrant*, I: 607, 740.

75. Lincoln, "Journal of a Treaty Held in 1793," 117; Wallace, ed., *Thirty Thousand Miles with John Heckewelder*, 299 ("a canoe"); Campbell, ed., *Life and Writings of De Witt Clinton*, 35; John Heckewelder to Samuel Miller, Feb. 26, 1801, Samuel Miller Papers, I, NYHS.

76. Smith, *Tour of Four Great Rivers*, 68 (all quotations); Smith, "Notes of a Tour," May 21, 30, and 31, and June 3, 1769, in Du Simitière MSS, LCP.

77. Johnson to Lords of Trade, Oct. 30, 1764 ("difficult matter"), in O'Callaghan, ed., *NYCD*, VII: 672.

78. For communal ownership of land, see John Tabor Kempe to Johnson, Aug. 12, 1765, *PSWJ*, XI: 889.

79. Warren Johnson, "Journal," 261; Dexter, ed., *Diary of David McClure*, 95 ("To destroy"). For the sharing of hunting and fishing territories with fictive kin, see Albers and Kay, "Sharing the Land," 47–91.

80. Sir William Johnson, Indian Journal, July 28, 1765 ("You should"), and Daniel Claus to Johnson, Aug. 30, 1765 ("common"), *PSWJ*, XI: 876, 918–19; Kahnawake chief (unnamed), speech, and Guy Johnson, reply, Sept. 17, 1773, MG 19 F 35, 1st Ser. (PSGIA), NAC.

81. Conoghquieson, speech, Mar. 4, 1768 ("When our"), in O'Callaghan, ed., *NYCD*, VIII: 38; Hamilton, ed., "Guy Johnson's Opinions," 326; Sir William Johnson, "Review of the Trade and Affairs of the Indians in the Northern District of America," Sept. 22, 1767, in O'Callaghan, ed., *NYCD*, VII: 959.

82. Sir William Johnson to Gen. Thomas Gage, Dec. 21, 1765 ("Grand Design"), *PSWJ*, XI: 983; Chief Hendrick, speech, July 5, 1754 ("Let us all"), quoted in Shannon, *Indians and Colonists*, 166.

83. Snyderman, "Concepts of Land Ownership," 28; Starna, "Aboriginal Title," 39–41.

84. Chicksagan, speech, Feb. 25, 1762, RG 10 (Indian Affairs), VI: 167, NAC; Sir William Johnson, "Journal to Detroit," July 16, 1761, *PSWJ*, XIII: 219; Gahswanyaroras, speech, Apr. 2, 1763,

RG 10 (Indian Affairs), IX: 316 (Reel C-1223), NAC; Johnson, "Indian Journal," n.d. March 1767 ("the Inhabitants"), *PSWJ*: XII: 288.

85. Schoolcraft, *Notes on the Iroquois*, 18 ("Adverse").

86. Conrad Weiser quoted in Merrell, *Into the American Woods*, 296 ("pay them" and "the Proprietors").

87. Sir William Johnson to Thomas Gage, Apr. 17, 1766, and Johnson to Goldsbrow Banyar, Sept. 22, 1766, and May 9, 1771 ("greater notions"), *PSWJ*, XII: 73, 192, 906; Johnson to Lord Adam Gordon, Feb. 18, 1771 ("The Indians"), William Leland Thompson Coll., Box 1, Albany Institute.

88. Cadwallader Colden to Lord Hillsborough, May 31, 1765, in "The Colden Letter Books," New-York Historical Society, *Collections for the Year 1877*, X (1878): 6; Abraham, speech, Apr. 9, 1767, in O'Callaghan, ed., *NYCD*, II: 847–48; Sir William Johnson to Goldsbrow Banyar, Apr. 27, 1767 ("If the Indians"), *PSWJ*, XII: 302.

89. Cadwallader Colden to Sir William Johnson, June 13, 1765, and Colden to Board of Trade, Dec. 6, 1765, in New-York Historical Society, *Collections*, X (1878): 21.

90. Sir William Johnson to William Denny, July 21, 1758 ("a solemn"), *PSWJ*, II: 879; Johnson to Lords of Trade, Nov. 13, 1763 ("encourage"), in O'Callaghan, ed., *NYCD*, VII: 578.

91. Anderson, *Crucible of War*, 565–71; Borrows, "Wampum at Niagara," 160; Royal Proclamation, Oct. 7, 1763, *PSWJ*, X: 981–84; Sir William Johnson to Thomas Gage, Dec. 23, 1763, *PSWJ*, X: 973.

92. Sir William Johnson to Thomas Gage, Apr. 1, 1767, Gage to Johnson, Sept. 21, 1767, and Johnson to Gage, Nov. 24, 1767, in O'Callaghan, ed., *DHSNY*, II: 844, 866, 886; Gage to Johnson, May 11, 1767, *PSWJ*, V: 548; Gage to Lord Sherburne, Jan. 22, 1768 ("the driving"), in Carter, ed., *Correspondence of General Thomas Gage*, I: 157.

93. Thomas King, speech, May 5, 1765 ("Let us"), Sir William Johnson to the Lords of Trade, Oct. 20, 1767, and Conoghquieson, speech, Mar. 8, 1768, in O'Callaghan, ed., *NYCD*, VII: 728, 987, VIII: 46; Johnson to Thomas Gage, Oct. 22, 1767, in O'Callaghan, ed., *DHSNY*, II: 881–82; Shoemaker, *Strange Likeness*, 35–60.

94. Sir William Johnson to Lords of Trade, Nov. 13, 1763 ("I can"), Johnson to Lords of Trade, May 24, 1765 ("large Tracts"), and Johnson, Indian Journal, May 2, 1765 ("Considerable"), in O'Callaghan, ed., *NYCD*, VII: 578, 717, 725; Thomas Penn to Johnson, Sept. 7, 1764, and Johnson, speech, Nov. 23, 1764, *PSWJ*, XI: 348, 481.

95. Thomas Gage to Lord Shelburne, June 13, 1767, and Jan. 22, 1768, in Carter, ed., *Correspondence of General Thomas Gage*, I: 142, 157; Gage to Sir William Johnson, Nov. 9, 1767 ("the new Lands"), May 8, 1768, and Apr. 3, 1769 ("I am"), *PSWJ*, XII: 376, 494, 709–10.

96. Sir William Johnson to Thomas Gage, Apr. 8, 1768, *PSWJ*, VI: 184–85. For Johnson's interest in the Carrying Place, see Johnson to Lord Adam Gordon, Apr. 4, 1769, *PSWJ*, XII: 711. For Johnson's allies among the land speculators, see Marshall, "Sir William Johnson and the Treaty of Fort Stanwix," 159–60, 169–71; Johnson to Baynton, Wharton & Morgan, Jan. 30, 1766, and George Croghan to Benjamin Franklin, Feb. 25, 1766, *PSWJ*, V: 16, 38–39; Johnson to Lords of Trade, Jan. 31, 1766, in O'Callaghan, ed., *NYCD*, VII: 809.

97. Lord Shelburne to Sir William Johnson, Jan. 5, 1768 ("without"), Lord Hillsborough to Sir Henry Moore, Feb. 25, 1768 ("finally settled"), and Lords of Trade, Report to the King, Mar. 7, 1768, in O'Callaghan, ed., *NYCD*, VIII: 2, 11, 20–23; Sosin, *Whitehall and the Wilderness*, 163–64, 169–70; Billington, "The Fort Stanwix Treaty of 1768," 183; Marshall, "Sir William Johnson and the Treaty," 166.

98. Sir William Johnson, Fort Stanwix Council Proceedings, Sept. 19–21 and Oct. 28 and 30, 1768, in O'Callaghan, ed., *NYCD*, VIII: 112, 120, 123; Indian Journal, Oct. 24, 1768, *PSWJ*, XII:

628; Johnson to Thomas Gage, Nov. 24, 1768, in O'Callaghan, ed., *DHSNY*, IV: 397; Johnson, Account Against the Crown, Dec. 9, 1768 ("Private presents"), *PSWJ*, XII: 665–68.

99. Sir William Johnson, speech, Oct. 28, 1768 ("I expect"), Fort Stanwix Council Proceedings, in O'Callaghan, ed., *NYCD*, VIII: 121; Sir William Johnson to Thomas Gage, Nov. 24, 1768 ("difficulties"), in O'Callaghan, ed., *DHSNY*, IV: 397.

100. Sir William Johnson to Sir Henry Moore, Aug. 17, 1768, in O'Callaghan, ed., *NYCD*, VIII: 92–93; Johnson to Goldsbrow Banyar, Mar. 21 and Sept. 4, 1769, *PSWJ*, XII: 707–8, 751.

101. Fort Stanwix Council Proceedings, Oct. 31, 1768, in O'Callaghan, ed., *NYCD*, VIII: 124–25; Sir William Johnson to Goldsbrow Banyar, Nov. 24, 1768, *PSWJ*, XII: 656–59.

102. Sir William Johnson to Lord Hillsborough, Nov. 18, 1768, and Fort Stanwix Council Proceedings, Oct. 31, 1768, in O'Callaghan, ed., *NYCD*, VIII: 110, 124–25; Johnson to Goldsbrow Banyar, Nov. 24, 1768 ("the Utmost" and "do assure"), and Jan. 5, 1769, *PSWJ*, XII: 656–59, 684–85; Johnson, "Account Against the Crown, Dec. 9, 1768, *PSWJ*, XII: 665–68.

103. Fort Stanwix Council Proceedings, Oct. 28, 1768, in O'Callaghan, ed., *NYCD*, VIII: 121–22.

104. Fort Stanwix Council Proceedings, Oct. 31, 1768, in O'Callaghan, ed., *NYCD*, VIII: 125–26; Billington, "Fort Stanwix Treaty," 189–93.

105. Fort Stanwix Council Proceedings, Nov. 1 and 4, 1768, in O'Callaghan, ed., *NYCD*, VIII: 127, 130.

106. Fort Stanwix Council Proceedings, Oct. 31 and Nov. 5–6, 1768, in O'Callaghan, ed., *NYCD*, VIII: 125–26, 133–37; Samuel Wharton to Benjamin Franklin, Dec. 2, 1768 ("the greatest"), in Labaree et al., eds., *Papers of Benjamin Franklin*, XV: 277; Ebenezer Cleaveland to Eleazar Wheelock, Nov. 21, 1768, EWP #768568.1, DCA.

107. Sir William Johnson to the Lords of Trade, Nov. 13, 1763, in O'Callaghan, ed., *NYCD*, VII: 572–75; Johnson to Thomas Gage, May 17, 1764, *PSWJ*: XI, 195; Johnson to Lord Dartmouth, Apr. 22, 1773, in O'Callaghan, ed., *NYCD*, VIII: 361–62.

108. Sir William Johnson to Thomas Gage, Aug. 30, 1769, Johnson to Thomas Wharton, Sept. 12, 1769, and Johnson to George Croghan, May 11, 1770, *PSWJ*, VII: 150–51, 167, 655; White, *The Middle Ground*, 351–53; Heckewelder, *History, Manners, and Customs of the Indian Nations*, 83–84; Gage to Johnson, Aug. 20 and 27, 1769, Alexander McKee to Johnson, Sept. 18, 1769, George Croghan to Johnson, Dec. 22, 1769, and Red Hawk, speech, n.d. [ca. Feb. 1770], *PSWJ*, VII: 107–8, 140, 184–85, 315–17, 407; Johnson, speech, July 22, 1770, in O'Callaghan, ed., *NYCD*, VIII: 236.

CHAPTER TWO: PATRONS

1. Wheelock, *Plain and Faithful Narrative* (1763), 40–41 ("*Indian*-fashion"); Patrick, "Life and Times of Samuel Kirkland," 4–9; Pilkington, ed., *Journals of Samuel Kirkland*, xv; Eleazar Wheelock to Sir William Johnson, Nov. 2, 1761 ("Worthy Minister"), *PSWJ*, III: 557.

2. Patrick, "Life and Times of Samuel Kirkland," 4–9, 12–13, 18–19, 23; Pilkington, ed., *Journals of Samuel Kirkland*, xv–xvii; Samuel Kirkland to John Kemp, Mar. 16, 1790 ("I contracted"), LFP, DCLSC; Eleazar Wheelock to George Whitefield, July 4, 1761, EWP #761404, DCLSC; William Whitwell and William Dawes to Wheelock, Nov. 9, 1761, EWP #761609.2, DCLSC.

3. Samuel Kirkland to Eleazar Wheelock, Oct. 25, 1760 [actually 1761] ("had relied"), and Jan. 20 and Apr. 27, 1763, EWP #760900.4, #763120.1, and #763277, DCLSC; Patrick, "Life and Times of Samuel Kirkland," 52.

4. Dexter, ed., *Literary Diary of Ezra Stiles*, II: 338 ("He had").

5. Hamilton, "Sir William Johnson's Wives," 24–26; Hamilton, *Sir William Johnson*, 33–34; Barbara Graymont, "Konwatsitsiaienni," *DCB*, IV (1771 to 1800): 416–17; Lord Adam Gordon to Sir William Johnson, July 2, 1765, *PSWJ*, XIII: 375; Stone, *Life and Times of Sir William Johnson*, II: 492–97.

6. Hamilton, "Sir William Johnson's Wives," 22–25; Hamilton, *Sir William Johnson*, 33–34; Kelsay, *Joseph Brant*, 52–53, 68–69; *PSWJ*, XII: 966n3; Graymont, "Konwatsitsiaienni," *DCB*, IV (1771 to 1800), 416–18 (colonist quoted, "daughter to" on 417); Tilghman, ed., *Memoir of Lieut. Col. Tench Tilghman*, 83 ("As she is").

7. Kelsay, *Joseph Brant*, 38–70; Klinck and Talman, eds., *Journal of Major John Norton*, 271; Wheelock, "A List of Charity Scholars," 1754–1765, EWP #765690, DCLSC.

8. Wheelock, "To the People of God in England, Scotland, & Ireland," Nov. 15, 1765, in Richardson, ed., *Indian Preacher in England*, 66 ("brutal Creation" and "Scourge and Terror"); McClure and Parish, *Memoirs of the Rev. Eleazar Wheelock*, 29–30; Wheelock, *Plain and Faithful Narrative* (1763), 10–11 ("Covenant-People"), 14. Although Wheelock dismissed Indian culture as devoid of science, he consulted "a doctor sqwaw" to relieve a sick daughter; and he sought Indian medicines to ease his wife in childbirth. See McCallum, *Eleazar Wheelock*, 18–19, 73.

9. McCallum, ed., *Letters of Eleazar Wheelock's Indians*, 16; McClure and Parish, *Memoirs of the Rev. Eleazar Wheelock*, 23; O'Brien, " 'Divorced' from the Land," 144–61.

10. Axtell, *Invasion Within*, 204–15; Sweet, *Bodies Politic*, 42–43, 53, 110, 116–18, 317–18.

11. Eleazar Wheelock to George Whitefield, July 4, 1761, EWP #761404, DCLSC; Wheelock to Sir William Johnson, May 27, 1761, and June n.d., 1761 ("the influence"), *PSWJ*, X: 272, 309. For the Warren Fund, see McCallum, *Eleazar Wheelock*, 143.

12. Klingberg, *Anglican Humanitarianism*, 79, 83, 101; Sir William Johnson to Lords of Trade, May 17, 1759, in O'Callaghan, ed., *DHSNY*, II: 783; Johnson to Jeffrey Amherst, Feb. 12, 1761 ("Ministers"), Daniel Claus to Johnson, May 24, 1761, Johnson to William Smith, et al., Dec. 9, 1761, and Johnson to Daniel Burton, Oct. 8, 1766, *PSWJ*, III: 330, 394, 585, V: 389.

13. Eleazar Wheelock to Sir William Johnson, Nov. 2, 1761 ("Joseph appears"), *PSWJ*, III: 556; Wheelock to George Whitefield, Mar. 5, 1763, EWP #763205.2, DCLSC; Wheelock, *Plain and Faithful Narrative*, 40–41; Wheelock to Rev. Andrew Gifford, Feb. 24, 1763 ("Sprightly Genius"), and (for Brant's gratitude) Joseph Johnson to Wheelock, Oct. 17, 1774, in McCallum, ed., *Letters of Eleazar Wheelock's Indians*, 70, 179. For the dispute over the costs charged for Brant, see McCallum, *Eleazar Wheelock*, 150; Wheelock, *Plain and Faithful Narrative*, 42–44.

14. Sir William Johnson to Eleazar Wheelock, Nov. 17, 1761, and Wheelock to Johnson, Oct. 24, 1764, in O'Callaghan, ed., *DHSNY*, IV: 305–6, 342; Wheelock to Andrew Oliver, Nov. 30, 1761 ("General Johnson"), EWP #761630.2, DCLSC; Wheelock, *Plain and Faithful Narrative*, 44; Johnson, speech, Jan. 28, 1762, RG 10 (Indian Affairs), VI: 153, NAC; Johnson to Wheelock, July 21, 1762, *PSWJ*, III: 832; McCallum, *Eleazar Wheelock*, 143, 147.

15. Eleazar Wheelock to Sir William Johnson, June 27, 1762, and Henry Barclay to Johnson, Oct. 5, 1763, *PSWJ*, X: 468–70 and XIII: 300; Charles Jeffery Smith to Johnson, Jan. 18, 1763, and Wheelock to Johnson, May 16, 1763, in O'Callaghan, ed., *DHSNY*, IV: 325–26, 330; Wheelock to Andrew Gifford, Feb. 24, 1763, in McCallum, ed., *Letters of Eleazar Wheelock's Indians*, 70; Kelsay, *Joseph Brant*, 83–85, 88–91.

16. Henry Barclay to Sir William Johnson, Oct. 5, 1763 ("when he can"), *PSWJ*, XIII: 300; Johnson to Barclay, Nov. 24, 1763, *PSWJ*, X: 935.

17. Kelsay, *Joseph Brant*, 96–102; Thomas Foster to Eleazar Wheelock, Feb. 17, 1764, EWP #764167, DCLSC; Wheelock to Sir William Johnson, Mar. 14, 1764, and Johnson to Wheelock, Apr. 25, 1764, *PSWJ*: XI, 102, 161; Wheelock to Johnson, Mar. 26, 1764 ("joyn'd himself"),

PSWJ, IV: 379–80; Robert Clelland to Wheelock, Sept. 15, 1763, EWP #763515, and William Gaylord to Wheelock, Sept. 18, 1763, EWP #763518, DCLSC.

18. Kelsay, *Joseph Brant*, 117–18; Joseph Johnson to Eleazar Wheelock, Oct. 17, 1774, in McCallum, ed., *Letters of Eleazar Wheelock's Indians*, 179.

19. Kelsay, *Joseph Brant*, 99–100, 109–10; Theophilus Chamberlain to Wheelock, July 29, 1765 ("handsome"), EWP #765429.1, DCLSC. For Isaac Dekayenensere, see Calloway, *American Revolution in Indian Country*, 112, 114–17; Smith, *Tour of Four Great Rivers*, 68. Barbara Graymont initially favored the alternative theory that Margaret and Susanna were the daughters of Skenandon, an Oneida chief, but Graymont later embraced Isaac Dekayenensere as the father. See Graymont, *Iroquois in the American Revolution*, 53; Graymont, "Joseph Brant," *DCB*, V: 804. Perhaps Skenandon was their grandfather or great-uncle.

20. Kelsay, *Joseph Brant*, 113–17, 122–23; Smith, *Tour of Four Great Rivers*, 60 (all quotations), 68–69, 84.

21. Eleazar Wheelock to "Mr. Kirtland's Benefactors," Oct. 13, 1762, EWP #762563.1, DCLSC; Patrick, "Life and Times of Samuel Kirkland," 29–33; Thorp, *Lives of Eighteen from Princeton*, 24–26; Pilkington, ed., *Journals of Samuel Kirkland*, xvii; John Brainerd to Wheelock, Mar. 31, 1764 ("very pretty"), in Thomas Brainerd, *Life of John Brainerd*, 343.

22. Patrick, "Life and Times of Samuel Kirkland," 33–34, 51–52; McLachlan, *Princetonians, 1748–1768*, 504; Kirkland to Eleazar Wheelock, Jan. 1, 1765 ("before"), in Wheelock, *Brief Narrative of the Indian Charity-School* (1767), 34; Pilkington, ed., *Journals of Samuel Kirkland*, 3–5, 43n2.

23. Pilkington, ed., *Journals of Samuel Kirkland*, 3–4.

24. Pilkington, ed., *Journals of Samuel Kirkland*, 5, 7–14, 22–36 (Johnson quoted: "Good God!" on 35), 37–39, 316; Patrick, "Life and Times of Samuel Kirkland," 60–64, 74–82; Eleazar Wheelock to George Whitefield, July 8, 1766, EWP #766408, DCLSC; Samson Occom to Wheelock, Dec. 6, 1765, in Richardson, ed., *Indian Preacher in England*, 75–76.

25. Patrick, "Life and Times of Samuel Kirkland," 82–88; Samuel Kirkland to Sir William Johnson, June 17, 1765 ("treat me"), in O'Callaghan, ed., *DHSNY*, IV: 358–59; Kirkland to Eleazar Wheelock, June 10, 1765, EWP #765360.3, DCLSC; Kirkland to Wheelock, Mar. 6, 1766, EWP #766206 ("God has"), DCLSC; David Fowler to Wheelock, Jan. 21, 1766, in McCallum, ed., *Letters of Eleazar Wheelock's Indians*, 100; Kirkland to Johnson, Feb. 21, 1766 ("They imagine"), *PSWJ*, XII: 26–27. For Iroquois dualism, see also Ralph Wheelock, journal, Mar. 31, 1768, EWP #768290, DCLSC.

26. Wheelock to John Smith, Mar. 19 and Aug. 16, 1765, and Wheelock to Kirkland, Mar. 7, 1766 ("Now is"), EWP #765219.4, #765466, and #766207.2, DCLSC; Wheelock, *A Continuation of the Narrative* (1765), 17 ("Mr. Kirtland"); Patrick, "Life and Times of Samuel Kirkland," 94–95.

27. Pilkington, ed., *Journals of Samuel Kirkland*, 40; Patrick, "Life and Times of Samuel Kirkland," 105–10; Eleazar Wheelock to George Whitefield, July 8, 1766, EWP #766408, DCLSC.

28. Beauchamp, *Aboriginal Place Names of New York*, 137, 139; Pilkington, ed., *Journals of Samuel Kirkland*, 44n24, 45n26; Tiro, "People of the Standing Stone," 39; Campisi, "Oneida," 481; Guy Johnson, Indian Journal, Nov. 30–Dec. 1, 1752, *PSWJ*, X: 584–87.

29. Patrick, "Life and Times of Samuel Kirkland," 109–10; Dexter, ed., *Diary of David McClure*, 12–13; Campisi, "Fur Trade and Factionalism," 38–39.

30. Tiro, "People of the Standing Stone," 38–39; Samuel Kirkland to unknown, Aug. 22, 1768 ("was treated"), SKP, Folder 3, HCA; Dexter, ed., *Diary of David McClure*, 16; Aaron Kinne to Eleazar Wheelock, June 13, 1768, and Thomas Huntington, journal, n.d. [ca. June 1769], EWP #768363.1 and #769390.1, DCLSC; Kirkland to Sir William Johnson, May 25, 1769,

and Johnson, Indian Journal, Aug. 10, 1770, *PSWJ*, VI: 774, XII: 836–37; Indian critics quoted in Kirkland to Andrew Oliver, Nov. 12, 1770 ("white people's"), SKP, Folder 12, HCA.

31. Pilkington, ed., *Journals of Samuel Kirkland*, 61–62 ("Their relations" and "flocked in"), 66 ("Constantly"), 69.

32. Samuel Kirkland quoted ("I have lain") in William De Loss Love, Jr., "An Account of the Christian Indians Who Were Associated with Rev. Samuel Kirkland in His Indian Missions," 28–29, HCA; Kirkland to David McClure, Dec. 2, 1766, in Willard Thorp, *Lives of Eighteen*, 34; Murray, ed., "*To Do Good to My Indian Brethren*," 62; Kirkland quoted in McLaclan, ed., *Princetonians, 1748–1768*, 504–5 ("seldom"); Kirkland to unknown, Aug. 22, 1768, SKP, Folder 3, HCA.

33. Samuel Kirkland to unknown, Aug. 22, 1768 ("such as"), SKP, Folder 3, HCA; Kirkland to Eleazar Wheelock, Feb. 15, 1770 ("from the Conduct"), SKP, Folder 6, HCA; Kirkland to Wheelock, Oct. 16, 1770, and Kirkland to John Thornton, Oct. 31, 1770, in SKP, Folder 11, HCA; Pilkington, ed., *Journals of Samuel Kirkland*, 71 (Oneidas quoted: "You are sent"); Kirkland to John Rodgers, June 4, 1771, SKP, Folder 19, HCA; Kirkland, "An Account of Some Extraordinary Charges," Oct. 6, 1770–Sep. 16, 1771, SKP, Folder 21, HCA; Kirkland to Thornton, June 5, 1773, SKP, Folder 42, HCA.

34. Samuel Kirkland to Andrew Eliot, Aug. 3, 1772 ("My house"), LFP, DCLSC; Patrick, "Life and Times of Samuel Kirkland," 217–18.

35. Oneidas quoted in Patrick, "Life and Times of Samuel Kirkland," 113–14 ("It is contrary"); Eleazar Wheelock to Nathaniel Whitaker, April. 16, 1767, in McClure and Parish, *Memoirs of the Rev. Eleazar Wheelock*, 274–75; Tiro, "People of the Standing Stone," 43.

36. Dexter, ed., *Diary of David McClure*, 13–14; Eleazar Wheelock to Nathaniel Whitaker, Apr. 16, 1767 ("This is" and "under Mr. Kirtland"), in McClure and Parish, *Memoirs of the Rev. Eleazar Wheelock*, 274; Joseph Johnson to Wheelock, Feb. 10, 1768, in McCallum, ed., *Letters of Wheelock's Indians*, 128–29; Thomas Huntington, journal, n.d. [ca. June 1769] ("I think"), EWP #769390.1 and #769359, DCLSC.

37. Samuel Kirkland to Eleazar Wheelock, Feb. 15, 1770, SKP, Folder 6, HCA; Kirkland to Wheelock, Oct. 16, 1770, SKP, Folder 11, HCA; Kirkland to Levi Hart, Jan. 17, 1771 ("would afford"), SKP, Folder 14, HCA.

38. Patrick, "Life and Times of Samuel Kirkland," 118–22, 126–28; Pilkington, ed., *Journals of Samuel Kirkland*, 100; Kirkland, sermon, July 1, 1773 ("total"), SKP, Sermons Folder, HCA.

39. Pilkington, ed., *Journals of Samuel Kirkland*, 61–62, 66 ("Every little" and "The Lord"), 69–70, 103; Patrick, "Life and Times of Samuel Kirkland," 123–24.

40. Samuel Kirkland, sermon, July 1, 1773 ("among" and "noble joy"), SKP, Sermons Folder, HCA.

41. Connecticut Board of Correspondents, minutes, July 1, 1767, and Hezekiah Calvin to Eleazar Wheelock, Jan. 29, 1768, in McCallum, ed., *Letters of Wheelock's Indians*, 45, 61–62; Richardson, *History of Dartmouth College*, I: 69–71; Wheelock, "A List of Charity Scholars," 1754–1765, and Wheelock to Whitaker, Nov. 15, 1766, EWP #765690 and #766615.1, DCLSC.

42. Eleazar Wheelock, "A List of Charity Scholars," 1754–1765, and Wheelock to Nathaniel Whitaker, Feb. 13, 1767 ("so lifted up"), EWP #765690, and #767163, DCLSC; McCallum, *Eleazar Wheelock*, 134–37; Axtell, *Invasion Within*, 207. Because Wheelock kept such poor records on his female students, and primarily treated them as domestic servants, I have not included them in the assessment.

43. Wheelock, *Continuation of the Narrative* (1771), 21; Wheelock to Nathaniel Whitaker, June 24, 1767, and Wheelock to Robert Keen, May 31, 1768, in Richardson, ed., *An Indian Preacher in*

England, 270, 339; Wheelock to Sarah Simon, June 27, 1768, in McCallum, ed., *Letters of Wheelock's Indians*, 226.

44. Sir William Johnson to Henry Barclay, Mar. 30, 1763 ("greatest Distortion"), *PSWJ*, IV: 73; Johnson to Thomas Barton, Dec. 2, 1766, *PSWJ*, V: 435–36; Johnson, "Review of the Trade and Affairs of the Indians in the Northern District of America," Sept. 22, 1767 ("generally appear" and "well-meaning"), in O'Callaghan, ed., *NYCD*, VII: 969–70.

45. Eleazar Wheelock to Samuel Adams, May 25, 1767, EWP #767325, DCLSC; Sir William Johnson to Henry Barclay, Mar. 30, 1763, *PSWJ*, IV: 73; Johnson to Samuel Auchmuty, Apr. 26, 1770, and Johnson to Charles Inglis, Sept. 4, 1770, *PSWJ*: VII; 584–85, 876; Johnson to Henry S. Conway, July 10, 1766, and Johnson to Daniel Burton, Oct. 8, 1766 ("the Members"), *PSWJ*, V: 325, 388; Upton, *Loyal Whig*, 62–63.

46. Guzzardo, "Superintendent and the Ministers," 255–56.

47. Eleazar Wheelock to Marquis of Lothian, July 7, 1763 ("The Savages"), EWP #763407.1, DCLSC; Wheelock, "Address to the Sachems and Chiefs of the Mohawk, Oneida, Tuscarora, and other Nations and Tribes of Indians," Apr. 29, 1765 ("This earth"), in O'Callaghan, ed., *DHSNY*, IV: 355.

48. Shoemaker, *Strange Likeness*, 105–24; Captain Onoonghwadekha, quoted in Pilkington, ed., *Journals of Samuel Kirkland*, 24 ("We shall").

49. Sir William Johnson to Daniel Burton, Oct. 8, 1766, Johnson to Samuel Johnson, Dec. 2, 1766, William Smith to Johnson, Mar. 16, 1767, and Johnson to William Smith, Apr. 10, 1767 ("As Hunters"), *PSWJ*, V: 389, 439, 511–12, 529–30; Johnson, "Review of the Trade and Affairs of the Indians in the Northern District of America," Sept. 22, 1767, in O'Callaghan, ed., *NYCD*, VII: 970; Johnson to Charlies Inglis, Nov. n.d., 1770, in O'Callaghan, ed., *NYCD*, IV: 428; Johnson to Arthur Lee, Mar. 28, 1772, *PSWJ*, XII: 951; Johnson to Charles Inglis, Apr. 26, 1770, *PSWJ*: VII, 599–600.

50. Sir William Johnson, "Review of the Trade and Affairs of the Indians in the Northern District of America," Sept. 22, 1767 ("design"), in O'Callaghan, ed., *NYCD*, VII: 970.

51. Eleazar Wheelock to Sir Jeffrey Amherst, Apr. 2, 1763, in O'Callaghan, ed., *DHSNY*: IV, 328; Wheelock, "A Plan for Introducing Religion, Learning, Agriculture, and Manufactures Among the Savages in America," July 7, 1763 ("such as Love" and "large farm"), EWP #763407.2, DCLSC.

52. Sir William Johnson to Samuel Auchmuty, Apr. 26, 1769, and Daniel Burton to Johnson, May 8, 1769, *PSWJ*, VI: 710, 746; Auchmuty to Johnson, June 5, 1769, Johnson to Auchmuty, Sept. 14, 1769, Johnson to Burton, Dec. 6, 1769, Johnson to Auchmuty, Apr. 15, 1770, Burton to Johnson, May 21, 1770, Johnson to Harry Munro, June 8, 1770, Daniel Burton to Johnson, Aug. 17, 1770, and Munro to Burton, Sept. 25, 1770, *PSWJ*, VII: 2–3, 169, 290–91, 543, 693, 720, 841, 962n2; Johnson to Thomas Barton, Feb. 28, 1771, and Henry Babcock to Miles Cooper, Aug. 11, 1773 ("brown Ladies"), in O'Callaghan, ed., *DHSNY*, IV: 438, 489; Johnson to Richard Hind, Nov. 25, 1773, *PSWJ*, VIII: 927–28.

53. McCallum, *Eleazar Wheelock*, 164; William Samuel Johnson to Dr. Benjamin Gale, July 31, 1767, in Boyd, ed., *Susquehannah Company Papers*, II: 320. Expenses reduced the net take to about £11,000.

54. Wheelock, *Continuation of the Narrative* (1771), 18–21, 27; McCallum, *Eleazar Wheelock*, 24, 176–80, 190–91.

55. McCallum, *Eleazar Wheelock*, 172–75, 194; McClure and Parish, eds., *Memoirs of the Rev. Eleazar Wheelock*, 48–51; Nathaniel Whitaker to Wheelock, Sept. 8, 1770, EWP #770508, DCLSC; Matthew Graves to Samuel Lloyd, Aug. 5, 1770 ("all a farce"), EWP #770455,

DCLSC; Chase, *History of Dartmouth College*, I: 238–44, 557–58; Wheelock, *Continuation of the Narrative* (1773), 20–27; Wheelock, *Continuation of the Narrative* (1775), 21–26.

56. David McClure to Wheelock, May 21, 1770, in Richardson, ed., *Indian Preacher in England*, 354–55; Samson Occom to Wheelock, July 24, 1771 ("I think," and "Indian Buck"), EWP #771424, DCLSC; Blodgett, *Samson Occom*, 135.

57. Richardson, *History of Dartmouth College*, 69; Robert Keen to Wheelock, Sept. 14, 1767 ("received"), in Richardson, ed., *Indian Preacher in England*, 297.

58. Eleazar Wheelock to Nathaniel Whitaker, Nov. 28, 1767 ("high Spirits"), in Richardson, ed., *Indian Preacher in England*, 321; McCallum, *Eleazar Wheelock*, 126; Pilkington, ed., *Journals of Samuel Kirkland*, 41; Richardson, *History of Dartmouth College*, 72; Dexter, ed., *The Literary Diary of Ezra Stiles*, I: 90: "Mr. Kirtland & Mr. Ralph Wheelock, Son of the Doctor, were at College together & there had a Difference."

59. Richardson, *History of Dartmouth College*, I: 71–72; McCallum, *Eleazar Wheelock*, 127–29; Ralph Wheelock quoted in Deacon Thomas, speech, June 5, 1772 ("Who do" and "the head"), in McCallum, ed., *Letters of Eleazar Wheelock's Indians*, 284–87.

60. Wheelock, *Continuation of the Narrative* (1771), 15–18; Eleazar Wheelock to Samuel Kirkland, Feb. 24, 1769, and Wheelock to George Whitefield, Apr. 24, 1769, EWP #769174.3 and #769274.2, DCLSC; McCallum, *Eleazar Wheelock*, 129–30; Kirkland to Andrew Elliot, Aug. 11, 1772, SKP, Folder 32, HCA.

61. Samuel Kirkland to Eleazar Wheelock, Feb. 15, 1770, SKP, Folder 6, HCA; Patrick, "Life and Times of Samuel Kirkland," 199–206, 213; Dexter, ed., *Literary Diary of Ezra Stiles*, I: 90; Kirkland to John Rodgers, June 4, 1771, SKP, Folder 19, HCA.

62. Samuel Kirkland to Eleazar Wheelock, Feb. 15, 1770, SKP, Folder 6, HCA; Patrick, "Life and Times of Samuel Kirkland," 204–6, 218–21; Wheelock to Kirkland, Feb. 24, 1769 ("I think"), and May 15, 1769, EWP #769174.3 and #769315, DCLSC.

63. Patrick, "Life and Times of Samuel Kirkland," 138–42, Kirkland quoted on 140 ("with nothing"); Kirkland to Andrew Elliot, Aug. 11, 1772, SKP, Folder 32, HCA.

64. Nathaniel Whitaker to Eleazar Wheelock, Aug. 28 and Oct. 16, 1769, and Charles Jeffrey Smith to Wheelock, Nov. 12, 1769 ("He is"), EWP #769478.2, #769566, and #769612, DCLSC.

65. Dexter, ed., *Diary of David McClure*, 22–23; Pilkington, ed., *Journals of Samuel Kirkland*, 88n13; Samuel Kirkland to Andrew Oliver, Oct. 4, 1770, and Kirkland to Eleazar Wheelock, Oct. 9, 1770, EWP #770554, #770559, DCLSC; Boston Board Meeting Minutes, Oct. 4, 1770, HGWAIP, Box 1, HUA; Kirkland to John Rodgers, June 4, 1771, SKP, Folder 19, HCA.

66. Samuel Kirkland to David McClure, Apr. 24, 1770 ("Honored Patron"), Kirkland and Wheelock, memorandum of understanding, Oct. 30, 1771, and Kirkland to Thornton, July 27, 1772 ("My refusing"), and Sept. 29, 1772, SKP, Folders 8, 22, 31, and 33, HCA.

67. Samuel Kirkland to Sir William Johnson, Feb. 21, 1766, #12875, NYSL; Records of St. Patrick's Lodge, I: 9, 25, copy in Milton Hamilton Papers, Box 3, Albany Institute; Charles Inglis to Daniel Burton, June 15, 1770, *PSWJ*, VII: 748.

68. Samuel Kirkland to Andrew Oliver, Nov. 12, 1770, Kirkland to John Thornton, June 5, 1773, and Kirkland to Oliver, Aug. 30, 1773, SKP, Folders 12 and 43, HCA; Pilkington, ed., *Journals of Samuel Kirkland*, 82–84 and 93; Guzzardo, "The Superintendent and the Ministers," 271–74; Oneida petition to Lord Dunmore, Dec. 31, 1770, *PSWJ*, XIII: 498–99; Dunmore to Lord Hillsborough, Mar. 9, 1771, in O'Callaghan, ed., *NYCD*, VIII: 265; Sir William Johnson to Dunmore, Mar. 16, 1771, *PSWJ*, VIII: 30.

69. Sir William Johnson quoted in Pilkington, ed., *Journals of Samuel Kirkland*, 67 ("much better"); Guzzardo, "The Superintendent and the Ministers," 273–75.

70. Sir William Johnson to Thomas Hutchinson, Aug. 21, 1771 ("missionary" and "Countenance"), *PSWJ*, VIII: 229–31; Guzzardo, "The Superintendent and the Ministers," 277; Samuel Kirkland to Andrew Eliot, Nov. 19, 1771, SKP, Folder 23, HCA.

71. Joseph Johnson to Eleazar Wheelock, May 2, 1768, in McCallum, ed., *Letters of Eleazar Wheelock's Indians*, 131; Tiro, "People of the Standing Stone," 91–95; Edward Wall to Sir William Johnson, May 16, 1771, *PSWJ*, VIII: 105; Pilkington, ed., *Journals of Samuel Kirkland*, 67–68.

72. Oneida Chiefs, speech, June 5, 1772, in McCallum, ed., *Letters of Eleazar Wheelock's Indians*, 131, 282; Pilkington, ed., *Journals of Samuel Kirkland*, 74–75 (Tagawaron quoted: "We don't think"), 77; David Avery, sermon, June 27, 1772, Samuel Kirkland to John Rodgers, June 20, 1772, Kirkland to Jerusha Kirkland, July 10, 1772 ("Religion"), and Kirkland to John Thornton, July 27, 1772, SKP, Folders 30–31, HCA.

73. Pilkington, ed., *Journals of Samuel Kirkland*, 93–94 ("the attention" and "generally practised").

74. Samuel Kirkland to John Thornton, June 5, 1773, and Kirkland to Andrew Oliver, Aug. 30, 1773, SKP, Folder 43, HCA; Pilkington, ed., *Journals of Samuel Kirkland*, 82–84.

75. Samuel Kirkland to John Thornton, June 5, 1773, SKP, Folder 42, HCA; Samuel Dunlap to the Boston Board, July 2, 1773 ("ravishing"), SKP, Folder 43, HCA; Pilkington, ed., *Journals of Samuel Kirkland*, 83–84, 93; Kirkland to Andrew Eliot, Nov. 19, 1773, Feb. 18 ("Things") and Apr. 24, 1774 ("The Cause"), SKP, Folders 45, 48, and 49, HCA; Samson Occom, diary, July 24, 1774 ("hopeful Prospect"), in Blodgett, *Samson Occom*, 155.

76. Samuel Kirkland to Andrew Eliot, Nov. 19, 1773 ("*scalp*"), and June 13, 1774, SKP, Folders 45 and 50, HCA; Pilkington, ed., *Journals of Samuel Kirkland*, 93.

77. Nammack, *Fraud, Politics, and the Dispossession of the Indians*, 23–24; Kelsay, *Joseph Brant*, 77–78, 123; Albany corporation, speech, Dec. 21, 1773, *PSWJ*, VIII: 955–59 (see also 936n2); Sir William Johnson to Sir Henry Moore, Aug. 5, 1768, and Johnson to John Bradstreet, Dec. 7, 1768, *PSWJ*, VI: 310, 520; Guy Johnson to Sir William Johnson, Mar. 2, 1772, and Feb. 2 and 10, 1773, Peter Silvester to Sir William Johnson, Mar. 22, 1773, Stephen DeLancey to Johnson, Dec. 4, 1773, and Albany Corporation, speech, Dec. 21, 1773, *PSWJ*, VIII: 410–11, 703, 710, 741, 936–37, 955–60; William Tryon to Lord Hillsborough, Aug. 31, 1772, and Johnson Hall Council Minutes, July 28, 1772, in O'Callaghan, ed., *NYCD*, VIII: 303, 306; Sabine, ed., *Historical Memoirs . . . of William Smith*, 139.

78. Sir William Johnson to Goldsbrow Banyar, Jan. 7 and Mar. 13, 1762, ("most troublesome") *PSWJ*, III: 603–4, 647.

79. Joseph [Brant], speech, July 28, 1772, and Sir William Johnson to Lord Dartmouth, Dec. 16, 1773, in O'Callaghan, ed., *NYCD*, VIII: 304–5; Kelsay, *Joseph Brant*, 136–37; Johnson to John Blackburn, May 27, 1774, *PSWJ*, VIII: 1160; George Klock, deposition, July 8, 1774 ("They said"), in Brant Papers, II: 53, Lyman C. Draper Coll., Wisconsin State Historical Society, Madison; Tekarihoga, speech, July 11, 1774, in O'Callaghan, ed., *DHSNY*, II: 1004–5; Guy Johnson to Cadwallader Colden, Aug. 2, 1774, *PSWJ*, VIII: 1192–93.

80. Graymont, *Iroquois in the American Revolution*, 49; Johnson Hall, Council Minutes, July 8, 1774, and Serihowane, speech, July 9, 1774 ("We are sorry" and "If this"), in O'Callaghan, ed., *NYCD*, VIII: 474–76.

81. Sir William Johnson, speeches, July 9 and 11, 1774, in O'Callaghan, ed., *NYCD*, VIII: 477–78.

82. Tekarihoga, speech, July 11, 1774 ("with pain"), in O'Callaghan, ed., *NYCD*, VIII: 478; Guy Johnson to Thomas Gage, Sept. 8, 1774 ("even those Nations"), *PSWJ*, XIII: 677.

83. Johnson Hall Council Minutes, July 11, 1774, in O'Callaghan, ed., *NYCD*, VIII: 479; Guy Johnson to John Penn, July 22, 1774 ("a Fit"), *PSWJ*, VIII: 1186; G. Johnson to Thomas Gage, Sept. 8, 1774, *PSWJ*, XIII: 677.

84. Thomas Gage to Lord Dartmouth, July 18, 1774 ("I should"), *PSWJ*, VIII: 1185.

85. Col. [John] Duncan to unknown, Nov. n.d., 1769 ("a great loss"), in O'Callaghan, ed., *DHSNY*, II: 957.

86. Guzzardo, "Sir William Johnson's Official Family," 130–32, 134–37, 162; Jonathan G. Rossie, "Guy Johnson," *DCB*, IV (1771–1800): 154, 393; Cadwallader Colden to Gage, July 28, 1774 ("showed"), *PSWJ*, XIII: 643–45; Hamilton, "An American Knight," 127–31, 138; Thomas, "Sir John Johnson," 352–53.

87. Feister and Pulis, "Molly Brant," 306–8; Tilghman, ed., *Memoir of Lieut. Col. Tench Tilghman*, 83–87 (all quotations).

88. Sir William Johnson to Thomas Gage, June 2, 1773, and Apr. 20, 1774, *PSWJ*, VIII: 813, 1128–30; Johnson to Lord Dartmouth, Apr. 17, 1774; Guy Johnson to Lord Dartmouth, July 12, 1774, Conoghquieson, speech, July 14, 1774, Tyerhansera, speech, July 14, 1774 ("*Great King*"), and Johnson Hall council minutes, July 16, 1774, in O'Callaghan, ed., *NYCD*, VIII: 419, 471, 480–81, 481–82, 484; Guy Johnson to John Penn, July 22, 1774, *PSWJ*, VIII: 1186; Thomas Gage to Dartmouth, July 18, 1774, in Carter, ed., *Correspondence of General Thomas Gage*, I: 360; Cadwallader Colden to William Tryon, Aug. 2, 1774, in "The Colden Letter Books," New-York Historical Society, *Collections for the Year 1877*, X (1878): 352.

89. George Croghan to Sir William Johnson, Oct. 10, 1767, and Johnson to John Watts, Oct. 20, 1767, *PSWJ*, V: 659, 745; Guy Johnson to Sir William Johnson, Nov. 28, 1771, and Sir William Johnson to Eyre Massey, June 15, 1773, *PSWJ*, VIII: 328, 823; Occom quoted in Blodgett, *Samson Occom*, 155 ("very Solitary").

90. Guy Johnson to Thomas Gage, Nov. 10, 1774, *PSWJ*, XIII: 691; Johnson to Lord Dartmouth, Dec. 14, 1774, and Johnson, speeches, Jan. 28 and Feb. 13, 1775 ("it was"), in O'Callaghan, ed., *NYCD*, VIII: 516, 541, 554–55; Johnson, speech, Jan. 23, 1775 ("I charge"), RG 10 (Indian Affairs), XI: 46, NAC.

91. Pilkington, ed., *Journals of Samuel Kirkland*, 95; Patrick, "Life and Times of Samuel Kirkland," 253 (Kirkland quoted: "Thus saith").

92. Calloway, *American Revolution in Indian Country*, 115–20; Pilkington, ed., *Journals of Samuel Kirkland*, 80–82, 96; Samuel Kirkland to Jerusha Kirkland, Mar. 24, 1773, SKP, Folder 39, HCA; Aaron Crosby to S. Kirkland, Jan. 25, 1774, SKP, Folder 47, HCA; Onoquaga Chiefs, speech, Oct. 14, 1774 ("to follow"), RG 10 (Indian Affairs), XI: 6, NAC; Kirkland to Rev. Andrew Eliot, Oct. 24, 1774, SKP, Folder 51, HCA.

93. Samuel Kirkland to Andrew Eliot, June 13, 1774 ("My heart"), SKP, Folder 50, HCA; Stephen West to Kirkland, Nov. 2, 1774 ("Every thing"), and Timothy Edwards to Kirkland, Nov. 14, 1774, SKP, Folder 52, HCA; Eliot to Kirkland, Feb. 12, 1775, SKP, Folder 53, HCA.

94. Samuel Kirkland to Albany Committee, June 9, 1775 ("I apprehend"), in Jones, *Annals and Recollections of Oneida County*, 853; Conoghquieson, speeches, Jan. 20, 1775 and Jan. 27, 1775, in O'Callaghan, ed., *NYCD*, VIII: 535–36, 541; Pilkington, ed., *Journals of Samuel Kirkland*, 104–11; Guy Johnson to Samuel Kirkland, Feb. 14, 1775, Kirkland to Johnson, Feb. 21, 1775, and Oneida Chiefs to Johnson, Feb. 23, 1775, SKP, Folder 53, HCA; Kirkland to Andrew Eliot, Mar. 28, 1775, SKP, Folder 54, HCA; Eliot to Kirkland, Apr. 7, 1775, SKP, Folder 55, HCA; Johnson to Lord Dartmouth, Mar. 16, 1775, in O'Callaghan, ed., *NYCD*, VIII: 548; Kirkland to Albany Committee of Correspondence, June 9, 1775, in Jones, *Annals and Recollections of Oneida County*, 853.

95. Kelsay, *Joseph Brant*, 131–33; Joseph Brant to Frederick Haldimand, May 21, 1783 ("messengers"), MG 11 (Colonial Office 42), XXXXIX: 3, NAC; Samuel Kirkland to Guy Johnson, Feb. 21, 1775, and Onoquaga Sachems, speech, Mar. 7, 1775, SKP, Folders 53 and 54, HCA.

96. Kelsay, *Joseph Brant*, 133, 140–41; Teyawarunte, speech, Dec. 1, 1774, in O'Callaghan, ed.,

NYCD, VIII: 519; Graymont, *Iroquois in the American Revolution*, 53; Graymont, "Joseph Brant," *DCB*, V: 804.

97. Graymont, *Iroquois in the American Revolution*, 62–63; Patrick, "Life and Times of Samuel Kirkland," 285; Kirkland, "Brandt Indian Warrior: Anecdotes," Andrews-Eliot Collection, MHS ("We think"); Kelsay, *Joseph Brant*, 146; Kirkland to Albany Committee of Safety, June 9, 1775, in Jones, *Annals and Recollections of Oneida County*, 853.

CHAPTER THREE: WAR

1. Countryman, *People in Revolution*, 131–32; Countryman, *American Revolution*, 106–24; Kammen, *Colonial New York*, 366–67; Colden quoted in Kierner, *Traders and Gentlefolk*, 207 ("all the confidence").

2. Campbell, *Annals of Tryon County*, 17–19; Guzzardo, "Sir William Johnson's Official Family," 319–20; Graymont, *Iroquois in the American Revolution*, 64–65; Kelsay, *Joseph Brant*, 149–50; Guy Johnson to Peter Van Burgh Livingston, July 8, 1775, Gansevoort-Lansing Coll., NYPL; Johnson to Lord Dartmouth, Oct. 12, 1775, in O'Callaghan, ed., *NYCD*, VIII: 636.

3. Guzzardo, "Sir William Johnson's Official Family," 333–45; Hanson and Frey, eds., *Minute Book of the Committee of Safety*, 25–30, 67–68, 137–38; Sir John Johnson to Daniel Claus, Sept. 10, 1775, and Jan. 20, 1777, in De Peyster, *Miscellanies by an Officer*, xlix; Gerlach, *Proud Patriot*, 99–101, 176–77; Campbell, *Annals of Tryon County*, 50; Philip Schuyler to George Washington, Aug. 18, 1776, in Force, ed., *American Archives*, 5th Ser., I: 1032; Lender and Martin, eds., *Citizen-Soldier*, 47–48, 59–60. The latter documents that of the 195 Loyalists rounded up, 52 went to jail in Albany.

4. Peter Silvester to Sir William Johnson, Mar. 22, 1773, Johnson to Albany Common Council, Feb. 16, 1774, *PSWJ*, VIII (1933): 741, 1037.

5. Palatine District Committee to Albany Committee, May 18, 1775 ("the Indians" and "made use"), in Campbell, *Annals of Tryon County*, 21–22; Lender and Martin, eds., *Citizen-Soldier*, 49; Schuyler quoted in Gerlach, *Proud Patriot*, 183 ("Entre nous").

6. Joseph Brant quoted in Calloway, *American Revolution in Indian Country*, 122 ("to defend"); Guy Johnson quoted in Campbell, *Annals of Tryon County*, 55 ("Are you").

7. Colley, *Captives*, 230–36; Countryman, "Indians, the Colonial Order, and the Social Significance of the American Revolution," 342–62; Gould, *Persistence of Empire*, 184–85.

8. Sosin, *Whitehall and the Wilderness*, 239–41; Neatby, *Quebec*, 135–42; "The Declaration of Independence," in Rhodehamel, ed., *American Revolution*, 130 ("for abolishing").

9. Sosin, *Whitehall and the Wilderness*, 241–50; Neatby, *Revolutionary Age*, 133–35, 142.

10. Colley, *Captives*, 234 ("evolved"); Hinderaker, *Elusive Empires*, 189, 268–70. For the composite empire, see Countryman, "Indians, the Colonial Order, and the Social Significance of the American Revolution," 342–62; Koenigsberger, "Composite States, Representative Institutions, and the American Revolution," 135–53.

11. Graymont, *Iroquois in the American Revolution*, 72–74; American Commissioners, speech, Aug. 28, 1775, in O'Callaghan, ed., *NYCD*, VIII: 619.

12. Patrick, "Life and Times of Samuel Kirkland," 287–95, 301; Tiro, "James Dean in Iroquoia," 394–99 (Gideon Hawley quoted on 397: "Indian boy"); Wheelock, *Continuation of the Narrative* (1771), 31.

13. Patrick, "Life and Times of Samuel Kirkland," 299–300, 309, 323; Ford, ed., *Journals of the Continental Congress*, III: 351, VII: 72–73, XV: 1181–82, XXVIII: 306, 407–8; Tilghman, ed., *Memoir of Lieut. Col. Tench Tilghman*, 95; Clinton, *Discourse Delivered Before the New-York Historical Society*, 36 ("Those who"), 39.

14. John Adams to James Warren, July 10, 1775, in Massachusetts Historical Society, *Warren-Adams Letters*, I: 79; Ford, ed., *Journals of the Continental Congress*, II: 187; Thomas Cushing to John Hancock, Aug. n.d., 1776, in Force, ed., *American Archives*, 5th Ser., I: 902–3; Tiro, "James Dean in Iroquoia," 402; Tilghman, ed., *Memoir of Tench Tilghman*, 94 ("put into"); Kirkland, diary, July 21, Aug 2, 14 ("some apology"), 15, 17, 24, and 31, 1775, LFP, DCLSC.

15. Gerlach, *Proud Patriot*, 49–53; Shannon, *Indians and Colonists*, 221–23; Nammack, *Fraud, Politics, and the Dispossession of the Indians*, 10–35, 58; Hamilton, *Sir William Johnson*, 26–31, 51–55; Graymont, *Iroquois in the American Revolution*, 71–72. For Oneida initiative in proposing Albany, see Philip Schuyler to Congress, June 29, 1775, PCC, Reel 172, p. 5, LC.

16. American Commissioners, speeches, Aug. 23, 1775 ("the descendants"), and Aug. 28, 1775 ("By this belt"), in O'Callaghan, ed., *NYCD*, VIII: 609, 619. The commissioners referred to twelve rather than thirteen united colonies because Georgia had not yet joined the Continental Congress.

17. Shannon, *Indians and Colonists*, 237–38; American Commissioners, speech, Aug. 28, 1775, and resolutions, Sept. 1, 1775, in O'Callaghan, ed., *NYCD*, VIII: 619, 627. Owing to illness, Hawley did not attend the Albany council.

18. Tilghman, ed., *Memoir of Tench Tilghman*, 88 ("plain to me").

19. Kelsay, *Joseph Brant*, 152; Graymont, *Iroquois and the American Revolution*, 3, 28, 32, 44, 47, 61, 69–70, 116–17; Captain John Deserontyon quoted in Charles M. Johnston, "John Deserontyon," *DCB*, V: 254 ("we thought"). For population levels, see Shannon, *Indians and Colonists*, 236.

20. Colonel Elias Dayton quoted in Lender and Martin, eds., *Citizen-Soldier*, 50 ("would burn"); Philip Schuyler to Samuel Kirkland, Jan. 5, 1776, SKP, Folder 62, HCA; Schuyler to John Hancock, June 8, 1776, PCC, Reel 172, p. 192, LC.

21. Tiro, "People of the Standing Stone," 111–12; Samuel Kirkland, diary, Aug. 14, 1775, LFP, DCLSC; Guy Johnson to Lord Germain, Jan. 26, 1776, in O'Callaghan, ed., *NYCD*, VIII: 657; James Dean to Philip Schuyler, Mar. 10 and Mar. 12, 1776, SKP, Folder 64, HCA; Kirkland to Schuyler, Mar. 12, 1776, in Force, ed., *American Archives*, 4th Ser., V: 772–73; Kirkland to Timothy Edwards, April. 8, 1776, SKP, Folder 65, HCA. For growing exasperation by other Iroquois with the Oneidas, see James Dean to Schuyler, Mar. 10, 1776, SKP, Folder 64, HCA.

22. Graymont, *Iroquois and the American Revolution*, 86–103; Samuel Kirkland to Timothy Edwards, Apr. 8, 1776, SKP, Folder 65, HCA; John Butler quoted in Oneidas to Philip Schuyler, May 22, 1776 ("He was born"), SKP, Folder 66, HCA; Kirkland to Schuyler, June 8, 1776, SKP, Folder 67, HCA.

23. Ford, ed., *Journals of the Continental Congress*, III: 366, VII: 127, XII: 1177–78, XIII: 363, XVI: 180–81 ("we should"); Samuel Kirkland to Philip Schuyler, Mar. 12, 1776, SKP, Folder 64, HCA; Schuyler to Congress, Jan. 7, 1777 ("My house"), in "Proceedings of a General Court Martial . . . for the Trial of Major General Schuyler, October 1, 1778," New-York Historical Society, *Collections for the Year 1879*, 60; Robert Yates to Henry Laurens, Jan. 12, 1778, PCC, Reel 183, p. 377, LC.

24. Stone, ed., *Memoirs, and Letters and Journals of Major General Riedesel*, II: 200–201 ("He conversed"); Daniel Claus, "Anecdotes of Capt. Joseph Brant," Sept. 1778, MG 19 F 1 (Claus Family Papers), II: 53, NAC.

25. Kelsay, *Joseph Brant*, 154–55; Graymont, *Iroquois in the American Revolution*, 66–69.

26. Sir Guy Carleton to Sir William Johnson, Mar. 27, 1767, Carleton to Johnson, Mar. 16, 1768, Daniel Claus to Johnson, Aug. 25, 1769, Johnson to Thomas Gage, Oct. 19, 1769, Claus to Johnson, May 5, 1770, and Daniel Campbell to Johnson, Aug. 3, 1770, *PSWJ*, V: 521–22, VI: 157–58, VII: 129, 222, 638–39, 819.

27. Kelsay, *Joseph Brant*, 157–58; Douglas Leighton, "John Campbell," *DCB*, IV: 129–31; Graymont, *Iroquois in the American Revolution*, 80–81.

28. Kelsay, *Joseph Brant*, 158–59; Allen, *His Majesty's Indian Allies*, 48–49; R. Arthur Bowler and Bruce G. Wilson, "John Butler," *DCB*, IV: 117–18.

29. Guy Johnson to Lord George Germain, Jan. 26, 1776 ("an attachment"), in O'Callaghan, ed., *NYCD*, VIII: 654–57; Kelsay, *Joseph Brant*, 162–65; Douglas Leighton, "Christian Daniel Claus," and Jonathan G. Rossie, "Guy Johnson," *DCB*, IV: 155, 394.

30. Joseph Brant, speech, Mar. 14, 1776 ("The Mohocks"), in O'Callaghan, ed., *NYCD*, VIII: 671.

31. Kelsay, *Joseph Brant*, 166–67; Joseph Brant to Lord George Germain, May 7, 1776, in O'Callaghan, ed., *NYCD*, VIII: 678.

32. Kelsay, *Joseph Brant*, 167–69; Graymont, *Iroquois in the American Revolution*, 105.

33. Kelsay, *Joseph Brant*, 163–73; Allen, *His Majesty's Indian Allies*, 49–50; Joseph Brant to Samuel Kirkland, Feb. 4, 1792 ("I have had"), SKP, Folder 143, HCA.

34. Kelsay, *Joseph Brant*, 174–76; Graymont, *Iroquois in the American Revolution*, 106.

35. Graymont, *Iroquois in the American Revolution*, 108–10; Kelsay, *Joseph Brant*, 184–87; Samuel Kirkland to Philip Schuyler, Jan. 25, 1777, SKP, Folder 72, HCA.

36. Joseph Brant to the Mohawks of the Lake of the Two Mountains, Dec. 28, 1776, MG 21 (Haldimand Papers), B39, 360–61, NAC; Cruikshank, "King's Royal Regiment of New York," 204; Daniel Claus to William Knox, Nov. 6, 1777, in O'Callaghan, ed., *NYCD*, VIII: 724; Kelsay, *Joseph Brant*, 187–88; Graymont, *Iroquois in the American Revolution*, 110–12.

37. Thomas S. Abler, "Kaienkwaahton," *DCB*, 404–6; Kelsay, *Joseph Brant*, 188; Abler, ed., *Chainbreaker*, 59–62.

38. Kelsay, *Joseph Brant*, 188–93; Hinman, *Onaquaga*, 24–30; Calloway, *American Revolution in Indian Country*, 122–23; McGinnis, "Loyalist Journal," 198.

39. Kelsay, *Joseph Brant*, 193–94 (Major James Gray quoted on 193: "refuse").

40. Graymont, *Iroquois in the American Revolution*, 115–17; Kelsay, *Joseph Brant*, 193–96.

41. Philip Schuyler to John Hancock, June 8, 1776 ("impress"), and Schuyler to George Washington, June 11, 1776, in Peter Force, ed., *American Archives*, 4th Ser., VI: 762–63, and 819; Gerlach, *Proud Patriot*, 185; Lender and Martin, eds., *Citizen-Soldier*, 73–76, 97–99; Graymont, *Iroquois in the American Revolution*, 106–8.

42. Kelsay, *Joseph Brant*, 196–203; Graymont, *Iroquois in the American Revolution*, 117–31; Tiro, "People of the Standing Stone," 114–16.

43. Daniel Claus to William Knox, Oct. 16, 1777, in O'Callaghan, ed., *NYCD*, VI: 719–21; Cruikshank, "King's Royal Regiment of New York," 209–11; Graymont, *Iroquois in the American Revolution*, 132–46; Kelsay, *Joseph Brant*, 203–8; Abler, ed., *Chainbreaker*, 86–91; Isabel T. Kelsay, "William Tekawironte," *DCB*, IV, 731.

44. Daniel Claus to William Knox, Nov. 6, 1777, in O'Callaghan, ed., *NYCD*, VI: 725; John Johnston to John Butler, Oct. n.d., 1777, MG 19 F 35 (PSGIA), Lot 688, NAC; Torok, "Tyendinaga Mohawks," 72; Abler, ed., *Chainbreaker*, 91; Charles M. Johnston, "John Deserontyon," *DCB*, V: 253–56; Kelsay, *Joseph Brant*, 208–9; Graymont, *Iroquois in the American Revolution*, 142, 146–49; Captain John Johnston to John Butler, Oct. n.d., 1777, MG 19 F 35 (PSGIA), Lot 688, NAC.

45. Campbell, *Annals of Tryon County*, 93–94, 100; Daniel Claus, "Remarks on the Management of the Northern Indian Nations," in O'Callaghan, ed., *NYCD*, VIII: 704; Cruikshank, "King's Royal Regiment of New York," 206, 213; Kelsay, *Joseph Brant*, 222–23; Mintz, *Seeds of Empire*, 156–64; Mason Bolton quoted in Calloway, *American Revolution in Indian Country*, 133 ("Scalps").

46. Campbell, *Annals of Tryon County*, 98, 104–5; Jacob Klock to George Clinton, June 22, 1778, in

Hastings, ed., *Public Papers of George Clinton*, III: 475–76; Halsey, *Old New York Frontier*, 211, 226; Kelsay, *Joseph Brant*, 215–24; Graymont, *Iroquois in the American Revolution*, 231.

47. Graymont, *Iroquois in the American Revolution*, 181–82; Kelsay, *Joseph Brant*, 228; Col. William Butler to George Clinton, Oct. 28, 1778 ("finest Indian town"), in Hastings, ed., *Public Papers of George Clinton*, IV: 222–31; Preston, "Journey to Harmony," 100–101.

48. Halsey, *Old New York Frontier*, 224, 234–43, 257–58; Graymont, *Iroquois in the American Revolution*, 183–91; Mason Bolton to Frederick Haldimand, Feb. 12, 1779 ("behaved with"), MG 21 (Haldimand Papers), NAC; Daniel Claus, "Observations of Jos. Brant's distinguished Genius & Character from other Indians," MG 19 F 1 (Claus Family Papers), II: 207 ("singular power"), NAC.

49. Daniel Claus to Frederick Haldimand, Oct. 12, and Nov. 20, 1778, and Mar. 17, 1779, MG 19 F 1 (Claus Family Papers), XXV: 82, NAC; Kelsay, *Joseph Brant*, 237–41. For Haldimand, see Neatby, *Quebec*, 172–73; Stuart R. J. Sutherland, Pierre Tousignant, and Madeleine Dionne-Tousignant, "Sir Frederick Haldimand," *DCB*, V: 887–904.

50. Frederick Haldimand, order, April 7, 1779 ("as soon"), MG 19 F 1 (Claus Family Papers), II: 89, NAC; Haldimand to Mason Bolton, May 23, 1779, MG 21 (Haldimand Papers), #21764, p. 17 ("intelligent"), NAC; Kelsay, *Joseph Brant*, 239–41; Haldimand to Lord Germain, quoted in Feister and Pulis, "Molly Brant," 311 ("whatever").

51. Kelsay, *Joseph Brant*, 278–79 (prisoner quoted on 279: "His dress").

52. Kelsay, *Joseph Brant*, 225, 274–77.

53. Kelsay, *Joseph Brant*, 260 (Walter Butler quoted: "more notice"), 273; H. Watson Powell to Haldimand, May 15, 1781 ("much happier"), MG 21 (Haldimand Papers), #21761, p. 74, NAC; Calloway, *American Revolution in Indian Country*, 139, 142 (Haldimand quoted: "the man").

54. Daniel Claus to Frederick Haldimand, Aug. 17, 1779 ("the late" and "promised"), in Riddell, "Was Molly Brant Married?" 151; Daniel Claus and Captain Malcolm Fraser quoted in Feister and Pulis, "Molly Brant," 309 ("prevented"), 313 ("far superior").

55. De Forest, ed., "Hannah Lawrence Shieffelin's Letter," 120–23; Guy Johnson quoted in Feister and Pulis, "Molly Brant," 312 ("Molly used"); Bond, "British Base at Carleton Island," 11; Riddell, "Was Molly Brant Married?" 152.

56. Captain John Johnston to John Butler, Apr. 1, 1779, MG 19 F 35, Ser. 1 (PSGIA), Lot 690, NAC; Frederick Haldimand to Sir John Johnson, Aug. 24, 1780 ("The Treachery"), in Cruikshank, "King's Royal Regiment of New York," 230–31, 236; Tiro, "People of the Standing Stone," 123–27. For Oneida restraint, see Tiro, "A Civil War?" 148–65. Samuel Kirkland calculated that at least two-thirds of the Oneidas allied with the Americans. See Dexter, ed., *Literary Diary of Ezra Stiles*, III: 76. For the special value of Oneida warriors, see also Marinus Willett to Lord Stirling, Nov. 2, 1781, PCC, Reel 177, p. 401, LC.

57. Philip Schuyler to the Oneidas, Mar. n.d., 1776 ("Be assured"), PCC, Reel 172, p. 93, LC; Schuyler to John Hancock, Oct. 30, 1776 ("such good Friends"), PCC, Reel 172, p. 471, LC; Samuel Kirkland to Schuyler, Jan. 3, 1777, PCC, Reel 173, p. 31, LC; Schuyler to Oneidas, May 11, 1778 ("partake"), PCC, Reel 189, p. 281, LC.

58. Philip Schuyler to Oneida Sachems and Warriors, Jan. n. d., 1777 ("wishing you"), SKP, Folder 72, HCA; Samuel Kirkland to Schuyler, Jan. 14, 1777, PCC, Reel 173, pp. 63–68, LC; Oneida Chiefs to Schuyler, Jan. 16, 1779, PCC, Reel 189, p. 108 ("makes us feel"), LC; Graymont, *Iroquois in the American Revolution*, 112; Dexter, ed., *Literary Diary of Ezra Stiles*, II: 140–42.

59. Cruikshank, "King's Royal Regiment of New York," 219; Quebec Council, minutes, Aug. 20, 1779, in O'Callaghan, ed., *NYCD*, VIII, 776–77; Graymont, *Iroquois in the American Revolution*, 196–99.

60. Tiouganda, speech, Dec. 11, 1782 ("these Rebels"), RG 10 (Indian Affairs), XV: 78, NAC; Graymont, *Iroquois in the American Revolution*, 192–96.

61. Abler, ed., *Chainbreaker*, 107–10, 113; Kelsay, *Joseph Brant*, 258–62; Graymont, *Iroquois in the American Revolution*, 194–214; Patrick, "Life and Times of Samuel Kirkland," 325–29. Guy Johnson, "Minutes of Indian Affairs," Sept. 4–7, 1779, RG 10 (Indian Affairs), XII: 21, NAC.

62. Henry Dearborn, journal, Aug. 11–Sept. 19, 1779, Dearborn Papers, MHS; R. W. G. Vail, ed., "The Western Campaign of 1779: The Diary of Quartermaster Sergeant Moses Sproule of the Third New Jersey Regiment in the Sullivan Expedition of the Revolutionary War, May 17–October 17, 1779," New-York Historical Society, *Quarterly* (Jan. 1957), 26–33; Abler, ed., *Chainbreaker*, 110–12; Graymont, *Iroquois in the American Revolution*, 212–18; Kelsay, *Joseph Brant*, 263–67; Mintz, *Seeds of Empire*, 103–14.

63. Graymont, *Iroquois in the American Revolution*, 219–20 (Gansevoort quoted on 219: "remarked").

64. Cruikshank, "King's Royal Regiment of New York," 220–25; Guy Johnson to Lord Germain, Sept. 5, 1779, in O'Callaghan, ed., *NYCD*, VIII: 775–76; Guy Johnson, "Minutes of Indian Affairs," Sept. 4–Oct. 4, 1779, RG 10 (Indian Affairs), XII: 21–33, NAC; Graymont, *Iroquois in the American Revolution*, 214.

65. Guy Johnson, "Minutes," Sept. 22, Oct. 6–7, 1779, RG 10 (Indian Affairs), XII: 29, 33–35, NAC; Abler, ed., *Chainbreaker*, 114; Graymont, *Iroquois in the American Revolution*, 221–22.

66. Guy Johnson, "Minutes," Oct. 14 ("very drunk"), and 21–24, 1779, RG 10 (Indian Affairs), XII: 38, 42–46, NAC; Guy Johnson to Lord Germain, Nov. 11, 1779, in O'Callaghan, ed., *NYCD*, VIII: 779–80.

67. Calloway, *American Revolution in Indian Country*, 137–41; Namias, ed., *Narrative of the Life of Mary Jemison*, 105; Cartwright, ed., *Life and Letters of the Late Hon. Richard Cartwright*, 46 ("The rebels").

68. Calloway, *American Revolution in Indian Country*, 141–42; Graymont, *Iroquois in the American Revolution*, 230–33, 236–41.

69. Frederick Haldimand quoted in Cruikshank, "King's Royal Regiment of New York," 220 ("right arm"); Abler, ed., *Chainbreaker*, 118, 144–45; Graymont, *Iroquois in the American Revolution*, 225–28; Tiro, "People of the Standing Stone," 126, 132.

70. Oneida speech, June 18, 1780, and Col. Cornelius Van Dycke to Governor George Clinton, July 3, 1780, in Hastings, ed., *Public Papers of George Clinton*, V: 883, 912; Samuel Kirkland to Jerusha Kirkland, June 20, 1780, SKP, Folder 81, HCA; Graymont, *Iroquois in the American Revolution*, 233–35; Guy Johnson, speech, July 3, 1780 ("What think you"), MG 19 F 35 (PSGIA), Lot 698, NAC; Guy Johnson to Lord Germain, July 26, 1780, in O'Callaghan, ed., *NYCD*, VIII: 796–97.

71. Graymont, *Iroquois in the American Revolution*, 234–35; Tiro, "A Civil War?" 162–63 (includes Daniel Claus quotation: "fixed"). For Jacob Reed, see Col. Frederick Wissenfels to George Clinton, Dec. 9, 1780, in Hastings, ed., *Public Papers of George Clinton*, VI: 480–82.

72. Chastellux, "Visit to Schenectady, 1780," 293–94; Gerlach, *Proud Patriot*, 441; Tiro, "People of the Standing Stone," 137–38; Samuel Kirkland, Memorandum on Peter Penet ("The devastation"), SKP, Letters Undated and Fragmentary File, HCA; Philip Schuyler to Samuel Huntington, Oct. 10, 1780 ("late incursions"), PCC, Reel 173, p. 541, LC; Schuyler to Henry Glen, Nov. 6, 1780, quoted in Graymont, *Iroquois in the American Revolution*, 242; Haldimand quoted in Cruikshank, "King's Royal Regiment of New York," 268–69 ("This opportunity"); Ford, ed., *Journals of the Continental Congress*, XVIII: 1067, XX: 465; Pierre Van Cortlandt to the New York congressional delegation, Jan. 17, 1781, in Judd, ed., *Correspondence of the Van*

Cortlandt Family, 400; and Marinus Willett to Lord Stirling, Nov. 2, 1781, PCC, Reel 177, p. 401, LC.

73. Cruikshank, "King's Royal Regiment of New York," 233–34, 252, 270; Graymont, *Iroquois in the American Revolution,* 230–58; Kelsay, *Joseph Brant,* 301–5; Daniel Claus to Mr. Blackburn, Nov. 16, 1780, in De Peyster, ed., *Miscellanies by an Officer,* xlviii; Hanson and Frey, eds., *Tryon County Committee of Safety,* xiii, iii; Bond, "British Base at Carleton Island," 13; George Clinton to George Washington, Oct. 18, 1780, and Clinton to James Duane, Oct. 29, 1780 ("Schenectady"), in Hastings, ed., *Public Papers of George Clinton,* VI: 306–7, 345–47. For supply problems and desertion at Fort Schuyler, see George Washington to Samuel Huntington, June 20, 1780, PCC, Reel 170, p. 615, LC.

74. Wilson, *Enterprises of Robert Hamilton,* 11; Allan MacLean to Frederick Haldimand, Aug. 8, 1783 ("the People"), in MG 21 (Haldimand Papers), #21763, pp. 225–26, NAC.

75. Calloway, *American Revolution in Indian Country,* 132–33 (Sayenqueraghta quoted: "your Business").

76. Cometti, ed., *American Journals of Lt. John Enys,* 119–20, 146; Allan MacLean to Frederick Haldimand, Mar. 29, 1783 ("a maxim"), MG 21 (Haldimand Papers), #21763, p. 32, NAC.

77. Calloway, *American Revolution in Indian Country,* 133–34, 137.

78. Frederick Haldimand to Sir John Johnson, Sept. 9, 1779, in Cruikshank, "King's Royal Regiment of New York," 222.

79. Calloway, *American Revolution in Indian Country,* 142–43 (includes Guy Johnson quotation: "blue Coat"); Johnson to Haldimand, July 3, 1780 ("Many of"), MG 21 (Haldimand Papers), #21170, p. 244, NAC; Kelsay, *Joseph Brant,* 272–74.

80. Guy Johnson quoted in Calloway, *American Revolution in Indian Country,* 143 ("must depend"); Guy Johnson to Board of Inquiry, Oct. 10, 1783, MG 21 (Haldimand Papers), #21170, p. 242, NAC.

81. Sayenqueraghta, speech, July 24, 1783 ("receive"), MG 11 (Colonial Office 42), XLIV: 270, NAC.

82. Calloway, *American Revolution in Indian Country,* 142, 145–52; O'Donnell, "Joseph Brant," 29–30; Guy Johnson to Daniel Claus, July 8, 1782, in Milton W. Hamilton Papers, Box 1, Folder 7, Albany Institute; Allan MacLean to Robert Matthews, May 17, 1783 ("Extravagant"), MG 21 (Haldimand Papers), #21763, pp. 114–15, NAC; Guy Johnson to Frederick Haldimand, May 20, 1783, MG 11 (Colonial Office 42), XLV: 136, NAC; Guy Johnson to Board of Inquiry, Oct. 10, 1783, MG 21 (Haldimand Papers), #21170, pp. 242–44; Kelsay, *Joseph Brant,* 299–300; Haldimand to Sir John Johnson, Oct. 20, 1783 ("reprehensible"), MG 21 (Haldimand Papers), #21175, p. 190, NAC. For Butler's good favor, see Robert Mathews to John Butler, May 19, 1782, in Cruikshank, "Records of Niagara, 1778–1783," 37; Haldimand to Lord North, Nov. 2, 1783, MG 11 (Colonial Office 42), XLV: 54, NAC.

83. Sir John Johnson to Daniel Claus, Mar. 21, 1782, in De Peyster, ed., *Miscellanies by an Officer,* lv; Kelsay, *Joseph Brant,* 328–30; Cruikshank, "King's Royal Regiment of New York," 283; unspecified Iroquois chief, speech, July 31, 1783 ("Our feelings" and "the Interference"), MG 11 (Colonial Office 42), XLIV: 275, NAC.

84. Frederick Haldimand to Sir John Johnson, Nov. 25, 1782, and Robert Matthews to Johnson, May 29, 1783, MG 19 F 2 (Sir John Johnson Papers), Box 3, NAC; Haldimand to Johnson, Dec. 5, 1782, Feb. 6 and Apr. 10, 1783, and Johnson to Haldimand, Apr. 17, 1783 ("will hold"), MG 21 (Haldimand Papers), #21175, pp. 38, 65, 104, 106, NAC.

85. Kelsay, *Joseph Brant,* 321–28; John Ross to Frederick Haldimand, June 27 ("I cannot"), and July 7, 1782, in Cruikshank, "King's Royal Regiment of New York," 280.

86. Cruikshank, "King's Royal Regiment of New York," 276–85 (Robert Mathews quoted on 285: "the Indians"); Kelsay, *Joseph Brant*, 321–28, 334; Frederick Haldimand to Sir John Johnson, Sept. 9, 1782, MG 21 (Haldimand Papers), #21175, p. 8, NAC; Haldimand to Guy Carleton, Sept. 18, 1782 ("are alarmed"), in "Haldimand Papers," Michigan Pioneer and Historical Society, *Collections*, XX (1892), 57–58.

87. Allan MacLean to Frederick Haldimand, Dec. 16, 1782, MG 21 (Haldimand Papers), #21762, p. 230, NAC; Sir John Johnson to Haldimand, Nov. 20 and Nov. 28, 1782, Haldimand to Johnson, Dec. 5, 1782, Joseph Brant to Johnson, Dec. 25, 1782 ("We think"), and Haldimand to Johnson, Feb. 6, 1783, MG 21 (Haldimand Papers), #21175, pp. 29, 37, 38, 49, 70, NAC; Haldimand to Sir John Johnson, Nov. 25, 1782, MG 19 F 2 (Sir John Johnson Papers), Box 3, NAC; Kelsay, *Joseph Brant*, 335; Cruikshank, "King's Royal Regiment of New York," XXVII: 288; Brant to Haldimand, May 21, 1783, MG 11 (Colonial Office 42), XLIX: 3, NAC.

88. Robert Mathews to John Ross, July 1, 1782 ("*Entre nous*"), MG 21 (Haldimand Papers), #21785, p. 40, NAC; Allan MacLean to Robert Mathews, May 13, 1783 ("Joseph knows"), MG 21 (Haldimand Papers), #21763, p. 108; MacLean to Frederick Haldimand, May 18, 1783 ("More Sensible"), in Johnson, ed., *Valley of the Six Nations*, 38.

89. Testimony of Archibald Thompson, Apr. 17, 1783 ("would kill"), Niagara Coroner's Inquiry, Apr. 18, 1783, and MacLean to Haldimand, Apr. 20 ("nothing else"), and Apr. 24, 1783, MG 21 (Haldimand Papers), #21763, pp. 48, 54–59, 64, NAC.

90. Allan MacLean to Frederick Haldimand, May 11, 1783, and MacLean to Robert Mathews, Aug. 18, 1783, in MG 21 (Haldimand Papers), #21763, pp. 104, 238, NAC; Calloway, *American Revolution in Indian Country*, 149; Calloway, *Crown and Calumet*, 60. In the last, Calloway mistakenly writes, "When Joseph Brant requested that the murderer of a drunken Delaware be hanged at Niagara, Haldimand complied and the guilty white man was executed on the site where the crime was committed." In fact, Pray was sent away and neither tried nor executed anywhere, as Brant later bitterly complained. See Brant to Joseph Chew, Oct. 27, 1791, F 47-1-1 (Simcoe Papers), Reel MS-1797, AO. I am indebted to Patricia Kennedy of the NAC for checking the Montreal sheriff's fiscal records for the negative evidence that Pray never cost the Crown for lodging there.

91. Joseph Brant to Joseph Chew, Oct. 27, 1791 ("We demanded"), F 47-I-1 (Simcoe Papers), Reel MS-1797, AO.

92. Graymont, *Iroquois in the American Revolution*, 259–91.

CHAPTER FOUR: PEACE

1. Graymont, *Iroquois in the American Revolution*, 259–62; Calloway, *Crown and Calumet*, 7–8; Frederick Haldimand to Baron von Riedesel, Apr. 26, 1783 ("My soul"), in Stone, ed., *Memoirs, and Letters and Journals of Major General Riedesel*, II: 168–69.

2. Lord Shelburne quoted in Graymont, *Iroquois in the American Revolution*, 261–62 ("the Indian nations"); Sayenqueraghta, speech, April 1, 1783 ("If we had"), MG 21 (Haldimand Papers), #21779, NAC.

3. Calloway, *Crown and Calumet*, 8–9; Kelsay, *Joseph Brant*, 339–40; George Clinton to George Washington, Apr. 13, 1783, and Clinton to Marinus Willett, Apr. 14, 1783, in Hastings, ed., *Public Papers of George Clinton*, VIII: 136, 136n; John Ross to Haldimand, Apr. 29 and May 14, 1783, MG 21 (Haldimand Papers), #21784, pp. 132, 134, NAC; Severance, "The Niagara Peace Mission," 118–22; Benjamin Lincoln to Ephraim Douglass, May 3, 1783 ("That all"), MG 11 (Colonial Office 42), XLIV: 225, NAC. Signed in Paris on March 3, 1783, the final treaty was identical to the preliminary treaty. See Ritcheson, *Aftermath of Revolution*, 50.

4. Captain John Deserontyon to Daniel Claus, Jan. 8, 1784 ("Our minds"), MG 19 F 1 (Claus Family Papers, XXIV: 15, NAC; Allan MacLean to Frederick Haldimand, May 18, 1783 ("They told" and "a free People" and Brant quoted: "England"), MG 21 (Haldimand Papers), #21763, p. 118.

5. Allan MacLean to Frederick Haldimand, May 11, 1783 ("We have been"), and June 22, 1783, and MacLean to Maj. DePeyster, June 26, 1783, in MG 21 (Haldimand Papers), #21763, pp. 104, 153, 164, NAC. For MacLean's previous strictures, see Calloway, *American Revolution in Indian Country*, 152; MacLean to Haldimand, Jan. 28, 1783, and MacLean to Robert Mathews, May 17, 1783, MG 21 (Haldimand Papers), #21763, pp. 6, 114, NAC.

6. Cometti, ed., *American Journals of Lt. John Enys*, 144 ("He is"); Mancall, *Deadly Medicine*, 85–100.

7. Allan MacLean to Maj. DePeyster, July 8, 1783, MG 21 (Haldimand Papers), #21763, p. 179, NAC; Sir John Johnson, speech, July 22, 1783, MG 11 (Colonial Office 42), XLIV: 270, NAC.

8. Frederick Haldimand to John Ross, Apr. 25, 1783, in Cruikshank, "King's Royal Regiment of New York," 292; Allan MacLean to Haldimand, May 13 and 18, 1783, MG 21 (Haldimand Papers), #21763, pp. 111, 118, NAC; Ross to Haldimand, May 14, 1783, MG 21 (Haldimand Papers), #21784, p. 134, NAC; Maj. A. Campbell to Col. Barry St. Leger, Aug. 6, 1785, in Cruikshank, ed., "Records of Niagara, 1784–7," 69. For the Indian numbers near Niagara, see John Butler, "Return of the Six Nation Indians and Confederates, June 24, 1783," RG 10 (Indian Affairs), Ser. A6, XV: 74, NAC. For the rotten state of Fort Niagara, see Gother Mann, report, Dec. 6, 1788, MG 11 (Colonial Office 42), LXX: 49, NAC.

9. Allan MacLean to Frederick Haldimand, May 13 and 18, 1783, MG 21 (Haldimand Papers), #21763, pp. 111, 118, NAC; John Ross to Haldimand, May 14, 1783, MG 21 (Haldimand Papers), #21784, p. 132, NAC; Haldimand to Lord North, May 12, 1784 ("prevent"), and Maj. A. Campbell to Col. Barry St. Leger, Aug. 6, 1785, in Cruikshank, ed., "Records of Niagara, 1784–7," 24–25, 69; Haldimand to Lord North, Aug. 30 and Nov. 27, 1783, MG 11 (Colonial Office 42), XLIII: 241, XLVI: 41, NAC; Haldimand to Sir John Johnson, June 14, 1784, MG 21 (Haldimand Papers), #21723, p. 131, NAC; Elbridge Gerry to Thomas Jefferson, Aug. 24, 1784, in Burnett, ed., *Letters of Members of the Continental Congress*, VII: 587; François de Barbé-Marbois to Comte de Vergennes, Sept. 30 and Oct. 30, 1784, in Giunta, ed., *Emerging Nation*, II: 451, 482–83.

10. Allen, *His Majesty's Indian Allies*, 56–57; Wright, *Britain and the American Frontier*, 20–26, 36, 42–43; Ritcheson, *Aftermath of Revolution*, 33–37, 59–69; Lord Sydney to Henry Hope, Apr. 6, 1788, in Cruikshank, ed., "Records of Niagara, 1784–7," 88; Kelsay, *Joseph Brant*, 371–72.

11. Ritcheson, *Aftermath of Revolution*, 4–6; Wright, *Britain and the American Revolution*, 16, 80–86; Samuel Adams to Richard Henry Lee, Dec. 23, 1784, in Cushing, ed., *Writings of Samuel Adams*, IV: 311–12; John Francis Mercer, Nov. 12, 1784, in Burnett, ed., *Letters of Members of the Continental Congress*, VII: 609–10; John Adams to Robert R. Livingston, June 23 and July 17, 1783, John Jay to Thomas Jefferson, July 13, 1785, and Adams to Jay, Aug. 25 ("They have"), Oct. 15 and Dec. 3, 1785, in Giunta, ed., *Emerging Nation*, II: 169–70, 195, 694, 774–75, 864–65, 938–41.

12. Allan MacLean to Frederick Haldimand, May 18, 1783, and Joseph Brant to Philip Schuyler, Oct. 22, 1783 ("contrary to"), MG 21 (Haldimand Papers) #21763, p. 118, and #21779, p. 147, NAC; Kelsay, *Joseph Brant*, 341–42. Schuyler offered an evasive reply to the Iroquois reiteration of the Fort Stanwix Line. See Schuyler, speech, Jan. 11, 1784, PSP, XIV, NYPL.

13. Graymont, *Iroquois in the American Revolution*, 262; Sir John Johnson, speech, July 22, 1783, MG 11 (Colonial Office 42), XLIV: 270, NAC; John Butler, speech, Oct. 4, 1783, MG 19 F 35, Ser. 1 (Papers of the Superintendent of Indian Affairs), Lot 708, NAC; Frederick

Haldimand to Lord North, Nov. 27, 1783 ("These People), quoted in Calloway, *Crown and Calumet*, 9.

14. Captain Aaron Hill, speech, Oct. 17, 1784 ("We are free"), in Craig, ed., *Olden Time*, II: 418; Frederick Haldimand to Lord North, Nov. 27, 1783, MG 11 (Colonial Office 42), XLVI: 41–42, NAC. Some historians miscast the buffer zone as a British initiative, thereby obscuring the catalytic Indian role. See, for example, Stuart, *United States Expansionism and British North America*, 7, 37–38. Stuart insists that the British "controlled Indian tribes linked with the fur trade." Rather than describing Indians as "controlled" by the British, it would be more accurate to say that the British and the Indians both *influenced* and *pressured* one another in a constant give-and-take to balance their mutual and their clashing interests.

15. Allan MacLean to Frederick Haldimand, July 31, 1783, MG 21 (Haldimand Papers), #21763, p. 211, NAC; Indian Confederacy to Congress, Dec. 18, 1786, and Nov. 16, 1792, *ASPIA*, I: 8–9, 323–24; Kelsay, *Joseph Brant*, 344–46, 403–4; Calloway, *Crown and Calumet*, 14; White, *Middle Ground*, 413–17, 433–43, 447–48; Samuel Kirkland, diary, July 7, 1788 ("that Congress"), LFP, DCSCL; Kirkland to Peter Thacher, June 8, 1791, #791358, DCSCL.

16. Allan MacLean to Frederick Haldimand, July 31, 1783, MG 21 (Haldimand Papers), #21763, p. 111, NAC; Wright, *Britain and the American Frontier*, 68; Samuel Kirkland, diary, July 7, 1788 ("unite"), LFP, DCSCL.

17. Calloway, *Crown and Calumet*, 51–52.

18. Allen, *His Majesty's Indian Allies*, 88; Calloway, *Crown and Calumet*, 64–71; Riddell, *La Rochefoucault-Liancourt's Travels in Canada*, 46; Lord Dorchester, Oct. 17, 1790 ("certain"), MG 11 (Colonial Office 42), LXIX: 215, NAC.

19. White, *Middle Ground*, 434–35.

20. Allen, *His Majesty's Indian Allies*, 67–68; Calloway, *Crown and Calumet*, 17; White, *Middle Ground*, 416–17; James Monroe to Thomas Jefferson, Nov. 1, 1784, in Hamilton, ed., *Writings of Monroe*, I: 43–44; John Adams to John Jay, Oct. 15 and Dec. 3, 1785, in Giunta, ed., *Emerging Nation*, II: 864–65, 940–41.

21. Philip Schuyler to the President of Congress, July 29, 1783 ("if driven"), PCC, Reel 173, p. 601, LC; George Washington to James Duane, Sept. 7, 1783, in Prucha, ed., *Documents of United States Indian Policy*, 1–2.

22. Committee on Indian Affairs, report, Oct. 15, 1783, in Ford, ed., *Journals of the Continental Congress*, XXV: 681–83; John Butler to Sir John Johnson, Mar. 17, 1784 ("This information"), MG 21 (Haldimand Papers), #21779, p. 156, NAC.

23. Philip Schuyler to the President of Congress, July 29, 1783 ("dwindle"), PCC, Reel 173, p. 601, LC; Campisi, "Oneida Treaty Period," 54–55. For the overwhelming numeric advantage of the Americans over the Six Nations in New York, see Samuel Kirkland, "A Statement of the Number & Situation of the Six United Nations of Indians in North America," Oct. 15, 1791, Misc. Bound MSS, MHS; Ellis, "Rise of the Empire State," 5–6; Macauley, *Natural, Statistical, and Civil History of the State of New-York*, I: 417–18; and the 1786 New York State census aggregates published in the *Albany Gazette*, Jan. 18, 1787.

24. Louis Guillaume Otto to Comte de Vergennes, Aug. 20, 1786, and Jay to Thomas Jefferson, Dec. 14, 1786, in Giunta, ed., *Emerging Nation*, III: 270 and 374; Thomas Proctor, diary, Apr. 27 and 28, 1791, in *ASPIA*, I: 156.

25. Patrick Murray to John Graves Simcoe, Dec. 23, 1791 ("We are"), MG 23 H-I-1, 3rd Ser. (Simcoe Transcripts), I: 367, NAC; Wright, *Britain and the American Frontier*, 2.

26. John Dease to Henry Hamilton, Sept. 16, 1785, in Cruikshank, ed., "Records of Niagara, 1784–7," 72; Alexander McKee, "Private Memorandum Relative to Indians," MG 23 H-I-1 (Simcoe Transcripts), 4th Ser., III, Folder Tt, p. 21, NAC; Sir John Johnson to John

Graves Simcoe, May 28, 1792, MG 23 H-I-1 (Simcoe Transcripts), 4th ser., I, Folder Ff, NAC.

27. Gen. Riedesel to Frederick Haldimand, Dec. 19, 1782, in "Haldimand Papers," *Michigan Pioneer and Historical Society, Collections*, XX (1892): 83; E. B. Littlehales to James Smith, Sept. 24, 1792, MG 23 H-I-1 (Simcoe Transcripts), 4th Ser., VII, Folder 9, p. 34, NAC; Capt. Schoedde to Francis Le Maistre, Sept. 28, 1792, RG 8 (Military Records), vol. 930, p. 105, NAC; Gen. Alured Clarke to John Graves Simcoe, Oct. 8, 1792, and Capt. David Shank to Maj. Littlehales, Sept. 11, 1794, in Cruikshank, ed., *Correspondence of Simcoe*, I: 232, III: 70; Riddell, ed., *La Rochefoucault-Liancourt's Travels in Canada*, 80–81; Turner, *Pioneer History of the Holland Purchase*, 393–94.

28. John Butler, "Return of the Six Nation Indians and Confederates, June 24, 1783," RG 10, (Indian Affairs), Ser. A6, XV: 74, NAC; Houghton, "History of the Buffalo Creek Reservation," 5–11, 114–16; Howland, "Seneca Mission at Buffalo Creek," 127–28; Ketchum, *Authentic and Comprehensive History of Buffalo*, I: 359–67; Thomas Proctor, diary, Apr. 27, 1791 ("far better"), *ASPIA*, I: 155.

29. Fenton and Tooker, "Mohawk," 466–80; Frederick Haldimand, "Means Suggested as the Most Probable to Retain the Six Nations and Western Indians in the King's Interest" ("preserve"), in Johnston, ed., *Valley of the Six Nations*, 53; Allan MacLean to Robert Mathews, May 13, 1783 ("If we"), and MacLean to Haldimand, May 18, 1783, MG 21 (Haldimand Papers), #21763, pp. 108, 119, NAC.

30. Allan MacLean to Frederick Haldimand, May 9, 1783 ("a brave fellow"), MacLean to Robert Mathews, May 13, 1783, and MacLean to Haldimand, May 18, 1783, MG 21 (Haldimand Papers), #21763, pp. 99, 108, 119, NAC; Haldimand to Sir John Johnson, May 27, 1783, and Mathews to Johnson, May 29, 1783, MG 21 (Haldimand Papers), #21775, pp. 124, 126, NAC; Kelsay, *Joseph Brant*, 340–42; Cruikshank, "King's Royal Regiment," 304, 310, 312.

31. Frederick Haldimand to Sir John Johnson, May 26, 1783, Haldimand to Arent Schuyler de Peyster, c. 1784, and Haldimand, "Means Suggested as the Most Probable to Retain the Six Nations and Western Indians in the King's Interest," in Johnston, ed., *Valley of the Six Nations*, 41, 51, 53; Haldimand to Johnson, Mar. 23, 1784, MG 19 F 2 (Sir John Johnson Papers), III, NAC; Haldimand to Lord Sydney, Mar. 16, 1785 ("abandon us,"), in Cruikshank, ed., "Records of Niagara, 1784–7," 55.

32. Sir John Johnson to Frederick Haldimand, May 19, 1783, Haldimand to Johnson, May 26, 1783, and Johnson to Haldimand, Mar. 11, 1784, MG 21 (Haldimand Papers), #21775, pp. 112, 122, 260, NAC; Robert Mathews to Joseph Brant, Apr. 12, 1784, MG 21 (Haldimand Papers), #21725, p. 9, NAC; Haldimand to Johnson, Apr. 22, 1784, RG 10 (Indian Affairs), XV: 121, NAC; Rev. John Stuart to the Society for the Propagation of the Gospel, May 25, 1784, in Johnston, ed., *Valley of the Six Nations*, 49; Arent Schuyler de Peyster to Haldimand, June 28, 1785, MG 21 (Haldimand Papers), #21763, p. 327, NAC; Brant, speech, Sept. 8, 1795, MG 23 H I 1 (Simcoe Transcripts), 4th Ser., III, Folder Zz, p. 8, NAC; Brant, speech, July 23, 1806, MG 19 F 35 (PSGIA), 2nd Ser., Lot 728, NAC; Kelsay, *Joseph Brant*, 343, 349–51; Siebert, "Loyalists and the Six Nation Indians," 93–94; Johnston, "Outline of Early Settlement," 44–47.

33. Siebert, "Loyalists and the Six Nations," 94; Frederick Haldimand to Sir John Johnson, Mar. 23, 1784, MG 19 F2 (Sir John Johnson Papers), III, NAC; Johnson to Haldimand, Apr. 8, 1784 ("Counteract"), MG 21 (Haldimand Papers) #21775, p. 272, NAC; Johnston, "An Outline of Early Settlement in the Grand River," 48–50; Haldimand to Arent Schuyler de Peyster, Nov. n.d., 1784, in Johnston, ed., *Valley of the Six Nations*, 51–52; Joseph Brant to Arent Schuyler de Peyster, May 30, 1785 ("to disappoint"), in De Peyster, ed., *Miscellanies by an Officer*, xv.

34. Sir John Johnson to Frederick Haldimand, Mar. 11, 1784, MG 21 (Haldimand Papers),

#21775, p. 260, NAC; John Deserontyon to Daniel Claus, Apr. 7, 1784, MG 19 F 1 (Claus Family Papers), XXIV: 17, NAC; Arent Schuyler De Peyster to Haldimand, June 28, 1785, MG 21 (Haldimand Papers), #21763, p. 327, NAC; John Stuart to the Society for the Propagation of the Gospel, May 25, 1784, in Johnston, ed., *Valley of the Six Nations*, 49; Siebert, "The Loyalists and the Six Nation Indians," 117; Torok, "Tyendinaga Mohawks," 70–73.

35. Frederick Haldimand to John Deserontyon, Oct. 29, 1784, and Haldimand to Major John Ross, Oct. 25, 1784, MG 21 (Haldimand Papers), #21725, pp. 110, 113, NAC; Robert Mathews to John Stuart, Oct. 30, 1784, in Johnston, ed., *Valley of the Six Nations*, 51; Deserontyon to Daniel Claus, Feb. 15, 1784, MG 19 F 4 (Claus Family Papers), IV: 69, NAC; Deserontyon to Maj. Potts, Jan. 12, 1785, James Givens Papers, Box 1, Folder 1, MTL; Torok, "Tyendinaga Mohawks," 74–76; Charles M. Johnston, "John Deserontyon," *DCB*, V: 253–56; John Collins to Lord Dorchester, Dec. 19, 1787, and John Stuart to Charles Inglis, July 6, 1788, in Preston, ed., *Kingston Before the War of 1812*, 126, 135–37; Johnston, "An Outline of Early Settlement," 47; Cruikshank, "Coming of the Loyalist Mohawks," 402; Cometti, ed., *American Journals of Lt. John Enys*, 301; Sir John Johnson to John Deserontyon, Apr. 21, 1788, RG 10 (Indian Affairs), XV: 207, NAC.

36. John Stuart to Robert Mathews, Apr. 12, 1784, MG 21 (Haldimand Papers), #21822, p. 224, NAC; John Stuart to the Society for the Propagation of the Gospel, May 25, 1784, in Johnston, ed., *Valley of the Six Nations*, 49; Stuart to Charles Inglis, July 6, 1788, in Preston, ed., *Kingston Before the War of 1812*, 135–37; "Memoir of the Rev. John Stuart, D.D.," O'Callaghan, ed., *DHSNY*, IV: 508–17.

37. Abler, ed., *Chainbreaker*, 167 ("wanted").

38. Abler, ed., *Chainbreaker*, 168 ("For it may be").

39. Siebert, "Loyalists and the Six Nation Indians," 93–94, 117–18; Johnston, "Outline of Early Settlement," 47–51; John Dease to Henry Hamilton, Sept. 16, 1785, in Cruikshank, ed., "Records of Niagara, 1784–7," 72; Joseph Brant to Patrick Langan, Mar. 20, 1788 ("We must"), in Stone, *Life of Joseph Brant*, II: 275. For an ethnic breakdown of the Grand River inhabitants, see "A Census of the Six Nations on the Grand River" (1785), in Johnston, ed., *Valley of the Six Nations*, 52. That census, however, gives an implausibly high total population of 1,843 at odds with all other estimates, which put the Grand River total at about 1,200. See, for example, [John Butler], "Return of the Number of the Six Nations of Indians," Nov. 15, 1789, F 47-1-1 (Simcoe Papers), AO.

40. Memorial of Hendrick Nelles, n.d., MG 21 (Haldimand Papers), #21765, p. 417, NAC; John Dease to Sir John Johnson, Sept. 18, 1784, in Cruikshank, "Records of Niagara, 1784–7," 47; Siebert, "Loyalists and the Six Nation Indians," 120; Johnston, *Brant County*, 7–11; Five Nations, deed, to Hendrick Nelles et al., Feb. 26, 1787, in Johnston, ed., *Valley of the Six Nations*, 70–71.

41. John Deserontyon, speech, Sept. 2, 1800, and Sir John Johnson, speech, Sept. 20, 1788, in Johnston, ed., *Valley of the Six Nations*, 54, 72; Captain Isaac Hill and Captain Aaron Hill, speech, Feb. 10, 1789, and Joseph Brant, speech, Feb. 10, 1789 (John Deserontyon quoted: "mere Slaves"), MG 19 F 35 (PSGIA), 2nd Ser., Lot 673, NAC; Johnson to Lord Dorchester, Jan. 28, 1790, MG 11 (Colonial Office 42), LXIX: 227, NAC.

42. Joseph Brant to Joseph Chew, Oct. 27, 1791 ("My Wishing" and "applied to"), F 47-1-1 (Simcoe Papers), Reel MS-1797, AO.

43. John Deserontyon, speech, Sept. 2, 1800, and Sir John Johnson, speech, Sept. 20, 1788 ("to the Six Nations"), in Johnston, ed., *Valley of the Six Nations*, 54, 72; Lord Dorchester to Lord Sydney, Oct. 14, 1788, MG 11 (Colonial Office 42), LXI: 102, NAC; Captain Isaac Hill and Captain Aaron Hill, speech, Feb. 10, 1789 ("we wish"), MG 19 F 35 (PSGIA), 2nd Ser., Lot 673,

NAC. For the release of the murderer, see Joseph Brant to Joseph Chew, Oct. 27, 1791, F 47-1-1 (Simcoe Papers), Reel MS-1797, AO.

44. Joseph Brant, speech, Feb. 10, 1789, and Fish Carrier, speech, Feb. 10, 1789, MG 19 F 35 (PSGIA), 2nd Ser., Lot 673, NAC; Lord Dorchester to Sir John Johnson, June 22, 1789, RG 10 (Indian Affairs), XV: 362, NAC; John Deserontyon to Johnson, Apr. 28, 1790, MG 19 F 35 (PSGIA), 2nd Ser., Lot 678, NAC.

45. Paulus to Daniel Claus, Aug. 7, 1785 ("that the land"), MG 19 F 1 (Claus Family Papers), XXIV: 24, NAC; Johnston, "An Outline of Early Settlement," 43–44, 50; "Memoir of the Rev. John Stuart, D.D.," in O'Callaghan, ed., *DHSNY*, IV: 518 ("I found"); Campbell, *Travels in the Interior*, 178 ("the finest").

46. Campbell, *Travels in the Interior*, 178–79 ("The habitations"); Johnston, ed., *Valley of the Six Nations*, xxvii, xl, and map facing lxxxvi; Klinck and Talman, eds., *Journal of Major John Norton*, 5, 283; E. B. Littlehales, journal, Feb. 7, 1793, in Cruikshank, ed., *Correspondence of Simcoe*, I: 289; Smith, *Short Topographical Description*, 122.

47. Kelsay, *Joseph Brant*, 521–23; Campbell, *Travels in the Interior*, 166 ("better"), 178–79 ("large quantities" and "as happy").

48. Sir John Johnson to Claus, Oct. 19, 1787 ("They have"), MG 19 F 1 (Claus Family Papers), XXIV: 24, IV: 167, NAC; John Stuart, report, July 2, 1788, in Johnston, ed., *Valley of the Six Nations*, 236; "Memoir of the Rev. John Stuart, D.D.," in O'Callaghan, ed., *DHSNY*, IV: 518 ("a handsome"); E. B. Littlehales, journal, Feb. 7, 1793, in Cruikshank, ed., *Correspondence of Simcoe*, I: 289; Campbell, *Travels in the Interior*, 166; Johnston, "Six Nations in the Grand River Valley," 174; Young, "Rev. Robert Addison," 175; Zeisberger, *Diary of David Zeisberger*, II: 374 ("in the school-house").

49. Gray, ed., "From Bethlehem to Fairfield," 120 ("a handsome"); Kelsay, *Joseph Brant*, 522–23.

50. Campbell, *Travels in the Interior*, 165–70 ("Tea," "served," "with silver," "King," "a brace," and "our beds"); [Anonymous], "Canadian Letters," 162.

51. Gray, ed., "From Bethlehem to Fairfield," 120; Stone, *Life of Joseph Brant*, II: 449 (Samuel Woodruff quoted: "five feet"), 457–58; Innis, ed., *Mrs. Simcoe's Diary*, 82 ("Capt. Brant"); Anonymous, "Canadian Letters," 162 ("His deportment").

52. Campbell, *Travels in the Interior*, 164–65 ("appeared" and "elegance"); Kelsay, *Joseph Brant*, 528–29.

53. Campbell, *Travels in the Interior*, 167–70 ("in their," "held the drum," and "much surprised"). Apparently, the schoolhouse windows got smashed during his frequent absences.

54. Allan MacLean to Frederick Haldimand, May 3, June 17, and July 19, 1783, MG 21 (Haldimand Papers), #21763, pp. 77 ("to Japan"), 121, 197, NAC; Zeichner, "Loyalist Problem in New York," 289–95; Cruikshank, "King's Royal Regiment of New York," 293–97.

55. Gentilcore and Wood, "Military Colony in a Wilderness," 32; Moore, "Disposition to Settle," 53–79; McLean, "Peopling Glengarry County," 151–73; Gates, *Land Policies of Upper Canada*, 11–15. For Loyalist numbers in Canada, see Henry Hope to the Commissioners for American Claims, Jan. 29, 1786, and John Craigie, "Abstract of the Number of Loyalists Settled in the Upper Parts of the Province of Quebec," Oct. 27, 1786, in Cruikshank, ed., "Records of Niagara, 1784–7," 80–81, 95.

56. Hansen and Brebner, *Mingling of the Canadian and American Peoples*, 60–62; Hunter, *Quebec to Carolina*, 70 ("It does"); Gates, *Land Policies of Upper Canada*, 15; Moore, "Disposition to Settle," 68–71; Cometti, ed., *American Journals of Lt. John Enys*, 298–301.

57. Smith, *Sacred Feathers*, 1–21; Smith, "Dispossession of the Mississauga Indians," 25; Rogers, "Southeastern Ojibwa," 760–64; Sir John Johnson, Return of the Mississauga, Sept. 23, 1787, RG 10 (Indian Affairs), XV: 197, NAC; Cometti, ed., *American Journals of Lt. John Enys*, 103,

150–52; Hughes, *Journal by Thos. Hughes*, 154; Campbell, *Travels in the Interior*, 158–60; Innis, ed., *Mrs. Simcoe's Diary*, 107 ("To see").

58. Rogers, "Southeastern Ojibwa," 760–61; Smith, "Dispossession of the Mississauga," 25; Cruikshank, "Coming of the Loyalist Mohawks," 399; Cometti, ed., *American Journals of Lt. John Enys*, 301; White, ed., *Lord Selkirk's Diary*, 306; Smith, *Sacred Feathers*, 3.

59. Smith, *Sacred Feathers*, 31; John Ross to Robert Mathews, June 9, 1782, MG 21 (Haldimand Papers), #21784, p. 30, NAC; Hunter, *Quebec to Carolina*, 97; Weld, *Travels Through the States of North America*, II: 84 ("They are"); Sir John Johnson to Patrick Langan, Sept. 20, 1789, and Patrick Langan, speech, Oct. 18, 1789, RG 1 E 3 (Upper Canada Executive Council, State Submissions), XXXVII: 35, 37–38, NAC; Chiefs of Sault S. Louis, speech, Dec. 16, 1791 ("Can you"), MG 19 F 35 (PSGIA), 2nd Ser., Lot 694, NAC.

60. John Ross to Frederick Haldimand, Oct. 9, 1783, in Cruikshank, ed., "King's Royal Regiment," 301; Sir John Johnson to Haldimand, Aug. 11, 1783 ("seem to have"), MG 21 (Haldimand Papers), #21775, p. 152, NAC; Smith, "Dispossession of the Mississauga," 29.

61. Sir John Johnson list of goods for the Mississaugas, Sept. 23, 1787, and John Butler to Johnson, Aug. 28, 1788, RG 10 (Indian Affairs), XV: 195, 413, NAC; Johnson to Daniel Claus, Oct. 19, 1787, MG 19 F 1 (Claus Family Papers), IV: 167, NAC; Butler to Johnson, Nov. 6, 1791, F47-1-1 (Simcoe Papers), AO; Smith, *Sacred Feathers*, 23–27.

62. John Collins, memorandum, Aug. 9, 1785 ("the Chiefs"), F 47-1-1 (Simcoe Papers), AO; Shawancoupaway, speech, Aug. 28, 1788 ("They say"), RG 1 E 3 (Upper Canada Executive Council, State Submissions), XXXVII: 50, NAC.

63. Smith, *Sacred Feathers*, 25–26; Smith, "Dispossession of the Mississauga," 29–32; Sir John Johnson to Daniel Claus, Oct. 19, 1787, MG 19 F 1 (Claus Family Papers), IV: 167, NAC.

64. Daniel Claus to Robert Mathews, July 17, 1783, MG 19 F 1 (Claus Family Papers), III: 237, NAC; Pokquan, speech, May 22, 1784 ("We are"), in Johnston, ed., *Valley of the Six Nations*, 47; Mathews to John Ross, June 24, 1784, MG 21 (Haldimand Papers), #21723, p. 137, NAC; Tekarihoga, speech, July 4, 1819, in Brymner, ed., *Report on Canadian Archives, 1896*, 18.

65. Smith, "Dispossession of the Mississauga," 33–34; Captain Richard Porter to John Graves Simcoe, May 3, 1794, in Preston, ed., *Kingston Before the War of 1812*, 359; William Chewitt to David W. Smith, Sept. 4, 1794 ("the English"), RG 1 (Crown Lands), A-I-1 (Letters Received by the Surveyor General), L: 580, AO.

66. Samuel Sherwood to Major Holland, Oct. 17, 1784, MG 21 (Haldimand Papers), #21822, p. 366, NAC; William Chewitt to David W. Smith, Sept. 4, 1794 ("take Cattle"), RG 1 (Crown Lands) A-I-1 (Letters Received by the Surveyor General), L: 580, AO; Pataquan Speech, Oct. n.d., 1801 ("with Hats"), in Upper Canada Executive Council Minutes, Oct. 20, 1791, MG 11 (Colonial Office #42), CCCXXXII: 17, NAC; Quinepenon, speech, Sept. 6, 1806 ("our Waters"), RG 10, Upper Canada Civil Control, Indian Affairs, I: 451, NAC.

67. Smith, "Dispossession of the Mississauga," 33–34; Smith, *Sacred Feathers*, 26–27; Innis, ed., *Mrs. Simcoe's Diary*, 117 ("almost starved").

68. [David Ramsey], Mississauga Memorial to John Graves Simcoe, n.d. 1793 ("the taking"), MG 23 H-I-1, 4th Ser. (Simcoe Transcripts), II, Folder Qq, NAC; Nauwagaseck, speech, Mar. 22, 1798, MG 19 F 35 (PSGIA), 2nd Ser., Lot 719, NAC; Quinepenon, speech, Aug. 1, 1805 ("Colonel Butler"), RG 10, Upper Canada Civil Control, Indian Affairs, I: 294, NAC.

69. Castiglioni, *Viaggio*, 80; Samuel Sherwood to Maj. Holland, Oct. 17, 1784, MG 21 (Haldimand Papers), #21822, p. 366, NAC; [David Ramsey], Mississauga Memorial to John Graves Simcoe, n.d. 1793, MG 23 H-I-1, 4th Ser. (Simcoe Transcripts), II, Folder Qq, NAC; Smith, "Dispossession of the Mississauga," 39–41; John Cameron to William Claus, Dec. 16, 1806 ("many of"), MG 19 F 1 (Claus Family Papers), IX: 156, NAC.

70. Mississauga chief, speech, July 8, 1820 ("You came"), in McOuat, ed., "Diary of William Graves," 10.

71. Kagondanayon, speech, Apr. 18, 1792, MG 11 (Colonial Office 42), XC: 166, NAC; Samuel Kirkland, "A Statement of the Number & Situation of the Six United Nations of Indians in North America," Oct. 15, 1791, Misc. Bound MSS, MHS.

72. Good Peter, speech for the Cayuga women, Feb. 19, 1789 ("Our Ancestors"), in Hough, ed., *Proceedings of the Commissioners*, II: 279. For the rise of the war chiefs, see Graymont, *Iroquois in the American Revolution*, 22–23, 110, 115–16; Calloway, *American Revolution in Indian Country*, 59–60.

73. Samuel Kirkland, "A Statement of the Number & Situation of the Six United Nations of Indians in North America," Oct. 15, 1791, Misc. Bound MSS, MHS. For the return to the Allegheny, see Richter, "Onas, the Long Knife," 131–33; Wallace, *Death and Rebirth of the Seneca*, 168–69.

74. Samuel Kirkland, "A Statement of the Number & Situation of the Six United Nations of Indians in North America," Oct. 15, 1791, Misc. Bound MSS, MHS; Bureau of the Census, *Heads of Families at the First Census*, 9; Israel Chapin, Jr., to Oliver Phelps, Mar. 16, 1791 ("People"), PGP, Box 18, NYSL; Captain Bowman, journal, Apr. 28, 1791 ("wished"), TPP, LXI: 190, MHS.

75. Lt. Col. Butler, memorandum, Sept. 20, 1788, and Robert Hamilton to John Graves Simcoe, Jan. 4, 1792 ("In extending"), F 47-1-1 (Simcoe Papers), AO; Sir John Johnson to Lord Dorchester, Sept. 13, 1790, MG 11 (Colonial Office 42), LXIX: 265, NAC; Simcoe to Gen. Alured Clarke, July 24, 1793, in Cruikshank, ed., *Correspondence of Simcoe*, I: 398.

76. Joseph Brant to Patrick Langan, Mar. 20, 1788 ("As for"), in Stone, *Life of Joseph Brant*, II: 275; Brant, speech, Aug. 19, 1788 ("The Americans"), MG 11 (Colonial Office 42), LXXXIII: 203, NAC; Brant, "Memorandum for Mr. Johnston," n.d. [ca. 1792] ("We must"), F 47-1-2-8 (Simcoe Papers), Reel Ms-1798, AO.

77. David and Aaron Hill to Sir John Johnson, Apr. 15, 1790, and Joseph Brant to Johnson, Nov. 8, 1790 ("have ever disapproved"), in Cruikshank, ed., "Records of Niagara, 1790–1792," 27, 80; Brant, speech, Aug. 19, 1791, and Brant to Joseph Chew, Jan. 19, 1792 ("I believe"), MG 11 (Colonial Office 42), LXXXIII: 203, XC: 148, NAC; Col. Adam Gordon to Francis Le Maistre, Apr. 14, 1792, MG 11 (Colonial Office 42), XC: 164, NAC; Alexander McKee, "Private Memorandum Relative to Indians," n.d. [c. 1792] ("not good policy" and "more dangerous"), MG 23 H-I-1, Ser. 4 (Simcoe Transcripts), III, Folder Tt, p. 21, NAC; Butler, speech, Apr. 8, 1790, MG 19 F 35 (PSGIA), Ser. 2, Lot 675, NAC; Lord Dorchester to Lord Sydney, Oct. 14, 1788, MG 11 (Colonial Office 42), LXI: 98, NAC; Dorchester to Sir John Johnson, May 31, 1790, and Francis Le Maistre to Col. Adam Gordon, Apr. 14, 1791, in Cruikshank, ed., "Records of Niagara . . . 1790–1792," 42 and 94; Butler addendum to speech by Kagondnayen (Onondaga), Apr. 18, 1792, F-47-1-2-2 (Simcoe Papers), Reel Ms-1792, AO.

78. William Perry, "An Account of the Damage Done in the German Flats and Kingsland District," 1783, Robert R. Livingston Papers, Reel 3, NYHS; Peter Sailly, "Diary of Peter Sailly on a Journey in America in the Year 1784," in Snow, Gehring, and Starna, eds., *In Mohawk Country*, 29 ("most beautiful"); Idzerda et al., eds., *Lafayette in the Age of the American Revolution*, V: 245–47; Wallace, ed., *Thirty Thousand Miles with John Heckewelder*, 299.

79. Horton, ed., "Mohawk Valley in 1791," 213 (James Kent: "The inhabitants"); Lincoln, "Journal of a Treaty Held in 1793," 120; Watson, ed., *Men and Times of the Revolution*, 312; Vanderkemp, "Extracts from the Vanderkemp Papers," 56 ("a number"); Abraham Cuyler and Henry Glen to George Clinton, June 28, 1784 ("the Inhabitants"), in Hough, ed., *Proceedings of the Commissioners*, I: 16.

80. Simon Desjardins, Pierre Pharoux, and Geoffrey Desjardins, "Castorland Journal," 117 ("begged"), AAS; Watson, ed., *Men and Times of the Revolution*, 309 ("He entered").

81. Watson, ed., *Men and Times of the Revolution*, 311 ("They looked"). Watson called the Indians "Mohawks," but the Indians attending the 1788 council were Oneidas.

82. Coventry, *Memoirs of an Emigrant*, I: 572; Lincklaen, *Travels in the Years 1791 and 1792*, 58 ("these people," "richer lands," and "covered"); Col. Thomas Proctor, journal extracts, Mar. 26, 1791 ("enjoined me"), #12841, NYSL.

83. Kingman, ed., *Early Owego*, 14–16, 34; Murray, *History of Old Tioga Point*, 237; McMaster, *History of the Settlement of Steuben County*, 54.

84. James Clinton to his wife, July 18, 1786, DWFP, Box 1, SULSC; James Kent, Travel Journal #3, June 21, 1798, JKP, Reel 6, Container 14, LC; McMaster, *History of the Settlement of Steuben County*, 47, 251–52; Jesse McQuigg quoted in Kingman, ed., *Early Owego*, 36 ("The deer").

85. Murray, *History of Old Tioga Point*, 241–46; Perkins, *Early Times on the Susquehanna*, 58–61; Kingman, ed., *Early Owego*, 1–11, 16, 20, 35–39; McMaster, *Steuben County*, 52–53.

86. Moses DeWitt to Jacob R. Dewitt, July 6 ("Treaty" and "very merry") and July 17, 1786 ("white People," and "I have been"), and Aug. 7, 1786, and James Clinton to his wife, July 18, 1786, DWFP, Box 1, SULSC.

87. Andrew Ellicott to Sally Ellicott, July 11, 1786 ("Contrary to") and Aug. 6, 1786 ("share in"), in Mathews, *Andrew Ellicott*, 58, 59; David Rittenhouse to Hannah Rittenhouse, Aug. 6, 1786, in [New York State], *Report of the Regents' Boundary Commission upon the New York and Pennsylvania Boundary*, 87.

88. Caty McMaster quoted in Kingman, ed., *Early Owego*, 20 ("wigwams"), see also 36; McMaster, *Steuben County*, 68–72; Fenton, ed., "Journal of James Emlen," 297; Way-Way quoted in Murray, *History of Old Tioga Point*, 169–70 ("very good").

89. Moses DeWitt to Jacob R. DeWitt, July 17, 1786, and James Clinton to unnamed wife, July 18, 1786, DWFP, Box 1, SULSC; Perkins, *Early Times on the Susquehanna*, 75–76; Murray, *History of Old Tioga Point*, 313.

90. Moses DeWitt, journal, July 10, 1786 ("very likely"), DWFP, Box 7, SULSC; Kent and Deardorff, eds., "John Adlum on the Allegheny," 468n47; [Andrew Ellicott], "Extract of a Letter from Chemung to a Gentleman in Baltimore," July 26, 1787 ("began to adopt," and "imposed"), *Albany Gazette*, Sept. 6, 1787.

91. Gridley, *History of the Town of Kirkland*, 36–37; McMaster, *Steuben County*, 242 ("lived in").

92. Moses DeWitt to Jacob R. DeWitt, June 7, 1787 ("The people"), DWFP, Box 1, SULSC. For population figures from the 1790 and 1800 censuses, see Hough, ed., *Census of the State of New-York, for 1855*, xiii–xiv.

93. McMaster, *Steuben County*, 243; Jesse McQuigg quoted in Kingman, ed., *Early Owego*, 38 ("He was afraid").

94. McMaster, *Steuben County*, 243, 251, 257.

95. Taylor, " 'Great Change Begins,' " 265–90.

96. Unnamed settler quoted in McMaster, *Steuben County*, 166 ("People now"); Turner, *Phelps and Gorham Purchase*, 352.

CHAPTER FIVE: STATE

1. Charles DeWitt to George Clinton, June 4, 1784 ("The whole World"), in "Letters of Charles DeWitt," *Olde Ulster*, V (1909): 149–50.

2. Young, *Democratic Republicans of New York*, 233–35; "An Act to Facilitate the Settlement of the

Waste and Unappropriated Lands Within This State . . ." (Chap. 66, passed Apr. 11, 1785), [New York State], *Laws of the State of New York* (1887), II: 114–16.

3. James Duane to George Clinton, June n.d., 1784 (all quotations), in Hastings, ed., *Public Papers of George Clinton*, VIII: 329–30.

4. New York Delegates to the New York Legislature, Mar. 31, 1779 ("cruel"), in Smith, ed., *Letters of Delegates to Congress*, XII: 269–70; "An Act to Appoint Commissioners to Represent This State in Any Treaty of Pacification That May Be Had with Any of the Nations of Indians Therein Mentioned," Oct. 23, 1779 (Chap. 29), [New York State], *Laws of the State of New York* (1887), I: 93.

5. "An Act for Indian Affairs," Mar. 25, 1783, [New York State] *Laws of the State of New York* (1887), I: 565; Henry Glen, Peter Schuyler, and Abraham Cuyler to George Clinton, Aug. 29, 1783, A 1823 (Assembly Papers, Indian Affairs, 1783–1809), Box 40, NYSA. For the federal guarantees to the Oneidas, see Report of the Committee on Indian Affairs, Oct. 15, 1783, in Ford, ed., *Journals of the Continental Congress*, XXV: 683; Campisi, "Oneida Treaty Period," 56.

6. Ford, ed., *Journals of the Continental Congress, 1774–1789*, IX: 996 ("It rejoices"), XXV: 687 ("that the lands"); Philip Schuyler, speech, May 11, 1778 ("you will"), PCC, Reel 189, p. 281, LC; Schuyler, speech, Jan. 11, 1784 ("have no right"), PSP, XIV, NYPL.

7. Philip Schuyler to the President of Congress, July 29, 1783, PCC, Reel 173, p. 601, LC; Tiro, "People of the Standing Stone," 139–43, 150; Pilkington, ed., *Journals of Samuel Kirkland*, 125; Kirkland to James Board, Jan. 14, 1785, SKP, Folder 91, HCA; Kirkland to Jerusha Kirkland, Sept. 10, 1785, SKP, Folder 97B, HCA; Samuel Kirkland, Memorandum on Peter Penet, n.d. SKP, Letters Undated and Fragmentary File ("Previous"), HCA.

8. Oneida speech to New York State Legislature, in *New-York Journal* (New York City), Mar. 20, 1788; Joseph Brant to Captain Fraser, Aug. 30, 1784 ("The Oneidas"), RG 10 (Indian Affairs), XV: 153, NAC; Chase, ed., *Our Revolutionary Forefathers*, 197.

9. Jones, *Stockbridge*, 85–86 (Kirkland quoted, p. 86).

10. Love, *Samson Occom and the Christian Indians*, 211–12, 222–23; Oneida speeches, Jan. 22 and 24, 1774, and Joseph Johnson to Eleazar Wheelock, in McCallum, ed., *Letters of Eleazar Wheelock's Indians*, 168–69, 171–72, 178–79; Peyer, *Tutor'd Mind*, 83–84; Blodgett, *Samson Occom*, 150–55, 160–61; Murray, ed., *To Do Good to My Indian Brethren*, 168–262.

11. Axtell, *The Invasion Within*, 163, 196–99; Tilghman, ed., *Memoir of Lieut. Col. Tench Tilghman*, 96; John Sergeant, "Case of [the] Stockbridge Indians," [Aug. 1776], in Force, ed., *American Archives*, 5th Ser., I: 903; Calloway, *American Revolution in Indian Country*, 86, 91–100; Taylor, "Captain Hendrick Aupaumut," 432–57; Frazier, *Mohicans of Stockbridge*, 194–205, 234–38; Hauptman, Dispersal of the River Indians," 244–60; Hendrick Aupaumut, speech, July 24, 1795, in Embree, "Some Account of a Visit Paid to the Indians Situated on the Frontiers of the State of New York," 20.

12. Love, *Samson Occom*, 225, 241–45; Peyer, *Tutor'd Mind*, 84–85; Blodgett, *Samson Occom*, 162–75; Frazier, *Mohicans of Stockbridge*, 234–41; Calloway, *American Revolution in Indian Country*, 101–4; Samson Occom to Solomon Welles, Sept. 26, 1784, DCA, #784526, DCLSC; Pilkington, ed., *Journals of Samuel Kirkland*, 160.

13. Peter the Quarter Master, speech, June 27, 1785, and the Great Grasshopper, speech, June 28, 1785 ("who turned" and Our Country"), in Hough, ed., *Proceedings of the Commissioners*, I: 104. For culture brokers, see Szasz, *Between Indian and White Worlds*; and Merrell, *Into the American Woods*, 19–41. For the Oneida buffer scheme, see Tiro, "James Dean in Iroquoia," 413.

14. Good Peter, speech, June 25, 1785 ("We look" and "Brothers!"), in Hough, ed., *Proceedings of the*

Commissioners, I: 92–93. For the Oneida refugee village in the Genesee country during the 1780s, see Turner, *Phelps and Gorham Purchase*, 329.

15. Oneida petition to the New York State Legislature, Jan. 10, 1793 ("We are old men"), A 4016 (Records of the Surveyor General), XXI: 97, NYSA.

16. Good Peter, speech, June 25, 1785 ("We have many friends"), in Hough, ed., *Proceedings of the Commissioners*, I: 92–93; Oneida chiefs to the New York State Legislature, *New-York Journal*, Mar. 20, 1788.

17. Oneida chiefs to William Colbrath, Aug. 6, 1792 ("old Mr. Clock"), #13426, HL; Good Peter, interview, April n.d., 1792, TPP, LX: 123, MHS; Samuel Kirkland, "Memoir of Negotiations Relative to Indian Lands Within the State of New York, 1786–1788," Manuscript #2140, HL; Oneida petition to Gov. Clinton, Dec. 6, 1788 ("Our Friend"), #13427, HL. For a similar rent, the Oneida leased a township to another silversmith, Abraham Van Eps, from Schenectady and Hezekiah Olcott, an Indian trader.

18. Lincklaen, *Travels in the Years 1791 and 1792*, 70, 112; Oneida indenture with Isaac Carpenter, Sept. 1, 1789, and Oneida indenture with Conrad Klock and sons, Aug. 14, 1794, PSP, Box 14, NYPL.

19. Good Peter, speech, June 25, 1785, in Hough, ed., *Proceedings of the Commissioners*, I: 91–93; Samuel Kirkland to Samuel Phillips, Jr., Aug. 15, 1785, SKP, Folder 96, HCA. For the leasing and prosperity of the Kahnawake, see Long, *Voyages and Travels*, 6–7; McOuat, ed., "Diary of William Graves," 23.

20. New York State Commissioners, council minutes, Sept. 1, 1784 ("private artifice"), in Hastings, ed., *Public Papers of George Clinton*, VIII: 350–51.

21. Pilkington, ed., *Journals of Samuel Kirkland*, 43n9; Hauptman, *Conspiracy of Interests*, 40; Eleazar Wheelock to George Whitefield, Feb. 24, 1764 ("an honest Man"), EWP #764174, DCLSC; Dexter, ed., *Diary of David McClure*, 15; Sir William Johnson, Pass for Good Peter, Feb. 20, 1765 ("Pious Indian"), in Flick, ed., *PSWJ*, IV: 648; Schuyler to Thomas Mifflin, Jan. 15, 1784 ("a man"), PSP, Box 14, NYPL. Aaron Crosby to Samuel Kirkland, Jan. 25, 1774, SKP, Folder 47, HCA. For Good Peter's lack of English literacy, see Isaac Dakayensere [Dekayenensere] and Gwedlhes Agwelondongwas to Wheelock, Nov. 12, 1764, EWP #764612.3, DCLSC. John Harper translated and Samuel Kirkland wrote the last document, which attests that Good Peter knew little English. See also Kirkland, diary, Aug. 24, 1791, LFP, DCLSC.

22. Calloway, *American Revolution in Indian Country*, 122, 125; Samuel Kirkland to Philip Schuyler, Jan. 25, 1777, SKP, Folder 72, HCA; Schuyler to Thomas Mifflin, Jan. 14 and 15, 1784, PSP, Box 14, NYPL; George Clinton to Peter Ryckman, Apr. 12, 1784 ("Peter"), in Hough, ed., *Proceedings of the Commissioners*, I: 12.

23. Griffith Evans, "Journal," 214; Lincklaen, *Travels in the Years 1791 and 1792*, 67–68; Samuel Kirkland to Peter Thacher, May 15, 1792, #792315, DCLSC; Kirkland to Timothy Pickering, Sept. 8, 1792, TPP, LXII: 60, MHS; Kirkland, diary, Sept. 26, 1791 ("His exhortation"), LFP, DCLSC; Kirkland, Memorandum regarding Peter Penet, SKP, "Letters Undated and Fragmentary" Folder, HCA ("There were").

24. Countryman, *People in Revolution*, 197–98, 210–12; De Pauw, *Eleventh Pillar*, 19–20; Kaminski, *George Clinton*, 1–110; Young, *Democratic Republicans of New York*, 23–25 (includes Schuyler quotation—"played his Cards"—on 24).

25. Countryman, *People in Revolution*, 21–12; De Pauw, *Eleventh Pillar*, 20–21; Young, *Democratic Republicans of New York*, 34–38 (includes the contemporary quotes: "matters," "old George," "circumspect," and "admired"); Schuyler to John Jay, May 30, 1785, in Johnston, ed., *Correspondence and Public Papers of John Jay*, III: 151.

26. Young, *Democratic Republicans*, 26, 29–31, 36–39, 54–56, 231–39; Francis Adrian Vanderkemp to Adam G. Mappa, July 27, 1792, in Vanderkemp, "Extracts from the Vanderkemp Papers," 54–55. For Clinton's frontier speculations see, Hastings, ed., *Public Papers of George Clinton*, X: 1033; Spaulding, *His Excellency George Clinton*, 228–33.

27. Lincoln, ed., *State of New York: Messages from the Governors*, II: 199 ("utmost encouragement"); Graymont, "New York State Indian Policy," 438–74.

28. George Clinton, speeches, Sept. 4 and 5, 1784, in Hastings, ed., *Public Papers of George Clinton*, VIII: 353–54, 363; Return of Provisions & Stores Issued & Delivered to the Indians at Fort Schuyler in August and September 1784, A 0802, Box 13, NYSA; Meeting, Sept. 14, 1784, in Hough, ed., *Proceedings of the Commissioners*, I: 66.

29. George Clinton, speech, Feb. 19, 1789 ("The Dish," "Sisters," and "express"), in Hough, ed., *Proceedings of the Comissioners*, II: 284; Clinton, *Discourse Delivered Before the New-York Historical Society*, 80.

30. George Clinton to the Mohawk, Onondaga, Cayuga, and Seneca sachems and warriors, Apr. 12, 1784, and Clinton to Peter Ryckman, Apr. 12, 1784 ("To Captain Brandt"), in Hough, *Proceedings of the Commissioners*, I: 10–11, 12–13; Clinton to Ryckman, Aug. 14, 1784 ("If you"), in Hastings, ed., *Public Papers of George Clinton*, VIII: 335; Joseph Brant to Clinton, Sept. 28, 1784 ("obligingly offered"), #12481, NYSL.

31. De Pauw, *Eleventh Pillar*, 8–12; Young, *Democratic-Republicans of New York*, 56–58; Kaminski, *George Clinton*, 59–111.

32. John Jay to George Clinton, Oct. 25, 1779, in Morris, ed., *John Jay*, 659–60; Charles DeWitt and Ephraim Paine to George Clinton, April 9, 1784 ("Massachusetts People"), DeWitt to Clinton, June 4, 1784 ("I believe"), and Hugh Williamson to James Duane, June 8, 1784 ("the seeds"), in Burnett, ed., *Letters of Members of the Continental Congress*, VII: 487–88, 545, 546.

33. Philip Schuyler to Pierre Van Cortlandt and Evert Banker, Jan. 29, 1780, in [New York State], *Report of the Regents of the University on the Boundaries of the State of New York*, 137–41; Charles DeWitt and Ephraim Paine to George Clinton, April 9, 1784, Paine to Clinton, Apr. 29, 1784, and DeWitt to Clinton, June 4, 1784 ("high time"), in Burnett, ed., *Letters of Members of the Continental Congress*, VII: 487–88, 504, 545; Frederick Haldimand to Lord North, May 12, 1784, in Cruikshank, ed., "Records of Niagara, 1784–7," 24–25; Kaminski, *George Clinton*, 88.

34. Campisi, "Oneida Treaty Period," 49–50; New York Delegates to George Clinton, Oct. 16, 1783, in Hastings, ed., *Public Papers of George Clinton*, VIII: 261–62.

35. Samuel Osgood to John Adams, Jan. 14, 1784 ("purchase"), in Burnett, ed., *Letters of Members of the Continental Congress*, VII: 415; John Hancock to Massachusetts General Court, May 27, 1784, in Goebel, ed., *Law Practice of Alexander Hamilton*, I: 567.

36. James Monroe to James Madison, Nov. 15, 1784 ("Whether" and "whose management"), in Hamilton, ed., *Writings of James Monroe*, I: 46–47; James Duane to George Clinton, n.d., [ca. 1784], in Hastings, ed., *Public Papers of George Clinton*, VIII: 328. See also Madison to Monroe, Nov. 27, 1784, in Hutchinson and Rachal, eds., *Papers of James Madison*, VIII: 156; Graymont, *Iroquois in the American Revolution*, 268–69.

37. James Duane to George Clinton, n.d. [ca. 1784] ("And if" and "There is"), in Hastings, ed., *Public Papers of George Clinton*, VIII: 328.

38. George Clinton to Arthur Lee and Richard Butler, Aug. 13, 1784 ("with Indians"), Lee and Butler to Clinton, Aug. 19, 1784 ("at the same time"), and New York State Commissioners, proceedings, Aug. 26, 1784, in Hough, ed., *Proceedings of the Commissioners*, I: 21, 29–30, 33.

39. Joseph Brant to Henry Glen, Aug. 11, 1784 ("more general Meeting"), in Hough, ed., *Proceedings of the Commissioners*, I: 26–27; Brant to Captain Fraser, Aug. 30, 1784, RG 10 (Indian Affairs), XV: 151, NAC.

40. George Clinton, speech, Sept. 5, 1784, and Joseph Brant, speech, Sept. 7, 1784 ("Here lies"), in Hough, ed., _Proceedings of the Commissioners_, I: 48–50, 54; Clinton, speech, Sept. 10, 1784, in Hastings, ed., _Public Papers of George Clinton_, VIII: 372; Aaron Hill, speech, Oct. 17, 1784, in Craig, ed., _Olden Time_, II: 419.

41. Campisi, "The Oneida Treaty Period," 55–56; John Butler to Sir John Johnson, RG 10 (Indian Affairs), XV: 109, NAC; Peter Ryckman to Henry Glen, Aug. 23, 1784, Jelles Fonda to Clinton, Aug. 31, 1784, New York State Commissioners, council minutes, Sep. 1, 1784, and George Clinton, speech, Sept. 4, 1784 ("This is not true") in Hastings, ed., _Public Papers of George Clinton_, VIII: 341, 348, 350–51, 354.

42. New York State Commissioners to Peter Schuyler, Sept. 11, 1784 ("any thing"), in Hough, ed., _Proceedings of the Commissioners_, I: 63; Campisi, "From Stanwix to Canandaigua," 53–54; François de Barbé-Marbois to Comte de Vergennes, Sept. 30, 1784, in Giunta, ed., _The Emerging Nation_, II: 452.

43. François de Barbé-Marbois, journal, Sept. 23, 1784, in Idzerda, ed., _Lafayette_, V: 248; Barbé-Marbois to Comte de Vergennes, Sept. 30, 1784, in Giunta, ed., _Emerging Nation_, II: 451; Joseph Brant, "Account of What Passed at Fort Stanwix Prior to the Treaty in October 1784," RG 10 (Indian Affairs), XV: 170, NAC.

44. Kelsay, _Joseph Brant_, 361; E. Leonard, "List of Indians at Fort Stanwix," Oct. 22, 1784, in Oliver Wolcott, Sr., Papers, III, Folder 5, CHS. My Oneida count includes the fifteen characterized on the list as "Col. Louis' family."

45. Evans, "Journal," 208 ("I now"), 213; Evans to John Nicholson, Oct. 5, 1784 ("Just returned"), John Nicholson Papers, Box 1, Folder 6, NYSL.

46. Oliver Wolcott, speech, Oct. 3, 1784 ("without"), and Wolcott, Richard Butler, and Arthur Lee to the President of Congress, Oct. 5, 1784, in Craig, ed., _Olden Time_, 406–7, 414; Monroe, _Autobiography of James Monroe_, 38–40.

47. François de Barbé-Marbois to Comte de Vergennes, Oct. 14, 1784, in Giunta, ed., _The Emerging Nation_, II: 472–74; Griffith Evans, "Journal," 207–11; Fort Stanwix Council Proceedings, Oct. 5 ("the Governor"), 6, 9, 11, and 12, in Craig, ed., _Olden Time_, 408–10, 412, 415.

48. Evans, "Journal," 212, 214 ("his assurance"); Aaron Hill, speech, Oct. 17, 1784, and Arthur Lee, speech, Oct. 20, 1784 ("are mistaken), in Craig, ed., _Olden Time_, 418, 424–25; John Dease to Major Fraser, Nov. 26, 1784 (Hill quoted: "were obliged"), RG 10 (Indian Affairs), XV: 158, NAC; Graymont, _Iroquois in the American Revolution_, 282; Arthur Lee to [unknown], Nov. 19, 1784 ("Animals"), in Potts, _Arthur Lee_, 270. For the seizure of hostages, see also Richard Butler, "Notes of Proceedings at Fort Stanwix," Oct. 18, 1784, in Lyman Draper Papers, Frontier War Ser., MSS 3 U, State Historical Society of Wisconsin.

49. Arthur Lee, Richard Butler, and Oliver Wolcott to Captain Lane, Oct. 26, 1784, in Oliver Wolcott, Sr., Papers, Box III, Folder 5, CHS; Ford, ed., _Journals of the Continental Congress_, XXVII: 659–60. For the gradual return of the prisoners by the Iroquois, see _Albany Gazette_, July 28, 1785. For the Pennsylvania treaty, see Evans, "Journal," 214; Richter, "Onas, the Long Knife," 136–44; Graymont, _Iroquois in the American Revolution_, 282. Pennsylvania paid $4,000 immediately and another $1,000 a year later. This total was less than half of what the state legislature had authorized their commissioners to expend for the purchase.

50. White, _Middle Ground_, 416–17; Richard Butler, "Fort Stanwix Proceedings," in Craig, ed., _Olden Time_, II: 413 ("sole power"), 425; Arthur Lee, Richard Butler, and Oliver Wolcott to Congress, Oct. n.d., 1784, Oliver Wolcott, Sr., Papers, III, Folder 5, CHS.

51. Graymont, _Iroquois in the American Revolution_, 282–84; Wallace, _Death and Rebirth of the Seneca_, 173–74; John Dease to Major Fraser, Nov. 20, 1784, RG 10 (Indian Affairs), XV: 159, NAC;

Tanawaneas, speech, Mar. 26, 1787, in Hough, ed., *Proceedings of the Commissioners*, I: 110; Arthur Lee to [unknown], Dec. 24, 1784, in Lee, *Life of Arthur Lee*, II: 389.

52. Fort Stanwix Council Proceedings, Oct. 20, 1784, in Craig, ed., *Olden Time*, 425–26 ("it does not become"); Campisi, "Oneida Treaty Period," 57–58; Arthur Lee, Richard Butler, and Oliver Wolcott to President of Congress, Oct. n.d., 1784, in Oliver Wolcott, Sr., Papers, Box III, Folder 5, CHS.

53. Samson Occom to [unknown], n.d. [ca. Oct. 27, 1784] (all quotations), in William Lane Griswold Papers, Box 2, Sterling Library, Yale University.

54. James Dean to the President of Congress, July 11, 1785 ("as head" and "The Oneidas"), PCC Reel 37, p. 479, LC. For the perfunctory response by Congress, see Ford, ed., *Journals of the Continental Congress*, XXIX: 619.

55. Gerlach, *Proud Patriot*, 53; Thomas Tillotson to Robert R. Livingston, May n.d., 1784, RRLP, Reel 3, NYHS; Philip Schuyler to Congress, Oct. 15, 1786 ("I had found"), PSP, Box 14, NYPL; Henry Knox to Congress, July 14, 1787, PCC, Reel 165, p. 271, LC.

56. Henry Knox to Congress, Sept. 12, 1785, and July 14, 1787, PCC, Reel 165, pp. 103, 271, LC; William Samuel Johnson to Roger Sherman, Apr. 20, 1785, in Smith, ed., *Letters of Delegates to Congress*, XXII: 349. For the growing poverty and weakness of the confederacy, see also Cochran, *New York in the Confederation*, 133–50, 163–68; Henry Knox to Congress, Mar. 31, 1788, in Carter, ed., *Territorial Papers of the United States*, II: 101. For the federal abandonment of a land claim within Iroquoia, see James Monroe to James Madison, Nov. 15, 1784, in S. M. Hamilton, ed., *Writings of Monroe*, I: 47. Nonetheless, the treaty obligated the federal government to protect the Iroquois claim to lands within the treaty boundary. See Samuel Hardy to the Governor of Virginia, Nov. 21, 1784, in Burnett, ed., *Letters of Members of the Continental Congress*, VII: 614; Ford, ed., *Journals of the Continental Congress*, XXIX: 806.

57. Gould, *History of Delaware County*, 11, 30–38; Campbell, *Annals of Tryon County*, 153.

58. Hough, *Proceedings of the Commissioners*, I: 73n1–74n1; [New York State], *Journal of the State Senate for 1785*, 10 (Feb. 5, 1785). For Harper's introduction of settlers onto the land, see William Guthrie et al., petition to the state legislature, June 6, 1787, Office of the Secretary of State, Indorsed Land Papers, XLIV: 29, NYSA.

59. Oneida Chiefs to New York Commissioners of Indian Affairs, Sept. 9, 1782 ("agreed"), #11621, HL; [New York State], *Journal of the State Senate for 1785*, 10, 80; [New York State], *Journal of the State Assembly for 1785*, 31–32 ("when").

60. "An Act to facilitate the Settlement of the Waste and Unappropriated Lands Within this State," Apr. 11, 1785 ("reasonable terms"), [New York State] *Laws of the State of New York* (1887), II: 114; Rufus King to Elbridge Gerry, Apr. 18, 1785 ("very unfair"), in Smith, ed., *Letters of Delegates to Congress*, XXII: 345.

61. Abraham Cuyler to George Clinton, May 14, 1785, and Cuyler, Henry Glen, and Peter Schuyler to the Oneida and Tuscarora Nations, May 13, 1785, in Hough, ed., *Proceedings of the Commissioners*, I: 70–74.

62. Abraham Cuyler and Henry Glen to George Clinton, May 27, 1785 ("Peculiar situation" and "well timed"), in Hough, ed., *Proceedings of the Commissioners*, I: 77–78.

63. George Clinton to the Commissioners for Indian Affairs, May 28, 1785, and Commissioners' proceedings, June 23, 1784, in Hough, ed., *Proceedings of the Commissioners*, I: 80, 84.

64. George Clinton to the Commissioners, May 1, 1785, Abraham Cuyler to Clinton, May 14, 1785, Clinton, speech, June 23, 1785 ("contiguous"), and Clinton, speech, June 26, 1785, in Hough, ed., *Proceedings of the Commissioners*, I: 68, 71, 86, 96; Good Peter, interview, n.d. [ca. April 1792] ("produced a heap"), TPP, LX: 122–122A, MHS.

65. Good Peter, speech, June 25, 1785 ("last Winter" and "we are however"), and George Clinton, speech, June 26, 1785 ("highly disagreeable"), in Hough, ed., *Proceedings of the Commissioners*, I: 92–93, 97 ("We are sorry"); Good Peter, interview, April n.d., 1792, TPP, LX: 122A, MHS.

66. George Clinton, speech, June 26, 1785 ("your Fault"), in Hough, ed., *Proceedings of the Commissioners*, I: 97; Good Peter, interview, April n.d., 1792, TPP, LX: 122A, MHS.

67. Good Peter, speech, June 27, 1785, and Peter the Quarter Master, speech, June 27, 1785, in Hough, ed., *Proceedings of the Commissioners*, I: 102–3. To reward the collaborating chiefs, the state commissioners spent £168.8.8 ($421) in "gratuities" at the Fort Herkimer council. See, Hough, ed., *Proceedings of the Commissioners*, I: 109.

68. George Clinton, speech, June 28, 1785, Great Grasshopper, speech, June 28, 1785, and Proceedings, June 29, 1785, in Hough, ed., *Proceedings of the Commissioners*, I: 105, 106, 108; Records of the Office of the Surveyor General (A 4002), Book of Land Sales, I, NYSA; Commissioners of the Land Office, notice, July 11, 1785, in *Albany Gazette*, July 28, 1785.

69. "An Act for the Speedy Sale of the Unappropriated Lands Within This State, and for Other Purposes Therein Mentioned," May 5, 1786, [New York State], *Laws of the State of New York* (1887), II: 334; Tiro, "James Dean in Iroquoia," 411–14.

70. Records of the Office of the Surveyor General (A 4002), Book of Land Sales, I, NYSA; Commissioners of the Land Office, notice, July 11, 1785, in *Albany Gazette*, July 28, 1785; James Bowdoin to George Clinton, July 18, 1785, in Hastings, ed., *Public Papers of George Clinton*, 393–95; Elbridge Gerry to Rufus King, Oct. 9, 1785, and Nathaniel Gorham to Caleb Davis, Feb. 23, 1786, in Smith, ed., *Letters of Delegates to Congress*, XXII: 673, XXIII: 161.

71. Goebel, ed., *Law Practice of Alexander Hamilton*, 575–77, 651; McNall, *Agricultural History of the Genesee Valley*, 11–13.

72. Samuel Osgood to John Adams, Jan. 14, 1784, in Burnett, ed., *Letters of Members of the Continental Congress*, VII: 415; Nathaniel Gorham to Caleb Davis, Feb. 23, 1786, in Smith, ed., *Letters of Delegates to Congress*, XXIII: 161; Gorham to James Warren, Mar. 6, 1786, in Massachusetts Historical Society, *Warren-Adams Letters*, II: 270; Oliver Ellsworth, speech, Jan. 4, 1788 ("What is to defend"), in Labaree, ed., *Public Records of the State of Connecticut from May, 1785, Through January, 1789*, 554.

CHAPTER SIX: LEASES

1. Samuel Kirkland, "Memoir of Negotiations Relative to Indian Lands Within the State of New York, 1786–1788," #2140, HL; Good Peter, narrative, April 5, 1792 ("And verily"), TPP, LX: 123–123A, MHS; John Tayler to George Clinton, June 8, 1788, and Joseph Brant, speech, June 18, 1788, in Hough, ed., *Proceedings of the Commissioners*, I: 145–46, II: 415–16. For Maj. Schuyler's standing, see George Clinton, speech, June 19, 1790, in Hough, ed., *Proceedings of the Commissioners*, II: 422–23. For the political prominence of the Lessees, see Hough, ed., *Proceedings of the Commissioners*, I: 119n–120n.

2. Murray, *History of Old Tioga Point*, 297; James Bryan to the New York State Legislature, Feb. 21, 1789, A 1823 (Assembly Papers, Indian Affairs, 1783–1809), Box 40, NYSA; Six Nations Chiefs to Congress, June 2, 1789, RG 10 (Indian Affairs), XV: 356, NAC; Joseph Brant to Timothy Pickering, Feb. 25, 1791, TPP, XLI: 197, MHS; John Livingston to Walter Livingston, Jan. 9, 1791 ("a particular friend"), RRLP, Reel 4, NYHS.

3. John Livingston and Caleb Benton to New York State Legislature, n.d., [New York State], *Journal of the Assembly . . . 1788*, 78; Hough, ed., *Proceedings of the Commissioners*, I: 120n–121n; Jonas Platt, Answers to Queries, in Jeremy Belknap, "Notes on a Journey to Oneida," 1796, Belknap Papers, Reel 11, MHS; Turner, *Phelps and Gorham Purchase*, 144. For the 360-year

term and estimate of 13 million acres, see Lewis Morris to Lewis Morris, Jr., Jan. 13, 1788, #15766, NYSL.

4. Livingston Lease from the Oneidas, Jan. 8, 1788, and John Tayler to George Clinton, April 9, 1788, in Hough, ed., *Proceedings of the Commissioners*, I: 120–24, 132–33; Good Peter, narrative, April 5, 1792 ("our advantage" and "must add"), TPP, LX: 123–123A, MHS.

5. John Tayler to George Clinton, Apr. 9, 1788, and May 16, 1788, in Hough, ed., *Proceedings of the Commissioners*, I: 131, 141. For the $2,000 in private payments to interest Oneida chiefs, see Clinton, speech, June 19, 1790, in Hough, ed., *Proceedings of the Commissioners*, II: 424.

6. An Oneida named Jacob was admitted to Wheelock's school on Oct. 5, 1765. See Eleazar Wheelock, school roster, Sept. 3, 1765–May 6, 1767, EWP #767306.6, DCA.; Frederick Wissenfels to George Clinton, Dec. 9, 1780, in Hastings, ed., *Public Papers of George Clinton*, VI: 480–82; Francis Adrian Vanderkemp to Adam G. Mappa, July 27, 1792 ("Captain Jacob Reed"), in Vanderkemp, "Extracts from the Vanderkemp Papers," 53; Ebenezer Caulking to Peter Thacher, June 4, 1794, #794354, DCLSC; Good Peter, speech, April n.d., 1792 ("who can talk"), TPP, LX: 121, MHS.

7. Jeremy Belknap, "Notes on a Journey to Oneida," 1796 ("can behave"), and John T. Kirkland, response to queries, 1796 ("hates"), in Belknap Papers, Reel 11, MHS; Pilkington, ed., *Journals of Samuel Kirkland*, 143.

8. Hough, ed., *Proceedings of the Commissioners*, I: 39–40; Barbara Graymont, "Atiatoharongwen," *DCB*, V: 39–41; Sizer, *Works of Colonel John Trumbull*, 50, and figures on 152–53 (Trumbull misconstrues the name as "Col. Joseph Lewis (or Louis), chief of the Oneida Indians"); Col. Louis to Thomas McKeen, Sept. 11, 1781, PCC, Reel 98, p. 489, LC; Chase, *History of Dartmouth College*, I: 345, 353.

9. John Tayler to George Clinton, Apr. 9, 1788, and May 16, 1788, in Hough, ed., *Proceedings of the Commissioners*, I: 131, 141.

10. Livingston Lease from the Oneida, Jan. 8, 1788, and John Tayler to George Clinton, April 9, 1788, in Hough, ed., *Proceedings of the Commissioners*, I: 120–24, 132–33; Good Peter, narrative, April 5, 1792, TPP, LX: 123–123A, MHS; [New York State], *Journal of the Assembly . . . 1788*, 76–77 (Feb. 16, 1788). The lands reserved for clients consisted of Brothertown (2 by 5 miles), New Stockbridge (6 by 6 miles), James Dean (2 by 2 miles), Col. Wemple (1 square mile), George and John Thornton Kirkland (1 square mile), Jedediah Phelps (6 by 6 miles), Jean-François Perache (14 square miles), and Archibald Armstrong (1 square mile).

11. Onuf, *Origins of the Federal Republic*; Onuf, "Settlers, Settlements, and New States," 179–213; Taylor, " 'To Man Their Rights,' " 231–57; Bouton, "A Road Closed," 855–87.

12. Joseph Sprague to Timothy Pickering, Feb. 20, 1787, and Pickering to George Clymer, Nov. 1, 1787 ("peculiar," and "final issue"), in R. J. Taylor, ed., *Susquehannah Company Papers*, IX: 64, 255–59.

13. R. J. Taylor, ed., *Susquehannah Company Papers*, VII: xv–xxxviii, VIII: xv–xxxix, IX: xv–xlii; Harvey, *History of Wilkes-Barre*, III: 1476–78; Timothy Pickering quoted in O. Pickering and Upham, *Life of Timothy Pickering*, II: 297–98 ("Men destitute").

14. Joseph Hamilton to John Franklin, Mar. 24, 1786, William Hooker Smith, Samuel Hover, and Abraham Westbrook to William Montgomery, May 14, 1786, William Judd to Zebulon Butler, June 1, 1786 ("Onaquaguah"), Timothy Pickering to Samuel Hodgdon, Aug. 9, 1787, Benjamin Franklin to George Clinton, Sept. 22, 1787, Mathias Hollenback to John Nicholson, Nov. 13, 1787, and Benjamin Earl, deposition, July 19, 1788, in R. J. Taylor, ed., *Susquehannah Company Papers*, VIII: 312–13, 326, 356–57, IX: 153–54, 202–3, 272, 420. For the overlapping membership and methods, see also R. J. Taylor, ed., *Susquehannah Company Papers*, VII: xv–xxxviii, VIII: xv–xxxix, IX: xv–xlii; Miller, *Historical Sketches of Hudson*, 77;

Harvey, *History of Wilkes-Barre*, III: 824–25n, 1498n, 1569n; Lipson, *Freemasonry in Federalist Connecticut*, 69–71, 88.

15. James Bryan to the New York State Legislature, Feb. 21, 1789, A 1823 (Assembly Papers, Indian Affairs, 1783–1809), Box 40, NYSA; "Assembly Proceedings," *New-York Journal*, Mar. 3, 1788; John Livingston and Caleb Benton to New York State Legislature, n.d., [New York State], *Journal of the Assembly . . . 1788*, 78 (Feb. 16, 1788), 82 (Feb. 20, 1788).

16. Lewis Morris to Lewis Morris, Jr., Jan. 13, 1788 ("great many" and "much envied"), #15766, NYSL; "A Citizen," *Albany Journal*, Feb. 9, 1788; Petitions to the New York State Legislature from Stephen Paddock et al., Philip Rockefeller et al., n.d. [Feb. 1788], and John Warren et al., [Feb. 1788], A 1823 (Assembly Papers, Indian Affairs, 1783–1809), Box 40, NYSA; Hough, ed., *Proceedings of the Commissioners*, I: 119n1, 124n–126n; Anonymous, *Columbia County*, 127, 255, 309, 314; Chernow, *Robert Morris*, 42–43; [New York State], *Journal of the Assembly . . . 1788*, 73 (Feb. 16, 1788) and 82–83 (Feb. 20, 1788). Eight members represented only about 9 percent of a legislature that had twenty-three state senators and sixty-four representatives. See Hough, ed., *The New York Civil List*, 127–28, 191.

17. William Wilson to Robert R. Livingston, Mar. 13, 1788, RRLP, Reel 3, NYHS; [New York State], *Journal of the Assembly . . . 1788*, 73 (Feb. 16, 1788) and 82–83 (Feb. 20, 1788); Governor George Clinton, "A Proclamation," Mar. 5, 1788, *Albany Journal*, Mar. 8, 1788; Clinton to Joseph Brant, Sept. 19, 1789 ("There never"), in Hough, ed., *Proceedings of the Commissioners*, II: 344–45.

18. Indian commissioners' proceedings, Mar. 3, 10, and 12, 1788, and John Tayler, speech, n.d. [ca. Apr. 1, 1788] ("and if they do"), in Hough, ed., *Proceedings of the Commissioners*, I: 117–18, 119, 129–30, 133–35; State Senate, proceedings, Feb. 20, 1788, in *Albany Gazette*, Mar. 27, 1788 ("if the said leases").

19. Oliver Phelps to James Sullivan, Jan. 23, 1788, Phelps to James Bull, May 3, 1788 ("Indian world"), and Phelps to James Wadsworth, June 6, 1788 ("well aware"), PGP, Box 2, NYSL; Phelps to Wadsworth, Apr. 5, 1788, Phelps to Gorham, Apr. 5, 14, and 22, 1788, and Phelps to Sullivan, Apr. 22, 1788, PGP, Letterbook II, NYSL; Articles of Agreement, Apr. 19, 1788, PGP, Box 59, NYSL; John Tayler to George Clinton, Apr. 9 and May 16, 1788, and Six Nations Chiefs to Clinton, May 14, 1788, in Hough, ed., *Proceedings of the Commissioners*, I: 132, 141, 148.

20. Oliver Phelps to Nathaniel Gorham, Apr. 14 and 22, May 13, and June 5, 1788, and Phelps to James Wadsworth, June 6, 1788, PGP, Box 2, NYSL; Bruce A. Parker, "Samuel Street," *DCB*, V: 781; Articles of Agreement, July 11, 1788, PGP, Box 2, NYSL; John Butler to Jelles Fonda, June 13, 1788, John Wyman Coll., Box 1, #96, NYSHA; Articles of Agreement, July 4, 1788, PGP, Box 79, NYSL; Butler quoted in William Johnston, "Account of the Transactions with Respect to the Sale of the Indian Lands," n.d., in Cruikshank, ed., "Records of Niagara, 1790–1792," 61 ("lease of the country"); Peter Hunter to Maj. Mathews, Sept. 23, 1788, F 47 (Simcoe Papers), Reel 1797, AO.

21. William Johnston, "Account of the Transactions with Respect to the Sale of the Indian Lands," in Cruikshank, ed., "Records of Niagara, 1790–1792," 61–63; Samuel Kirkland, "Memoir of Negotiations Relative to Indian Lands Within the State of New York, 1786–1788," #2140, HL; Articles of Agreement, Apr. 19, 1788, PGP, Box 59, NYSL; Elisha Lee, affidavit, July 4, 1791, Phelps Family Papers, Box 1, OCHS; Samuel Kirkland, affidavit, n.d. ("should not be"), Kirkland File, OCHS; Hough, ed., *Proceedings of the Commissioners*, I: 160n1. For Buffalo Creek, see Kirkland, diary, June 26 and July 1, 1788, LFP, DCLSC; Kirkland, "A Statement of the Number & Situation of the Six United Nations of Indians in North America," Miscellaneous Bound, MHS.

22. Samuel Kirkland, diary, July 3, 1788, LFP, DCLSC; Elisha Lee, affidavit, May 27, 1791, PGP, Box 18, NYSL; Elisha Lee, affidavit, July 4, 1791, Phelps Family Papers, Box 1, OCHS; William Johnston, affidavit, Mar. 18, 1791, PGP, Box 18, NYSL; Brant to Timothy Pickering, Feb. 25, 1791, TPP, LXI: 197, MHS; Red Jacket, speech, Nov. 21, 1790, HORC, XV, NYHS; Phelps and Gorham to Kirkland, Aug. 21, 1788, LFP, DCLSC; and Phelps to Brant, Oct. 6, 1788 ("Elegant"), PGP, Box 2, NYSL; Patrick, "Life and Times of Samuel Kirkland," 411–14.

23. John Butler quoted in Ralph Clench to Sir John Johnson, Aug. 28, 1790 ("that the Dish"), MG 11 (Colonial Office 42), LXIX: 277, NAC; Elisha Lee, affidavit, May 27, 1791, PGP, Box 18, NYSL; Elisha Lee, affidavit, July 4, 1791, Phelps Family Papers, Box 1, OCHS; William Johnston, affidavit, Mar. 18, 1791, PGP, Box 18, NYSL; Oliver Phelps and Six Nations, deed, July 8, 1788, HORC, XV, NYHS; Joseph Brant to George Clinton, July 9, 1788, in Hough, ed., *Proceedings of the Commissioners*, I: 160–67.

24. Oliver Phelps and Six Nations, deed, July 8, 1788, HORC, XV, NYHS; Phelps to Israel Chapin, Jr., May 18, 1795 ("too small" and "so as to"), HORC, XI, NYHS; Red Jacket, speech, Nov. 21, 1790 ("all that"), HORC, XV, NYHS; Cornplanter, speech, Dec. 31, 1790, RG 10 (Indian Affairs), VIII: 8148, NAC; Phelps to Henry Champion, Jr., Aug. 9, 1788, PGP, Letterbook II, NYSL; Phelps to Samuel Kirkland, Nov. 14, 1790, SKP, Folder 130, HCA; John Livingston to Walter Livingston, Jan. 9, 1791, RRLP, Reel 4, NYHS; Turner, *Phelps and Gorham*, 476–77; Joseph Brant to Timothy Pickering, Feb. 25, 1791, TPP, XLI: 197, MHS; William Johnston, "Account of the Transactions with Respect to the Sale of the Indian Lands," and Samuel Kirkland, deposition, May 5, 1792, in Cruikshank, ed., "Records of Niagara, 1790–1792," 139–40. Upon investigating the controversy, the federal commissioner Timothy Pickering sided with Phelps. See Pickering to Phelps, July 16, 1791, in Cruikshank, ed., *Correspondence of Simcoe*, V: 4.

25. Oliver Phelps to Henry Champion, Jr., Aug. 9, 1788 ("well pleased"), PGP, Letterbook II, NYSL; Phelps to Hugh Maxwell, Aug. 7, 1788 ("killed me"), PGP, Letterbook II, NYSL; *Albany Gazette*, Aug. 10, 1789 ("highly gratified").

26. Johnston, "Account of the Transactions," in Cruikshank, "Records of Niagara, 1790–1792," 60–62.

27. Johnston, "Account of the Transactions," in Cruikshank, "Records of Niagara, 1790–1792," 64; Samuel Street to Oliver Phelps, Aug. 4, 1788, Phelps Family Papers, Box 1, OCHS; Lord Dorchester to Lord Sydney, Oct. 14, 1788, MG 11 (Colonial Office 42), LXI: 98, NAC; Lord Grenville to Lord Dorchester, Oct. 20, 1789 ("no less than"), in Cruikshank, "Records of Niagara, 1784–9," 95.

28. Lord Grenville to Lord Dorchester, Oct. 20, 1789, in Cruikshank, "Records of Niagara, 1784–9," 95; A. Fraser to Evan Nepean, Oct. 31, 1789 ("Suspected persons"), MG 11 (Colonial Office 42), LXVI, Misc. MSS, NAC.

29. John Tayler to George Clinton, Apr. 9, May 16, June 8, and June 17, 1788, and John Livingston quoted in Onyigat, speech, Sept. 3, 1788 ("Do not listen" and "The Governor's Business"), in Hough, ed., *Proceedings of the Commissioners*, I: 132, 141, 145, 151, 182–83; John Tayler to George Clinton, June 8, 1788, in Hough, ed., *Proceedings of the Commissioners*, I: 147; Col. Hugh Maxwell, in Charles F. Milliken, "Western New York—Highlights in its History," p. 64 ("many Indians"), typescript at OCHS.

30. Hough, ed., *Proceedings of the Commissioners*, 148n1; Oliver Phelps to Nathaniel Gorham, June 5, 1788, PGP, Box 2, NYSL; Anonymous, "Extract," Aug. 8, 1792 ("idle persons"), Massachusetts Historical Society, *Collections*, 1st Ser., I: 285; Watson, ed., *Men and Times of the Revolution*, 354 ("troubled"); James K. Garnsey to William Walker, Sept. 21, 1793 ("French conjurer"), Walker Papers, Box 1, NYHS.

31. John Tayler to George Clinton, June 8, 1788 ("seem to think"), and Clinton to Six Nations Chiefs, June 16, 1788, in Hough, ed., *Proceedings of the Commissioners*, I: 145, 149.

32. George Clinton to Six Nations, June 16, 1788 ("The Business"), in Hough, ed., *Proceedings of the Commissioners*, I: 149.

33. Oneida warrior, information, Sept. 8, 1788, and Samuel Kirkland quoted in Commissioners, minutes, Dec. 15, 1788 ("kept"), in Hough, ed., *Proceedings of the Commissioners*, I: 187–92, II: 258–59; Oliver Phelps to William Walker, Oct. 3, 1788 ("be tyed"), PGP, Box 2, NYSL; Kirkland, journal, Oct. 6, 1788, in Ketchum, *History of Buffalo*, 98–99.

34. Blau, Campisi, and Tooker, "Onondaga," 495–96; Hough, ed., *Proceedings of the Commissioners*, I: 180, 183–201; Six Nations Chiefs to Congress, June 2, 1789, William Walker Papers, Box 2, NYHS; Six Nations Chiefs to George Clinton, June 2, 1789, in Hough, ed., *Proceedings of the Commissioners*, II: 331. For the Onondaga numbers at the lake, see Lincklaen, *Travels in the Years 1791 and 1792*, 67; Samuel Kirkland, diary, June 19, 1788, LFP, DCLSC.

35. Jacob Reed et al. to the New York State Legislature, Mar. 12, 1788 ("surprized"), in Hough, ed., *Proceedings of the Commissioners*, I: 125n1; *New York Journal*, Mar. 20, 1788; John Tayler to George Clinton, July 6, 1788, in Hough, ed., *Proceedings of the Commissioners*, I: 153; Good Peter, narrative, Apr. 5, 1792, TPP, LX: 126, MHS.

36. John Tayler to George Clinton, July 6, 1788, Good Peter, Louis Cook, and John Skenandon to Governor Clinton, June 27, 1788 ("If not"), and Tayler to Clinton, July 16, 1788, in Hough, ed., *Proceedings of the Commissioners*, I: 153, 154, 156; Good Peter, narrative, Apr. 5, 1792, TPP, LX: 126, MHS. For Penet's influence, see John Tayler to George Clinton, Apr. 9 and May 16, 1788, Good Peter, speech, Sept. 22, 1788, and Penet in 1787, quoted by Oneida warriors to George Clinton, Aug. 23, 1789, in Hough, ed., *Proceedings of the Commissioners*, I: 132, 141, 235, II: 346–47.

37. New York State Indian Commissioners, proceedings, Sept. 16, 1788 ("a cession"), in Hough, ed., *Proceedings of the Commissioners*, I: 215–16; Samuel Latham Mitchell to Stephen Van Rensselaer, Sept. 19, 1788, #20280, HL.

38. George Clinton, speech, Sept. 20, 1788 ("of such Extent"), in Hough, ed., *Proceedings of the Commissioners*, I: 223–26.

39. Good Peter, speech, Sept. 20, 1788 ("It is just so"), in Hough, ed., *Proceedings of the Commissioners*, I: 227. For Clinton's persistent patronage for the Harpers of Harpersfield, see Council of Appointment, Record Book II (1786–93): 231, NYSA; Council of Appointment Files, Box 3, NYSA; Hastings, ed., *Military Minutes of the Council of Appointment*, I: 213.

40. Col. Louis, speech, Sept. 20, 1788 ("You have"), in Hough, ed., *Proceedings of the Commissioners*, I: 229–30.

41. Pilkington, ed., *Journals of Samuel Kirkland*, 219 ("I find"); Brissot de Warville, *New Travels in the United States*, 75 ("He danced") and 75n ("was about" and "lucky"); Watson, ed., *Men and Times*, 314–16; Lincklaen, *Travels in the Years 1791 and 1792*, 69.

42. Good Peter, narrative, Apr. 5, 1792, TPP, LX: 126–126A, MHS.

43. Treaty of Fort Schuyler, Sept. 22, 1788 ("make Provision"), in Hough, ed., *Proceedings of the Commissioners*, I: 242–43.

44. Col. Louis, speech, Sept. 20, 1788, and Treaty of Fort Schuyler, Sept. 22, 1788, in Hough, ed., *Proceedings of the Commissioners*, I: 230–31, 243–44. The state legislature subsequently restored Brothertown to township dimensions (6 by 6 miles), thanks to successful lobbying by Rev. Samson Occom. See "An Act for the Sale and Disposition of Lands, Belonging to the People of This State," Feb. 25, 1789, [New York State] *Laws of the State of New York* (1887), III: 65–70. For Jedediah Phelps, see Oneida chiefs to George Clinton, Dec. 6, 1788, #13427, Huntington

Library; [New York State], *Journal of the Assembly . . . 1789*, 70 (Jan. 19, 1789), 130 (Feb. 19, 1789).

45. "An Act for Vesting a Certain Tract of Land in Trustees for the Benefit of Peter Otsequette," Mar. 18, 1791, [New York State], *Laws of the State of New York* (1887), III: 232. Watson, ed., *Men and Times*, 314 ("Ten days ago"); Lincklaen, *Travels in the Years 1791 and 1792*, 69; Thomas Morris, "Recollections," in Morris Papers, Folder 2, OCHS.

46. Treaty of Fort Schuyler, Sept. 22, 1788, in Hough, ed., *Proceedings of the Commissioners*, I: 242–43.

47. Campisi, "Oneida Treaty Period," 52–53; Lehman, "The End of the Iroquois Mystique," 524–47.

48. Treaty of Fort Schuyler, Sept. 22, 1788, in Hough, ed., *Proceedings of the Commissioners*, I: 244; Good Peter, narrative, Apr. 5, 1792, TPP, LX: 126A, MHA. For Oneida population, see Samuel Kirkland, "A Statement of the Number & Situation of the Six United Nations of Indians in North America," Oct. 15, 1791, Misc. Bound MSS, MHS.

49. "An Act for the Sale and Disposition of Lands Belonging to the People of This State," Feb. 25, 1789, [New York State], *Laws of the State of New York Passed at the Sessions of the Legislature*, III: 65–66.

50. Samuel Latham Mitchell to Stephen Van Rensselaer, Sept. 19, 1788 ("By means"), #20280, HL; Good Peter, speech, Sept. 19, 1788 ("we chose"), in Hough, ed., *Proceedings of the Commissioners*, I: 219.

51. Good Peter, narrative, Apr. 11, 1792 ("the Governor" and "again converse"), TPP, LX: 127A, MHS; Campisi, "Oneida Treaty Period," 52–54; Lehman, "End of the Iroquois Mystique," 544.

52. Lehman, "End of the Iroquois Mystique," 544; Good Peter, narrative, Apr. 11, 1792 ("This alarmed"), TPP, LX: 128A, MHS; James Livingston to George Clinton, Aug. 30, 1789, and Oneida Chiefs to G. Clinton, Jan. 27, 1790, in Hough, ed., *Proceedings of the Commissioners*, II: 349, 361.

53. Oriske Chiefs to Gov. George Clinton, Jan. 26, 1790 ("be happy"), and Oneida Chiefs to Governor George Clinton, Jan. 27, 1790 ("We find" and "somewhere"), in Hough, ed., *Proceedings of the Commissioners*, II: 359–60, 361; Lehman, "End of the Iroquois Mystique," 544–45. The delegates included Honyery, Capt. Jacob Reed, Col. Louis, and Nicholas Jourdan. For Clinton's financial interest in the Oriskany Patent, see Hastings, ed., *Public Papers of George Clinton*, X: 1033; and Henry Brockholst Livingston to William Livingston, Feb. 16, 1790, in Prince, *Papers of William Livingston*, V: 424. In September 1784, at the state council of Fort Schuyler, Good Peter had broached the Oriske issue, but Clinton had summarily dismissed their request. See Good Peter, speech, Sept. 4, 1784, and Clinton, speech, Sept. 10, 1784, in Hough, ed., *Proceedings of the Commissioners*, I: 47, 59.

54. New York State Indian Commissioners, proceedings, Feb. 13–15, 1789 ("without Foundation" and "fully satisfied"), in Hough, ed., *Proceedings of the Commissioners*, II: 364–67; Henry Brockholst Livingston to William Livingston, Feb. 16, 1790 ("appeared no ways"), in Prince et al., eds., *Papers of William Livingston*, V: 424; James Pemberton to John Pemberton, Feb. 16, 1790 ("make slaves"), quoted in Lehman, "End of the Iroquois Mystique," 545. The state did pay the delegates' bill for food and lodging (£27.18.8), as well as a small present of cloth and blankets worth £20.8.0.

55. For the prosecutions, see Oliver Phelps to Samuel Street, Feb. 16, 1789, PGP, Letterbook III, NYSL; Montgomery County Court of Oyer & Terminer, Minute Book I, Sept. 9, 1788, July 7, 1789, and Nov. 15–18, 1790, Box 572, Montgomery County Archives, Fonda, N.Y. For

the buyout, see Oliver Phelps to Nathaniel Gorham, Sept. 10 and 30, 1788, PGP, Letterbook II, NYSL; Phelps to Gorham, Feb. 5, 1789, and Phelps to Samuel Street, Feb. 16, 1789, PGP, Letterbook III, NYSL.

56. Meeting, Feb. 14, 1789, in Hough, ed., *Proceedings of the Commissioners*, II: 269; [New York State], *Journal of the Assembly . . . 1789*, 121; *Albany Gazette*, Mar. 13, 1789; John and Henry Livingston to Stephen Van Rensselaer and Leonard Gansevoort, Apr. 27, 1789, Misc. MSS, NYHS.

57. Peter Ryckman and Seth Reed to George Clinton, Oct. 7, 1788, and Reed to Clinton, Jan. 13, 1789, in Hough, ed., *Proceedings of the Commissioners*, II: 258, 265; David Smith, affidavit, Oct. 31, 1789, Thomas Sisson, affidavit, Oct. 31, 1789, and Peter Bortel, affidavit, Oct. 31, 1789 ("most able"), Indorsed Land Papers, Office of the Secretary of the State of New York, A 0272 (Applications for Land Grants, 1642–1803), XLIX: 120, 121, 123, NYSA.

58. Clinton to Reed and Ryckman, Dec. 16, 1788, Reed and Ryckman to Clinton, Jan. 13, 1789, Resolutions, Feb. 11, 1789, and Toneaghas, speech, Feb. 21, 1789 ("Brother Governor"), in Hough, ed., *Proceedings of the Commissioners*, II: 261–64, 265–67, 290. For Cayuga numbers near Niagara, see Sir John Johnson, "Descriptive Return of the Number of Indians," Dec. 10, 1786, JGSP, Reel 1797, AO. For Cayuga numbers at the lake, see Samuel Kirkland, "A Statement of the Number & Situation of the Six United Nations of Indians in North America," Oct. 15, 1791, Miscellaneous Bound MSS, MHS. Kirkland's estimate of 130 Cayugas at the lake exceeds all other calculations, which fall short of 100.

59. Good Peter, speeches for the Cayugas, Feb. 19 and 23, 1789, in Hough, ed., *Proceedings of the Commissioners*, II: 279, 292–93.

60. Good Peter, speech, Feb. 23, 1789, Clinton, speeches, Feb. 23 and 24, 1789, and Cayuga Deed of Cession, Feb. 25, 1789, in Hough, ed., *Proceedings of the Commissioners*, II: 292, 297–98, 302–5, 306–10. In addition to the 100-square-mile reservation, the Cayugas retained a detached square mile on a river to sustain their eel fishery. For the bounds, see [New York State], *Report of Special Committee to Investigate the Indian Problem of the State of New York*, 216–20.

61. Good Peter, speeches, Feb. 19 ("watch over" and "bad Men"), and Feb. 24 ("We had"), 1789, Hough, ed., *Proceedings of the Commissioners*, II: 280, 304.

62. Cayuga Deed of Cession, Feb. 25, 1789, State Commissioners, minutes, Feb. 9, 1790, and George Clinton to Abraham Hardenbergh, Oct. 4, 1789, in Hough, ed., *Proceedings of the Commissioners*, II: 258n2, 308, 357–58, 457; Seth Reed to George Clinton, Oct. 15, 1790, Joel Prescott, affidavit, Aug. 24, 1789, James Manning Reed, affidavit, Aug. 25, 1789, Albert Ryckman, affidavit, Aug. 27, 1789, Samuel Kirkland, affidavit, Sept. 24, 1789, Indorsed Land Papers, Office of the Secretary of the State of New York, A 0272 (Applications for Land Grants, 1642–1803), XLIX: 115, 116, 118, 119, 131, NYSA.

63. Peter Ryckman, deed, Aug. 10, 1791, Book of Deeds, I, 173, Ontario County Archives (Hopewell, N.Y.); Peter Ryckman to Oliver Phelps, Aug. 21, 1791, PGP, Box 18, NYSL.

64. Moses DeWitt, journal, May 20, 1789, and Moses DeWitt to Jacob R. DeWitt, June 8, 1789, DWFP, Box 6, SULSC.

65. Samuel Kirkland, journal, Oct. 18, 1788, in Ketchum, *History of Buffalo*, II: 101–2; Samuel Street to Oliver Phelps, June 23, 1789, Phelps Family Papers, Box 1, OCHS; Job Smith to Moses DeWitt, June 15, 1789, and DeWitt to John Cantine, June 27, 1789, DWFP, Box 1, SULSC; Hezekiah Olcott to John Tayler, June 28, 1789, and Brant to George Clinton, July 30, 1789 ("those who remain"), in Hough, ed., *Proceedings of the Commissioners*, II: 327, 340; Fish Carrier, speech, Aug. 15, 1789 ("Artifice"), RG 10 (Indian Affairs), XV: 366, NAC; John Butler to Samuel Kirkland, Nov. 24, 1789, SKP, Folder 119, HCA; William Johnston, "Account of the Transactions," in Cruikshank, ed., "Records of Niagara, 1790–1792," 61 ("where the business").

66. Six Nations to George Clinton, June 2, 1789 ("We did not"), in Hough, ed., *Proceedings of the Commissioners*, II: 331; Six Nation Chiefs to Congress, June 2, 1789 ("a small Number"), RG 10 (Indian Affairs), XV: 354, NAC.

67. Steel Trap, speech, June 3, 1789, and Six Nations to George Clinton, June 2, 1789 ("We expect"), in Hough, ed., *Proceedings of the Commissioners*, II: 324–25, 331.

68. Oneida Chiefs to George Clinton, June 30, 1789 ("We are threatened"), and Abraham Hardenbergh to Clinton, July 5 and 17, 1789, in Hough, ed., *Proceedings of the Commissioners*, II: 328, 433–36, 446–47; Moses DeWitt, journal, July 8, 1789, DWFP, Box 6, SULSC; Oliver Phelps to Nathaniel Gorham, July 14, 1789, PGP, Box 2, NYSL.

69. Storke and Smith, *History of Cayuga County*, 392–93; Yawger, *Indian and the Pioneer*, II: 9, 28–29; Coventry, *Memoirs of an Emigrant*, I: 597–98; Steel Trap, speech, June 3, 1789, and Simeon DeWitt to George Clinton, July 17, 1789, in Hough, ed., *Proceedings of the Commissioners*, II: 324–26, 445; Moses DeWitt to Jacob R. DeWitt, Sept. 7, 1789 ("Our Business"), DWFP, Box 1, SULSC.

70. Moses DeWitt, journal, July 6–7, 1789, DWFP, Box 6, SULSC; Abraham Hardenbergh to Simeon DeWitt, July 5, 1789 ("For if we"), George Clinton to Hardenbergh, July 14, 1789, Clinton to DeWitt, July 14, 1789, and Hardenbergh to Clinton, Sept. 3, 1789, in Hough, ed., *Proceedings of the Commissioners*, II: 436–37, 438–39, 443, 449–51; Moses DeWitt to Jacob R. DeWitt, Sept. 11, 1789, DWFP, Bos 1, SULSC.

71. Abraham Hardenbergh to George Clinton, Sept. 3, 1789 ("afford"), in Hough, ed., *Proceedings of the Commissioners*, II: 451; Cayuga Chiefs to New York State Legislature, Mar. 8, 1791, John McKesson Papers, NYHS.

72. Commissioners, minutes, May 6, 1790, Governor Clinton, proclamation, May 7, 1790, and Clinton to Abraham Hardenbergh, June 21, 1790 ("on Pain"), in Hough, ed., *Proceedings of the Commissioners*, II: 373–74, 459, 459–60; Moses DeWitt to Jacob R. DeWitt, July 11, 1790, DWFP, Bos 2, SULSC. For the Cayuga numbers, see Lincklaen, *Travels in the Years 1791 and 1792*, 65.

73. Commissioners, minutes, June 4, 1790, George Clinton, speech, June 14, 1790, Onondaga Nation, Instrument of Ratification, June 16, 1790, Clinton, speech, June 19, 1790, Cayuga Nation, Instrument of Ratification, June 22, 1790, and Joseph Brant to Clinton, Mar. 4, 1791, in Hough, ed., *Proceedings of the Commissioners*, II: 380, 391, 400, 421–24, 428–30, 469; Cayuga Chiefs to New York State Legislature, Mar. 8, 1791, John McKesson Papers, NYHS.

74. Cayuga Nation and John Richardson, indenture, July 16, 1791, HORC, VI, NYHS; Timothy Pickering, journal, July 17, 1791, Abraham Hardenbergh to Pickering, July 22, 1791, and Brinton Paine to Pickering, Sept. 20, 1791, TPP, LX: 112, LXI: 257, 273, MHS; Hardenbergh to George Clinton, July 26, 1791, and Pickering to Henry Knox, Aug. 16, 1791, McKesson Papers, NYHS. For Clinton's oral promise, see Richardson to Pickering, Feb. 21, 1792, TPP, LXII, 6, MHS. For Richardson's conduct in 1789, see Hardenbergh to Clinton, July 17, 1789, in Hough, ed., *Proceedings of the Commissioners*, II: 447.

75. Cayugas quoted in Samuel Kirkland, diary, Sept. 1, 1791 ("of the Cayuga nation"), LFP, DCLSC; Kirkland to John Tayler, Sept. 1, 1791, and William Colbrath to Clinton, Oct. 15, 1791, John McKesson Papers, NYHS; Joseph Kinney to Timothy Pickering, Oct. 24, 1791, TPP, LXI: 278, MHS; Yawger, *Indian and the Pioneer*, II: 9 (Hannah Gore Durkee quoted: "our food"), 31–32; John Harris to New York State Legislature, n.d. [ca. Nov. 1792], and Steel Trap, Broken Log, and George Steel Trap to New York State Legislature, n.d. [ca. Nov. 1792], A 1823 (Assembly Papers, Indian Affairs, 1783–1809), Box 40, NYSA. For the western Cayuga outrage, see Israel Chapin to Pickering, July 17, 1792, TPP, LXII: 58, MHS; George Clinton to New York State Assembly, Dec. 13, 1792, A 3189 (Governor's Official Letterbook),

104, NYSA. Colbrath calculated that 2 to 3 families resided in some of the 25 cabins, which suggests a total of 50 families with 4 persons per family, making for about 200 people. He reported 22 Indians, by which he may have meant families. For an estimate of 20 Cayuga families on September 1, 1791, see Lincklaen, *Travels in the Years 1791 and 1792*, 65.

76. Montgomery County Court of Oyer & Terminer, Minutes I, Sept. 9, 1788, July 7, 1789, and Nov. 15–18, 1790, Box 572, Montgomery County Archives, Fonda, N.Y.; Oliver Phelps to Samuel Street, Feb. 16, 1789, PGP, Letterbook III, NYSL; Moses DeWitt, journal, Dec. 9, 1789, DWFP, Box 7, SULSC; DeWitt to Bozaleel Seely, Feb. 23, 1790, DWFP, Box 1, SULSC; "An Act for the Relief of Henry Haydock and others," Mar. 9, 1790, [New York State] *Laws of the State of New York* (1887), III: 138; George Clinton, speech, Sept. 16, 1788 ("we will severely"), in Hough, ed., *Proceedings of the Commissioners*, I: 213.

77. Hough, ed., *Proceedings of the Commissioners*, I: 126n1; Turner, *History of the Pioneer Settlement of Phelps and Gorham Purchase*, 109; Ellicott, *Refutation of the Claim of John Livingston*, 20–25 (Hathorn quoted on 23: "to sell"). The decision to reward the Lessees appalled the prominent lawyer and politician Jonas Platt. See Platt, answers to queries, in Jeremy Belknap, "Notes on a Journey to Oneida," 1796, Belknap Papers, Reel 11, MHS.

78. Dangerfield, *Chancellor Robert R. Livingston*, 250; Kaminski, *George Clinton*, 203–4; John Livingston to Walter Livingston, Nov. 13, 1791 ("approaching Election"), Feb. 16, 1792, and Mar. 7, 1792 ("I love"), RRLP, Reel 4, NYHS.

79. Robert C. Livingston to John Livingston, Apr. 27, 1792 ("Moderate"), RRLP, Reel 4, NYHS; Hough, ed., *Proceedings of the Commissioners*, I: 126n1–127n1; County Judiciary, meeting, Nov. 8, 1793 ("a Number"), PGP, Box 20, NYSL; Thomas Morris to Robert Morris, Nov. 10, 1793, HORC, XV, NYHS; Turner, *Phelps and Gorham Purchase*, 109–10; Boyd, "Attempts to Form New States," 266–67.

80. Turner, *Pioneer History of the Holland Purchase*, 365n ("this was"); Turner, *Phelps and Gorham Purchase*, 378–79; Porter, "Narrative of Early Years in the Life of Judge Augustus Porter," 282–83 ("the Indian method").

81. Nathaniel Gorham to Oliver Phelps, April 5, 1789 ("I have not"), PGP, Box 17, NYSL. Gorham wrote "that the Doctor was killed at Canadasaga by the Indians." In 1795, Big Skies, an Onondaga chief, recalled the "Murder of Docter Vanderwort & party five Year[s] past on their way to the falls of this [Genesee] River." See Big Skies, speech, quoted in Nicholas Rosencrantz to Oliver Phelps, Aug. 20, 1795, Phelps Family Papers, XLIV, Folder 403, OCHS.

82. Turner, *Phelps and Gorham*, 379n; Turner, *Holland Purchase*, 365n ("the object").

83. Good Peter, speech, June 3, 1788 ("so faint"), in Hough, ed., *Proceedings of the Commissioners*, II: 317; Pilkington, ed., *Journals of Samuel Kirkland*, 164, 167 ("almost starved"), 168.

84. Pilkington, ed., *Journals of Samuel Kirkland*, 160 ("the uncommon"), 167 (Oneida father quoted: "I have been"); Benjamin Young to Benjamin Rush, June 2, 1789 ("The people"), Benjamin Rush Papers, XXXII: 87, LCP; Mancall, *Valley of Opportunity*, 172. For a more thorough exploration of this widespread hunger, see Taylor, "The Hungry Year," 145–81.

85. Horatio Hickock, "Of the Hessian Fly," in Board of Agriculture of the State of New York, *Memoirs* (Albany, N.Y.: Packard & Van Benthuysen, 1823), II: 169–70; *New-York Journal*, June 4 and 5, and July 10, 1788; Phineas Bond to Lord Carmathen, Oct. 1 and Nov. 3, 1788 ("The ravages"), and Jan. 20, 1789, in "Letters of Phineas Bond . . ." American Historical Association, *Annual Report*, I (1896): 576, 580, 592; Thomas Jefferson, Notes on the Hessian Fly, June n.d., 1791, in Boyd, ed., *Papers of Thomas Jefferson*, XX: 457; Lamb, *Climate, History, and the Modern World*, 237; Taylor, "Hungry Year," 153–56.

86. Henry Ruttan, "Reminiscences," in Talman, ed., *Loyalist Narratives from Upper Canada*, 300; Coventry, *Memoirs of an Emigrant*, I: 213; *Vermont Gazette* (Bennington), June 8, 1789; Taylor, "Hungry Year," 157–60.

87. Cooper, *Guide in the Wilderness*, 16; Guillet, *Early Life in Upper Canada*, 210, 213; Gridley, *History of the Town of Kirkland*, 32; Jones, *History of Agriculture in Ontario*, 17–18; Taylor, "Hungry Year," 161–62.

88. John Tayler, report, July 8, 1789, in Hough, ed., *Proceedings of the Commissioners*, II: 316–19; Oliver Phelps to Nathaniel Gorham, July 14, 1789, PGP, Box 2, NYSL; Porter, "Narrative of Early Years in the Life of Judge Augustus Porter," 283; Colt, "Judah Colt's Narrative," 339 ("They came").

89. Oneida Chiefs to George Clinton, June 30, 1789 ("If hunger"), in Hough, ed., *Proceedings of the Commissioners*, II: 328–29.

90. [New York State], *Journal of the Assembly . . . 1790*, 4 ("distresses"), 19–20; Clinton to the Oneidas, July 14, 1789, and Meeting of the Commissioners, July 15, 1789 ("a testimony"), in Hough, ed., *Proceedings of the Commissioners*, II: 334–35.

91. Brant to Clinton, June 18, 1789, and Clinton to Brant, July 14, 1789, in Ketchum, *Authentic and Comprehensive History of Buffalo*, I: 387–88; Jelles Fonda to Brant, June 16, 1790, Fonda Papers, NYHS; Kelsay, *Joseph Brant*, 432, 540.

92. Simeon DeWitt, report to the State Senate, Mar. 6, 1834 ("were conducted"), Senate Document #88, NYSA. In 1800, the state assessed $9,303 in property taxes in the three counties carved out of former Oneida lands. See [New York State], *Journal of the Assembly of the State of New-York, At their Twenty-Fourth Session . . . 1800*, App. A.

93. The table derives from data in the annual reports of the state treasurer in [New York State], *Journal of the Assembly of the State of New-York, Fourteenth Session*, 9; [New York State], *Journal of the Assembly of the State of New-York, Fifteenth Session*, 7–8; [New York State], *Journal of the Assembly of the State of New-York, Sixteenth Session*, 113–14; [New York State], *Journal of the Assembly of the State of New-York, . . . Seventeenth Session*, 63–64; [New York State], *Journal of the Assembly of the State of New-York, . . . Eighteenth Session*, 23–25; [New York State], *Journal of the Assembly of the State of New-York, . . . Nineteenth Session*, 15–17. See also, Young, *Democratic Republicans of New York*, 593. The treasurer's figures in the New York pound have been converted to dollars at the rate of 8 shillings to a dollar (and rounded to the nearest dollar). Land sales in 1791 consisted of three categories: (1) lands sold by various officials, £534.5.8 ($1,336); (2) lands sold by the commissioners of the land office, £48,277.0.7 ($120,693); (3) lands sold by the surveyor general, £740.1.3 ($1,850.16). Land sales in 1792 consisted of two types: (1) lands sold by the commissioners of the land office, £126,529.19.1 ($316,325); (2) lands sold by the surveyor general, £3,740.16.0 ($9,352).

94. The table derives from data in the annual reports of the state treasurer in [New York State], *Journal of the Assembly of the State of New-York, Fourteenth Session*, 9; [New York State], *Journal of the Assembly of the State of New-York, Fifteenth Session*, 7–8; [New York State], *Journal of the Assembly of the State of New-York, Sixteenth Session*, 113–14; [New York State], *Journal of the Assembly of the State of New-York, . . . Seventeenth Session*, 63–64; [New York State], *Journal of the Assembly of the State of New-York, . . . Eighteenth Session*, 23–25; [New York State], *Journal of the Assembly of the State of New-York, . . . Nineteenth Session*, 15–17. The treasurer's figures in the New York pound have been converted to dollars at the rate of 8 shillings to a dollar (and rounded to the nearest dollar). For 1790, the commissioners of Indian affairs drew £3,640 ($9,100) but refunded £811.8.10 ($2,028.60), for a net of $7,071. For want of a distinct budget line for the Indian annuities in 1790, they must have been accounted for under the commis-

sioners of Indian affairs. For 1790, the land costs include £500.0.0 ($1,250) for surveys plus £4,225.4.9 ($10,563.09) "to prevent intrusions on lands, and punish infractions," which refers to the state efforts to defeat the Livingston Lessees, making a total of $11,813 for the category of Surveys, &c. In 1791, the Indian commissioners drew £669.19.0 ($1,675), but returned £7.4.0 ($18), for a net of $1,657. In 1792, the costs of Indian administration appear as two categories: (1) £640 ($1,600) for annuities to the Oneidas, Onondagas, and Cayugas, and (2) £37.16.0 ($94.50) to the commissioners of Indian affairs. In 1793, Indian administration costs appear in two categories: (1) £640 ($1,600) in annuities to the Oneidas, Onondagas, and Cayugas; (2) £1,400 ($3,500) to the commissioners of Indian affairs. In 1794, Indian administration costs appear in two categories: (1) £640 ($1,600) in annuities to the Oneidas, Onondagas, and Cayugas; and (2) £1,143.10.2 ($2,858.75) paid to John Tayler as the state's Indian agent. But this category also received a credit of £540.4.11 ($1,351) refunded by the commissioners of Indian affairs. In 1795, Indian administration costs included (1) a charge of £8,453.19.6 ($21,134.94) by the commissioners of Indian affairs; (2) £640 ($1,600) in annuities to the Oneidas, Onondagas, and Cayugas.

CHAPTER SEVEN: FATHERS

1. Philip Schuyler to John Hancock, Oct. 30, 1776, PCC, Reel 173, p. 471, LC; Samuel Kirkland to Schuyler, Jan. 14, 1777, PCC, Reel 173, p. 63, LC. For Nicholas Jourdan, see Chase, ed., *Our Revolutionary Forefathers*, 191–93 ("lead"); Samuel Kirkland, memorandum on Peter Penet, in SKP, Letters Undated File, HCA. Jourdan was probably the subject of the French officer who described the visit of an Oneida delegation to the French army at Newport, Rhode Island, in 1780: "The one who seemed to be in command and who addressed us was a Canadian who spoke French and who likes being associated with them." See Rice and Brown, eds., *American Campaigns of Rochambeau's Army*, I: 19n12.

2. Gottschalk, *Lafayette Joins the American Army*, 143–46, 190; Graymont, *Iroquois in the American Revolution*, 162–65; Patrick, "Life and Times of Samuel Kirkland," 318–20; Ojistalale, speech, Apr. 24, 1778 ("reach the Ears"), PCC, Reel 95, p. 157, LC; Philip Schuyler to the Oneidas, May 11, 1778, PCC, Reel 189, p. 281, LC.

3. Gerlach, *Proud Patriot*, 420; Rice and Brown, eds., *American Campaigns of Rochambeau's Army*, I: 19, 121–22.

4. Oneida chiefs, speech, Aug. 29, 1780 ("O my Father"), in Rice and Brown, eds., *American Campaigns of Rochambeau's Army*, I: 121.

5. Lyon, *The Man Who Sold Louisiana*, 45; Chase, ed., *Our Revolutionary Forefathers*, 22.

6. François Barbé de Marbois to Comte de Vergennes, Oct. 14, 1784 ("an old man"), in Giunta, ed., *The Emerging Nation*, II: 472–73; Lyon, *The Man Who Sold Louisiana*, 18–49; Sieur De La Forest to Marquis de Castries, Aug. 15, 1786, French Foreign Affairs Archives Transcripts, Consular Series, Vol. 909, pp. 165–66, NA; Marbois, journal, Sept. 23, 1784 ("These savages"), in Idzerda et al., eds., *Lafayette*, V: 251–52.

7. Evans, "Journal of Griffith Evans," 207–8; François Barbé de Marbois, journal, Sept. 23, 1784, and Marquis de Lafayette, speech, Oct. 3, 1784, in Idzerda et al., eds., *Lafayette*, V: 251–52, 256; James Madison to Thomas Jefferson, Oct. 17, 1784, in Hutchinson and Rachal, eds., *Papers of James Madison*, VIII: 118–20. For Lee's Francophobia, see Potts, *Arthur Lee*, 244, 269.

8. John Dease to Maj. Fraser, Nov. 20, 1784, RG 10 (Indian Affairs), XV: 160, NAC; Marquis de Lafayette to Adrienne de Noailles de Lafayette, Oct. 4, 1784 ("very weary" and "pleasure"), in Idzerda et al., eds., *Lafayette*, V: 256, 260–61; Gottschalk, *Lafayette Between the American and the French Revolutions*, 96–106, 141, 433–34. Gottschalk argues that Lafayette took a different boy,

named Kayenlaha, in 1784 and that Otsequette traveled to France a year later, but this seems to be a misunderstanding, for Kayenlaha was Lafayette's own adoptive name in Oneida.

9. Patrick, "Life and Times of Samuel Kirkland," 359.

10. Samuel Kirkland to Philip Schuyler, Jan. 14, 1777 ("Your seasonable"), PCC, Reel 173, pp. 63–68, LC.

11. Ford, ed., *Journals of the Continental Congress*, III: 351, VII: 72–73, XV: 1181–82, XXVIII: 306, 407–8; Patrick, "Life and Times of Samuel Kirkland," 305–6, 317, 320–39.

12. Samuel Kirkland to Jerusha Kirkland, Sept. 10, 1785 ("The most"), SKP, Folder 97, HCA.

13. Pilkington, ed., *Journals of Samuel Kirkland*, 125; Patrick, "Life and Times of Samuel Kirkland," 383, 392; Ford, ed., *Journals of the Continental Congress*, III: 351, VII: 72–73, XV: 1181–82, XXVIII: 306, 407–8.

14. Samuel Kirkland, journal, Jan. 14, 1789 ("lovers"), SPGP, Box 1, MHS; Samson Occom to John Bailey, n.d. [ca. June 1783] ("went with"), Samson Occom Papers, Reel 79998, Frame 307, CHS; Occom to Rev. Samuel Buell, n.d. [ca. 1784] ("coldly received"), Samson Occom Papers, Reel 79998, Frame 314 CHS.

15. Patrick, "Life and Times of Samuel Kirkland," 384–86, 389–92.

16. Samuel Kirkland to Rev. Kemp, Mar. 16, 1790 ("most undissembled," and "There is something"), LFP, DCLSC; Patrick, "Life and Times of Samuel Kirkland," 393–95; Pilkington, ed., *Journals of Samuel Kirkland*, 163, 170 ("general course").

17. Tuscarora and chiefs quoted in Pilkington, ed., *Journals of Samuel Kirkland*, 163 ("*two persons*"), 173 ("the Lord's day"); Samuel Kirkland, diary, Nov. 27, 1787 ("exercises"), LFP, DCLSC.

18. Pilkington, ed., *Journals of Samuel Kirkland*, 170 ("mourn and sigh"); Samuel Kirkland, diary, Mar. 25, 1790, LFP, DCLSC.

19. Samuel Kirkland, diary, Nov. 21, 1787, and Dec. 9, 1787, SPGP, Box 1, MHS; Samuel Kirkland, journal, Sept. 2, 1787 ("This creature" and "They appeared"), SPGP, Box 1, MHS. For the association of Iroquois witchcraft beliefs with social and cultural stress, see Wallace, *Death and Rebirth of the Seneca*, 254–62.

20. Samuel Kirkland, diary, Jan. 1, 1787 ("would soon"), LFP, DCLSC; Patrick, "Life and Times of Samuel Kirkland," 396–97.

21. Samuel Kirkland, diary, Nov. 21, 1787 ("The more"), Dec. 3, 1787 (Good Peter quoted: "Father"), SPGP, Box 1, MHS; Pilkington, ed., *Journals of Samuel Kirkland*, 201, 205; Lincklaen, *Travels in the Years 1791 and 1792*, 67–68.

22. Patrick, "Life and Times of Samuel Kirkland," 400–401, 406–7, 410; Pilkington, ed., *Journals of Samuel Kirkland*, 180; Samuel Kirkland, diary, May 7, 1788, LFP, DCLSC; Kirkland, journal, Jan. 23, 1788 ("She was"), SGP, Box 1, MHS.

23. Samuel Kirkland to David McClure, Apr. 24, 1770, Kirkland and Eleazar Wheelock, memorandum of understanding, Oct. 30, 1771, and Kirkland to John Thornton, July 27 and Sept. 29, 1772, SKP, Folder 8, 22, 31, and 33, HCA; Patrick, "Life and Times of Samuel Kirkland," 358–59, 414, 419–21; Kirkland, journal, Jan. 14, 1789, SPGP, Box 1, MHS.

24. Oneida Sachems to the Society for Promoting Christian Knowledge, Jan. 29, 1794 ("told us" and "that if he could"), SKP, Folder 164, HCA; Patrick, "Life and Times of Samuel Kirkland," 414; "An Act for the Speedy Sale of the Unappropriated Lands Within this State," May 5, 1786, [New York State], *Laws of the State of New York* (1887), II: 334; Tiro, "James Dean in Iroquoia," 413.

25. James Dean quoted in John Sergeant, Jr., to Timothy Pickering, Jan. 3, 1795 ("Mr. Kirkland"), TPP, LXII: 200, MHS.

26. Kirkland quoted in John Tayler to George Clinton, May 16, 1788 ("his Thoughts" and "his Ideas"), in Hough, ed., *Proceedings of the Commissioners*, I: 131, 141; Livingston Lease from the

Oneida, Jan. 8, 1788, in Hough, ed., *Proceedings of the Commissioners*, I: 120–24; Kirkland quoted in "Assembly Proceedings," *New-York Journal*, Mar. 3, 1788 ("good order").

27. Samuel Kirkland, affidavit, n.d. ("should not be"), Kirkland File, OCHS; Hough, ed., *Proceedings of the Commissioners*, I: 160n1; Kirkland, diary, June 26–July 3, 1788, LFP, DCLSC; Oliver Phelps and Nathaniel Gorham to Kirkland, Aug. 21, 1788 ("consideration"), LFP, DCLSC; Pilkington, ed., *Journals of Samuel Kirkland*, 183.

28. Treaty of Fort Schuyler, Sept. 22, 1788, in Hough, ed., *Proceedings of the Commissioners*, I: 243–44; "An Act for the sale and disposition of lands, belonging to the people of this State," Feb. 25, 1789 ("meritorious Services"), [New York State], *Laws of the State of New York* (1887), III: 70; Samuel Kirkland to George Clinton and the State Indian Commissioners, Dec. 18, 1788 ("would bind me"), SKP, Folder III, HCA. Evidently, Samuel Kirkland remained controversial for his earlier assistance to the Livingston Lessees, for on Feb. 19 the state assembly initially defeated his proposed land grant by a vote of 26 no to 23 yes, but reconsidered later that day by 35 yes to 18 no. See [New York State], *Journal of the Assembly*, 12th Sess. (1789), 130.

29. John Cozens Ogden to Dr. Hunter, Aug. 8, 1796 ("In America"), in Cameron, ed., *Papers of Loyalist Samuel Peters*, 131.

30. Patrick, "Life and Times of Samuel Kirkland," 402–3, 446; Jacob Reed to Society for the Promotion of Christian Knowledge, Sept. 5, 1791, #791505, DCLSC; Oneida Sachems and Warriors to the Society for the Promotion of Christian Knowledge, Jan. 29, 1794 ("Scarcely see"), TPP, LXII: 82–83; MHS.

31. Editorial note and Peter Penet to Benjamin Franklin, Aug. 3, 1776 ("no other Interest"), in Wilcox, ed., *Papers of Benjamin Franklin*, XXII: 311–12, and 543–47; Hough, *Notices of Peter Penet*, 4–7.

32. Peter Penet to Benjamin Franklin, Aug. 3, 1776 ("the Honour"), in Wilcox, ed., *Papers of Benjamin Franklin*, XXII: 546, 547n3; see also editorial note in ibid., XXIII (1983): 357; Hough, *Notices of Peter Penet*, 7; Ford, ed., *Journals of the Continental Congress*, VI: 869–70.

33. Benjamin Franklin, Silas Deane, and Arthur Lee to Congress, Jan. 17, 1777 ("At the same time"), and Jonathan Williams, Jr., to Franklin, Dean, and Lee, Jan. 18, 1777, in Wilcox, ed., *Papers of Benjamin Franklin*, XXIII: 195, 208.

34. Wilcox, ed., *Papers of Benjamin Franklin*, XXIV, 284n5, XXVII, 362–63; Thomas Jefferson, credentials for Peter Penet, July 15, 1779, Jefferson to Benjamin Harrison, Oct. 30, 1779, Philip Mazzei to Jefferson, Apr. 20, 1780 ("a mixture"), and Peter Penet to Jefferson, May 20, 1780 in Boyd, ed., *Papers of Thomas Jefferson*, III: 36, 125, 358–59, 383.

35. Benjamin Franklin to Robert Morris, Dec. 14, 1782 ("broke" and "We have"), in Boyd, ed., *Papers of Thomas Jefferson*, IV: 147n; Burgermeisters of Hamburg to Congress, Mar. 29, 1783 ("Mr. Penet), in Giunta, *The Emerging Nation*, II: 78, 79n1.

36. Hough, *Notices of Peter Penet*, 11; Penet quoted in Oneida Warriors to George Clinton, Aug. 23, 1789 ("You are"), in Hough, ed., *Proceedings of the Commissioners*, II: 346–47; Samuel Kirkland, Memorandum on Peter Penet ("an agency"), in SKP, Letters Undated File, HCA.

37. Samson Occom, diary, Aug. 4, 1788, in Blodgett, *Samson Occom*, 202; Samuel Kirkland, Memorandum on Peter Penet ("to make out"), in SKP, Letters Undated File, HCA.

38. Peter Penet quoted in Oneida warriors to George Clinton, Aug. 23, 1789 ("I come"), in Hough, ed., *Proceedings of the Commissioners*, II: 346–47; Samuel Kirkland, Memorandum on Peter Penet ("The King"), in SKP, Letters Undated File, HCA.

39. John Tayler to George Clinton, May 16, 1788 ("They have discovered"), in Hough, ed., *Proceedings of the Commissioners*, I: 141; Pilkington, ed., *Journals of Samuel Kirkland*, 142–43 ("abusive treatment").

40. Good Peter, speech, Sept. 22, 1788, in Hough, ed., *Proceedings of the Commissioners*, I: 234–36; Good Peter, narrative, Apr. 11, 1792, TPP, LX: 129, MHS; Peter Penet, speech, Oct. 19, 1788 ("the great secrets"), French Foreign Affairs Archives Photostats, Mémoires et Documents (États-Unis), III: 70, LC.

41. Thomas Jefferson to James Madison, Oct. 8, 1787, and Madison to Jefferson, Dec. 8, 1788 ("cunning disciple"), in Smith, ed., *Republic of Letters*, I: 494, 579; Malone, *Jefferson and the Rights of Man*, 197–98; Rice, *Barthelemi Tardiveau*, 13–15; De Conde, *This Affair of Louisiana*, 77.

42. Samuel Kirkland, Memorandum on Peter Penet, in SKP, Letters Undated File, HCA; Pilkington, ed., *Journals of Samuel Kirkland*, 143 ("They appear").

43. Samuel Kirkland, memorandum on Peter Penet, in SKP, Letters Undated File, HCA; Pilkington, ed., *Journals of Samuel Kirkland*, 143; Comte de Moustier, to the Oneida Chiefs, Nov. 1, 1788 ("agent general"), French Foreign Affairs Archives Photostats, Mémoires et Documents (États-Unis), III: 77–80, LC.

44. Good Peter, speech, Sept. 22, 1788 ("When our Business" and "You also"), in Hough, ed., *Proceedings of the Commissioners*, I: 234–36; Good Peter, narrative, Apr. 11, 1792, TPP, LX, 129, MHS.

45. Hough, *Notices of Peter Penet*, 11–12 ("his Benevolence"); Pilkington, ed., *Journals of Samuel Kirkland*, 175.

46. Samuel Kirkland, Memorandum on Peter Penet ("art & address" and "hoodwinked"), in SKP, Letters Undated File, HCA.

47. Peter Penet, speech, Oct. 19, 1788 ("to make"), Comte de Moustier to Oneida Chiefs, Nov. 1, 1788, and Moustier to unknown, February n.d., 1789, French Foreign Affairs Archives Photostats, Mémoires et Documents (États-Unis), III: 70, 77–80, 87–88B, LC. Moustier described the plan as his in conception, but Penet must have developed the elaborate details.

48. Peter Penet, speech, Oct. 19, 1788 ("I did look"), French Foreign Affairs Archives Photostats, Memoires et Documents (États-Unis), III: 70B, LC; Penet, "Plan of Government adopted by the Oneida Nation," Oct. 25, 1788, in Hough, *Notices of Peter Penet*, 24–29.

49. Peter Penet, "Plan of Government Adopted by the Oneida Nation," Oct. 25, 1788 ("true and trusty"), in Hough, *Notices of Peter Penet*, 24–29.

50. Comte de Moustier to Oneida Chiefs, Nov. 1, 1788, French Foreign Affairs Archives Photostats, Mémoires et Documents (États-Unis), III: 77–80; "The Plan of Government adopted by the Oneida Nation," *Albany Gazette*, Feb. 6, 1789.

51. Peter Penet, "Plan of Government Adopted by the Oneida Nation," Oct. 25, 1788 ("to overlook"), in Hough, *Notices of Peter Penet*, 27–29.

52. Peter Penet, "Plan of Government Adopted by the Oneida Nation," Oct. 25, 1788 ("to travel"), in Hough, *Notices of Peter Penet*, 27–29.

53. Wallace, *Death and Rebirth of the Seneca*, 239–340; Wallace, "Origins of the Longhouse Religion," 442–48.

54. Pilkington, ed., *Journals of Samuel Kirkland*, 144; Richter, *Ordeal of the Longhouse*, 255–280.

55. Pilkington, ed., *Journals of Samuel Kirkland*, 144. For emphasis on an enduring Oneida polarity between sachems and warriors, see Campisi, "Fur Trade and Factionalism," 37–46.

56. Jacob Reed to Samuel Kirkland, Feb. 14, 1789, in Campisi and Chrisjohn, eds., "Two Eighteenth-Century Oneida Letters," 41–42; Kirkland to Dr. Edward Wigglesworth, Mar. 7, 1789, #789207, DCLSC. For a sachem (Akeandyakhon or Coulense) defecting from the French party in June of 1789, see Pilkington, ed., *Journals of Samuel Kirkland*, 168.

57. Pilkington, ed., *Journals of Samuel Kirkland*, 145; Kirkland, journal, Nov. 30, 1788, SPGP, MHS; Kirkland, diary, May 17, 1791, LFP, DCLSC.

58. Pilkington, ed., *Journals of Samuel Kirkland*, 143, 167–68; Hough, *Notices of Peter Penet*, 21.

59. John Tayler, speech, June 3, 1789, and George Clinton to the Oneida Warriors, Sept. 12, 1789 ("Mr. Penet" and "nothing to do"), in Hough, ed., *Proceedings of the Commissioners*, II: 320–21, 350.

60. Peter Penet, deed to John Duncan, Jan. 23, 1789, Harmanus Bleecker Papers, #278, NYSL; John Tayler, speech, June 3, 1789, in Hough, ed., *Proceedings of the Commissioners*, II: 321; Hough, *Notices of Peter Penet*, 22–23.

61. Good Peter, speech, June 3, 1789 ("our Mother"), in Hough, ed., *Proceedings of the Commissioners*, II: 320; James Madison to Thomas Jefferson, Dec. 8, 1788, in Smith, ed., *Republic of Letters*, I: 579; Malone, *Jefferson and the Rights of Man*, 189.

62. Oneida Chief Warriors to Governor Clinton, Aug. 23, Sept. 20, and Oct. 28, 1789 (Colonel Louis quoted: "You think"), in Hough, ed., *Proceedings of the Commissioners*, II: 346–48, 352, 353; Pilkington, ed., *Journals of Samuel Kirkland*, 174, 176, 184.

63. Oneida Warriors to George Clinton, Sept. 20, 1789, in Hough, ed., *Proceedings of the Commissioners*, II: 352; Penet quoted in Good Peter, narrative, Apr. 24, 1792 ("where I can"), TPP, LX: 129A–130, MHS; Pilkington, ed., *Journals of Samuel Kirkland*, 175–76 ("the best land").

64. Oneida Warriors to Gov. George Clinton, Aug. 23, 1789, in Hough, ed., *Proceedings of the Commissioners*, I: 346–48; Honyery to Clinton, Apr. 11, 1791, John McKesson Papers, NYHS; Pilkington, ed., *Journals of Samuel Kirkland*, 207. For the relocation of the Oriske villagers that spring, see Horton, ed., "The Mohawk Valley in 1791," 211–12; Coventry, *Memoirs of an Emigrant*, I: 548. For the ouster of Penet's men, see George Clinton to William Colbrath, Apr. 13, 1791, and Colbrath to Clinton, Oct. 15, 1791, John McKesson Papers, NYHS; Colbrath, affidavit, Feb. 9, 1796, #11840, NYSL; Good Peter, narrative, Apr. 24, 1792, TPP, LX: 130A–131A, MHS; Clinton to Col. Louis Cook, Nov. 13, 1791, TPP, LXII: 209, MHS.

65. Oneida lease to Peter Penet, Oct. 8, 1791, HORC, VI, NYHS; Good Peter, narrative, Apr. 24, 1792, TPP, LX: 131A, MHS; Timothy Pickering to Penet, May 4, 1792, TPP, LXII: 42, MHS; Samuel Kirkland to Peter Thacher, June 30, 1792, SKP, Folder 149, HCA.

66. Simon Desjardins et al., "Castorland Journal," trans. Franklin B. Hough, 106, 108, 109, 216–17, and 225–26, AAS.

67. Samuel Kirkland, journal, Nov. 13, 1790, SPGP, Box 1, MHS; Pilkington, ed., *Journals of Samuel Kirkland*, 210 ("I find"); Kirkland to Timothy Pickering, June 14, 1792, TPP, LXII: 57, MHS; Captain John quoted in Kirkland, diary, May 17, 1791 ("brink"), LFP, DCLSC; Kirkland to Peter Thacher, June 30, 1792, #792380, DCLSC. In late 1791, Colonel Louis apparently still resided on the reservation. See George Clinton to Louis Cook, Nov. 13, 1791, TPP, LXII: 209, MHS. For Good Peter's reconciliation, see Pilkington, ed., *Journals of Samuel Kirkland*, 201, 215–16.

68. Patrick, "Life and Times of Samuel Kirkland," 550–51; Belknap, "Journal to Oneida, 1796," 409; Belknap, "Notes on a Journey to Oneida," 1796 ("He has," and "It was"), Belknap Papers, Reel 11, MHS; Moss Kent, Jr., to James Kent, Oct. 24, 1796 ("old Gentleman"), JKP, Reel 1, LC; Town of Paris, Assessment Roll, 1799, NYSA.

69. Stephen West to Samuel Kirkland, Apr. 18, 1789, SKP, Folder 114 ("the danger"), HCA; Kirkland to Rev. Peter Thacher, Jan. 14, 1791, DCA #791114 ("inveterate" and "nevertheless true"), DCLSC.

70. Samuel Kirkland to John Kemp, Mar. 16, 1790 ("It matters not"); LFP, DCLSC.

71. Kirkland to Peter Thacher, n.d. [ca. 1791], SKP, Undated Letters File, HCA.

72. Samuel Kirkland to Peter Thacher, Jan. 14, 1791 ("I received"), #791114, DCLSC.

73. Bagg, *Pioneers of Utica*, 14–18; "Guide to the Microfilm Edition of the Peter Smith Papers," 1–2, SULSC; James Kent, "Travel Journal #2: Tour of the Western Circuit, 1798" ("very avaricious"), JKP, Reel 6, Container 14, LC; Jones, *Annals of Oneida County*, 85, 451 ("anecdote").

74. Thomas Herring to Peter Smith, Aug. 28, 1801 ("your harshness" and "only serves"), Peter Smith to James Livingston, Jr., Sept. 15, 1801, and Elizabeth Smith to Peter Smith, Mar. 5, 1807 ("You write" and "Don't try"), PSmP, Box 1, SULSC.

75. Peter Smith, speech, ca. Oct. 1792 ("My house"), New Petersburgh Land Book, 1, PSmP, Box 11, SULSC; Ebenezer Caulkins to Peter Smith, May 10, 1793, PSmP, Box 1, SULSC; Oneida lease to Peter Smith, Jan. 15, 1793 ("peaceable"), TPP, LXII: 75, MHS. The leased land lay in the present-day towns of Augusta in Oneida County and Stockbridge, Smithfield, Fenner, and Cazenovia in Madison County. In 1794, James Emlen calculated the size of Smith's leased tract as 61,440 acres. See Fenton, ed., "Journal of James Emlen," 300. But Peter Smith's own records calculated the tract at 45,793 acres. See Smith, New Petersburgh Land Book, 154–57, PSmP, Box 12, SULSC.

76. Jacob Reed to Peter Smith, Oct. 20, 1792, and Feb. 22, 1793 ("It must be"), and Samuel Kirkland to Smith, Oct. 17, 1801 ("I have made" and "in private"), in PSMP, Box 1, SULSC. For Kirkland's previous business dealings with Smith, see Kirkland to Smith, July 30, 1792, and Aug. 9, 1792, Smith Family Papers, NYPL.

77. Peter Smith, New Petersburgh Land Book, 1, PSmP, Box 11, SULSC; Oneida lease to Peter Smith, Jan. 15, 1793, and Jacob Reed et al. to Timothy Pickering, May 14, 1794, TPP, LXII: 67, 75, MHS; Smith to Israel Chapin, Jan. 24, 1793, and Smith to Jacob Reed, Feb. 25, 1793, HORC, IX, NYHS; Capt. John, speech, Oct. 13, 1794, TPP, LX: 229, MHS; Jacob Atawanokta et al. to the New York State Legislature, Feb. 15, 1794 ("you told us"), in A 1823 (Assembly Papers), Box 40 (Indian Affairs, 1783–1809), 199, NYSA.

78. Peter Smith, New Petersburgh Land Book, 1 (Jan. 15, 1793), PSmP, Box 11, SULSC; Oneida lease to Peter Smith, Jan. 15, 1793, and Jacob Reed et al. to Timothy Pickering, May 14, 1794, TPP, LXII: 67, 75, MHS; Oneida Chiefs and Warriors to the New York State Legislature, Jan. 10, 1793 ("free liberty" and "to make"), A 4016 (Records of the Surveyor General), XXI: 97, NYSA; Treaty of Fort Schuyler, Sept. 22, 1788 ("Provision by law"), in Hough, ed., *Proceedings of the Commissioners*, I: 243. The schoolteacher Ebenezer Caulkins drafted the Oneida petition to the legislature; he signed that petition as a witness.

79. "An Act relative to the Lands appropriated by this State, to the use of the Oneida, Onondaga, and Cayuga Indians," Mar. 11, 1793, [New York State], *Laws of the State of New York* (1797), III: 73–74. At 250,000 acres, the Oneida reservation had 391 square miles.

80. Simon Desjardins et al., "Castorland Journal," Nov. 2, 1793, trans. Franklin B. Hough, 108, AAS.

81. Simeon DeWitt to Moses DeWitt, Sept. 28, 1793 ("most important", DWFP, Box 3, SULSC; Simeon DeWitt and John Cantine to Gov. Clinton, n.d. [ca. Nov. 1793] ("connection"), A 4016 (Records of the Surveyor General), XXI: 120, NYSA; Simeon DeWitt to Moses DeWitt, Oct. 14, 31, 1793, DWFP, Box 4, SULSC; Simon Desjardins et al., "Castorland Journal," Nov. 2, 1793, trans. Franklin B. Hough, 108, AAS. For their exertions as interpreters, Dean received £42.18.8 ($107.35), while Kirkland got $36. See A 0832 (State Comptrollers' Indian Annuity Claims, Receipts and Related Documents), XV: 86, NYSA. The legislature initially appointed a third commissioner, Israel Chapin, but he declined, recognizing the conflict with his duty as a federal official.

82. Simeon DeWitt, speech, Nov. 4, 1793 ("for the State"), A 4016 (Records of the Surveyor General), XXI: 116, NYSA.

83. Capt. Jacob Reed, speech, Nov. 4, 1793 ("We were misled"), and Capt. Peter, speech, Nov. 5, 1793 ("no application"), A 4016 (Records of the Surveyor General), XXI: 116, NYSA.

84. Simeon DeWitt, speeches, Nov. 5, 1793 ("Whenever" and "beneath") and Nov. 6, 1793 ("destitute," and "would it be"), in A 4016 (Records of the Surveyor General), XXI: 92ff., NYSA.

85. Capt. John, speech, Nov. 5, 1793 ("Now it appears"), and Capt. Peter, speech, Nov. 5, 1793 ("It seems"), A 4016 (Records of the Surveyor General), XXI: 92ff., NYSA

86. Simeon DeWitt and John Cantine, report, Nov. n.d., 1793, A 4016 (Records of the Surveyor General), XXI: 120, NYSA; Samuel Desjardins et al., "Castorland Journal," Nov. 3, 1793 (Skenandon quoted: "that his advice"), trans. Franklin B. Hough, 110, AAS.

87. Simeon DeWitt and John Cantine, report, Nov. n.d., 1793 (Capt. Peter quoted: "if the Rent"), A 4016 (Records of the Surveyor General), XXI: 120, NYSA; Simeon DeWitt to Moses DeWitt, Oct. 31, 1793, DWFP, Box 3, SULSC. For lease rates in New York during the 1790s, see Alexander, *A Revolutionary Conservative*, 218; and Strickland, *Journal of a Tour*, 112.

88. Capt. Peter, speech, Feb. 17, 1794 ("We tell you"), A 1823 (Assembly Papers), Box 40 (Indian Affairs, 1783–1809), 192, NYSA.

89. Capt. Peter, speech, Nov. 7, 1793 ("The U.S."), A 4016 (Records of the Surveyor General), XXI: 98, NYSA.

CHAPTER EIGHT: CHIEFS

1. Meginness, *Otzinachson*, 678–80; "Description of the Indian Murderers," Aug. 19, 1790 ("brought up" and "fond of"), and People v. Samuel Doyle, Northumberland County Court of Oyer & Terminer, Nov. 12, 1790, in *Pennsylvania Archives*, 1st Ser., XI: 721, 744; John Robinson to Thomas Proctor, Aug. 17, 1790, *Pennsylvania Archives*, 1st Ser., XI: 719. None of the sources name the two dead Indians. The Northumberland County indictment referred to each as an Indian "whose Name is to the Inquest unknown."

2. Meginness, *Otzinachson*, 679; Lt. Bernard Hubley to Thomas Mifflin, July 12, 1790, Hubley to Robert Fleming et al., July 12, 1790 in *Pennsylvania Archives*, 1st Ser., XI: 709–10.

3. Meginness, *Otzinachson*, 680; Genesee Seneca Chiefs to the Governor and Council of Pennsylvania, Aug. 12, 1790 ("Where you will meet," "your Governor," and "Our young"), TPP, LXI: 1–1A, MHS; Oliver Phelps to Nathaniel Gorham, Aug. 7, 1790 ("I never saw"), in Turner, *Pioneer History of the Holland Purchase*, 332.

4. Pennsylvania General Assembly, resolution, Sept. 2, 1790, TPP, LXI: 5, MHS; George Washington to Timothy Pickering, Sept. 4, 1790, *PGW-PS*, VI: 393–96; Pickering to the Seneca Chiefs, Sept. 4, 1790, TPP, LXI: 12A, MHS.

5. Ben-Atar and Oberg, eds., *Federalists Reconsidered*; Elkins and McKitrick, *Age of Federalism*.

6. Henry Knox, report, Jan. 22, 1791 ("embarrassed" and "critically"), *ASPIA*, I: 112; Onuf, "Settlers, Settlements, and New States," 171–96; Cayton, "Radicals in the 'Western World,' " 80–82.

7. Henry Knox, report, Jan. 22, 1791 ("Government"), *ASPIA*, I: 112–13; Rohrbough, *Land Office Business*, 15; Cayton, *Frontier Republic*, 12–32; Madison quoted ("a mine") in Cayton, "Radicals in the 'Western World,' " 80; Jones, *License for Empire*, 163; Horsman, *Expansion and American Indian Policy*, 42–43.

8. Prucha, *Great Father*, 59–61; White, *Middle Ground*, 457–58; Henry Knox, report, June 15, 1789 ("the right"), *ASPIA*, I: 13.

9. Royster, *Revolutionary People at War*, 79–95, 353–57; Taylor, "From Fathers to Friends of the People," 465–91; Cayton, *Frontier Republic*, 18, 43; Gardiner, *Early Recollections of Robert Hallowell Gardiner*, 107 ("in the style").

10. Henry Knox, reports, June 15, 1789 ("system," "blood," and "a sum"), July 7, 1789, Jan. 4, 1790, and Dec. 29, 1794, *ASPIA*, I: 12–14, 53–54, 60, 543–44; Jones, *License for Empire*, 157–79.

11. Henry Knox, reports, July 7, 1789 ("practice"), and Jan. 4, 1790 ("the cheapest"), *ASPIA*, I: 54, 60; Timothy Pickering to George Washington, Jan. 8, 1791, and Washington to Pickering, Jan. 20, 1791, *PGW-PS*, VII: 204–7, 257; Washington to the Senate, Mar. 23, 1792, *ASPIA*, I: 225.

12. Henry Knox, reports, July 7, 1789 ("the Indians"), and Dec. 29, 1794, *ASPIA*, I: 53, 544.

13. Cayton, "Radicals in the 'Western World,'" 77–96; Taylor, "Land and Liberty on the Post-Revolutionary Frontier," 81–108.

14. George Washington to James Duane, Sept. 7, 1783, in Fitzpatrick, ed., *Writings of George Washington*, XXVII: 133–40; Henry Knox, reports, June 15 ("As the settlements") and July 7, 1789, *ASPIA*, I: 12–14, 53–54; Benjamin Lincoln to Jeremy Belknap, Jan. 21, 1792 ("precipitate"), in Massachusetts Historical Society, *Collections*, 6th Ser., IV (1891): 512–16; Lincoln, "Journal of a Treaty Held in 1793," 138–41; Lincoln to John Heckewelder, Nov. n.d., 1793 ("those slow"), SPGP, Box 2, MHS; Prucha, *Great Father*, 60.

15. Henry Knox, reports, June 15, and July 7, 1789, *ASPIA*, I: 12–14, 53–54; Benjamin Lincoln to Jeremy Belknap, Jan. 21, 1792 ("time will" and "very nature"), in MHS, *Collections*, 6th Ser., IV (1891): 513–16; Lincoln, "Journal of a Treaty Held in 1793," 138–41; Timothy Pickering, "Remarks on the Proposed Instructions to the Commissioners," TPP, LIX: 28, MHS.

16. Benjamin Lincoln to John Heckewelder, Nov. n.d., 1793, SPGP, Box 2, MHS; Timothy Pickering to George Washington, Jan. 8, 1791 ("They will find"), and Washington to Pickering, Jan. 20, 1791, *PGW-PS*, VII: 204–7, 257.

17. Rufus King to Alexander Hamilton, Mar. 24, 1791, in Syrett, ed., *Papers of Alexander Hamilton*, VIII: 213; Hamilton to Washington, Mar. 27, 1791 ("You are"), *PGW-PS*, VIII: 10–11.

18. Horsman, *Expansion and American Indian Policy*, 53–65, 84–103; Prucha, *The Great Father*, 50–60; Prucha, *American Indian Policy*, 41–50.

19. Samuel Kirkland to Henry Knox, Jan. 27, 1792 ("happy circumstance"), SKP, Folder 144, HCA.

20. George Clinton to Henry Knox, Apr. 27, 1791 ("those nations"), *ASPIA*, I: 167; Timothy Pickering to Knox, Aug. 10, 1791, TPP, LX: 115, MHS.

21. Henry Knox, report, July 7, 1789 ("independent nations"), *ASPIA*, I: 53.

22. Prucha, *American Indian Policy*, 45–50, 144–45; John Sergeant, Jr., to Timothy Pickering, Jan. 3, 1795, TPP, LXII: 199, MHS; Capt. Peter, speech, Nov. 7, 1793, A 4016 (Records of the Surveyor General), XXI: 98, NYSA.

23. George Washington to Timothy Pickering, Sept. 4, 1790, *PGW-PS*, VI: 393–94; and Pickering to the Seneca Chiefs, Sept. 4, 1790, TPP, XLI: 12A, MHS.

24. O. Pickering and Upham, eds., *Life of Timothy Pickering*, II: 452; Phillips, "Timothy Pickering at His Best," 166–67. Pennsylvania's representative delivered the appropriate speech acknowledging federal supremacy in Indian affairs. See Col. Wilson, speech, Nov. 19, 1790, TPP, LXI: 74, MHS.

25. Phillips, "Timothy Pickering at his Best," 167–69; O. Pickering and Upham, *Life of Timothy Pickering*, II: 464–67; Pickering, Tioga Council Journal, Nov. 15 and 22, 1790, TPP, LXI: 64A, 91A, MHS; Red Jacket, speech, Nov. 20, 1790 ("in the time of" and "the mind"), and Little Billy, speech, Nov. 23, 1790 ("first time"), TPP, LXI: 80, 96, MHS; Pickering to George Washington, Dec. 4, 1790, *PGW-PS*, VII: 27–29.

26. Farmer's Brother, speech, Nov. 21, 1790, Red Jacket, speeches, Nov. 21 and 23, 1790, Little Billy, speech, Nov. 23, 1790, and Timothy Pickering, report, Dec. 24, 1790, TPP, LXI: 85, 85A–86, 93, 97, 113, MHS.

27. Henry Knox to Timothy Pickering, Dec. 27, 1790 ("conducted"), George Washington to Pickering, Dec. 31, 1790 ("entire Approbation"), and Pickering to Washington, Dec. 31, 1790 ("I was"), *PGW–PS*, VII: 114n2, 157–58, 158n; Philips, "Timothy Pickering at His Best," 171.

28. Bernard Hubley, Jr., to Timothy Pickering, Sept. 9, 1790, TPP, LXI: 21, MHS; Pickering to George Washington, Dec. 4, 1790 (all quotations), *PGW-PS*, VII: 27–29; People v. Samuel Doyle, Northumberland County Court of Oyer & Terminer, Nov. 12, 1790, in *Pennsylvania Archives*, 1st Ser., XI: 744–46. There is a plausible tradition that Doyle and one of the Walkers later resurfaced in Steuben County, New York, where in 1807 Walker killed at least one more Indian hunter, successfully secreting the body with Doyle's help. See, Meginness, *Otzinachson*, 682–85; McMaster, *History of the Settlement of Steuben County*, 245.

29. Ensign John Jeffers quoted in Kent and Deardorff, eds., "John Adlum on the Allegheny," 452n27 ("might be"); Henry Knox to George Washington, Dec. 27, 1790, *PGW-PS*, VII: 126; Pickering, "Remarks on the Proposed Instructions to the Commissioners," [1793] ("if the Indians"), TPP, LIX: 29, MHS.

30. Asa Danforth to Israel Chapin, July [*sic*; August] 7, 1792, HORC, VIII, NYHS; William Colbrath to George Clinton, Aug. 6, 1792, #11248, NYSL; Moses DeWitt to DeWitt Clinton, Aug. 12, 1792, DeWitt Clinton Papers, Reel 1, Columbia University; Clinton to John Graves Simcoe, Aug. 17, 1792, and Simcoe to Clinton, Sept. 20, 1792, in Cruikshank, ed., *Correspondence of Simcoe*, I: 198, II: 65; George Clinton, Proclamation, Aug. 16, 1792, *Albany Gazette*, Aug. 23, 1792; Killian K. Van Rensselaer to Oliver Phelps, Aug. 23, 1792, PGP, Box 19, NYSL; Gatcontegachte, speech, Feb. 15, 1794 ("tho' our people"), and George Clinton, speech, Feb. 15, 1794 ("who went up"), A 1823 (Assembly Papers), Box 40 (Indian Affairs, 1783–1809), 183, 187, NYSA.

31. James McHenry to Israel Chapin, Jr., Sept. 13, 1796, and Mar. 9, 1797, HORC, XII, NYHS; Captain O'Bail (Cornplanter) to Chapin, Jun. 18, 1794, and Jun. 16, 1798, HORC, X and XIII, NYHS; Samuel Dexter to Chapin, Feb. 17, 1801, HORC, XIV, NYHS; Prucha, *American Indian Policy*, 202.

32. Graymont, *Iroquois in the American Revolution*, 236, 283–84; Wallace, *Death and Rebirth of the Seneca*, 170; Pilkington, *Journals of Samuel Kirkland*, 209 ("uncommon genius"); Henry Knox to George Washington, Dec. 27, 1790, *PGW-PS*, VII: 124; Kent and Deardorff, eds., "John Adlum on the Allegheny," 268–70.

33. Wallace, *Death and Rebirth of the Seneca*, 168–69, 185–91; Kent and Deardorff, eds., "John Adlum on the Allegheny," 294n72; Thomas Proctor, diary, Apr. 21, 1791 ("This figure"), *ASPIA*, 154–55.

34. Thomas Mifflin to Cornplanter, May 10, 1790, *Pennsylvania Archives*, 4th Ser., IV: 99; Wallace, *Death and Rebirth of the Seneca*, 169–71; Richter, "Onas, the Long Knife," 133, 145, 154–55.

35. Wallace, *Decline and Rebirth of the Senecas*, 156–59, 169–70; Henry Knox to George Washington, Dec. 27, 1790, *PGW-PS*, VII: 122; Richter, "Onas, the Long Knife," 153–54; *Pennsylvania Archives*, 1st Ser., XII: 86–87, 361–62; Thomas Proctor, diary, Apr. 6, 9, and 12, 1791, *ASPIA*, I: 152–53.

36. Richter, "Onas, the Long Knife," 155; Thomas Mifflin to Cornplanter, Nov. 3, 1790, and Mifflin to the Pennsylvania General Assembly, Jan. 21, Feb. 5, 1791, in *Pennsylvania Archives*, 4th Ser., IV: 112, 160–61, 166; Timothy Pickering, report, Dec. 24, 1770, TPP, LXI: 114, MHS; Cornplanter, speech, Dec. 1, 1790, Henry Knox to George Washington, Dec. 27, 1790, and Cornplanter, speech, Jan. 10, 1791, *PGW-PS*, VII: 7–15, 123, 218–21; Pilkington, ed., *Journals of Samuel Kirkland*, 208–9.

37. Henry Knox to George Washington, Dec. 27, 1790 ("fittest," "almost," and "besides"), *PGW-PS*, VII: 121–28.

38. Henry Knox to George Washington, Dec. 27, 1790, and Washington, speeches, Dec. 29, 1790 ("Here then" and "You possess"), and Jan. 19, 1791, *PGW-PS*, VII: 121–28, 146–50, 252–54.

39. Henry Knox to George Washington, Dec. 27, 1790 ("attach"), Washington, speech, Dec. 29, 1790, and Cornplanter, speech, Feb. 7, 1790 ("open their Eyes"), *PGW-PS*, VII: 121–28, 149, 322; Pilkington, ed., *Journals of Samuel Kirkland*, 209.

40. Cornplanter to George Washington, Mar. 17, 1791, Knox to Washington, Mar. 27 and Apr. 10, 1791, *PGW-PS*, VII: 590–91, VIII: 14–17, 80–81; James Jeffers to Richard Butler, Aug. 16, 1791, MG 19 F 35 (PSGIA), 1st Ser., Lot 734, NAC.

41. Rufus King to Alexander Hamilton, Mar. 24, 1791, in Syrett, ed., *Papers of Alexander Hamilton*, VIII: 213; George Washington to Hamilton, April 4, 1791 ("What must"), *PGW-PS*, VIII: 57–58.

42. Henry Knox to George Washington, Feb. 22 and April 10, 1791 ("Every exertion"), Timothy Pickering to Washington, May 2, 1791, and Knox to Washington, May 30, 1791, *PGW-PS*, VII: 402–13, VIII: 80–81, 150–51, 223; Horsman, *Expansion and American Indian Policy*, 86–89. For Iroquois dread in western New York, see Captain Bowman, journal, May 3, 1791, TPP, LXI: 190, MHS; Nathaniel Gorham, Jr., to Oliver Phelps, May 9, 1791, PGP, Box 18, NYSL.

43. Henry Knox to George Washington, Feb. 22 and April 10, 1791, Thomas Jefferson to Washington, Apr. 17, 1791, Timothy Pickering to Washington, May 2, 1791, and Knox to Washington, May 30, 1791, *PGW-PS*, VII: 402–13, VIII: 80–81, 114–15, 150–51, 223; Knox to Pickering, May 2, and June 13, 1791, *ASPIA*, I: 165–66, 166; Jasper Parrish to Pickering, June 13, 1791, TPP, LXI: 231, MHS. As editor of *The Papers of Thomas Jefferson*, Julian P. Boyd indulged in a conspiracy theory to find an ulterior motive behind the convening of a Six Nations council in 1791. Conceding that he lacked any direct evidence, Boyd speculates that the council met no federal need but served as a cover for the land speculator Robert Morris, who in March procured the Massachusetts preemption right (formerly held by Oliver Phelps and Nathaniel Gorham) to 4 million acres in western New York. Boyd insinuates that Knox and Hamilton concocted the federal council to permit Morris to pressure the Senecas into a land cession. Given the crucial importance of the Senecas and their adamant opposition to further land cessions, made abundantly clear at Tioga Point and by Cornplanter in Philadelphia, such conduct by Knox and Hamilton would have betrayed the president's entire Indian policy. Given Knox's abundantly documented commitment to avoiding war by mollifying the Six Nations, such a conspiracy theory strains credulity—especially in the absence of any evidence. Nor is it conceivable that Knox would so readily betray the confidence of the president, whom he revered. And for a land speculator's supposed ploy, there could have been no worse choice than Timothy Pickering as the treaty commissioner, given his manifest sympathy for the Senecas expressed after the Tioga council. Indeed, at that council Pickering outraged Morris by honoring a Seneca request to vest some of the coveted land in their favorite, Ebenezer Allan. In fact, the federal government had pressing reasons to convene the Six Nations to confirm their neutrality. For the conspiracy theory, see Boyd, ed., *The Papers of Thomas Jefferson*, XX: 127–32. For Seneca opposition to Morris's land bid, see Thomas Proctor, diary, Apr. 27–28, 1791, *ASPIA*, I: 156.

44. *PGW-PS*, VIII: 434n1; Thomas Morris, "Recollections," Morris Papers, Folder 2, OCHS.

45. Henry Knox to Timothy Pickering, May 2 and June 13, 1791, *ASPIA*, I: 165–66; Pickering, speeches, July 4 and 6, 1791, Red Jacket, speech, July 10, 1791 ("We wish"), Pickering, speech, July 13, 1791 ("Observing"), and Red Jacket, speech, July 14, 1791, TPP, LX: 82, 84, 93, 99A–102, 106, MHS.

46. Densmore, *Red Jacket*, xiii–xix, 3–36; Graymont, *Iroquois in the American Revolution*, 185, 215–16; Wallace, *Death and Rebirth of the Seneca*, 26, 135, 139, 180–83, 199, 204–6.

47. Thomas Morris, "Recollections," Morris Papers, Folder 2 ("a cunning" and "very fluent"), OCHS; Thomas S. Abler, "Shakoyewatha," *DCB*, VI: 703–4.

48. Thomas Morris, "Recollections," Morris Papers, Folder 2, OCHS; Savery, "Journal," 357; Dwight, *Travels*, IV: 144–45; Turner, *Phelps and Gorham Purchase*, 487–88.

49. Thomas Morris, "Recollections" (Red Jacket quoted: "when a Seneca speaks"), Morris Papers, Folder 2, OCHS; Red Jacket, speeches, July 14 and 15, 1791, and Pickering, speech, July 15, 1791, TPP, LX: 106, 110a, 111, MHS; Philips, "Timothy Pickering at His Best," 175.

50. Good Peter, speech, July 10, 1791 ("'Tis the mind"), and Pickering to Knox, July 16, 1791, TPP, LX: 91, 112A, MHS.

51. George Washington, speech, Dec. 29, 1790 ("That you possess"), *PGW-PS*, VII: 146–50; Timothy Pickering, journal, July 15 and 17, 1791, TPP, LX: 60, 110–112, 112, MHS; Cayuga Lease to John Richardson, July 16–17, 1791, HORC, VI, NYHS.

52. Timothy Pickering, journal, July 15 and 17, 1791, TPP, LX: 60, 110–112, 112, MHS; Cayuga Lease to John Richardson, July 16–17, 1791, HORC, VI, NYHS; Pickering to Henry Knox, Aug. 16, 1791 ("reviving"), John McKesson Papers, NYHS.

53. Red Jacket, speech, July 14, 1791, Timothy Pickering, speech, July 17, 1791 ("Let us"), and Pickering to Henry Knox, July 16 and Aug. 10, 1791 ("we parted"), TPP, LX: 106, 110A, 112A, 117, MHS.

54. Abraham Hardenbergh to George Clinton, July 26, 1791, John McKesson Papers, NYHS; John Richardson to Timothy Pickering, July 30, 1791, TPP, LXI: 266, MHS; Henry Knox to Clinton, Aug. 17, 1791, *ASPIA*, I: 169; Pickering to Knox, Aug. 16, 1791 ("solemn assurances"), John McKesson Papers, NYHS; Knox to George Washington, Aug. 17, 1791, and Washington to the United States Senate, Oct. 26, 1791, *PGW-PS*, VIII: 433, IX: 118–19; William J. Vredenburgh to Moses De Witt, Oct. 5, 1791, DWFP, Box 2, SULSC. Some Clinton supporters insinuated that Pickering had a financial interest in the Cayuga lease, but there is no evidence for this. For the insinuation, see William Colbrath to Clinton, Oct. 15, 1791, McKesson Papers, NYHS. For a denial, see Pickering to Samuel Kirkland, Apr. 24, 1792, and Kirkland to Pickering, May 10, 1792, TPP, LXII: 16, 43, MHS.

55. Henry Knox to George Washington, Aug. 17, 1791 ("the Commissioner"), and Washington to the United States Senate, Oct. 26, 1791, *PGW-PS*, VIII: 433, IX: 118–19; Washington to Knox, Oct. 26, 1791, TPP, LXI: 280, MHS; O. Pickering and C. Upham, *Life of Timothy Pickering*, II: 496–97; Phillips, "Timothy Pickering at his Best," 177–78.

56. Henry Knox to Congress, Sept. 12, 1785, in Giunta, ed., *The Emerging Nation*, II: 812–13.

57. Kelsay, *Joseph Brant*, 352, 377, 379–82; Allen, *His Majesty's Indian Allies*, 65–66; Henry Hope to Sir John Johnson, Oct. 30, 1785, MG 19 F 2 (Sir John Johnson Papers), III, NAC; Patrick Langan to Daniel Claus, Dec. 15, 1785, and Joseph Brant to Lord Sydney, Jan. 4, 1786, MG 11 (Colonial Office 42), XLIX: 1, 25, NAC.

58. Calloway, *Crown and Calumet*, 101; Joseph Brant to Lord Sydney, Jan. 4, 1786, MG 11 (Colonial Office 42), XLIX: 1, NAC; Brymner, ed., "Private Diary of Gen. Haldimand," 157, 159–61; Kelsay, *Joseph Brant*, 382–94.

59. Henry Hope to Lord Sydney, June 26, 1786 ("I was sorry"), and Robert Mathews to Frederick Haldimand, Aug. 9, 1786 ("did not" and "Blockhead"), both quoted in Kelsay, *Joseph Brant*, 395; Mathews, journal, May 27, 1787, MG 23 J 9 (Mathews Papers), NAC.

60. Patrick Langan to Daniel Claus, June 29, 1786 ("Subtlety" and "add to"), and Dec. 14, 1786, MG 19 (Claus Family Papers), IV: 109, 133, NAC; Major Campbell to Henry Hope, July 19, 1786 ("very great" and "I cannot"), MG 11 (Colonial Office 42), XLIX: 369, NAC; Hope to Lord Sydney, Aug. 17, 1786, in Cruikshank, "Records of Niagara, 1784–7," 92; Sir John Johnson to Brant, Mar. 22, 1787, in Stone, *Life of Joseph Brant*, II: 267–68.

61. Kelsay, *Joseph Brant*, 431; Joseph Brant to Robert Mathews, Sept. 23, 1789 ("Dear friend"), in Cruikshank, "Records of Niagara, 1784–9," 92–93.

62. Kelsay, *Joseph Brant*, 431; Sir John Johnson to Lord Dorchester, Jan. 28, 1790, MG 11 (Colonial Office 42), LXIX: 227, NAC.

63. Joseph Brant to George Clinton, June 18, 1789, and Clinton to Brant, July 14, 1789, in Ketchum, *History of Buffalo*, I: 387–88; Jelles Fonda to Brant, June 16, 1790, Fonda Papers, NYHS; Kelsay, *Joseph Brant*, 432; Brant to Clinton, July 21, 1790 ("I am at a loss"), Clinton to Brant, Sept. 1, 1790, Clinton to George Washington, Nov. 26, 1790 ("a Man"), and Brant to Clinton, Mar. 4, 1791, in Hough, ed., *Proceedings of the Commissioners*, II: 460–61, 462, 465, 470.

64. Samuel Kirkland to Peter Thacher, Jan. 24, 1791, and June 8, 1791, #791374 and #791358, DCLSC; Kirkland to Joseph Willard, June 24, 1791, Harvard Indian Papers, 1720–1810, Folder 12, HUA; Joseph Brant to Sir John Johnson, Mar. 24, 1791, MG 11 (Colonial Office 42), LXXIII, 145, NAC; Kirkland to Henry Knox, Apr. 22, 1791, SKP, Folder 135, HCA; Knox to George Clinton, Apr. 12, 1791 ("Your Excellency"), and Clinton to Knox, Apr. 27, 1791 ("enable me"), *ASPIA*, 167, 168.

65. Joseph Brant to Samuel Kirkland, Mar. 8, 1791 ("call a general"), SKP, Folder 134, HCA.

66. Joseph Brant to Sir John Johnson, Mar. 24, 1791 ("from the"), MG 11 (Colonial Office 42), LXXIII: 145, NAC.

67. Henry Knox to Timothy Pickering, May 2 and May 18, 1791, *ASPIA*, I: 166; Kelsay, *Joseph Brant*, 446; Joseph Brant to Sir John Johnson, June 4, 1791, Old Thomas, speech, June 29, 1791, Cornplanter, speech, July 4, 1791, and De Barge to Jacob Slough, July 5, 1791, MG 11 (Colonial Office 42), LXXXII: 359, LXXXIII: 112, LXXXIX: 180, 182, NAC.

68. Joseph Brant to Major Smith, July 9, 1791, MG 11 (Colonial Office 42), LXXXIII: 184, NAC; Kelsay, *Joseph Brant*, 446–48.

69. Kelsay, *Joseph Brant*, 450–52; Joseph Brant, speech, Aug. 14, 1791, MG 19 F 35 (PSGIA), 2nd Ser., Lot 693, NAC; Lord Dorchester, speech, Aug. 15, 1791, and Brant, speech, Aug. 19, 1791 ("It is a Grievous thing"), MG 11 (Colonial Office 42), LXXXIII: 184, 203. For Dorchester's copy sent to Philadelphia, see *PGW-PS*, IX: 51n1–52n1.

70. Farmer's Brother, speech, Oct. n.d., 1791, F 47-1-1 (Simcoe Papers), Reel 1797, AO; John Butler to Sir John Johnson, Oct. 19, 1791, MG 23, H-I-1, Ser. 4 (Simcoe Transcripts), II, Folder Rr, 3, NAC; Kelsay, *Joseph Brant*, 455.

71. Kelsay, *Joseph Brant*, 454–57; White, *Middle Ground*, 454; Henry Knox, report, Dec. 26, 1791, *PGW-PS*, IX: 318. For the Senecas and Cayugas in the battle, see Alexander McKee to Sir John Johnson, Dec. 5, 1791, F 47-1-1 (Simcoe Papers), Reel 1797, AO; Samuel Kirkland to Knox, Jan. 17, 1792, and Israel Chapin to Knox, July 17, 1792, *PGW-PS*, IX: 525–26, X: 639–40; Coventry, *Memoirs of an Emigrant*, I: 853–54.

72. Kelsay, *Joseph Brant*, 457; Robert Hamilton to unknown, Nov. 24, 1791, in Cruikshank, ed., "Records of Niagara, 1790–1792," 128–29; Samuel Kirkland to Henry Knox, Dec. 28, 1791, and Feb. 13, 1792, SKP, Folders 142 and 145, HCA; Joseph Brant to Sir John Johnson, Dec. 30, 1791, F 47-1-1 (Simcoe Papers), Reel 1797, AO; Kirkland to Knox, Jan. 17, 1792 ("I am"), in *PGW-PS*, IX: 525–26; Shawnee emissary's speech, quoted in Kirkland to Knox, Feb. 13, 1792 ("You chief Mohawk"), SKP, Folder 145, HCA.

73. Johnston, *Valley of the Six Nations*, xxxiii–xli; Johnston, "Joseph Brant, the Grand River Lands, and the Northwest Crisis," 268–69; John Butler to the Grand River Chiefs, Oct. 2, 1791, Joseph Brant to Ralfe Clench, Oct. 8, 1791, Col. Gordon to Joseph Brant, Oct. 18, 1791, Butler to Sir John Johnson, Oct. 19, 1791, Brant to Joseph Chew, Oct. 27, 1791 ("We have"), F 47-1-1 (Simcoe Papers), Reel 1797, AO; Wilson, *Enterprises of Robert Hamilton*, 52. Wilson writes that

two whites were killed in 1791, but the documents indicate only one murdered man. None of the documents reveal his name.

74. Col. Gordon to Joseph Brant, Oct. 18, 1791 ("Had the murder"), and Brant to Joseph Chew, Oct. 27, 1791 ("This is by no means"), in F 47-1-1 (Simcoe Papers), Reel 1797, AO.

75. Col. Gordon to Joseph Brant, Oct. 18, 1791, F 47-1-1 (Simcoe Papers), Reel 1797, AO.

76. Sir William Johnson "Articles of Peace Concluded with the Seneca Indians," Apr. 3, 1764, and Johnson, "Articles of Peace with the Chenussio Indians and other Enemy Senecas," Aug. 6, 1764, in O'Callaghan, ed., *NYCD*, VII: 621–23, 652–53.

77. Frederick Haldimand to Sir William Johnson, Dec. 1, 1773, Johnson to Haldimand, Dec. 17, 1773, and Apr. 21, 1774, and Haldimand to Johnson, Apr. 27, 1774, *PSWJ*, VIII: 934, 952, 1131–32, 1135; Lord Dartmouth to Johnson, Apr. 6, 1774, Sayenqueraghta, speech, Apr. 18, 1774, Johnson Hall, Council Minutes, July 8, 1774, and Serihowane, speech, July 9, 1774, in O'Callaghan, ed., *NYCD*, VIII: 416, 425–26, 474, and 475–76.

78. Joseph Brant to Joseph Chew, Oct. 27, 1791 ("What gives rise"), F 47-1-1 (Simcoe Papers), Reel MS-1797, AO.

79. Sir John Johnson to Thomas Aston Coffin, Nov. 17, 1791, and Brant to Johnson, Dec. 30, 1791 ("confidence" and "to Exercise"), in F 47-1-1 (Simcoe Papers), Reel 1797, AO; Preston, ed., *Kingston Before the War of 1812*, 176n53; John Graves Simcoe to Lord Dorchester, Dec. 6, 1793, in Cruikshank, ed., *Correspondence of Simcoe*, II: 115.

80. John White to Samuel Shepherd, June 30, 1792 ("two Iroquois"), MG 23 H-I-5 (White-Shepherd Papers), II: 1, NAC; Edith G. Firth, "John White," *DCB*, IV: 766–67.

81. John Graves Simcoe, speech, Jan. 12, 1793 ("Brothers"), F 47-1-1 (Simcoe Papers), Reel 1797, AO; Colgate, "Diary of John White," 154–55.

82. John Graves Simcoe to Alured Clarke, July 3, 1792, Simcoe Letterbook, 61, #558, HL; Clarke to Simcoe, July 12, 1792, and Simcoe to Clarke, July 29 and Aug. 9, 1792, in Cruikshank, ed., *Simcoe Papers*, I: 179–80, 184, 192; Hesse District Grand Jury Indictment, Sept. 6, 1792 ("kicked & stomped"), RG 22, Ser. 138 (Court of King's Bench Criminal Filings, 1792–1819), Box 1, AO.

83. John Graves Simcoe to Alured Clarke, July 3, 1792, Simcoe Letterbook, 61, #558, HL; Clarke to Simcoe, July 12, 1792, and Simcoe to Clarke, July 29 and Aug. 9, 1792, in Cruikshank, ed., *Simcoe Papers*, I: 179–80, 184, and 192; John White to Simcoe, July 3, 1792, and William Osgoode to Simcoe, July 27, 1792, in Preston, ed., *Kingston Before the War of 1812*, 357, 358; Simcoe to Osgoode, July 28, 1792 ("I am sorry"), in F 47-1-1 (Simcoe Papers), Reel 1797, AO.

84. Riddell, *Michigan Under British Rule*, 333, 336, 454n5; Preston, ed., *Kingston Before the War of 1812*, 357–58.

85. Colgate, ed., "Diary of John White," 160; John Graves Simcoe to Lord Dorchester, Dec. 6, 1793 (all quotations), in Cruikshank, ed., *Simcoe Papers*, II: 115; Simcoe, speech in council, Jan. 12, 1793, F 47, Ser. 1-1 (Simcoe Papers), Reel MS-1797, AO; Firth, "John White," *DCB*, IV: 766–67.

CHAPTER NINE: CRISIS

1. Lord Grenville to George Hammond, Sept. 1, 1791, John Graves Simcoe to Henry Dundas, Feb. 16, 1792, and Dundas to Simcoe, Aug. 15, 1792, in Cruikshank, ed., *Correspondence of Simcoe*, I: 58–59, 114, 196.

2. Montreal Merchants to John Graves Simcoe, Dec. 9, 1791 ("In place"), Henry Dundas to Alured Clarke, Mar. 16, 1792, Dundas to Simcoe, May 5, 1792, and Simcoe and Alexander McKee to George Hammond, June 21, 1792, in Cruikshank, ed., *Correspondence of Simcoe*, I:

91–92, 125, 151, 173; Wright, *Britain and the American Frontier*, 69–72; Samuel Kirkland to Henry Knox, Feb. 25, 1792, and Thomas Jefferson, memorandum, Mar. 9, 1792, *PGW-PS*, X: 48n, 69–72.

3. Henry Dundas to Alured Clarke, Mar. 16, 1792, Dundas to John Graves Simcoe, May 5, 1792, and George Hammond to Lord Grenville, June 8, 1792, in Cruikshank, ed., *Correspondence of Simcoe*, I: 125, 151, V: 15; Lord Grenville to George Hammond, Mar. 17, 1792, in Syrett, ed., *Papers of Alexander Hamilton*, XIX: 117n6; Thomas Jefferson, memorandum, Mar. 9, 1792, and George Washington to Gouverneur Morris, June 21, 1792 ("The United States"), *PGW-PS*, X: 69–72, 489–90.

4. Thomas Jefferson, memorandum, Mar. 9, 1792, and George Washington to Gouverneur Morris, June 21, 1792, *PGW-PS*, X: 69–72, 489–90; George Beckwith to Lord Dorchester, Jan. 14, 1793, in Cruikshank, ed., *Correspondence of Simcoe*, I: 298. For an example of effective Indian pressure on the British, see the Indian confederacy speech of May 16, 1792, in Cruikshank, ed., *Correspondence of Simcoe*, I: 157.

5. Horsman, *Expansion and American Indian Policy*, 90–94; White, *Middle Ground*, 457; Knox to Anthony Wayne, Aug. 7 and Sept. 7, 1792, in Knopf, *Anthony Wayne*, 61 ("Another conflict"), 83.

6. Henry Knox, report, Dec. 26, 1791, and George Washington to Knox, Sept. 24, 1792, *PGW-PS*, IX: 319–21, XI: 149–50; Knox to Anthony Wayne, Sept. 7, 1792, in Knopf, ed., *Anthony Wayne*, 83–84; Horsman, *Expansion and American Indian Policy*, 90–94; White, *Middle Ground*, 457–58; Indian Confederacy to Washington, n.d. [ca. Jan. 1793] ("you hold"), in Cruikshank, ed., *Correspondence of Simcoe*, I: 283.

7. Col. Louis Cook to Timothy Pickering, May 3, 1792 ("runners"), *PGW-PS*, X: 340–41; Aupaumut, answers to questions, Feb. 5, 1793, TPP, LIX: 40A–41, MHS. For Colonel Louis at Akwesasne, see Alured Clarke to John Graves Simcoe, Apr. 15, 1793, in Cruikshank, ed., *Correspondence of Simcoe*, I: 313.

8. John Graves Simcoe to Sir Joseph Banks, Jan. 8, 1791 ("I am"), Simcoe to Henry Dundas, Aug. 12 and Aug. 26, 1791, Simcoe to Alured Clarke, Aug. 20, 1792, and April 5, 1793, and Simcoe to the Duke of Portland, Dec. 20, 1794, in Cruikshank, ed., *Correspondence of Simcoe*, I: 17, 43, 52–53, 199–204, 310, III: 233; Simcoe, *Military Journal*, 62; Simcoe, "Remarks on the Travels of the Marquis de Chastellux," 18–19; Riddell, *Life of John Graves Simcoe*, 58–59; Craig, *Upper Canada*, 15–19. For the Patriot hatred of Simcoe, see William Livingston to Elisha Boudinot, Nov. 2, 1779, and Livingston to William Churchill Houston, Nov. 5, 1779, in Prince et al., eds., *Papers of William Livingston*, III: 190, 195.

9. John Graves Simcoe to Sir Joseph Banks, Jan. 8, 1791, Simcoe to Henry Dundas, June 30, 1791, Simcoe to James Bland Burges, Aug. 21, 1792, and Simcoe to the Lords of Trade, Sept. 1, 1794, in Cruikshank, ed., *Correspondence of Simcoe*, I: 18, 28, 205, III: 60; Peter Russell to Simcoe, Aug. 16, 1791, F 47-1-2-7 (Simcoe Papers), Reel 1797, AO.

10. John Graves Simcoe, "Remarks on the Relative Situation of the Indians, British & States Interests," n.d. [ca. 1792] ("Swindling Transactions"), MG 23 H-I-1, 4th Ser. (Simcoe Transcripts), I, Packet Cc, NAC; William Hartshorne, diary, May 30, 1793, NYPL; Simcoe to Samuel Ogden, Aug. 31, 1793, in Cruikshank, ed., *Correspondence of Simcoe*, IV: 356.

11. E. B. Littlehales, journal, Mar. 2, 1793, John Graves Simcoe to Alured Clarke, Apr. 1, 1793, Simcoe to Henry Dundas, Sept. 20, 1793, and Simcoe to Lords of Trade, Sept. 1, 1794 ("all due form" and "to repose"), in Cruikshank, ed., *Correspondence of Simcoe*, I: 293, 309, II: 60–61, III: 63.

12. Duke of Portland to Peter Russell, Nov. 4, 1797, and Nov. 5, 1798, and Joseph Brant to Russell, June 11, 1799, in Cruikshank, ed., *Correspondence of Russell*, II: 3, 300, III, 227.

13. Timothy Pickering to Henry Knox, Aug. 10, 1791 ("I have no"), TPP, LX: 116, MHS; *PGW-PS*, IX: 588n; Knox to Samuel Kirkland, Dec. 20, 1791, and Jan. 7, 1792, SKP, Folders 142 and 144, HCA.

14. Othniel Taylor to Oliver Phelps, Jan. 15, 1792 ("I think" and "You must"), PGP, Box 19, NYSL; Pittsburgh Committee to Governor Thomas Mifflin, Dec. 11, 1791, *PGW-PS*, IX: 310n1; Samuel Kirkland to Henry Knox, Jan. 5, 1792, SKP, Folder 144, HCA.

15. *PGW-PS*, IX: 588n; Henry Knox to Samuel Kirkland, Dec. 20, 1791, and Kirkland to Knox, Jan. 5 ("to see"), Jan. 19, Jan. 27, and Feb. 25, 1792, SKP, Folders 142, 144, and 145, HCA; Kirkland to Knox, Jan. 17, 1792, *PGW-PS*, IX: 525–26; Pilkington, ed., *Journals of Samuel Kirkland*, 216, 219–22; Red Jacket and Good Peter, speeches, Mar. n.d., 1792, TPP, LXII: 10, MHS.

16. Samuel Kirkland to Henry Knox, Mar. 10, 1792, and S. Kirkland to John T. Kirkland, Apr. 5, 1792, SKP, Folders 146 and 147, HCA; Turner, *Red Men Calling on the Great White Father*, 3–16; Thomas Jefferson, memorandum, Mar. 9, 1792, and Knox to Tobias Lear, Mar. 19, 1792, *PGW-PS*, X: 69, 134.

17. Timothy Pickering to George Washington, Mar. 21, 1792 ("the knowledge"), Washington, speech, Mar. 23, 1792, and Washington to the United States Senate, Mar. 23, 1792, *PGW-PS*, X: 141–42, 148–49, and 151–52; Phillips, "Timothy Pickering at his Best," 179–80.

18. Red Jacket, speech, Mar. 31, 1792 ("The President"), *PGW-PS*, X: 192.

19. George Washington, speech, Dec. 29, 1790, and Red Jacket, speech, Mar. 31, 1792, *PGW-PS*, VII: 146–50, X: 192.

20. Samuel Kirkland to Peter Thacher, May 15, 1792 ("The manners" and "The Senekas"), #792315, DCLSC; Israel Chapin to Henry Knox, June 2, 1792, HORC, VIII, NYHS.

21. Amos Hall to Oliver Phelps, Apr. 9, 1792 ("Indian disturbances"), PGP, Box 19, NYSL; Benjamin Allen to Phelps, May 16, 1792, Phelps Family Papers, Box 1, OCHS; Israel Chapin to Henry Knox, July 17, 1792 ("The chiefs"), *ASPIA*, I: 242; Chapin to Pickering, July 17, 1792 ("reconciled"), TPP, LXII: 59, MHS.

22. William Colbrath to Gov. George Clinton, Aug. 6, 1792 ("The Indians"), #11248, NYSL; Oneida Chiefs to Israel Chapin, Sept. 29, 1792 ("we understand"), Chicago Historical Society.

23. Timothy Pickering to Israel Chapin, Apr. 29, 1792 ("one who" and "You know"), TPP, LXII: 26, MHS.

24. Samuel Kirkland to Oliver Phelps, Jan. 6, 1791 ("on account" and "tells me"), SKP, Folder 132, HCA; Timothy Pickering to George Washington, Jan. 15, 1791, and Washington to Pickering, Jan. 20, 1791, *PGW-PS*, VII: 234–36, 257; Kirkland to Israel Chapin, May 30, 1792 ("troublesome"), HORC, VIII, NYHS. For the rejected bid by Thomas Reese, see Pickering to Knox, July 16, 1791, TPP, LX: 112A–114A, MHS.

25. Campbell, *Travels in the Interior*, 207–8 ("an agreeable"); Israel Chapin to Oliver Phelps, Feb. 6, 1792, and Hezekiah Chapman to Phelps, Mar. 30, 1792, PGP, Box 19, NYSL; Chapin to Timothy Pickering, Feb. 26, 1792 ("Reasonable"), TPP, LXII: 8, MHS; Chapin to Samuel Kirkland, Mar. 21, 1792, and Knox to Chapin, Apr. 28, 1792, SKP, Folders 146 and 147, HCA.

26. Henry Knox to Israel Chapin, Apr. 23, 1792, HORC, VIII, NYHS; Timothy Pickering to Chapin, Apr. 29, 1792, and Chapin to Pickering, June 2, 1792 ("be persuaded"), TPP, LXII: 27, 49A, MHS; Chapin to Knox, July 17, 1792 ("I am"), *ASPIA*, I: 242; Chapin, Account with the United States, Sept. 18, 1792, HORC, VII, NYHS; Chapin to Knox, Nov. 17, 1792, and Knox to Chapin, Dec. 12, 1792, HORC, VIII, NYHS.

27. John Graves Simcoe to Alured Clarke, Apr. 21, 1793 ("I observed"), in Cruikshank, ed., *Correspondence of Simcoe*, I: 317; Israel Chapin to Henry Knox, Apr. 29 ("Confirmed them") and July 30, 1794 ("The Expences"), in HORC, X, NYHS.

28. John Jeffers to Richard Butler, Aug. 16, 1791 ("Black Rascals" and "flinging away"), MG 19 F 35 (PSGIA), 1st Ser., Lot 734, NAC.

29. Samuel Kirkland to Henry Knox, Feb. 13, 1792 ("should esteem" and "few Gentlemen"), SKP, Folder 145, HCA.

30. Henry Knox to Samuel Kirkland, Dec. 20, 1791, Kirkland to Joseph Brant, Jan. 3, 1792 ("my honor" and "general government"), and Feb. 16, 1792, SKP, Folders 142, 144, and 145, HCA; Pilkington, ed., *Journals of Samuel Kirkland*, 218; Knox to Brant, Feb. 25, 1792, and Brant to Kirkland, Feb. 4, 1792, *PGW-PS*, IX: 588–89n1, X: 310–12; Knox to Kirkland, Feb. 25, 1792 ("as flattering"), *ASPIA*, I: 228; Kelsay, *Joseph Brant*, 458–61.

31. Othniel Taylor to Oliver Phelps, Apr. 9, 1792, PGP, Box 19, NYSL; Andrew Gordon to Alured Clarke, Apr. 19, 1792, Gordon to Joseph Brant, May 20, 1792, Brant to Alexander McKee, May 23, 1792 ("the evasive"), Brant to Gordon, May 21, 1792, MG 11 (Colonial Office 42), XC: 158, 162, 196, 197, and 198, NAC; Brant to Matthew Elliot, May 22, 1792, MG 19 F 35 (PSGIA), Ser. 2, Lot 697, NAC.

32. Israel Chapin to Timothy Pickering, June 2, 1792, TPP, LXII: 49, MHS; Chapin to Henry Knox, June 2, 1792, and Chapin, Account with the United States, June 3, 1792, William Mathews, bill, June 19, 1792, and Knox to Chapin, June 22 and 27, 1792, HORC, VIII, NYHS; Richard Varick to Knox, June 19, 1792, #22867, HL; Kelsay, *Joseph Brant*, 466–68; Thomas Jefferson to James Madison, June 21, 1792, in Smith, ed., *Republic of Letters*, II: 732; Knox to Brant, June 27, 1792, in Cruikshank, ed., *Correspondence of Simcoe*, V: 18–20; Brant to Knox, July 26, 1792 ("the politeness"), *ASPIA*, I: 245.

33. John Graves Simcoe to Alured Clarke, Aug. 6, 1792, Simcoe Letterbook, 69, number 558, HL; Simcoe to Lord Dorchester, Dec. 6, 1793, in Cruikshank, ed., *Correspondence of Simcoe*, II: 116; Henry Knox to Israel Chapin, Dec. 23, 1793 ("services"), HORC, IX, NYHS; Timothy Pickering to James McHenry, Mar. 10, 1796 ("I know"), TPP, LXII: 239, MHS.

34. Thomas Jefferson to James Madison, June 29, 1792, in Smith, ed., *Republic of Letters*, II: 735; Samuel Kirkland to Oliver Phelps, July 21, 1792 ("No Person"), PGP, Box 19, NYSL; Stone, *Life of Joseph Brant*, II: 329–30; Kelsay, *Joseph Brant*, 474; Joseph Brant to Sir John Johnson, Mar. 24, 1791 ("that deep"), MG 11 (Colonial Office 42), LXXIII: 145, NAC.

35. Kelsay, *Joseph Brant*, 471–73, 478–82; Henry Knox to Anthony Wayne, Aug. 7, 1792, in Knopf, ed., *Anthony Wayne*, 59; John Stuart to Rev. Dr. White, July 17, 1792 ("I fear"), and Joseph Brant, speech, Oct. 28, 1792 ("General Washington"), in Cruikshank, ed., *Correspondence of Simcoe*, I: 180; Brant to Chapin, Dec. 11, 1792, HORC, VIII, NYHS.

36. John Graves Simcoe to George Hammond, Jan. 23, 1793 ("This Cunning"), in Cruikshank, ed., *Correspondence of Simcoe*, V: 29; Joseph Brant to David W. Smith, Dec. 28, 1792 ("I have"), F 47-1-2-7 (Simcoe Papers), Reel 1798, AO.

37. John Graves Simcoe to Henry Dundas, Sept. 20, 1793 ("I believe"), in Cruikshank, ed., *Correspondence of Simcoe*, II: 59; Joseph Brant to Israel Chapin, Jr., Jan. 2, 1795, Misc. Mss, NYHS.

38. *PGW-PS*, XI: 3–6; Henry Knox to George Washington, Sept. 15, 1792, and Washington to Knox, Sept. 24, 1792, *PGW-PS*, XI: 115–16, 149–50; Wallace, *Death and Rebirth of the Seneca*, 164–65 ("very coward"); Horsman, *Expansion and American Indian Policy*, 92–95; Densmore, *Red Jacket*, 39–40; Indian Confederacy to Washington, n.d., [ca. Jan. 1793], Knox to Indian Confederacy, Feb. 28, 1793, and Indian Confederacy, speech, Feb. 27, 1793, in Cruikshank, ed., *Correspondence of Simcoe*, I: 284, 295, V: 34–35.

39. Anthony Wayne to Henry Knox, Aug. 24, 1792, and Knox to Indian Confederation, Dec. 12, 1792, *PGW-PS*, XI: 63–64, 500n1; Horseman, *Expansion and American Indian Policy*, 95–97; Knox to Wayne, Jan. 5, 1793, in Knopf, ed., *Anthony Wayne*, 164–67; Thomas Jefferson, notes,

Feb. 25, 1793, in Cruikshank, ed., *Correspondence of Simcoe*, I: 297; Knox to Benjamin Lincoln, Beverly Randolph, and Timothy Pickering, Apr. 26, 1793, *ASPIA*, I: 340.

40. Red Jacket, speech, Nov. 16, 1792 ("sensible"), *PGW-PS*, XI: 477–78; Densmore, *Red Jacket*, 40; *ASPIA*, I: 337; Horsman, *Expansion and American Indian Policy*, 96–97; Pilkington, ed., *Journals of Samuel Kirkland*, 254; Lincoln, "Journal of a Treaty Held in 1793," 121; Lindley, "Account of a Journey," 566; Benjamin Lincoln to James Dean, May 6, 1793, John Parrish, William Savery, John Ellicott, and William Hartshorne to Lincoln, Timothy Pickering, and Beverly Randolph, June 17, 1793, and Lincoln, Pickering, and Randolph to Henry Knox, June 20, 1793, TPP, LIX: 149–50, 181, LX, 150, MHS. The last letter estimated that 116 Iroquois would accompany the commissioners to Sandusky: 14 Oneidas, 16 Onondagas, 15 Cayugas, and 71 Senecas.

41. Lindley, "Account of a Journey," 583 ("There were"); Lincoln, "Journal of a Treaty," 138–41 ("I cannot").

42. Phillips, "Timothy Pickering at his Best," 185–87; Lincoln, "Journal of a Treaty," 122–23; Benjamin Lincoln to John Graves Simcoe, Aug. 22, 1793, MG 23 H-I-1, 4th Ser. (Simcoe Transcripts), I, Folder Ff, NAC; William Hartshorne, diary, May 30, 1793, NYPL; Simcoe to Alured Clarke, June 14 ("low Craft"), and July 26, 1793 ("You may"), in Cruikshank, ed., *Correspondence of Simcoe*, I: 354–55, 399; Lincoln, Pickering, and Randolph to Knox, June 20, 1793, TPP, LX: 149A, MHS. For American criticism of Simcoe as two-faced, see "Lansingburgh," *Albany Gazette*, July 29, 1793. For a forced attempt to vindicate Simcoe as resolutely pro-peace, see Burt, *The United States, Great Britain, and British North America*, 127.

43. John Graves Simcoe to George Hammond, Jan. 21, 1793, Alured Clarke to Henry Dundas, Mar. 2, 1793, Simcoe to Clarke, Apr. 1, 1793, Clarke to Simcoe, May 19, 1793, Simcoe to Benjamin Lincoln, Timothy Pickering, and Beverly Randolph, June 7, 1793, Simcoe to Clarke, June 14, 1793, and Simcoe to Alexander McKee, June 22 and 28 and July 5, 1793, in Cruikshank, ed., *Correspondence of Simcoe*, I: 277, 297–98, 308, 321, 350–51, 354–55, V: 50, 52, 56; Joseph Chew to Simcoe, May 29, 1793, MG 23 H-I-1, 4th Ser. (Simcoe Transcripts), II, Folder Mm, NAC.

44. Alexander McKee to John Graves Simcoe, July 1, 1793, in Cruikshank, ed., *Correspondence of Simcoe*, I: 374; Lindley, "An Account," 603, 623, 625.

45. Lindley, "Account of a Journey," 618–20; United States Indian Commissioners to the General Indian Council, July 31, 1793 ("a large sum" and "You are men"), *ASPIA*, I: 352–54; John Heckewelder, "Estimate . . . of the Settlers North of the Ohio," 1793, TPP, LIX: 31, MHS; Phillips, "Timothy Pickering at His Best," 184, 188–90.

46. General Indian Council to the United States Commissioners, Aug. 13, 1793 ("You have talked" and "As no consideration"), *ASPIA*, I: 356–57. Believing Indians too primitive to develop such a sophisticated proposal, the American commissioners dismissed it as the work of British traders. In fact, the distinction between traders and Indians was elusive among the Shawnees who developed the proposal. See Lindley, "Account of a Journey," 627; Phillips, "Timothy Pickering at His Best," 191; White, *Middle Ground*, 455; Wallace, ed., *Thirty Thousand Miles with John Heckewelder*, 319. It is significant that similar sentiments appeared in a speech by Messquakenoe, a Shawnee orator speaking on behalf of the Indian confederation two years earlier. See Messquakenoe, speech, Oct. 7, 1792, in Cruikshank, ed., *Correspondence of Simcoe*, I: 227. For the role of class conflict in driving American frontier expansion, see Morgan, *American Slavery, American Freedom*, 328–32.

47. Doddridge, *Notes on the Settlement and Indian Wars*, 190, 194; Slaughter, *Whiskey Rebellion*, 133–42.

48. United States Indian Commissioners to the General Indian Council, Aug. 16, 1793, *ASPIA*, I: 357; Lindley, "Account of a Journey," 627–28; Phillips, "Timothy Pickering at His Best," 191–92; Robert Woolsey, Jr., to John Edwards, Nov. 2, 1793 ("The Americans"), in Cruikshank, ed., *Correspondence of Simcoe*, II: 96.

49. Zeisberger, *Diary*, II: 323; Joseph Brant to John Graves Simcoe, July 28, 1793, Brant, journal, Aug. 9, 1793, Simcoe to Lord Dorchester, Nov. 10, 1793, Simcoe to Henry Dundas, Nov. 10, 1793, and Simcoe to Dorchester, Dec. 6, 1793, in Cruikshank, ed., *Correspondence of Simcoe*, I: 402, II: 13, 101–2, 103–4, 115; Kelsay, *Joseph Brant*, 493–505; White, *Divided Ground*, 461–64; Brant to Alexander McKee, Mar. 23, 1793, in Cruikshank, ed., *Correspondence of Simcoe*, V: 37; Brant to McKee, Aug. 4, 1793, MG 23 H-I-1, 4th Ser. (Simcoe Transcripts), VI, Folder A 15, NAC; Brant, journal, June 3 and July 21 ("I was") and 26, RG 10 (Indian Affairs), VIII: 8442, 8446, 8457–8461, NAC.

50. Joseph Brant, journal, Aug. 9, 1793, and Brant to John Graves Simcoe, Sept. 2, 1793, in Cruikshank, ed., *Correspondence of Simcoe*, II: 13–17, 47; Brant, journal, Sept. 10, 1793, RG 10 (Indian Affairs), VIII: 8475, NAC; Brant to Simcoe, Sept. 28, 1793, and William Osgoode to Simcoe, Oct. 1, 1793, MG 23 H-I-1, 4th Ser. (Simcoe Transcripts), IV, Folder A4, and V, Folder A7, NAC; Zeisberger, *Diary*, II: 335; Kelsay, *Joseph Brant*, 484.

51. Alexander McKee to John Graves Simcoe, Aug. 22, 1793, and Simcoe to George Hammond, Sept. 8, 1793, in Cruikshank, ed., *Correspondence of Simcoe*, II: 34–35, 49; Nelson, *A Man of Distinction Among Them*, 166–67.

52. Nelson, *A Man of Distinction Among Them*, 162–67; Wise, "The Indian Diplomacy of John Graves Simcoe," 39–43; John Graves Simcoe to Lord Dorchester, Nov. 10 and Dec. 6, 1793 ("is true"), and Simcoe to Alexander McKee, Sept. 8, 1793, in Cruikshank, ed., *Correspondence of Simcoe*, II: 102–3, 116, V: 72; Kelsay, *Joseph Brant*, 496–97.

53. Wright, *Britain and the American Frontier*, 87–88; Werner, "War Scare and Politics in 1794," 324–34; George Hammond to Lord Dorchester, Mar. 16, 1794, in Cruikshank, ed., *Correspondence of Simcoe*, V: 84; John Jay to George Washington, July 21, 1794, in Johnston, ed., *Correspondence and Public Papers of John Jay*, IV: 33–34.

54. Lord Dorchester to the Seven Nations of Lower Canada, Feb. 10, 1794 ("All their approaches"), and Dorchester to Simcoe, July 11, 1794 ("the King's Rights"), in Cruikshank, ed., *Correspondence of Simcoe*, II: 149–50, and 318; George Davison to Simcoe, Aug. 1, 1794, MG 23 H-I-1, 4th Ser., (Simcoe Transcripts), II, Folder Oo, NAC. It slowly dawned on some in the borderland that Dorchester had overreacted, creating the crisis. In July, Detroit's commandant worried, "We don't see anything from home that justifies His Excellency's Speech to the Indians, or taking the [Maumee] Post that seems to Court [American] offence." See Richard England to Simcoe, July 22, 1794, in Cruikshank, ed., *Correspondence of Simcoe*, II: 334.

55. Lord Dorchester to John Graves Simcoe, Feb. 17, 1794, Dorchester to Henry Dundas, Feb. 24, 1794, Joseph Chew to Thomas Aston Coffin, Feb. 27, 1794, Simcoe to Dorchester, Apr. 29, 1794, Alexander McKee to Joseph Chew, May 8, 1794 ("has given"), Simcoe to Dorchester, July 10, 1794, Simcoe to George Hammond, July 18, 1794, Joseph Brant to John Smith, July 19, 1794, John Jay to George Washington, July 21, 1794, and Simcoe to Alexander McKee, June 4, 1789, in Cruikshank, ed., *Correspondence of Simcoe*, II: 154, 160, 164, 220, 234, 315, 324–25, 326, 333, V: 89; White, *Middle Ground*, 465–66; Israel Chapin to Henry Knox, Apr. 29, 1794 ("took pains"), HORC, X, NYHS; Thomas Morris to George Clinton, Aug. 18, 1794, and Charles Williamson to Clinton, Aug. 19, 1794, in Assembly Papers, Box 45, Folder 113, NYSA; Kelsay, *Joseph Brant*, 507–8.

56. Edmund Randolph to George Hammond, May 20, 1794, and Hammond to Randolph, May 22, 1794, in Manning, ed., *Diplomatic Correspondence of the United States*, I: 66–68, 411–12; Randolph to Hammond, Sept. 1, 1794, in Cruikshank, ed., *Correspondence of Simcoe*, III: 27; George Washington to John Jay, Aug. 30, 1794 ("irregular" and "all the difficulties"), in Johnston, ed., *Correspondence of John Jay*, IV: 55–56.

57. Flick, "How New York Won and Lost an Empire," 371; Ebenezer Denny to Thomas Mifflin, May 2, 1794, and Iroquois deed to Pennsylvania, Jan. 9, 1789, *ASPIA*, I: 505, 513; Mifflin to William Irvine, Andrew Ellicott, and Albert Gallatin, Mar. 1, 1794, *Pennsylvania Archives*, 2nd Ser., VI: 635; Kent and Deardorff, eds., "John Adlum," 267–68; Matthews, ed., *Andrew Ellicott*, 107–13.

58. Joseph Brant, speech, Apr. 21, 1794 ("Brother"), HORC, X, NYHS; Ebenezer Denny to Thomas Mifflin, June 29, 1794, *ASPIA*, I: 516; Andrew Ellicott to Thomas Mifflin, June 29 and July 19, 1794 ("would find"), *Pennsylvania Archives*, 2nd Ser., VI: 728–29, 748–49; Kelsay, *Joseph Brant*, 508.

59. Joseph Brant to Thomas Talbot, May 30, 1794, MG 23 H-I-1, 4th Ser. (Simcoe Transcripts), I, Folder Jj, NAC; Cornplanter, speech, July 4, 1794, *Pennsylvania Archives*, 2nd Ser., VI: 735–36; Kent and Deardorff, eds., "John Adlum," 268, 304 ("The young Indians"); Israel Chapin to Henry Knox, May 5, and June 7, 12, and 26, 1794, and Cornplanter (Capt. O'Bail), speech, June 18, 1794, HORC, X, NYHS; John Graves Simcoe to Lord Dorchester, June 15, 1794, and July 10, 1794, in Cruikshank, ed., *Correspondence of Simcoe*, II: 266, 315–16; Kelsay, *Joseph Brant*, 508–9; Fenton, *Great Law and the Longhouse*, 648–49.

60. George Washington to Henry Knox, Apr. 4, 1794 ("General Chapin"), in Fitzpatrick, ed., *Writings of George Washington*, XXXIII: 313–14; John Wilkins, Jr., to Clement Biddle, Apr. 25, 1794, and Henry Knox to Thomas Mifflin, May 24, 1794, *ASPIA*, I: 504, 518–19; Mifflin to Presque Isle Commissioners, May 25, 1794, Mifflin to Washington, July 15 and 22, 1794, and Ebenezer Denny to Timothy Pickering, Mar. 11, 1795, *Pennsylvania Archives*, 2nd Ser., VI: 671, 742, 753, 815; Israel Chapin to Joseph Brant, July 10, 1794, and Chapin to Knox, Aug. 12, 1794, HORC, X, NYHS; Fenton, *Great Law and the Longhouse*, 649–52.

61. John Graves Simcoe to Duke of Portland, Oct. 23, 1794 ("Admitting"), in Cruikshank, ed., *Correspondence of Simcoe*, III: 143.

62. Joseph Brant to Joseph Chew, Apr. 24, 1794 ("more Compact"), in Cruikshank, ed., *Correspondence of Simcoe*, II: 214; Brant to Maj. Littlehales, Aug. 7, 1794, in F 47-1-2-7 (Simcoe Papers), Reel #1799, AO; John Adlum to Thomas Mifflin, Aug. 31, 1794 ("I think"), *Pennsylvania Archives*, 2nd Ser., VI: 764–67; Kent and Deardorff, eds., "John Adlum," 444–45.

63. John Butler to Joseph Chew, Apr. 27, John Graves Simcoe to Henry Dundas, Aug. 5, 1794, Butler to Chew, Aug. 7, 1794, and Simcoe to Duke of Portland, Oct. 23, 1794, in Cruikshank, ed., *Correspondence of Simcoe*, II: 218, 353, 361, III: 143; Othniel Taylor and Phinehas Pierce to George Clinton, May 5, 1794, A 1827 (Assembly Papers), Box 45, Folder 9, NYSA; Commissioners to Fortify the Western and Northern Frontiers, minutes, June 27, 1794, A 1827 (Assembly Papers), Box 45, Folder 71, NYSA; Turner, *Pioneer History of the Holland Purchase*, 339; Samuel Kirkland to Peter Thacher, June 3, 1794, #794353, DCLSC; Israel Chapin to Henry Knox, July 30, 1794, HORC, X, NYHS; Kirkland to Pickering, Dec. 8, 1794 ("two suits"), TPP, LXII: 119–20, MHS.

64. George Washington to John Jay, Aug. 30, 1794, in Johnston, ed., *Correspondence of John Jay*, IV: 55–56; Edmund Randolph to George Hammond, Sept. 1, 1794 ("It has"), and John Graves Simcoe to Hammond, Oct. 20, 1794 ("incompatible"), in Cruikshank, ed., *Correspondence of*

Simcoe, III: 27, 134; Israel Chapin and Thomas Morris to Pickering, Apr. 29, 1794, TPP, XIX: 312, MHS.

65. MacLeod, "Fortress Ontario or Forlorn Hope?" 158.

66. Ojibwa chief quoted in Zeisberger, *Diary*, II: 361 ("set on"); John Graves Simcoe to Henry Dundas, July 5, 1794, Richard England to Simcoe, July 22, 1794, Wyandot Chiefs, speech, Aug. 5, 1794 ("We hope"), England to Simcoe, Aug. 6, 1794, and England, speech, Aug. 6, 1794, in Cruikshank, ed., *Correspondence of Simcoe*, II: 303–5, 334, 357, 359, 360; White, *Middle Ground*, 466.

67. John Graves Simcoe to Lord Dorchester, July 23, 1794 ("Upper Canada"), Simcoe to Henry Dundas, Aug. 5, 1794, Simcoe to Dorchester, Aug. 16, 1794, Simcoe, diary, Sept. 27, 1794, in Cruikshank, ed., *Correspondence of Simcoe*, II: 336, 353, 382–83, III: 98; MacLeod, "Fortress Ontario," 158, 161–67.

68. John Jay to George Washington, July 21, 1794, in Johnston, ed., *Correspondence of John Jay*, IV: 33–34; Wright, *Britain and the American Frontier*, 92–95; Henry Dundas to John Graves Simcoe, July 4, 1794 ("a perfect"), Lord Grenville to George Hammond, July 17, 1794, and Duke of Portland to Simcoe, Sept. 5, 1794, in Cruikshank, ed., *Correspondence of Simcoe*, II: 300, 322, III: 39; Simcoe to McKee, Aug. 6, 1794, in Cruikshank, ed., *Correspondence of Simcoe*, V: 99; Simcoe to Robert Pratt, July 20, 1794, MG 23 H-I-1, 4th Ser. (Simcoe Transcripts), I, Folder Cc, NAC. News of Dundas's dispatches reached Montreal on September 7. See William Osgoode to Simcoe, Sept. 7, 1794, MG 23 H-I-1, 4th Ser. (Simcoe Transcripts), V, Folder A 7, NAC; White, *Middle Ground*, 467.

69. Robert Pratt to E. B. Littlehales, Aug. 10, 1794, and Alexander McKee to Joseph Chew, Aug. 27, 1794, in Cruikshank, ed., *Correspondence of Simcoe*, II: 364, III: 8; Kelsay, *Joseph Brant*, 509–11; Anthony Wayne to Henry Knox, Aug. 14, 1794, *ASPIA*, I: 490; White, *Middle Ground*, 467–68; Kelsay, *Joseph Brant*, 510–11. For the fate of the traders, see Thomas Morris to [unknown], Sept. 20, 1794, #11203, NYSL.

70. Wright, *Britain and the American Frontier*, 95–97; White, *Middle Ground*, 468; Zeisberger, *Diary*, II: 376, 378 ("Thou hast"), 393; Joseph Brant to Joseph Chew, Oct. 22, 1794, and Richard England to John Graves Simcoe, Dec. 13, 1794, in Cruikshank, ed., *Correspondence of Simcoe*, III: 140, 219.

71. Robert England to Francis Le Maistre, Oct. 28, 1794, Duke of Portland to John Graves Simcoe, Nov. 19, 1794, in Cruikshank, ed., *Correspondence of Simcoe*, III: 156–57, 185; White, *Middle Ground*, 474–75.

72. George Washington to Henry Knox, Apr. 4, 1794, in Fitzpatrick, ed., *Writings of George Washington*, XXXIII: 313–14; Fenton, *Great Law and the Longhouse*, 645–59; Knox to Israel Chapin, July 25, 1794, HORC, X, NYHS; Fenton, ed., "The Journal of James Emlen," 279–85. For the Iroquois request for Pickering as commissioner, see Chapin to Pickering, July 9, 1794, TPP, LIX: 267, MHS.

73. Israel Chapin to Henry Knox, Sept. 17, 1794, HORC, X, NYHS; Six Nations to Timothy Pickering, Sept. 17, 1794, and Pickering to Six Nations, Sept. 27, 1794 ("all your" and "Sir William Johnson"), MG 23 H-I-1, 4th Ser. (Simcoe Transcripts), I, Folder Jj, NAC; Thomas Morris to [unknown] Sept. 20, 1794, #11203, NYSL; Pickering to Henry Knox, Oct. 8, 1794, TPP, LX: 203A, MHS; Fenton, *Great Law and the Longhouse*, 655–58, 661–63.

74. Anonymous, "Extract," Aug. 8, 1792, 285; Fenton, ed., "Journal of James Emlen," 291.

75. Timothy Pickering to Henry Knox, Sept. 27 and Oct. 15, 1794, TPP, LX: 202, 204; Phillips, "Pickering at His Best," 194–96; Israel Chapin to Oliver Phelps, Oct. 13, 1794, Israel Chapin

File, OCHS; Chapin to Knox, Oct. 18, 1794, HORC, X, NYHS; Fenton, ed., "Journal of James Emlen," 301–2; Savery, "Journal," 353 ("drew up" and "They made").

76. Savery, "Journal," 354–55 ("He wiped"); Fenton, *Great Law and the Longhouse*, 671–72.

77. Six Nations Chiefs to John Butler, Sept. 17, 1794 ("We think"), MG 23 H-I-1, 4th Ser. (Simcoe Transcripts), I, Folder Jj, NAC; White, *Middle Ground*, 470; Phillips, "Timothy Pickering at His Best," 196–97; Timothy Pickering, speech, Oct. 25, 1794 ("Brothers"), TPP, LX: 233A–241, MHS; Pickering to Brant, Oct. 26, 1794, TPP, LX: 211, MHS; Fenton, ed., "Journal of James Emlen," 308–11; Savery, "Journal," 357; Fenton, *Great Law and the Longhouse*, 680–82.

78. Timothy Pickering to Henry Knox, Oct. 15, 1794 ("if they suffer"), TPP, LX: 204A–205; Fenton, ed., "Journal of James Emlen," XII: 305 (Seneca matrons quoted: "had found themselves"), 306–7 (Pickering quoted: "too much reason"); Savery, "Journal," 356, 358.

79. Henry Knox to Thomas Mifflin, July 21, 1794, *Pennsylvania Archives*, 2nd Ser., VI: 751–52; Mifflin to Pennsylvania General Assembly, Sept. 2, 1794, *Pennsylvania Archives*, 4th Ser., IV: 306; Fenton, ed., "Journal of James Emlen," XII: 314–16; Timothy Pickering to Henry Knox, Oct. 28, Nov. 7 and 12, 1794, TPP, LX: 206, 207–9, 209; Savery, "Journal," 358–60, 364–65; William Johnston to John Butler, Nov. 29, 1794, MG 23 H-I-1, 4th Ser. (Simcoe Transcripts), NAC; Fenton, *Great Law and the Longhouse*, 693–98.

80. Treaty of Canandaigua, Nov. 11, 1794 ("until they choose"), *ASPIA*, I: 545; Savery, "Journal," 367; Wallace, *Death and Rebirth of the Seneca*, 173–78; Timothy Pickering to Henry Knox, Nov. 12, 1794, TPP, LX: 207A, MHS; Fenton, *Great Law and the Longhouse*, 700–701.

81. Timothy Pickering to Henry Knox, Nov. 12, 1794 ("great object"), and Israel Chapin to Pickering, Feb. 6, 1794 ("Our treaty"), TPP, LX: 207A, LXII: 212, MHS; Timothy Hosmer to Oliver Phelps, Jan. 19, 1795, PGP, Box 20, NYSL.

82. William Ewing to Israel Chapin, Sept. 17, 1794, in Turner, *Phelps and Gorham Purchase*, 486; John Wilkins, Jr., to Thomas Mifflin, Oct. 10, 1794, *Pennsylvania Archives*, 2nd Ser., VI: 781; Kent and Deardorff, eds., "John Adlum," 460n35; Savery, "Journal," 357 ("The Indians").

83. Fenton, *Great Law and the Longhouse*, 706.

84. Timothy Pickering to Six Nations, Mar. 31, 1795 ("an evidence"), in Jemison and Schein, eds., *Treaty of Canandaigua, 1794*, 306.

85. Treaty of Canandaigua, Nov. 11, 1794 ("within"), *ASPIA*, I: 545; Joseph Brant to Israel Chapin, Sept. 2, and Nov. 2, 1794, HORC, X, NYHS; William Ewing to Chapin, Sept. 17, 1794, in Turner, *Phelps and Gorham Purchase*, 485–87; John Graves Simcoe to Duke of Portland, Oct. 24, 1794, in Cruikshank, ed., *Correspondence of Simcoe*, III: 147; Brant to Timothy Pickering, Nov. 5, 1794 ("As a Free"), TPP, LX: 214–15, MHS; Samuel Kirkland to Pickering, Dec. 8, 1794, TPP, LXII: 120, MHS; Fenton, *Great Law and the Longhouse*, 663–64.

86. Timothy Pickering to Joseph Brant, Nov. 17, 1794, TPP, LX: 212A; Pickering to Brant, Nov. 20, 1794 ("As one"), HORC, X, NYHS.

87. Andrew Ellicott to Sally Ellicott, Sept. 11, 1795 ("We have"), in Mathews, ed., *Andrew Ellicott*, 124.

88. Combs, *The Jay Treaty*, 159–90; Duke of Portland to John Graves Simcoe, Nov. 19, 1794, Simcoe to Portland, May 20, 1795, Lord Dorchester to Simcoe, July 31, 1795, and Simcoe to Portland, Oct. 30, 1795, in Cruikshank, ed., *Correspondence of Simcoe*, III: 184, IV: 14, 55, 118; Kelsay, *Joseph Brant*, 517–18.

89. Treaty of Greenville, Aug. 3, 1795, and Treaty of Greenville Minutes, June 16–Aug. 10, 1795, *ASPIA*, I: 562–63, 564–82; Jones, *License for Empire*, 174–75; White, *Middle Ground*, 472–73; Horsman, *Expansion and American Indian Policy*, 99–103.

90. Timothy Pickering to Anthony Wayne, Apr. 15, 1795 ("When a peace"), in Knopf, ed.,

Anthony Wayne, 407; Horsman, *Expansion and American Indian Policy*, 99–101; Rohrbough, *The Trans-Appalachian Frontier*, 63–65; Joseph Brant to Joseph Chew, Jan. 19, 1796 ("the distressed"), *Michigan Historical Collections*, XX: 434.

91. Wright, *Britain and the American Frontier*, 92–98.

CHAPTER TEN: BOUNDS

1. Capt. James Bruff, speech, Sept. 21, 1796 ("Lines"), and Bruff to unknown, Sept. 25, 1796, HORC, XV, NYHS.

2. Red Jacket, speech, Sept. 23, 1796 ("You are"), HORC, XV, NYHS.

3. Williamson, "Description of the Settlement of the Genesee Country," 1141.

4. Israel Chapin, Jr., to Timothy Pickering, May 6, 1795 ("The Oneidas"), HORC, XI, NYHS; Belknap and Morse, "Report on the Oneida, Stockbridge, and Brotherton Indians," 36 ("Once we coveted").

5. Israel Chapin to Timothy Pickering, June 2, 1793, and Jacob Reed to Chapin, Feb. 10, 1793, HORC, IX, NYHS; Pickering to Samuel Kirkland, Dec. 24, 1793 ("Something"), SKP, Folder 163A, HCA.

6. Kirkland, "Answers to Queries," 71 ("The origin").

7. For Capt. Peter, see Ebenezer Caulkins to Israel Chapin, Feb. 23, 1793, HORC, IX, NYHS; Pilkington, ed., *Journals of Samuel Kirkland*, 356–57, 389; Belknap, "Journal to Oneida," 1796, 414; and Belknap and Morse, "Report on the Oneida, Stockbridge, and Brotherton Indians," 14–15. For Capt. John, see Embree et al., "Some Account of a Visit Paid to the Indians," 803; Pilkington, ed., *Journals of Samuel Kirkland*, 225–30 ("Capt. John," on 228), 249.

8. Capt. John, speeches, Oct. 11 ("really believe"), and Oct. 13, 1794 ("The restoration"), TPP, LX: 219A, 230, MHS.

9. Timothy Pickering, memorandum, Oct. 11, 1794, and Pickering, speech, Oct. 13, 1794 ("They pretend" and "every such farm"), TPP, LX: 218, 224–26A, MHS; Savery, "Journal," 351–53.

10. Timothy Pickering, speech, Oct. 13, 1794 ("I am"), TPP, LX: 224–26A, MHS.

11. Savery, "Journal," 353; John Sergeant, Jr., to Timothy Pickering, Jan. 3, 1795 ("As to"), TPP, LXII: 199A, MHS.

12. Timothy Pickering, speech, Oct. 13, 1794 ("I know," "The land," and "advice"), TPP, LX: 228–28a, MHS.

13. Treaty of Canandaigua, Nov. 11, 1794, *ASPIA*, I: 545; Pilkington, ed., *Journals of Samuel Kirkland*, 275–77.

14. Oneidas to the New York State Legislature, Feb. 27, 1795, A 1823 (Assembly Papers), XL (Indian Affairs, 1783–1809), 221, NYSA; Capt. Israel Chapin, Jr., to Timothy Pickering, Mar. 10, 1795, HORC, XI, NYHS.

15. [New York State], *Journal of the Assembly*, Mar. 31, 1795; "An Act for the Better Support of the Oneida, Onondaga, and Cayuga Indians," Apr. 9, 1795, [New York State], *Laws of the State of New York* (1797), III: 236–39.

16. John Livingston to Peter Smith, Feb. 20, 1795, and DeWitt Clinton to Smith, May 25, 1795 ("The Governor"), PSmP, Box 1, SULSC. Having reconciled with George Clinton and his party, Livingston sought Smith's support for Robert Yates, the Republican candidate to succeed Clinton as governor. But leading Federalists also helped Smith and solicited his support of John Jay. See Elisha Kane to Smith, Apr. 14, 1795, PSmP, Box 1, SULSC. Smith attended the legislative session, Jan. 4–Mar. 26, 1795, and spent £80 wooing legislators. See Smith, New Petersburgh Land Book, 6 (Nov. 1795), PSmP, Box 12, SULSC.

17. "An Act for the Better Support of the Oneida, Onondaga, and Cayuga Indians," Apr. 9, 1795

("sole benefit"), [New York State] *Laws of the State of New York*, (1797), III: 236–39; [New York State] *Journal of the Assembly*, Apr. 9, 1795; George Clinton, message, April 9, 1795 ("three-fourths"), in Lincoln, ed., *State of New York: Messages from the Governors*, II: 356–57; Graymont, "New York Indian Policy," 462–65; Jonas Platt, answers to queries, 1796 ("a stain"), JBP, Reel 11, MHS.

18. Rev. John Sergeant, Jr., to Timothy Pickering, Apr. 26, 1795 ("Unless"), TPP, LXII: 226, MHS; William Bradford to Pickering, June 16, 1795 ("cannot be"), Pickering to Israel Chapin, Jr., June 29, 1795, and Chapin to Pickering, July 31, 1795, HORC., XI, NYHS; Graymont, "New York State Indian Policy," 465–67.

19. Hauptman, *Conspiracy of Interests*, 68–69, 75; Belknap and Morse, "Report on the Oneida, Stockbridge, and Brotherton Indians," 10.

20. Capt. John, speech, Aug. 8, 1795, PSP, Box 15, NYPL; Philip Schuyler to Congress, Oct. 15, 1786 ("I had found"), PSP, Box 14, NYPL; Hauptman, *Conspiracy of Interests*, 68–69, 75.

21. Philip Schuyler, speech, Aug. 6, 1795, and Capt. John, speech, Aug. 8, 1795 ("We hoped"), PSP, Box 15, NYSL.

22. Philip Schuyler, speech, Aug. 6, 1795, and Capt. John, speech, Aug. 8, 1795 ("Brother"), PSP, Box 15, NYPL.

23. Capt. John, speeches, Aug. 10 ("full value") and 11, and Philip Schuyler, speeches, Aug. 10 and 11, 1795, PSP, Box 15, NYPL; Israel Chapin, Jr., to Timothy Pickering, Aug. 19, 1795, HORC, XI, NYHS.

24. James Dean to Philip Schuyler, Aug. 16, 1795 ("asserted"), and Oneida Chiefs to the New York State Commissioners, Aug. 16, 1795, PSP, Box 15, NYPL; Tiro, "James Dean in Iroquoia," 415. For Dean's special tie to the matrons, see Tracy, *Notices of Men and Events*, 17. Like Schuyler, Dean adeptly displayed a genial face to the Oneidas, masking the disgust for them that he expressed in confidence to other whites. He told one visitor that Indians "are not of the same species which we are." See John T. Kirkland, response to queries, 1796, JBP, Reel 11, MHS; and Ripley, *Bank of Faith and Works*, 87 ("are not"). For the influence by Van Eps, see Philip Schuyler et al., report, n.d. [ca. Sept. 15, 1795], #13491, HL.

25. John T. Kirkland, answers to queries, 1796 ("Capt. John"), JBP, Reel 11, MHS. Ordinarily temperate, Capt. John had previously had drunken lapses. See, for example, Michael Myers to Israel Chapin, Oct. 5, 1792, HORC, VIII, NYHS. Those lapses had not then cost him his leadership. Capt. John did put his mark to the message sent by the Oneida chiefs to the state commissioners on August 16, but that mark appeared toward the end of the document, indicating his diminished status. See Oneida Chiefs to the New York State commissioners, Aug. 16, 1795, PSP, Box 15, NYPL.

26. James Dean to Philip Schuyler, Aug. 16, 1795, and Schuyler to Dean, Aug. 24, 1795 ("dispatch"), PSP, Box 15, NYPL; Schuyler et al., report, n.d. [ca. Sep. 15, 1795], #13491, HL. At Canandaigua in western New York, Israel Chapin, Jr., first heard of the September 15 transaction in early October: three weeks too late. See Chapin to Timothy Pickering, Oct. 9, 1795, HORC, XI, NYHS.

27. Tall William, speech, Sept. 12, 1795, and Philip Schuyler, speech, Sept. 14, 1795, PSP, Box 15, NYPL; Schuyler et al., report, n.d. [ca. Sept. 15, 1795], #13491, HL; Oneida Treaty, Sept. 15, 1795, [New York State], *Report of Special Committee to Investigate the Indian Problem*, 241–49; Graymont, "New York State Indian Policy," 470; Simeon DeWitt to Philip Schuyler, Jan. 10, 1797, PSP, Box 15, NYPL.

28. John Cantine, speech, Sept. 16, 1795, PSP, Box 15, NYPL; "Albany," *Albany Gazette*, Sept. 18 and 21, 1795; Samuel Kirkland to John T. Kirkland, Apr. 20, 1792 ("All business"), SKP, Folder 147, HCA. Peter Otsequette died on March 19, 1792, which suspended discussions until

March 23. At the state council with the Oneidas in 1788 at Fort Schuyler, there was a similar prolonged suspension to honor an Indian who died from drinking; see Hough, ed., *Proceedings of the Commissioners*, I: 217–18.

29. Skenandon and Martinus each got £100 ($250); Peter Bread and Tall William received £83.2.8 ($208) apiece; and Jacob Reed collected £50 ($125). See "Money to Van Eps and who received it," Sept. 16, 1795, A 0832 (State Comptrollers' Indian Annuity Claims, Receipts, and Related Documents), Box 1, Folder 5, NYSA; "An Act Supplementary to the Act Entitled an Act for the Better Support of Oneida, Onondaga, and Cayuga Indians," and "An Act for the Relief of the Tenants of Peter Smith and Others," [New York State], *Laws of the State of New York* (1797), III: 310–14 and 460–61; Evans, *Journal of the Life*, 126 ("Some of "); Peter Smith, New Petersburgh Land Book, 154, PSmP, Box 12, SULSC; Simeon DeWitt to Smith, Oct. 10, 1797, Smith Family Papers, NYPL; DeWitt Clinton, "Private Canal Journal, 1810," in Campbell, ed., *Life and Writings of DeWitt Clinton*, 189 ("Peter Smith").

30. Timothy Pickering to Israel Chapin, Jr., June 29, 1795, HORC, XI, NYHS; John Jay to Pickering, July 13 and 18, 1795, John Jay Papers, Pickering File, Columbia University; Pickering to George Washington, July 21, 1795, George Washington Papers, 4th Ser., LC.

31. George Washington to Timothy Pickering, July 27, 1795 ("any further"), in Fitzpatrick, ed., *Writings of George Washington*, XXXIV: 250–51; Pickering to Israel Chapin, Jr., Aug. 26, 1795 ("right to inform"), and Chapin to Pickering, Oct. 9, 1795, HORC, XI, NYHS. At Canandaigua in western New York, Chapin first heard of the state treaty in early October.

32. Wallace, *Death and Rebirth of the Seneca*, 172–98; John Dean to Henry Drinker and John Parrish, Apr. 2, 1801, Drinker to Robert Bowne and John Murray, Jr., Oct. 3, 1801, John Dean to the Philadelphia Yearly Meeting's Indian Committee, Oct. 19, 1801, Oneida Chiefs to the U.S. Congress, Feb. 13, 1802, and John Dean to Henry Drinker, Nov. 21, 1802, PYMICR, Box 1, Quaker Collection, Haverford College.

33. Graymont, "New York State Indian Policy," 470; *ASPIA*, I: 616–20; Kaminski, *George Clinton*, 255–61; J. Wingate, Jr., to Senate, Jan. 26, 1802, RG 233 (Unbound Records, U.S. Senate), NA; Thomas Jefferson to the U.S. Senate, Mar. 9, 1802, *ASPIA*, I: 663. Jay's other two compliant treaties were held in May 1796, to purchase lands in northern New York from the Akwesasne and Kahnawake Iroquois (known as "the Seven Nations of Canada") and in March 1797, to extinguish Mohawk claims within the state. The ratification process for the state's 1802 treaty with the Oneidas was never completed. On December 27, 1802, President Jefferson sent the Oneida treaty to the Senate along with three Seneca treaties also attended and certified by John Tayler as the federal treaty commissioner. In two of those deals, both concluded on June 30, the Senecas sold tracts to private land speculators holding the Massachusetts "preemption right" in western New York: Oliver Phelps & Co. and the Holland Land Company. On August 20, in Albany, the state purchased Seneca lands along the Niagara River. The United States Senate approved all four treaties, acting on the Oneida cession on December 31. The president, however, ratified only the two Seneca deals with private interests, signing and promulgating both. He neither signed nor promulgated the two state treaties: of June 4 with the Oneidas and of August 20 with the Senecas. The surviving record does not reveal his reasons for leaving those two treaties incomplete. See Thomas Jefferson to the U.S. Senate, Dec. 27, 1802, RG 233 (Unbound Records, U.S. Senate), 7th Cong., Sen. 7B-D3, Folder 1, NA; [United States Senate], *Senate Executive Journal*, Apr. 29 and Dec. 20, 27, 30, and 31, 1802.

34. "An Act Authorizing the Governor to Appoint Commissioners to Treat with the Oneida Indians for the Purchase of Part of Their Lands," Feb. 26, 1798, [New York State], *Laws of the State of New York* (1887), IV: 163; Samuel Jones to Robert McClellan, Apr. 12, 1798, New York

State Comptroller's Records, Onondaga County Historical Society; John Jay to Timothy Pickering, Apr. 23, 1798, President Adams to the Senate, May 3, 1798, and Joseph Hopkinson to Pickering, June 26, 1798, ASPIA, I: 636, 642, 643; Pickering to Hopkinson, May 5, 1798, TPP, VIII: 405, MHS; [New York State], *Report of the Special Committee to Investigate the Indian Problem of the State of New York*, 249–59; Joseph Annin, "Field Book of the Purchase Made of the Oneida Nation of Indians in the Year . . . 1802," in A 4019 (Records of the Surveyor General, Field Books), XIII, NYSA. The $.54 price comes from the principal value of $5,900 ($900 up front, plus the $5,000 reserved to generate $300 per year at 6 percent interest).

35. Williamson, "Description of the Settlement of the Genesee Country," 1141; Robert Morris to George Washington, Aug. 25, 1796, HORC, XV, NYHS; Israel Chapin to Timothy Pickering, May 5, 1791, TPP, LXI: 187, MHS; Robert Morris to Oliver Phelps, June 13, 1791, R. Morris to George Washington, Aug. 25, 1796, Red Jacket, speech, Sept. 23, 1796 ("great Eater"), and R. Morris to Thomas Morris and Charles Williamson, Aug. 1, 1797, HORC, XV, NYHS.

36. Chernow, *Robert Morris*, 61–69; James Kent, journal, Dec. 1793 ("He has"), JKP, Reel 1, LC.

37. Chernow, *Robert Morris*, 84–117, 148–89; Theophile Cazenove to Joseph Ellicott, July 25, 1797, in Bingham, *Reports of Joseph Ellicott*, I: 3–5; Wallace, *Death and Rebirth of the Seneca*, 179–80; Syrett et al., eds., *Papers of Alexander Hamilton*, XVIII: 295–99, XX: 447n1.

38. Parrish, "The Story of Jasper Parrish," 527–29; Allen, "Personal Recollections of Captains Jones and Parrish," 541; Turner, *Holland Purchase*, 292–93; Kent and Deardorff, eds., "John Adlum," 298n79, 450.

39. Seneca Chiefs, speech, Nov. 21, 1798 ("Brothers" and "wished"), HORC, XIII, NYHS.

40. Harris, "Life of Horatio Jones," 387–94, 416–20 (Jones quoted: "Cousin").

41. Timothy Pickering for Heautenhtonk to Jonathan DeLong, Nov. 19, 1790 ("When my uncle"), TPP, LXI: 73, MHS.

42. Harris, "Life of Horatio Jones," 465–77; Namias, ed., *Narrative of the Life of Mary Jemison*, 119–20; Kent and Deardorff, eds., "John Adlum," 450n24; Thomas Proctor, diary, Apr. 9, 1791, ASPIA, I: 153; Turner, *Holland Purchase*, 289–90 ("unrestrained liberty").

43. Harris, "Life of Horatio Jones," 475–85; Namias and Seaver, eds., *Narrative of Mary Jemison*, 99.

44. Turner, *Phelps and Gorham Purchase*, 349–50; Oliver Phelps to Joseph Brant, Sept. 13, 1789 ("Smith & Jones"), PGP, Box 2, NYSL.

45. Harris, "Life of Horatio Jones," 491–93.

46. John Graves Simcoe to the Lords of Trade, Sept. 1, 1794 ("hourly" and "Prisoners"), in Cruikshank, ed., *Correspondence of Simcoe*, III: 64.

47. Thomas Morris to Robert Morris, May 13, 1796, R. Morris to George Washington, Aug. 25, 1796, T. Morris to R. Morris, Sept. 9, 1796 ("he shall"), T. Morris to R. Morris, May 29, 1797, R. Morris to T. Morris, July 20, 1797, and T. Morris, "Personal Memoir," 1852, HORC, XV, NYHS.

48. Robert Morris to Alexander Hamilton, Mar. 3, 1797 ("The moment"), in Syrett et al., eds., *Papers of Alexander Hamilton*, XX: 529; R. Morris to Thomas Morris, July 6 and Aug. 1, 1797, and T. Morris, "Personal Memoir," 1852, HORC, XV, NYHS; Chernow, *Robert Morris*, 211–13; Densmore, *Red Jacket*, 50–51.

49. Red Jacket, speech, Sept. 3, 1797 ("We are" and "we could"), in Thomas Morris, journal, Sept. 3–7, 1797, and T. Morris, "Personal Memoir," 1852, HORC, XV, NYHS.

50. Thomas Morris, journal, Sept. 6–7, 1797 ("told them" and "This had"), and Sept. 10–16, and T. Morris, "Personal Memoir," 1852, HORC, XV, NYHS; Wallace, *Death and Rebirth of the Seneca*, 181–82. For the landed authority of clan mothers, see also Kent and Deardorff, eds., "John Adlum," 311n102.

51. Thomas Morris, journal, Sept. 16, 1797, Joseph Ellicott, Reservation List, Sept. 16, 1797, and T. Morris, "Personal Memoir," 1852 ("The importance"), HORC, XV, NYHS; Bingham, ed., *Reports of Joseph Ellicott*, I: 52–55; Wallace, *Death and Rebirth of the Seneca*, 182–84. For the annuities, see also, Jasper Parrish, certificate, Apr. 26, 1799, HORC, XIII, NYHS.

52. Thomas Morris, journal, Sept. 3, 1797, and T. Morris, "Personal Memoir," 1852 ("because" and "would not do"), HORC, XV, NYHS; Wallace, *Death and Rebirth of the Seneca*, 181–82.

53. Theophile Cazenove to P. and C. Van Eeghen, Sept. 28, 1797 ("Such complete" and "gratifications"), in Buffalo Historical Society, *Publications*, XXVIII (1924): 193; Wallace, *Death and Rebirth of the Seneca*, 183.

54. Robert Morris to Alexander Hamilton, Jan. 17, 1798 ("Martyr"), in Syrett et al., eds., *Papers of Alexander Hamilton*, XXI: 336–37; Chernow, *Robert Morris*, 216–22.

55. Allen, "Personal Recollections of Captains Jones and Parrish," 539–42; Wallace, *Death and Rebirth of the Seneca*, 179–83.

56. Israel Chapin, Jr., memorandum, Mar. 26, 1800, HORC, XIII, NYHS.

57. Theophile Cazenove to Joseph Ellicott, May 10, 1798, and Ellicott to Cazenove, Sept. 25, 1798, in Bingham, ed., *Reports of Joseph Ellicott*, I: 23–27, 42–43. For the interpreter's background, see William Johnston, petition, July 13, 1797, and John Powell, certificate, July 14, 1797, in Cruikshank, ed., "Petitions for Grants of Land in Upper Canada, Second Series, 1796–99," 225; Cruikshank, ed., "Records of Niagara, 1790–1792," 62; Severance, ed., "Joseph Ellicott's Letter Books," 68; Bingham, *Cradle of the Queen City*, 132–33; Ketchum, *Authentic and Comprehensive History of Buffalo*, I: 372, II: 61–62. The latter source reports the impossible tradition that Johnston was the son of Sir William by Molly Brant.

58. Bigelow, *Journal of a Tour to Niagara Falls*, 51; Bingham, *Cradle of the Queen City*, 133–35.

59. Campbell, ed., *Life and Writings of DeWitt Clinton*, 136–37; Melish, *Travels Through the United States of America*, II: 312; Turner, *Pioneer History of the Holland Purchase*, 390.

60. Israel Chapin, Jr., to James McHenry, Oct. 18, 1797 ("has united"), HORC, XII, NYHS.

61. Turner, *Phelps and Gorham Purchase*, 411; James Kent, Travel Journal, June 15, 1798 ("The melancholy"), and June n.d., 1802 ("harmless race"), JKP, Reel 6, LCP; Thomas Morris, "Personal Memoir," 1852 ("the Indians" and "became"), HORC, XV, NYHS; Severance, ed., "Teacher Among the Senecas," 245 (Rev. Jabez Hyde: "despondency" and "circumstances").

62. Charles Augustus Murray quoted in Harris, "Life of Horatio Jones," 506–7 ("I found").

63. Belknap, "Journal of a Tour to Oneida," 407n; "Communication," *Whitestown Gazette*, Aug. 23, 1796 ("a duty").

64. Israel Chapin, Jr., to James McHenry, Sept. 4, 1796 ("the Americans"), HORC, XII, NYHS.

65. Treaty of Canandaigua, Nov. 11, 1794, *ASPIA*, I: 544–45 ("United States").

66. James Dean to Timothy Pickering, Aug. 22, 1796, TPP, LXII: 246; Belknap and Morse, "Report on the Oneida, Stockbridge, and Brotherton Indians," 15, 31; Belknap, "Journal to Oneida," 407n; *Upper Canada Gazette* (Niagara), Nov. 9, 1796; Joseph Brant to Israel Chapin, Jr., July 26, 1796 ("belongs"), and Chapin to James McHenry, Sept. 4, 1796 ("the next murder"), HORC, XII, NYHS. For Saucy Nick see also, *New York Herald*, Oct. 5, 1796; Jones, *Annals and Recollections of Oneida County*, 874–78.

67. Israel Chapin, Jr., to James McHenry, Sept. 4, 1796, John Jay to Chapin, Sept. 19, 1796, Josiah Ogden Hoffman to Chapin, Sept. 24, 1796 ("a question"), and James McHenry to Chapin, Sept. 23 and Oct. 1, 1796, HORC, XII, NYHS; "Communication," *Whitestown Gazette*, Aug. 23, 1796; James Dean to Timothy Pickering, Aug. 22, 1796 ("should be"), TPP, LXII: 246. For Dean's fear of Indian retaliation, see Pilkington, ed., *The Journals of Samuel Kirkland*, 332–33 ("in the course").

68. For Ayamonte's acquittal, see James Dean to Timothy Pickering, Aug. 22, 1796, TPP, LXII:

246; "Communication," *Whitestown Gazette*, Aug. 23, 1796. For Saucy Nick's acquittal, see *Albany Chronicle*, July 17, 1797. For his subsequent move to Canada, see Turner, *Phelps and Gorham Purchase*, 475. The fate of Captain Kee is uncertain, but there is no record of his execution in Hearn, *Legal Executions in New York State*. For the George Peters case, see Pilkington, ed., *Journals of Samuel Kirkland*, 402n6; Jones, *Annals of Oneida County*, 43–44; Love, *Samson Occom and the Christian Indians of New England*, 356; Johnson, *Reports of Cases Adjudged in the Supreme Court of Judicature*, II: 344; Hearn, *Legal Executions in New York State*, 29.

69. Israel Chapin, Jr., to Henry Dearborn, Aug. 1, 1802, HORC, XIV, NYHS; Red Jacket, speeches, Aug. 18 and 20, 1802, in A 1823 (Assembly Papers), XL (Indian Affairs, 1780–1809), 395, NYSA.

70. Red Jacket, speech at Canandaigua, quoted in Stone, *Life and Times of Red-Jacket*, 175 ("Did we" and "We now"); Red Jacket, speech, Aug. 18, 1802 ("We always thought"), A 1823 (Assembly Papers), XL (Indian Affairs, 1780–1809): 395, NYSA; George Clinton to Henry Dearborn, Aug. 21, 1802 ("repugnant"), *ASPIA*, I: 667.

71. Prucha, *Great Father*, 31 (Jefferson quoted: "We presume"), 76–78, 191–200; Horsman, *Expansion and American Indian Policy*, 104–57; Sheehan, *Seeds of Extinction*; White, *The Jeffersonians*, 496–512.

72. George Clinton to Henry Dearborn, Aug. 21, 1802 *ASPIA*, I: 667; Dearborn to Clinton, Feb. 14, 1803 ("killed" and "good effect"), and Ontario County Grand Jurors to New York State Legislature, Feb. 25, 1803 ("the White"), A 1823 (Assembly Papers), XL (Indian Affairs, 1780–1809): 389, NYSA; People v. George, a Seneca Indian, Feb. 22, 1803, Ontario County Court of Oyer & Terminer, Record Book for 1797–1847, p. 20, Ontario County Archives, Hopewell, N.Y.; Lincoln, ed., *State of New York: Messages from the Governors*, II: 531 ("extenuating" and "considerations"); "An Act to Pardon George, a Seneca Indian," [New York State], *Laws of the State of New York* (1803), 64. On August 17, 1804, the state executed John Delaware, a resident of the Cayuga reservation, for killing a local farmer. He was the first denizen of an Iroquois reservation to suffer execution by the state. See Hearn, *Legal Executions in New York State*, 29.

73. Stone, *Life and Times of Red Jacket*, 317–22; Densmore, *Red Jacket*, 95–97. I am also indebted to an unpublished essay on the Tommy-Jemmy case by Matthew Dennis, generously provided by the author.

74. Red Jacket, speech, Oct. 30, 1799, Reel C-1194, RG 1 E 3 (Upper Canada State Papers), XXXIX: 14, NAC; Charles D. Cooper, Oliver Phelps, and Ezra L'Hommedieu to Gov. George Clinton, July 12, 1802, and Red Jacket, speech, Aug. 19, 1802, both in A 1823 (Assembly Papers), XL (Indian Affairs, 1780–1809): 395, NYSA; New York State treaty with the Senecas, Aug. 20, 1802, *ASPIA* I: 664; Elisha Jenkins to Erastus Granger, Oct. 22, 1806, in Snyder, ed., *Red and White on the New York Frontier*, 36; Chap. LXXII, "An Act relative to the Purchase of the Cayuga Reservation . . . and for other Purposes," Mar. 27, 1807, in [New York State], *Laws of the State of New York* (1809), 89.

75. Henry Dearborn to Israel Chapin, Jr., June 15, 1802, and Chapin to Dearborn, July 6, 1802 ("lame Widow" and "the Indians"), HORC, XIV, NYHS; Joseph Brant to Oliver Phelps, Aug. 17, 1802, PGP, Box 59, Brant Folder, NYSL.

76. Henry Dearborn to Israel Chapin, Jr., June 15, 1802 ("glaring outrage"), and Chapin to Dearborn, July 6, 1802, HORC, XIV, NYHS.

77. Erastus Granger, notes, Oct. 11, 1810, and Red Jacket, speech, Feb. 13, 1810, in Snyder, ed., *Red and White on the New York Frontier*, 31 and 40; Red Jacket, speech, July 8, 1812, in Cruikshank, ed., *Documentary History of the Campaign on the Niagara Frontier in 1812*, 110. For the removal agitation, see Densmore, *Red Jacket*, 88–89; Hauptman, *Conspiracy of Interests*, 144–61.

78. Hauptman, *Conspiracy of Interests*, 133–34.

79. Charles D. Cooper, Oliver Phelps, and Ezra L'Hommedieu to Gov. George Clinton, July 12, 1802, and Red Jacket, speech, Aug. 19, 1802, A 1823 (Assembly Papers), XL (Indian Affairs, 1780–1809), NYSA; New York State Treaty with the Senecas, Aug. 20, 1802, John Tayler to Henry Dearborn, July 19 and Aug. 23, 1802, and George Clinton to Dearborn, Aug. 21, 1802 ("mutual protection"), *ASPIA*, I: 664, 666–67.

CHAPTER ELEVEN: BLOCKS

1. John Graves Simcoe to Lord Dorchester, June 18, 1796 ("All proper"), in Cruikshank, ed., *Correspondence of Simcoe*, IV: 304; MacLeod, "Fortress Ontario or Forlorn Hope?" 160–61.

2. John Graves Simcoe to Lords of Trade, Sept. 1, 1794 ("habits"), MG 23 H-I-1 (Simcoe Transcripts), 4th Ser., VII, Folder II, 29. For the relative populations of Upper Canada and New York, see McCalla, *Planting the Province*, 249; Hough, *Census of the State of New-York for 1855*, xii.

3. Peter Russell to John Graves Simcoe, Apr. 5, 1795, William Johnson Chew to Joseph Chew, Apr. 11, 1795, Simcoe to Lord Dorchester, July 9 and Oct. 9, 1795, W. J. Chew to J. Chew, Nov. 23, 1795, and Simcoe to Dorchester, Dec. 22, 1795, in Cruikshank, ed., *Correspondence of Simcoe*, III: 342, 343, IV: 38, 101–2, 145, 164.

4. Gray, ed., "From Bethlehem to Fairfield—1798," 118–19; Peter Russell to John Graves Simcoe, Apr. 5, 1795, John Butler to Joseph Chew, Apr. 8, 1795, William Johnson Chew to Joseph Chew, Apr. 11, 1795, Simcoe to Lord Dorchester, July 9, 1795, in Cruikshank, ed., *Correspondence of Simcoe*, III: 342, 343, 344, IV, 38; Joseph Brant in 1795 recalled and quoted in William Dummer Powell to Peter Russell, Jan. 3, 1797 ("it would be seen"), in Cruikshank, ed., *Correspondence of Russell*, I: 123. For Isaac Brant's bad reputation, see Richard G. England to Alexander McKee, Aug. 18, 1793, in Cruikshank, ed., *Correspondence of Simcoe*, V: 68; Stone, *Life of Joseph Brant*, II: 464–66; Kelsay, *Joseph Brant*, 280, 529.

5. William Johnson Chew to Joseph Chew, Nov. 23, 1795, John Graves Simcoe to Lord Dorchester, Dec. 22, 1795 in Cruikshank, ed., *Correspondence of Simcoe*, IV: 145, 164; Simcoe to Dorchester, May 5, 1795, and Simcoe to Joseph Brant, Nov. 6, 1795, F 47-1-1 (Simcoe Papers), Reel 1797, AO; William Dummer Powell to Peter Russell, Jan. 3, 1797 ("personal opinion"), in Cruikshank, ed., *Correspondence of Russell*, I: 123; Kelsay, *Joseph Brant*, 563–65.

6. William Jarvis to Samuel Peters, Nov. 10, 1795 ("peevish"), John Graves Simcoe to Duke of Portland, Dec. 1, 1795, Portland to Simcoe, Apr. 9, 1796, Simcoe to Phineas Bond, July 1, 1796, E. B. Littlehales to Peter Russell, July 14, 1796, and Simcoe to Russell, July 18, 1796, in Cruikshank, ed., *Correspondence of Simcoe*, IV: 139, 152, 240, 321, 332, 335.

7. Edith G. Firth, "Peter Russell," *DCB*, V: 729–32.

8. Firth, "Administration of Peter Russell," 163–81; Craig, *Upper Canada*, 42, 49.

9. Allen, *His Majesty's Indian Allies*, 89–91; Peter Russell to Robert Prescott, Aug. 20, 1796, and Russell to the Duke of Portland, Sept. 28, 1796, in Cruikshank, ed., *Correspondence of Russell*, I: 29, 48.

10. John Graves Simcoe to Peter Russell, July 20, 1796, Russell to Robert Prescott, Aug. 29, 1796, and Russell to Simcoe, Nov. 24, 1796, and Sept. 13, 1797, in Cruikshank, ed., *Correspondence of Russell*, I: 15, 33, 90, 280.

11. Firth, ed., *Town of York*, xxxi–xl, lxxvii; Craig, *Upper Canada*, 56–57; O'Brien, *Speedy Justice*, 23–25.

12. Allen, *His Majesty's Indian Allies*, 90–92; Sir John Johnson to William Claus, July 6, 1797 ("Invidious"), in Cruikshank, ed., *Correspondence of Simcoe*, I: 207–8; Red Jacket, speech, July 27, 1797, MG 19 F 35 (PSGIA), 2nd Ser., Lot 717, NAC.

13. Robert Prescott to Peter Russell, Apr. 26, 1797, Duke of Portland to Russell, May 10, 1797, Russell to Alexander McKee, Sept. 22, 1797, Russell to Portland, Oct. 7, 1797, and Prescott to Portland, Dec. 27, 1797, in Cruikshank, ed., *Correspondence of Russell*, I: 166, 173, 296, 297, II: 48.

14. Red Jacket, speech, July 27, 1797 ("As we now"), and Russell, speech, July 27, 1797 ("immediate"), MG 19 F 35 (PSGIA), 2nd Ser., Lots 717 and 718, NAC; Joseph Brant to Peter Russell, Nov. 5, 1798, in Cruikshank, ed., *Correspondence of Russell*, I: 179–80.

15. Joseph Brant, speech, May 16, 1796, in Cruikshank, ed., *Correspondence of Simcoe*, IV: 265–66; Kelsay, *Joseph Brant*, 568; Robert S. Allen, "William Claus," *DCB*, VI: 151–53.

16. Reginald Horsman, "Alexander McKee," *DCB*, IV: 499–500; Nelson, *Man of Distinction Among Them*, 178–87; John Clarke, "Thomas McKee," *DCB*, V: 535–36.

17. Johnston, "Joseph Brant, the Grand River Lands, and the Northwest Crisis," 268–69; John Graves Simcoe to Lord Dorchester, Mar. 9, 1795, in Cruikshank, ed., *Correspondence of Simcoe*, III: 323.

18. Joseph Brant to Peter Russell, June 19, 1797, in Cruikshank, ed., *Correspondence of Russell*, I: 190; Thomas Aston Coffin to Sir John Johnson, June 21, 1790, F 47-1-1 (Simcoe Papers), Reel MS-1797, AO; Brant to Lord Dorchester, Mar. 24, 1791, and Henry Motz to Johnson, May 9, 1791, in Johnston, ed., *Valley of the Six Nations*, 57–58; Brant, speech, Aug. 14, 1791, MG 19 F 35 (PSGIA), 2nd Ser., Lot 693, NAC; Kelsay, *Joseph Brant*, 556–57; Romney, *Mr. Attorney*, 30. For Brant's title expectations, see Brant to John Graves Simcoe, Dec. 13, 1792, MG 23 H-I-1 (Simcoe Transcripts), Box 5, Folder A 8, p. 21, NAC; Brant to John Butler, Dec. 28, 1792 ("better than"), F 47-1-2-7 (Simcoe Papers, Official Correspondence), Reel MS-1798, AO. Brant was not entirely consistent, for in his speech to Dorchester of August 14, 1791, he had sought "a Patent [such] as the King gives for other Lands with a clause that [it] is never to be sold, but to remain [the] Sole & entire property of the Indians for Ever."

19. John Graves Simcoe to James Smith, Nov. 13, 1791, Simcoe Letter Book, 25, #558, HL; Patent of the Grand River Lands to the Six Nations, Jan. 14, 1793, in Johnston, ed., *Valley of the Six Nations*, 73–74; Colgate, ed., "Diary of John White," 159–60; Romney, *Mr. Attorney*, 30; Simcoe, speech, Jan. 12, 1793 ("Brothers"), MG 23 H-I-1 (Simcoe Transcripts), 4th Ser., I, Packet Cc, NAC; Hannah Jarvis to Samuel Peters, Jan. 15, 1793, in Young, ed., "Letters from the Secretary of Upper Canada and Mrs. Jarvis," 29; Simcoe to Alured Clarke, Mar. 20, 1793, Simcoe to Henry Dundas, Sept. 20, 1793, and Simcoe to Lord Dorchester, Dec. 6, 1793 ("great tumult"), in Cruikshank, ed., *Correspondence of Simcoe*, I: 303, II: 58–59, 114–15.

20. Joseph Brant to Alexander McKee, Feb. 25, 1793 ("It hurt"), in Johnston, ed., *Valley of the Six Nations*, 75; John Graves Simcoe to Lord Dorchester, Dec. 6, 1793 (Joseph Brant quoted: "to be fools"), in Cruikshank, ed., *Correspondence of Simcoe*, II: 114–15; Brant to David W. Smith, Apr. 3, 1796 ("It seems"), in Cruikshank, ed., *Correspondence of Russell*, I: 2–3.

21. Samuel Street and William Dickson, memorandum, Mar. 29, 1793, in F 47-1-2-10 (Simcoe Official Correspondence), Reel MS-1798, AO; Joseph Brant to Joseph Chew, Feb. 24 and Mar. 5, 1795, in Cruikshank, ed., *Correspondence of Simcoe*, III: 310, 314; Brant to Sir John Johnson, Nov. 25, 1796 ("My sole" and "I hope"), MG 19 F 35 (PSGIA), Lot 713, NAC.

22. John Graves Simcoe to Henry Dundas, Sept. 20, 1793 ("their Women"), and Joseph Brant to Joseph Chew, Mar. 5, 1795, in Cruikshank, ed., *Correspondence of Simcoe*, II: 58, III: 314; John Norton, Memorial of the Six Nations, 1804 ("leasing" and "received"), in Johnston, ed., *Valley of the Six Nations*, 272.

23. Joseph Brant to Maj. Littlehales, Feb. 24, 1795, MG 23 H-I-1 (Simcoe Transcripts), 4th Ser., Box VI, Folder A 17, p. 31, NAC; Gouverneur Morris to John Jay, July 14, 1799 ("His Great Object"), Jay Papers, Box 45, Columbia University.

24. Joseph Brant to James Green, Dec. 10, 1797 ("King's subjects" and "tie us down"), in Cruikshank, ed., *Correspondence of Russell*, II: 39.

25. Kelsay, *Joseph Brant*, 561–62; John Graves Simcoe to Lord Dorchester, Mar. 3, 1794 ("utmost"), Joseph Brant to Joseph Chew, Mar. 5, 1795, and Peter Russell to Simcoe, Apr. 5, 1795, in Cruikshank, ed., *Correspondence of Simcoe*, II: 174, III: 314, 342; Brant to John Butler, Aug. 10, 1795 ("I have"), MG 23 H-I-1 (Simcoe Transcripts), 4th Ser., VI, Folder A 17, p. 38, NAC.

26. Ebenezer Allen to Ira Allen, Mar. 29, 1795 ("Gardon"), in Duffy, ed., *Ethan Allen and His Kin*, II: 437. For the dimensions and price of the purchases (and anticipated annuity), I have followed Joseph Brant, memorandum, July 22, 1797, in Cruikshank, ed., *Correspondence of Russell*, I: 223. For other calculations that place the sales acreage at 320,000 to 350,000, see Johnston, "An Outline of Early Settlement in the Grand River Valley," 53; Gates, *Land Policies of Upper Canada*, 49; and Johnston, ed., *Valley of the Six Nations*, lv. For the Oneida annuity, see Belknap and Morse, "Report," 31–32.

27. Joseph Brant to Sir John Johnson, Nov. 25, 1796 ("even should"), MG 19 F 35 (PSGIA), 2nd Ser., Lot 713, NAC; Johnston, ed., *Valley of the Six Nations*, lv.

28. For the backgrounds of the speculators, see Johnston, ed., *Valley of the Six Nations*, 86n24, 97nn30–35. For American speculators investing in Grand River, see James Smedley to Joseph Brant, Apr. 22, 1795, MG 23 H-I-1 (Simcoe Transcripts), Box 6, Folder A 17, p. 34, NAC; Robert Hamilton to Colin McGregor, Mar 27, 1796, James Caldwell Papers, Box 1, Albany Institute; Gates, *Land Policies of Upper Canada*, 49; Brant to Israel Chapin, Jr., July 11, 1796, and Nov. 22, 1796, HORC, XII and XV, NYHS; Peter Russell to John Graves Simcoe, Sept. 22, 1796, and Jan. 30, 1797, in Cruikshank, ed., *Correspondence of Russell*, I: 40, 136; Moses Cleaveland to Chapin, July 22, 1801, HORC, XIV, NYHS. For Simcoe's opposition, see Russell to Simcoe, Apr. 5, 1795, and E. B. Littlehales to Brant, Aug. 7, 1795, in Cruikshank, ed., *Correspondence of Simcoe*, III: 342, IV: 67; Brant, speech, Nov. 24, 1796, in Cruikshank, ed., *Correspondence of Russell*, I: 93–94.

29. Lord Dorchester to John Graves Simcoe, Jan. 25, 1796 ("I see"), Simcoe to Duke of Portland, Feb. 27, 1796, Simcoe to Brant, Mar. 2, 1796, and Brant to Joseph Chew, May 17, 1796, in Cruikshank, ed., *Correspondence of Simcoe*, IV: 182, 201, 206, 268–69; Jonathan Sewell to Lord Dorchester, Jan. 25, 1796, in Brymner, ed., "Note A—Indian Lands on the Grand River," 17; Proposed deed, Apr. 29, 1796, MG 19 F 35 (PSGIA), 2nd Ser., Lot 707, NAC.

30. Joseph Chew to Alexander McKee, Sept. 26, 1796 ("Five Nations"), and John White to Peter Russell, Sept. 26, 1796, in Cruikshank, ed., *Correspondence of Russell*, I: 43, 46; Romney, *Mr. Attorney*, 30; Joseph Brant to Israel Chapin, Jr., May 17, 1796 ("Chose to Settle"), HORC, XII, NYHS; Kelsay, *Joseph Brant*, 565–66.

31. Peter Russell to John Graves Simcoe, Sept. 22, 1796 ("very heart" and "throw open"), Russell to the Duke of Portland, Jan. 28, 1797 ("so large"), and Russell to Simcoe, Jan. 30, 1797 ("If Brant"), in Cruikshank, ed., *Correspondence of Russell*, I: 40, 134–35, 136–37; Sir John Johnson to Joseph Brant, Aug. 17, 1797, MG 19 F 6 (Brant Family Papers), I: 15, NAC.

32. Grand River chiefs, power of attorney to Joseph Brant, Nov. 2, 1796, in Johnston, ed., *Valley of the Six Nations*, 79–80; Brant, speech, Nov. 24, 1796 ("As many"), in Cruikshank, ed., *Correspondence of Russell*, I: 94; Brant to Sir John Johnson, Nov. 25, 1796, MG 19 F 35 (PSGIA), 2nd Ser., Lot 713, NAC.

33. Peter Russell to Duke of Portland, Jan. 28, 1797, and Russell to John Graves Simcoe, Jan. 30, 1797, Robert Liston to David Shank, Mar. 28, 1797, Liston to Robert Prescott, Apr. 8, 1797, and Liston to Lord Grenville, July 19, 1797, in Cruikshank, ed., *Correspondence of Russell*, I: 131–34, 136, 157, 160, 218; Kelsay, *Joseph Brant*, 574–75; Israel Chapin, Jr., to James McHenry, Feb. 6, 1797, HORC, XV, NYHS.

34. Robert Liston to David Shank, Mar. 28, 1797, Liston to Robert Prescott, Apr. 8, 1797 ("he would offer"), and Liston to Lord Grenville, July 19, 1797, in Cruikshank, ed., *Correspondence of Russell*, I: 157, 160, 218; Aaron Burr to Theodosia Burr, Feb. 28, 1797 ("He is"), in Stone, *Life of Joseph Brant*, II: 455–56; Kelsay, *Joseph Brant*, 575–76; Parmet and Hecht, *Aaron Burr*, 116–17.

35. Kelsay, *Joseph Brant*, 540–41; Nammack, *Fraud, Politics, and the Dispossession of the Indians*, 23–24; Johannes Crine, petition, n.d. [ca. Jan. 1786], and Nicholas Onwawennarongengh et al., petition, Jan. 12, 1788, in A 1823 (Assembly Papers), XL (Indian Affairs, 1783–1809): 17, 41, NYSA; Philip Schuyler to unknown, Jan. 13, 1786, John Wyman Coll., Box 1, NYSHA; Abraham Schuyler, deposition, Oct. 5, 1786, A 0272 (Indorsed Land Papers, Office of the Secretary of State), XLVII: 20, NYSA; Johannes Crine, notice, *Albany Gazette*, Oct. 12, 1786; Israel Chapin, Jr., to James McHenry, Apr. 29, 1796, Israel Chapin, Jr., to Brant, Apr. 30, 1796, and John Jay to Chapin, Aug. 1, 1796, HORC, XII, NYHS; *ASPIA*, I: 636.

36. Jeromus Johnson to William Leete Stone, Dec. 1, 1837 (Brant quoted: "would never"), in Stone, *Life of Joseph Brant*, II, App. P, xliv; Stone, *Life of Joseph Brant*, 454, 459; Kelsay, *Joseph Brant*, 576–77.

37. James McHenry to Israel Chapin, Jr., June 8, 1797, and Chapin to McHenry, June 29, 1797, HORC, X, NYHS; Brant to unknown, July 2, 1797, HORC, XII, NYHS; Kelsay, *Joseph Brant*, 579–82.

38. Peter Russell to Robert Prescott, Aug. 20, 1796, Russell to Duke of Portland, Sept. 28, 1796, and Thomas Welch to D. W. Smith, June 12, 1797, in Cruikshank, ed., *Correspondence of Russell*, I: 29, 48, 187; Brant to unknown, July 2, 1797, HORC, XII, NYHS; William Dummer Powell to John Askin, May 7, 1798 ("In such Case"), in Quaife, ed., *John Askin Papers*, II: 139; Kelsay, *Joseph Brant*, 583–84; Zeisberger, *Diary*, II: 483; Horsman, *Matthew Elliott*, 123–25.

39. Joseph Brant to Israel Chapin, Jr., June 16, 1797, HORC, XII, NYHS; Chapin to James McHenry, June 29, 1797, Israel Chapin File, NYHS; Mathew Elliott to Sir John Johnson, June 23, 1797, and William Dummer Powell, "Memoir," Nov. 1, 1797, in Cruikshank, ed., *Correspondence of Russell*, I: 194, II: 19–21; Kelsay, *Joseph Brant*, 584; Reginald Horsman, "Matthew Elliott," *DCB*, V: 301–3.

40. Peter Russell to Joseph Brant, June 10, 1797 ("to adjust"), Russell to David W. Smith, June 23, 1797 ("This is"), and Russell to the Executive Council, June 29, 1797 ("the present"), in Cruikshank, ed., *Correspondence of Russell*, I: 185, 195, 198–99.

41. Duke of Portland to Peter Russell, Mar. 10, 1797, Executive Council, minutes, July 16, 1797, Russell to Robert Prescott, July 16, 1797 ("Dangerous dilemma"), Russell to Portland, July 21, 1797 ("I confess" and "This Speech"), and July 29, 1797 (Brant quoted: "declared"), in Cruikshank, ed., *Correspondence of Russell*, I: 155, 215, 216, 219–22, 227–28; Russell, speech, July 26, 1797, MG 19 F 35 (PSGIA), 2nd Ser., Lot 716, NAC. To explain Russell's concessions in July 1797, some historians suggest that Brant prevailed by threatening to attack York. This version takes too literally two partisan accounts, one written in November 1797 by William Dummer Powell and the other in November 1803 by Lord Selkirk. Powell sought to advance his own career by sending a memoir to the home government faulting Russell's land and Indian management. According to Powell, Brant brought "three hundred Warriors" to York to intimidate the Executive Council. Lord Selkirk subsequently reported gossip (perhaps derived from Powell) that Brant "frightened poor Russel into compliance by threats of attacking York." No other contemporary documents support such a threat, and Brant was too subtle to render his intimidation that blunt and crude. Brant denounced the rumors of his threat to Russell as insulting and preposterous. See Powell, memoir, Nov. 1, 1797, in Cruikshank, ed., *Correspondence of Russell*, II: 21; White, ed., *Lord Selkirk's Diary*, 148 ("frightened"); Johnston,

ed., *Valley of the Six Nations*, 1–11; Brant to Lord Dorchester, Oct. 10, 1800, RG 8, C Ser. (British Military), CCLIII (Indians, 1800–1801): 230, NAC.

42. Joseph Brant to David W. Smith, Dec. 15, 1797, in Cruikshank, ed., *Correspondence of Russell*, II: 41–42; Brant, speech, July 25, 1797, MS-234, Peter Russell Copy Book of Indian Correspondence, AO; Johnston, ed., *Valley of the Six Nations*, 111i; Kelsay, *Joseph Brant*, 592–95.

43. For contemporary criticisms of Brant's sales as corrupt, see White, ed., *Lord Selkirk's Diary*, 48 ("rogue"); Francis Gore, "Brief Notices of a View of the Political Situation of Upper Canada in 1808," MG 11 (Colonial Office 42), CCCL: 13, 18, NAC; [Cartwright], *Letters from an American Loyalist*, 76. For Brant's refutation, see Brant to Edward Walsh, May 3, 1805, MG 19 F 10 (Walsh Papers), Folder 1, p. 15, NAC. For a vigorous and effective defense of Brant's conduct, see Kelsay, *Joseph Brant*, 639–40. When Selkirk got away from the officials at York, he heard a far more positive version of Brant's transactions from the Hatt brothers. See White, ed., *Lord Selkirk's Diary*, 303. For historians critical of Brant's land sales, see Johnston, "Joseph Brant, the Grand River Lands, and the Northwest Crisis," 270–71; Allen, *His Majesty's Indian Allies*, 93; Harring, *White Man's Law*, 37.

44. Manuel Overfield, indenture, Apr. 21, 1803, MG 19 F 1 (Claus Family Papers), IX: 131, NAC; William Claus to Peter Hunter, Jan. 19, 1805, RG 8 (British Military), MCCXII (MSL, 1804–1805): 276; Kelsay, *Joseph Brant*, 601. For the festivals, see Brant, account, 1805, MG 19 F 35 (PSGIA), 2nd Ser., Lot 725, NAC. For Brant's efforts at regulating alcohol on the reserve, see Gray, ed., "From Bethlehem to Fairfield," 119; *Niagara Herald*, Feb. 13, 1802.

45. Klinck and Talman, eds., *Journal of Major John Norton*, 285; John Stuart to the Society for the Propagation of the Gospel, Oct. 9, 1797 ("to divide"), in Johnston, "An Outline of Early Settlement in the Grand River Valley," 48; Stuart to the S.P.G., Oct. 11, 1798 ("sensible" and "judiciously"), in Johnston, ed., *Valley of the Six Nations*, 65–66.

46. Gray, ed., "From Bethlehem to Fairfield," 119 ("On muster"); *Upper Canada Gazette* (Newark), May 12, 1798 ("many loyal" and "together").

47. Gray, ed., "From Bethlehem to Fairfield," 119; *Upper Canada Gazette* (Newark), May 12, 1798 ("firing" and "invitation").

48. Firth, ed., *Town of York, 1793–1815*, 84–85; Donald B. Smith, "Wabakinine," *DCB*, IV: 755–56; Peter Russell to John Graves Simcoe, Sept. 28, 1796, in Cruikshank, ed., *Russell Papers*, I: 49–50.

49. O'Brien, *Speedy Justice*, 45–46; Peter Russell to John Graves Simcoe, Sept. 28, 1796, in Cruikshank, ed., *Russell Papers*, I: 49–50; *Upper Canada Gazette* (Newark), Dec. 14, 1796 ("not having").

50. For the conspiracy theory, see O'Brien, *Speedy Justice*, 45–53. For evidence of Mississauga reluctance to cooperate, see Wabenip, speech, Sept. 26, 1796, in Cruikshank, ed., *Russell Papers*, I: 44; White, ed., *Lord Selkirk's Diary*, 162.

51. Peter Russell to John Graves Simcoe, Dec. 31, 1796, in Cruikshank, ed., *Russell Papers*, I: 117; O'Brien, *Speedy Justice*, 49. For the Indian aversion to public disagreement see Merrell, *Into the American Woods*, 183–84; Wallace, *Death and Rebirth of the Seneca*, 42–43. For a scholar of the Mississaugas who accepts that they chose not to testify at Wabakinine's trial, see Smith, "Dispossession of the Mississauga," 23–51.

52. Smith, "Dispossession of the Mississauga Indians," 38; Kelsay, *Joseph Brant*, 569, 604; William Chewett to E. B. Littlehales, Aug. 31, 1794, in Cruikshank, ed., *Correspondence of Simcoe*, III: 24; Keuebegon, speech, Nov. 25, 1796, Peter Russell to John Graves Simcoe, Dec. 31, 1796, Musquakie (Yellow Head), speech, Sept. 4, 1797, and Joseph Brant to James Givens, July 24, 1798 ("I do not"), in Cruikshank, ed., *Correspondence of Russell*, I: 98, 117, 287, II: 233; William

Dummer Powell to John Askin, May 7, 1798 ("They say"), in Quaife, ed., *John Askin Papers*, II: 139–40; Joseph Brant, memorandum, Apr. 3, 1802, RG 10 (Indian Affairs), XXVI: 15415, NAC; White, ed., *Lord Selkirk's Diary*, 161.

53. William Dummer Powell, memoir, Nov. 1, 1797, and Peter Russell to Duke of Portland, Mar. 21, 1798, in Cruikshank, ed., *Correspondence of Russell*, II: 21, 123; Gates, *Land Policies*, 50.

54. Wabanip, speeches, May 1 ("the sole" and "transact") and 17, 1798 ("become"), Peter Russell to Robert Prescott, Sept. 20, 1798 ("shaving"), and Russell to the Duke of Portland, Nov. 8, 1798 ("at the Head"), in Cruikshank, ed., *Correspondence of Russell*, II: 186, 187–88, 261, 310.

55. John Elmsley, report, Oct. 22, 1798 ("the Aborigenes," "Slow as," and "that foresight"), in Cruikshank, ed., *Correspondence of Russell*, II: 290–91; White, ed., *Lord Selkirk's Diary*, 303.

56. John Graves Simcoe to John King, Sept. 7, 1797 ("the jealousy"), Duke of Portland to Peter Russell, Sept. 11, 1797, and Portland to Robert Prescott, Dec. 6, 1798, in Cruikshank, ed., *Correspondence of Russell*, I: 274, 277–78, III: 22.

57. John Graves Simcoe to John King, Sept. 7, 1797 ("nurtured"), William Dummer Powell, Memoir, Nov. 1, 1797 ("the Mischiefs"), and Peter Russell to Duke of Portland, Mar. 21, 1798 ("Brant's conduct"), in Cruikshank, ed., *Correspondence of Russell*, I: 274, II: 21, 123.

58. John Graves Simcoe to John King, Sept. 7, 1797, Duke of Portland to Peter Russell, Sept. 11, 1797, Russell, speech, Sept. 12, 1797, Russell to Duke of Portland, Mar. 21, 1798, Russell to Robert Prescott, June 15, 1798, Joseph Brant to James Givens, June 6, 1798, Russell to Brant, July 29, 1798, Russell to Prescott, Aug. 9, 1798, Quineponen, speech, Nov. 5, 1798 ("We have taken"), Brant to Russell, Nov. 5, 1798, and Russell to Portland, Nov. 8, 1798, in Cruikshank, ed., *Correspondence of Russell*, I: 274–75, 277–78, 289, II: 122–23, 185, 199, 232, 234, 306, 307, 310.

59. Joseph Brant to James Givens, Aug. 3, 1798, Brant to Joseph Chew, Aug. 30, 1798 ("Dear friend"), Brant, speech, Aug. 26, 1798, Peter Russell to Brant, Sept. 28, 1798, Russell to Robert Prescott, Oct. 12, 1798, and Russell to Comte de Puisaye, June 11, 1799 ("That Indians") in Cruikshank, ed., *Correspondence of Russell*, II: 235, 249, 264–65, 271–72, 278–79, III: 211.

60. Peter Russell to Robert Prescott, Sept. 20, 1798, in Cruikshank, ed., *Correspondence of Russell*, II: 261; Fenton and Tooker, "Mohawk," 466–75; Hough, *History of St. Lawrence and Franklin Counties*, 125–29.

61. "Albany," *Albany Gazette*, Oct. 9, 1795; William Gray, speech, May 23, 1796 ("Those Mohawks" and "just people"), and New York commissioners, speech, May 26, 1796, A 1823 (Assembly Papers), XL (Indian Affairs, 1783–1809): 301, NYSA.

62. New York Commissioners, speech, May 26, 1796, A 1823 (Assembly Papers), XL (Indian Affairs, 1783–1809): 301, NYSA; New York State Treaty with the Seven Nations of Canada, May 31, 1796, in Hough, ed., *History of St. Lawrence and Franklin Counties*, 145; John Jay, address to the New York State Legislature, Nov. 1, 1796, *Albany Gazette*, Nov. 7, 1796. For a refutation of the state's use of those documents, see Joseph Brant, speech, Aug. 26, 1798, in Cruikshank, ed., *Correspondence of Russell*, II: 262–63.

63. Hough, *History of St. Lawrence and Franklin Counties*, 192–93; Colonel Louis quoted in Timothy Pickering to Henry Knox, Feb. 13, 1793 ("my enemy"), TPP, LIX: 50, MHS; Joseph Brant to Israel Chapin, Jr., Nov. 22, 1796, HORC, XII, NYHS; Brant to James Givens, July 24, 1798 ("Black fellow"), in Cruikshank, ed., *Correspondence of Russell*, II: 233.

64. Peter Russell to Robert Prescott, Mar. 21, 1798, and Joseph Brant to William Claus, Apr. 5, 1798, in Cruikshank, ed., *Correspondence of Russell*, II: 124, 135; Sabathy-Judd, ed., *Moravians in Upper Canada*, 140; Brant to Israel Chapin, Jr., June 7, 1798, John Jay to Chapin, June 18, 1798, Brant to Chapin, Aug. 31, 1798 ("backwardness"), and Jan. 14, 1799, HORC, XIII, NYHS; Brant to Thomas Morris, Apr. 4, 1799 ("skin a flint"), in Stone, ed., *Life of Joseph Brant*, II: 412–13.

65. Joseph Brant to George Clinton, Jan. 11, 1799, John Wyman Coll., Box 1, #101, NYSHA; Brant to Oliver Phelps, Jan. 11, 1799, PGP, Box 59, NYSL; Brant to Thomas Morris, Apr. 4, 1799, in Stone, ed., *Life of Joseph Brant*, II: 412–13.

66. Peter N. Moogk, "Joseph-Genevieve de Puisaye," *DCB*, VI: 618–21.

67. Kelsay, *Joseph Brant*, 606–7; Joseph Brant to Peter Russell, Apr. 10, 1799, in Cruikshank, ed., *Correspondence of Russell*, III: 168.

68. Peter Russell to Comte de Puisaye, June 11, 1799 ("chearfully"), in Cruikshank, ed., *Correspondence of Russell*, III: 211; Executive Council, minutes, May 28, 1799 ("would certainly"), RG 1 E 3 (Upper Canada Executive Council, State Submissions), XII: 11, NAC.

69. Kelsay, *Joseph Brant*, 607–8; John Elmsley, report, Oct. 22, 1798 ("dictate"), Executive Council, minutes, Feb. 27–28, 1799, Joseph Brant to Sir John Johnson, May 10, 1799, Peter Russell to Duke of Portland, May 26, 1799, and Russell to Robert Prescott, May 26, 1799, in Cruikshank, ed., *Correspondence of Russell*, II: 290, III: 121–23, 195, 205, 209; Executive Council Minutes, May 28, 1799 ("assent to"), RG 1 E 3 (Upper Canada Executive Council, State Submissions), XII: 11, NAC.

70. Horsman, *Matthew Elliott*, 128–41; Robert Prescott to Peter Russell, Oct. 5, 1798, Russell to Prescott, Nov. 2, 1798 ("dangerous cloud"), Joseph Brant to Russell, Jan. 27, 1799, Russell to Prescott, Jan. 31, 1799, Executive Council Minutes, Jan. 31, 1799, Executive Council, minutes, Feb. 1, 1799, Russell to Duke of Portland, Feb. 3, 1799, Russell to Robert Liston, Feb. 11, 1799, and Russell to Prescott, Feb. 14, 1799 ("Indian Allies"), in Cruikshank, ed., *Correspondence of Russell*, II: 272–73, 294–96, III: 69–70, 73, 77, 86, 93–94, 102, 109.

71. Robert Prescott to Duke of Portland, Mar. 5, 1799, Robert Liston to Peter Russell, Mar. 8, 1799, Hector McLean to James Green, Mar. 21, 1799, Thomas McKee to Russell, Mar. 18, 1799, Russell to McLean, Apr. 5, 1799 ("only confirmed me"), and Russell to Portland, Apr. 25, 1799, in Cruikshank, ed., *Correspondence of Russell*, III: 127–29, 131, 144–45, 149, 163, 181; Maj. J. J. Ulrich Rivardi to Alexander Hamilton, Mar. 21, 1799, Alexander Hamilton Papers, Reel 9, LC; Joseph Brant to Sir John Johnson, Apr. 3, 1799, Brant File, J. J. Tallman Regional Coll., University of Western Ontario Library; Kelsay, *Joseph Brant*, 608. For Brant's intervention on Elliott's behalf, see Joseph Brant to John Graves Simcoe, Jan. 22, 1799, MG 11 (Colonial Office 42), LXXXVIII: 422, NAC; Russell to Robert Prescott, Feb. 1, 1799, in Cruikshank, ed., *Correspondence of Russell*, III: 82–83.

72. Peter Russell to Robert Prescott, June 22, 1799 ("Altho"), in Cruikshank, ed., *Correspondence of Russell*, III: 248–49.

73. William Dummer Powell, "First Days in Upper Canada," MG 23 H-I-4 (Powell Papers), III: 1050, NAC; Duke of Portland to Peter Hunter, Oct. 4, 1799 ("Whatever credit" and "as separate"), MG 11 (Colonial Office 42), CCCXXIV: 213, NAC.

74. Frances G. Halpenny and Jean Hamelin, "Peter Hunter," *DCB*, V: 439–43; Cruikshank, "A Memoir of Lieutenant-General Peter Hunter," 5–32; O'Brien, *Speedy Justice*, 22.

75. Halpenny and Hamelin, "Peter Russell," *DCB*, V: 440–41 (includes Todd quotation: "verry exact"); Gates, *Land Policies of Upper Canada*, 67–74; William Dummer Powell, "First Days in Upper Canada," MG 23 H-I-4 (Powell Papers), III: 1051–52; White, ed., *Lord Selkirk's Diary*, 147–51; O'Brien, *Speedy Justice*, 23–24; Hannah Jarvis to Samuel Peters, Sept. 28, 1805 ("For my part"), MG 23 H-I-3 (Jarvis Family Papers), II: 157, NAC.

76. Joseph Brant to Peter Hunter, Sept. 6, 1799, RG 10 (Indian Affairs), Upper Canada Civil Control, I: 268; William Dummer Powell, "First Days in Upper Canada," MG 23 H-I-4 (Powell Papers), III: 1050; Kelsay, *Joseph Brant*, 619, 628; James Green to Sir John Johnson, Dec. 2, and Dec. 9, 1799, and Green to Johnson, June 9, 1800, RG 8 (British Military), MCCVIII (MSL, 1799–1800): 103, 104, 236, NAC; Hunter to Duke of Portland, Mar. 8,

1800 ("Captain Brant's aim"), MG 11 (Colonial Office 42), CCCXXV: 111, NAC; Brant to Johnson, Sept. 10, 1801, MG 19 F 6 (Brant Family Papers), I: 34, NAC.

77. James Green to Thomas Talbot, June 26, 1801, RG 8 (British Military), MCCIX (MSL, 1800–1802): 213, NAC; Quinepenon, speeches, Aug. 1 and 2, 1805 ("Although"), in William Claus, council minutes, Aug. 1–2, 1805, and Mississauga Treaty of Cession, Aug. 1, 1805, RG 10 (Indian Affairs), Upper Canada Civil Control, I: 296–98, NAC; Surtees, "Land Cessions, 1763–1830," 110–11.

78. Quinepenon, speech, Aug. 1, 1805 ("generosity"), in William Claus, council minutes, Aug. 1–2, 1805, and Claus to Alexander Grant, Oct. 28, 1805 ("in former"), and Nov. 15, 1805 ("the pity-ful"), RG 10 (Indian Affairs), Upper Canada Civil Control, I: 296–98, NAC; Requisition, Nov. 16, 1805, RG 10 (Indian Affairs), XXVI: 15595, NAC. On November 23, 1805, Claus endorsed the requisition of November 16 for the original price of goods worth just £1,000.

79. Peter Hunter to Earl of Camden, Feb. 1, 1805 ("highly disgraceful"), RG 8 (British Military), MCCXII (MSL, 1804–1805): 252, NAC; James Green to William Claus, July 17, 1800, RG 8 (British Military), MCCVIII (MSL, 1799–1800): 289, NAC; Joseph Brant to Sir John Johnson, n.d. [ca. early 1801] ("that we are not"), MG 19 F 6 (Brant Family Papers), I: 30, NAC.

80. James Green to William Claus, July 17, 1800, RG 8 (British Military), MCCVIII (MSL, 1799–1800): 289, NAC; Joseph Brant to Sir John Johnson, n.d. [ca. early 1801] ("When I find"), MG 19 F 6 (Brant Family Papers), I: 30, NAC; Klinck and Talman, eds., *Journal of Major John Norton*, 284–85 ("His latter Days").

81. Sir John Johnson to Peter Hunter, Dec. 16, 1799 ("the uncommon"), MG 11 (Colonial Office 42), CCCXXV: 23, NAC; William Claus, speech, Feb. 25, 1801 ("one of the last"), RG 10 (Indian Affairs), XXVI: 15361, NAC; Kelsay, *Joseph Brant*, 624.

82. Kelsay, *Joseph Brant*, 633; Joseph Brant, speech, Aug. 17, 1803, and William Claus, speech, Aug. 17, 1803, in Johnston, ed., *Valley of the Six Nations*, 133–35; Claus to Peter Hunter, Jan. 19, 1805 ("The manner"), RG 8 (British Military), MCCXII (MSL, 1804–1805): 277, NAC.

83. Kelsay, *Joseph Brant*, 621–22, 624–25; Joseph Brant, speech, May 1, 1802, RG 8 (British Military), MCCXII (Military Secretary's Letterbook, 1804–1805): 271, NAC.

84. Joseph Brant, speech, May 1, 1802, RG 8 (British Military), MCCXII (Military Secretary's Letterbook, 1804–1805): 271, NAC; Kelsay, *Joseph Brant*, 621–22, 624–25; Brant, speech, n.d. [ca. 1804] ("important services"), in Stone, *Life of Joseph Brant*, II: 418–19.

85. Tchaosennoghts, speech, ca. 1804 ("The divisions"), in Stone, *Life of Joseph Brant*, II: 421.

86. Pilkington, *Journals of Samuel Kirkland*, 364–65 ("Upholder"); Kelsay, *Joseph Brant*, 611–12; Dr. Edward Walsh, "Indians," 1804, MG 19 F 10 (Walsh Papers), Folder 3, pp. 133–34, NAC.

87. Informant quoted in Gates, "Roads, Rivals, and Rebellion," 245 ("American Government"); John Elmsley to Peter Hunter, Feb. 1, 1802 ("That the plan"), and Apr. 14, 1802, Elmsley Letterbook (1800–1802), Baldwin Room, MTL. For a fuller discussion of this plot, see A. Taylor, "A Northern Revolution of 1800?" 383–409.

88. Gates, *Land Policies of Upper Canada*, 30–31; Gates, "Roads, Rivals, and Rebellion," 235–37; Asa Danforth, Jr., to Elisha Beaman, Mar. 2, 1802, RG 5 A 1 (Civil Secretary's Correspondence, Upper Canada Sundries), II: 708, NAC; *Niagara Herald*, May 16, 1801.

89. Judd, *Hatch and Brood of Time*, 98–101, 121–32; E. A. Cruikshank, ed., "Petitions for Grants of Land: Second Series, 1796–1799," 270; Joseph Brant to Sir John Johnson, Dec. 15, 1797, and to John Elmsley, n.d. [ca. 1799], in Stone, *Life of Joseph Brant*, II: 433, 434; Peter Russell to Bishop Jacob Mountain, Feb. 22, 1798, Russell to Brant, May 14, 1798, and Mountain to Russell, June 12, 1798 ("Spiritual Instructor"), in Cruikshank, ed., *Correspondence of Russell*, II: 98, 153, 180; Peter Hunter to Elmsley, Oct. 3, 1799, RG 8 (British Military), MCCVIII (MSL, 1799–1800): 28, NAC.

90. Joseph Brant to Aaron Burr, May 7, 1800, in Stone, *Life of Joseph Brant*, II: 436–38; Kelsay, *Joseph Brant*, 547 (Duke of Portland quotation: "neither have been"); Burr to Theodosia Burr Alston, Aug. 20 and Nov. 3, 1801, Brant to Captain Isaac Chapin, Jr., May 7, 1801 ("religion and morality"), and Davenport Phelps to Burr, Dec. 15, 1801, in Davis, ed., *Memoirs of Aaron Burr*, II: 152, 155, 163–64; Davenport Phelps to John Elmsley, Apr. 8, 1802, and James Green for Peter Hunter to William Claus, May 28, 1802, in RG 8 (British Military), MCCX (Military Secretary's Letterbook, 1800–1802): 38, NAC.

91. Joseph Brant to Sir John Johnson, n.d. [ca. early 1801], MG 19 F 6 (Brant Family Papers), I: 30, NAC; Kelsay, *Joseph Brant*, 625.

92. Joseph Brant to Thomas Morris, Dec. 26, 1800 ("Secret," "protection," and "great jealousy"), in Stone, *Life of Joseph Brant*, II: 405; Brant to Israel Chapin, Jr., May 7, 1801, in Davis, ed., *Memoirs of Aaron Burr*, II: 164; Kelsay, *Joseph Brant*, 620–21. Kelsay dismisses the charge that Brant was disloyal, insisting that Brant "said all these things with his tongue very much in his cheek. Joseph had not the remotest idea of leaving Upper Canada, but buying land to make a settlement had a better sound to it than buying land to sell and make a profit." Kelsay argues that Brant was simply conning American politicians into providing lands for his profitable speculation. But, if put in the context of the other evidence, including his approach to Burr and the bishop of New York on behalf of Davenport Phelps, this bid for Ohio land in 1800–1801 makes the most sense as a contingency plan in the event that circumstances worsened in Upper Canada. This is not to say that Brant *wanted* to move to Ohio, for he hoped to have his way within Upper Canada. For his earlier bid to procure an American reservation, see Joseph Brant to Israel Chapin, Jr., Jan. 19, 1796, HORC, XII, NYHS.

93. Joseph Brant to David W. Smith, Sept. 20, 1800, Smith Unbound Correspondence, Folder B7, p. 259, Baldwin Room, MTL; Stone, *Life of Joseph Brant*, II: 469–73; Kelsay, *Joseph Brant*, 608–10; Benjamin Sumner to John Wheelock, Oct. 24, 1800, McClure Coll., #800574, DCLSC.

94. John Wheelock to David McClure, Jan. 12, 1801, McClure Coll., #801112, DCLSC; Wheelock to the Earl of Dartmouth, May 1, 1801, DCA #801301, DCLSC; Chase, *History of Dartmouth College*, I: 618–19. For the withheld funds, see also John Kemp to Peter Thacher, Feb. 5, 1794, Society in Scotland to Thacher, Oct. 28, 1796, and Kemp to Thacher, Aug. 28, 1797, DCA #794155, #796653, and #797478, DCLSC.

95. John Wheelock to Jonathan Freeman, Dec. n.d., 1800 ("In regard" and "Pray consider"), and Jan. 6, 1801 ("great magnitude"), DCA #800690 and #801106.1, DCLSC.

96. Kelsay, *Joseph Brant*, 622–23; Aaron Burr to Theodosia Burr Alston, Aug. 20 and Nov. 3, 1801, Brant to Captain Isaac Chapin, Jr., May 7, 1801, and Davenport Phelps to Aaron Burr, Dec. 15, 1801, in Davis, ed., *Memoirs of Aaron Burr*, II: 152, 155, 163–64.

97. Thomas McKee to William Claus, Sept. 14, 1801, and Chippewa (i.e., Ojibwa) Council to McKee, n.d., RG 10 (Indian Affairs), XXVI: 15378, 15382, NAC; Brant quoted in Makonce, speech, Oct. 30, 1801 ("ungrateful nation" and "I have traveled"), RG 8 (British Military) MCCXII (MSL, 1804–1805): 269, NAC; Executive Council, minutes, Sept. 30, 1801, MG 11 (Colonial Office 42), CCCXXXII, 16–18, NAC.

98. Old Thomas Dewataogharanegen and H. Brant to William Claus, Sept. 24, 1801 ("to the States"), RG 8 (British Military), MCCXII (MSL, 1804–1805): 265, NAC. On February 1, 1805, Peter Hunter forwarded a copy of this 1801 letter to the home government to discredit Brant. For official reaction to this news, see Executive Council, minutes, Sept. 30, 1801, and William Claus to John Elmsley, Oct. 20, 1801, MG 11 (Colonial Office 42), CCCXXXII: 16, 18, NAC; James Green to William Claus, Oct. 22, 1801, RG 8 (British Military), MCCIX (MSL, 1800–1802): 314, NAC; Joseph Brant, speech, May 1, 1802 ("It is said"), in Peter

Hunter to the Earl of Camden, Feb. 1, 1805, RG 8 (British Military), MCCXII (MSL, 1804–1805): 271, NAC. For Norton's presence in Albany, see Joseph Brant to James Caldwell, Feb. 17, 1802, Thomas Addison Emmett Coll., #4623, NYPL.

99. Asa Danforth, Jr., to Timothy Green, Feb. 17, 1801, Danforth File, Misc. Coll., NYHS; McCalla, *Planting the Province*, 13–29, 250; Greenwood, *Legacies of Fear*, 102–3; Wallot, *Intrigues Françaises et Américaines au Canada*, 43.

100. Perkins, *The First Rapprochement*, 129–32; Jefferson to Madison, Sept. 18, 1801 ("I think"), in Smith, ed., *The Republic of Letters*, II: 1199; Wallot, *Intrigues*, 43. For Jefferson's cooling attitude toward the French Revolution, see Onuf, " 'To Declare Them a Free and Independent People,' " 31.

101. Asa Danforth, Jr., to Richard Cockrell, June 26, 1802, RG 5 A 1 (Civil Secretary's Correspondence, Upper Canada Sundries), II: 759, NAC; Caniff, *History of the Settlement of Upper Canada*, 226; Peter Russell to William Osgoode, July 22, 1802 ("a tissue"), F 46 (Peter Russell Papers), Reel Ms-75/5, AO; Judd, *Hatch and Brood*, 135; Gates, "Roads, Rivals, and Rebellion," 250–51.

102. For the attempt to oust Brant, see Executive Council, minutes, Sept. 30, 1801, and William Claus to John Elmsley, Oct. 14, 1801, in RG 1 E 1 (Upper Canada Executive Council, State Minute Books), C (1800–1804): 146, 149–50, NAC; Joseph Brant, speech, May 1, 1802, RG 8 (British Military), MCCXII (MSL, 1804–1805): 271, NAC; Six Nations Matrons, speech, and Brant's reply, May 22, 1802, in Stone, *Life of Joseph Brant*, II: 443–44; Kelsay, *Joseph Brant*, 628–29; White, ed., *Lord Selkirk's Diary*, 161. For Brant's retreat to Burlington Bay, see Klinck and Talman, eds., *Journal of Major John Norton*, 285; Kelsay, *Joseph Brant*, 597–601.

103. Klinck and Talman, eds., *Journal of Major John Norton*, 285; Kelsay, *Joseph Brant*, 597–601; William C. Bryant quoted in Hamilton, "Joseph Brant Painted by Rigaud," 251 (all quotations).

104. Rev. Reed quoted in Carroll, *Case and His Contemporaries*, I: 165 ("immediate vicinity"). For acquisition of the Burlington Bay tract, see Joseph Brant to Lord Dorchester, Aug. 27, 1790, RG 1 (Crown Lands) A-1-1 (Letters Received by the Surveyor General), LII: 1022, AO; Brant to David W. Smith, Dec. 28, 1792, F 47-1-2-7 (Simcoe Papers), Reel MS-1798, AO; Kelsay, *Joseph Brant*, 540, 598–601; Lord Dorchester to Simcoe, Jan. 24, 1796, and E. B. Littlehales to Brant, Feb. 6, 1796, in Cruikshank, ed., *Correspondence of Simcoe*, IV: 180, 191; Cruikshank, ed., "Petitions for Grants of Land, 1792–6,", 30; D. W. Smith, memorandum, Aug. 3, 1797, in Cruikshank, ed., *Correspondence of Russell*, I: 240.

105. Peter Hunter, proclamation, Nov. 10, 1802, in *Upper Canada Gazette* (York), Nov. 20, 1802; Joseph Brant, petition, Jan. 1, 1803, in Fraser, ed., *Sixth Report of the Bureau of Archives for the Province of Ontario, 1909*, 360; Joseph Brant, speech, Aug. 17, 1803 ("to a line"), RG 1 E 1 (Upper Canada Executive Council, State Minute Books), C: 396, NAC; Brant, speech, Oct. 8, 1803 ("Should we"), in Johnston, ed., *Valley of the Six Nations*, 104–5; John Norton, memorial, c. 1804, MG 11 (Colonial Office 42), CCCXXXVI: 255, NAC; White, ed., *Lord Selkirk's Diary*, 304 ("fine improvements"). For a Brant lease, see Amos Sturgis, indenture, Oct. 1, 1801, F 547 (Samuel Street Papers), Reel MS-500, AO.

106. Kelsay, *Joseph Brant*, 629; James Green to William Claus, Jan. 17, 1804 ("the Lieut. General"), RG 8 (British Military), MCCXI (MSL, 1803–1804): 321, NAC.

107. James Green to William Claus, Dec. 11, 1804 ("that Captain"), RG 8 (British Military), MCCXII (MSL, 1804–1805): 209, NAC.

108. Kelsay, *Joseph Brant*, 632–33; Klinck and Talman, eds., *Journal of Major John Norton*, xli–li.

109. Klinck and Talman, eds., *Journal of Major John Norton*, xxiv–xl; Klinck, "John Norton," *DCB*,

VI: 550–53; Cruikshank, "Petitions for Grants of Land in Upper Canada, Second Series, 1796–99," 262–63; James Green to William Claus, Aug. 7, 1800, RG 8 (British Military), MCCVIII (MSL, 1799–1800): 342, NAC; Claus to Peter Hunter, Jan. 19, 1805, RG 8 (British Military), MCCXII (MSL, 1804–1805): 278; Francis Gore to Viscount Castlereagh, Sept. 4, 1809, MG 11 (Colonial Office 42), CCCXLIX: 88, NAC.

110. James Green to John Norton, July 6, 1801 ("With respect"), RG 8 (British Military), MCCIX (MSL, 1800–1802): 220–21; Francis Gore to Viscount Castlereagh, Sept. 4, 1809, MG 11 (Colonial Office 42), CCCXLIX: 88, NAC; [Cartwright], *Letters From an American Loyalist in Upper Canada*, 77. For dubious scholars, see Kelsay, *Joseph Brant*, 538, 635; Fogelson, "Major John Norton as Ethnologist," 250. For scholars who accept Norton's claim of Cherokee paternity, see Klinck and Talman, eds., *Journal of Major John Norton*, xxiv–xl; Klinck, "John Norton," *DCB*, VI: 550–53; Johnston, "William Claus and John Norton," 101; Johnston, *Brant County*, 19; Benn, *Iroquois in the War of 1812*, 8–9. Samuel Kirkland reported an alternative theory from the circuit of Indian gossip: that Norton's father was British but his mother was Indian. But Kirkland's version erroneously reported that the father was an officer who had commanded at Niagara and the mother was a Shawnee or Mohawk. See Pilkington, ed., *Journals of Samuel Kirkland*, 417.

111. Kelsay, *Joseph Brant*, 633; Klinck and Talman, eds., *Journal of Major John Norton*, xli–li, cviii; White, ed., *Lord Selkirk's Diary*, 243; Joseph Brant to Earl of Moira, Feb. 20, 1804, MG 11 (Colonial Office 42), CCCXXXVI: 173, NAC.

112. Duke of Northumberland to Joseph Brant, May 5, 1806 ("converting us"), in Stone, *Life of Joseph Brant*, II: 427.

113. John Norton, memorial, n.d. 1804, MG 11 (Colonial Office 42), CCCXXXVI: 175, NAC.

114. Earl of Camden to Peter Hunter, Aug. 2, 1804, Lord Hobart to Hunter, Aug. 3, 1804, and John Norton to Camden, Sept. 18, 1804, MG 11 (Colonial Office 42), CCCXXXVI: 41, 42, 258, NAC; James Green to William Claus, Jan. 1, 1805, RG 8 (British Military), MCCXII (MSL, 1804–1805): 224, NAC; Hunter to Earl of Camden, Feb. 1, 1805, Claus to Hunter, Jan. 19, 1805, and Green to Claus, Feb. 25, 1805, RG 8 (British Military), MCCXII (MSL, 1804–5): 278, 280, 297, NAC; Claus to Prideaux Selby, Feb. 1, 1805, MG 19 F 1 (Claus Family Papers), IX: 76–77, NAC; Claus, speech, Sept. 23, 1806 ("White man"), MG 19 F 35 (PSGIA), 2nd Ser., Lot 728, NAC; Claus to Hunter, Apr. 13, 1805, RG 8 (British Military), MCCXII (MSL, 1804–5): 336, NAC; Kelsay, *Joseph Brant*, 636–37.

115. William Claus to Peter Hunter, Apr. 13, 1805, and Red Jacket, speech, Apr. 8, 1805, RG 8 (British Military), MCCXII (MSL, 1804–5): 336, 338–39, NAC; Kelsay, *Joseph Brant*, 627–28, 636–37; Stone, *Life and Times of Red-Jacket*, 179–81.

116. William Claus to Peter Hunter, Apr. 13, 1805, and Red Jacket, speech, Apr. 8, 1805 ("We the Six Nations" and "put Captain Brant"), RG 8 (British Military), MCCXII (MSL, 1804–5): 336, 338–39, NAC.

117. Kelsay, *Joseph Brant*, 637–38; Klinck and Talman, eds., *Journal of Major John Norton*, xliii, cviii.

118. Joseph Brant, speech, May 1, 1805, and Brant to Edward Walsh, May 3, 1805, MG 19 F 10 (Walsh Papers), Folder 1, pp. 15, 17–20, NAC; Brant to unknown, undated draft, MG 19 F 6 (Brant Family Papers), I: 38, NAC; Brant, speech, July 23, 1806, MG 19 F 35 (PSGIA), 2nd Ser., Lot 728, NAC; Kelsay, *Joseph Brant*, 638–39; Brant to William Claus, Nov. 9, 1806, RG 10 (Indian Affairs), Correspondence of the Deputy Superintendent General, XXVII: 15670, NAC.

119. Aikins [*sic*; Askins], "Journal of a Journey from Sandwich to York," 17; Merriman, "Upper Canada Land Petitions, 'G' Leases #88," 328–29. The thirty-three farm-sized tracts

amounted to 7,392 acres and promised to pay £4,203.16.0. In making these calculations, I reduced to £90 three leases of 200 acres listed at an implausible £900 each, out of line with the standard price of £100–£120 for almost all other tracts of that size.

120. Carol Whitfield, "Alexander Grant," *DCB*, V: 363–67; Alexander Grant to John Askin, Oct. 24, 1805, in Quaife, ed., *John Askin Papers*, II: 486; Romney, *Mr. Attorney*, 40; Joseph Brant to Grant, Feb. 12, and 13, 1806, RG 10 (Indian Affairs), Upper Canada Civil Control, I: 323, 326, NAC.

121. S. R. Mealing, "Francis Gore," *DCB*, VIII (1985): 336–40; Joseph Brant to Francis Gore, Aug. 24, 1806, RG 10 (Indian Affairs), Upper Canada Civil Control, I: 436, NAC; Gore to the Six Nations Chiefs, Sept. 2, 1806, RG 10 (Indian Affairs), Correspondence of the Deputy Superintendent General, XXVII: 15657, NAC; Klinck and Talman, eds., *Journal of Major John Norton*, xciv; Kelsay, *Joseph Brant*, 646; William Claus, speech, Sept. 23, 1806, RG 1 E 3 (Upper Canada Executive Council State Submissions), XII: 140–49, NAC; Gore to Isaac Brock, Nov. 20, 1806, RG 8 (British Military), C Series, CCLIV: 71, NAC.

122. Guest, "Upper Canada's First Political Party," 275–96; Craig, *Upper Canada*, 59–63; G. H. Patterson, "Robert Thorpe," *DCB*, VII: 864–65.

123. Joseph Brant, petition to the assembly, Feb. 14, 1806, in Cruikshank, ed., "Records of Niagara, 1805–1811," 24–25; Kelsay, *Joseph Brant*, 642–43; Wilson, *Enterprises of Robert Hamilton*, 157; William Claus, journal, July 19–22, and Brant, speech, July 23, 1806, MG 19 F 35 (PSGIA), 2nd Ser., Lot 728, NAC; Claus to Alexander Grant, July 24, 1806, RG 10 (Indian Affairs), Upper Canada Civil Control, I: 409, NAC; Prideaux Selby to Robert Kerr, Aug. 4, 1806, RG 10 (Indian Affairs), Correspondence of the Deputy Superintendent General, XXVII: 15630, NAC; Claus, speech, Sept. 23, 1806, MG 19 F 35 (PSGIA), 2nd Ser., Lot 728, NAC. Claus's letters of July 24, and Selby's of August 4, indicate that Brant's speech occurred on July 23. An extract from Brant's speech of July 23 appears misdated as July 28, in Johnston, ed., *Valley of the Six Nations*, 105–9, and in Klinck and Talman, eds., *Journal of Major John Norton*, cix–cx.

124. William Allan to Francis Gore, Jan. 5, 1807, in Brymner, ed., "Political State of Upper Canada," 69; Guest, "First Political Party," 284–89; Firth, ed., *The Town of York*, 173–74; Francis Gore to Viscount Castlereagh, Sept. 4, 1809 ("if they are"), and Samuel Thompson to Robert Thorpe, Dec. 24, 1806, MG 11 (Colonial Office 42), CCCXLIX: 90, CCCL: 262, NAC.

125. Guest, "First Political Party," 291–92; Craig, *Upper Canada*, 62.

126. Francis Gore to Viscount Castlereagh, Sept. 4, 1809, and Joseph Brant to Gore, Apr. 14, 1807, MG 11 (Colonial Office 42), CCCXLIX: 90, 98, NAC.

127. William Claus, speech, May 29, 1807, RG 1 E 3 (Upper Canada Executive Council State Submissions), XXV: 93, NAC; Alexander MacDonell to Earl of Selkirk, Mar. 18, 1808, MG 19 E 1 (Selkirk Papers), LIV: 14424–25, NAC.

128. Stone, *Life of Joseph Brant*, II: 498–99; Kelsay, *Joseph Brant*, 651; Klinck and Talman, eds., *Journal of Major John Norton*, 284 ("an Example"); Robert Addison to Society for Propagating the Gospel, Jan. 2, 1808 ("fell"), in Young, "The Rev. Robert Addison and St. Mark's Church," 181. Stone states that Brant was sixty-four years and eight months old, but a year before, Brant stated that he turned sixty-two in April of 1806, which would make him sixty-three and nine months at his death. See Brant to William Halton, Nov. 3, 1806, RG 10 (Indian Affairs), Vol. 782, p. 65, NAC.

129. Sir John Johnson to William Claus, Dec. 16, 1807 (all quotations), MG 19 F 1 (Claus Family Papers), IX: 166, NAC.

130. Joseph Brant quoted in Stone, *Life of Joseph Brant*, 499 ("Have pity").

CHAPTER TWELVE: ENDS

1. Samuel Kirkland to Israel Chapin, May 30, 1792, HORC, VIII, NYHS; Kirkland to Timothy Pickering, Jan. 17, 1794, Mar. 11, 1795 ("order"), LXII: 79, 220, MHS.

2. Kirkland, "A Plan of Education for the Indians, Particularly of the Five Nations," Oct. 4, 1791 ("After"), in Ibbotson, ed., *Documentary History of Hamilton College*, 30.

3. Pilkington, ed., *Journals of Samuel Kirkland*, 157–58 ("Education" and "introduce").

4. Kirkland, diary, June 7, 1791, LFP, DCLSC; Kirkland, "A Plan of Education for the Indians, Particularly of the Five Nations," Oct. 4, 1791 ("the principles" and "the doctrines"), and Kirkland, "Plan for the Academy," n.d. [ca. Dec. 1792], in Ibbotson, ed., *Documentary History of Hamilton College*, 27–28, 55.

5. Samuel Kirkland to John Wheelock, Oct. 12, 1791, DCA #791562 ("worthy founder" and "laudable"), DCLSC; Kirkland, "A Plan of Education for the Indians, Particularly of the Five Nations," Oct. 4, 1791 ("necessary"), in Ibbotson, ed., *Documentary History of Hamilton College*, 27–28.

6. Kirkland, "A Plan of Education for the Indians, Particularly of the Five Nations," Oct. 4, 1791, Thomas Casety to Kirkland, Apr. 27, 1792, and Subscription List, 1792–93, in Ibbotson, ed., *Documentary History of Hamilton College*, 28–29, 41–42, 61–62; Pilkington, *Hamilton College*, 25–30; Belknap and Morse, "Report on the Oneida, Stockbridge, and Brotherton Indians, 1796," 38.

7. Subscription List, 1792–93, in Ibbotson, ed., *Documentary History of Hamilton College*, 28–29, 41–42, 61–62; Pilkington, *Hamilton College*, 25–30; Hamilton Oneida Academy Trustees to the Society for Propagating Christian Knowledge, Jan. 2, 1794 ("those prejudices"), SKP, Folder 164, HCA.

8. Pilkington, ed., *Journals of Samuel Kirkland*, 232, 270, 273–74 ("envious"); Pilkington, *Hamilton College*, 31–33. For Ebenezer Caulkins's diversion, see John Sergeant, Jr., to Peter Thacher, Mar. 12 and Sept. 6, 1794, SKP, Folders 166 and 171, HCA; Caulkins to Thacher, June 4, 1794, DCA #794354, DCLSC.

9. John Sergeant, Jr., to Peter Thacher, Jan. 10 and Mar. 12, 1794, SKP, Folders 164 and 166 HCA; Sergeant to Timothy Pickering, Jan. 3, 1795, TPP, LXII: 200, MHS; Sergeant to Jedediah Morse, Feb. 18, 1800, Morse Family Papers, Box 3, Stirling Library, Yale University; Pickering to Kirkland, Dec. 4, 1791 ("plain learning"), in Ibbotson, ed., *Documentary History of Hamilton College*, 35–36.

10. Samuel Kirkland to Stephen Van Rensselaer, Feb. 24, 1795, SKP, Folder 176, HCA; Pilkington, *Hamilton College*, 35, 39–44; Belknap, "Journal to Oneida, 1796," 409 ("nothing more"); Dwight, *Travels in New England and New York*, III: 129.

11. Pilkington, ed., *Hamilton College*, 35, 39–44; Belknap, "Journal to Oneida, 1796," 409; Pilkington, ed., *Journals of Samuel Kirkland*, 312.

12. Pilkington, ed., *Journals of Samuel Kirkland*, 190, 231, 266, 299; Samuel Kirkland to Peter Thacher, Dec. 26, 1792, DCA #792676, DCLSC; Samuel Kirkland to John Thornton Kirkland, Apr. 15 and Sept. 30, 1795 ("hard"), and Apr. 30, 1796, SKP, Folders 178, 183, and 189, HCA; S. Kirkland to the Harvard Corporation, May 1, 1799 ("the peculiar"), HGWAIP, Box 1, Folder 12, HUA.

13. Pilkington, ed., *Journals of Samuel Kirkland*, 290 ("The whole night"), 292–94 ("You have").

14. Ebenezer Caulkins to Israel Chapin, Dec. 26, 1792 ("absent"), and Feb. 23, 1793, HORC, VIII, NYHS.

15. Pilkington, ed., *Journals of Samuel Kirkland*, 269, 275 ("may add"); Oneida Chiefs to Timothy

Pickering, Jan. 29, 1794 ("Our father"), and Hendrick Aupaumut to Timothy Pickering, Jan. 30, 1794, TPP, LXII: 82A, 84A, MHS.

16. Oneida Chiefs to the Commissioners for Propagating the Gospel, Jan. 29, 1794 ("We believe" and "whether you"), SKP, Folder 164, HCA; Hendrick Aupaumut to Timothy Pickering, Jan. 30, 1794, TPP, LXII: 84A, MHS; Jeremy Belknap, "Notes on a Journey to Oneida," 1796, JBP, Reel 11, MHS; John Sergeant, Jr., to Peter Thacher, Mar. 12, 1794, SKP, Folder 166, MHS; Sergeant to Timothy Pickering, Jan. 3, 1795 ("faithfully"), TPP, LXII: 199A, MHS; Sergeant to Thacher, Aug. 22, 1796, DCA #796472, DCLSC.

17. Pilkington, ed., *Journals of Samuel Kirkland,* 223–24, 301, 312; [John McDonald], "Extract," Aug. 8, 1792, Massachusetts Historical Society, *Collections,* 1st Ser., I: 287–88; Pilkington, *Hamilton College,* 17–18 (McDonald quoted in John Kemp to Peter Thacher, Oct. 5, 1792: "I cannot"), 32–33, 39–41; Belknap, "Journal to Oneida," 394; John Kemp to Peter Thacher, Feb. 5, 1794, Thacher to the Oneida Chiefs, Apr. 25, 1794, and Jeremy Belknap, report, May 1, 1794, DCA #794155, #794275, and #794275, DCLSC; Kemp to Samuel Kirkland, Feb. 5, 1794, and Thacher to Kirkland, Apr. 11 and May 16, 1794, SKP, Folders 165, 167, and 168 HCA; Kirkland to John Thornton Kirkland, Dec. 5, 1798, SKP, Folder 207, HCA.

18. Samuel Kirkland to Peter Thacher, Mar. 13, 1794, SKP, Folder 166, HCA; Kirkland to Thacher, June 3, 1794, and Hendrick Aupaumut to Thacher, July 28, 1795, DCA #794353, DCLSC.

19. Belknap, "Journal to Oneida," 395, 418 ("the warm").

20. Pilkington, ed., *Journals of Samuel Kirkland,* 312–13 ("the *influence*"); J. T. Kirkland, "Answers to Queries," 73, 74 ("they shall be").

21. J. T. Kirkland, "Answers to Queries," 63; Philip Schuyler quoted in Jeremy Belknap, "Notes on a Journey to Oneida," 1796 ("They answered"), JBP, Reel 11, MHS; Belknap and Morse, "Report," 22–23.

22. Philip Schuyler quoted in Jeremy Belknap, "Notes on a Journey to Oneida," 1796 ("They allow"), JBP, Reel 11, MHS; Samuel Kirkland, diary, Aug. 6, 1803 ("perishing" and "an instance"), LFP, DCLSC.

23. Jeremy Belknap, "Notes on a Journey to Oneida," 1796 ("The Oneidas"), JBP, Reel 11, MHS; Belknap and Morse, "Report," 10, 16; Belknap, "Journal to Oneida," 411–14; J. T. Kirkland, "Answers to Queries," 72–73 ("Their villages"); Pilkington, ed.; *Journals of Samuel Kirkland,* 363.

24. J. T. Kirkland, "Answers to Queries," 71; Pilkington, ed., *Journals of Samuel Kirkland,* 312–13; Belknap and Morse, "Report," 11–13 ("never indulges"); Samuel Kirkland quoted in Jeremy Belknap, "Notes on a Journey to Oneida," 1796 ("If once"), JBP, Reel 11, MHS.

25. Rev. Asahel Norton, answers to queries, 1796 ("His new friends" and "the ridicule"), JBP, Reel 11, MHS; Belknap and Morse, "Report," 35–36.

26. John Sergeant, Jr., answers to queries, 1796 ("As an Independent"), and Samuel Kirkland, extract, in Jeremy Belknap, "Notes on a Journey to Oneida," 1796, JBP, Reel 11, MHS.

27. Belknap, "Journal to Oneida," 409 ("found him"); Peter Thacher to Samuel Kirkland, Sept. 3, 1796 ("groundless"), SKP, Folder 191, HCA.

28. John Kemp to Peter Thacher, Dec. 3, 1796, Thacher to Samuel Kirkland, Apr. 1, 1797, and Kemp to Thacher, Aug. 28, 1797 ("deeply disappointed"), DCA #796653, #797251, and #797478, DCLSC.; Samuel Kirkland to John Thornton Kirkland, Nov. 24, 1796, SKP, Folder 193, HCA; S. Kirkland to Thacher, May 2, 1797, SPGP, Box 3, Folder 3, PEI; Pilkington, ed., *Journals of Samuel Kirkland,* 300–301.

29. Pilkington, ed., *Journals of Samuel Kirkland,* 300–301 ("calculated").

30. Samuel Kirkland to George W. Kirkland, Aug. 14, 1789 ("their abuse"), and to John Thornton Kirkland, Jan. 11, 1796 ("delightful *task*"), SKP, Folders 117 and 187, HCA.

31. Patrick, "Life and Times of Samuel Kirkland," 525–27, 539–40; Dartmouth College Trustees and President, resolution, Aug. 23, 1790, DCA #792490, DCLSC; Pilkington, *Hamilton College*, 34; Samuel Kirkland to John T. Kirkland, Nov. 16, 1795, Jan. 16 ("George has") and Mar. 24, 1796, SKP, Folders 185 and 187, HCA; Pilkington, ed., *Journals of Samuel Kirkland*, 280.

32. Samuel Kirkland to John T. Kirkland, Mar. 24, 1796, and April 30, 1796, SKP, Folder 188, HCA. For the ubiquity of manic land speculation, see Royster, *Fabulous History of the Dismal Swamp Company*.

33. John T. Kirkland to George W. Kirkland, Oct. 14, 1796 ("Where are"), SKP, Folder 192, HCA; Thomas R. Gold to Samuel Kirkland, Nov. 25, 1796, SKP, Hamilton Oneida Academy Trustees Folder, HCA; Pilkington, *Hamilton College*, 35, 39–44; Belknap, "Journal to Oneida, 1796," 409; Dwight, *Travels in New England and New-York*, III: 129.

34. George Kirkland to Samuel Kirkland, Nov. 18, 1796 ("about to"), Dec. 31, 1796, and May 1, 1797 ("My usefulness" and "My enemies"), and S. Kirkland to John T. Kirkland, Aug. 5, 1797, SKP, Folder 193, 194, and 198, HCA.

35. Pilkington, ed., *Journals of Samuel Kirkland*, 280; Samuel Kirkland to John T. Kirkland, Oct. 31, 1797, SKP, Folder 202, HCA; George W. Kirkland to Peter Smith, Dec. 1, 1797 ("If I am"), PSmP, Box 1, SULSC; Patrick, "Life and Times of Samuel Kirkland," 559–60, 580–81, 594n75. For the military career, see Colonel William Smith to Hamilton, Mar. 5, 1800 ("few months"), in Syrett, ed., *Papers of Alexander Hamilton*, XXIV: 293 (see also XXII: 98 and XXIV: 295n5); Rosewell Welles to John Jenkins, Feb. 20, 1802, in R. J. Taylor, ed., *Susquehannah Company Papers*, XI: 295; Robinson, *Life of Miranda*, I: 299–320. Pilkington dates George's death to 1806, but Patrick argues for 1810.

36. Pilkington, ed., *Journals of Samuel Kirkland*, 280, 310; Samuel Kirkland to Oliver Phelps, Oct. 31, 1797, S. Kirkland to Charles and George Webster, May 30, 1798, and S. Kirkland to John T. Kirkland, Dec. 5, 1798 ("keeps me"), SKP, Folders 202, 204, and 207, HCA; George W. Kirkland to Peter Smith, Dec. 1, 1797, Thomas Herring to Smith, June 28, 1798, and S. Kirkland to Smith, Oct. 17, 1801, PSmP, Box 1, SULSC; S. Kirkland to Phelps, May 30, 1798, PGP, Box 59, NYSL.

37. Samuel Kirkland to John T. Kirkland, Oct. 31, 1797 ("sorest trial"), and Dec. 5, 1798 ("To be arrested"), SKP, Folder 202, HCA; Barent Sanders, journal, Aug. 31, 1800 ("I find"), NYHS.

38. Thomas Herring to Smith, June 28, 1798, and S. Kirkland to Smith, Oct. 17, 1801, PSmP, Box 1, SULSC; Judd, *More Lasting than Brass*, 83–87.

39. Pilkington, ed., *Journals of Samuel Kirkland*, 245 ("a tender"); John T. Kirkland to Samuel Kirkland, July 12, 1792 ("love" and "talents"), and S. Kirkland to O. Phelps, Aug. 18, 1792, PGP, Box 19, NYSL; Judd, *More Lasting than Brass*, 84–86; William Eustis to Aaron Burr, May 25, 1804 ("Please name"), in Kline, ed., *Political Correspondence and Public Papers of Aaron Burr*, II: 869.

40. Samuel Kirkland to Dr. Willard, n.d. [ca. Oct. 1802] ("indescribable affliction"), HGWAIP, Box 1, HUA; Thomas Herring to Peter Smith, Sept. 19, 1802, and Nov. 2, 1802 ("in perfect"), PSmP, Box 1, SULSC; Judd, *More Lasting than Brass*, 86–87; Patrick, "Life and Times of Samuel Kirkland," 580.

41. Samuel Kirkland to John T. Kirkland, July 15 and Aug. 6, 1797 ("Oh how"), SKP, Folders 197 and 198, HCA; Patrick, "Life and Times of Samuel Kirkland," 561, 567–68; Samuel Kirkland to Alexander Miller, May 24, and June 7, 1800, HGWAIP, Box 1, Folder 12, HUA; Pilkington, ed., *Journals of Samuel Kirkland*, 376–77; John T. Kirkland to Eliphalet Nott, Sept. 20,

1803, SKP, Folder 225, HCA; S. Kirkland, diary, July 10, 1802, and Apr. 2, 1806 ("*Martyrdom*"), LFP, DCLSC.

42. Samuel Kirkland, diary, June 23, 1805 ("black bug" and "This animal"), LFP, DCLSC; Patrick, "Life and Times of Samuel Kirkland," 579.

43. Samuel Kirkland to James Sullivan, Sept. 14, 1803, and Kirkland to Joseph Willard, Sept. 24, 1803, HGWAIP, Box 1, Folder 6, HUA; Northern Missionary Society, *Meeting . . . 1804*, 2.

44. Samuel Kirkland to John T. Kirkland, Aug. 6, 1797 ("May I trust"), S. Kirkland to Peter Thacher, Dec. 16, 1798, and S. Kirkland to J. T. Kirkland, Mar. 14, 1799, SKP, Folders 198, 207, and 208, HCA; S. Kirkland to the Harvard Corporation, May 1, 1799, and to Dr. Willard, n.d. [ca. Oct. 1802] ("trials"), HGWAIP, Box 1, Folder 12, HUA.

45. Pilkington, ed., *Journals of Samuel Kirkland*, 305–6 ("Alas!"), 308, 316.

46. John Sergeant, Jr., journal, Feb. 7, 1794 ("very industrious"), HUA; Pilkington, ed., *Journals of Samuel Kirkland*, 312, 315 ("a man"); Jones, *Annals and Recollections of Oneida County*, 865–66; Gridley, *History of the Town of Kirkland*, 46–48; Hauptman, *Conspiracy of Interests*, 42.

47. Pilkington, ed., *Journals of Samuel Kirkland*, 315; Embree et al., "Some Account of a Visit Paid to the Indians Situated on the Frontiers of the State of New York," VI (1853): 3; Skenandon quoted in Gridley, *History of the Town of Kirkland*, 47 ("Drink no"); Hauptman, *Conspiracy of Interests*, 43–44. Hauptman depicts Skenandon as Kirkland's passive dupe: "Whatever the missionary advised him to do, Skenandoah, the faithful son, complied." In fact, Skenandon was independent enough to sign the 1794 petition that denounced Kirkland's neglect. See Oneida Chiefs to the Commissioners for Propagating the Gospel, Jan. 29, 1794, SKP, Folder 164, HCA.

48. "The Six Nations," *Friends Review: A Religious, Literary, and Miscellaneous Journal*, V (1852), 501; Pilkington, ed., *Journals of Samuel Kirkland*, 314–15, 345–49; Campbell, ed., *Life and Writings of De Witt Clinton*, 188–89; Old Blacksmith quoted in Ripley, *Bank of Faith and Works*, 80 ("friendly"); Wallace, *The Death and Rebirth of the Seneca*, 272, 275–77.

49. Ripley, *Bank of Faith and Works United*, 112 ("acted," "Indian women" and "next woman"); Samuel Kirkland, diary, July 12, 1805 ("judicious") and July 18, 1805 ("much pleased"), LSP, DCLSC.

50. Pilkington, ed., *Journals of Samuel Kirkland*, 418 ("a mongrel breed").

51. Pilkington, ed., *Journals of Samuel Kirkland*, 359–60, 365, 373; Samuel Kirkland to Israel Chapin, Jr., Mar. 17, 1800, SKP, Folder 209, HCA; Ripley, *Bank of Faith and Works United*, 80–81. For the traditionalists numbering 250 and comprising a third of the Oneidas, see John Sergeant, Jr., to Solomon Williams, Nov. 20, 1805, Misc. MSS, NYHS.

52. Pilkington, ed., *Journals of Samuel Kirkland*, 359–60, 365; Samuel Kirkland to Israel Chapin, Jr., Mar. 17, 1800, SKP, Folder 209, HCA; Kirkland to Alexander Miller, May 24 ("serious" and "their feasts") and June 7, 1800 ("Most"), HGWAIP, Box 1, Folder 12, HUA.

53. Wallace, "Origins of the Longhouse Religion," 442–48; Wallace, *Death and Rebirth of the Seneca*, 277–85, 298–99; Samuel Kirkland, diary, Aug. 5, and 15, 1804, LFP, DCLSC; Pilkington, ed., *Journals of Samuel Kirkland*, 412–13, 418; Patrick, "Life and Times of Samuel Kirkland," 577.

54. Wallace, *Death and Rebirth of the Seneca*, 201, 236, 255–61; Samuel Kirkland, diary, Aug. 5 and 15, 1804, LFP, DCLSC; Ripley, *Bank of Faith and Works United*, 95; Jones, *Annals and Recollections of Oneida County*, 864. The latter mistakenly dates the killings to 1805.

55. Samuel Kirkland, diary, Mar. 26 ("exhorted") and 28 ("for blood"), and April 17 ("A general" and "most solemn"), 1804, Lothrop Family Papers, MHS.

56. Pilkington, *Journals of Samuel Kirkland*, 325, 328–38, 351–52, 354, 391–92.

57. James Kent, "Tour of the Western Circuit, 1798," June 8, 1798 ("The Oneidas"), JKP, Reel 6, Container 14, LC.

58. Andreani, "Travels of a Gentleman from Milan, 1790," 325 ("dark and dense"); James Kent, "Tour of the Western Circuit, 1798," June 8, 1798 ("The Forests"), JKP, Reel 6, Container 14, LC; Simon Desjardins et al., "Castorland Journal," Nov. 2, 1793 ("We can"), trans. and ed. Franklin B. Hough, 107–8, AAS.

59. Belknap, "Journal to Oneida," 412 ("Were the country"); Simon Desjardins et al., "Castorland Journal," Nov. 2, 1793 ("the best"), 107–8, AAS.

60. Simon Desjardins et al., "Castorland Journal," Nov. 2, 1793 ("The Indians"), 111, AAS; Coventry, *Memoirs of an Emigrant*, II: 756–57; James Kent, "Tour of the Western Circuit, 1798," June 8, 1798 ("one vast"), JKP, Reel 6, Container 14, LC.

61. James Kent, "Tour of the Western Circuit, 1798," June 8, 1798 ("The entrance" and "The Plains"), JKP, Reel 6, Container 14, LC; Simon Desjardins et al., "Castorland Journal," Nov. 2, and Nov. 4, 1793, 108, 111, AAS; Embree et al., "Some Account of a Visit Paid to the Indians Situated on the Frontiers of the State of New York," V (1852): 803 ("over a compass"); Andreani, "Travels of a Gentleman from Milan," 319.

62. Andreani, "Travels of a Gentleman from Milan," 323; Belknap, "Journal to Oneida," 411; J. T. Kirkland, "Answers to Queries," 71–72; Belknap, "Journal to Oneida," 411–12; Coventry, *Memoirs of an Emigrant*, I: 609; Simon Desjardins et al., "Castorland Journal," Nov. 2, 1793, 106–8, AAS; Ripley, *Bank of Faith and Works United*, 76 ("a good").

63. Coventry, *Memoirs of an Emigrant*, I: 756–57; James Kent, "Tour of the Western Circuit, 1798," June 8, 1798, JKP, Reel 6, Container 14, LC; Maude, *Visit to the Falls of Niagara*, 38 ("dress as").

64. Hough, ed., *Census of the State of New-York, for 1855*, xxi–xxv. For Oneida population, see Samuel Kirkland, "A Statement of the Number & Situation of the Six United Nations of Indians in North America," Oct. 15, 1791, Misc. Bound MSS, MHS; Kirkland to [Rev. Alexander Miller], June 7, 1800, HGWAIP, Box 1 (1770–1810), HUA.

65. "An Act Supplementary to the Act Entitled An Act for the Better Support of Oneida, Onondaga, and Cayuga Indians . . ." Apr. 1, 1796, [New York State], *Laws of the State of New York*, (1797), III: 310; Maude, *Visit to the Falls of Niagara*, 35; Benjamin De Witt, "A Sketch," Society for the Promotion of Useful Arts, *Transactions* (1807), 190 ("the contrast").

66. Maude, *Visit to the Falls of Niagara*, 35; Melish, *Travels Through the United States of America*, II: 382.

67. James Kent, "Tour of the Western Circuit, 1798," (1808 addendum: "alteration"), and "Western Circuit Journal, 1802" ("resembled"), JKP, Reel 6, Container 14, LC.

68. Campbell, ed., *Life and Writings of De Witt Clinton*, 185; Bigelow, *Journal of a Tour to Niagara Falls*, 21; Melish, *Travels Through the United States of America*, II: 381. For the populations of Lenox and Sullivan, see Hough, ed., *Census of the State of New-York for 1855*, xxiii.

69. Coventry, *Memoirs of an Emigrant*, I: 607 ("marked") and II: 1118.

70. Simeon DeWitt and Ezra L'Hommedieu, report, Jan. 13, 1802, A 1823 (Assembly Papers), XL (Indian Affairs, 1780–1809), NYSA; Oneida and Onondaga Chiefs to Congress, Feb. 13, 1802 ("we are" and "we Sepos"), PYMICR, Box 1, Quaker Coll., Haverford College.

71. Niemcewicz, "Journey to Niagara, 1805," 95 ("In front"); Grew, *Journal of a Tour from Boston*, 45; Bigelow, *Journal of a Tour to Niagara Falls*, 22–23; Ripley, *Bank of Faith and Works*, 75–77; Campbell, ed., *Life and Writings of De Witt Clinton*, 187–88; Wallace, ed., " 'From the Windows of the Mail Coach,' " 279–80. A rare exception was the Englishman Thomas Moore, who so disliked Americans that he praised Skenandon's intelligence and manners as a proof that "the savages are the only well-bred gentlemen in America." See Thomas Moore, *Memoirs, Journal, and Correspondence of Thomas Moore*, I: 168–69.

72. Pilkington, ed., *Journals of Samuel Kirkland*, 350 ("very peaceable"), 390–91 (Captain Peter quoted: "Whiteskins" and "I don't"); James Dean, answers to queries, 1796, Rev. Asahel Norton, answers to queries, 1796 ("very few exceptions"), JBP, Reel 11, MHS; Northern Missionary Society, *Annual Meeting . . . 1808*, 2–3.

73. "An Act Relative to the Unappropriated Lands of This State, to Prevent Intrusions, and for Other Purposes," Apr. 5, 1802, [New York State], *Laws of the State of New York . . . Twenty-Fifth Session*, 259–60. In 1802, state agents found squatters intruded prior to that year's cession on seventeen of the fifty-three lots within their surveys (including all seven of the lots directly on the highway). See Joseph Annin, "Field Book of the Purchase Made of the Oneida Nation of Indians in the Year . . . 1802," and Charles Brodhead, "A Survey of Part of the Lands Purchased from the Oneida Indians in 1802 Lying Along the North Side of the Seneca Turnpike Road," May 1805, in A 4019 (Records of the Surveyor General, Field Books), XIII, NYSA.

74. Grew, *Journal of a Tour from Boston*, 43; Schultz, *Travels on an Inland Voyage*, 22; Ann Mifflin, journal, 15–17 ("Their sale"), HSP; Erastus Granger to Henry Dearborn, Oct. 12, 1805, Granger Papers, Buffalo and Erie County Historical Society, Buffalo, N.Y.; Wallace, *Death and Rebirth of the Seneca*, 199–201.

75. Skenandon quoted in Pilkington, ed., *Journals of Samuel Kirkland*, 385 ("drank" and "not only").

76. Samuel Kirkland, diary, Jan. 24, 1805, LFP, DCLSC; Report of the Surveyor General, n.d. [ca. Jan. 1810] ("that the white people"), A 4016 (Records of the Surveyor General), 2nd Ser., XXIV: 138, NYSA.

77. Blacksmith quoted in Ripley, *Bank of Faith and Works United*, 81 ("thought").

78. Pilkington, ed., *Journals of Samuel Kirkland*, 382–87; Samuel Kirkland, diary, Feb. 11 and Aug. 6, 1803, July 10, 1805, and Aug. 1, 1806 ("Many of them"), LFP, DCSCL; Oneida South Party to Gov. Daniel D. Tompkins, Jan. 30, 1810, A 4016 (Records of the Surveyor General), 2nd Ser., XXIV: 150, NYSA.

79. Oneida South Party to Gov. Daniel D. Tompkins, Jan. 30, 1810, A 4016 (Records of the Surveyor General) 2nd Ser., XXIV: 150, NYSA; Tompkins to the State Legislature, Feb. 20, 1813, in Hastings, ed., *Public Papers of Daniel D. Tompkins*, III: 260–61; Tiro, "People of the Standing Stone," 207–8.

80. Oneida Chiefs and Warriors to Gov. George Clinton, n.d. [ca. Feb. 1803], A 1823 (New York State Assembly Papers), XL (Indian Papers, 1783–1809): 349, NYSA. For the partition, see Pilkington, ed., *Journals of Samuel Kirkland*, 399, 415; Samuel Kirkland, diary, Jan. 24 and Apr. 20, 1805, LFP, DCSCL; Oneida Chiefs to Gov. Morgan Lewis, Jan. 24, 1805, SKP, Folio 235, HCA; Oneida Christian Party and Pagan Party, treaty, Mar. 21, 1805, in [New York State], *Report of the Special Committee to Investigate the Indian Problem of the State of New York*, 259–61.

81. On March 13, 1807, the Christian Party sold over 14,000 acres to the state at $.75 per acre to procure $600 down and a $644.86 boost to their annuity, but the deal also set aside 1,144 acres for Angel De Ferriere, who had conducted the chiefs to Albany, and another 20 acres for Zaccheus P. Gillett. See Oneida Christian Party Treaty, Mar. 13, 1807, in [New York State], *Report of the Special Committee to Investigate the Indian Problem of the State of New York*, 263–69. Because the annuity was pegged at 6 percent of the principal value, the $10,750, at $.75 per acre, meant a cession of 14,333 acres. On February 16, 1809 the Christian Party sold its Fish Creek lands (7,500 acres) for $.50 per acre, reserving 300 acres for the merchant Abraham Van Eps "being in full for all his demands against the said Christian Party and of every individual belonging to the Same to this day." The Christian Party threw in another 400 acres for De Ferriere along the coveted Genesee turnpike. For this deal, the Christian

Party got unspecified debt relief from Van Eps and De Ferriere, as well as $600 immediately, another $1,000 in June, and a $120 boost to the annuity. Five days later, the Pagan Party made its own bad deal with the state, forsaking 11,681 acres east of Oneida Creek and north of Mud Creek for $1,000 down and a 6 percent annuity on the principal value calculated at $.56 per acre. In both cases, state payments to prominent Christian chiefs greased the deals: $80 each to Lewis Denny, Jr., Jacob Dockstader, Cornelius Dockstader, Skenandon, and Martinus; $70 for Henry Platcop, Captain Peter, and Queder Tolanoget; $10 each to Paulus and Nicholas Sharp. The state also paid Zaccheus P. Gillett $50 for his "services." For the 1809 transactions, see Oneida Christian Party Treaty, Feb. 16, 1809, and Oneida Pagan Party Treaty, Feb. 21, 1809, in [New York State], *Report of the Special Committee to Investigate the Indian Problem of the State of New York*, 266–72. For the private payments, see Daniel D. Tompkins, receipts, Feb. 1809, A 0832 (State Comptrollers' Indian Annuity Claims, Receipts, and Related Documents), Box 4, Folder 5, NYSA. For the dimensions of the Pagan cession, see James Geddes, "Field Book of the First Pagan Purchase," Nov. and Dec. 1809, A 4019 (Surveyor General's Office, Field Books), Vol. 0, NYSA.

82. Oneida Christian Party to Gov. Daniel D. Tompkins, Feb. 1, 1810 ("number of" and "But at last"), A 4016 (Records of the Surveyor General) 2nd Ser., XXIV: 138, NYSA. The missionary Rev. William Jenkins, who had succeeded the late Samuel Kirkland, witnessed this petition and it is probably written in his hand.

83. The Oneidas received $11,500 in 1785 at the Treaty of Fort Herkimer; another $5,500 at the Treaty of Fort Schuyler in 1788; plus $600 in annuities for seven years, 1789–95 ($4,200); another $2,952 paid down in the 1795 Treaty of Albany, which also raised the annuity to $3,552, so that the Oneidas received $10,656 in annuity during the three years 1796–1798. Another sale in 1799 garnered $500 and increased the annuity to $4,252, so that the Oneidas received another $8,504 during the two years 1799 and 1800. That makes for a grand total of $21,852 for 1785–1800. See Proceedings, June 29, 1785, and Treaty of Fort Schuyler, Sept. 22, 1788, in Hough, ed., *Proceedings of the Commissioners*, I: 108, 242–43; [New York State], *Report of Special Committee to Investigate the Indian Problem of the State of New York*, 241–52. For the real estate valuations for Chenango ($2,203,510), Herkimer ($1,550,704), and Oneida ($5,149,988) counties, see [New York State], *Journal of the Assembly of the State of New-York, At their Twenty-Fourth Session . . . 1800*, Appendix A.

84. Morse, *Report to the Secretary of War*, App., p. 89 ("are so far"); and Rev. John Sergeant, Jr., to Rev. Jedediah Morse, Mar. 30, 1818, in ibid., App., p. 113 ("They buy").

85. Belknap and Morse, "Report," 32–33; Pilkington, ed., *Journals of Samuel Kirkland*, 311 ("flocked" and "It was").

86. Pilkington, ed., *Journals of Samuel Kirkland*, 305, 311, 316 ("The State" and "Civilization"); John Jay to Peter Thacher, Apr. 25, 1797, DCA #797275, DCLSC; Patrick, "The Life and Times of Samuel Kirkland," 573–74.

87. Hauptman, *Conspiracy of Interests*, 58–81.

88. Pilkington, ed., *Journals of Samuel Kirkland*, 305, 311, 316; Hendrick Aupaumut, speech, July 24, 1795 ("For every time"), in George Embree et al., "Some Account of a Visit Paid to the Indians Situated on the Frontiers of the State of New York," VI (1853): 20; Knapp, *Life of Thomas Eddy*, 112–14; Mohican, Tuscarora, and Oneida Chiefs to the New York State Legislature, Feb. 4, 1799 ("We united"), and Mohican Chiefs to the legislature, Jan. 21, 1800, in A 1823 (Assembly Papers), XL (Indian Affairs, 1783–1809): 323–24, 331, NYSA; John Sergeant, Jr., journal, Feb. 20, 1800, and Samuel Kirkland to Alexander Miller, May 24, 1800, HGWAIP, Box 1, Folder 12, HUA; [New York State], *Laws of the State of New York* (1887), IV: 573.

89. Samuel Kirkland to Alexander Miller, May 24, 1800 ("Skenendon's life"), HGWAIP, Box 1, Folder 12, HUA; Myndert Wemple et al. to the New York State Legislature, Jan. 16, 1802 ("has Created"), and Oneida petition to Governor George Clinton, n.d. [ca. Feb. 1802] ("We are able"), in A 1823 (Assembly Papers), XL (Indian Affairs, 1783–1809): 353, 355, NYSA; Ripley, *Bank of Faith and Works*, 87. The legislature renewed the law in 1813. See [New York State], *Laws of the State of New York . . . Thirty-Sixth Session* (1813), 153–54.

90. Ripley, *Bank of Faith and Works*, 104–6 ("very solemn," "remarked" and "if thou").

91. Samuel Kirkland, diary, Nov. 28 and Dec. 11, 1803, and Apr. 2, 1806 ("wavering"), LFP, DCLSC; Pilkington, ed., *Journals of Samuel Kirkland*, 391–99.

92. Oneida petition, n.d. [ca. 1805] ("We need"), SKP, Folder of Kirkland Papers from the Library of Thornton K. Lothrop, HCA.

93. Pilkington, ed., *Journals of Samuel Kirkland*, 375 ("I know"); Oneida Chiefs, speech, May 2, 1802, SKP, Folder 216, HCA; Samuel Kirkland, diary, July 10, 1802, LFP, DCLSC.

94. Pilkington, ed., *Journals of Samuel Kirkland*, 419–20; Patrick, "Life and Times of Samuel Kirkland," 581; Samuel Kirkland, diary, Apr. 2, 1806 ("I love"), LFP, DCLSC.

EPILOGUE: SARAH AINSE

1. Hamil, "Sally Ainse, Fur Trader," 5; John Clarke, "Sarah Ainse," *DCB*, VI: 7–9. A dubious theory attributes her last name to marriage to a French-Canadian interpreter, Joseph Ainse of Michilimackinac; if she ever did cohabit with Ainse, it was so short-lived (limited to part of 1774) that his last name was unlikely to endure as hers in subsequent decades.

2. For Ainse's Conoy connection, see Merrell, *Into the American Woods*, 346n72. For her service as an interpreter of Conoy, see Indian Journal, Mar. 11, 1757, *PSWJ*, IX: 633–34. For the Conoys, see Feest, "Nanticoke and Neighboring Tribes," 240–52. For her relationship to Skenandon, who was related to Brant's first two wives, see Pilkington, ed., *Journals of Samuel Kirkland*, 34. For her identification as an Ojibwa, see Harring, *White Man's Law*, 306n2; Skenandon was originally a Conestoga adopted by the Oneida. For Skenandon, see Hauptman, *Conspiracy of Interests*, 42. For her late-life claim to be an Oneida, see Sarah Ainse to Francis Gore, July 9, 1808, RG 5 A 1 (Upper Canada Civil Secretary's Sundries), VIII: 3298, NAC. For the fluidity of native identities, see White, " 'Although I am dead, I am not entirely dead. I have left a second of myself,' " 404–18; and Hirsch, "Indian, *Metis*, and Euro-American Women on Multiple Frontiers," 66–67.

3. Hamil, "Sally Ainse," 4; Linda Sabathy-Judd, ed., *Moravians in Upper Canada*, 159 ("She understands").

4. Hamil, *Valley of the Lower Thames*, 14; Hamil, "Sally Ainse," 4. For Madame and Andrew Montour, see Darlington, ed., *Christopher Gist's Journals*, 159–75; Hagedorn, " 'Faithful, Knowing, and Prudent,' " 44–60; Hirsch, "The 'Celebrated Madame Montour,' " 81–112; Lewin, "A Frontier Diplomat: Andrew Montour," 153–86; Merrell, " 'The Cast of His Countenance,' " 13–39; Merrell, *Into the American Woods*, 54–56, 69–71, 75–77; Wallace, *Conrad Weiser*, 139–40, 339–40, 371–72.

5. Merrell, " 'The Cast of His Countenance,' " 29–34; Conrad Weiser to Richard Peters, Sept. 13, 1754 ("Says" and "Stocking"), in Wallace, *Conrad Weiser*, 371; Merrell, *Into the American Woods*, 298–300.

6. Hamil, *Valley of the Thames*, 14; Hamil, "Sally Ainse," 4, 20; Richard Peters to Richard Hockley, Feb. 6, 1753 ("Andrew"), *PMHB*, XXXIX (1915): 239; Merrell, *Into the American Woods*, 99–100; Hagedorn, "Andrew Montour," 48, 58; Thomas Butler to Sir William Johnson,

Apr. 3, 1757, *PSWJ*, IX: 661. For Montour's death, see Lewin, "Andrew Montour," 186. Sarah had Nicholas baptized in the Dutch church at Albany on October 31, 1756.

7. Hamil, "Sally Ainse," 4; Pilkington, ed., *Journals of Samuel Kirkland*, 34. For Indian women as traders, see Hirsch, "Indian, *Metis*, and Euro-American Women," 72–75.

8. Sally Ainse quoted in Hamil, *Valley of the Lower Thames*, 14 ("being" and "requested"); Nicholasera, speech, Aug. 12, 1762 ("Sarah Montour"), *PSWJ*, X: 480–81; Oneida sachems, memorandum, July 10, 1793, #22693, HL.

9. Oneida sachems, memorandum, July 10, 1793, #22693, HL. For Johnson's help in procuring the Oneida title to lands around Fort Stanwix, see Sir William Johnson to Henry White, Aug. 18, 1772, William Leland Thompson Coll., Box 1, Albany Institute; New York Council, minutes, Aug. 21, 1772, and Jelles Fonda, affidavit, July 18, 1785, A 0272 (Indorsed Land Papers, Office of the Secretary of State), XXXIX: 58, 60; Nelson, *William Tryon and the Course of Empire*, 109.

10. Hamil, *Valley of the Lower Thames*, 14; Benjamin Roberts to Sir William Johnson, Dec. 24, 1766, MG 19 F 35 (PSGIA), 1st Ser., Lot #651, NAC; Hamil, "Sally Ainse," 6, 12; Clarke, "Sarah Ainse," 8.

11. Chippewa Chiefs, speech, July 13, 1791 ("their sister" and "she had"), RG 5 A 1 (Upper Canada Civil Secretary's Sundries), VIII: 3259, 3260, 3262, NAC.

12. Good Peter, speech, Sept. 22, 1788, in Hough, ed., *Proceedings of the Commissioners*, I: 239; Oneida sachems, memorandum, July 10, 1793, #22693, HL; Hamil, "Sally Ainse," 8–9 (Ainse quoted: "her friends"); Sarah Montour (Ainse) to Skenandon, Apr. 19, 1794, SKP, Folder 167, HCA. For Skenandon's temptation to move to Upper Canada, see Samuel Kirkland to Pickering, Dec. 8, 1794, TPP, LXII: 119–20, MHS.

13. Coventry, *Memoirs of an Emigrant*, I: 859 ("Going down").

14. Hamil, "Sally Ainse," 7–9 (Ainse quoted: "one Indian"); Hamil, *Valley of the Lower Thames*, 22–23; Alexander McKee to David W. Smith, Mar. 30, 1792, Hesse District Land Board, minutes, Apr. 6, 1792, and Chippewa Chiefs, speech, July 13, 1791, RG 5 A 1 (Upper Canada Civil Secretary's Sundries), VIII: 3259, 3260, 3262, NAC.

15. E. B. Littlehales to Detroit Land Board, Oct. 23, 1792, Littlehales to Col. Richard England, Nov. 14, 1792, and Detroit Land Board to Upper Canada Executive Council, Aug. 23, 1792 RG 5 A 1 (Upper Canada Civil Secretary's Sundries), VIII: 3270, 3271, 3272–73, NAC; R. England to David W. Smith, Nov. 4, 1792 ("occasion"), RG 1 (Crown Lands), A-I-1 (Letters Received by the Surveyor General), L: 640, AO; Hamil, "Sally Ainse," 9–11.

16. John Graves Simcoe to David W. Smith, July 25, 1793 ("I am"), RG 1 (Crown Lands), A-I-1 (Letters Received by the Surveyor General), XLIX: 189, AO; E. B. Littlehales to David W. Smith, Nov. 3, 1793, in Cruikshank, ed., *Correspondence of Simcoe*, IV: 356–57; Patrick McNiff to Richard England, Dec. 5, 1793 ("I do not"), RG 5 A 1 (Upper Canada Civil Secretary's Sundries), VIII: 3282, NAC.

17. Sarah Ainse to David W. Smith, Mar. 26, 1794 ("Though I am"), RG 5 A 1 (Upper Canada Civil Secretary's Sundries), VIII: 3282–83, NAC. For Smith's covert support for the intruders on Ainse's land, see Richard England to Smith, Nov. 4, 1792, RG 1 (Crown Lands), A-I-1 (Letters Received by the Surveyor General), L, 540, AO; Isaac Dolson to Smith, Jan. 6, 1795, and John Dodemead to Smith, Nov. 5, 1795, RG 1 (Crown Lands), A-I-6 (Letters Received by the Surveyor General), Reel #563/1, pp. 421, 588, AO.

18. Joseph Brant to E. B. Littlehales, Sept. 21, 1794, MG 23 H-I-1 (Simcoe Transcripts), 4th Ser., VI, Folder A 17, NAC; Brant to Alexander McKee, Jan. 14, 1795, Sarah Ainse to Aguishua, Jan. 26, 1795, Ainse to Brant, Feb. 5, 1795, Brant to Joseph Chew, Feb. 24, 1795, Chew to

Thomas Aston Coffin, Mar. 26, 1795, Brant to John Butler, June 28, 1795, and Grand River Chiefs, speech, July 13, 1795, in Cruikshank, ed., *Correspondence of Simcoe*, III: 258, 274, 287–88, 310, IV: 33, 43; Brant to David W. Smith, Apr. 3, 1796 ("You very well"), in Cruikshank, ed., *Correspondence of Russell*, I: 2.

19. Joseph Chew to Thomas Aston Coffin, Mar. 26, 1795, Lord Dorchester to John Graves Simcoe, Nov. 5, 1795 ("opened"), and E. B. Littlehales to Joseph Brant, Apr. 8, 1796, in Cruikshank, ed., *Correspondence of Simcoe*, III: 334, IV: 126, 238; Hamil, "Sally Ainse," 15–16; Sarah Ainse to Brant, Feb. 20, 1796, MG 23 H-I-1 (Simcoe Transcripts), III, Folder Zz, p. 20, NAC; Executive Council, minutes, Apr. 9, 1798, in Cruikshank, ed., *Correspondence of Russell*, II: 137; Hamil, "Sally Ainse," 17–18.

20. Sabathy-Judd, ed., *Moravians in Upper Canada*, 159 ("She came"); John Askin quoted in Hamil, "Sally Ainse," 18 ("I don't").

21. Sabathy-Judd, ed., *Moravians in Upper Canada*, 159 ("She visited"), 220; Zeisberger, *Diary*, II: 148–49.

22. Nathan Bangs quoted in Stevens, *Life and Times of Nathan Bangs*, 138 ("in the house"); Sabathy-Judd, ed., *Moravians in Upper Canada*, 297 ("very old").

23. Chewitt & Ridout, report, Aug. 10, 1808, and Sarah Ainse to Francis Gore, July 9, 1808, RG 5 A 1 (Upper Canada Civil Secretary's Sundries), VIII: 3254, 3298, NAC; Hamil, "Sally Ainse," 18–20.

24. Samuel Kirkland, undated memorandum regarding Peter Penet ("The Indians"), SKP, "Letters Undated and Fragmentary" File, HCA.

25. Hinderaker, *Elusive Empires*, 267; White, *The Middle Ground*, 518–23; Benn, *Iroquois in the War of 1812*, 123–73.

26. Countryman, "Indians, the Colonial Order, and the Social Significance of the American Revolution," 357–59.

27. Good Peter, interview with Timothy Pickering, April n.d., 1792 ("Brother"), TPP, LX: 121–22, MHS.

28. Smith, "The INS and the Singular Status of North American Indians," 131–54; Jolene Rickard, "The Indian Defense League of America," *Akwesasne Notes*, I, No. 2 (1995): 48–54 ("sense of freedom" on 53). I am grateful to Steven Paul McSloy for directing me to these sources. For contemporary boundary and identity issues on a continental scale, see DePalma, *Here*, especially 139–63, 281–87.

Bibliography

Abbott, W. W., et al., eds. *The Papers of George Washington, Presidential Series.* 12 vols. to date. Charlottesville: University of Virginia Press, 1987–.

Abler, Thomas S., ed. *Chainbreaker: The Revolutionary War Memoirs of Governor Blacksnake.* Lincoln: University of Nebraska Press, 1989.

Adelman, Jeremy, and Stephen Aron. "From Borderlands to Borders: Empires, Nation-States, and the Peoples in Between in North American History." *American Historical Review,* CIV (June 1999): 814–41.

———. "Of Lively Exchanges and Larger Perspectives." *American Historical Review,* CIV (Oct. 1999): 1235–39.

Aikins [*sic*; Askins], Charles. "Journal of a Journey from Sandwich to York in the Summer of 1806." Ontario Historical Society, *Papers and Records,* VI (1905): 15–20.

Albers, Patricia, and Jeanne Kay. "Sharing the Land: A Study in American Indian Territoriality." In Thomas E. Ross and Tyrel G. Moore, eds., *A Cultural Geography of North American Indians,* 47–92. Boulder, Colo.: Westview Press, 1987.

Alexander, Edward P. *A Revolutionary Conservative: James Duane of New York.* New York: Columbia University Press, 1938.

Allen, Orlando. "Personal Recollections of Captains Jones and Parrish." Buffalo Historical Society, *Publications,* VI (1903): 539–42.

Allen, Robert S. *His Majesty's Indian Allies: British Indian Policy in the Defence of Canada, 1774–1815.* Toronto: Dundurn Press, 1992.

American State Papers: Documents, Legislative and Executive, of the Congress of the United States, Class II: Indian Affairs. 2 vols. Washington, D.C.: Gales & Seaton, 1832.

Anderson, Benedict. *Imagined Communities: Reflections on the Origins and Spread of Nationalism.* London: Verso, 1983.

Anderson, Fred. *Crucible of War: The Seven Years' War and the Fate of Empire in British North America, 1754–1766.* New York: Knopf, 2000.

Andreani, Paolo. "Travels of a Gentleman from Milan, 1790." In Dean R. Snow, Charles T. Gehring, and William A. Starna, eds., *In Mohawk Country: Early Narratives About a Native People,* 318–33. Syracuse, N.Y.: Syracuse University Press, 1996.

Anonymous. "Canadian Letters: Description of a Tour thro' the Provinces of Lower and Upper Canada in the Course of the Years 1792 and '93." *Canadian Antiquarian and Numismatic Journal,* 3rd ser., IX (July–Oct. 1912): 85–168.

———. *Columbia County at the End of the Century.* 2 vols. Hudson, N.Y.: Record Printing & Publishing Co., 1900.

―――. "Extract," Aug. 8, 1792. Massachusetts Historical Society, *Collections*, 1st ser., I: 285.

Aquila, Richard. *The Iroquois Restoration: Iroquois Diplomacy on the Colonial Frontier, 1701–1754.* Detroit: Wayne State University Press, 1983.

Axtell, James. *The Invasion Within: The Contest of Cultures in Colonial North America.* New York: Oxford University Press, 1985.

―――. "The White Indians of Colonial America." *William and Mary Quarterly*, 3rd. ser., XXXII (Jan. 1975): 55–88.

Bagg, Moses M. *The Pioneers of Utica.* Utica, N.Y.: Curtiss & Childs, 1877.

Beauchamp, William M. *Aboriginal Place Names of New York.* Albany: New York State Education Department, 1907.

Belknap, Jeremy. "Journal to Oneida, 1796." Massachusetts Historical Society, *Proceedings*, XIX (1881–82): 393–423.

Belknap, Jeremy, and Jedediah Morse. "Report on the Oneida, Stockbridge, and Brotherton Indians, 1796." *Indian Notes and Monographs*, no. 54 (1955): 1–39.

Ben-Atar, Doron, and Barbara Oberg, eds. *Federalists Reconsidered.* Charlottesville: University of Virginia Press, 1998.

Benn, Carl. *The Iroquois in the War of 1812.* Toronto: University of Toronto Press, 1998.

Bigelow, Timothy. *Journal of a Tour to Niagara Falls in the Year 1805.* Boston: John Wilson & Co., 1876.

Billington, Ray A. "The Fort Stanwix Treaty of 1768." *New York History*, XXV (Apr. 1944): 182–94.

Bingham, Robert W. *The Cradle of the Queen City: A History of Buffalo to the Incorporation of the City.* Buffalo: Buffalo Historical Society, 1931.

―――. ed. *Reports of Joseph Ellicott.* 2 vols. Buffalo: Buffalo Historical Society, 1937, 1941.

Blau, Harold; Jack Campisi; and Elisabeth Tooker. "Onondaga." In Bruce G. Trigger, ed., *Handbook of North American Indians, XV: Northeast*, 491–99. Washington, D.C.: Smithsonian Institution, 1978.

Blodgett, Harold W. *Samson Occom.* Hanover, N.H.: Dartmouth College Publications, 1935.

Bond, C. C. J. "The British Base at Carleton Island." *Ontario History*, LII (Mar. 1960): 1–16.

Bonomi, Patricia U. *A Factious People: Politics and Society in Colonial New York.* New York: Columbia University Press, 1971.

Borrows, John. "Wampum at Niagara: The Royal Proclamation, Canadian Legal History, and Self-Government." In Michael Asche, ed., *Aboriginal and Treaty Rights in Canada: Essays on Law, Equity, and Respect for Difference*, 155–72. Vancouver: University of British Columbia Press, 1997.

Bouton, Terry. "A Road Closed: Rural Insurgency in Post-Independence Pennsylvania." *Journal of American History*, LXXXVII (Dec. 2000): 855–87.

Boyd, Julian P. "Attempts to Form New States in New York and Pennsylvania, 1786–1796." New York State Historical Association, *Quarterly Journal* XII (July 1931): 257–70.

―――, ed. *The Susquehannah Company Papers.* 4 vols. Ithaca, N.Y.: Cornell University Press, 1962.

Boyd, Julian P., et al., eds. *The Papers of Thomas Jefferson.* 30 vols. to date. Princeton, N.J.: Princeton University Press, 1950–.

Brissot de Warville, J. P. *New Travels in the United States of America, 1788.* Cambridge, Mass.: Harvard University Press, 1994.

Brymner, Douglas, ed. "Note A—Indian Lands on the Grand River." *Report on Canadian Archives, 1896*, 1–23. Ottawa: S. E. Dawson, 1897.

―――, ed. "Political State of Upper Canada in 1806–7." *Report on Canadian Archives, 1892*, 32–135. Ottawa: S. E. Dawson, 1893.

―――, ed., *Report on Canadian Archives, 1896.* Ottawa: S. E. Dawson, 1897.

Burnett, Edmund C., ed. *Letters of Members of the Continental Congress.* 8 vols. Washington, D.C.: U.S. Government Printing Office, 1921–36.

Burt, Alfred Leroy. *The United States, Great Britain, and British North America from the Revolution to the Establishment of Peace After the War of 1812.* New Haven, Conn.: Yale University Press, 1940.

Bushman, Richard L. *King and People in Provincial Massachusetts.* Chapel Hill: University of North Carolina Press, 1992.

Calloway, Colin G. *The American Revolution in Indian Country: Crisis and Diversity in Native American Communities.* New York: Cambridge University Press, 1995.

———. *Crown and Calumet: British-Indian Relations, 1783–1815.* Norman: University of Oklahoma Press, 1987.

Cameron, Kenneth Walter, ed., *The Papers of Loyalist Samuel Peters. . . .* Hartford: Transcendental Books, 1978.

Campbell, Patrick. *Travels in the Interior Inhabited Parts of North America in the Years 1791 and 1792.* Edited by H. H. Langton. Toronto: Champlain Society, 1937.

Campbell, William W. *Annals of Tryon County; or, the Border Warfare of New York, During the Revolution.* New York: Dodd, Mead, & Co., 1924, reprint of 1831 original.

———, ed. *The Life and Writings of De Witt Clinton.* New York: Baker & Scribner, 1849.

Campisi, Jack. "From Stanwix to Canandaigua: National Policy, States' Rights, and Indian Land." In Christopher Vecsey and William A. Starna, eds., *Iroquois Land Claims,* 49–65. Syracuse, N.Y.: Syracuse University Press, 1988.

———. "Fur Trade and Factionalism of the Eighteenth-Century Oneida Indians." In Nancy Bonvillain, ed., *Studies on Iroquoian Culture,* 37–46. Rindge, N.H.: Man in the Northeast, Occasional Publications No. 6, 1980.

———. "The Iroquois and the Euro-American Concept of a Tribe." *New York History,* LXXVIII (Oct. 1997): 455–72.

———. "Oneida." In Bruce G. Trigger, ed., *Handbook of North American Indians, Volume 15: Northeast,* 481–90. Washington, D.C.: Smithsonian Institution, 1978.

———. "The Oneida Treaty Period, 1783–1838." In Campisi and Laurence M. Hauptman, eds., *The Oneida Indian Experience: Two Perspectives,* 48–64. Syracuse, N.Y.: Syracuse University Press, 1988.

Campisi, Jack, and Richard Chrisjohn, eds. "Two Eighteenth-Century Oneida Letters." In Marianne Mithun and Hanni Woodbury, eds., *Northern Iroquoian Texts,* 41–42. Chicago: University of Chicago Press, 1980.

Caniff, William. *History of the Settlement of Upper Canada with Special Reference to the Bay of Quinte.* Toronto, 1869.

Carroll, John. *Case and His Contemporaries; or, The Canadian Itinerants' Memorial.* 2 vols. Toronto: Samuel Rose, 1867.

Carter, Clarence Edwin, ed. *The Correspondence of General Thomas Gage with the Secretaries of State, 1763–1775.* 2 vols. New Haven, Conn.: Yale University Press, 1931.

Carter, Clarence Edwin, ed. *The Territorial Papers of the United States.* 28 vols. Washington, D.C.: U.S. Government Printing Office, 1934–75.

Cartwright, Conway E., ed. *Life and Letters of the Late Hon. Richard Cartwright.* Toronto: Belford Brothers, 1876.

[Cartwright, Richard]. *Letters from an American Loyalist in Upper Canada to His Friend in England. . . .* Kingston: n.d. [ca. 1810].

Castiglioni, Luigi. *Viaggio: Travels in the United States of North America, 1785–87.* Edited by Antonio Pace. Syracuse, N.Y.: Syracuse University Press, 1983.

Cayton, Andrew R. L. *The Frontier Republic: Ideology and Politics in the Ohio Country, 1780–1825.* Kent, Ohio: Kent State University Press, 1986.

————. "Radicals in the 'Western World': The Federalist Conquest of Trans-Appalachian North America." In Doron Ben-Atar and Barbara Oberg, eds., *Federalists Reconsidered*, 77–96. Charlottesville: University of Virginia Press, 1998.

Chase, Eugene Parker, ed. *Our Revolutionary Forefathers: The Letters of François, Marquis de Barbé-Marbois, 1779–1785*. Freeport, N.Y.: Books for Libraries Press, 1929.

Chase, Frederick. *A History of Dartmouth College and the Town of Hanover, New Hampshire*. 2 vols. Cambridge, Mass.: John Wilson & Son, 1891.

Chastellux, Marquis de. "Visit to Schenectady, 1780." In Dean R. Snow, Charles T. Gehring, and William A. Starna, eds., *In Mohawk Country: Early Narratives About a Native People*, 292–94. Syracuse, N.Y.: Syracuse University Press, 1996.

Chernow, Barbara Ann. *Robert Morris: Land Speculator, 1790–1801*. New York: Arno Press, 1978.

Clayton, Daniel W. *Islands of Truth: The Imperial Fashioning of Vancouver Island*. Vancouver, B.C.: UBC Press, 2000.

Clinton, DeWitt. *Discourse Delivered Before the New-York Historical Society, at Their Anniversary Meeting, 6th December 1811*. New York: James Eastburn, 1812.

Cochran, Thomas C. *New York in the Confederation: An Economic Study*. Philadelphia: University of Pennsylvania Press, 1932.

Colgate, William, ed. "The Diary of John White, First Attorney General of Upper Canada (1791–1800)." *Ontario History*, XLVII (Autumn 1955): 147–70.

Colley, Linda. *Captives: Britain, Empire, and the World, 1600–1850*. London: Jonathan Cope, 2002.

Colt, Judah. "Judah Colt's Narrative." Buffalo Historical Society, *Publications*, VII (1904): 331–59.

Combs, Jerald A. *The Jay Treaty: Political Battleground of the Founding Fathers*. Berkeley: University of California Press, 1970.

Cometti, Elizabeth, ed. *The American Journals of Lt. John Enys*. Syracuse, N.Y.: Syracuse University Press, 1976.

Countryman, Edward. *The American Revolution*. New York: Hill & Wang, 1985.

————. "Indians, the Colonial Order, and the Social Significance of the American Revolution." *William and Mary Quarterly*, 3rd ser., LIII (April, 1996): 342–62.

————. *A People in Revolution: The American Revolution and Political Society in New York, 1760–1790*. Baltimore: Johns Hopkins University Press, 1981.

Coventry, Alexander. *Memoirs of an Emigrant: The Journal of Alexander Coventry, M.D.* 2 vols. Albany, N.Y.: Albany Institute, 1978.

Craig, Gerald M. *Upper Canada: The Formative Years, 1784–1841*. Toronto: McClelland & Stewart, 1963.

Craig, Neville B., ed. *The Olden Time*. 2 vols. Pittsburgh: Wright & Charlton, 1848.

Cronon, William. *Changes in the Land: Indians, Colonists, and the Ecology of New England*. New York: Hill & Wang, 1983.

Cruikshank, E. A. "Coming of the Loyalist Mohawks to the Bay of Quinte." Ontario Historical Society, *Papers and Records*, XXVI (1930): 390–403.

————, ed. *The Correspondence of the Honourable Peter Russell*. 3 vols. Toronto: Ontario Historical Society, 1932–36.

————, ed. *The Correspondence of Lieut. Governor John Graves Simcoe, with Allied Documents Relating to His Administration of the Government of Upper Canada*. 5 vols. Toronto: Ontario Historical Society, 1923–31.

————, ed. *Documentary History of the Campaign on the Niagara Frontier in 1812*. Welland, Ont.: Lundy's Lane Historical Society, 1907.

————. "The King's Royal Regiment of New York." Ontario Historical Society, *Papers and Records*, XXVII (1931): 193–323.

————. "A Memoir of Lieutenant-General Peter Hunter." Ontario Historical Society, *Papers and Records*, XXX (1934): 5–32.

————, ed. "Petitions for Grants of Land, 1792–6." Ontario Historical Society, *Papers and Records*, XXIV (1927): 17–144.

————, ed. "Petitions for Grants of Land in Upper Canada, Second Series, 1796–99." Ontario Historical Society, *Papers and Records*, XXVI (1930): 97–379.

————, ed. "Records of Niagara, 1778–1783." Niagara Historical Society, *Publications*, XXXVIII (1927): 3–72.

————, ed. "Records of Niagara, 1784–7." Niagara Historical Society, *Publications*, XXXIX (1928): 3–134.

————, ed. "Records of Niagara, 1784–9." Niagara Historical Society, *Publications*, XL (1929): 3–100.

————, ed. "Records of Niagara, 1790–1792." Niagara Historical Society, *Publications*, XLI (1930): 3–146.

————, ed. "Records of Niagara, 1805–1811." Niagara Historical Society, *Publications*, XLII (1931): 3–132.

Cushing, Harry Alonzo, ed. *The Writings of Samuel Adams*. 4 vols. New York: Putnam, 1908.

Dangerfield, George. *Chancellor Robert R. Livingston of New York, 1746–1813*. New York: Harcourt, Brace, 1960.

Darlington, William M., ed. *Christopher Gist's Journals, with Historical, Geographical, and Ethnological Notes and Biographies of his Contemporaries*. New York: Arno Press, 1966, reprint of 1893.

Davis, Matthew L., ed. *Memoirs of Aaron Burr with Miscellaneous Selections from His Correspondence*. New York: Harper Brothers, 1837.

De Conde, Alexander. *This Affair of Louisiana*. New York: Scribner, 1976.

De Forest, L. Effingham, ed. "Hannah Lawrence Shieffelin's Letter." *New York Genealogical and Biographical Record*, LXXII (April 1941): 120–23.

Densmore, Christopher. *Red Jacket: Iroquois Diplomat and Orator*. Syracuse, N.Y.: Syracuse University Press, 1999.

DePalma, Anthony. *Here: A Biography of the New American Continent*. New York: Public Affairs, 2001.

De Pauw, Linda Grant. *The Eleventh Pillar: New York State and the Federal Constitution*. Ithaca, N.Y.: Cornell University Press, 1966.

De Peyster, John Watts, ed. *Miscellanies by an Officer (Colonel Arent Schuyler de Peyster, B.A.), 1774–1813*. New York: A. E. Chasmer & Co., 1888.

Dexter, Franklin Bowditch, ed. *Diary of David McClure, Doctor of Divinity, 1748–1820*. New York: Knickerbocker Press, 1899.

————, ed. *The Literary Diary of Ezra Stiles. . . .* 3 vols. New York: Scribner, 1901.

Doddridge, Joseph. *Notes on the Settlement and Indian Wars of the Western Parts of Virginia and Pennsylvania, from 1763 to 1783, Inclusive*. Pittsburgh: John S. Ritenour & William T. Lindsey, 1912.

Dowd, Gregory Evans Dowd. *War Under Heaven: Pontiac, the Indian Nations & the British Empire*. Baltimore: Johns Hopkins University Press, 2002.

Druke, Mary A. "Iroquois Treaties: Common Forms, Varying Interpretations." In Francis Jennings, ed., *The History and Culture of Iroquois Diplomacy: An Interdisciplinary Guide to the Treaties of the Six Nations and Their League*, 85–98. Syracuse, N.Y.: Syracuse University Press, 1985.

————. "Linking Arms: The Structure of Iroquois Intertribal Diplomacy." In Daniel K. Richter and James H. Merrell, eds., *Beyond the Covenant Chain: The Iroquois and their Neighbors in Indian North America, 1600–1800*, 29–39. Syracuse, N.Y.: Syracuse University Press, 1987.

Duffy, John J., ed. *Ethan Allen and His Kin: Correspondence, 1772–1819*. 2 vols. Hanover, N.H.: University Press of New England, 1998.

Dunbar, John R., ed. *The Paxton Papers*. The Hague: Martinus Nijhoff, 1957.

Dwight, Timothy. *Travels in New England and New York*. Edited by Barbara Miller Solomon. 4 vols. Cambridge, Mass.: Harvard University Press, 1969, reprint of 1822 original.

Eliades, David K. "Two Worlds Collide: The European Advance into North America." In Thomas E. Ross and Tyrel G. Moore, eds., *A Cultural Geography of North American Indians*, 33–46. Boulder, Colo.: Westview Press, 1987.

Elkins, Stanley, and Eric McKitrick. *The Age of Federalism*. New York: Oxford University Press, 1993.

Ellicott, Joseph. *Refutation of the Claim of John Livingston, Esquire, to Lands in the Western District of the State of New York, Under Certain Leases*. N.p., 1811.

Ellis, David Maldwyn. "The Rise of the Empire State, 1790–1820." *New York History*, LVI (Jan. 1975): 5–27.

Embree, George, et al. "Some Account of a Visit Paid to the Indians Situated on the Frontiers of the State of New York." *Friends Review: A Religious, Literary, and Miscellaneous Journal*, V (1852) and VI (1853).

Evans, Griffith. "Journal of Griffith Evans, 1784–1785." *Pennsylvania Magazine of History and Biography*, LXV (April 1941): 202–33.

Evans, Joshua. *A Journal of the Life, Travels, Religious Exercises, and Labours in the Work of the Ministry*. Byberry, Pa.: John & Isaac Comly, 1837.

Feest, Christian F. "Nanticoke and Neighboring Tribes." In Bruce G. Trigger, ed., *Handbook of North American Indians, Volume 15: Northeast*, 240–52. Washington, D.C.: Smithsonian Institution, 1978.

Feister, Lois M., and Bonnie Pulis. "Molly Brant: Her Domestic and Political Roles in Eighteenth-Century New York." In Robert S. Grumen, ed., *Northeastern Indian Lives, 1632–1816*, 295–320. Amherst: University of Massachusetts Press, 1996.

Fenton, William N. *The Great Law and the Longhouse: A Political History of the Iroquois Confederacy*. Norman: University of Oklahoma Press, 1998.

———, ed. "The Journal of James Emlen Kept on a Trip to Canandaigua, New York. . . ." *Ethnohistory*, XII (Fall 1965): 279–342.

———. "Northern Iroquoian Culture Patterns." In Bruce G. Trigger, ed., *Handbook of North American Indians, Volume 15: Northeast*, 296–321. Washington, D.C.: Smithsonian Institution, 1978.

———. "Structure, Continuity, and Change in the Process of Iroquois Treaty Making." In Francis Jennings, ed., *The History and Culture of Iroquois Diplomacy: An Interdisciplinary Guide to the Treaties of the Six Nations and Their League*, 3–36. Syracuse, N.Y.: Syracuse University Press, 1985.

Fenton, William N., and Elisabeth Tooker. "Mohawk." In Bruce G. Trigger, ed., *Handbook of North American Indians, Volume 15: Northeast*, 466–80. Washington, D.C.: Smithsonian Institution, 1978.

Firth, Edith. "The Administration of Peter Russell, 1796–1799." *Ontario History*, XLVIII (1956): 163–81.

———, ed. *The Town of York, 1793–1815: A Collection of Documents of Early Toronto*. Toronto: Champlain Society, 1962.

Fitzpatrick, John C., ed. *The Writings of George Washington*. 39 vols. Washington, D.C.: U.S. Government Printing Office, 1931–44.

Flick, Alexander C. "How New York Won and Lost an Empire." *New York History*, XVIII (Oct. 1937): 361–77.

Fogelson, Raymond D. "Major John Norton as Ethnologist." *Journal of Cherokee Studies*, III (Fall 1978): 250–55.

Force, Peter, ed. *American Archives*. 9 vols. Washington, D.C.: U.S. Congress, 1837–53.

Ford, Worthington C., ed. *Journals of the Continental Congress, 1774–1789*. 34 vols. Washington, D.C.: Government Printing Office, 1904–37.

Fraser, Alexander, ed. *Sixth Report of the Bureau of Archives for the Province of Ontario, 1909*. Toronto: L. K. Cameron, 1911.

Frazier, Patrick. *The Mohicans of Stockbridge*. Lincoln: University of Nebraska Press, 1992.

Gardiner, Robert Hallowell. *Early Recollections of Robert Hallowell Gardiner, 1782–1864*. Hallowell, Maine, 1936.

Gates, Lillian F. *Land Policies of Upper Canada*. Toronto: University of Toronto Press, 1968.

Gates, Lillian F. "Roads, Rivals, and Rebellion: The Unknown Story of Asa Danforth, Jr." *Ontario History*, LXXVI (Sep. 1984): 233–54.

Gentilcore, R. Louis, and John David Wood. "A Military Colony in a Wilderness: The Upper Canada Frontier." In Wood, ed., *Perspectives on Landscape and Settlement in Nineteenth-Century Ontario*, 32–58. Toronto: McClelland and Stewart, 1975.

Gerlach, Don R. *Proud Patriot: Philip Schuyler and the War of Independence, 1775–1783*. Syracuse, N.Y.: Syracuse University Press, 1987.

Giunta, Mary A., ed. *The Emerging Nation: A Documentary History of the Foreign Relations of the United States Under the Articles of Confederation, 1780–1789*. 3 vols. Washington, D.C.: National Historical Publications and Records Commission, 1989.

Goebel, Julius, Jr., et al., eds. *The Law Practice of Alexander Hamilton: Documents and Commentary*. 5 vols. New York: Columbia University Press, 1964–81.

Gottschalk, Louis. *Lafayette Between the American and the French Revolutions, 1783–1789*. Chicago: University of Chicago Press, 1950.

———. *Lafayette Joins the American Army*. Chicago: University of Chicago Press, 1937.

Gould, Eliga H. *The Persistence of Empire: British Political Culture in the Age of the American Revolution*. Chapel Hill: University of North Carolina Press, 2000.

Gould, Jay. *History of Delaware County, New York*. Roxbury, N.Y., 1856.

Grant, Francis. "Journal from New York to Canada, 1767." *New York History*, LIII (April 1932): 181–96.

Gray, Elma E., and Leslie R. Gray. *Wilderness Christians: The Moravian Mission to the Delaware Indians*. Ithaca, N.Y.: Cornell University Press, 1956.

Gray, Leslie R., ed. "From Bethlehem to Fairfield—1798." *Ontario History*, XLVI (Spring and Winter 1954): 37–61 and 107–30.

———, ed. "From Fairfield to Schonbrun—1798." *Ontario History*, XLIX (Winter 1957): 63–96.

Graymont, Barbara. *The Iroquois in the American Revolution*. Syracuse, N.Y.: Syracuse University Press, 1972.

———. "New York State Indian Policy After the Revolution." *New York History*, LVII (Oct. 1976): 438–74.

Greenwood, F. Murray. *Legacies of Fear: Law and Politics in Quebec in the Era of the French Revolution*. Toronto: Osgoode Society, 1993.

Grew, John. *Journal of a Tour from Boston to Niagara Falls and Quebec, 1803*. N.p., privately printed, n.d.

Gridley, Amos Delos. *History of the Town of Kirkland, New York*. New York: Hurd & Houghton, 1874.

Gross, Robert. *The Minutemen and Their World*. New York: Hill & Wang, 1976.

Guest, Harry H. "Upper Canada's First Political Party." *Ontario History*, LIV (Dec. 1962): 275–96.

Guillet, Edwin C. *Early Life in Upper Canada*. Toronto: Ontario Publishing Co., 1933.

Guzzardo, John Christopher. "Sir William Johnson's Official Family: Patron and Clients in an Anglo-American Empire, 1742–1777." Ph.D. diss., Syracuse University, 1975.

———. "The Superintendent and the Ministers: The Battle for Oneida Allegiances, 1761–1775." *New York History*, LVII (July 1976): 255–84.

Gwyn, Julian. "Sir William Johnson." *Dictionary of Canadian Biography, IV: 1771 to 1800,* 394–98. Toronto: University of Toronto Press, 1979.

Haefeli, Evan. "A Note on the Use of North American Borderlands." *American Historical Review,* CIV (Oct. 1999): 1222–25.

Hagedorn, Nancy. " 'Faithful, Knowing, and Prudent': Andrew Montour as Interpreter and Cultural Broker, 1740–1772." In Margaret Connell Szasz, ed., *Between Indian and White Worlds: The Cultural Broker,* 44–60. Norman: University of Oklahoma Press, 1994.

Halsey, Francis Whiting. *The Old New York Frontier: Its Wars with Indians and Tories, Its Missionary Schools, Pioneers, and Land Titles, 1614–1800.* New York: Scribner, 1912.

Hamil, Fred Coyne. "Ebenezer Allan in Canada." Ontario Historical Society, *Papers and Records,* XXXVI (1944): 83–93.

———. "Sally Ainse, Fur Trader." Algonquin Club, *Historical Bulletin,* III (Jan. 1939): 1–21.

———. *The Valley of the Lower Thames, 1640 to 1850.* Toronto: University of Toronto Press, 1951.

Hamilton, Milton W. "An American Knight in Britain: Sir John Johnson's Tour, 1765–1767." *New York History,* XLII (Apr. 1961): 119–23.

———, ed. "Guy Johnson's Opinions on the American Indian." *Pennsylvania Magazine of History and Biography,* LXXVII (July 1953): 311–27.

———. "Joseph Brant Painted by Rigaud." *New York History,* XL (July 1959): 250–52.

———. *Sir William Johnson: Colonial American, 1715–1763.* Port Washington, N.Y.: Kennikat Press, 1976.

———. "Sir William Johnson's Wives." *New York History,* XXXVIII (Jan. 1957): 18–28.

Hamilton, Stanislaus M., ed. *The Writings of James Monroe,* 7 vols. New York: Putnam, 1898–1903.

Hansen, Marcus Lee, and John Bartlett Brebner. *The Mingling of the Canadian and American Peoples.* New Haven, Conn.: Yale University Press, 1940.

Hanson, J. Howard, and Samuel Ludlow Frey, eds. *The Minute Book of the Committee of Safety of Tryon County, the Old New York Frontier.* New York: Dodd, Mead, 1905.

Harring, Sidney L. *White Man's Law: Native People in Nineteenth-Century Canadian Jurisprudence.* Toronto: Osgoode Society, 1998.

Harris, George H. "The Life of Horatio Jones: The True Story of Hoc-Sa-Go-Wah, Prisoner, Pioneer, and Interpreter." Buffalo Historical Society, *Publications,* VI (1903): 383–514.

Harvey, Oscar Jewell. *A History of Wilkes-Barre, Luzerne County, Pennsylvania.* 4 vols. Wilkes-Barre, Pa.: Raeder Press, 1927.

Hastings, Hugh, ed. *Military Minutes of the Council of Appointment of the State of New York, 1783–1821.* 4 vols. Albany, N.Y.: James B. Lyon, 1901.

———, ed. *Public Papers of Daniel D. Tompkins, Governor of New York: 1807–1817.* 3 vols. Albany, N.Y.: Wynkoop, Hallenbeck & Crawford, 1898.

———, ed. *Public Papers of George Clinton, First Governor of New York, 1777–1795, 1801–1804.* 10 vols. Albany: New York State Printers, 1899–1914.

Hauptman, Laurence M. *Conspiracy of Interests: Iroquois Dispossession and the Rise of New York State.* Syracuse, N.Y.: Syracuse University Press, 1999.

———. "The Dispersal of the River Indians: Frontier Expansion and Indian Dispossession in the Hudson Valley." In Hauptman and Jack Campisi, eds., *Neighbors and Intruders: An Ethnohistorical Exploration of the Indians of Hudson's River,* 244–60. Ottawa: National Museum of Man, 1978.

Hearn, Daniel Allen. *Legal Executions in New York State: A Comprehensive Reference, 1639–1963.* Jefferson, N.C.: McFarland, 1997.

Heckewelder, John C. *History, Manners, and Customs of the Indian Nations Who Once Inhabited Pennsylvania and the Neighboring States.* Philadelphia: Historical Society of Pennsylvania, 1876, reprint of 1819 original.

Herzog, Lawrence A. *Where North Meets South: Cities, Space, and Politics on the U.S.-Mexico Border.* Austin, Tex.: Center for Mexican American Studies, 1990.

Hinderaker, Eric. *Elusive Empires: Constructing Colonialism in the Ohio Valley, 1673–1800.* New York: Cambridge University Press, 1997.

Hinman, Marjory Barnum. *Onaquaga: Hub of the Border Wars.* Binghamton, N.Y.: Valley Offset, 1975.

Hirsch, Alison Duncan. "The 'Celebrated Madame Montour': 'Interpretress' Across Early American Frontiers." *Explorations in Early American Culture,* IV (2000): 81–112.

———. "Indian, *Metis,* and Euro-American Women on Multiple Frontiers." In William A. Pencak and Daniel K. Richter, eds., *Friends and Enemies in Penn's Woods: Indians, Colonists, and the Racial Construction of Pennsylvania,* 63–84. University Park: Pennsylvania State University Press, 2004.

Horsman, Reginald. *Expansion and American Indian Policy, 1783–1812.* East Lansing: Michigan State University Press, 1967.

———. *Matthew Elliott, British Indian Agent.* Detroit: Wayne State University Press, 1964.

Horton, John T., ed. "The Mohawk Valley in 1791." *New York History,* XXII (Apr. 1941): 208–13.

Hough, Franklin B., ed. *Census of the State of New-York, for 1855.* Albany, N.Y.: Charles Van Benthuysen, 1857.

———. *A History of St. Lawrence and Franklin Counties, New York* Albany, N.Y.: Little & Co., 1853.

———, ed. *The New York Civil List, Containing the Names and Origin of the Civil Divisions, and the Names and Dates of Election or Appointment of the Principal State and County Officers.* Albany, N.Y.: Weed, Parsons & Co., 1855.

———. *Notices of Peter Penet and of His Operations Among the Oneida Indians.* Lowville, N.Y.: Franklin B. Hough, 1866.

———, ed. *Proceedings of the Commissioners of Indian Affairs Appointed by Law for the Extinguishment of Indian Titles in the State of New York.* 2 vols. Albany, N.Y.: Joel Munsell, 1861.

Houghton, Frederick. "The History of the Buffalo Creek Reservation." Buffalo Historical Society, *Publications,* XXIV (1920): 3–181.

Howland, Henry R. "The Seneca Mission at Buffalo Creek." Buffalo Historical Society, *Publications,* VI (1903): 125–61.

Hughes, Thomas. *A Journal by Thos. Hughes for his Amusement. . . .* Cambridge: University of Cambridge Press, 1947.

Hunter, Robert, Jr. *Quebec to Carolina in 1785–1786, Being the Travel Diary and Observations of Robert Hunter, Jr., a Young Merchant of London.* Edited by Louis B. Wright and Marion Tinling. San Marino, Calif.: Huntington Library, 1943.

Hutchinson, William T., and William M. E. Rachal, eds. *The Papers of James Madison.* 17 vols. Chicago: University of Chicago Press, 1962–91.

Ibbotson, Joseph D., ed. *Documentary History of Hamilton College.* Clinton, N.Y.: Hamilton College, 1922.

Idzerda, Stanley J., et al., eds. *Lafayette in the Age of the American Revolution: Selected Letters and Papers, 1776–1790.* 6 vols. Ithaca, N.Y.: Cornell University Press, 1977–83.

Innis, Mary Quale, ed. *Mrs. Simcoe's Diary.* Toronto: Macmillan, 1965.

Jacobs, Wilbur R. *Wilderness Politics and Indian Gifts: The Northern Colonial Frontier, 1748–1763.* Lincoln: University of Nebraska Press, 1966.

Jemison, G. Peter, and Anna M. Schein, eds. *Treaty of Canandaigua, 1794: 200 Years of Treaty Relations Between the Iroquois Confederacy and the United States.* Santa Fe: Clear Light Publishers, 2000.

Jennings, Francis, ed. *The History and Culture of Iroquois Diplomacy: An Interdisciplinary Guide to the Treaties of the Six Nations and Their League.* Syracuse, N.Y.: Syracuse University Press, 1985.

———. "Iroquois Alliances in American History." In Jennings, ed., *The History and Culture of Iro-*

quois Diplomacy: An Interdisciplinary Guide to the Treaties of the Six Nations and their League, 37–65. Syracuse, N.Y.: Syracuse University Press, 1985.

Johnson, Warren. "Journal of Warren Johnson, 1760–1761." In Dean R. Snow, Charles T. Gehring, and William A. Starna, eds., *In Mohawk Country: Early Narratives About a Native People*, 250–73. Syracuse, N.Y.: Syracuse University Press, 1996.

Johnson, William. *Reports of Cases Adjudged in the Supreme Court of Judicature of the State of New-York; from January Term 1799–January Term 1803.* 3 vols. New York: Isaac Riley, 1808–12.

Johnston, Charles M. *Brant County: A History, 1784–1945.* Toronto: Oxford University Press, 1967.

———. "William Claus and John Norton." *Ontario History*, LVII (June 1965): 101–8.

———. "Joseph Brant, the Grand River Lands, and the Northwest Crisis." *Ontario History*, LV (Dec. 1963): 267–82.

———. "An Outline of Early Settlement in the Grand River Valley." *Ontario History*, LIV (Mar. 1962): 43–67.

———, ed. *The Valley of the Six Nations: A Collection of Documents on the Indian Lands of the Grand River.* Toronto: Champlain Society, 1964.

Johnston, Henry P., ed. *The Correspondence and Public Papers of John Jay.* New York: Putnam, 1891.

Jones, Dorothy V. *License for Empire: Colonialism by Treaty in Early America.* Chicago: University of Chicago Press, 1982.

Jones, Electa. *Stockbridge, Past and Present; or, Records of an Old Mission Station.* Springfield, Mass.: Samuel Bowles & Co., 1854.

Jones, Pomroy. *Annals and Recollections of Oneida County.* Rome, N.Y.: Pomroy Jones, 1851.

Jones, Robert Leslie. *History of Agriculture in Ontario, 1613–1880.* Toronto: University of Toronto Press, 1946.

Judd, Jacob, ed. *Correspondence of the Van Cortlandt Family of Cortlandt Manor, 1748–1801.* Tarrytown, N.Y.: Sleepy Hollow Restoration, 1977.

Judd, Peter. *The Hatch and Brood of Time.* Boston: Newbury Street Press, 1999.

———. *More Lasting Than Brass: A Thread of Family from Revolutionary New York to Industrial Connecticut.* Boston: Newbury Street Press, 2004.

Kaminski, John P. *George Clinton: Yeoman Politician of the New Republic.* Madison, Wis.: Madison House, 1993.

Kammen, Michael. *Colonial New York: A History.* New York: Oxford University Press, 1975.

Kawashima, Yasuhide. *Puritan Justice and the Indian: White Man's Law in Massachusetts, 1630–1763.* Middletown, Conn.: Wesleyan University Press, 1986.

Kelsay, Isabel. *Joseph Brant, 1743–1807: Man of Two Worlds.* Syracuse, N.Y.: Syracuse University Press, 1984.

Kent, Donald K., and Merle H. Deardorff. eds. "John Adlum on the Allegheny: Memoirs for the Year 1794." *Pennsylvania Magazine of History and Biography*, LXXXIV (July and Oct. 1960): 266–324 and 435–80.

Ketchum, William. *An Authentic and Comprehensive History of Buffalo.* 2 vols. Buffalo: Rockwell, Baker & Hill, 1864–65.

Kierner, Cynthia A. *Traders and Gentlefolk: The Livingstons of New York, 1675–1690.* Ithaca, N.Y.: Cornell University Press, 1992.

Kingman, Leroy Wilson, ed. *Early Owego.* Owego, N.Y.: Tioga County Historical Society, 1987.

Kirkland, John T. "Answers to Queries Respecting the Western Indians." Massachusetts Historical Society, *Collections*, 1st ser., IV (1795): 67–74.

Klinck, Carl F., and J. J. Talman, eds. *Journal of Major John Norton, 1816.* Toronto: Champlain Society, 1970.

Kline, Mary-Jo, ed. *Political Correspondence and Public Papers of Aaron Burr.* 2 vols. Princeton, N.J.: Princeton University Press, 1983.

Klingberg, Frank J. *Anglican Humanitarianism in Colonial New York.* Philadelphia: Church Historical Society, 1940.

Knapp, Samuel L. *The Life of Thomas Eddy.* New York: Conner & Cooke, 1834.

Knopf, Richard C., ed. *Anthony Wayne, A Name in Arms: The Wayne-Knox-Pickering-McHenry Correspondence.* Pittsburgh: University of Pittsburgh Press, 1960.

Koenigsberger, H. G. "Composite States, Representative Institutions, and the American Revolution." *Historical Research,* LXII (1989): 135–53.

Labaree, Leonard W., ed., *The Public Records of the State of Connecticut from May, 1785, through January, 1789.* Hartford: State of Connecticut, 1945.

Labaree, Leonard W., et al., eds. *The Papers of Benjamin Franklin.* 32 vols. to date. New Haven, Conn.: Yale University Press, 1959–.

LaDow, Beth. *The Medicine Line: Life and Death on a North American Borderland.* New York: Routledge, 2001.

Lamb, H. H. *Climate, History, and the Modern World.* London: Methuen, 1982.

Lecker, Robert, ed. *Borderlands: Essays in Canadian-American Relations.* Toronto: E.C.W. Press, 1991.

Lee, Richard Henry. *Life of Arthur Lee, LL.D.* Boston: Wells & Lily, 1829.

Lehman, J. David. "The End of the Iroquois Mystique: The Oneida Land Cession Treaties of the 1780s." *William and Mary Quarterly,* 3rd ser., XLVIII (Oct. 1990): 524–47.

Lender, Mark E., and James Kirby Martin, eds. *Citizen-Soldier: The Revolutionary War Journal of Joseph Bloomfield.* Newark: New Jersey Historical Society, 1982.

Lepore, Jill. *The Name of War: King Philip's War and the Origins of American Identity.* New York: Knopf, 1998.

Lewin, Howard. "A Frontier Diplomat: Andrew Montour." *Pennsylvania History,* XXXIII (1966): 153–86.

Limerick, Patricia Nelson. *The Legacy of Conquest: The Unbroken Past of the American West.* New York: Norton, 1987.

Lincklaen, John. *Travels in the Years 1791 and 1792 in Pennsylvania, New York, and Vermont.* New York: Putnam, 1897.

Lincoln, Benjamin. "Journal of a Treaty Held in 1793 with the Indian Tribes North West of the Ohio by Commissioners of the United States." *Massachusetts Historical Society, Collections,* 3rd ser., V (1836): 109–76.

Lincoln, Charles Z., ed. *State of New York: Messages from the Governors.* 11 vols. Albany, N.Y.: J. B. Lyon & Co., 1909.

Lindley, Jacob. "Account of a Journey to Attend the Indian Treaty Proposed to be Held at Sandusky in the Year 1793." Michigan Pioneer and Historical Society, *Collections,* XVIII (1890): 565–632.

Lipson, Dorothy A. *Freemasonry in Federalist Connecticut, 1789–1835.* Princeton, N.J.: Princeton University Press, 1977.

Long, John. *Voyages and Travels of an Indian Interpreter and Trader.* Toronto: Coles Publishing Co., 1971, reprint of London, 1791.

Love, William DeLoss. *Samson Occom and the Christian Indians of New England.* Boston: Pilgrim Press, 1899.

Lyon, E. Wilson. *The Man Who Sold Louisiana: The Career of François Barbé-Marbois.* Norman: University of Oklahoma Press, 1942.

McAnear, Beverly, ed. "Personal Accounts of the Albany Congress of 1754." *Mississippi Valley Historical Review,* XXXIX (Mar. 1953): 727–46.

Macauley, James. *The Natural, Statistical, and Civil History of the State of New York.* . . . 3 vols. New York: Gould & Banks, 1829.

McCalla, Douglas. *Planting the Province: The Economic History of Upper Canada, 1784–1870.* Toronto: University of Toronto Press, 1993.

McCallum, James Dow. *Eleazar Wheelock: Founder of Dartmouth College.* Hanover, N.H.: Dartmouth College Publications, 1939.

―――, ed. *Letters of Eleazar Wheelock's Indians.* Hanover, N.H.: Dartmouth College Publications, 1932.

McClure, David, and Elijah Parish. *Memoirs of the Rev. Eleazar Wheelock.* New York: Arno Press, 1972, reprint of 1811 original.

McCusker, John J., and Russell R. Menard. *The Economy of British America, 1607–1789.* Chapel Hill: University of North Carolina Press, 1985.

McGinnis, Richard. "A Loyalist Journal." *New York Genealogical and Biographical Record,* CV (Oct. 1974): 197–200.

McLachlan, James, ed. *Princetonians, 1748–1768: A Biographical Dictionary.* Princeton, N.J.: Princeton University Press, 1976.

McLean, Marianne. "Peopling Glengarry County: The Scottish Origins of a Canadian Community." In J. K. Johnson and Bruce G. Wilson, eds. *Historical Essays on Upper Canada: New Perspectives,* 151–73. Ottawa: Carleton University Press, 1989.

McLeod, Malcolm. "Fortress Ontario or Forlorn Hope? Simcoe and the Defence of Upper Canada." *Canadian Historical Review,* LIII (June 1972): 149–78.

McMaster, Guy H. *History of the Settlement of Steuben County, New York.* Bath, N.Y.: R. S. Underhill, 1853.

McNall, Neill Adams. *An Agricultural History of the Genesee Valley, 1790–1860.* Philadelphia: University of Pennsylvania Press, 1952.

McOuat, Donald F., ed. "The Diary of William Graves." Ontario Historical Society, *Papers and Records,* XLIII (Jan. 1951): 1–26.

Malone, Dumas. *Jefferson and the Rights of Man.* Boston: Little, Brown, 1951.

Mancall, Peter C. *Deadly Medicine: Indians and Alcohol in Early America.* Ithaca, N.Y.: Cornell University Press, 1995.

―――. *Valley of Opportunity: Economic Culture Along the Upper Susquehanna, 1700–1800.* Ithaca, N.Y.: Cornell University Press, 1991.

Manning, William R., ed. *Diplomatic Correspondence of the United States: Canadian Relations, 1784–1860.* 3 vols. Washington, D.C.: Carnegie Endowment for International Peace, 1940.

Marshall, Peter. "Sir William Johnson and the Treaty of Fort Stanwix, 1768." *Journal of American Studies,* I (1971): 149–79.

Massachusetts Historical Society. *Warren-Adams Letters: Being Chiefly a Correspondence Among John Adams, Samuel Adams, and James Warren.* 2 vols. Boston: Massachusetts Historical Society, 1917, 1925.

Mathews, Catharine Van Cortlandt. *Andrew Ellicott, His Life and Letters.* New York: Grafton Press, 1908.

Maude, John. *Visit to the Falls of Niagara in 1800.* London: Longman, Rees & Green, 1826.

Meginness, John F. *Otzinachson: A History of the West Branch Valley of the Susquehanna.* Williamsport, Pa.: Gazette & Bulletin Printing House, 1889.

Melish, John. *Travels Through the United States of America, in the Years 1806 & 1807 and 1809, 1810 & 1811.* 2 vols. Philadelphia: T. & G. Palmer, 1812.

Merrell, James H. " 'The Cast of His Countenance': Reading Andrew Montour." In Ronald Hoffman, Mechal Sobel, and Fredrika J. Teute, eds. *Through a Glass Darkly: Reflections on Personal Identity in Early America*, 13–39. Chapel Hill: University of North Carolina Press, 1997.

———. *The Indians' New World: Catawbas and Their Neighbors from European Contact Through the Era of Removal.* Chapel Hill: University of North Carolina Press, 1989.

———. *Into the American Woods: Negotiators on the Pennsylvania Frontier.* New York: Norton, 1999.

Merriman, Brenda. "Upper Canada Land Petitions, 'G' Leases #88." Ontario Genealogical Society, *Families*, XXII, no. 4 (1983): 328–29.

Miller, Stephen B. *Historical Sketches of Hudson.* Hudson, N.Y.: Bryan & Webb, 1862.

Mintz, Max M. *Seeds of Empire: The American Revolutionary Conquest of the Iroquois.* New York: New York University Press, 1999.

Monroe, James. *Autobiography of James Monroe.* Edited by Stuart G. Brown. Syracuse, N.Y.: Syracuse University Press, 1959.

Moore, Christopher. "The Disposition to Settle: The Royal Highland Emigrants and Loyalist Settlement in Upper Canada, 1784." In J. K. Johnson and Bruce G. Wilson, eds., *Historical Essays on Upper Canada: New Perspectives*, 53–79. Ottawa: Carleton University Press, 1989.

Moore, Thomas. *Memoirs, Journal, and Correspondence of Thomas Moore.* 8 vols. London: Longman, Brown, Green & Longmans, 1853.

Morgan, Edmund S. *American Slavery, American Freedom: The Ordeal of Colonial Virginia.* New York: Norton, 1975.

Morris, Richard B., ed. *John Jay: The Making of a Revolutionary: Unpublished Papers, 1745–1780.* New York: Harper & Row, 1975.

Morse, Jedediah. *A Report to the Secretary of War of the United States, On Indian Affairs, Comprising a Narrative of a Tour Performed in the Summer of 1820. . . .* New Haven, Conn.: S. Converse, 1822.

Murray, Laura J., ed. *To Do Good to My Indian Brethren: The Writings of Joseph Johnson, 1751–1776.* Amherst: University of Massachusetts Press, 1998.

Murray, Louise Welles. *A History of Old Tioga Point and Early Athens, Pennsylvania.* Wilkes-Barre, Pa.: Rader Press, 1908.

Namias, June, ed. *Narrative of the Life of Mary Jemison by James Seaver.* Norman: University of Oklahoma Press, 1992.

Nammack, Georgiana C. *Fraud, Politics, and the Dispossession of the Indians: The Iroquois Land Frontier in the Colonial Period.* Norman: University of Oklahoma Press, 1969.

Neatby, Hilda. *Quebec: The Revolutionary Age, 1760–1791.* Toronto: McClelland & Stewart, 1966.

Nelson, Larry L. *A Man of Distinction Among Them: Alexander McKee and the Ohio Country Frontier, 1754–1799.* Kent, Ohio: Kent State University Press, 1999.

Nelson, Paul David. *William Tryon and the Course of Empire: A Life in British Imperial Service.* Chapel Hill: University of North Carolina Press, 1990.

New-York Historical Society. *Collections for the Year 1879.* New York: New-York Historical Society, 1880.

[New York State]. *Journal of the Assembly of the State of New-York, at Their Twelfth Session, . . . 1788.* Albany, N.Y.: Samuel & John Loudoun, 1788.

———. *Journal of the Assembly of the State of New-York, the Second Meeting of the Thirteenth Session . . . 1789.* New York: Francis Childs & John Swaine, 1789.

———. *Journal of the Assembly of the State of New-York, Fourteenth Session.* New York: Francis Childs & John Swaine, 1791.

———. *Journal of the Assembly of the State of New-York, Fifteenth Session.* New York: Francis Childs & John Swaine, 1792.

————. *Journal of the Assembly of the State of New-York, Sixteenth Session.* New York: Francis Childs & John Swaine, 1792.

————. *Journal of the Assembly of the State of New-York, at Their Seventeenth Session . . . 1794.* Albany, N.Y.: Charles R. & George Webster, 1794.

————. *Journal of the Assembly of the State of New-York, at Their Eighteenth Session . . . 1795.* New York: Francis Childs, 1795.

————. *Journal of the Assembly of the State of New-York, at Their Nineteenth Session . . . 1796.* New York: John Childs, 1796.

————. *Journal of the Assembly of the State of New-York, at Their Twenty-Fourth Session . . . 1800.* Albany, N.Y.: Loring Andrews, 1801.

————. *Laws of the State of New York . . . from the 15th to the 20th Session, Inclusive.* 4 vols. New York: Thomas Greenleaf, 1797.

————. *Laws of the State of New York Passed at the Twenty-Fifth Session of the Legislature.* Albany, N.Y.: John Barber, 1802.

————. *Laws of the State of New York Passed at the Twenty-Sixth Session of the Legislature.* Albany, N.Y.: John Barber, 1803.

————. *Laws of the State of New York, Containing All the Acts Passed at the 30th, 31st, and 32nd Sessions of the Legislature.* Albany, N.Y.: Websters & Skinner, 1809.

————. *Laws of the State of New York, Revised and Passed at the Thirty-Sixth Session of the Legislature.* Albany, N.Y.: H. C. Southwick & Co., 1813.

————. *Laws of the State of New York Passed at the Sessions of the Legislature.* Albany, N.Y.: Weed, Parsons & Co., 1887.

————. *Report of the Regents of the University on the Boundaries of the State of New York.* Albany, N.Y.: Argus Co., 1874.

————. *Report of the Regents' Boundary Commission upon the New York and Pennsylvania Boundary.* Albany, N.Y.: Weed, Parsons & Co., 1886.

————. *Report of the Special Committee to Investigate the Indian Problem of the State of New York, Appointed by the Assembly of 1888* [commonly known as *The Whipple Report*]. Albany, N.Y.: Troy Press Co., 1889.

Niemcewicz, Julian Ursyn. "Journey to Niagara, 1805," edited by Metchie J. E. Budka, *New-York Historical Society Quarterly*, XLIV (Jan. 1960): 72–113.

Northern Missionary Society. *Annual Meeting of the Northern Missionary Society, of the State of New-York, Holden in the Presbyterian Church at Troy, 7th Sept. 1808.* N.p., 1808.

Northern Missionary Society. *Meeting of the Northern Missionary Society of the State of New-York, Held in the Town of Troy, 5th Sept. 1804.* Troy, N.Y., 1804.

O'Brien, Brendan. *Speedy Justice: The Tragic Last Voyage of His Majesty's Vessel Speedy.* Toronto: University of Toronto Press, 1992.

O'Brien, Jean M. " 'Divorced' from the Land: Resistance and Survival of Indian Women in Eighteenth-Century New England." In Colin G. Calloway, ed., *After King Philip's War: Presence and Persistence in Indian New England*, 144–61. Hanover, N.H.: University Press of New England, 1997.

O'Callaghan, E. B., ed. *The Documentary History of the State of New York.* 4 vols. Albany, N.Y.: Weed, Parsons & Co., 1849–51.

————. *Documents Relative to the Colonial History of the State of New York.* 15 vols. Albany, N.Y.: Weed, Parsons & Co., 1853–87.

O'Donnell, James. "Joseph Brant." In R. David Edmunds, ed. *American Indian Leaders: Studies in Diversity*, 21–40. Lincoln: University of Nebraska Press, 1980.

Onuf, Peter. " 'To Declare Them a Free and Independent People': Race, Slavery, and National Identity in Jefferson's Thought." *Journal of the Early Republic*, XVIII (Spring 1998): 1–46.

———. *The Origins of the Federal Republic: Jurisdictional Controversies in the United States, 1775–1787.* Philadelphia: University of Pennsylvania Press, 1983.

———. "Settlers, Settlements, and New States." In Jack P. Greene, ed., *The American Revolution: Its Character and Limits*, 179–213. New York: New York University Press, 1987.

Parmet, Herbert S., and Marie B. Hecht. *Aaron Burr: Portrait of an Ambitious Man.* New York: Macmillan, 1967.

Parrish, Jasper. "The Story of Jasper Parrish." Buffalo Historical Society, *Publications*, VI (1903): 527–38.

Patrick, Christine Sternberg. "The Life and Times of Samuel Kirkland, 1741–1808: Missionary to the Oneida Indians, American Patriot, and Founder of Hamilton College." Ph.D. diss., State University of New York at Buffalo, 1993.

Pennsylvania Archives. 1st ser. 12 vol. Philadelphia: Joshua Severns & Co., 1852–56.

Perkins, Bradford. *The First Rapprochement: England and the United States, 1795–1805.* Philadelphia: University of Pennsylvania Press, 1955.

Perkins, Julia Anna Shepard. *Early Times on the Susquehanna.* Binghamton, N.Y.: Herald Co., 1906.

Peyer, Bernd C. *The Tutor'd Mind: Indian Missionary-Writers in Antebellum America.* Amherst: University of Massachusetts Press, 1997.

Phillips, Edward H. "Timothy Pickering at His Best: Indian Commissioner, 1790–1794." Essex Institute, *Historical Collections*, CII (July 1966): 163–202.

Pickering, Octavius, and Charles W. Upham. *The Life of Timothy Pickering.* 2 vols. Boston: Little, Brown, 1867–73.

Pilkington, Walter. *Hamilton College: 1812–1962.* Clinton, N.Y.: Hamilton College, 1962.

———, ed. *The Journals of Samuel Kirkland.* Clinton, N.Y.: Hamilton College, 1980.

Porter, Augustus. "Narrative of Early Years in the Life of Judge Augustus Porter." Buffalo Historical Society, *Publications*, VII (1904): 277–330.

Potts, Louis. *Arthur Lee: A Virtuous Revolutionary.* Baton Rouge: Louisiana State University Press, 1981.

Preston, Richard A., ed. *Kingston Before the War of 1812: A Collection of Documents.* Toronto: Champlain Society, 1959.

Preston, Samuel. "Journey to Harmony." In Patricia H. Christian and Eleanor H. Keesler, eds., *Samuel Preston, 1789–1989: From Buckingham to Buckingham.* Equinunk, Pa.: Equinunk Historical Society, 1989.

Prince, Carl, et al., eds. *The Papers of William Livingston.* 5 vols. Trenton, N.J.: Rutgers University Press, 1979–88.

Prucha, Francis Paul. *American Indian Policy in the Formative Years: The Indian Trade and Intercourse Acts, 1790–1834.* Cambridge, Mass.: Harvard University Press, 1962.

———, ed. *Documents of United States Indian Policy.* Lincoln: University of Nebraska Press, 1990.

———. *The Great Father: The United States Government and the American Indians.* Lincoln: University of Nebraska Press, 1984.

Quaife, Milo M., ed. *The John Askin Papers.* 2 vols. Detroit: Detroit Library Commission, 1928–31.

Recht, Michael. "The Role of Fishing in the Iroquois Economy, 1600–1792," *New York History*, LXXVIII (Oct. 1997), 429–54.

Reid, John Phillip. *Patterns of Vengeance: Crosscultural Homicide in the North American Fur Trade.* Pasadena, Calif.: Ninth Judicial Circuit Historical Society, 1999.

Resendez, Andres. *Changing National Identities at the Frontier: Texas and New Mexico, 1800–1850*. New York: Cambridge University Press, 2005.

Rhodehamel, John, ed. *The American Revolution: Writings from the War of Independence*. New York: Library of America, 2001.

Rice, Howard C. *Barthelemi Tardiveau: A French Trader in the West*. Baltimore: Johns Hopkins University Press, 1938.

Rice, Howard C., Jr., and Anne S. K. Brown, eds. *The American Campaigns of Rochambeau's Army: 1780, 1781, 1782, 1783*. 2 vols. Princeton, N.J.: Princeton University Press, 1972.

Richardson, Leon Burr. *History of Dartmouth College*. 2 vols. Hanover, N.H.: Dartmouth College Publications, 1932.

———, ed. *An Indian Preacher in England* Hanover, N.H.: Dartmouth College Publications, 1933.

Richter, Daniel K. *Facing East from Indian Country: A Native History of Early America*. Cambridge, Mass.: Harvard University Press, 2001.

———. "Onas, the Long Knife: Pennsylvanians and Indians, 1783–1794." In Frederick E. Hoxie, Ronald Hoffman, and Peter J. Albert, eds., *Native Americans and the Early Republic*, 125–61. Charlottesville: University of Virginia Press, 1999.

———. *The Ordeal of the Longhouse: The Peoples of the Iroquois League in the Era of European Colonization*. Chapel Hill: University of North Carolina Press, 1992.

Richter, Daniel K., and James H. Merrell, eds. *Beyond the Covenant Chain: The Iroquois and Their Neighbors in Indian North America, 1600–1800*. Syracuse, N.Y.: Syracuse University Press, 1987.

Riddell, William Renwick, ed. *La Rochefoucault-Liancourt's Travels in Canada, 1795*. Toronto: Ontario Bureau of Archives, 1917.

———. *The Life of John Graves Simcoe, First Lieutenant Governor of the Province of Upper Canada, 1792–96*. Toronto: McClelland & Stewart, 1926.

———. *Michigan Under British Rule: Law and Law Courts, 1760–1796*. Lansing: Michigan Historical Commission, 1926.

———. "Was Molly Brant Married?" Ontario Historical Society, *Papers and Records*, XIX (1922): 147–57.

Ripley, Dorothy. *The Bank of Faith and Works United*. Philadelphia: J. H. Cunningham, 1819.

Ritcheson, Charles R. *Aftermath of Revolution: British Policy Toward the United States, 1783–1795*. Dallas: Southern Methodist University Press, 1969.

Robinson, William Spence. *The Life of Miranda*. 2 vols. Chapel Hill: University of North Carolina Press, 1929.

Rogers, E. S. "Southeastern Ojibwa." In Bruce G. Trigger, ed., *Handbook of North American Indians: Northeast*, 760–71. Washington, D.C.: Smithsonian Institution, 1978.

Rohrbough, Malcolm J. *The Land Office Business: The Settlement and Administration of American Public Lands, 1789–1837*. New York: Oxford University Press, 1968.

Romney, Paul. *Mr. Attorney: The Attorney General for Ontario in Court, Cabinet, and Legislature, 1791–1899*. Toronto: Osgoode Society, 1986.

Royster, Charles. *The Fabulous History of the Dismal Swamp Company: A Story of George Washington's Times*. New York: Knopf, 2000.

———. *A Revolutionary People at War: The Continental Army and American Character, 1775–1783*. Chapel Hill: University of North Carolina Press, 1979.

Sabathy-Judd, Linda, ed. *Moravians in Upper Canada: The Diary of the Indian Mission of Fairfield on the Thames, 1792–1813*. Toronto: Champlain Society, 1999.

Sabine, William H. W., ed. *Historical Memoirs from 16 March 1763 to 9 July 1776 of William Smith. . . .* New York: Colburn & Tegg, 1956.

Sahlins, Peter. *Boundaries: The Making of France and Spain in the Pyrenees.* Berkeley: University of California Press, 1989.

Salisbury, Neal. *Manitou and Providence: Indians, Europeans, and the Making of New England, 1500–1643.* New York: Oxford University Press, 1982.

Savery, William. "Journal of William Savery." *Friends' Library,* I: 324–459. Philadelphia: Joseph Rakestraw, 1837.

Schoolcraft, Henry R. *Notes on the Iroquois; or, Contributions to American History, Antiquities, and General Ethnology.* Albany, N.Y.: Erastus H. Pease, & Co., 1847.

Schultz, Christian. *Travels on an Inland Voyage.* New York: Isaac Riley, 1810.

Severance, Frank H., ed. "Extracts from Joseph Ellicott's Letter Books and Early Correspondence." Buffalo Historical Society, *Publications,* XXVI (1922): 49–166.

———. "The Niagara Peace Mission of Ephraim Douglass in 1783." Buffalo Historical Society, *Publications,* XVIII (1914): 115–42.

———, ed. "A Teacher Among the Senecas: Narrative of Rev. Jabez Hyde, 1811–1820." Buffalo Historical Society, *Publications,* VI (1903): 239–74.

Shannon, Timothy J. "Dressing for Success on the Mohawk Frontier: Hendrick, William Johnson, and the Indian Fashion." *William and Mary Quarterly,* 3rd ser., LIII (Jan. 1996): 13–42.

———. *Indians and Colonists at the Crossroads of Empire.* Ithaca, N.Y.: Cornell University Press, 2000.

Sheehan, Bernard. *Seeds of Extinction: Jeffersonian Philanthropy and the American Indian.* Chapel Hill: University of North Carolina Press, 1973.

Shoemaker, Nancy. *A Strange Likeness: Becoming Red and White in Eighteenth-Century North America.* New York: Oxford University Press, 2004.

Siebert, W. H. "The Loyalists and the Six Nation Indians in the Niagara Peninsula." Royal Society of Canada, *Transactions,* 3rd ser., IX (1915–16), Sec II, 79–128.

Simcoe, John Graves. "Remarks on the Travels of the Marquis de Chastellux (1787)." *Magazine of History,* XLIII, Extra No. 172, 8–49. Tarrytown, N.Y.: William Abbott, 1931.

———. *Simcoe's Military Journal.* Toronto: Baxter Publishing Co., 1962.

Sizer, Theodore. *The Works of Colonel John Trumbull: Artist of the American Revolution.* New Haven, Conn.: Yale University Press, 1967.

Slaughter, Thomas P. *The Whiskey Rebellion: Frontier Epilogue to the American Revolution.* New York: Oxford University Press, 1986.

Smith, David W. *A Short Topographical Description of His Majesty's Province of Upper Canada, in North America.* London: W. Paden, 1799.

Smith, Donald B. "The Dispossession of the Mississauga Indians: A Missing Chapter in the Early History of Upper Canada." In J. K. Johnson and Bruce G. Wilson, eds., *Historical Essays on Upper Canada: New Perspectives,* 23–51. Ottawa: Carleton University Press, 1989.

———. *Sacred Feathers: The Reverend Peter Jones (Kahkewaquonaby) and the Mississauga Indians.* Toronto: University of Toronto Press, 1987.

Smith, James Morton, ed. *The Republic of Letters: The Correspondence Between Thomas Jefferson and James Madison, 1776–1826.* 3 vols. New York: Norton 1995.

Smith, Marian L. "The INS and the Singular Status of North American Indians." *American Indian Culture and Research Journal,* XXIV (1997): 131–54.

Smith, Paul H., ed. *Letters of Delegates to Congress, 1774–1789.* 25 vols. Washington, D.C.: Library of Congress, 1976–.

Smith, Richard. *A Tour of Four Great Rivers: The Hudson, Mohawk, Susquehanna, and Delaware in 1769.* Edited by Francis W. Halsey. Port Washington, N.Y.: Ira J. Friedman, 1964.

Smolenski, John. "The Death of Sawantaeny and the Problem of Justice on the Frontier." In

William A. Pencak and Daniel K. Richter, eds. *Friends and Enemies in Penn's Woods: Indians, Colonists, and the Racial Construction of Pennsylvania*, 104–28. University Park: Pennsylvania State University Press, 2004.

Snow, Dean R. *The Iroquois*. Cambridge, Mass.: Blackwell Publishers, 1994.

Snow, Dean R.; Charles T. Gehring; and William A. Starna, eds. *In Mohawk Country: Early Narratives About a Native People*. Syracuse, N.Y.: Syracuse University Press, 1996.

Snyder, Charles M., ed. *Red and White on the New York Frontier: A Struggle for Survival*. Harrison, N.Y.: Harbor Hill Books, 1978.

Snyderman, George S. "Concepts of Land Ownership Among the Iroquois and their Neighbors." In William N. Fenton, ed., *Symposium on Local Diversity in Iroquois Culture*, Bureau of American Ethnology, Bulletin No. 149, 13–34. Washington, D.C.: U.S. Government Printing Office, 1951.

Sosin, Jack M. *Whitehall and the Wilderness: The Middle West in British Colonial Policy, 1760–1775*. Lincoln: University of Nebraska Press, 1961.

Spaulding, E. Wilder. *His Excellency George Clinton, Critic of the Constitution*. New York: Macmillan, 1938.

Starna, William A. "Aboriginal Title and Traditional Iroquois Land Use: An Anthropological Perspective." In Starna and Christopher Vecsey, eds. *Iroquois Land Claims*, 31–48. Syracuse, N.Y.: Syracuse University Press, 1988.

———. "The Oneida Homeland in the Seventeenth Century." In Jack Campisi and Laurence M. Hauptman, eds. *The Oneida Indian Experience: Two Perspectives*, 9–22. Syracuse, N.Y.: Syracuse University Press, 1988.

Steele, Ian K. *Betrayals: Fort William Henry & the "Massacre."* New York: Oxford University Press, 1990.

———. *Warpaths: Invasions of North America*. New York: Oxford University Press, 1994.

Stevens, Abel. *The Life and Times of Nathan Bangs, D.D.* New York: Carlton & Porter, 1863.

Stone, William L. *The Life of Joseph Brant—Thayendanegea, Including the Indian Wars of the American Revolution*. 2 vols. New York: Alexander V. Blake, 1838.

———. *Life and Times of Red-Jacket, or Sa-Go-Ye-Wat-Ha: Being the Sequel to the History of the Six Nations*. New York: Wiley & Putnam, 1841.

———. *The Life and Times of Sir William Johnson, Bart.* 2 vols. Albany, N.Y.: 1865.

———, ed. *Memoirs, and Letters and Journals of Major General Riedesel, During His Residence in America*. 2 vols. Albany, N.Y.: J. Munsell, 1868.

Storke, Elliot G., and James H. Smith. *History of Cayuga County, New York, with Illustrations and Biographical Sketches of Some of Its Prominent Men and Pioneers*. Syracuse, N.Y.: D. Mason & Co., 1879.

Strickland, William. *Journal of a Tour in the United States of America, 1794–95*. New York: New-York Historical Society, 1971.

Stuart, Reginald C. *United States Expansionism and British North America, 1775–1871*. Chapel Hill: University of North Carolina Press, 1988.

Sullivan, James, et al., eds. *The Papers of Sir William Johnson*. 14 vols. Albany: University of the State of New York, 1921–1965.

Surtees, Robert J. "Land Cessions, 1763–1830." In Edward S. Rogers and Donald B. Smith, eds., *Aboriginal Ontario: Historical Perspectives on the First Nations*, 92–121. Toronto: Dundurn Press, 1994.

Sutcliff, Robert. *Travels in Some Parts of North America, in the Years 1804, 1805 & 1806*. York, Eng.: W. Alexander, 1815.

Sweet, John Wood. *Bodies Politic: Negotiating Race in the American North, 1730–1830*. Baltimore: Johns Hopkins University Press, 2003.

Syrett, Harold C., et al., eds. *The Papers of Alexander Hamilton.* 27 vols. New York: Columbia University Press, 1961–87.

Szasz, Margaret. *Between Indian and White Worlds: The Cultural Broker.* Norman: University of Oklahoma Press, 1994.

Talman, James J., ed. *Loyalist Narratives from Upper Canada.* Toronto: Champlain Society, 1946.

Tanner, Helen Hornbeck, ed. *Atlas of Great Lakes Indian History.* Norman: University of Oklahoma Press, 1987.

Taylor, Alan. *American Colonies: The Settling of North America.* New York: Penguin, 2001.

———. "Captain Hendrick Aupaumut: The Dilemmas of an Intercultural Broker." *Ethnohistory,* XLIII (Summer 1996): 432–57.

———. "From Fathers to Friends of the People: Political Personas in the Early Republic." *Journal of the Early Republic,* XI (Winter 1991): 465–91.

———. " 'The Great Change Begins': Settling the Forest of Central New York." *New York History,* LXXVI (July 1995): 265–90.

———. " 'The Hungry Year': 1789 on the Northern Border of Revolutionary America." In Alessa Johns, ed. *Dreadful Visitations: Confronting Natural Catastrophe in the Age of Enlightenment,* 145–81. New York: Routledge, 1999.

———. "Land and Liberty on the Post-Revolutionary Frontier." In David T. Konig, ed., *Devising Liberty: Preserving and Creating Freedom in the New American Republic,* 81–108. Stanford, Calif.: Stanford University Press, 1995.

———. " 'To Man Their Rights': The Frontier Revolution." In Ronald Hoffman, ed., *The Transforming Hand of Revolution: Reconsidering the American Revolution as a Social Movement,* 231–57. Charlottesville: University of Virginia Press, 1995.

———. "A Northern Revolution of 1800?: Upper Canada and Thomas Jefferson." In James Horn, Jan Ellen Lewis, and Peter S. Onuf, eds. *The Revolution of 1800: Democracy, Race & the New Republic,* 383–409. Charlottesville: University of Virginia Press, 2002.

Taylor, Robert J., ed. *The Susquehannah Company Papers.* Vols. V–XI. Ithaca, N.Y.: Cornell University Press, 1968–71.

Thorp, Willard. *The Lives of Eighteen from Princeton.* Princeton, N.J.: Princeton University Press, 1946.

Tilghman, Oswald, ed. *Memoir of Lieut. Col. Tench Tilghman, Secretary and Aid to Washington.* Albany, N.Y.: J. Munsell, 1876.

Tiro, Karim Michel. "A Civil War?: Rethinking Iroquois Participation in the American Revolution." *Explorations in Early American Culture,* IV (2000): 148–65.

———. "James Dean in Iroquoia," *New York History,* LXXX (Oct. 1999): 397–422.

———. "People of the Standing Stone: The Oneida Indian Nation from Revolution Through Removal, 1765–1840." Ph.D. diss., University of Pennsylvania, 1999.

Tooker, Elisabeth. "The League of the Iroquois: Its History, Politics, and Ritual." In Bruce G. Trigger, ed. *Handbook of North American Indians, Volume 15: Northeast,* 418–41. Washington, D.C.: Smithsonian Institution, 1978.

Torok, Charles H. "The Tyendinaga Mohawks." *Ontario History,* LVII (1965): 69–77.

Tracy, William. *Notices of Men and Events Connected with the Early History of Oneida County.* Utica, N.Y.: R. Northway, Jr., 1836.

Trigger, Bruce G., ed. *Handbook of North American Indians, Volume 15: Northeast.* Washington, D.C.: Smithsonian Institution, 1978.

Turner, Frederick Jackson. "The Significance of the Frontier in American History." In Turner, *The Frontier in American History,* 1–38. New York: Holt, 1920.

Turner, Katharine C. *Red Men Calling on the Great White Father.* Norman: University of Oklahoma Press, 1951.

Turner, Orsamus. *History of the Pioneer Settlement of Phelps and Gorham Purchase and Morris Reserve.* Rochester, N.Y.: W. Atting, 1852.

———. *Pioneer History of the Holland Purchase of Western New York.* Buffalo: George H. Derby & Co., 1850.

Turpin, Morley Bebee. "Ebenezer Allan." In Edward R. Foreman, ed., *Centennial History of Rochester, New York.* 4 vols. Rochester, N.Y.: Rochester Historical Society, 1931–34.

United States, Bureau of the Census. *Heads of Families at the First Census of the United States Taken in the Year 1790: New York.* Baltimore: Genealogical Publishing Co., 1966.

[United States]. *Documents, Legislative and Executive, of the Congress of the United States: Class II: Indian Affairs.* 42 vols. Washington, D.C.: Gales & Seaton, 1834–56. [Cited as *ASPIA.*]

———. *Journal of the Executive Proceedings of the Senate of the United States.* 143 vols. to date. Washington, D.C.: U.S. Government Printing Office, 1805–.

Upton, L. F. S. *The Loyal Whig: William Smith of New York & Quebec.* Toronto: University of Toronto Press, 1969.

Vanderkemp, Francis Adrian. "Extracts from the Vanderkemp Papers." Buffalo Historical Society, *Publications,* II (1880): 33–105.

Wainwright, Nicholas B., ed. "The Opinions of George Croghan on the American Indian." *Pennsylvania Magazine of History and Biography,* LXXI (April 1947): 152–59.

Wallace, Anthony F. C. *The Death and Rebirth of the Seneca.* New York: Knopf, 1970.

———. "Origins of the Longhouse Religion." In Bruce G. Trigger, ed., *Handbook of North American Indians: Northeast,* 442–48. Washington, D.C.: Smithsonian Institution, 1978.

Wallace, David H., ed. " 'From the Windows of the Mail Coach': A Scotsman Looks at New York State in 1811." *New-York Historical Society Quarterly,* XL (July 1956): 264–96.

Wallace, Paul A. W. *Conrad Weiser: Friend of Colonist and Mohawk.* Philadelphia: University of Pennsylvania Press, 1945.

———, ed. *Thirty Thousand Miles with John Heckewelder.* Pittsburgh: University of Pittsburgh Press, 1958.

Wallot, Jean-Pierre. *Intrigues Françaises et Américaines au Canada, 1800–1802.* Montreal: Éditions Leméac, 1965.

Watson, Winslow C. ed. *Men and Times of the Revolution; or, Memoirs of Elkanah Watson. . . .* Elizabethtown, N.Y.: Crown Point Press, 1968, reprint of 1856 original.

Weber, David J. "Turner, the Boltonians, and the Borderlands." *American Historical Review,* XCI (Feb. 1986): 66–81.

Weld, Isaac. *Travels Through the States of North America and the Provinces of Upper and Lower Canada During the Years 1795, 1796, and 1797.* 2 vols. London, 1807.

Werner, Raymond C. "War Scare and Politics in 1794." New York State Historical Association, *Quarterly Journal,* XI (Oct. 1930): 324–34.

Wheelock, Eleazar. *A Brief Narrative of the Indian Charity-School in Lebanon in Connecticut, New England.* London: J. & W. Oliver, 1767.

———. *A Continuation of the Narrative of the State, &c. of the Indian Charity-School at Lebanon, in Connecticut; From Nov. 27th, 1762 to Sept. 3d, 1765.* Boston: Printed by Richard & Samuel Draper, 1765.

———. *A Continuation of the Narrative of the Indian Charity-School at Lebanon, in Connecticut; From the Year 1768 to the Incorporation of It with Dartmouth-College. . . .* Hartford: Ebenezer Watson, 1771.

———. *A Continuation of the Narrative of the Indian Charity-School, Begun in Lebanon, in Connecticut;*

Now Incorporated with Dartmouth-College, in Hanover, in the Province of New-Hampshire. Hartford: Ebenezer Watson, 1773.

————. *A Continuation of the Narrative of the Indian Charity-School, Begun in Lebanon, in Connecticut; Now Incorporated with Dartmouth-College, in Hanover, in the Province of New-Hampshire.* Hartford: Ebenezer Watson, 1775.

————. *A Plain and Faithful Narrative of the Original Design, Rise, Progress and Present State of the Indian Charity-School in Lebanon.* Boston: Printed by Richard & Samuel Draper, 1763.

White, Leonard D. *The Jeffersonians: A Study in Administrative History, 1801–1829.* New York: Macmillan, 1956.

White, Patrick C. T., ed. *Lord Selkirk's Diary, 1803–1804: A Journal of His Travels in British North America and the Northeastern United States.* Toronto: Champlain Society, 1958.

White, Richard. "'Although I Am Dead, I Am Not Entirely Dead, I Have Left a Second of Myself': Constructing Self and Persons on the Middle Ground of Early America." In Ronald Hoffman, Mechal Sobel, and Fredrika J. Teute, eds., *Through a Glass Darkly: Reflections on Personal Identity in Early America,* 404–18. Chapel Hill: University of North Carolina Press, 1997.

————. *The Middle Ground: Indians, Empires, and Republics in the Great Lakes Region, 1650–1815.* New York: Cambridge University Press, 1991.

————. "The Nationalization of Nature." *Journal of American History,* LXXXVI (Dec. 1999): 976–86.

Williams, Robert A., Jr. *Linking Arms Together: American Indian Treaty Visions of Law and Peace, 1600–1800.* New York: Oxford University Press, 1997.

Williamson, Charles. "Description of the Settlement of the Genesee Country, in the State of New-York." In E. B. O'Callaghan, ed., *The Documentary History of the State of New York.* 4 vols. Albany, N.Y.: Weed, Parsons & Co., 1849, II: 1129–68.

Wilson, Bruce G. *The Enterprises of Robert Hamilton: A Study of Wealth and Influence in Early Upper Canada, 1776–1812.* Ottawa: Carleton University Press, 1983.

Wise, S. F. "The Indian Diplomacy of John Graves Simcoe." Canadian Historical Association, *Report, 1953,* 36–44. Ottawa: Canadian Historical Association, 1954.

Wraxall, Peter. *An Abridgment of the Indian Affairs Contained in Four Folio Volumes, Transacted in the Colony of New York, from the Year 1678 to the Year 1751.* Edited by Charles Howard McIlwain. Cambridge, Mass.: Harvard University Press, 1915.

Wright, J. Leitch, Jr. *Britain and the American Frontier, 1783–1815.* Athens: University of Georgia Press, 1975.

Wunder, John R., and Pekka Hamalainen. "Of Lethal Places and Lethal Essays." *American Historical Review,* CIV (Oct. 1999): 1229–34.

Yawger, Rose N. *The Indian and the Pioneer: An Historical Study.* 2 vols. Syracuse, N.Y.: C. W. Bardeen, 1893.

Young, A. H., ed. "Letters from the Secretary of Upper Canada and Mrs. Jarvis, to Her Father, the Rev. Samuel Peters." Women's Canadian Historical Society of Toronto, *Transactions,* XXIII (1922–23): 11–63.

————. "The Rev. Robert Addison and St. Mark's Church." Ontario Historical Society, *Papers and Records,* XIX (1922): 158–91.

Young, Alfred F. *The Democratic Republicans of New York: The Origins, 1763–1797.* Chapel Hill: University of North Carolina Press, 1967.

Zeichner, Oscar. "The Loyalist Problem in New York after the Revolution." *New York History,* XIX (July 1940): 284–302.

Zeisberger, David. *Diary of David Zeisberger: A Moravian Missionary Among the Indians of Ohio.* Edited by Eugene F. Bliss. 2 vols. Cincinnati: Historical and Philosophical Society of Ohio, 1885.

Acknowledgments

The generosity of friends and scholars enriches a writer's life. For research assistance, I am grateful to several graduate students (past or present) at the University of California at Davis: Kyle Bulthuis, Ruma Chopra, Bridget Ford, Kelly Hopkins, Jill Hough, Ken Miller, Sherri Patton, and Seth Rockman. I also learned a great deal from reading draft work on the northern borderland by Greg Wigmore and Andy Young. And I benefited from three undergraduate interns, who performed wonders: Tiffany Edwards, Julie Hong, and Beth Lew. For leads and insights, I am also grateful to Jason Acton, Caroline Judge, Steven Paul McSloy, David Reiser, Michael Smith, and Paul Thomas. I am especially indebted to Thomas B. Mason, whose passion for underdogs (past and present) is belied by an inexplicable devotion to the minions of George Steinbrenner.

This book depends on the professionalism and courtesy of archivists and curators at the Albany Institute of History and Art, the American Antiquarian Society, the Archives of Ontario, the Hamilton College Archives, the Library of Congress (Manuscript Division), the Massachusetts Historical Society, the National Archives of Canada, the New-York Historical Society, the New York Public Library, the New York State Archives, the New York State Library, the Oneida County Historical Society, the Peabody-Essex Institute, and the Syracuse University Library (Special Collections). I am especially grateful to Thomas Knoles of the American Antiquarian Society, Peter Drummey of the Massachusetts Historical Society, James D. Folts of the New York State Archives, Stefan Bielinski and Tricia Barbagallo of the New York State Library, Sarah Hartwell of Dartmouth College, and Frank Lorenz of Hamilton College. For expert guidance into Canadian sources, I relied on Patricia Kennedy of the National Archives of Canada. To find dozens of the most obscure (but invaluable) published works, I would have been lost without Marie Lamoureux's immense knowledge of the vast holdings at the American Antiquarian Society.

For help with illustrations, I am grateful to Richie Allen (Library and Archives Canada); Gigi Barnhill and Jackie Donovan (American Antiquarian Society); Fred Bassett (New York State Library); Clark Bernat (Niagara Historical Society & Museum); Jere Brubaker (Old Fort Niagara Association, Inc.); Wanda Burch (Johnson Hall State Historic Site); Anne Ricard Cassidy (New York State Office of Parks, Recreation, and Historic Preservation); Katherine Collett (Hamilton College Library Archives); Michele Dale (Archives of Ontario); Paul D'Ambrosio and Shelly L. Stocking (New York State Historical Association); Linda-Anne D'Anjou (Montreal Museum of Fine Arts); Brian Dunnigan and Clayton Lewis (William L. Clements Library); James D. Folts (New York State Archives); Megan Gillespie (Albany Institute of History & Art); Andrea C. Ashby Leraris (Independence National Historical Park); Suz Massen (Frick Art Reference Library); Kathleen P. O'Malley (Hood Museum of Art); Jill Reichenbach (New-York Historical

Society); Patricia M. Virgil (Buffalo & Erie County Historical Society); Alan Walker (Toronto Public Library); Suzanne Warner (Yale University Art Gallery); Susanna White (Emerson Gallery, Hamilton College); and Nicola Woods (Royal Ontario Museum). I am especially indebted to Jeffery L. Ward for his superb work in preparing the maps for this book.

Several historians generously shared their expertise in suggesting lines of inquiry or in fielding queries. They include Carl Benn, who led me through the intricacies of Canadian Iroquois history; Edward Countryman, who always considers the big picture; Nancy Shoemaker, who showed the way; John Smolenski, who shared his forthcoming work on natives and colonists in Pennsylvania; and Tony Wonderley, who provided expert guidance on the Oneida landscape and historical sources. For writing on my behalf, I am grateful to Eric Foner, Laurel Thatcher Ulrich, and David Weber. Richard White's scholarship provided a model and his personal generosity and scholarly seminar enriched my year at Stanford. I have also borrowed early and often from the expansive and innovative work (and conversation) of James Brooks. I also thank Karim Tiro, who is a paragon of scholarly generosity and wisdom.

I benefited from the opportunity to present my scholarship at the University of Toronto, University of Western Ontario, and York University. For their help and advice on those occasions (and others), I am grateful to Heidi Bohaker, Marc Egnal, Allan Greer, Adrienne Hood, Michelle Leung, Linda Sabathy-Judd, Ian Steele, and Sylvia Van Kirk. I also benefited from the feedback received at the University of Oklahoma during a visit arranged with aplomb by my amigo Paul "Pablo" Gilje. I am also grateful for the help and responses of Rob Griswold, Albert Hurtado, Cathy Kelly, David Levy, Josh Piker, Don Pisani, and Bob Shalhope.

A Mellon Fellowship from the American Antiquarian Society supported a year of my research. For a wonderful sojourn at that unmatched library, I thank Gigi Barnhill, Nancy Burkett, Joanne Chaison, Ellen Dunlap, John Hench, and Caroline Sloat. And Nina Dayton, Jim Boster, Warren Leon, Cynthia Robinson, and Lance and Melissa Schachterle were the most generous of friends during my year in Worcester.

Another fellowship, from a bequest by Reverend Marta S. Weeks, permitted me to write this book at the Stanford Humanities Center. For leadership there, I am grateful to John Bender and Beth Wahl. For innumerable favors, I thank the staff, especially Chi Elliott, Pei-Pei Lin, Gwen Lorraine, and Susan Sebbard. During that year, I learned much from my fellow fellows, particularly Jared Farmer, Zephyr Frank, and Gavin Wright. For many other acts of Stanford friendship, I thank Gordon Chang, Denise Gigante, Beverly Purrington, Gavin Jones, and Judith Richardson (and Eli).

At the University of California at Davis, I am blessed with colleagues who sustain both morale and mind by their friendship and example. I am especially grateful to my peers in the "Borders and Borderlands" research group: Lorena Oropeza, Andres Resendez, Chuck Walker, and Louis Warren. For his most regal friendship and many acts of noblesse oblige, I will always be indebted to Clarence Walker. Susan Mann has been an exemplary department chair and a true friend. The wonderful staff at the history department rescued me innumerable times. For that and their good cheer, I thank Kevin Bryant, Elvira Hack, Charlotte Honeywell, Debbie Lyon, Eteica Spencer, and Heidi Williams. For support for my research and writing, I am grateful to Steve Roth, assistant dean, and Steve Sheffrin, dean of social sciences.

For literary representation, I thank Andrew Wylie and Elena Schneider, especially for helping to renew my working relationship with Jane Garrett, the most sage of editors at Alfred A. Knopf. For shepherding the book so professionally, I am indebted to Jane and her assistant, Emily Owens Molanphy.

In developing a project in Canadian history, my ulterior motive was to spend more time with

Sheila McIntyre and Michael Von Herff (and Will and Silas and Maggie), who have provided the best of times and of basements during my visits to Ottawa. Jack Crowley and Marian Binkley warmed my stay in Halifax. When sojourning at Hamilton College, I similarly benefited from the thoughtful hospitality of Kevin Grant and Lisa Trivedi. Visits to Boston are always a special delight because of the contrarian friendship of Jim McCann, who tries to keep me honest (and drinking good wine). Kevin Convey is responsible for all references to pirates in this book. In New York City (and at their country estate, "Oscarwald"), I have enjoyed the generous friendship of Barbara Brooks, David Jaffee, Isadora Brooks Jaffee, and Oscar Handlin Jaffee. Nothing can compare to a visit to Oneonta thanks to the loving friendship of Peter and Shelley Wallace. In Maine, Wendy Hazard always has more energy and hope than seems possible in these fallen times. And who could write a book without the support of amigos? For that, I always thank Pablo Gilje, Jan Lewis, Annette Gordon-Reed, Pedro Onuf, and David "El Jefe" Konig.

Closer to home, I have benefited from the intertwined gifts of friendship and insight offered by Emil and Rosamaria Tanghetti, and Louis Warren. Thanks also to Spring Warren for letting me pretend to be her book agent and to Sam Warren for sharing my delight in Canadian history. Emily Albu remains a saint of human kindness, when not humbling my friends on the pool table. Our life has been enriched by the best of friends: Alessa Johns, Chris Reynolds, and Gabriel Johns Reynolds.

I dedicate this book to my sister, Carole Goldberg, who has been so loving and supportive, and to her husband, Marty, who is a prince among men (despite his devotion to baseball's evil empire).

Index

ALSO BY ALAN TAYLOR

*"An absorbing account of . . . a change so fundamental that it
shaped the American character."*
—The Boston Globe

WILLIAM COOPER'S TOWN

*Power and Persuasion on the Frontier
of the Early American Republic*

An innovative work of biography, social history, and literary
analysis, this Pulitzer Prize–winning book presents the
story of two men, William Cooper and his son, the novelist
James Fennimore Cooper, who embodied the contradictions
that divided America in the early years of the Republic. In
William Cooper's Town, Alan Taylor dramatizes the clash
between gentility and democracy that was one of the principal consequences of the American Revolution, a struggle
that was waged both at the polls and on the pages of our
national literature. Taylor shows how Americans resolved
their revolution through the creation of new social forms
and new stories that evolved with the expansion of our
frontier.

History/United States/978-1-4000-7707-6

VINTAGE BOOKS
Available at your local bookstore, or call toll-free to order:
1-800-793-2665 (credit cards only).

Printed in the United States
by Baker & Taylor Publisher Services